CONTENTS

ACKNOWLEDGMENTS

It's tough to write an acknowledgments section for a book of this magnitude. Obviously a lot of people helped to bring this book to print, and to assure that the quality was top-notch. First and foremost, I would like to thank my technical editor, C. Thomas Woodford of Factory Tour in Rainbow, California. This book is basically a collection of his years of knowledge put into print. Without his assistance, I'm sure that many people would be putting their 911 engines together backwards.

Gill Paszek was also extremely helpful. Gill spent hours helping me cut out a lot of the BS in the book, and also helped to focus the theoretical information. Walt Watson of Competition Engineering volunteered his services and knowledge many times. Not only is Walt a great machinist, but he's also a super-nice guy. Peter Bodensteiner was my very patient editor on this book, and his tenacity in keeping content from getting cut definitely helped to keep this book very close to my original concept. He also put up with my egotistical whining over font sizes and other trivial things. I also would like to thank James Bricken for reading through and editing a lot of the book. Finally, I would like to thank my wife Nori. Without her constant patience and understanding, this book surely would never have been completed.

Also on my list are John Walker, of John Walker's Workshop in Seattle. If you're in Seattle, I recommend that you take your Porsche to John's shop. Special thanks to Richard Clewett of Clewett Engineering. Richard is the foremost expert on Electromotive engine management systems for Porsches. Also very helpful was Steve Weiner of Rennsport Systems in Oregon. Steve is an expert on just about anything and everything having to do with the 911. Special thanks to Bruce Anderson, author of *Porsche 911 Performance Handbook*. I recommend his engine rebuilding class as a good hands-on learning experience, in addition to this book.

Special thanks to Jerry Woods, who co-teaches the engine rebuild class with Bruce. Also helpful were Bill Duncan and Dick Nuss from Engine Machine Service (EMS) in Los Angeles. I recommend EMS and Competition Engineering as the two top Porsche machine shops in the US.

Special thanks are due to Alex Wong, of Precision Tech Motorsports for allowing me to take some photos of his top-secret engine, and to Dave Darling for providing tech support and content. I'd like to thank Tom Wilson (even though I've never met or spoken with him), for giving me such a good model to follow with his book, *How to Rebuild your VW Air-cooled Engine*.

Also helpful were Darren Bond, Tom Gould, Bev Frohm, Alan Halpern, Jerry Murray, Cris Huergas, Mark Hargett, Becky Pagel, Zack Miller, Kirk Haight and Peter Visser of Electromotive, Brian Perry of S-Car-Go, Juan Lopez, Peter and Arnold at Andial, Kurt Williams, William Yowell, Mikko Kosonen, Alan Drayson, John Luetjen, Steven Kaspar of Imagine Auto, Mario Lusardi, Noah Pollak, Bruce Brown of SSF, and of course Mom and Dad. My apologies to anyone I may have forgotten.

Approximately 99% of the photos in this book were shot with the Sony Mavica CD-300. It is by far the best camera that I have ever owned, and I highly recommend it. This particular camera writes all of the images to a miniature CD-ROM drive that is contained within the camera itself. This not only allows you to shoot as many images as you can fit onto the discs, but it also creates what I call a digital negative. The miniature CD-ROM will hold store your images indefinitely, similar to a traditional film negative. You needn't worry about storage space on your computer's hard drive because the images are permanently archived to the CD-ROM format.

Few machines in this world have garnered as much respect and admiration as the 911 engine. For more than 25 years, the basic design of the engine remained unchanged from its original 1963 incarnation. In a testament to the ingenuity of this unique design, subsequent upgrades and tweaks were all that was needed to turn the original 130-horsepower six-cylinder engine into the 800-plus horsepower variant used in the legendary Porsche 935.

Unique in so many details, the 911 engine has created an air of mystery that surrounds the mechanics trained to work on them. In a role commensurate with automotive royalty, the Porsche engine mechanic has been revered for the intimate knowledge that can only be learned at the Porsche factory in Stuttgart. To have your engine treated by one of the great factory-trained mechanics required a lengthy wait, or even worse, rejection because the good doctor was too busy restoring that original Carrera RS.

Well, to heck with all that! By buying this book, you have taken your first steps toward breaking the myths associated with the 911 engine. For many years, useful information on the 911 engine has existed only in the heads of those trained at the Porsche factory. The tips, tricks, and the secrets of the inner circle have remained a closely guarded treasure trove that only a chosen few have had access to. Well, that has all come to an end now. Like the popular television series, "Magician's Secrets Revealed," this book exposes all of the undocumented laws and formulas for rebuilding, restoring and modifying your Porsche 911 engine.

So who should be reading this book? This book exists for anyone who owns a Porsche 911 and has an interest in learning about what goes on within the engine compartment. This book is designed to be the definitive resource and guide to rebuilding your engine—regardless of whether you do it yourself, or have a mechanic perform the rebuild. All of the notes, information and technical specifications that are contained in the depths of the factory workshop manuals are included in this book. As principal technical writer for Pelican Parts, I have had the opportunity to collaborate with some of the finest Porsche engine rebuilders in the world. All the knowledge and lessons learned over their years of collective experience are compiled here.

Do you need a Ph.D. from MIT to rebuild your engine? Certainly not! If you can read, follow directions carefully, and turn a wrench, then there is no reason why you can't rebuild your own engine. This book is written in the same easy-to-understand style that I wrote with in my first book, *101 Projects for Your Porsche 911*. If you can perform even the most basic projects in *101 Projects*, then you can certainly tackle the job of rebuilding your 911 engine. The key is to have patience, work carefully and cleanly, and don't rush or cut corners. Follow my advice in this book, and you will have a strong-running, leak-free engine that will run well and last a very long time.

Are you planning on taking your 911 in to have the engine rebuilt? Great—then this book will help you to ask the right questions of your mechanic, and will help ensure that your 'baby' will get all the proper care and upgrades that she needs. If your mechanic doesn't know what an oil bypass modification is, then he certainly shouldn't be rebuilding your engine. I will arm you with all the questions that you need to ask your mechanic to decide if he is worthy enough to work on your car. Too many of my Pelican Parts customers have been suckered by mechanics claiming to be experts, when in reality they have never rebuilt a Porsche engine before. It doesn't matter if they've rebuilt thousands of American big block engines or even Volkswagen motors—the Porsche 911 engine is completely different. It's like a Swiss watch that must be assembled with complete precision, attention to detail, and the knowledge of years of experience—which I provide in this book.

This book is not necessarily about rebuilding your 911 engine, but more about restoring it. Very often these engines have become old and have not been treated with the best of care. Restoring the engine compensates for years of heat cycles, previous incorrect rebuilds, the effects of dirty oil, high mileage, racing, and just plain abuse. This restoration is performed through careful machine work, parts replacement, improved assembly procedures, and extreme attention to detail while utilizing all of the factory recommended updates and upgrades.

So why is the Porsche 911 engine so special? The difference lies in the engineering and precision. The 911 contains many race-designed components that are taken for granted: a dry-sump system, the natural balance of six horizontally opposed cylinders, a single rod per throw, single-overhead chain-driven camshafts, and air-cooled cylinders to name a few. It's an honor and a challenge to rebuild one of these engines—elements of their race heritage can be seen in just about all aspects of their design.

With that in mind, let me take a moment to walk through each chapter of the book. Chapter One addresses the issues surrounding the question, "When to Rebuild?" It's a simple question that's often asked, yet the answer can be complex and confusing. I've had customers who think that they needed a rebuild, only to find out that a tiny piece of carbon stuck against a valve was causing all of their problems. In this chapter I detail the tests, evaluations, and items to look for to determine if your engine actually needs to be rebuilt. No use tearing down your engine if it can be easily repaired in some other way.

I detail the engine teardown process in Chapter Two. Detailed photos document each step of the teardown and cataloging process. It's important to stay organized during this step, as you don't want to misplace or lose any of your important engine pieces. I show you what to look for, where to find it, and most importantly how to take things apart without damaging them. Disassembly is a fun process where you can actually learn about how the engine works from the outside in.

In the next chapter, I discuss the mysterious processes that are performed on your parts when you send them off to the machine shop for refurbishment. Can you reuse this part? How much wear is acceptable? Which parts should be scrapped? It's all detailed in this chapter, along with the machining processes you should have performed on your parts. Should you hone your cylinders or not? Which head studs should you use? It's all in Chapter Three.

Chapter Four is an immense collection of never-before-published information. I've separated this one into three distinct sections. The first section describes in detail what parts you should definitely replace on your engine. These are the parts that wear out in your engine, and their replacement is the main reason why you are tearing the engine down to begin with. In section two, I detail my recommendations for reliability upgrades. These additions won't give you any more horsepower, but they will increase the longevity of your engine and help ensure many miles of problem-free driving. Section three exists in the land of unlimited budgets. Everything from twin-plugging to engine management systems are detailed and explained. This is where you ask yourself, "what if…" and then go check the balance in your checking account!

Chapter Five can be called the fruit filling of this book. Step-by-step, this chapter guides you through the assembly process, avoiding the snake pits and sand traps that can lead to costly mistakes later on. Follow the instructions and you will end up with a leak-free, superbly running engine when you're finished. Two hundred photos document the assembly process, clearly pointing out every single detail so you won't make any mistakes.

In the final chapter I detail the break-in process and include a bonus section on dyno testing. In Appendix A, I've compiled a lengthy list of tolerances and specifications that you need to rebuild your engine. Appendix B is a comprehensive parts diagram listing complete with all the part numbers for all parts used on the 1965-89 engines.

I chose to focus this book primarily on the 1965-89 911 engine family because there are so many similarities and common parts throughout this year range. The 1989 and later 3.6 engines are similar, yet different enough to require vastly differing assembly procedures. I am currently working on the 3.6 supplement to this book—see http://www.101projects.com for more details.

In a detailed how-to book like this one, it's important to distinguish literally which way is up. The 911 engine can be confusing because it's located in the rear of the car, and oriented backwards from most other engines. When I refer to the front of the engine, I will be talking about the area towards the front of the car, where the flywheel is located. Conversely, the back of the engine refers to where the fan and pulley are mounted. Left and right refer to the left and right side of the engine as it is installed in the engine compartment of the 911. I also refer to locations by cylinder numbers. The diagram nearby displays the cylinder numbers for the 911 engine. Cylinder numbers one through three are located on the left; cylinder numbers four through six are located on the right. Refer back to this diagram if you have any question as to where a particular cylinder is located.

As with any big how-to project, information is key to success. Although I have tried to include every single scrap of information you may need to rebuild your engine in this book, there are some elements of the process that I just did not have enough space to include. A lot of this material is already published in my first book, *101 Projects for Your Porsche 911*. I recommend picking up a copy of that book to use in conjunction with this one if you don't already have it.

In addition, I have some recommendations for supplemental material that may help on topics like particular fuel injection or exhaust systems. I recommend picking up some of these sources of information in addition to this book as I have learned that multiple viewpoints on the same topic can be invaluable if you are having trouble understanding something. See the next page for some of my personal recommendations.

I hope that you enjoy this book, as I have spent a lot of hours documenting each element of the rebuild process. If you have any questions or comments, feel free to contact me at this book's official website, http://www.101projects.com, which is also shared with the *101 Projects* book. Enjoy!

You can never have too much information. Although this book contains just about everything that you need to rebuild your engine, there are some additional resources that might give you a slightly different viewpoint on a confusing topic. I'll describe them starting clockwise from the upper left corner. The Bentley workshop manuals are an excellent guide to the 911. Available for the 1978-83 911 SC, and the 1984-89 Carreras, they contain a wealth of information on the whole car. In the upper center of the photo are the factory workshop manuals—very handy, although lacking in a lot of details. On the right is the Haynes manual, a good value for only fifteen dollars. The book with the blue 911 on the cover is a Porsche factory publication with parts diagrams and part numbers for all 911s from 1974-89. Below that is the Pelican Parts CD-ROM, which contains hundreds of technical articles on everything from clutch replacement to detailing your engine compartment. Along the bottom are the factory spec books, which are very hard to find these days. Keep a lookout for them at swap meets and other events, as they contain a tremendous amount of technical information. Bruce Anderson's Porsche 911 Performance Handbook is a great reference tool for such procedures as the calculation of compression chamber sizes. I also recommend taking Bruce Anderson's 911 overhaul class. It is taught by both himself and Jerry Woods, who is well known as a premier rebuilder of 911 race engines. Last but not least is my other book, 101 Projects for Your Porsche 911. I refer to this book throughout all the chapters, as there are many projects that should be performed while the engine is out of the car.

CHAPTER 1
WHEN TO REBUILD

"When should you rebuild your engine?" Indeed, this is a very common question, and one that is often not easily answered. Obviously, if the end of a rod is sticking out of your engine case, it's time for a rebuild. With subtler problems, however, such as noises, smoking, and poor performance, the rebuild decision may not be crystal clear. In this section, I will provide you with some questions to ask yourself, and dispel some common myths, to help you determine whether your engine needs to be rebuilt.

For any serious medical condition, it's always wise to get a second opinion. The same is true with 911 engine rebuilds. I have heard many stories of unscrupulous or simply over-meticulous Porsche mechanics who have recommended, or even insisted on, a rebuild when not all of the signs pointed in that direction. Keep in mind that no matter how good your mechanic's intentions may be, he may have a vested financial interest in seeing you rebuild your engine. Of course, not knowing that you're armed with this book and prepared to do it yourself, he might recommend a full rebuild. Rebuilding engines is a good business, and will guarantee about 40 hours of labor for a complete job.

My recommendation is that you take your car to a second, independent mechanic, and pay to have the car evaluated. Have him perform a leak-down test on the engine (see later in this chapter), and let him know up-front that you have a master mechanic friend waiting in the wings to rebuild the engine for you. The goal is to try to get an independent, unbiased expert view of the condition of your engine. Many of the problems with 911 engines can be somewhat subtle, and difficult for a novice to detect and decipher. I'll give you some hints, tips, procedures, and clues to help you in the following sections, but getting at least two expert opinions is always a wise idea.

HIGH MILEAGE ENGINES

Each derivative of the 911 has its own quirks and problems. Some of the engines are known for their longevity, and some are decidedly not. Just because your 911 engine has a lot of miles on it doesn't mean that it's automatically time for a rebuild. With proper care and maintenance, certain 911 engines can easily last 250,000 miles or more. Of course, some model years have had better track records than others, but the basic rules apply: if the engine was well cared for, and not abused, then it should last a long time, and gradually wear out. In general, the rule of thumb is that high-mileage is not a good measurement of engine condition. The way the car was treated and maintained during its life affect the condition of the engine much more than the total mileage driven.

High mileage engines often show signs of their age in compression and leak-down tests, described later in this chapter. As the engines age and mileage increases, the small tolerances within the engine slowly become larger. While this usually doesn't result in a catastrophic breakdown, high-mileage engines will gradually decline in performance as the mileage increases. An engine in this condition is often referred to as "tired."

Stock engines almost always last longer than modified engines. Higher compression ratios, aftermarket turbos, or superchargers add heat and stress that will make an engine wear out more quickly. Engines driven constantly on the track may especially show signs of wear. Race engines have such a typically short lifespan that their usage is usually tallied in hours run, rather than miles traveled.

1-1 *The 911 engine is truly a unique beast. Porsche has built its reputation on the 911 engine and the many engines derived from the original platform. The venerable 917, the successful 935 and 956 are all built on the basic engine design initially revealed in 1964. Given proper maintenance and care, any 911 engine can easily last 100,000 miles or more. Subsequent rebuilds can result in even longer life. The key to this longevity is meticulous attention to the details during the rebuild. The 911 engine is very unforgiving of mistakes—there isn't too much room for error. However, armed with the right information, you can rebuild your own engine, and make it last many, many years.*

STOCK ENGINE RELIABILITY

The 1978–89 engines are probably best known for having the longest life. It's not uncommon to find a good, well-maintained 3.0-liter engine running strong with more than 200,000 miles on the clock. Then again, I have seen 3.0-liter engines with many broken head studs and barely 100,000 miles on the odometer. It's really a combination of maintenance and the luck-of-the-draw as to whether your 1978–89 engine will be one of the good ones that last. Just to give you a reality check, in the late-seventies and early eighties, there were very few cars that lasted significantly past 100,000 miles, so the Porsche 911 engine was indeed way ahead of its time. The 911 Turbo engines are also known for long life, despite the added stress placed on them.

The 1974-77 engines are the least reliable of the bunch. It's very rare to find a stock 2.7-liter engine over 100,000 miles that has not been rebuilt. The 2.7-liter engines suffered from a host of problems: pulled head studs, worn valve guides, over-stressed cases, and overheating problems caused by thermal reactors used on the exhaust system. Fortunately, the design flaws that plagued these engines can be overcome with proper repairs and maintenance. Once their problems are properly addressed, the 2.7-liter engine should be able to last as long as its 1978-89 brethren. We'll discuss these problems and the methods used to repair them in Chapter 4.

The 1969-73 engines were generally more reliable than the 2.7-liter engines. Despite using the weaker magnesium case, these engines didn't stress the limits of the case, and were generally long-lived. The 911 T engines, in particular, with their lower compression pistons, seem to just run forever. The higher compression "S" models tend to wear out a little faster, but they are still probably good for 110,000 miles or so. With today's improved motor oils, the life expectancy of these early engines is actually increasing.

One of the items hampering the durability of the 1969-73 engines was the biral cylinders, which don't last nearly as long as the Nikasil cylinders sometimes used on 1974-89 models. Again, the longevity of these later engines was unprecedented, and helped Porsche earn its reputation for excellent engineering.

FAILED SMOG TESTS

Out in sunny California, we have one of the strictest emissions tests in the world. Cars are held to high standards that seem to get higher each year. Recently the California Air Resources Board (CARB) instituted a dynometer test where the wheels of the car are placed on a roller and tested for emissions at a specific speed. In addition, the tests monitor hydrocarbons, carbon monoxide, and nitrogen oxides (NOx). These tests are designed to monitor the emissions for engine conditions that might produce smog. Unfortunately, as the tests get tougher and tougher to pass, more 911 engines tend to fail. In some cases, the tests hold the cars to emissions standards that they were never designed to meet.

Just because your car fails the smog test doesn't necessarily mean that its engine needs to be rebuilt. In fact, a recently rebuilt engine will most certainly fail the test if it hasn't been fully run-in yet. The best thing that you can do to get your car to pass a smog test is to make sure that it is running perfectly. Most of the time a non-passing car simply has its timing set incorrectly, or has a fuel injection problem. You must make sure that all of your fuel injection and ignition components are working 100 percent properly before you can assume that the engine mechanicals may be suspect. A compression or leak-down test should be able to let you know if your failure to pass a smog test is caused by internal engine wear.

The graphical output from the smog station is also very useful to a trained expert – he can often determine the likely cause of failure simply by looking at the charts.

POOR PERFORMANCE & POOR GAS MILEAGE

When rings and valve guides begin to wear, they allow oil into the combustion chamber, where it burns along with the air-fuel mixture. This burnt oil is a contaminant in the combustion chamber that interferes with the combustion process. Worn rings and guides also reduce engine compression and impair combustion. For the driver, these conditions produce poor performance and reduced fuel economy.

There are plenty of other factors that can affect fuel economy and power. Most notably, the fuel injection system must be performing perfectly in order for the engine to achieve maximum power and efficiency. Before deciding on a rebuild, make sure that neither the fuel system nor the ignition system is causing your problems. Also try to isolate and fix other obscure problems that may contribute to the trouble. For example, improper suspension alignment can seriously reduce performance, as can improper tire inflations. Brake problems (especially with the emergency hand brake) can create some pretty significant drag.

The other book I've written, *101 Projects for Your Porsche 911*, has more information on fixing these problems.

STRANGE ENGINE NOISES

Air-cooled engines are designed to expand and contract as they heat and cool. It is very difficult to diagnose strange engine noises that occur when the engine is cold. A stone cold engine can make some unusual tapping or knocking noises right after you start it. The strange noises to watch out for are the ones the engine makes when it's warm and running. All engines tend to grow noisier as they age and clearances between parts inside the engine become larger.

Engine noises are indeed difficult to hear at times. A loud noise coming from one area of the engine may be inaudible from another angle. Sometimes while sitting inside the car, you will hear more of the lower pitched noises, as the higher pitched ones are filtered out by the car's insulation. Closing your eyes when listening to the engine helps to eliminate potential distractions, and allows you to concentrate on isolating the engine noises from one another.

An automotive stethoscope is a useful tool for listening closely to the engine. This tool works best when placed against a solid piece of the engine. Local sounds from troubled components can be heard better through the stethoscope because it helps to isolate outside noise. A long wooden dowel is a good alternative to the stethoscope, but be careful not to stick it in your ear, as intermittent engine vibrations can sometimes knock it into the inside of your ear. A piece of rubber vacuum hose will work as well.

There are four basic types of noises that can come from the 911 engine. Intermittent noises occur at irregular intervals and seem to have no reasonable pattern to them. An example would be something rattling around inside one of the valve covers. There are noises linked to the crankshaft that occur once every revolution. Then there are valvetrain noises that come and go once every two revolutions (the valvetrain operates at half the speed of the crankshaft). Such noise would include rocker and valve sounds. This is probably the most common noise heard on the 911 engine, and the fix may be simply to adjust the valves.

You may also hear a loud squeaky noise while the engine is running. Such a noise can often be caused by worn alternator bearings. Take the fan belt off, and run the engine for no more than 10 to 15 seconds. If the noise disappears, you know the problem is with your fan, fan housing, or alternator.

Another common noise is piston slap. This is the sound that the piston makes on its power stroke when clearances between the piston and the cylinder are somewhat excessive. It's a dull thud-clunk that can be heard every two rotations of the crankshaft. Piston slap is most commonly heard when the engine is warming up, before the piston-to-bore clearances have decreased due to the pistons expanding.

There are a whole host of noises associated with problems such as rod knock, noisy valves, broken rings, chain tensioner failure, detonation, and broken or pulled head studs. Unfortunately, I have discovered that it's nearly impossible to describe these noises accurately in writing so that someone can diagnose them. The best suggestion would be to take your car to your mechanic and have him listen to the engine. The 911 engine can be loud and noisy, and if you haven't listened to a whole lot of them, your imagination can get the best of you. Listening to finely tuned 911 engines in cars owned by your friends will give you an idea of how a normal 911 should sound.

OIL CONSUMPTION & SMOKING

As your engine ages, it will consume more oil. When the engine is brand new, all of the clearances inside the engine are easily filled with a thin film of oil. As the surfaces wear, the clearances enlarge and oil begins to slip by them. This oil is then burned in the combustion chamber as it seeps past the valve guides and piston rings. The wider the clearances, the more oil will be burned away. Also, some oils have different viscosities and tend to burn at a higher rate than others. In general, thinner, lighter weight oils have a tendency to flow more easily past worn parts in the engine. Using a heavier weight oil in a tired engine may help to slightly reduce oil consumption.

In addition, excess clearances mean that the oil films that float the crankshaft bearings require more oil to work properly. Looser gap clearances between bearings means

1-2 *The oil level can only be checked with the engine running at idle and at operating temperature. About two quarts of oil added to the tank will make the oil level on the dipstick rise from the low mark to the high mark (shown by red arrows). The oil gauge in the dashboard of the 911 is one of the most dangerous gauges ever created. It gives unknowing owners a false sense of security, and often reads incorrectly. Check the oil on the dipstick only, and do not depend on the oil gauge to give accurate results. When recording oil consumption, make regular notes of the odometer and oil dipstick level readings. Also record exactly how much oil you are adding to the oil tank. A regular maintenance record can be extremely valuable in determining your engine's total oil consumption.*

that oil flows more easily around the bearing journals. The result is that more oil is required to do the same task, and there is a corresponding drop in oil pressure and an increase in wear. If you carefully observe your oil pressure readings over the life of an engine, you may be able to notice this small drop in oil pressure. In general, excessive oil consumption, coupled with decreased oil pressure, is a sure-fire sign that the clearances in the engine have increased, and the engine needs to be rebuilt.

The presence of oil in the combustion chamber may also have an adverse effect on the combustion process. Oil tends to lower the effective octane rating of the fuel mixture, thus making the engine a bit more prone to harmful detonation.

So how much oil should your 911 engine be consuming? One quart per 1,000 miles is about the standard amount for the 911 engine. Newly rebuilt engines with about 5,000 miles on them will usually burn this amount. If your engine is consuming significantly more oil than this, you have a problem. Consumption of two quarts per 1,000 miles is certainly cause for concern. Curiously, the factory technical specification books list the consumption levels at about 1.5 liters per 1,000 km. This translates to about 1.5 quarts every 620 miles, which I have found to be excessive. If your engine is consuming that much oil, then there is something wrong with it.

Air-cooled engines expand significantly as they warm up during operation. It's not uncommon for the entire engine to expand more than 1/8 of an inch side-to-side when heated from stone cold to operating temperature.

This means that certain clearances that are designed to be optimum at operating temperature are sometimes not ideal when the engine is cold.

There are two places where oil can be lost internally: past the piston rings, or through the valve guides. Oil seepage when the engine is cold is considered normal. It's not uncommon for a 911 engine to smoke when it's started, primarily because some oil has seeped into the combustion chamber as the engine cooled down from its last running. This smoking is not necessarily a sign that the engine needs to be rebuilt. If the smoking is sustained even after the car has warmed up, however, then a significant amount of oil is burning in the engine's combustion chambers.

What smoke should you look for? White smoke is typically caused by condensation in the engine, and is generally harmless when seen on an air-cooled engine. Black smoke means that there is a lot of unburned fuel in the combustion chamber and may be a sign that the car is running too rich. In general, blue, sooty smoke is caused by burning oil. If your engine puts out a big puff of bluish smoke when you pull away from a stoplight, it's probably a sign that the rings are significantly worn.

Worn rings also produce what is known as blow-by. Just as oil can get past the rings and enter the combustion chamber, exhaust gases can be blown the other way into the crankcase when the cylinder fires. Such blow-by often comes out of the crankcase through the breather hose on the top front of the engine. This hose connects to the oil tank, and the exhaust gases are recirculated back into the engine through the filler neck on the oil tank. On other cars, blow-by is typically funneled back into the air filter through the positive crankcase ventilation (PCV) valve.

Worn valve guides can also contribute to oil loss, although typically less than worn rings. In the mid-1970s, Porsche experimented with new types of valve guides that did not hold up well. As a result, many of the 1974-77 engines had to have their guides replaced at about 60,000 miles. Most of these engines have had this repair done. However, if you find that your engine has not, then you can expect that your guides will be well worn. Worn guides not only leak compression, but also can cause the valve heads to overheat and break off. This is because close valve guide clearances are necessary for proper cooling of the valve. It should be noted that puffs of smoke on deceleration are usually a sign of worn guides and valve seals.

In addition to the oil burned naturally by the engine, your 911 engine can also lose a lot of oil due to leaks. Many 911 oil leaks drip onto the heat exchangers and are burned off by the high heat. Sometimes it's very difficult to gauge exactly how much oil is being burned by the engine, and how much is being lost to leaks.

Air-cooled engines are infamous for oil leaks. Whether it's a Porsche 911 engine or a Volkswagen engine, air-cooled owners will fondly describe that burning oil smell that is characteristic of these cars. To be fair, the air-cooled cars must get their passenger compartment heat from heat exchangers that wrap around the exhaust pipes. If there is an oil leak onto these pipes, then the smell of burning oil will waft up into the passenger compartment. This is the reason why many air-cooled owners diligently try to chase down and repair oil leaks in their engines.

The 911 engine can leak oil from many different places. Fortunately, many of these oil leaks can be repaired without tearing down and rebuilding the engine. Project 21 from the book, *101 Projects for Your Porsche 911*, details all of the common leaks that can be easily fixed without engine disassembly. If your main goal of rebuilding the engine is to fix some of these major oil leaks, I suggest that you read that section first.

There are a few major leaks that cannot be fixed without major engine work. Crankcase parting line leaks require disassembly, as do leaks between the heads and the camshaft housing. Leaks from between the chain housing and the camshaft housing also require major disassembly. Many times a leak will appear to be coming from one of these places when in fact it is leaking from a different point that is significantly easier to fix. Wash the underside of the car and track down all of the easy oil leaks before you decide that it's time for a rebuild.

HEAD STUD PROBLEMS

One of the most common failures associated with the 911 engine is the head studs either breaking or pulling out. These are long, shanked studs that are thinner in the middle than on the end sections where the threads are located. Shanked studs are typically designed in this manner to achieve a

1-3 *This engine is suffering from pulled head studs. This particular engine case has been worked on before, and has had what are known as Time-Serts installed. Time-Serts are similar to case-savers, except for the fact that they are typically weaker, and can damage the case when installed. Whereas Time-Serts can still pull out of the case, as the green arrow in this photo clearly shows, case-savers are less prone to this type of failure.*

strong, coarse thread while keeping the center diameter of the stud at the optimum thickness—often designed with thermal considerations. When you remove your valve covers, you should do a quick inspection of your head studs. The head studs can be seen by looking deep down into the heads in the areas where the spark plugs are located.

The 1974-77 magnesium cases are most known for their pulled head studs. Magnesium is softer and lighter than aluminum. On 1973 and earlier cars, the engine didn't stress the limits of the magnesium case too much. But 2.7-liter engines from the mid-1970s faced additional stresses, from both increased displacement and higher operating temperatures. To increase displacement, Porsche engineers removed crucial material near where the cylinder head studs are mounted. In addition, new emissions restrictions in the mid-1970s required the engines to run hotter, because hotter thermal reactors on the exhaust give off fewer emissions. This heat caused the engines to expand farther, but they now had less strength where the head studs mounted. The result is that the metal threads in the magnesium case yield, and the studs begin to pull out.

Once the engine cools down to its normal operating state, the stress subsides, but the studs remain pulled out of the magnesium case. The result is that the barrel nuts on the end of the studs become loose and fall off. Subsequent attempts to re-torque the nuts almost always results in further pulling of the stud. The appropriate torque for the heads can no longer be maintained, and as a result, the heads become loose. This often creates a distinctive exhaust leak at the interface between the head and the cylinder. This *phat-phat-phat* sound is typical of a 2.7-liter engine with pulled head studs. This sound is most clearly heard at startup with a cold engine.

How can you tell if you have a pulled head stud? Simply pull off the valve covers (upper and lower), and check to see if you have any head stud barrel nuts floating around inside the spark plug area. If you do, then chances are good that your magnesium case has pulled at least one stud. If the barrel nuts are still attached to the head studs, take a 10mm Allen-head tool, and attempt to tighten them to factory specs (see Appendix A for the specification for your engine). If the nuts simply spin and spin, then you have a pulled head stud. Don't keep tightening it, as you can pull the stud so far out of the hole that it will be difficult to remove the nut later on when you disassemble the engine.

The repair involves a complete teardown of the engine, as you cannot easily and effectively repair the case without the use of a precision milling machine or drill press. The fix for pulled head studs is to install "case-savers." These double-threaded steel inserts screw into the engine case. The head studs then thread into the case-savers. Because the case-saver's outer diameter is larger than the original head stud, it has more material to grip on the engine case,

which results in the threads being stronger than the bare metal threads within the case. In addition, the case-saver has a larger, coarser thread, which means that there is more material between each thread. More material translates into greater strength along the axis of the head stud.

In simple terms, the case-saver creates a new hole for the head stud that is stronger and tougher than the original one in the case. Case-savers can still pull out of the case; however, this usually happens only in high-stress, high-compression race motors, or if the engine has been overheated. Otherwise, head studs reinforced with case-savers should be more than strong enough for street and most racetrack use. I recommend case-savers over Time-Serts, a similar product used to fix pulled head studs, because case-savers don't stress the magnesium case during installation. I talk more about case-savers in Chapter 3.

The 1978-89 engine cases were manufactured out of aluminum. Porsche realized that the magnesium cases, although lighter in weight, were more susceptible to the heat and stress of larger displacement engines. However, with the stronger case arose a new point of failure for the infamous head studs. Attempting to better balance the stress of the engine from hot to cold, Porsche used a new steel alloy called Dilavar for the construction of its head studs on the exhaust side of the engine (intake and exhaust for 911 Turbo engines). These studs were designed to have tensile (strength) properties similar to the earlier steel studs, but to expand and contract more like an aluminum alloy. Matching the expansion and contraction properties of the Dilavar stud to the overall engine would decrease the stress on the case and the cam towers.

1-4 *Looking at the bank of pistons and cylinders, it is obvious why this motor is coming apart. The arrows point to broken head studs. Surrounding the head studs is sludge that is leftover from oil leaking out of the heads. Theoretically, there shouldn't be any oil in this area, but this motor had other problems as well. The Dilavar studs used in 1982 seemed like a good idea at the time, but the seven broken studs on this motor (five on the opposite side) tell a different story. If you are shopping for a 911 SC or a 3.0-liter engine, insist that your mechanic remove the valve covers during the pre-purchase inspection to check for broken head studs.*

It was a good plan; however, the Dilavar studs did not hold up. Particularly in harsh climates, the studs are prone to snapping. With most engines this occurs only on the lower row of head studs because the top row are standard steel. Porsche used two materials on non-turbo engines because the temperature gradients on the exhaust side were much greater than on the top of the engine. Turbo engines used Dilavar on both rows.

The Dilavar studs were somewhat susceptible to the environment. Condensation in the air combined with scratches on the studs can create small pockets of corrosion that form what are known as stress concentrations. These are weak points where the stresses exerted on the stud will cause increasing damage, leading to failure. This process is similar to opening a bag of potato chips. The bag itself cannot be easily torn or punctured. However at the top there is a small notch in the material that allows you to tear it open from that point. The v-shaped notch creates what is known as a stress concentration in the material, and makes it easier to break and shear the material apart. In a similar manner, rust or abrasions on the studs can create stress concentrations in the studs. It is not uncommon to see a broken head stud that has snapped at a rusty scratch on the surface.

Stress concentrations aside, the Dilavar studs were not robust enough to hold up to the stress exerted by the larger displacement 3.0-liter and 3.2-liter engines. So the big question that many people ask is "what stud do I use?" Based on the consensus of Porsche engine rebuilding experts that I've asked, it would seem that the original steel studs used on the early cars are the best bet for use in rebuilding any 1965-89 engine. It is very rare to see these original steel studs snap. They have also been used in many 3.0-liter and 3.2-liter engines without any reported problems.

Another solution to the head stud problem is to use aftermarket RaceWare or ARP head studs. These aftermarket head studs are very effective, very strong, and also very expensive (about $550 per set). If you have the money, or are building a high-compression race motor, then the RaceWare head stud set would be a good bet. However, in most cases, the early steel head studs should be more than adequate.

The repair procedure for the broken studs doesn't involve a full rebuild, but instead can be performed only by removing the top end. Unfortunately, the top end accounts for about 80 percent of the engine, so if you've gone this far, you might as well tear down the bottom end as well. Removing the old studs can be a big problem, as the aluminum case combined with the red Loctite used to install the studs creates a pretty tight grip. Special tools and a torch are required to remove the studs, but we'll talk about this problem in Chapter 3.

Okay, so you've read about the head studs. You've checked and you've found that you're one of the many 911 SC owners out there driving around with a broken lower head stud. Many 911 owners have a panic attack when they see this, and many Porsche mechanics will instantly recommend a full top-end rebuild to repair the stud. I have heard of engines that will run fine for a very long time with one or two broken head studs. However, the chances of further damaging your engine increase if you drive the car in this condition. While finding a broken head stud doesn't mean that the car will be damaged if you drive it for another 100 miles or so, prolonged use can cause irreversible damage to your cylinder heads and cylinders. If you find a broken head stud in your motor, then you should start planning for a rebuild in the near future.

If two studs break on the same head, then it's definitely time for an immediate rebuild. In addition, if you can hear an exhaust popping noise when accelerating, it's time to rebuild. Driving the car with an exhaust leak can cause the head and cylinder to vibrate and knock against each other. If this problem is left unresolved, then the exhaust leak can end up damaging the head and the piston. In general, if you have an exhaust leak at the junction between the head and the cylinder, it's best not to drive the car.

READING SPARK PLUGS

The spark plug is really the best way to "see" what is going on inside your combustion chamber. You need to pull out all of the spark plugs to perform a compression test, so you might as well take a close look at them while they're out.

While today's modern fuels make plug-reading much more difficult, you can still glean a lot of information from looking at them. A good, well-balanced engine will produce a plug that is light brown in color, and dry. If the engine is running too rich, the plug will often be coated with a lot of extra carbon. Keep in mind that the rest of your combustion chamber probably looks the same. An engine running too lean will have a powdery white coating on it, and the outer porcelain ring may have a burned appearance.

1-5 *Spark plugs can give you a quick glance into the inside of your combustion chamber. The spark plug on the left shows a finely tuned engine. Note the light brown color, and no residue on the outside of the plug. The spark plug on the right shows an engine that is burning oil in the combustion chamber. This plug is wet with black, burned oil. This is a sign that there is a problem with either the rings or the valve guides, and that the engine needs to be rebuilt.*

When reading spark plugs, pay close attention to the white porcelain ring around the plug. This white area will give you an excellent background to inspect the color of deposits on the plug, and to help determine how your combustion chamber looks inside.

If the plug is wet with oil, then there is significant leakage into the combustion chamber past either the valve guides or the piston rings. This is generally a bad sign, and an indicator that your compression test may not yield good results.

COMPRESSION TESTS

One of the most common tests to determine an engine's condition is the standard compression test. This particular test measures the amount of pressure that is built up inside the combustion chamber when the engine is turned over. The typical compression tester is a pressure gauge that is attached via a short hose to a plug that is screwed into the spark plug hole. As the engine turns over, the compression gauge will read the maximum pressure exerted within the combustion chamber. The overall value provides a good indication of the condition of the rings or valves.

Your 911 needs to be set up properly before you start the compression test. If the valves are not opening or closing at the correct time, for example, one cylinder may read vastly different from another. Make sure that your valves are adjusted properly prior to performing the test. For the complete procedure on adjusting your valves with the engine inside the car, take a look at Project 18 in the book, *101 Projects for Your Porsche 911*. Premature camshaft wear can also lead to variances in compression readings; however, this type of wear is not normally common on the 911 engine.

With the engine cold, loosen the spark plugs with a spark plug socket and extension. Then tighten them up just a bit. You want to test the engine when it's warm, yet removing tight plugs from a hot engine can cause damage to the threads in the heads. Loosening the plugs a bit when the engine is cold will minimize any damage you could possibly do to the threads in the heads. (Although you might think that it's good practice to use anti-seize compound on the plug threads, Porsche specifically recommends against this; the compound seems to interfere with proper grounding of the plugs.) Also, temporarily remove any heater hoses that might get in the way of removing the spark plugs.

Warm the car up to operating temperature and then turn it off. Wait about 5 minutes or so, as head temperatures tend to spike right after you turn the engine off. At this point, the engine fan has stopped, and the heat tends to build up with no place to dissipate to. Removing the spark plugs immediately after turning off the engine can cause the threads in the aluminum to gall. After about five minutes, remove the spark plugs from their holes. Now, disconnect the cable from the capacitive discharge (CD) unit (1969-1983 911 and all Turbos). If you're working on a 1965-68 911, then simply disconnect the power line (+) from the coil. If you're testing a 1984-89 911 Carrera, then remove the small square DME relay from under the driver's seat. Doing this will disable the car's ignition system, and prevent the spark plug wires from firing. It's also a wise idea to remove the fuel pump relay at this time (for 1969-83 911s). You are going to be cranking the engine over several times, and you don't want raw fuel to be dumped into the system.

Having a helper around is useful, as you can watch the gauge while he or she cranks the engine. I recommend that you attach a charger to your battery to avoid running it down. Don't fire it up at 50 amps, but instead leave it on about 10 amps, which should help it recover when it's not cranking.

With the engine warm, install the compression tester into the spark plug hole. A bit of patience and skill are required in order to properly manipulate and screw in the compression tester so that you don't cross-thread the plug hole and damage the threads in the cylinder heads. With the compression tester installed, crank the engine over 12 to 16 times. Make sure that you place your foot all the way down on the throttle. This will allow maximum airflow into the engine; otherwise your compression readings will be off. The engine should make six to eight full complete compression strokes (12 to 16 turns of the crankshaft). You can tell when the engine is on a compression stroke because the compression gauge will jump and show an increase when the cylinder is compressed. Carefully watch how the compression tester gauge increases, and record the maximum value when you have completed the last compression stroke. The gauge will jump at first, and then increase slowly until cranking the engine over more has no additional effect on the reading. Remove the compression tester and repeat for each of the other cylinders.

So what do you do with the results? In general, compression tests are limited in what they can tell you. It is important to remember that different compression testers may give different readings as well. Cranking the engine faster (with a stronger battery or high-powered starter) may also skew readings. The most useful piece of information that you can glean from them is how each cylinder compares to the others. Little deviation across all of the cylinders generally indicates an engine in good health. A good rule of thumb is that each cylinder should read a minimum of 85 percent of the value of the highest cylinder. So, if the highest reading is 150 pounds per square inch (psi), then the minimum acceptable reading for any other cylinder would be about 128 psi.

It is important to note that while this range is acceptable, it is not ideal. In a motor that is in excellent condition the compression variation between the highest and lowest cylinders typically will not be more than 5 to 10 psi. On a newly assembled and run-in motor, compression numbers are usually within this range. As the engine ages and certain parts wear faster than others, one or more cylinders may experience a bit more wear than the others. This will definitely show up in the compression tests. Needless to say, if you have all of your cylinders in the 150 psi range, and one cylinder is down around 120 psi, that should give you cause for concern. The important thing to remember is that you want to gather consistent readings across all of the cylinders, without focusing on the actual values. If a reading is significantly off, go back and test that cylinder again to make sure that the first measurement was not a fluke, which is often the case.

So what causes variations in compression tests, and why can't they be used as the final word on engine rebuilds? The problem is that there are several factors that affect the final pressure read by the tester. Engines running with very aggressive camshafts have a tendency to give low compression readings. This is because there is significant overlap between the intake and the exhaust stroke on the cam. During high-rpm operation, this overlap works to give the engine more power. However, when turning the engine at a low RPM, as with a compression test, the overlap causes some of the pressure in the combustion chamber to leak out before the valve is closed. An early 911 S engine, for example (with its high-overlap cams), has a tendency to give lower compression readings than the 911 CIS engines (1974-83), despite having a higher compression ratio. This is caused by the aggressive camshaft overlap.

Altitude and temperature also affect the compression readings. Manufacturers' specifications are almost always given at a specific altitude (14.7 psi at sea level), and 59 degrees Fahrenheit. Both temperature and barometric pressure change as you go up in altitude, so you will need to correct your measurements if you wish to compare it with a factory specification. The following chart provides conversion factors for correctly compensating for changes in altitude:

Compression Test

Altitude Compensation Factors	Altitude Factor
500	0.987
1500	0.960
2500	0.933
3500	0.907
4500	0.880
5500	0.853
6500	0.826
7500	0.800
8500	0.773

A standard compression reading of about 150 psi at sea level in Los Angeles would measure significantly less in the surrounding mountains. For example, at an elevation of 6,000 feet, the expected reading would be 150 psi x .8359 = 125 psi. The cylinders would be reading low if compared to sea level measurements, yet perfectly fine at this altitude.

You can determine if the rings are causing low compression readings by squirting about a tablespoon of standard 10W-30 engine oil into the cylinder. Crank the engine two to three times to spread the oil around inside the combustion chamber. Then retest the compression. If the readings shoot up significantly (45 psi or so), then the problem is most likely with the piston rings seating to the cylinders. Squirting the oil inside the combustion chamber in this manner allows the rings temporarily to seal quite a bit more than they would dry. If the compression readings do not change, then the most likely culprit is a leaky valve.

LEAK-DOWN TESTING

Without a doubt, the most comprehensive test that you can perform on your engine is a leak-down test. While somewhat similar to the compression test, it eliminates nearly all of the extraneous variables that may alter the final compression readings in a typical compression test. In simple terms, the leak-down test involves pressurizing the cylinder and measuring the amount of air that is leaked out past either the rings, the valves, or a gap between the heads and the cylinder.

The leak-down test equipment uses an external air compressor to pressurize the cylinder. The engine is held stationary, and the test is not dependent upon outside variables

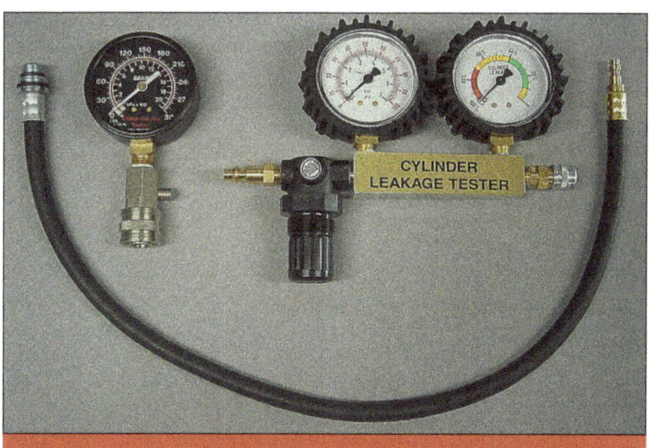

1-6 *A leak-down test is the best test that you can perform on your engine. Most home mechanics lack either the test equipment or the air compressor required to run the test. Most shops, however, have the equipment, and will perform the leak-down test for a nominal fee. Leakage is typically measured in the volume percentage lost. Good running engines will typically have leakage less than 10%. Engines with significant problems will exhibit leakage of 30% or more. The leak-down test is very effective because it eliminates all of the other extraneous factors that might influence and skew the results of a compression test. The leakdown tester is shown on the right. A standard compression tester gauge is shown on the left.*

like the cranking speed, altitude, temperature, or the camshaft overlap. In fact, the leak-down test can be performed on just about any engine, whether it's inside the car or not—though the engine must be warmed up for the test to be most accurate.

Unfortunately, the leak-down test equipment is somewhat specialized, requires an air compressor, and is not exactly inexpensive. Most local repair shops have a leak-down tester, but it's not common to find one in your neighbor's garage. The good news is that most shops will be able to perform a leak-down test on your engine for a nominal fee. The 911 engine doesn't require any special leak-down adapters, so any good foreign auto repair shop should be able to do the test for you. Similar to the compression test, the leak-down test should give you information on the condition of the rings and valves, but from a slightly different perspective.

The leak-down test is performed by initially setting the warmed-up engine to top dead center (TDC) on the compression stroke for the piston that you are checking. Make sure that it's exactly at TDC, otherwise the engine will begin to turn over as soon as you pressurize the cylinder. You want to make sure that both the intake and exhaust valves are completely closed (as they should be at TDC) otherwise air will immediately leak out of the cylinder. To make sure that you are at TDC for cylinder number 1, remove the distributor cap, and rotate the engine clockwise until the rotor is lined up with the small notch.

When you are running the test, it is a wise idea to make sure that the crank doesn't turn at all. Have an assistant hold the crank steady with a socket and driver placed on the pulley bolt or place a flywheel lock on the engine if it's out of the car. Connect the leakage tester to the engine in the same manner that you would with the compression tester. Pump up the cylinder and let the leakage tester measure the amount of air lost. The gauge on the tester should give readings in percentage numbers.

A newly rebuilt engine should have total leak-down percentages of around 3 to 5 percent. An engine in good running condition should show 10 percent or less. Numbers around 20 percent indicate some wear, but are still adequate for good engine operation. Leakage numbers of around 30 percent indicate that there are problems brewing, and that a rebuild may be necessary. Needless to say a large leakage amount like 90 percent indicates that there is a hole in the combustion chamber, and the engine is probably not firing on this cylinder at all. Rotate the engine crankshaft clockwise 120 degrees when you're done, and check the next cylinder. Repeat the process for each of the six cylinders, following the firing order (1-6-2-4-3-5).

Another good quality of the leak-down test is its ability to pinpoint the exact problem with the engine. When the cylinder is compressed with air, you can usually hear where the air is releasing from. Leakage past the intake valves can be heard at the intake manifolds through the fuel injection. Exhaust valve leakage can be heard through the tailpipe. Leakage past the rings can sometimes be heard in the crankcase breather hoses. The most obvious leakage occurs when the cylinder head studs have broken or pulled, and the air leaks directly out of the combustion chamber in between the cylinder and the head.

While the leak-down test is probably the best indicator of engine condition, it shouldn't be the final word in your evaluation. I have heard from many people about great running engines that for one reason or another do not test well on the leak-down tester. It's important to remember that the leak-down tester does not test the engine when it's running—it only does a static evaluation. As with any air-cooled motor, its operating characteristics vary widely. Use the leak-down test as one indicator and back it up with other tests and observations.

CARBON DEPOSITS

I thought it important to mention some things about carbon deposits built up inside engines. Just about every single engine I have ever seen torn open has had a significant layer of carbon buildup on the pistons and the inside of the

1-7 *Carbon deposits, like death and taxes, are a fact of life. You don't need to rebuild your engine in order to clean out your combustion chamber though. Deposits can build up on the heads and get caught in the valves, creating a stuck valve that may result in compression and performance loss. Before tearing open your engine, make sure that you're simply not suffering from carbon buildup in your combustion chamber. Of course, if your engine is relatively aged, and showing other signs of wear, then a carbon-removal treatment will probably not work too well.*

heads and valves. Particularly with today's ever-changing formulations of gasoline, the additional carbon buildup appears to be a problem in almost all air-cooled engines.

The 911 engine has a few problems of its own, specifically related to carbon build-up. Carbon deposits form naturally inside the combustion chamber as a by-product of the combustion process. Both engine oil and gasoline are hydrocarbons, so burning either of them incorrectly can result in a buildup of excess carbon deposits. These deposits are often caused by excessive oil burning in the combustion chamber, which is a sign that your engine needs a rebuild. A rich mixture setting can also introduce more of the black soot that creates the carbon buildups in the engine. Short-trip driving and extended idling (not ideal running conditions for an engine) can also increase the buildup rate. While excess carbon deposits can be cleaned and removed without a complete overhaul, very often they are yet another sign that something else on the engine needs attention (like rings and guides).

Carbon deposits can cause the engine's valves to become shrouded, and covered with carbon. In an opposite manner to porting and polishing the heads, the carbon buildup actually disrupts the flow of fuel mixture, and can restrict the airflow into the combustion chamber. The horizontal boxer layout of the 911 engine also lends itself to problems with carbon deposits. It is not uncommon to find that a 911 engine that has not been run for a long time has low compression. Even if the engine has had a relatively short number of miles put on it since its last rebuild, you may discover that it has very low or zero compression in one of its cylinders. Often the reason for this is carbon deposits. When an engine is left idle for a long period of time, moisture can get into the combustion chamber, where it gets absorbed by the carbon deposits. This absorption causes the carbon to become loose and flake off. Because the 911's exhaust valves are located at the bottom of the engine, carbon deposits that flake off have a bad habit of getting lodged between the exhaust valve and its seat. This creates a compression leak in the combustion chamber.

It's important not to drive the car for extended periods of time (thousands of miles) if you think that a piece of carbon might be lodged between the exhaust valve and its seat. The reason for this is simple. The exhaust valve (unlike the intake valve) becomes very hot, and needs to cool by coming in contact with its valve seat, which serves as a heat sink. If the valve doesn't seat properly, then it will overheat. The heat from prolonged driving in this condition will burn a pie-piece shaped notch in the valve. Valves damaged in this manner are basically destroyed, and will not seat properly even if the carbon is removed. In the worst-case scenario, the valve head will become so hot that it breaks off. Having the head of a valve dance around the inside of your combustion chamber will usually destroy the piston and send chunks of metal circulating throughout your motor. Needless to say, this is not a good thing.

As mentioned previously, worn valve guides or worn-out rings allow excess oil into the combustion chamber, which vastly increases carbon buildup. Of course, the solution to this problem is a full rebuild, or at best a top-end valve job. Excess carbon deposits can often be "burned out" by driving on the highway for about an hour or so. This should allow the combustion chamber to heat up enough to burn away the carbon deposits.

If your engine has been sitting for an extended period of time, you may want to try a gasoline additive. Berryman B-12 Chemtool and Techron both have good reputations for helping to dissolve and remove deposits. One of the best things to do is to take your 911 on an extended, spirited drive of at least an hour or more along the freeway. Try to vary your RPMs, but make sure that you keep them relatively high to help raise cylinder head temps. The cleaning additive, combined with the heated cylinder heads, should be enough to remove any excess deposits. When you return from your drive, run the compression or leak-down test again, and you may be surprised at the improvement in the numbers!

REBUILD COSTS

Okay, so you've determined that it's time for an engine rebuild for your 911. One of the big questions is, "how much is it going to cost me?" The actual number depends upon a lot of different factors—which engine you have, what condition it is in, are you assembling it yourself or having someone else do it for you?

Rebuild costs can vary greatly depending on these factors. For example, a 911 SC engine that is tired with about 125,000 miles, has no broken head studs, and Nikasil cylinders, can probably be rebuilt for about $2,000 if you assemble it on your own. This is, of course, assuming that there is no damage to the engine, the engine already has the Carrera pressure-fed chain tensioners installed, and you are able to reuse your pistons and cylinders. Suppose, though, that you have a broken head stud that damaged one cylinder. Then you will have to go find a good used cylinder. Or suppose that your 3.0 liter has non-reusable Alusil cylinders (it's the luck of the draw on these). Then you will have to purchase a new set for about $3,000.

On the other side of the spectrum is the 2.7-liter engines. The machine work to repair and strengthen the case itself runs about $1,000. Additional work on the heads can run about $125 to $150 per head (total $750 to $950), not including new valves. Reconditioning the rods adds another $200, and to balance the engine runs about $300.

The bottom line is that you need to be prepared to spend the money to do the job correctly. The total cost of most rebuilds is roughly divided into three sections—machine work, parts, and labor. The thirty-dollar investment that you

Parts costs

	Cost	Qty	Total
Main Bearing Set	$108.70	1	$108.70
Rod Bearing Set	$43.60	1	$43.60
Engine Gasket Set	$214.10	1	$214.10
Connecting Rod Bolt	$6.96	12	$83.52
Connecting Rod Nut	$2.43	12	$29.16
Flywheel Bolt, 6 per car, each	$9.60	6	$57.60
Flywheel Pilot Bearing	$15.50	1	$15.50
Oil Pressure Switch	$10.70	1	$10.70
Inner Intermediate Shaft Bearings	$17.30	1	$17.30
Outer Intermediate Shaft Bearings	$16.20	1	$16.20
1974-77, 2.7 liter CIS, Nikasil Piston & Clyinder Set	$1,403.10	1	$1,403.10
Intake Valve, 46mm	$33.00	2	$66.00
Exhaust Valve, 40mm, sodium filled	$52.70	1	$52.70
Rocker Arm Shaft Inner Seal (used originally on RSR cars only)	$1.50	1	$1.50
One-piece Timing Chain	$39.00	1	$39.00
Chain Ramp Kit (all needed ramps)	$33.00	1	$33.00
Chain Wheel Support, right (1980-89)	$68.10	1	$68.10
Chain Wheel Support, left (1980-89)	$68.10	1	$68.10
1965-89 911 OEM Oil Return Tube	$9.10	4	$36.40
Alternator or Air Pump Belt	$4.95	1	$4.95
TOOLS:			
Heavy Duty Engine Holding Fixture, P201	$214.95	1	$214.95
Flywheel Lock. This flywheel lock is for the engine yoke only.	$27.40	1	$27.40
Allen Head Nut Removal Tool (10mm)	$31.30	1	$31.30
Allen Heat Exchanger Nut Removal Tool (8mm)	$20.30	1	$20.30
Clutch Alignment Tool, 911 (1972-98)	$8.80	1	$8.80
12-Point/12mm Flywheel Socket	$31.00	1	$31.00
Dial Gauge Holder, Z Block	$34.10	1	$34.10
Cam Socket, with 1/2 Drive	$38.95	1	$38.95
46mm Crows Foot, 1/2 Cap Drive	$78.50	1	$78.50
Chain Tensioner Clamping Tool	$17.60	1	$17.60
		Total:	$2,872.13

made in this book was a good step toward saving you the $2,500 in assembly costs that most mechanics will charge. However, you will still need to have all the machine work properly performed, and you will have to replace the parts that are worn out on your engine. The basic estimate that I use for a 911 rebuild is about $8,000 if you have a mechanic rebuild it, or about $6,000 if you do it yourself.

Don't believe me? Many people don't when I tell them that figure. See the nearby tables for a breakdown of the machining costs and the parts using actual invoices for the engine rebuilt for this particular book. It's a 1974 911 S engine rebuilt to a completely stock configuration. The engine had pulled head studs (pulled Time-Serts) and also had piston/cylinder/head damage from an exhaust leak at the head-to-cylinder interface. The engine needed new pistons and cylinders, and needed two intake valves and one exhaust valve. This engine already had the Carrera pressure-fed chain tensioners installed, so it did not require the purchase of the upgrade kit.

REBUILD YOURSELF?

Ok, so you've now gone through the previous section, and you've unfortunately determined that your 911 engine would benefit from a rebuild. The question you're now asking is, "can I do it?" For most people, the answer is yes. You will need a few special tools, a bunch of hours, and a lot of careful, meticulous planning, but the rebuild process is indeed one that the average weekend mechanic can perform in his garage. The most difficult part is finding all of the hints, tips, and clues that you need—and you already solved that problem when you purchased this book.

You will, however, need a fair amount of patience, and meticulous attention to detail. The 911 engine is a precise machine, and very unforgiving of sloppy work. It has unique

Machine shop costs

Invoice from Competition Engineering

Qty	Labor	Unit Price	Total
1	Inspect & Evaluate 1974 Crank Case	$50.00	$50.00
1	Standard Cut Linebore	$495.00	$495.00
1	Install Case Savers–Case had old Time-Certs	$350.00	$350.00
1	Oil system bypass modification	$130.00	$130.00
1	Spot-face through bolt holes	$145.00	$145.00
1	Flush & test piston squirters	$50.00	$50.00
3	Repair damaged motor mount threads	$15.00	$45.00
1	Inspect & Evaluate 2.7-liter Heads (1X junk)	$50.00	$50.00
12	R&R Valve Guides	$16.50	$198.00
1	Complete Valve Job	$350.00	$350.00
6	Resurface heads–.25mm	$40.00	$240.00
2	Install Exhaust Studs	$5.00	$10.00
1	Inspect & Evaluate 911 2.7-liter crankshaft–std./std.	$35.00	$35.00
1	Polish & Clean Crankshaft	$110.00	$110.00
6	Recondition & resize rods	$45.00	$270.00
12	Recondition rocker arms w/bushings	$19.00	$228.00
1	Balance engine	$300.00	$300.00

Qty	Parts (from machine shop)	Unit Price	Total
1	Set of Perimeter inserts	$23.00	$23.00
29	10x1.5 Case-Saver inserts	$1.00	$29.00
12	Rocker arm bushings	$3.25	$39.00
2	Exhaust studs	$2.00	$4.00
12	Valve guides	$5.50	$66.00
1	Misc Chemicals	$15.00	$15.00
12	Viton valve stem seals	$2.25	$27.00
6	Connecting rod bushings	$5.25	$31.50
		Total:	$3,290.50
2	Camshafts Reconditioned (Web Cam)		$335.00

Projects for Your Porsche 911. In addition, any special tools that you need will be documented in this book, along with good sources to purchase them from.

It takes a good mechanic about 40 hours to rebuild a 911 engine. Count on it taking you at least twice as much if you've never done it before. Doing all of the labor yourself will save you anywhere from $2,000 to $4,000 in labor costs. Buying the parts from places other than your mechanic will also save you money, as shops have a tendency to charge the suggested list price for most parts. Pelican Parts (www.pelicanparts.com) has an excellent resource catalog for finding all of the parts and tools referenced in this book. In addition, rebuilding your own engine will give you an unparalleled sense of pride knowing that you completed this difficult task yourself. I have designed this book with the same easy-to-follow formula as the *101 Projects* book. Every step of the process is covered here—you shouldn't have any problems or questions.

Okay, so what if you're still not up to the task? Not a problem, as many people just don't have the time, the garage space, or the tools to complete a full rebuild. This book will also tell you what you need to know about having a 911 engine rebuilt by a professional. Keeping you informed and armed

design features not found in conventional engines. Small errors in assembly can result in complete destruction of the engine, or at best, messy oil leaks. As the rebuilder, you must be willing to follow directions exactly, take your time, double check everything, and pay attention to details. There are critical procedures (setting valve timing, sealing case halves) not found in other engines. You must also be willing to spend the money to purchase the proper tools and parts for rebuilding your engine. Rebuilding a 911 engine with substandard or worn-out parts will only result in a poor running or leaky engine.

To rebuild your engine, you will need an appropriate garage and a decent set of tools. For more information on the basic tool sets I recommend, please see my other book, *101*

with the right questions to ask will ensure that you pick the proper mechanic to work on your engine. Read through the chapters and ask the rebuilder you're considering the difficult questions. Has he rebuilt other air-cooled engines, and particularly 911 engines? How many? Can you get references so that you can speak to other customers? If the shop you're considering doesn't know the answers to basic 911 engine questions, you should question their ability to adequately perform the rebuild for you. What is the agreed upon price? It's very difficult for someone to give you fixed pricing for an engine rebuild without opening up the case. Be wary of people who quote you costs when they don't know exactly what is wrong with the engine. Most of the time, this number will be low, and there will be many, many additional costs involved.

1-8 *Do it yourself, or have your mechanic rebuild it? It's all about who you are, your personality, the garage space you have, and also your time. Saving money is also a huge benefit, as you can lop about 40 to 50 hours of your mechanic's labor right off of the bill. You'll still need to purchase new replacement parts, but you can effectively cut your rebuild cost in half or more. It really takes no special talent to rebuild a 911 engine—all you need is the right information, which I've provided for you in this book.*

Expensive parts like pistons and cylinders ($3,000 cost for a 3.0-liter engine) can sometimes be reused, yet often need to be replaced. It's really impossible to tell until you're inside the case looking at the parts. A shop familiar with 911 engines will typically need to tear into it, and then give you a price quote based on what it has learned by examining your parts.

Beware of bargain-basement rebuilders. With 911 engines, you really do get what you pay for. It's rare that the lowest-price rebuilder is the best. The engine may work fine when you get it back, but it may leak oil, may smoke, or have some other small problem with it. It's very difficult to go back to a shop to get small problems corrected. Also make sure that you check with your local Better Business Bureau if you are unsure about a particular shop. The electronic bulletin board at Pelican Parts (http://forums.pelicanparts.com) is a great place to ask fellow 911 owners about recommendations on engine rebuilders.

One option you might want to consider is removing the engine yourself, taking it to the machine shop, and then having an expert assemble it. This will save you some time, and also keep the total costs for the entire project down. You don't need to pay an expert to perform the relatively simple task of lowering the engine and tearing down the fuel injection and accessories of the engine. Besides dropping the engine on your foot, there really isn't too much damage that you can do!

Another important note to make is to beware of companies offering complete "rebuild packages" that contain "all the parts that you need to rebuild your engine." When you're rebuilding your engine, there's no telling what you'll need (except for the parts on my must-replace list). Packages that claim to contain ALL the parts that you need typically contain parts that you might not need, and are lacking many parts that you do need. It's better to purchase smaller kits that you can mix and match as necessary. Check out the official website for this book at http://www.101projects.com (also the official site for the *101 Projects* book) for more details on where to get exactly the parts that you need to rebuild your 911 engine.

CHAPTER 2

ENGINE TEARDOWN

The first step in rebuilding your 911 engine is, of course, to remove it from the car. If you've ever worked on big American muscle cars before, then you might have to adjust your thinking to the German Porsche way. The engine is installed from underneath the car—a practice that at first glance sounds difficult, but in reality simplifies a lot of the tasks. The engine can be "dropped" out of the car using normal weekend mechanic's tools, and can even be performed single-handedly—although this is not recommended if this is your first time dropping a Porsche engine.

I had originally planned to include a lengthy chapter on removing the engine from your 911, but instead, I decided to devote this book to more technical information on the rebuild process. For information on dropping your engine, you can reference my other book, *101 Projects for Your Porsche 911*, or you can look at the original engine removal chapter and photos on this book's official website: www.101projects.com.

Okay, by the time that you get to this step, the engine should be out of the car, sitting on your furniture cart, and you will probably be covered in grease! Resisting the urge to take a shower, you should now take the effort to get the engine lifted on to your engine stand. Doing so requires a lot of effort, and will also make you very greasy again, so I recommend doing it right away.

2-1 After you have your engine out of your car, you will want to make sure that you place it on an engine stand. It's very important that you use an engine stand yoke (the part that attaches to the engine) that is specifically made for a Porsche engine. Some yokes are manufactured for VW engines, and will fit as well, but may not be able to support all of the extra weight of a 911 engine. Using the universal engine mount that comes with your engine stand is not a wise idea, as you can damage or tweak the case if you don't mount the engine correctly. With an engine weighing 400 to 500 lbs., you don't really want to take too many chances. Make sure that the engine yoke is securely fastened to the engine case studs, and always attach it to the right side of the engine, on the same side as the oil cooler.

Engine Stand

You can use a plain vanilla engine stand that you can purchase at any local auto parts store. However, you want to make sure that you use the special 911 engine-mount adapter yoke, shown in Figure 2-1. This adapter attaches where the transmission normally mounts, and holds the engine securely to the engine stand. Although the bolt pattern may be the same, I don't recommend using VW engine stand yokes—get one specifically made for the 911. The problem with the VW yokes is that they are not constructed to hold the extra weight of the 911 engine. Make sure that the yoke you purchase has five spokes holding onto the fixture ring, and is specifically rated to hold a minimum of 800 pounds. The typical 911 engine with fuel injection and exhaust weighs in at about 350 to 450 pounds, but you want that extra margin just to be safe. Keep in mind that the 911 Turbo engines will weigh quite a few pounds more with all their extra fuel injection and exhaust components.

Don't attempt to use the standard universal engine mount fixture that comes with most engine stands—this can be dangerous and cause damage to your engine case as well.

Plastic Bags

A few more important items that you need are four boxes of Ziploc freezer storage bags and some permanent markers. I like the 1-quart and the 1-gallon sizes. These bags are made out of thicker plastic, they won't tear or leak, and you can easily write descriptions on the white portion of the bag with a permanent marker. Also very useful are a few cupcake baking trays—they make excellent holding trays for small parts and hardware. It's very important to keep all your hardware and parts together, even if you're not going to be reusing some nuts and bolts. With the excitement of disassembling the engine, it's very easy to mix various mounting hardware together, making it a difficult process to sort out the mess later on. Keep everything in the Ziploc bags, and make sure that you have plenty of them on hand (100 or so) to avoid accidentally mixing up parts and hardware. Organize your parts by major assembly group (e.g., tin, injection, heads, pistons/cylinders) on shelves or stored neatly in big cardboard boxes.

Camera

An often overlooked tool is a camera. I recommend you take pictures of the entire disassembly process (particularly the fuel injection and vacuum hoses), so you can easily figure out where everything goes when it's time to re-assemble. This doesn't dismiss you from actually labeling each hose and wire. This is a step where you can't be too redundant. For example, in the case of the 911 SC, the plug connection for the cold start valve and air flow sensor are the same color and there is no easy way to tell them apart.

There are no books available that cover every conceivable fuel injection setup, and yours may be slightly different from ones used in other years. If your fuel injection was working well when you removed your engine, then you are probably going to want to put it back exactly the way it was originally configured.

I prefer digital cameras because you can shoot a virtually unlimited number of photos and be sure that you have a record of everything important. Digital cameras and Polaroids are also great because they let you know instantly if the picture that you took is good enough to tell you everything you need to know in the re-assembly phase. Film cameras can work too, but there is some risk that you will move on not knowing if you got a clear photo.

The most important parts to photograph are the intake systems and the exhaust (especially if you have a Turbo). These systems varied significantly over the years, and I don't have the room in this book to cover the reassembly procedures for all of these systems. Take careful notes—you will be relying on them later on.

Oil Pans

Even though you have emptied the engine of all its oil by this time, there will most certainly be some left in the sump, chain housings, and oil cooler. It's a smart idea to get a large oil drip pan that you can place under the engine stand to catch any excess that may seep out of the engine while you are disassembling it. Also have a few smaller coffee cans or round pans handy to catch specific drips that find their way outside of your large oil drip pan.

MOUNTING THE ENGINE

If you haven't already done so, disconnect the transmission from the engine case. Be aware that the transmission weighs about 80 to 175 pounds, depending upon which model you have, and can be difficult to remove from the engine without the help of a second person.

Once you have the transmission disconnected, remove the two pieces of sheet metal that are located on either side of the flywheel and clutch. They interfere with the engine stand adapter. I also recommend removing the rear and side sheet metal pieces, which have a tendency to get in the way when you are lifting the engine onto the engine stand.

Attaching the engine stand adapter yoke to the crankcase is an important process. The engine yoke fastens to the two studs that normally hold the transmission on either the left or right side of the case. At first, this may seem counterintuitive, but attaching the adapter yoke in this manner means that it attaches to only one half of the case—necessary for disassembling the block later on. The yoke should be strong enough to support the engine from any angle, allowing you to rotate the engine upside down or 360 degrees while you are working on it.

The studs that mount the transmission to the engine case are typically too long for the engine stand adapter yoke, so you need to fit some spacers in between the mounting nuts and the yoke. I prefer to use larger nuts that will simply act as washers or spacers. Place the adapter yoke on the right side of the engine—the side that the oil cooler is located on. The oil pump is mounted to this side of the case, making it easier to lift off and remove the opposite side of the case when the time comes to separate the two halves. Tighten down the nuts on the studs to about 48 Nm (35 ft-lbs.). (This is the torque specification for the engine to transmission nuts.) You certainly don't want this to be a loose connection when you have a 450-pound engine sitting on the stand.

Now comes the difficult part. Since it takes at least three strong men to lift the engine onto the engine stand, you should start buddying up to your neighbors a week or so in advance. The only small trick that I can suggest for helping to lift the motor is to jack it up as high as you can before you lift it. Be sure it's secure on the jack as you do this. Also make sure that the floor around the engine is dry and not slippery and that you wear boots and gloves. If something starts to slip, let go and get out of the way! It's far easier to replace a 911 engine than it is to replace a foot (even if it's your neighbor's foot). If you can't muster at least three

2-2 Shown here is the 2.7-liter engine that occupies the starring role in this book. The 2.7-liter engine is one of the more complicated 911 engine rebuilds, as there are many modifications and assembly concerns that need to be heeded to have a good-running motor free of oil leaks. This particular motor is a genuine 911 engine that had been transplanted into a 914. Note that the heat exchangers have been replaced with 914-6 headers, and the front engine mount bar is significantly shorter. Other minor differences include the right-angle bend in the oil line that is attached to the oil cooler, an early 911 flywheel, the 914-6 engine mount and some minor modifications to the fuel injection connectors. This particular engine lost a fan belt and overheated, contributing to pulled Time-Serts and head studs.

strong people willing to pick up a greasy motor, you can always rent or borrow an engine hoist. But be careful. I've had bad luck with engine hoists slipping at the wrong time.

The engine should be firmly mounted on the engine stand, as is shown in Figure 2-2. Now would be a good time to place a drip pan or large piece of cardboard under the engine to catch any oil that may leak out while you're disassembling it.

FUEL INJECTION & EXHAUST REMOVAL

Once you have the engine securely mounted on your engine stand, you can start the disassembly process. The first thing to remove is the fuel injection. On the earlier cars with carburetors, this is an easy process. Because of their linkages and fuel lines, Mechanical Fuel Injection (MFI) cars are a bit more difficult. Continuous Injection System (CIS) and Motronic engine management systems can usually be easily removed as one piece. It's a wise idea to keep all of your fuel injection components together and assembled—especially if the fuel system was working properly before the rebuild.

One tip that I would like to reiterate here is that you should take many, many pictures of the disassembly process. Digital cameras are great here, as they afford you the opportunity to take many pictures of items that might not seem of interest now, but can be used as a most useful reference later on. Photograph the wiring, the fuel lines, and basically where everything goes. You will be amazed at how little you remember when you try to put everything back together several months down the road.

The CIS fuel injection can easily be removed as a single unit. Simply remove all the nuts that hold the intake manifolds to the heads (Figure 2-3), and the additional damper

bracket at the front of the engine near the accelerator linkage mount. With a little bit of coaxing, the entire assembly should simply lift off of the engine. Make sure that no wires get in the way, and also be sure that you disconnect all electrical connectors (Figure 2-4). While you have the fuel injection out and exposed (Figure 2-5), I recommend that you freshen up and clean the system. Replace the CIS intake manifold hoses. If you have carburetors, rebuild them. For more information on fuel injection overhaul

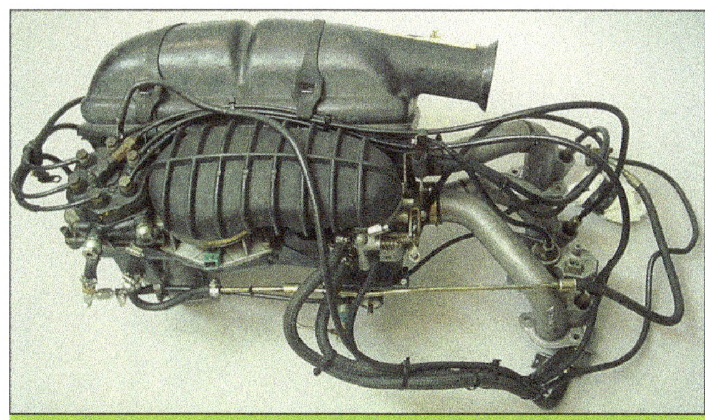

projects, see the book, *101 Projects for Your Porsche 911*. One good tip is to not take anything apart that doesn't have to come apart—at least until you're ready to work on that part of the system.

Exhaust

After you've removed the fuel injection (Figure 2-6), you can now remove the exhaust. Carefully rotate the engine 180 degrees on your engine stand and you will have access to the bottom of the heads. One of the reasons you want to have removed the fuel injection before you remove the exhaust is to minimize spilling any fuel that might still be trapped in the system. The first step is to disconnect the muffler straps and remove the muffler. This will take some of the load off of the exhaust studs.

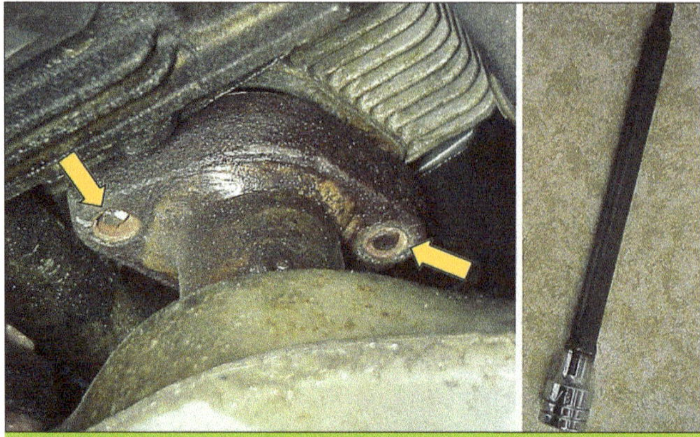
2-7 *Shown here are the exhaust studs that screw into the head, and the tool that is required to remove the barrel nuts that attach to them. In this particular picture, the studs have become brittle and tempered from heating and cooling, and have broken off during an effort to remove the heat exchangers. If you are tearing apart the engine, this is not a terribly big problem, as you can always remove the broken studs later on. However, if this happens with the engine in the car, then you're in trouble, as you will have to find some alternative means to remove the studs from the heads. (See Project 95 in* 101 Projects for Your Porsche 911.*)*

which has a tendency to temper the metal. This makes them very brittle and prone to breaking when you try to remove them (Figure 2-7). It is not abnormal to break one or two studs when you remove the exhaust on an older 911. Using an oxy-acetylene torch to heat up the nuts on the exhaust studs may help the removal process as well.

Two special tools can simplify the removal of the exhaust nuts. The first tool is a long 8mm Allen-head driver that attaches to your standard 3/8-inch socket. This tool allows you to remove the six barrel nuts through the special access holes in the heat exchangers. You also may need

2-6 *Here is a shot of the engine without the fuel injection installed. Remaining on the top of the motor are the fan shroud, accelerator linkage, and the electrical harness. If you choose to do so, you can remove the fuel injection, the fan shroud, alternator, fan housing, and fan as a single unit. I would recommend this only if you are planning on placing the fuel injection system back on the motor without any cleaning or modifications.*

Removing the heat exchangers is a tricky process. Very often, the exhaust nuts will be severely rusted and difficult to remove. If they are indeed rusted and stuck, I recommend soaking them in a penetrant oil like Liquid Wrench overnight to try to loosen them up. Penetrant oil is not one of those things that you can rush—make sure that you let the nuts sit overnight. An additional problem is that these studs are heated and cooled many times over their life,

2-8 *Shown in this picture is the 911 engine with its exhaust completely removed. You can see that one or two of the exhaust studs have screwed out (but did not break off) of the heads. This is not a problem, as you will replace them later on. You will also notice that one of the oil return tubes has been replaced with a collapsible type—a sign that someone attempted to stop an oil return tube leak. The big dent in one of the tubes is also a bad sign, as it restricts the flow of oil back to the engine.*

an angled 12mm or 13mm wrench to reach the other six exhaust nuts, although sometimes you can get by with some semi-standard wrenches in your toolbox. Swivel sockets do come in handy for this task.

As an alternative to tearing it down one piece at a time, you can remove the entire system as a single unit. This will probably require the help of another person to lift and maneuver it off of the engine. Keep in mind that over the 25-plus year lifespan of the 911 engine, there were many different exhaust systems, so you will have to use a little bit of common sense when figuring out what to disconnect. For 911 Turbo owners, removing both the fuel injection and the exhaust can take an afternoon. These owners, especially, should photograph the setup of their exhaust system before and during the disassembly process. The 911 engine with the exhaust removed is shown in Figure 2-8.

FAN, SHROUD, AND ACCESSORY REMOVAL

At this point, your 911 engine will be looking slightly naked without the exhaust and fuel injection. For the remainder of the disassembly process, I will detail the steps and proper order for removing items from the engine. Many items can be removed at different stages of the process; however, there are a few items that need to be removed before further disassembly. In general, if you follow the steps laid out here, you shouldn't have any problems.

Engine Wiring Harnesses

The next step is to disconnect and remove all of the wiring from your engine. If you haven't already done so, unplug the spark plug wires from their respective plugs. It's also a great time to remove the spark plugs from the engine, because it makes it easier to rotate the engine when they are removed. Then disconnect the distributor cap. I usually remove the entire cap, leaving the wires attached, so that it makes it easier to reconnect everything later on (Figure 2-9). Unbolt the coil from the side of the fan housing. Carefully label all of the wires that you are disconnecting. Double check that you disconnected all of the sensors located on the chain housing covers, the temperature sender near the lower right of the fan, and the oil pressure sensor. Make sure that every electrical connection is disconnected, except for the large part of the harness that goes through the fiberglass fan shroud and connects to the alternator behind the fan.

2-9 To remove the entire electrical harness, you need to remove all of the spark plug wires from the spark plugs (white arrow), the distributor cap from the distributor (green arrow), all electrical connections (red arrow), and the coil from the fan housing (yellow arrow). Make sure that you don't twist or tweak the wiring harness, as the old copper wiring can become stiff and brittle with age.

A note of caution here. With engines that are 10 to 20 years old or more, there is a tendency for the wiring in the engine compartment to become "work hardened." The repeated heating and cooling of the copper wire within the engine compartment can cause the wires to loose their malleability and become increasingly brittle. When handling your wiring harness, it is important that you don't bend any of the wires or connections at sharp angles. Be very careful

2-10 Begin by removing the pulley using the Porsche pulley tool (always included in the 911 factory toolkit that should have come with the car). Use a 24mm non-deep socket to remove the nut. The fan-housing strap is held on with either one or two bolts that need to be loosened (yellow arrows). The strap is the only hardware attaching the fan to the top of the engine case. Once the strap is loosened, you will be able to tip the fan backward to access the connections to the alternator.

handling the harness, and store it in a large box, where it won't get bent or tangled. Careful inspection of the wiring harness is important to any rebuild process, but we'll cover more of that in the reassembly stage.

Fan & Shroud

Once the wiring is free, it's time to remove the fiberglass fan shroud. Start by removing the left and right air funnel plates on either side of the fan. These are attached to the shroud with tapered screws and mounted to the case with standard machine screws. Now remove the fan belt and the pulley (Figure 2-10). The pulley-half (as it is called) is held on with a 22mm nut. Using the factory tool for holding the pulley, loosen up the nut. Do not use a screwdriver stuck in the fan blades to hold the fan steady. The fan is a somewhat fragile magnesium casting, and you can easily break blades off of it. (A new fan is about $250.) If you have an impact wrench, you can simply zap the nut off as well. Make sure that you keep the nut, pulley-half, retainer piece, and any shims together—it can be difficult to find replacements for some of these parts.

Alternator

With the fan belt disconnected, loosen and disconnect the one or two bolts that strap the fan and housing down to the case. The fan will be loose once these are disconnected. There is a nut and a bolt that has to be removed from the top of the fan housing. On a 911SC there is a separate plate that mounts the coil, and a bolt on the other side of the fan housing that also holds a retainer for the heater

hose. Carefully rock the fan backward and you will be able to see the air guide that is attached to the rear of the alternator. Six 10mm nuts secure the air guide. Remove them, and you should be able to see the connections to the alternator. I would suggest taking a picture of these connections, as labels have a tendency to come off as the wires are pulled through the shroud opening when you remove the harness (Figure 2-11). Be sure to remove the ground strap that connects the alternator to the case.

Carefully label the wires, then disconnect them and pull the harness through the back of the shroud. You will now be able to remove the wiring harness from the engine, and place it in the big box you set aside for it. At this point the fan housing will be loose and can be easily removed.

Now, move to the shroud and remove all of the machine screws (10mm socket) that attach it to the engine. Also remove the plastic piece that covers the oil cooler. Then, disconnect and remove the accelerator linkage mount from the top of the engine (Figure 2-12). You will now be able to lift the shroud off of the engine. There is a support that fits underneath the accelerator linkage mount. Make sure that you grab this piece (it is held in by the bolt or stud that secures the linkage mount) and place it with the linkage mount and its hardware. The long metal strip that holds on the fan can be fed through the openings in the case and removed. Try not to bend it any more than you have to, as new ones are somewhat expensive (about $35).

An alternative method that many veteran engine builders use is to simply remove the fuel injection, fan, housing, fan shroud, and wiring harness as one huge assembly. You can do this by removing the fan shroud mounting screws, the fan housing strap, the accelerator linkage mount, and the other small accessories that get in the way. Removing everything at once is a good idea if you are simply going to bolt it back on again without replacing or cleaning any of the fuel injection parts.

2-13 *Congratulations, you now have the engine down to what is called the long block. All accessories, fuel injection, and other support components have been removed, and all you have left is the main core engine. The yellow arrow shows the accelerator linkage standoff, which is loose now that the accelerator linkage mount has been removed. Simply grab it off of the top of the engine and make sure that you keep it with the rest of the linkage assembly pieces.*

Before going on to the next step, you probably want to remove the engine mount bar. Although very useful as a handle to help rotate the engine, it will get in the way when you remove the front chain housing covers. The engine mount bar is bolted to the rear of the engine and attached with four large nuts. The bare engine should resemble Figure 2-13 at this time.

2-14 *Four 10mm nuts hold the crankcase breather cover to the top of the engine. It is located toward the front of the engine and straddles the engine case parting line. A leaky gasket, or broken hose at the front of the engine, can create a messy, hard-to-find oil leak.*

CAMSHAFT HOUSING, HEAD, PISTON & CYLINDER REMOVAL

At this point, you will be staring at the long block—basically the core engine without any of the accessories. Now comes the interesting part, where we actually tear into the engine. It's important during this process to pay careful attention to the engine as you take it apart. Look at the components—see which ones are wearing and try to determine why. Record your observations with a notepad, and take plenty of pictures.

Start on the top of the engine by removing the crankcase breather cover, as shown in Figure 2-14. Then remove the oil pressure switch from the front of the engine, and the pressure sensor from the rear of the engine (Figure 2-15). Now, remove the oil thermostat by removing the two nuts that hold it to the case, and gently pry it up using a large screwdriver (Figure 2-16). The top of the thermostat has a lip on it for just this purpose, so you should be able to pry it out of the case. Your workbench should be neatly organized at this

2-15 *Remove the oil pressure sending unit, located at the rear of the engine. Make sure that you use a wrench on the adapter fitting of the sending unit. Don't tweak the case of the unit, as these have a tendency to fail and leak.*

2-16 *After you remove the two small 10mm nuts that attach it to the engine case, the thermostat can be easily pried from its hole. Use a large screwdriver to get underneath the lip of the thermostat and gently pry upward. The thermostat usually requires some wriggling to get it out of its mounting hole in the case. Often, the o-ring grips the side of the case, and creates some resistance.*

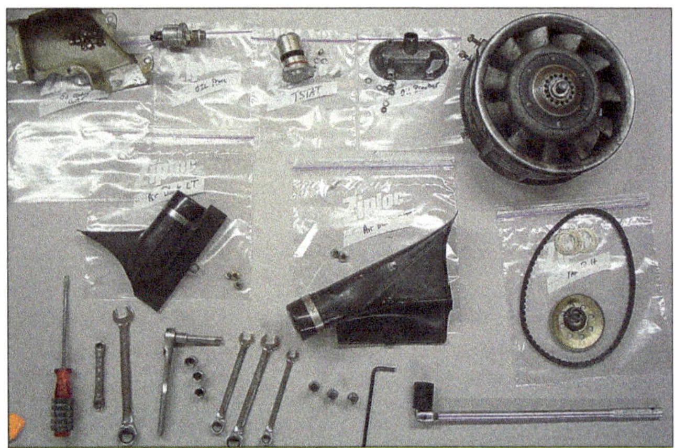

2-17 Here's what the workbench next to your engine should look like at this point. Keep your tools organized and all the parts, accessories, and mounting hardware for everything that you've removed in one place with labeled Ziploc bags. There is no such thing as being too organized, as it is way too easy to remove a piece from the engine and then simply forget where it goes, or what the mounting hardware looks like.

2-18 The oil cooler is mounted with four 13mm nuts (studs shown with green arrows). Remove them and the cooler will simply pull off of the engine case. Beware that a little bit of oil may leak out from the holes in the case. The oil cooler may have a significant amount of oil left inside of it as well, so make sure you quickly place it inside a plastic bag.

2-19 Rotate the engine so that the valve covers are pointing up toward the ceiling. We're now ready to start the removal of the valve covers and the entire camshaft housings. It's easiest to work on the engine in this configuration, and easy enough to rotate it so that you can work at this angle.

2-20 Remove the upper valve cover and gently peel off the gasket underneath. Repeat the process for the lower valve covers, making sure that excess oil doesn't leak out onto your garage floor. Don't worry about tearing the gaskets, as you will be installing new ones when you reassemble your engine.

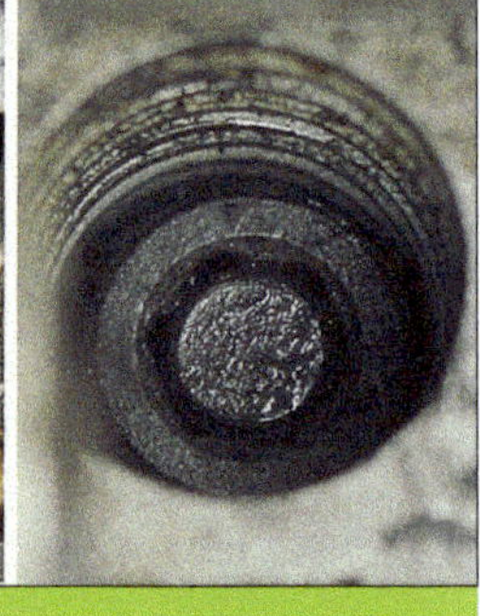

2-21 The infamous head stud problem. Opening up your valve covers and finding a loose barrel nut like the one shown in this photo (red arrow) is not a good sign. This usually means that there is a corresponding pulled or broken head stud to accompany the loose nut. In the photo on the right, you can see the danger in overtightening your head studs. This stud has pulled out so far that it is impossible to get an Allen wrench inside the barrel nut. In most cases, this nut would be loose regardless; but if it's tight, it can be very difficult to remove.

time, and the parts that you are removing should be sorted and ready to be bagged (Figure 2-17).

Four nuts are all that secure the oil cooler—it slides right off after they are removed (Figure 2-18). Now, rotate the engine slightly so that the right side is up in the air, as shown in Figure 2-19. Now remove the valve covers. Use a 13mm socket to zip these off. Valve cover gasket kits typically come with new hardware, so don't be too concerned about saving the nuts and washers. Remove the upper and lower covers, and the valve cover gaskets located underneath the covers (Figure 2-20). At this time, you'll see any head stud problems like the ones discussed in Chapter 1 (Figure 2-21).

will see when you remove it, the bolt is bored out in the center in order to allow oil to flow through it. Remove the oil pressure sensor that is attached to the end of the oil line that is attached to the case. Make sure that you remove the sensor by placing a wrench on the bottom adapter piece and not by clamping its housing. The housings can become stressed and leak if they are removed improperly.

Now remove the front chain housing cover. Several 10mm nuts hold this onto the chain housing. If you have a very early 911 with a mechanical fuel pump, you will need to

2-22 *Turn your attention to the front cam oil lines. Disconnect the oil lines from their connection points as shown by the white arrows. Place the lines in a plastic bag for use on reassembly. You will want to reuse the metal lines if you have the Carrera pressure-fed chain tensioners. The combination rubber/metal oil lines should not be reused.*

Turn your attention now to the cam oil line towards the rear of the engine. These lines (one on each side) may look slightly different depending upon whether your car has the Carrera chain tensioner upgrade option installed. The right-side cam oil line is attached at two points (three for the Carrera upgrade). Remove the line by loosening up the "hollow" bolt that is attached to the rear of the camshaft housing, the bolt that attaches the line to the case, and the hollow bolt that also attaches the line to the chain tensioner, if you have the Carrera chain tensioners installed (Figure 2-22). As you

2-24 *You need to remove the distributor from the left side of the engine before you can remove the left cam oil line. Simply remove the single nut that holds on the distributor and lift it out of its mount in the case. Place the distributor in a plastic bag for safe keeping. Once the distributor is removed, you will be able to easily access the point where the left cam oil line is attached to the engine case (yellow arrow).*

remove the pump before you remove the timing chain covers. Removing the chain housing cover reveals the chain, tensioner, camshaft sprockets, and the idler arms (Figure 2-23).

Flip the engine over so that the left side now is pointed up toward you. Be careful, as there may be some excess oil trapped in the chain housings that will leak out when you turn the motor over. Loosen up and remove the nut that secures the distributor. Gently pull the distributor out of its hole in the engine case (Figure 2-24). As you did with the right side, remove the cam oil line, the valve covers, and the left-side chain housing. You can now look inside the chain housings of your engine, as shown in Figure 2-25.

Clutch

Now is a good time to remove the pressure plate. Using a 13mm socket, remove each of the pressure plate bolts. Be careful not to drop the pressure

2-23 *After you remove the cam oil lines, you can then remove the front chain housing cover. This affords us a good look into the internals of the engine near the timing chain components. Shown in this photo are the chain (blue arrow), the chain tensioner (white arrow), the camshaft (orange arrow) and camshaft sprocket (green arrow), the idler arms (red arrow), and a chain ramp (yellow arrow).*

2-25 *Here is the front shot of the 911 engine as it should look now—with both the front timing chain covers and valve covers removed. You can see firsthand how the overhead cam and timing chain system of the 911 engine works. If you're curious, rotate the engine using a socket placed on the pulley nut and watch how the crankshaft, timing chain, camshafts, and rockers all move in conjunction with each other.*

2-26 *Once the pressure plate bolts are removed, the plate itself falls right off of the flywheel. Make sure that you catch it, as it has a tendency to fall on your foot if you're not aware of it. You shouldn't need to lock the flywheel to keep the plate from spinning when you loosen the nuts. Shown here is an early 911 flywheel, which has the outer ring gear integrated as part of the flywheel (yellow arrow). Later model engines will have a separate ring gear.*

2-27 *The flywheel can be locked using a conventional flywheel lock that fits between the engine stand and the flywheel teeth, or you can make your own. This flywheel lock consists of a piece of metal with two slots in it. The lock attaches to the flywheel and then to one of the studs in the case. There is a little bit of backlash in the lock, but it doesn't matter for our purposes.*

plate on your foot, as it has a tendency to fall out when you release the last bolt. The clutch disc should drop out with the pressure plate (Figure 2-26). You can use a commercially available flywheel lock tool, or you can simply make your own. A flat piece of steel with two large holes in it will suffice. Use one of the pressure plate bolts to hold the lock to the flywheel, while you wrap it around one of the engine studs, as shown in Figure 2-27. This configuration will keep the flywheel from turning. Using the flat-steel flywheel lock allows you to remove both the pressure plate and ring gear and place them out of the way. You can also use the flywheel lock that integrates with your engine yoke.

Camshafts

The next part is perhaps the trickiest and most difficult part of the engine disassembly process. Rotate the engine so that it's facing in its normal orientation (top of the engine facing up). Make sure that you lock the engine holding fixture into the engine stand. The large nut that fastens the timing chain sprocket to the camshaft needs to be loosened in order to remove the camshaft. On pre-1980 911s, removal of the camshafts requires the use of two special tools: a Porsche camshaft holder tool (P202) and a 46mm crowfoot wrench. Both tools are absolutely necessary to remove the cams—don't try to get around using them. So much force will be required to remove the large 46mm nut that you will probably need an assistant, and even then it might be difficult.

In the early 1980s, Porsche updated the hardware used to attach the camshaft to the engine. The newer style hardware requires the Porsche tool 9191 rather than the original P202. The Porsche tool 9191 fits over the cam sprocket and holds it using the small outer holes that are drilled into the sprocket. A 19mm bolt in the center of the cam is all that needs to be loosened to remove the camshaft, and the crowfoot wrench is no longer required. As with the earlier models, it is nearly impossible to remove the camshaft without the use of the P9191 tool. Porsche documentation seems to contradict itself on exactly when this change took place. Although the change in camshafts was supposed to take place in 1980, the 1982 911 SC engine I rebuilt for the book *101 Projects for Your Porsche 911* has the old-style retaining nut installed. The important thing to note here is to check your camshaft before you spend your hard-earned money on the wrong tool.

Again, it is important that you obtain these tools—trust me, it's practically impossible to remove the retaining nut without them. Even with the tools, loosening and removing this nut is a very difficult job. After you complete this task, you will probably agree that there is no other practical method.

At this point, you want to check that the flywheel lock is attached to the engine and holding the crankshaft secure. As a precaution, use a 13mm wrench to loosen each valve adjustment lock nut and back off each valve adjustment

screw as far as you can go. Backing off this screw will minimize the likelihood of the valves hitting the tops of the pistons when you are rotating the crankshaft with the chains detached. Back the screw off so that the swivel foot on the end of the screw just touches the tip of the rocker. Loosening this screw beyond this point can force the swivel foot off the end of the rocker, damaging the adjustment screw.

Starting with the left side of the engine, attach the camshaft holding tool to the end of the camshaft and wrap the crowfoot wrench around the large 46mm nut. For post-1980 cars, insert the camshaft holding tool into the small holes in the camshaft sprocket and place a socket on the bolt in the center of the camshaft. While holding the camshaft steady, slowly apply force in a counterclockwise motion, as shown in Figure 2-28. The nut or bolt should gently break free and loosen. It is important to note that you shouldn't use the timing chain as a method of holding the sprocket steady. For one, the chain can stretch and possibly break, and you can also end up damaging some parts of your engine.

Tensioners & Housing

Once you have the nut or bolt loosened, you can remove it, the spring washer, the sprocket, and the toothed spacer piece that fits behind it. Be aware of the small dowel pin that goes between the sprocket and the toothed spacer—it will fall out when you remove the assembly. You can pluck it out in advance with the tip of a used spark plug. Now, repeat the entire process and remove the cam sprocket nut assembly from the right side of the engine. Once these are removed, you can disconnect both chain tensioners—only one nut holds it in place. The chain tensioner sprocket will easily slide off as well, once the tensioner is removed.

Behind the toothed sprocket is the cam thrust plate, also called the camshaft end cover. Using a small screwdriver, carefully pry out and remove the small woodruff key from the camshaft. After removing the three screws that attach the plate to the camshaft housing, you can pry the camshaft end cover out of the chain housing in order to remove the chain housing from the engine (Figure 2-29). When you remove the end cover, a number of shims will fall off of the camshaft. The o-ring between the plate and the housing will offer some resistance as you pull it out. These are important for the alignment of the camshaft sprockets, and you should keep track of how many shims were used on each side.

Now you can loosen the chain housing. Five nuts (one on top, two inside the housing, and two below) fasten the housing to the engine case. Remove these five nuts and tap the edge of the housing with a rubber mallet. The housing should now almost come off of its studs. You may have to remove the chain ramp to negotiate the chain so that you can remove the chain housing from the engine. The chain

2-29 *Once the chain tensioner, idler arm, sprocket, and associated hardware are removed, take a small screwdriver and gently pry the camshaft backing plate away from the back of the chain housing. The backing plate is stuck into the chain housing and has a large o-ring (blue arrow) that will offer some resistance.*

2-30 *With a small screwdriver, carefully pry up the bottom end of the oil return tube so that it no longer sticks inside of the engine case. If necessary, crimp and crush the oil return tubes, as this will loosen them up, making it easier to pull off the camshaft housings and heads. Don't worry about damaging the return tubes—they are on my list of recommended replacement parts.*

ramp simply snaps off of the two posts that it is attached to. Don't worry about breaking it—the chain ramps are on the list of must-replace parts. The steel locating sleeves that connect the case to the housings should stay in the case. If they don't, then your chain housing may just not have enough clearance to be removed. This is not a major problem, as you will just have to lift up the camshaft housing/head assembly before you can completely remove the chain housing.

Camshaft Housings/Heads

Removal of the camshaft housing/head assembly is relatively straightforward. Rotate the engine so that the camshaft housings are facing directly up to the ceiling (90-degrees clockwise if standing at the back of the engine). Using a long 10mm Allen-head tool, loosen up all of the head stud barrel nuts. Then reach down into the heads and pick each one out using a pair of 6-inch long tongs or tweezers or a magnetic pickup tool. Place the nuts and washers in a bowl of motor oil—this will prevent them from rusting. Place all of these nuts together in a plastic bag for use when reinstalling the heads. I also recommend that you unseat the oil return tubes from the engine case. You can do this by using a screwdriver wedged along the edge of the hole where the tubes enter the engine case as shown in Figure 2-30. The oil return tubes have a tendency to get stuck in the engine case and make the process of pulling off the camshaft housing/head assembly a bit more difficult. By twisting the oil return tubes and unseating them, you're basically just loosening them up so that they can be easily disconnected. Don't worry about destroying the oil return tubes—these are parts that I recommend you replace when rebuilding the engine.

Once all the nuts have been removed, you will be able to raise the camshaft housing/head assembly about 1 inch. This will give you adequate clearance to remove the chain housing if it's still attached to the engine (Figure 2-31).

Once you have the chain housing removed from the engine, you should be able to pull the entire camshaft housing/head assembly off of the engine. Just carefully lift it straight off. It may get slightly caught on some of the

2-31 *Lift the camshaft housing and head assembly off of the engine by about 1 inch. With this clearance, you will be able to remove the chain housing from the engine. With the chain housing out of the way, pull the entire camshaft housing/head assembly off of the engine and place it in a safe place off to the side.*

2-32 *While the engine is tilted up in the air, remove the bottom sump plate. Underneath the sump plate is a metal screen that covers the bottom of the engine and filters out debris so that it isn't sucked into the oil pump. In late 1983, Porsche began to use an oil pump with a built-in screen and thus used a case that doesn't have a removable sump plate.*

head studs—just jiggle it as you lift it off and it should come free. The whole assembly weighs about 20 to 25 pounds. When you lift the assembly off, the washers that were located under the barrel nuts will be loose. Capture all of them and place them in a plastic bag. Place it in a safe place off to the side—we'll disassemble the heads, rockers, and camshaft housings later on.

While you have the engine tilted at a 90-degree angle, it's a good time to remove the bottom oil sump plate and screen (Figure 2-32). Simply remove the eight nuts that hold it on, and the plate will slide right off. Visible without the plate in place is the bottom of the crank, and also the pickup tube for the oil pump.

After you've removed the left-side camshaft housing/head assembly, take some old half-inch drive sockets and use them as spacers on the cylinder head studs. Take three of the barrel nuts that you removed and place them on one cylinder head stud for each of the three cylinders that are now exposed. The reason for this is that you will be turning over the engine in the next step and, although unlikely, you want to make sure that your cylinders won't fall off of your engine when they are upside down, or get pushed out of the case when you are rotating the crankshaft. Fasten the barrel nuts onto the end of the head studs just tight enough so that they will keep the cylinder from moving away from the case. There is a special Porsche tool just for this purpose (P241); however, the method of using sockets as spacers works just as well.

Now rotate the engine on your engine stand 180 degrees so that the opposite side of the engine is facing upwards and repeat the procedure for removing the camshaft housings. Removing both sets of camshaft housings at this point will eliminate the chances of the valves hitting the tops of your pistons as you rotate the engine.

Cylinders

With both camshaft housings removed, you can now remove each of the cylinders (Figure 2-33). Begin by removing the engine cooling sheet metal that is located on each side of the cylinders. Small spring clips that span the tops of the cylinders secure the sheet metal. Simply unclip them and you can easily remove the four pieces of sheet metal. Later cars have an additional piece of cooling tin located on the upper side of the engine.

When you're ready to remove the cylinders, first label plastic bags with the numbers 1 through 6 so that you can make sure that you keep your pistons with their respective cylinders. Start with whichever piston is currently recessed lowest in its cylinder. Scribe the cyclinder number (1 through 6) onto a non-mating area on the top of the cylinder. Also scribe a tiny mark into the top of each piston. Using a soft rubber mallet, gently tap the sides of the cylinder away from the engine case. The cylinder should slide up easily over the pistons, as shown in Figure 2-34. If it gives you some difficulty, then alternating taps from each side will help lift it off of the case.

After the cylinder is free, place it in your Ziploc bag and put it in a safe spot. The inside of your engine is usually coated with oil, which prevents rusting of the cylinders. I have seen cylinders that have been taken out of

2-33 *This photo shows the 911 engine with camshaft housings and heads removed. Shown here is the bank of pistons and cylinders ready to be removed. Notice the amount of carbon buildup on the piston domes (orange arrow). This is quite normal for the 911 engine.*

2-34 *Cylinder removal is accomplished by simply pulling up on the cylinder while the piston is at its lowest point of travel. Rotate the crankshaft so that the piston reaches this point. Use a soft rubber mallet to loosen the cylinder if it resists your attempts to remove it.*

engines and carelessly left on a shelf to rust. Placing them in the plastic bag will minimize any corrosion while you're working on your engine rebuild. When labeling the bag, use the diagram in the introduction section to figure out exactly which cylinder number you removed. I usually like to store the cylinders in a sturdy cardboard box on a low shelf, so that they will not be accidentally knocked over.

Removal of the other cylinders is very similar; however, I usually like to rotate the piston down to its lowest level before I pull off each cylinder. Cylinders may be particularly difficult to remove if you have a magnesium case that has been stressed and tweaked. Moving the piston to its lowest level minimizes the amount of force that is required to remove the cylinder. Using a 17mm socket on the pulley, rotate the crankshaft very slowly until one of the other exposed pistons has reached its lowest level. Make sure that you have removed the flywheel lock before attempting to turn the crankshaft. When you pull off the remaining two cylinders, make sure that you label them properly and place them in the Ziploc bags.

If you have Alusil cylinders on your engine (read ahead to Chapter 3) and you are planning on reusing them, then it is important not to remove the pistons from inside the cylinders. Instead, gently pull up on the cylinders until you can just get clearance of the piston pin, or wrist pin. The trick is then getting the piston pin out. For cylinder number six, start with removing the wrist pin retaining circlip that is located closest to the oil cooler. You should then be able to pull out the piston pin. Can't get it out because you don't have anything to hook it with? These pins are usually not pressed in very tightly. You can use a hooked screwdriver. Insert it down the center of the pin, and hook it around the edge. Then use a small hammer to tap the handle of the screwdriver in the direction of the oil cooler. The pin should come out. Remove the entire piston/cylinder assembly, place it in a plastic bag, and put it away safely on your shelf until it's time to reassemble the engine.

Pistons

Now, you can remove the pistons. Rotate the crankshaft so that one of the pistons reaches its maximum height. Then, using a screwdriver and a pair of needle-nose pliers, snap off the small wrist pin retaining circlips from both sides of the piston, as shown in Figure 2-35. Tap the screwdriver into the small groove at the top of the piston pin bore, and use the pliers to ensure that the clip doesn't fall into the recesses of the engine. Wear safety glasses at this point, as these little rings seem to fly off if you don't catch them just right. Also try to avoid having them fall into the engine. If they do get lost inside the crankcase, don't worry too much about it, as we will be opening it up shortly.

Once the small retaining clips have been removed, take the handle end of a small screwdriver and use it to push out the wrist pins. Using a small hammer, lightly tap on the blade end of the screwdriver until the wrist pins begin to come out of the piston (Figure 2-36). They shouldn't require too much force to get moving. Only push the pin out as far as needed to remove it from the rod. When the piston is loose, take it and place it with its appropriate cylinder, which will be in one of your labeled plastic bags. Repeat this procedure, carefully rotating the crankshaft to raise and lower the pistons so that you can reach each wrist pin retaining clip. It's a smart idea to scribe a small indicator mark on each cylinder and piston as you remove it so they won't get mixed up later on.

Once you have all of the pistons removed on this side of the case, simply flip the engine over and repeat the removal process for the pistons and cylinders on the other side. Remove the spacers and barrel nuts that you attached previously before attempting to remove the cylinders. Also

2-35 *The pistons are held onto the rods with wrist pins, which are retained by small circlips at the end of each rod (blue arrow). Using a small screwdriver and a pair of needle-nose pliers, carefully remove each circlip. Make sure that you wear safety glasses when removing the pins, as they can sometimes fly off at a high rate of velocity. Also try not to drop them into the inside of your engine—they can be difficult to fish out later on.*

2-36 *Using the plastic handle of a small screwdriver, gently tap out the wrist pins from each piston. Only tap each one far enough to allow you to remove the piston from the rod. Leave the wrist pin with each piston. As you pull off each piston, make sure that you place it with its corresponding cylinder.*

be aware that as you turn the crankshaft with the rods on the other side hanging free, you might experience one of them hanging up on the inside of the engine case. Simply lift them up and make sure that they are free. You can keep this from happening by working on the engine with one side facing directly up to the ceiling. The engine internals should hang directly down and not grab on any areas of the case. A good rule of thumb is to never use any force when turning your crankshaft. There should be no reason why it cannot turn freely. If you encounter any resistance, investigate before you apply more force.

At this point, you should be staring at the short block with all the heads, camshaft housings, pistons, and cylinders removed.

HEAD STUD REMOVAL

Now it's time for another potentially tough job—head stud removal. Let's talk for a moment first about whether you really need to remove your head studs. As mentioned in Chapter 1, the 2.7L engines from 1974-77 are notorious for pulled head studs. Without a doubt, you should install case-savers into these cases when performing a rebuild. Skip this step and your studs will pull out of the case when the engine is reassembled. So for the 1974-77 cars, you must pull out the original studs. If your 1974-77 magnesium case has already been rebuilt, then there is a chance that it might already have Time-Serts or case-savers installed.

If you own an earlier magnesium case (basically any pre-1978 case except the very early 1965-1968 1/2 911 aluminum cases, and the 1976-77 Turbo and Carrera cases), then I recommend that you install the case-savers as well. Although not as prevalent as with the infamous 2.7-liter head studs, the earlier engines can also experience the head stud pulling problem in the magnesium material. If your engine case becomes stressed, such as with an over-

heating problem, then having the case-savers installed will give you extra margin to weather any pulled stud problems. Again, check your case carefully to see if the case has already had the case-savers installed.

What about the 1978-89 aluminum cases? These are the engines with the infamous snapping exhaust-side head studs. I recommend that you pull these and replace them as well. The Dilavar exhaust head studs are basically a ticking time bomb that may eventually go off and ruin your rebuild. How do you know if the cylinder head studs have already been replaced? The original steel head studs are magnetic, whereas the Dilavar studs are not. Also, if you have a few broken studs on the lower exhaust side of the engine, then they most certainly are the original Dilavar ones. I have never seen an original, standard steel stud that has broken like the Dilavar ones.

Remember that with these engines, the only troublesome cylinder head studs are the ones on the lower exhaust side of the engine—the upper studs were the standard steel type used on the early motors. Turbo owners are less fortunate, as the upper and lower studs are both Dilavar studs, and all of them should be replaced.

Before you remove your head studs, contact your machine shop. Most shops will charge a nominal fee for removal of the head studs. In many cases, it's easier to let a machine shop tackle the difficult struggle of removing the head studs. Find out if the removal and replacement of the head studs is included in the work that you will have performed on your engine case.

So, what is the best way to remove the head studs? In this particular step, the weakness of the magnesium cases actually works to your advantage. Removing studs from magnesium cases is generally much easier than removal from the aluminum cases. The tool that I recommend using is a collet-type stud removal tool available from Snap-On (part number CG500 with collet number CG500-43, M10x1.5). This tool contains a threaded collet that screws onto the stud, as shown in Figure 2-37. The collar is then tightened down around the collet, squeezing the stud along its threads. If attached properly, the tool allows you to remove the stud without damaging the threads. There are other stud removers out there, and I have tried them. Some of them will work, some of them won't, but I have found that the Snap-On tool works the best.

The magnesium cases don't put up too much of a fight when it comes to giving up their head studs. Despite a healthy dose of Loctite on the threads, the studs can usually be backed out using the Snap-On tool. The proper way to use the Snap-On tool is with an impact wrench (either air or electric). Thread the collet onto the stud until all of the threads are mated inside the collet. Using a large wrench, hold the base steady while you use an impact wrench to tighten the collet in the base collar (Figure 2-38).

2-37 *The Snap-On stud removal collet tool is probably the best tool for this difficult job. The inner collet (red arrow) screws onto the outer threads of the stud. Then the outer shell (yellow arrow) clamps the collet onto the stud. The result is a tight connection that does not damage the threads of the stud. Most of the time this tool does its job and works very well.*

2-38 *The best way to use the Snap-On stud remover is in conjunction with an impact wrench and socket (shown attached in photo). Using the impact wrench, zap the collet around the stud while holding the entire tool stationary. Then using a larger impact socket, zap off the stud and the tool together. This makes a powerful combination that is difficult to beat with another tool. Keep in mind that the collet and the tool have non-metric nuts, so you will probably need a standard-sized impact socket set.*

studs are often weakened by the time you get to this point. Very often, you will find that the studs break when you are trying to remove them from the case. If this happens, then the collet stud remover is of no use, and you'll have to try using another type of stud remover that doesn't rely on clamping down on the stud's threads. You can try grinding down flat spots on the head studs in order to get a grip from a set of vise-grips or channel locks. A pipe wrench can also sometimes work well depending upon the surface texture of the stud. Welding a nut to the Dilavar stud won't work either, as the material responds poorly to welding.

One useful tool, particularly with the aluminum cases, is a propane torch. You can usually buy one at your local hardware store, and simply attach it to one of those propane canisters that are often used for camping. Do not use an oxy-acetylene torch, as it is difficult to determine how hot the case is getting. You can melt the aluminum

2-39 *It's bad news if you see this. As mentioned previously, this engine had overheated. As you can see here, the case was properly repaired during a previous rebuild. However, the added stress of overheating seemed to have caused the previously installed Time-Serts to pull out of the case. If your Time-Serts pull out like this, then your only recourse is to install case-savers, which have a larger outer diameter thread.*

While you are tightening the collet, it is good practice to let the impact wrench turn and tighten the stud into the hole about a quarter turn. This will help the stud break free of any Locite sealant that may be securing it within the hole. At this point, you can stop the impact wrench and simply unscrew the stud from the hole. Figure 2-39 shows the collet tool actually pulling a Time-Sert out of the magnesium case—still attached to the stud!

The 1978-89 aluminum cases are a lot more difficult than the magnesium cases. The good news is that you only need to remove the bottom row (exhaust) of studs, for all engines other than the 911 Turbo. The bad news is that they are usually screwed in very tight, and the Dilavar

case, or worse, if working on a magnesium case, set it on fire. Heat the case locally inside the cylinder bore nearest to the stud. This will help to melt some of the Loctite and loosen the head stud in the case. Propane takes quite a long time to heat up the case—point the torch at the base of the stud (inside the cylinder spigot, where the cylinder mates with the engine case) for about 10 to 15 minutes. While this may seem like a long time, propane burns relatively cool on the scale of flames, and you will be surprised at how easily the rest of the case can dissipate the heat.

Make sure that you use the torch in a well-ventilated area, as the propane will give off carbon monoxide as a by-product of combustion. Also make sure that you don't point the torch at the stud itself—as you want to heat the case (to make it expand), and keep the stud cool (so it doesn't expand). Keep the heat on the case while you are turning the stud for a couple of turns, or until the stud feels like it will come all the way out without binding again, forcing you to reheat the case.

Another useful trick is to cool the stud while you're heating the case. Office supply stores usually sell what is known as compressed air-in-a-can. This is typically not normal atmospheric air, but a semi-inert gas that compresses and expands a bit more easily than normal air. (Confirm that it is not flammable, as you'll be using it along with a torch.) The gas in the can is a liquid that quickly becomes a gas when released from the can. Elementary thermodynamics dictates that when the liquid becomes a gas, it will absorb heat. Holding the can upside down and pressing the trigger will cause the contents to leak out as a super-cooled liquid. If you drip this onto the stud, it will quickly absorb heat and cool the stud very rapidly. Heating the case and cooling the stud will make the case expand and the stud contract, making it easier to remove the stud. Make sure that you wear gloves and safety glasses, as the liquid can "freeze-burn" your hands and also burn your eyes.

Manipulating the torch and the can of compressed air while trying to remove the stud at the same time can be nearly impossible. In this case, it's a wise idea to have a helper manage at least one of the tasks. Make sure that you cool the stud but don't freeze it or get it too cold, because this can make the Dilavar studs even more brittle and prone to breaking.

FLYWHEEL & PULLEY

Replace the flywheel lock on the engine, and use a 17mm or 19mm socket to remove the nut that holds on the rear crankshaft pulley (Figure 2-40). It's easier to remove if you have an impact wrench. Now, move to the front of the engine where the flywheel is located. The flywheel bolts are torqued to a very high setting, and are usually very difficult to remove. This is another area of the engine disassembly where you can run into trouble. If you don't use the proper tool there is a chance that you will strip out the bolts that hold the flywheel. They are large 12-point "star" bolts, and are quite shallow, which means that there isn't too much material on the bolts to grab with the tool (Figure 2-41). The tool I used is manufactured to high-quality standards, and doesn't slip on the bolts.

If by chance the tool strips out the bolt, then you will have to grind off the head of the bolt. This is a very messy, loud, tiring process, and one that I recommend you try to avoid at all costs. Make sure that your tool is in good condition, and don't use an impact wrench with it. Instead, attach the tool to a long breaker bar, and slowly apply pressure to

the end of the bar with your hand. With your opposite hand, grip the end of the tool and make sure that it is exactly perpendicular to the flywheel and well seated in the bolt. If the tool is angled when you apply force to the breaker bar, there is a good chance that the tool will slip, and the bolt will strip. Grinding off your flywheel bolts is very difficult to do without seriously damaging your flywheel. Think twice before attempting this process without the proper high-quality tool.

Once you have all the bolts off, you should be able to remove the flywheel from the end of the crankshaft. You may have to tug a little at it, or use a large screwdriver wedged between the case and the flywheel to nudge it off

2-40 *Removal of the front pulley is straightforward. Simply lock the flywheel and use a large breaker bar to loosen the nut. The pulley will simply pull off after the nut has been removed.*

2-41 *Removal of flywheel bolts is a difficult job and it is very easy to make a mistake during this process. Make sure that you only use the proper tool, as the bolts are torqued to a very high level, and will usually strip if an improper tool is used, or if the tool is not held squarely and firmly in the bolt. Make sure that the tool is not damaged, and has good clear indentations for removal of the bolts. A mistake here usually means having to grind off the flywheel bolts.*

of the crank. Be careful not to drop the flywheel on your foot, as it is heavy, and has a tendency to seem stuck on the crank—only to fall off a few seconds later.

SPLITTING THE CASE & CRANK/RODS

Okay, now for the fun part: splitting the case. Begin by removing the small intermediate plate from the rear of the engine (Figure 2-42). It is held on with 10mm nuts, and should be easily pried off when the nuts are removed. Then remove the small bolts that hold the chain ramps to the inside of the case. The ramps should simply lift out of the case. Next, loosen and remove the nuts that hold the through-bolts onto the side of the engine case. These bolts extend the width of the case, and help to clamp it together. Removal requires a 15mm deep socket to get over the tops of the caps on the nuts. Since these through-bolts actually extend into oil passages, the nuts on the end of each are capped to prevent oil leaks. There are also o-rings on each side of each bolt. Once the nuts are off, you can tap the bolts out with a small hammer. They may slightly resist, as the o-ring can easily get caught in the case—pry out the o-rings with a pick before you try to remove the bolts. There are 11 of these through-bolts to remove.

An additional two M10 nuts are located in the area where the oil cooler mounts. Although they use the same cap-style nuts as the through-bolts, these are studs that are embedded to the case, and don't need to be tapped out.

If you made a mistake and mounted the wrong case half to your engine stand, now is the time to correct it. Although the engine is still very heavy at this point, two people can easily lift it off of the engine stand to reposition the engine stand mount.

2-42 In preparation for splitting the case, you will need to remove the remaining chain ramps. The ramps are attached to the case using two bolts each. Simply remove the bolts, and the ramps will fall right off (left photo). Don't forget to remove the rear intermediate plate (right photo). It straddles the engine case parting line, and will prevent you from splitting the case if you forget to remove it.

Case Nuts

Now you can start removing the nuts that hold the case together. There are a total of twenty-two 13mm nuts that need to be removed from the case, all of them shown in Figure 2-43. Three are located inside the rear of the engine case near the flywheel seal. When you think you have all the fasteners removed, double-check to make sure that you didn't miss any. With so many on the case, and some of them hidden by oil and grime, it's easy to overlook one. Needless to say, the case doesn't want to come apart too easily with an overlooked fastener still attached. The last remaining fastener is hidden in the left timing chain housing, and can be removed using a 15mm socket with an extension.

2-43 Shown in this photo are all the nuts and fasteners that you need to remove from the case in order to begin splitting it. The blue arrows show all the nuts on the outside studs. The orange arrows indicate where there are two nuts on the opposite side that need to be removed. The red arrows indicate the through-bolts that need to be removed. The yellow arrow shows the 15mm nut that is hidden inside the timing chain housing area. Remove this nut and place it in a safe location—it is typically a relatively rare M10x1 nut and can be difficult to replace. The green arrow shows two nuts on the opposite side of the case that also need to be removed. Double check to make sure that you didn't miss any hidden ones before you start hitting your case with the rubber mallet.

Case Separation

Start by tapping the left case half with a rubber mallet. Use the fan-housing mount as a good location to tap on the case, but don't pound on it aggressively, as excessive force can break the ears. The case should immediately begin to separate, and you will see some cracking of the oil grime at the seams. Use a breaker bar as an extension of the rubber hammer and tap the case evenly around its "four corners," as shown in Figure 2-44. Rotating your taps around the case in an even fashion should yield some progress (Figure 2-45).

Race engine cases that have been shuffle pinned can be notoriously difficult to separate. The shuffle-pin process involves installing extra sets of dowel pins around the main bearings to make sure that the bearing surfaces are precisely aligned when the case is closed. If your case has had this procedure, then you will have to work extra hard to get the case apart.

As tempting as it may be, don't ever use a screwdriver or pry bar to separate the case halves. The 911 engine case is a precision machined part and does not have a gasket that goes in-between the case halves. It's a metal-to-metal joint, and any scratches or indentations on the case parting line can cause serious oil leaks later on. If you have come to your rope's end and need to pry the case apart with a sharp tool, make sure that you use the parting line that is located inside the oil breather housing. Even if you damage the parting line in this location, it is internal to the engine, so oil leaks are not an issue.

You can flip the case upside down so that the weight of the case actually helps separate it. Although the 911 engine case does not simply fall apart, I would take precautions and attach

2-45 *Eureka! After many hours and quite a few impatient taps with the hammer, the case is finally beginning to separate. Don't be tempted to use a screwdriver to pry the case apart. It is a precision casting that does not use a gasket at the parting line. Scratching the parting line surface will ensure that you have an oil leak later on.*

a small nut to one of the studs just to catch the left case half in case it happens to fall out. Just remember to remove this "safety stud" when you get the case cracked open far enough.

When the case parting lines are about a half-inch apart, you will be able to simply lift the left half of the case off of the right half. Make sure that the right case half is facing up to the ceiling, as you don't want your crank to fall out of the case. You may have to wiggle the case back and forth in order to get it to loosen completely from the studs in the other half. Lift it straight up, and off of the right case half, then place it in a safe place off to the side.

CASE INTERNALS

For those who haven't seen the inside of a 911 engine before, this is the point where you can go "oooh" and "ahh" (Figure 2-46). After you're done admiring the inside of your engine, grab the crank by two of the rods and lift it out of the case. It will pull right out with a minimal amount of effort. Lift it straight up and place it in a safe place.

The oil pump is attached to the case with three nuts that have safety tabs on them. These are thin washers with tabs that bend up and prevent the nuts from accidentally backing out. Push down these little tabs with a small screwdriver and remove the nuts. You will then be able to reach into the case and remove the oil pump, driveshaft, intermediate shaft, and the two timing chains as an assembly, as shown in Figure 2-47. Make sure that you don't drop anything, as these components are not attached to each other. Use one hand on the oil pump, and one hand on the intermediate shaft to carry it to a safe place.

2-44 *There are a few safe places on the case where you can tap to separate the case halves. Underneath the engine near the flywheel is a flange in the bottom corner. Toward the rear of the engine, there is an identical flange underneath the area where the pulley mounts. Towards the top rear of the engine, use one of the flanges that normally mount the fan housing. On the top front, you can lightly tap inside the oil crankcase breather housing—be careful though as too much force can crack and break off the side of the housing.*

2-46 *This is perhaps the most gratifying step, similar to opening the entrance of a tomb. Inside are the crankshaft, rods, oil pump, intermediate shaft, and a lot of excess oil. Take stock in the sight for a moment, and then gently grab your crank and rods and lift them out of the case.*

2-47 *The intermediate shaft and oil pump should be lifted out of the case as an assembly. Use two hands (unlike this photo, in which the other hand is holding the camera) to lift the entire assembly out of the case. The intermediate shaft and oil pump are not joined together, and will simply slip out and fall apart if you don't use two hands to carry them as an assembly.*

Crank & Rods

The crank and rods disassembly process is quite straightforward. I recommend that you use two used flywheel bolts to attach the flywheel to the crank, making a handy disassembly stand. Start by removing the number eight bearing, as shown in Figure 2-48. It will simply lift off of the crankshaft. Next, disconnect each rod from the crankshaft by unbolting the rod bolts, as shown in Figure 2-49. You do not need to keep track of which rod was used on a particular cylinder, but do put each rod cap back on the rod it was attached to. Each rod and cap have a number stamped into the side where they mate together. Although you need to replace the rod bolts and nuts with brand new ones, the machine shop will need the old ones to hold your rod and cap together when they are machining and resizing each rod.

If you happen to own a large gear puller, then you can remove the crankshaft gear from the crankshaft. Before you do this, you should probably make sure that it is absolutely necessary. Most machine shops recommend

leaving the gear alone unless it or the distributor drive gear are damaged. If you want to change out the distributor drive gear (something you might need to do if you're running a different distributor), then you need to remove this gear.

Removal is not easy, as the gear is pressed on there quite tightly. Remove the large, stiff circlip that holds the gear onto the crankshaft. Then attach the gear puller and remove the crankshaft gear and distributor drive gear together, as shown in Figure 2-50. If you feel your gear puller is not strong enough, it's a relatively simple task for your machine shop to remove the gear.

2-48 *The number eight nose bearing simply lifts off of the nose of the crankshaft. From the appearance of oil on the outer end of the bearing, it would be a good guess that the orange O-ring inside the bearing wasn't performing its job very well.*

2-49 *With the crankshaft mounted to the flywheel, the removal of the rod bolts is made much easier. Make sure that you keep the rods and their caps together when you remove them. Also keep the old rod nuts and rod bolts, as your machine shop will need these when they recondition and resize your rods.*

CAMSHAFT HOUSING AND HEAD DISASSEMBLY

Now that you have the case completely disassembled, you can move to the heads (Figure 2-51). Make sure that you pick up the proper camshaft housing side (you don't want to confuse them). I usually like to scribe the number of the head onto an inconspicuous surface, or if you have a set of punches, that works well too. Make sure that you do not mark the heads on the flat surface where they mate with the camshaft housings. I have seen many heads have their cylinder numbers scratched on this delicate and important mating surface. Place the entire assembly combustion chamber side down on your bench. Have a whole set of large and small Ziploc bags handy, as you want to make sure that you carefully label all your rocker arms so that you know from which port and cylinder they came.

Rocker Shaft Removal

Begin the disassembly process by loosening the small bolt that holds the outer rocker in place using a 5mm Allen socket or Allen key. Remove it and the nut from the rocker assembly, as shown in Figure 2-52. Use an 8mm Allen-head socket to hold the opposite side steady while you loosen up the rocker retaining screw. Once the screw is loose, you should be able to remove it from the rocker. Don't leave the screw, nut, or cone washer in the rocker shaft when you remove it. Pushing on the end of the cone can expand the shaft slightly and compress it into the bore while you're trying to remove it, with the potential to damage the camshaft housing. At this time, you will be able to take the fat end of a 3/8-inch extension and tap out the rocker shaft, as shown in Figure 2-53. Tap the rocker shaft out, preferably through the shallower end—not the deeper,

dirtier side of the rocker shaft bore. The rocker will fall out shortly afterward.

Take the rocker, rocker shaft, screw, nut, and conical collar and place them in a Ziploc bag labeled with the cylinder number, and the port type. Example: Exhaust, Cylinder #3. It is important that you install the rockers and their shafts in the same holes that they came out of. In some cases, the rockers have a tendency to deform the camshaft housings, and this can lead to leaks later on. Putting the rocker arms back into their original positions can minimize leaks. In addition, if you are planning on reusing your rocker arms and camshafts without having them reconditioned, you must make sure that you reinstall your rockers in their original positions. This is because both the rockers and the camshafts are hardened, and if you mix and match the existing wear patterns between different rockers and different spots on the cam, you will wear out your camshaft a lot faster than normal. If you replace your rockers, you must replace or regrind your camshafts. This costs a good amount of money, so you may want to stick with the old units if replacement is not strictly necessary.

2-53 *Use a 3/8-inch extension and a small hammer to gently tap the rocker arm shaft out of its bore in the camshaft housings. Make sure that the inner nut and bolt are completely loose before tapping on the shaft. If there is significant resistance, try tapping from the opposite direction.*

2-54 *The inside rocker arm shafts can be reached easily by using long extensions on your ratchet driver.*

2-55 *With all of the rockers removed, the camshaft can simply be pulled out of the camshaft housings. This is an example of a three-bearing camshaft. In 1978, Porsche added a fourth bearing to the configuration to strengthen the assembly. The fourth bearing is located in the long section between the four cam lobes.*

Repeat the rocker removal procedure for each of the six rocker arms on the shaft, using an extension where necessary (Figure 2-54). Double-check to make sure that you place each rocker into its appropriate bag. When you're finished, you can slide the cam out of the camshaft housing, as shown in Figure 2-55. Don't use any force to remove it—it should simply slide out. If necessary, rotate the cam a bit to help it to slide out. You don't have to mark the cam left or right, as they are different for each side and it's relatively easy to tell which one is which by looking at them. If you have a 911 with mechanical fuel injection, then you will have to remove the MFI gear on the end of the camshaft and push the camshaft out of the camshaft housing.

2-56 *Shown here is a typical C-clamp type valve spring compressor. The spring compressor braces itself on the head of the valve while clamping down on top of the valve keeper. Make sure that you wear safety glasses when compressing the springs, as they sometimes pop loose and can fling objects like valve keepers across the room.*

2-57 *The spring compressor clamps down on the valve spring retainer and allows for the release of the valve keepers, shown separated here (orange arrows). Simply pick them out with a pair of needle-nose pliers. Resist the temptation to grab them with your fingers, because if the spring compressor slips, you may crush your fingertips. The valve keeps are cylindrical, and are designed so that the valve can rotate ever so slightly under normal operation.*

Now, remove all of the 13mm nuts that attach the heads to the camshaft housing. Then, remove the three barrel nuts that are located at the top of the camshaft housings. At this point, you will be able to take a small hammer and tap the studs that are attached to the heads. The heads should simply fall away from the camshaft housing. Repeat the entire process for the other camshaft housing, remembering to carefully label each head and rocker assembly.

Head Disassembly

You can perform the disassembly process if you'd like; however, most machine shops assume that you will be sending in your heads as a single unit and include the charge for disassembly in the reconditioning price. Disassembly of each head can only be achieved if you happen to have a valve spring compressor. Acting like a giant C-clamp, the compressor grips the face of the valve, and then allows you to press down on the retainers (Figure 2-56). Make sure that you wear safety glasses at this point, as these valve springs are pretty heavily loaded. Compress the valve down, and you will be able to remove the small valve keepers at the end of the valve stem.

Carefully release the pressure on the spring compressor, and you now will be able to take apart the entire assembly. The valve can be removed by pushing it out toward the combustion side of the head. The springs and retainer simply fall off, as shown in Figure 2-57. Pry the valve-stem seal off with a small screwdriver (Figure 2-58). The valve spring seal can be removed using a pair of needle-nose pliers. Finally, the shims that sit in the head and are used to adjust

the height of the spring can be easily removed by using a small magnet to grab them, as shown in Figure 2-59. Keep all the parts for each valve together with the valve in a labeled Ziploc bag (Figure 2-60).

Well, there you have it. By now, you will have your entire engine disassembled. Not too difficult, huh? Now you need to take a look at the parts that you have, and package them to be taken off to your machine shop. You also need to start thinking about which parts need to be replaced, and which ones need to be reused. We'll talk about that a little more in Chapter 3.

2-59 *A handy trick for removing the valve spring shims is to use a magnet to grab them out of the head.*

2-58 *Removal of the spring and retainer shows the valve stem seal and the spring seat. The seal can now be removed simply by prying it off with a small, flat-tipped screwdriver.*

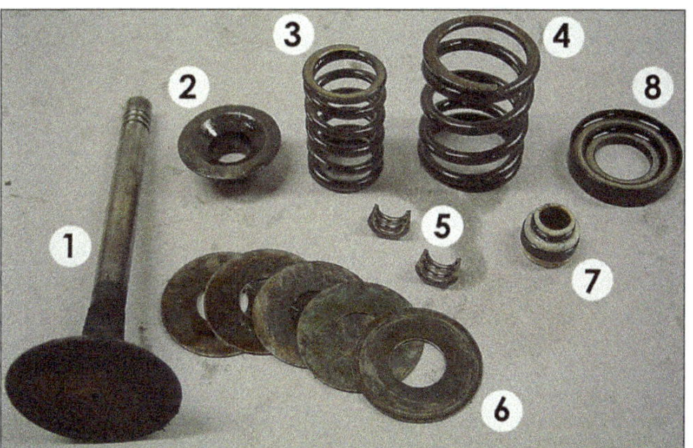

2-60 *Shown here are all the parts that are contained in the cylinder head. They are 1- valve, 2- valve spring retainer, 3- inner valve spring, 4- outer valve spring, 5- valve keepers, 6- valve spring shims, 7- valve stem seal, 8- valve spring seat. You only need to disassemble the heads for curiosity reasons. Most machine shops will factor in the cost of disassembly in their reconditioning price.*

CHAPTER 3
INSPECTION & MACHINE SHOP

Now that you have completely disassembled your engine, you can take a close look at the parts to see which ones need refurbishment or replacement. Each part of the engine has different wear patterns, and there are various techniques and methods for rebuilding all your parts. Remember that the key difference between a newly rebuilt engine and a worn-out one is the clearances between all the parts. It's your goal to inspect all of the parts and then have them brought back to their original clearances, either through machine shop work or replacement of the parts with new ones. We'll take a look at each part of the engine here, and discuss the various options for bringing these clearances back to their original specifications.

Let's first talk about which parts of your engine should be taken to your machine shop. Parts that specifically need to be machined according to Porsche quality standards and specifications should be taken to a machine shop specializing in the repair and refurbishment of Porsche engines. Parts that simply need to be cleaned or bead-blasted don't have to be mailed off to the Porsche experts. They can be taken to a local machine shop that is equipped with a bead-blaster and a large parts cleaner. The parts that specifically should be sent to the Porsche shop are the rods, crankshaft, engine case, heads, pistons, and cylinders. You might also want to take your oil cooler to have it cleaned and pressure tested to make sure that there are no leaks. The remaining parts (timing chain housings, sheet metal, fan and shroud, etc.) can all be taken to your local shop for standard cleaning and bead-blasting.

CRANKSHAFT

The 911 crankshaft is generally very robust, and can usually tolerate a lot of punishment. It's rare to see a crankshaft that has been broken or seriously damaged due to an engine failure. The most common major problems associated with crankshafts are damage from spun bearings, a bent crankshaft, microscopic cracks, or a bearing surface that has been damaged or scratched by dirty motor oil.

The most common crankshaft reconditioning work involves only cleaning and polishing. Typically, excessively dirty oil is hard on the main bearings and not the crankshaft. The bearings are manufactured out of a much softer material and will have a tendency to wear before the crankshaft journals. However, even the crankshaft has its limits. Exceptionally dirty oil will scratch and score the hardened material surfaces of the crankshaft. Even more destructive are small pieces of metal that circulate throughout the engine like the carnage that results from a dropped valve.

3-1 *Here is a 911 2.7-liter crank on a V-block test stand being checked for straightness. Using a dial indicator placed against the crank, you can check for a bent crank by spinning the crank. The dial indicator will not move at all if the crank is straight and unbent. Using the same fixture, you can check the main bearing surfaces for out-of-round conditions.*

Bent Crankshafts

Let's first talk about bent crankshafts. The crank can only become bent when really large, extraneous forces are placed on it. Because the 911 case supports the crank with eight bearings, it is very difficult to damage the crank without seriously damaging the case as well. You will most likely find that your crank is perfectly fine. The amount of bend in the crankshaft is called runout, and is measured in the distance that the center journal wobbles when you rotate the crankshaft (Figure 3-1).

You can measure your crankshaft runout by using your crankcase. Install the number eight and number one bearings in the case. Use some assembly lube on the inside of the number eight bearing, and also on the surface of the number one bearing. The crank should spin freely supported on these bearings. Rotate the crank by hand to detect if the crank is straight or bent. A dial indicator placed against bearings number 4, 8, or the outer edge of the center flange will display how much the center of the crank wobbles when it's rotated. The amount that the dial indicator moves is the crankshaft runout. If the indicator doesn't move, then crank is straight. Maximum runout for a 911 crankshaft should be 0.04mm. You can measure the runout on the flange instead of the bearing journal because the journal may be oblong and out-of-round, and may not give an accurate reading.

Spun Bearings

If your engine has spun a bearing, then you will probably have a damaged crank journal. A spun bearing is when one of the main or rod bearings becomes loose and rotates around the crank. This will damage both the case and the crank as the bearing wears grooves in both. In this case, it may be necessary to regrind your crank.

Regrinding is not a process that I recommend. The original cranks were hardened with a nitriding process that is no longer performed. The crankshaft can still be rehardened, just not as well as it was when it was new from the factory. It is better to locate and use a crankshaft that has not been reground, as opposed to a crankshaft that requires a grind. Used crankshafts are described by their bearing journals—both the main bearings and the rod bearings. A good used crankshaft that has not been reground would be called a Standard/Standard (Std/Std), meaning that it takes standard sized bearings for both the main bearings and the rod bearings. At the time of this writing, you can still easily find good used cranks at reasonable prices—especially for the 2.0 to 2.7-liter engines. The cost of a good-quality used crank is usually less than the cost of regrinding and rehardening an undersized crank.

The crank may also have a bearing journal that has become oval shaped, or what is commonly called out-of-round. While not too common to find with the 911 cranks, an out-of-round journal will require that the crank be reground or replaced. Unfortunately, since bearings are sold in sets, you will need to regrind all of the bearing journals on the crankshaft to the same size. This is true regardless of whether the crankshaft is badly scored or out-of-round.

Regrinds

If your crankshaft needs to be reground and you can't find a good used one that doesn't, then I suggest that you take it to a place that does a quality job. There are many machine shops out there that will simply regrind the crank without rehardening it. These cranks will undoubtedly wear out much faster, and generally are not worth the money required to regrind them, especially when good-quality used ones are still available. In addition, a regrind will require a complete cleaning of the crankshaft. You will need all of the aluminum plugs in the crankshaft replaced, as the rehardening process has a tendency to loosen them.

A reground crankshaft will require you to run undersized bearings. The crankshaft should be ground to either 0.25mm or 0.50mm undersize. If not, then the replacement bearings will not fit properly. This is yet another reason to use a Porsche-specific machine shop, as I have seen cranks that have been improperly ground to non-metric sizes. American engines typically are ground to English specification units, which are completely incorrect for European cars.

Inspection

Before you send your crankshaft to your machine shop, I suggest that you measure and inspect the bearing journals. Using a high-quality micrometer, you can determine the journal size, and figure out if your crank has already been ground. If it has, I would suggest that you find yourself a good used one that is standard/standard—that is, one that has not been reground.

Check the crankshaft for taper—it occurs when a bearing journal wears unevenly across its surface, and the dimension on one end of the bearing is different from the other side. Taper is usually not a problem on 911 cranks. However, you should perform this measurement anyway to make sure that your crank doesn't need to be reground. A taper of about .001 inch (.025mm) would be considered excessive enough to warrant regrinding.

The 911 crankshaft has no end-play adjustment because bearing number one is a thrust bearing. This means that it constrains axial play of the crankshaft. Wear can occur if unusual axial loads are placed on the crankshaft such as by a misaligned clutch that pulls on the crankshaft.

Also inspect the bearing journal surfaces themselves. Run your fingernail across the surface of each journal. Slight scratches are okay, but if your fingernail catches any significant grooves, then you may have a crankshaft that needs to be reground or scrapped (Figure 3-2).

The brass distributor drive gear should be inspected and replaced if there is any visible wear. It's important to note that the distributor drive gear on all 911 SCs and 911 Turbos (1978-89) turns the distributor in a counter-clockwise direction, which is backwards from all other years. The 1965–77, 911SC and Turbo, and 1984-later years are all different. The bottom line is, if replacing your crankshaft, the distributor and drive gear should be matched year-for-year.

3-2 Here are two photos of the same crank. This engine has been sitting for many years, and the result is an oil stain that can be seen on this crank journal in the photo on the left (green arrow). This is only a stain and does not affect the condition or performance of the crank. On the right, we see a different story. Clearly caused by dirty oil, the scratching and deep grooves cut into this crankshaft indicate that it has led a hard life (yellow arrow). Although this damage isn't terminal, it's a sign that the engine was not well cared for in its previous life.

The number eight bearing should be inspected and compared to the allowable tolerances listed in Appendix A. Most of the time, this bearing can be reused, as it doesn't typically experience a lot of wear. New ones cost between $65 and $100. Make sure that the small channel groove cast into the bearing is clean and clear of dirt—this is an oil flow channel (see arrow in Chapter 5 Figure 3-15).

Out-Of-Round

Bearing surfaces do not tend to wear evenly. This is because of the force profile placed on the crankshaft when the engine is running. The side of the bearing that is facing opposite of the piston tends to get the most wear, because the rod is pushing on it with a huge amount of force when the cylinder is fired. This is especially true of the rod bearings, since they transmit 100 percent of the load from combustion to the crankshaft. On the opposite side of the power stroke, the same rod pulls the piston and rod assembly back toward the crankshaft, creating wear on the opposite side. These push-pull forces on the crankshaft bearings are exactly opposite each other, and create wear patterns on opposite sides of the bearing journals.

You can check for this out-of-round condition by measuring the diameter of each journal at various positions around its circumference. If the bearing journal is perfectly round, then you should be able to take one measurement, and rotate your micrometer around the bearing without changing its setting. Out-of-round is measured by subtracting the minor dimension (smallest measurement) from the major dimension (the largest measurement). For the 911 crankshaft, this should not exceed 0.008 inch (0.15mm). If it exceeds this number, then your crank will need to be reground or replaced.

Magnafluxing

Magnafluxing is the most common task associated with crankshaft inspection. This process exposes all the flaws in the crankshaft, including microscopic cracks in its surface. You should have your crankshaft (and connecting rods) magnafluxed, if you are planning to re-use it (Figure 3-3).

The process of magnafluxing is relatively simple. The crankshaft is initially magnetized using a large circular magnet. The magnetic field is applied to the crankshaft at a 45 degree angle so that the process will detect cracks that run both parallel and perpendicular to the length of the crankshaft. Then the technician sprays the crankshaft with a magnetic powder suspended in a special liquid. If there are any cracks in the surface, the two sides will take on opposite polarity, concentrating the magnetic powder along the crack. To view any cracks identified by the powder, the technician examines the crankshaft under an ultraviolet (black) light in total darkness. Under the black light, the

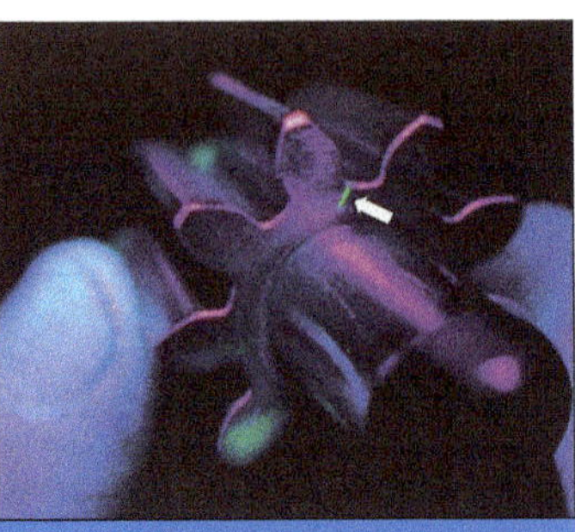

3-3 *The magnaflux process is quite interesting to watch. The crankshaft (or any metal object) is magnetized by the large electromagnetic coil, as shown on the left. Then a magnetic powder solution that can only be viewed under an ultraviolet light is sprinkled on the crankshaft. The solution is then blown off of the surfaces. The powder will find its way into any hidden cracks on the surface and can be seen when the UV light is shined on the crankshaft. On the right is shown a VW Type IV oil pump gear with a crack near the base of one of the gear teeth. The crack shows up as a green line under the UV light (white arrow).*

cracks will clearly show as bright lines in the surface. A 911 crankshaft rarely cracks. However, when it does, the failure typically occurs at the point where the bearing journal meets a center flange.

After the crankshaft is tested, it is demagnetized and then washed in solvent to remove any of the magnaflux material. It's very important to make sure that the crankshaft is demagnetized; otherwise, tiny bits of metal that accumulate in your engine oil will stick to the crankshaft bearing journals.

Polishing

A good, reusable crankshaft should have its bearing journals micropolished smooth. When performed properly, the polishing process should not reduce the outer diameter of the bearing surfaces, and will improve the flow of oil around the bearings. The oil creates a thin film between the bearing and the crank. Polishing the crank eliminates any friction or grooves that may impede or disrupt the flow of oil. Make sure that you check the final dimensions of the bearing journals when you get the crank back from being polished, as a bad polishing job may remove excess material from the metal. If the crank was severely grooved, this may result in a final journal dimension that is out-of-spec. Always use new bearings with your polished crank— keep new surfaces against other new surfaces.

Cleaning

When you get your crankshaft back, I suggest that you clean the entire unit with brake or carburetor cleaner (Figure 3-4). Do not remove the oil passage plugs for this process, as it is very easy to damage them, which can result in them falling out later on. Use a can or two of the cleaner with a small plastic attachment hose. Spray the inside passages completely to rid them of any dirt and grime that may

3-4 *When the crankshaft comes back from the machine shop, you should thoroughly clean out all of the oil passages inside. Using brake or carburetor cleaner, spray all of the passages and make sure that there is no debris from the machining processes trapped inside. A good polishing job isn't worth anything if all the dirt and grime from the job gets flushed out into the bearings when the engine is started.*

have been left over from the polishing process. A micro-polish job and new bearings are useless if the grit from the process remains inside the crankshaft—ready to be flushed out into the bearings when the engine is started.

Take a look at the oil holes. If the crank was reground, the oil holes should have a nice beveled chamfer around their outer surface. Also check the journal fillets. This is the area where the bearing journal meets the flange. This should have a nice small radius connecting the bearing journal and the crankshaft flange. This radius is specified at between 0.2mm and 0.5mm. If you happen to have a radius gauge, give it a look before you put together your engine. Too sharp a radius caused by overzealous grinding will cause sharp corners and stress concentrations. These stress concentrations can lead to cracks later on. Check for scratches caused by careless grinding as well.

Make sure that you purchase the correct bearings to match your crankshaft, rods, and case. Do not purchase bearings until you have all of your machined parts back from the machine shop. The crank can be ground undersize, and the case can be machined to accept larger bearings. It is sometimes a good idea to have the machine shop supply the bearings, as they can test fit them, and they will know exactly what the specifications are on the case, crank, and rods.

RODS

The connecting rods, like the crankshaft, are pretty robust parts. Rods typically become damaged when a more basic problem, like low oil pressure caused by high heat or simply low oil levels, causes the rod bearings to run dry. The rod bearing journals are one of the last places to receive oil and thus are one of the first to run dry when the engine oil level runs low. The result is catastrophic failure, as the rod itself crushes and squeezes the rod bearings against the crankshaft.

Other rod failures occur when there is a dropped valve or any other type of failure that causes the piston to suddenly

stop moving. The rod can become bent in many directions, and is basically destroyed. Such rod damage is generally easy to see, as you will usually find a rod sticking out of the engine case when you tear it down. Needless to say, damage on this magnitude usually renders just about everything in the engine completely destroyed.

Sizing

The most common problem for rods is the deformation of the big end. As the rod is thrust downward on each compression stroke, the force squeezes the rod against the crankshaft. As a result, the rod tends to become oblong or egg shaped at its larger end. The most common rod reconditioning involves resizing of the rods to bring them back to the desired size.

To bring the rods back to their original size, the rod and rod cap are ground down slightly on their mating surfaces, which removes a few thousandths of material and makes the rod increasingly egg-shaped (Figure 3-5). The rod bolts are installed and torqued to their final specification. Then, the inside of the rod bearing bore is machined round again on a precision hone. This brings the bearing bore of the rod back to perfect roundness. The result is then checked and verified with a precision bore gauge.

When you send your rods out to your machine shop make sure that you include your old rod nuts and bolts. The machine shop will use them to bolt your rods together and machine the bearing bore. Be careful that you don't use these nuts in your final assembly, as they are designed to be torqued down only once. If you are using aftermarket rod

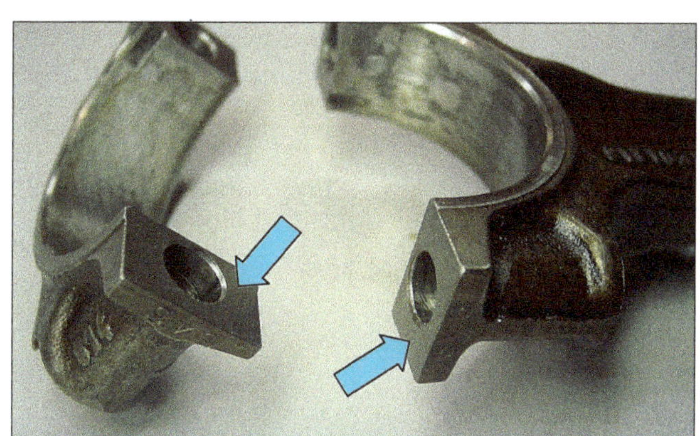

3-5 *The rod is resized by removing material from both the rod and its cap (blue arrows). When mounted back together, the inside bore will be slightly smaller and egg shaped. The original diameter bore is then rehoned into the rod, and the rod is resized back to its original bore size. Make sure that you send your used rod nuts and bolts with your rods as the machine shop will need these when resizing your rods. If you are using aftermarket rod bolts and nuts, send them along too as they have a tendency to affect the rod sizing process.*

nuts and bolts, like ones from ARP or RaceWare, make sure that you give them to your machine shop as well, as these rod bolts will affect the final dimensions of the rod. The machine shop will need to torque down the rods with these aftermarket bolts in order to achieve the proper bearing bore sizing. Unlike the Porsche factory parts, aftermarket nuts and bolts can be used more than once.

Bent Rods

You also need to check to see if your rods are bent. Because the 911 engine is horizontally opposed, rods seldom bend unless something catastrophic happened to the engine. Your machine shop will be able to determine if there is any bend or twist to any of the rods in your set. Although bent rods can be straightened, the supply of good used rods is ample enough. You can purchase a good, straight used rod for about $100.

Rod Weight

All of the Porsche connecting rods are classified by weight groups. If you need to replace one of the rods in your engine, make sure that you select one from the correct group. A good precision scale like the one you used in high school chemistry class should be accurate enough to measure the rod weights. Porsche recommends that there be no more than 9 grams of deviation between your heaviest and lightest rod. If you decide to have your engine balanced, the machine shop performing the work will carefully grind metal from five of the rods to bring them all to the same weight as the lightest rod in the set. These rods should then be within 0.5 grams end-for-end (all small ends weigh the same, all big ends weigh the same) and total weight.

Bushing Replacement

Piston pin bushing replacement is a standard procedure for rebuilding rods. The new bushing is pressed into the tip of the rod, and then honed to the proper dimension. The bushing must be carefully pressed into the rod using an arbor press, and requires a significant amount of pressure to insert. If it doesn't require enough pressure to insert the bushing, then the bushing is loose in the bore. If the bushing happens to rotate when the engine is running, the bushing may block the oil hole in the piston pin and starve the bearing of oil.

The piston pin bushing has a relatively thick outer diameter and can be machined in an offset manner. When the rod and its cap are ground, reassembled, and honed to the correct dimension, there is a possibility that the two bore centers (which affects the total length of the rod throw) are no longer the correct distance apart. Offset boring of the piston pin bushing involves honing the hole so that it is closer to the top or bottom of the rod and not centered in the hole in the rod. Honing the bushing in this manner allows the bearing-to-

bearing centerline distance to remain exactly the same, with no downside in performance or reliability.

Offset boring the rods also allows you to "stretch" the rods. The piston pin bushing can be machined closer to the top of the rod, effectively lengthening the rod, as shown in Figure 3-6. This has the effect of reducing the combustion chamber size, while maintaining the exact same stroke. The total effect is an increase in the compression ratio. This is just one of many techniques that can be used to incrementally increase your engine's compression ratio. If the center-to-center distance is not the same for all the rods, then you may end up with some cylinders having a higher compression ratio than others. Cylinders with higher compression will be more likely to experience detonation.

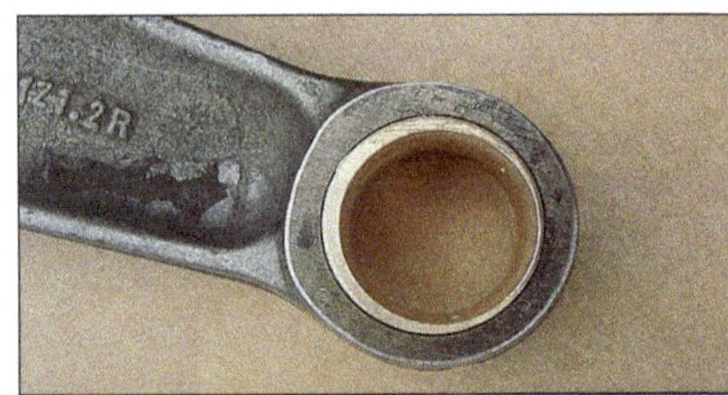

3-6 *The piston pin bushing that is installed in the small end of the rod is very thick. As a result, you can "stretch" the rods by offset boring this bushing. This is an easy way to increase your engine's compression ratio or correct some machining tolerance buildups. The offset bore can effectively increase or decrease the throw of the rod, and doesn't have any adverse affects on reliability.*

Rod bearings must be matched to the crank. If you're using a crankshaft with reground rod journals, then you will have to use oversized rod bearings. Understand and measure your rod journals on your crank before you order any replacement rod bearings.

CRANKCASE

Without a doubt, the engine crankcase is the most complex part in the engine. Porsche produced two families of engines with two distinctly different engine cases. The first one has a smaller crankshaft end, and was used from 1965-77 (Figure 3-7). The second generation of cases used the crankshafts with the larger flywheel mounting points (1978-89). Of course, there were some notable exceptions to this rule. The very early cases from 1965-68 were manufactured out of aluminum and did not have bearing inserts for the intermediate shaft. The 1976-77 911 Turbo and European Carrera used a unique and rare case that was manufactured out of aluminum and used the crank with the smaller sized flywheel end, but had the cylinder spigot spacing of the later cases.

The magnesium cases are generally referred to by the last digits of their casting numbers. The strongest of these are the 7R cases introduced in 1973. These had all of the

3-7 *The two different style crankshafts used on the 911 engine. The photo on the left shows the 1978 and later crankshaft with the larger flywheel mounting end. The photo on the right shows the early-style crank with the six-bolt flywheel pattern.*

3-8 *The early cases from 1965-69 used an intermediate shaft that rotated against the bare metal of the case. While this was adequate for the early aluminum case shown in the photo, the 1968 1/2 and later style magnesium cases were not robust enough to support this configuration. The fix for these magnesium cases is to have the case machined to accept the later-style intermediate shaft bearings or simply replace the case with a later one.*

improvements, and are the least likely to suffer from the problems associated with the weaker magnesium material. The 1973 1/2 911 T engine was equipped with a relatively rare 7R case. This is the only 7R case that has the cylinder spigot spacing for the 2.0/2.2/2.4-liter cylinders. As a result, this case is highly sought after by racers who want to have a stronger case but maintain a displacement of 2.4 liters or less. For these race engines, the early aluminum cases are also very desirable; however, they require extensive machining to install the upgrades that are present in the 7R cases.

Depending upon which case you are starting with, you will need to have a variety of inspection tasks performed on it. In the following section, I'll cover just about everything that needs to be done to each case, starting with the early cases.

Intermediate Shaft Bearings

As mentioned previously, the very early aluminum cases (1965-68) did not utilize bearings for the intermediate shafts. They ran in the bare aluminum, similar to how the camshafts run in the camshaft housings (Figure 3-8). Aluminum by itself actually makes for a very good bearing surface, when the loads are generally low. If you are looking to purchase an early aluminum case, it's important that you buy one with a matching intermediate shaft and end cover as well. These two parts are unique to this case, and can be costly and difficult to locate.

In mid-1968, Porsche began to manufacture all of their engine cases out of magnesium. However, they did not update the design of the case to reflect the weaker material properties of the magnesium. As a result, the early magnesium cases that don't use intermediate shaft bearings need to have their bores reamed and machined to accept the later style intermediate shaft and bearings. In most cases, the magnesium will be worn at the surface where the intermediate shaft rides in the case, necessitating this upgrade.

If you wish to install intermediate bearings in the early 1965-68 aluminum cases, you will need to weld up the bores and have them machined to accept the later style intermediate shaft. I don't recommend this procedure because it is very expensive (about $750) and also unnecessary. The intermediate shaft can run fine in the bare aluminum bore for both street and race engines.

Main Bearings

From 1975-1977, the factory switched the location of the tangs on the bearings. As a result, you must use bearings specific to that year, or have your case machined to accept the previous years' bearings. The machining process involves cutting notches for the bearing tangs into both sides of the main bearing webs. This is not a difficult process, but sometimes it is less expensive and easier to locate and use an engine case from a different year. I have also seen pre-1975 cases with the bearing tangs switched. No one can quite explain this—one theory is that these are factory replacement crankcases. Double-check your case before you purchase your main bearings.

Piston Squirters

The early cases up through 1970 did not have piston squirters. These small jets are mounted on the outboard surfaces of the main bearing webs and supply the inside of the piston crowns with a steady stream of oil (Figure 3-9). This helps to reduce piston temperatures by about 100 degrees or more, which is very significant. Installing the piston squirters will increase the life of your engine and are required if you want to run the later style Nikasil or Alusil pistons and cylinders. The squirters should be installed by your machine shop when your case is overhauled. The part number for the piston squirters is 911.101.011.01 (911 1974-89) and

49

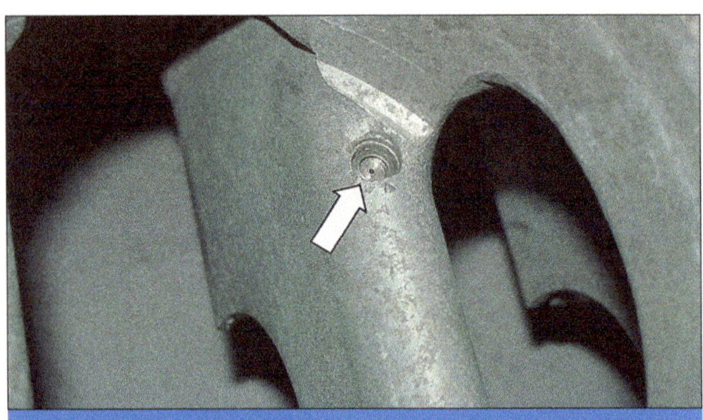

3-9 *In 1971, Porsche installed piston squirters in their engine cases. This was a significant upgrade, as it reduced the piston crown temperatures by as much as 100 degrees Fahrenheit. These piston squirters are an excellent upgrade if your case doesn't have them, and are required if you want to run the later-style Nikasil and Alusil pistons and cylinders.*

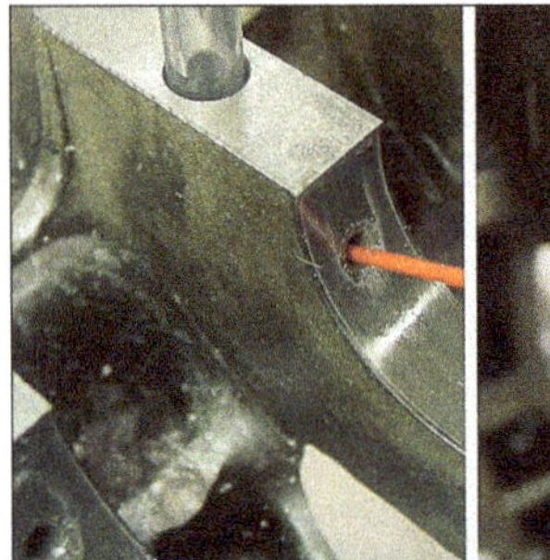

3-10 *The piston squirters should be thoroughly cleaned out before you assemble your case. On the case half with cylinders four through six, there is no practical method to access the squirters except through the main bearing oil holes. As shown in the left photo you need to use a small piece of rubber fuel line to block the intersection of the squirter supply while you spray through the main bearing holes. On the other case half, you can access the oil holes for the piston squirters directly inside the through-bolt holes.*

930.101.015.00 (911 Turbo). The 911 Turbo squirters may be used as an upgrade for high-performance engines.

When the case is brought to the machine shop, the piston squirters already installed should be blown out and cleaned. There is a trick for blowing out the piston squirters. On the right case half, you cannot directly access the holes that supply the piston squirters. If you try to clean them out, the cleaner will spray right back at you from the through-bolt holes. The trick is to insert a small piece of rubber hose into the through-bolt holes and block off the outlet that empties into these bores. Then, you can spray carburetor or brake cleaner into the hole that supplies oil to the main bearings and force out the piston squirters (Figure 3-10).

The left case half is a bit easier to access, as the supply holes for the piston squirters can be reached with a flexible plastic extension on your can of cleaner. Simply blow the cleaner through the access holes, and it should spray out of the squirters. When cleaning the squirters, you should see the cleaner exit in a spray pattern, not dribble out. Dribbling cleaner is a sign that your passages and squirters are clogged. Keep cleaning it until you have a nice even spray.

Re-Plane Cylinder Spigots

On the magnesium cases, the engine has a tendency to warp the entire case across the line of cylinder spigots. (The spigot is the cylindrical base where the cylinders mate with the engine case.) As a result, the center spigot can be as much as .020 inch below the ones on either side. Obviously, this makes for a gap somewhere in the center cylinder head assembly if not corrected while the case is apart. The solution is to have the machine shop level and plane all three spigots. The case is set on a precision milling machine, and all of the spigots are machined to be exactly level with each other.

Case Resizing

Very often, the engine case has a bearing that is out of round or has become oversized due to the forces placed on it (Figure 3-11). Particularly with the magnesium cases, it is very common to find center bearing bores that are no longer in spec. Previously, the fix for this problem was to align-bore the case out to the next larger bearing size. While you can have this machine work performed without any problems, you will end up with a case that requires oversized bearings, which are not ideal to use. They can be expensive and difficult to locate.

Another solution, used by Competition Engineering of Lake Isabella, California, involves machining and resizing the case in a similar manner to how the rods are machined.

3-11 *A dial-bore gauge is one of the more useful tools in the machine shop. Not only can it accurately measure the distances inside the case bearing journals, but it can also be used to determine if a journal is out of round. The dial-bore gauge is a precision tool that you usually only find at machine shops; however, it can be a particularly valuable asset for your own shop as well.*

The case is separated, all the studs are removed, and each case half is precision ground along the parting line to remove material from all mating surfaces. Then the case is reassembled and torqued together. Finally, the center bores are align-bored using a special boring bar that cuts the original bearing surfaces back to their original size. The case is then refitted with new studs. The effect on the compression ratio, chain tension, and fit of the chain housings is minimal if only a small amount of material is removed.

This resizing method is very popular for the magnesium cases, which can become somewhat distorted because they're not strong enough to support the stresses placed on the case. As the case is exposed to thermal cycles and combustion forces, it will deform in many different directions, bending, stretching and twisting across many axes and planes. The case-bearing saddles will become egg-shaped and the entire case itself will twist. In addition, the magnesium case will relax and deform farther after it has been disassembled. The stresses placed upon the material have a tendency to create hidden stresses on the case that are not apparent until the case is split. When the case is bolted together, the two halves support each other and help to keep the proper structure of the case.

You can sometimes observe this when you separate your case halves. Before you split the case, make sure that the crankshaft can turn freely in its bearings. Split the case and let it sit overnight. Then retorque the case halves together with the crankshaft and bearings installed. It is not uncommon for the crank to become stuck and offer resistance to being rotated. This is because the case halves—no longer supporting each other—have relaxed into their natural, deformed orientations. Resizing the case and correcting any other case deformities brings the case back into its original specifications.

Rebore Spigots

The weaker magnesium cases also have a tendency to warp around the piston spigots. When disassembling the case, you might have a difficult time removing the cylinders from their bores. This is usually not the case with the aluminum crankcases. The magnesium cylinder spigots warp so that they are no longer round. This warping has a tendency to affect the center spigot most of all, since there is less material and less support in the center of the case. The cure for warped spigots is to rebore them so they are brought back to round again.

Spot-Facing Through-Bolt Surfaces

On some magnesium cases, you can see the case warping by simply looking at the through-bolt holes (Figure 3-12). Very often they will appear oblong to the naked eye. While this out-of-round condition does not affect the operation of

3-12 *The magnesium cases bend and deform. This can be clearly seen in some magnesium cases where the through-bolt holes have been stretched and are now oblong. Although this doesn't affect the performance or reliability of the case, the outside surface where the bolts mount needs to be spot faced flat in order to prevent oil leaks. The hole appears oblong in the magnesium case shown in this photo.*

the engine, the pulling of these through-bolts in the case will have a tendency to distort the mounting surface for the through-bolt washers. The through-bolts occupy an area of the case that is used for oil transportation and supply. As a result, the through-bolts have an o-ring that is installed under a beveled washer. If this surface is not perfectly level, the case may leak at this interface. The cure is to slightly cut each surface with a fly cutter and plane them so they are all smooth, level, and at the same height. This creates a flat surface that the through-bolt o-ring will mount to.

Case-Savers

Adding case-savers is perhaps the most common upgrade or repair you can perform on your case. The threads in the soft magnesium material used to manufacture the early cases are not strong enough to secure the studs when the case is stressed. As a result, the studs pull out of the case. This is most prevalent with the cylinder head studs, although other studs in the case also have a tendency to pull out. As mentioned in Chapter 1, if you have a case with pulled head studs, it requires a full rebuild. Aluminum cases are strong enough that they don't suffer from the same head-stud problem. However, the magnesium cases manufactured from 1969 through 1977 will encounter these problems eventually. Particularly as the case ages and is exposed to an increased quantity of temperature cycles, the magnesium will weaken and the studs will pull.

Many shops repair pulled studs by inserting what are known as Time-Serts into the case. These are threaded steel inserts that are larger than the diameter of the original studs. The hole in the case is tapped and the Time-Sert is installed with a special insert tool. The tool helps press the Time-Sert into the case, creating an interference fit. This fit is what locks the Time-Sert so that it will not back out of the case if you try to remove a stud.

51

However, I have personally had problems using Time-Serts with a magnesium case. Although Time-Serts have been successfully used in many Porsche 911 engines, they can pull out if the engine is stressed. Figure 2-39 in Chapter 2 shows a properly installed Time-Sert that has been pulled out of the case. Because the Time-Sert creates an interference fit, it actually pushes out into the case to maintain its grip. Because the magnesium material is weak, this force has a tendency to deform the material around the case. This deformation actually makes the case weaker, and increasingly prone to having the studs pull out.

Instead of using Time-Serts to repair your case, I recommend that you use what are known as case-savers (Figure 3-13). Competition Engineering uses these steel inserts, which are specially manufactured for installation into 911 engine cases. The inserts are not an interference fit and install into the case without damaging the material. They have a larger outer diameter than the Time-Serts, so they can even be installed on a case that has had Time-Serts pulled out of it.

The case-savers have a very coarse pitch on their outer threads. Most engineering books will tell you a fine thread will give you greater strength than a coarse thread. However, this is not the case with weaker materials like magnesium. The coarser threads actually maintain a stronger grip in the magnesium because there is more material to grab onto. A fine-threaded case-saver would pull out very easily, whereas the coarse-threaded ones don't. The opposite is true with aluminum because the material is much stronger.

You should install case-savers for every cylinder head stud, as well as for the long 8mm stud that is close to the intermediate shaft on the inside of the case. In addition, it's sometimes wise to reinforce the studs that hold the engine to the transmission (Figure 3-14). If you really want to treat your case right, you can have all the small outer case studs removed, all of the holes reinforced with helicoil inserts, and have brand-new studs installed. This is the standard procedure for magnesium cases at Competition Engineering. It's very difficult to pull a case-saver out of the magnesium—with the added strength, you should be able to put together a high-compression, high-performance engine.

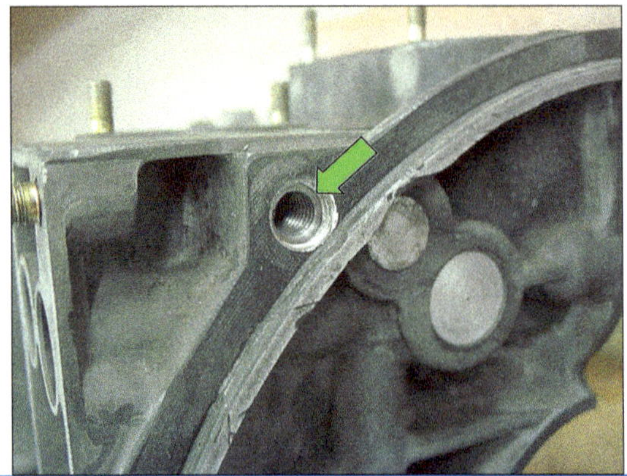
3-14 *The studs that mount the transmission can also pull out of the case. The threads on the case should be checked for damage and replaced with a case-saver (green arrow) or helicoil insert where necessary.*

At the same time that you are checking all of the threads on your case, check the cam oil line threads as well. These sometimes become galled or cross-threaded, and may need to have an insert or case-saver installed in their bore.

Oil Pump Bypass Modification

I talk about this modification in Chapter 4's discussion of performance upgrades, but I thought it worthy of mention here, too. Every case that doesn't have it should receive this upgrade at the machine shop. The bypass modification was instituted by the factory in mid-1976, and it is also a very popular upgrade, so your case may already be modified. The process involves plugging an oil outlet in the case and drilling a hole that connects two other oil passages (Figure 3-15). The result is that oil flow and pressure is increased. It's a simple modification with no real downside. See the full description in Chapter 4.

Case Cleaning

This is perhaps the most important step in preparing your case for assembly. The case has many hidden oil passages and nooks and crannies for dirt, oil, and debris to hide. The case should be cleaned in a parts washer by your machine shop, and then re-cleaned with brake cleaner when you get it back from the shop. Use a couple of cans of carburetor or brake cleaner, and spray the inside and outside of the case thoroughly in order to remove any dirt or grime that may have been left out of the machine shop cleaning process. Be sure to remove the oil pressure relief pistons and springs from the case before you send it out to be cleaned. The cleaning process can corrode the piston and make it stick in its bore. The piston on the side is a safety relief valve, the bottom controls the oil pressure. You can reach the bottom piston with a long screwdriver from the oil pressure sender mounting hole. Use compressed air to blow the cleaner out of the oil passages so it doesn't dilute the oil when you initially start

3-13 *This little device, called a case-saver, is better than the standard Time-Sert because it doesn't install with an interference fit. Similar to installing a wood screw into a piece of wood, the Time-Sert relies on expansion into the metal to secure its fit. While this may work for some materials, I wouldn't recommend it for the relatively soft magnesium cases.*

the engine. Carefully inspect and clean all case bores and oil passages using liberal amounts of cleaner. Using lint-free wipes, carefully clean out every surface, nook, and cranny that you can see, and even the ones that you can't see. Wrap the case up in plastic when you're not cleaning it so that dirt and dust don't find their way in. One sure-fire way to get off on the wrong foot with your engine rebuild is to start out with a dirty case. Cleanliness is vital to preventing oil leaks and also necessary to ensure that your bearings, rings, and all your other parts seat and mate properly. If you don't spend a total of about 3-5 hours cleaning your case, you probably have not done an adequate job.

INTERMEDIATE SHAFT & OIL PUMP

Your intermediate shaft assembly needs to be inspected for wear after it has been removed from the engine. The primary spot for wear will be around the aluminum gear teeth. Particularly if there was a catastrophic engine failure, you may find that the teeth are ground up or, even worse, missing.

It's also important to remember to clean out the central bore of the intermediate shaft. This often-overlooked shaft can hide dirt and grime. There is a small circlip that secures a small aluminum plug inside the intermediate shaft. Remove this circlip and clean out the dirt and debris inside the shaft. The internals of this shaft are directly exposed to the engine oil, and you might be surprised at how much dirt and debris can end up inside (Figure 3-16).

The second spot for wear is around the timing chain sprockets. If the chain was loose or even too tight (as is the case when running mechanical, non-spring-loaded tensioners), then you may find wear on the outer edges of the sprocket teeth. The entire shaft assembly can be disassembled and the sprockets replaced.

The oil pump is a tough one to inspect from the outside. Inspect the gears by carefully looking through the large holes in the side of the housing. Look for pitting in the gears and also check to see if there is any slop or significant backlash. If it's been sitting for a while, spray some oil into the pump to free up the gears. I don't recommend disassembling your oil pump. The gears of the pump wear together, because each tooth on each gear will always mate with the same tooth on the opposite gear. If the pump is disassembled, the gears must be reassembled exactly in the same orientation as when they were taken apart, otherwise the pump can bind.

I don't recommend reusing pumps that have been pulled from engines that have suffered a catastrophic failure. Small metallic particles that can get flushed through the system can damage the oil pump gears beyond repair. If your oil pump does not turn freely, or if you see pitting or gouges on the oil pump gear surfaces, then find yourself another pump. Damage to the oil pump here will result in decreased oil pressure when the engine is running.

PISTONS & CYLINDERS

Since 1965, Porsche has used four different types of cylinders in their production 911 engines. The early cars used either completely cast-iron cylinders or a biral cylinder that was manufactured out of cast-iron and had outer aluminum fins cast onto it. From 1968-73, Porsche used a completely cast-iron cylinder on the 911 T engines to help reduce production costs.

Nikasil vs. Alusil Cylinders

In 1973 Porsche introduced a new type of cylinder on the 911 2.7 Carrera RS. Engineered by German manufacturer Mahle, Nikasil cylinders are manufactured out of a dense, aluminum alloy that is centrifugally cast in a mold. The cylinder bore is then electroplated with a very thin layer of nickel-silicon carbide. Originally designed and used on the venerable 917 in 1971, these cylinders provide several unique advantages over the older style ones. The primary advantage is that the micro-thin layer is extremely durable and allows for thinner cylinder wall thickness. As a result, the piston bores can be enlarged without changing the original cylinder head stud bolt pattern. In addition, the reduced friction along the cylinder walls combined with the surface properties of the nickel-silicon coating creates a tighter seal between the piston rings and cylinder wall. The result is a slight increase in overall horsepower due to the increased efficiency.

Nikasil cylinders are the most durable of any of the production cylinders and are highly sought after for engine rebuilds. These cylinders can be retrofitted to the earlier cars; however, you will need to install the updated piston squirters in your early case (1970 and earlier) if it doesn't already have them. The piston squirters lower the piston crown temperatures so that you can run the close clearances used by Nikasil or Alusil pistons and cylinders. It's also important to note that Mahle makes replacement Nikasil pistons and cylinders for 2.2-liter and 2.4-liter engines.

In 1974, Porsche introduced a less expensive alternative to Nikasil—Alusil cylinders, manufactured by Kolbenschmidt. These cylinders are manufactured out of a special 390 eutectic aluminum-silicon alloy, and are used with a special iron-plated, ferrocoat piston. Like the Nikasil cylinders, they have a special coating on their inside bore. This coating is electrically etched to leave a microscopic layer of silicon particles exposed on the cylinder wall. The iron-plated piston and the silicon cylinder walls operated together to create a durable combination. In addition, the Alusil cylinders have the same thin-wall construction of the Nikasil cylinders, meaning that they too can maintain the same head-stud spacing pattern.

So what are the main differences between all of the available pistons and cylinders? The early biral cylinders can be honed and reused just like other cast-iron cylinders on non-Porsche cars (Figure 3-17). Starting in 1974, Porsche mixed and matched the Alusil and Nikasil sets, so it's really the luck of the draw as to which set you have in your car. For the most part, Porsche used mostly Alusil in the 2.7-liter and 3.0-liter engines because of their lower production cost. The Alusil cylinders, unfortunately, cannot be honed. The honing process destroys the etched layer and renders them useless. In fact, a general rule of thumb is that the Alusil cylinders are a one-time-use product, and should not be used again if the engine is re-

3-17 *The honing machine cuts a crisscross pattern on the inside of the cylinders that helps the rings seat and also controls the oiling of the cylinder wall. Also useful is a "grape hone," which can place a slight roughness on the inside of the cylinders.*

built. The basic rule of thumb is that Alusil piston and cylinder sets have a soft-walled cylinder and a hard piston, whereas Nikasil sets have a hard cylinder and a soft piston. You cannot mix and match Alusil and Nikasil components together (i.e., Alusil pistons will not work with Nikasil cylinders).

Alusil cylinders cannot be reliably re-ringed. This indeed is a common misconception in some Porsche circles. Of course, throwing out your current pistons and cylinders leads to the large expense of new ones, so a lot of people reuse them anyway. In some cases, the new set of rings seat fine, and they indeed can be reused successfully. However, you cannot hone these cylinders, nor predict whether the rings will seat properly. The correct action to take is to purchase new pistons and cylinders; otherwise you may be tearing down your engine again in less than 1,000 miles.

These Alusil cylinders typically have a "KS" Kolbenschmidt logo cast into their base, although for a time Mahle also made Alusil cylinders. The coating on the Alusil cylinders is non-magnetic, while the Nikasil coating is ever so slightly magnetic. So you should be able to tell the difference between them with a simple refrigerator magnet.

If you are tearing apart your engine for reasons other than worn-out rings or valve guides, then you might opt to reuse your Alusil cylinders. This would be the case, for example, if you were tearing down a low-mileage engine to replace broken or pulled head studs. In that situation, I would recommend that you take your pistons and cylinders off of the engine, put them on a shelf, and don't touch them until you are ready to reassemble: don't pull the pistons out of the cylinders and don't dislodge or disturb the rings. Of course, you are taking a risk here that you will have worn rings in the near future. However, if your engine is a 3.0 liter with 100,000 miles on the odometer, and otherwise in good condition, then there is a good chance that you can get 100,000 additional miles or more out of your rings, cylinders, and pistons. I don't necessarily recommend playing the odds like this, but if you're rebuilding a good-running engine with excellent leak-down numbers for the purpose of replacing head studs or some other non-wear problem, then it might be a good bet.

The Nikasil cylinders can be honed and reused. They typically have a "MAHLE" stamp on the lower side of the cylinder. The nickel-carbide surface needs to be lightly honed with a special silica impregnated tool, or what is commonly known as a grape or flex hone. The surface properties are too hard for normal tool steel honing machines. You should only have an expert familiar with the Nikasil cylinders perform the honing process.

Pistons

For the most part, Porsche used cast pistons in all its production cars. The notable exceptions have been the 911 S model (2.0 liter, 2.2 liter, 2.4 liter), the 911 2.7 RS, and a spate of high-performance and racing engines. For these applications, Porsche used a forged piston. As any Porsche wheel connoisseur will tell you, Porsche Fuchs factory alloys are almost exclusively forged, not cast. The forging process creates a much stronger part that will not be as susceptible to cracks and damage. In a similar manner, the Porsche forged pistons are the strongest of their type. Fortunately, for most street uses, the cast pistons are perfectly fine. It's only when an engine revs consistently above 6,700 rpm that the strength of the cast pistons comes into question.

For the past 30 years, Mahle has manufactured the best and most reliable pistons for Porsche. Their unique ability to forge an alloy piston with a high silicon content means that the piston expands less when hot. The result is that tighter piston/cylinder clearances can be used without the fear of the pistons seizing when hot. These tighter clearances translate into better ring sealing, less noise, and increased performance.

Until very recently, the Mahle pistons were basically the only game in town. However, another company has begun manufacturing similar high-quality pistons that can be used in the 911 engine. JE Pistons, of Huntington Beach, California, is now able to manufacture high-performance, custom replacement pistons for just about any 911 engine, as shown in Figure 3-18. The advantages of this are two-fold. Whereas previously you had to purchase an entire set of pistons and cylinders together, now you can choose to replace only your pistons if your cylinders are still reusable. In addition, when you purchase your new pistons, JE can custom build them so that you can create just about any compression ratio you desire. No longer handcuffed to complete piston and cylinder sets, you can purchase these pistons to upgrade your application. For example, in the past if you wanted to upgrade your engine to 911 2.7 RS specifications, you had to spend a lot of money purchasing the 2.7 RS piston and

3-18 *This photo shows a brand-new JE piston. The JE pistons are a great alternative to purchasing a new set of pistons and cylinders. Because they can be custom made for any application, you no longer need to purchase pistons and cylinders as a set. The JE pistons are manufactured with quality equal to their German counterparts and should work very well in any 911 engine.*

cylinder set from Mahle. Now you can use standard Nikasil 2.7-liter cylinders and have the pistons custom-made to 2.7 RS specifications by JE. This can result in a cost savings of about 65 percent off of a new set of pistons and cylinders. It is important to note, however, that JE does not manufacture exact replacement pistons for CIS or 3.2-liter engines. The JE pistons do not have the distinctive swirled piston domes that are characteristic of these engines.

Sometimes engine rebuilders are forced to reuse pistons and cylinders that are beyond their useful life because their customer cannot afford the $3,000 that may be required for a new set. Rebuilders and car owners alike should avoid such shortcuts because they will not provide a long-term solution to performance problems, such as excessive oil burning and low compression. One of the primary areas of piston wear is the first ring land where the piston rings sit (Figure 3-19). If this ring groove is too wide (it tends to stretch from millions of cycles), then installing new rings may result in premature ring failure. The failure is caused by the ring wobbling back and forth in the ring groove and is exacerbated by the installation of brand-new rings. These new rings can have such a stiff "bite" on the cylinder walls that they have a tendency to rock the rings back and forth in their loose grooves. The result of this vibration is ring failure after only a few thousand miles. Of course, this only happens with used pistons that have a worn piston ring groove. The solution is to purchase a new set of pistons (either along with the cylinders from Mahle, or just the pistons from JE) and solve the problem properly. You can also purchase individual replacement pistons and cylinders from Mahle if you find that one or two in your set are out of spec.

Some people will recommend running your old rings to avoid placing such a strong load on the worn ring

3-19 *You can check the ring side clearance using a feeler gauge and a new piston compression ring (yellow). Gently rotate the feeler gauge and ring around the piston and check to make sure that the gauge doesn't grab at all around the circumference. Compare the maximum clearance to the specifications given in Appendix A. Installing new rings with pistons that have worn ring grooves can lead to premature ring breakage.*

grooves. While this may work fine for several thousand miles, the piston rings are one of the two primary wear points in the engine. Reusing the old rings will guarantee that your rebuild life will be significantly shorter. Choosing not to replace the rings because your pistons are worn out is downright foolish. If you're going to be rebuilding your engine, you should be prepared to do it properly. You must replace your worn-out pistons in order to achieve a quality rebuild—that's the bottom line.

If by chance one of your pistons or cylinders is damaged, then you may have the option of finding a good used one as a replacement. It's important to note that the cylinders are all manufactured and sorted to height groups as they come out of the factory. Therefore, if you are replacing one of your cylinders, you must make sure that the replacement belongs to the same height group. The marker for the height group is located on the bottom of the cylinder inside of a triangle and is usually a 5 or a 6. Along the same lines, all pistons are sorted and sold by weight groups. If you are replacing one or two pistons out of your set, be sure to obtain replacement pistons that are part of the same weight group. Keeping all the pistons in the same group will help when it's time to have your engine balanced. See Appendix A for more information.

Clearances

After you remove your pistons and cylinders, you can perform a few inspections on them to see if they are still usable. If you don't have the proper tools, then you can always send your pistons and cylinders to your machine shop; they will be able to inspect them and tell you what you need to do to recondition them.

Perhaps the most important measurement that you can perform on your pistons is the ring groove clearance, or ring side clearance. This is easily measured with a set of

feeler gauges placed inside the ring groove. In order to measure this distance accurately, though, you will need a set of new rings or you will need to measure the thickness of your older, used rings precisely. If you do decide to measure this with the old rings (assuming that you haven't decided whether your pistons are reusable), make sure that you account for the fact that the older, used rings themselves are thinner than new replacement ones.

Install the ring around the piston and use a feeler gauge to check that the clearances are not greater than the values indicated in Appendix A. The ring lands are probably bent or damaged if you notice any lack of smoothness. If you find that the feeler gauge fits snugly, then you should check the piston-ring side clearance. This is the gap between the ring and the upper surface of the groove and should be measured with a new compression ring. If you don't have a new ring, simply use one of your old rings, but make sure that you compensate for the difference in thickness between the old ring and the new ring when you determine the clearance. The older ring will be thinner than the new ring and thus will produce a piston-ring side clearance measurement that is too large. This dimension should be within the specifications indicated in Appendix A. If not, then you will have to replace your pistons. Excessive piston-ring side clearance can lead to excess ring wear and premature ring breakage. The lower oil ring is usually well lubricated and doesn't wear as much as the compression rings. Check it for visible damage—if the groove looks fine, then it shouldn't give you any problems.

Your machine shop will be able to measure your pistons and internal cylinder bore size. The internal cylinder walls can be accurately measured using a dial-bore gauge. Pistons can be measured using a micrometer. Both need to meet the specifications for out-of-round and allowable clearance between the piston and cylinder as detailed in Appendix A.

Check the inside of your cylinders for scuffing from a piston scraping against it. This is often caused by engine overheating but can also be seen when the engine has had low oil pressure or a bent rod. Finding this type of damage usually means that significant wear has been inflicted on the piston and cylinder, and that they both need to be replaced. In a normally operating engine, the piston skirts will heat and expand until the piston-to-bore clearance has reached its optimal dimension. However, on an overheated engine, the piston will expand until this clearance becomes zero. As the piston begins to scuff the piston wall, it becomes even hotter, thus exacerbating the situation and accelerating the wear. When the engine cools down, the skirts will have been permanently damaged, and thus have a tendency to pull away from the cylinder walls. When the engine is started up again, this additional clearance is sometimes heard as piston slap, when the piston is slammed against the cylinder wall during each power stroke.

CYLINDER HEADS

Porsche 911 cylinder heads are unique animals that should only be taken to a machine shop that knows all about the intricacies of reconditioning them. Unlike their 356 or Volkswagen counterparts, 911 heads are remarkably robust. They don't suffer from the typical heat and cracking problems that the 4-cylinder cars are very prone to. It's a testament to Porsche's robust design that the 911 air-cooled head has basically remained unchanged from 1965 through 1998, long after the VW heads had been retired.

Disassembly

Most machine shops don't expect customers to have their own spring compressors and, as a result, factor disassembly of the heads into most price sheets. You do not need to disassemble your heads before you send them off to the shop. However, if you're curious, you can purchase a spring compressor (typically thirty dollars or so) and remove the valves yourself. Doing so, you can educate yourself on how the heads are assembled, and also get a feel for the tolerances associated with the valve guides.

I've detailed the procedure for disassembly of the heads at the end of Chapter 2. If you do want to take your heads apart, keep each valve with its respective head—it may make it easier to identify problems with the heads. Don't sandblast or clean the heads until you have the valves removed. Clean each part separately, and not as an assembly. Also, wear safety glasses when you disassemble your heads. The valve springs are very strong, and can fling pieces of your valve assembly around the room if the spring compressor happens to slip.

Valve Seats

The valve seats are the steel inserts that are embedded into the cylinder heads. These seats seal to the head of the valve when the valve is closed. On VW engines, it's not unheard of for a seat to become loose and fall out. This is commonly called a dropped valve seat and usually results in catastrophic damage to the engine. The 911 heads rarely drop seats as they are not as stressed as their 4-cylinder counterparts.

When reconditioning the heads, the valve seat must be ground down with a special tool that matches the angles that are ground into the valve. The angle on the seats, the angle on the valves, and the angle of the valve within the valve guide must be precisely matched for the valve to seat properly and seal against compression loss. A special tool is used to grind and machine the valve seat to mate perfectly with the bore in the valve guide. This tool indexes off of the center bore of the guide itself and ensures that the seat is ground precisely in alignment with the guide (Figures 3-25 and 3-26).

A standard Porsche valve grind is called a three-angle grind. The three-angle grind allows air to flow smoothly into the combustion chamber while providing a level and durable surface for the valve to mate to. Typically the tool that is used to grind the seat is pre-cut to the correct angles required for the standard three-angle grind.

For performance engines, some machine shops will perform a five-angle grind. With the five-angle grind, the edge of the valve seat has more of a rounded profile, allowing air to enter the combustion chamber more freely. This five-angle grind has three radiuses on its edge, which gives the valve a much narrower seat to mate to. The 45-degree angle surface found on the five-angle grind is typically too thin and wears out a lot faster. Also, the narrower seat doesn't transfer heat from the valve head to the seat as efficiently. However, for racers looking to gain that extra bit of horsepower, the freer flowing valve seat does seem to improve performance slightly. The bang for your buck is real small, though, on this particular upgrade.

If the seat is ground down from its original level, then the valve will naturally sit slightly more recessed into the head. This means that the valve stem will stick out farther into the rocker arm area. If too much material is removed from the seats, then the rocker arm angle may be changed. In order to prevent this from happening, and to keep the range of motion on the rocker arm at normal levels, the end of the valve can be ground down. By changing the stem height, you can ensure that the overall height of the valve stem remains the same after a seat is machined.

Using a slightly recessed valve seat also lengthens the total spring compression length because the valve stem keepers now sit farther away from the head. To take back this extra spring length, you will need to install additional shims underneath the spring seats. This will ensure that the overall spring height remains the same, and your spring compression is absolutely correct. Checking the spring height and compression force is standard operating procedure at all reputable machine shops. It's also important to note that different camshafts require different amounts of shims underneath the valve springs. The factory specifications for the valve springs vary whether you're running a T, E, or S camshaft. See Appendix A for details.

When a valve seat has been ground down too many times, it becomes necessary to replace it. Most machine shops will manufacture their own valve seats, as Porsche does not provide a replacement valve seat that is oversized. The proper method for replacing the valve seat involves heating the heads and removing the existing seats. Then the seat bore in the head is slightly enlarged by counterboring to fit the oversized replacement seat. The new seat is pressed into the head after the heads are heated up. This is also the same procedure that is used to add bigger valves to a cylinder head.

Valve Springs

On higher horsepower engines, you can add more shims underneath the valve spring seats. This will have the effect of preloading the springs to a higher compression and will make them spring back quicker. This is necessary only in high-revving race engines where you wish to avoid valve float. Valve float occurs when the engine is revving so high and the valves are moving so fast that the valve spring does not have enough force to pull the valve and rocker arm back in time to accurately follow the camshaft. Valve float is only seen in very high-revving 911 engines (8,000 to 9,000-plus rpm) with large valve sizes and is almost never a problem on the stock engines. The downside to adding more shims is that it will increase the load on your camshafts and rockers and will cause them to wear more quickly. Increased valve spring force will also steal some horsepower as the engine works harder to compress the stiffer springs. As an alternative to using shims, you can also substitute higher compression springs for the stock ones and increase your total spring rate.

Springs should always be inspected and checked on a calibrated spring compressor, shown in Figure 3-20. Your machine shop should definitely use one of these to check the total spring rate of your valve spring pair. Spring rate for the pair is not linear, and should be carefully measured at varying lengths of spring compression. I don't recommend reusing springs. As with any material designed to flex, they will fatigue on a microscopic level. Even if the spring measures perfectly fine on the spring compressor, you may not be aware of weaknesses that have developed inside the material after millions of cycles. It's best to replace your springs while you have the opportunity to do so. Valve stem keepers and valve spring retainers can be reused. Most machinists will tell you from experience that only one brand-new spring out of about 10,000 does not properly pass the spring specification test.

Valve Guides

When you remove your valves from the heads, you can often determine if your valve guides are worn simply by seeing how loose the valve rides in the guide (Figure 3-21). New, in-spec guides should be close fitting, and you shouldn't be able to wiggle the valves in them. Of course, nothing is better than a set of precision bore gauges for determining the condition of your guides. Most home mechanics don't have these, though, so it's best to let your machine shop determine whether your guides need to be replaced.

To remove your old guides, a machine shop will pull them out of the head. The guide is bored out, tapped, and threaded, and then a cap screw is used to grip the guide and drive it out of the head, as shown in Figure 3-22. Walt Watson of Competition Engineering uses custom valve guides designed by Technovance that are specifically manufactured for varying sizes of valve guide bores in the heads. The aluminum heads can warp, stretch, and change their inside valve guide bore dimension over many years of use. The Technovance guides that Walt uses are manufactured in oversized varieties, so that the guides can be perfectly matched to the bore. Pressing in the perfectly matched valve guide does not stress the guide or the aluminum boss, which helps retain the guide's alignment with the valve seat (Figures 3-23 and 3-24).

3-20 Not quite a household item, the spring tester checks both the large and small spring stogether. New springs are usually very reliable and only one in about 10,000 do not pass the test. Still, it is a regular procedure to check them on the spring compressor. As the compressor pushes the springs down, the resulting force is shown on the dial indicator.

3-21 You can assess the condition of the valve guides simply by placing a new valve in them and seeing how much the valve wobbles. If it doesn't move around too much, then further measuring of the valve guide wear will be required. In most cases, the valve will wobble, indicating that the guides are worn and should be replaced.

Once the valve guides are pressed into the head, they are precision machined to their proper inside diameter using a precision reamer. The tolerances between the valve stems

3-22 *The valve guides are removed from the heads by threading them and then inserting a cap screw into them. The screw and valve guide can then be easily removed from the head.*

3-23 *The old and new valve guides are placed side by side here for comparison. Valve guide design and materials used over the years have improved. In particular, the valve guides from the 2.7-liter motors used from 1974-77 were known to wear out in less than 60,000 miles. Newer advances in materials can increase that wear time up to 250,000 miles or more.*

3-24 *Walt Watson of Competition Engineering has his valve guides custom-made to fit the bore inside the head. The use of these special valve guides, manufactured by Technovance, reduces the stress on the head and the guide. The small bosses that support the guide can crack if a valve guide that is too large is forced into the bore.*

and the guides are very important to overall cooling and valve wear, and must be precisely maintained. The precision location of the valve guide is then used as an index to align the tool that machines the valve seats (Figures 3-25 and 3-26). The valve seats are machined precisely in line with the valve guides to ensure that the valve will seat properly when closed.

Valves

Valves usually take a lot of abuse and need to be inspected carefully. As mentioned previously, you can disassemble the heads yourself or have your machine shop do it for you. Most shops factor in the cost of disassembling the heads, so you should probably only disassemble your heads if you are curious about the condition of the valves. Also, much of the combustion chamber will be coated with carbon, which makes diagnosing the condition of your valves difficult. The machine shop will be able to blast all of the carbon off of the valves before inspecting them.

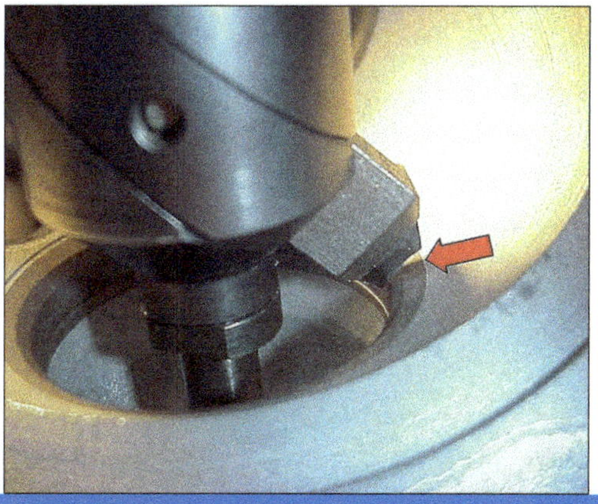

3-25 *The heads are machined on a jig that is aligned to cut the valve seats to match the valves exactly. A cutting tool cuts the angle of the seats (red arrow) while the machine holds the heads aligned to the inner bore of the valve guide.*

3-26 *The tool used for grinding the valve seats is made of tool steel and is ground to reflect the desired profile and angle of the seats.*

Sodium-Filled Exhaust Valves

The 911 engine uses steel valves for the intake ports, and sodium-filled valves for the exhaust ports. The sodium-filled valves are specially manufactured to help disperse heat away from the head and the combustion chamber. These valves have a hollow stem, which is partially filled with sodium. The sodium is a solid at room temperature, but quickly melts and becomes a liquid when the engine warms up. As the valve opens and closes, the sodium picks up heat from the head of the valve and conducts it away toward the stem. The stem is always in contact with the valve guide, and the heat from the stem is transported out through the guide. The guide then conducts the heat into the cylinder head, which is cooled by the flow of air through the cylinder cooling fins. You can identify the sodium-filled valves by the small divot located in the center of the valve head. This is where the sodium is added to the valve stem during the manufacturing process. One additional note: the Porsche factory technical specifications book for the 1984-87 Carrera (WKD-423-020) states that the exhaust valves used on 3.2-liter engines are not sodium filled. The spec book for 1982-83 states that they are sodium filled. However, the 1974-89 Parts and Technical Reference Catalog (PNA-000-147) says that all exhaust valves are the same from 1978-89. This is a clear example of the inaccuracies of factory documentation that has plagued Porsche owners since the 1950s. My point? Don't trust the factory documentaion as the final word.

Valve Stem Wear

Valves themselves need to be checked for wear. There are five major dimensions associated with valves. These are the valve length, the stem diameter, the margin on the head, the diameter of the head, and the angle of the face that mates with the seat located in the cylinder head (Figure 3-27). We'll talk first about the valve stem. Although the newer style valve guides are manufactured out of a soft, bronze alloy that is stronger than materials used earlier, the valves will still wear along the valve stem. The outer diameter of the valve will actually tend to taper, especially if the guides are heavily worn. The outer ends of the valve stem farthest from the valve head have a tendency to wear a bit more than the inside, creating this taper. The valve must be within spec across its entire length to be suitable for reuse. Since this spec is pretty tight, most valves that are measurably tapered will need to be replaced with new ones.

If the valve stem is out of spec, then you will have excess clearance between the valve guide and the stem. Under the best circumstances, this will cause oil consumption to increase and power to decrease. Under the worst-case scenario, the valve stem to guide clearance will become so large that it no longer dissipates heat from the valve head. The head of the valve will overheat and possibly break off, causing catastrophic engine failure. If the valve doesn't meet the specification across the *entire* length of the valve stem, you will need to replace it.

Valve Margin

Every valve has a head with a specific amount of material located on the edge that can be removed by grinding

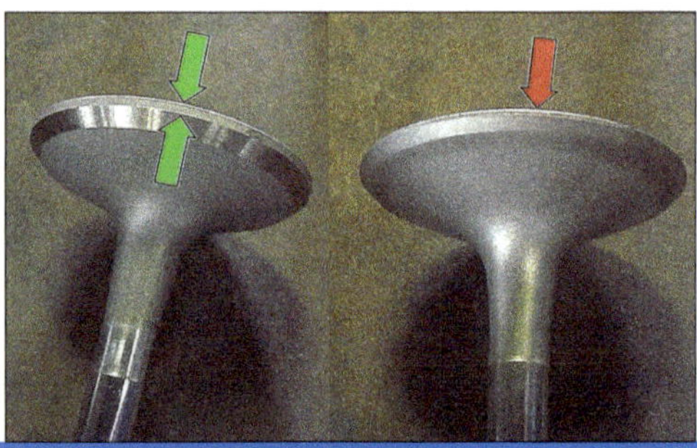

3-28 *Valves can usually be reused if there is enough material on the edge for a regrind (green arrows). The valve on the left is a brand-new one; the one on the right doesn't have enough margin left on its edge for another regrind (red arrow). Intake valves can usually be used again with no problems, but the exhaust valves should only be used once, unless they are the more expensive sodium-filled ones (standard equipment on 911s). These exhaust valves dissipate heat much better than ordinary steel ones and thus have a longer life.*

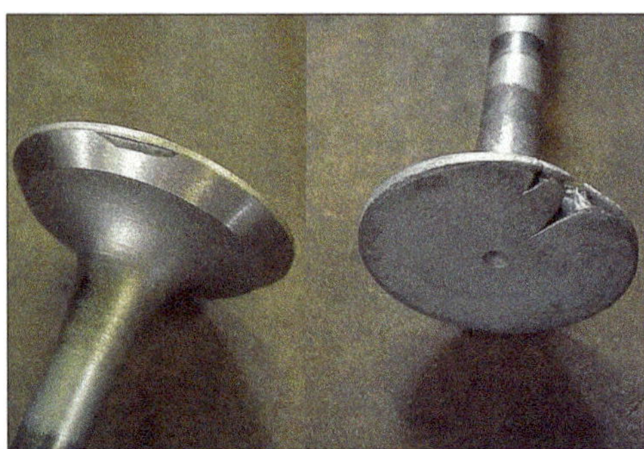

3-29 *Here are two valves that have seen better days. The valve on the left has been ground so thin that its edge has cracked off. The valve on the right came from an engine that exhibited signs of the valve getting too hot. If the seat and the valve don't mate perfectly, then hot spots will build up in the valve, causing cracks like the ones in this valve.*

3-27 *There are five major valve dimensions. **A-** overall valve length, **B-** valve stem diameter, **C-** valve head margin, **D-** face angle, **E-** head diameter. All of these dimensions need to be within the desired specifications in order for you to reuse the valve in your rebuild.*

(Figure 3-28). This is the distance from the valve head surface to the outer edge of the valve face, or in other terms, the thickness of the head at its largest diameter. The normal process of valve reconditioning includes a regrind of this area in order to restore fresh sealing surfaces on the valve so that it will mate snugly with the seat in the head. If a valve has been reground many times, then there may not exist enough margin to safely grind and recondition the valve. If this margin becomes too thin, then the valve may crack at its outer edge or overheat and burn, as shown in Figure 3-29. It is important that your machine shop is aware of and acknowledges the limits that the 911 valves can be ground to.

If there is enough surface left, then the machine shop can use a precision grinder to refinish this angled surface. The valve is placed in a special grinding machine that rotates the

valve while removing a very small amount of material. Typically less than 0.010 inch (0.25mm) is removed for each grind—just enough to remove small irregularities in the valve surface. Removing too much material here will reduce the cooling properties of the valve. If the valve is damaged or oblong, then this will show immediately during the grinding process (Figure 3-30). Following the grinding process, the tip is slightly chamfered to remove any sharp edges or burrs.

When the entire head is reassembled with the valve spring, the assembly is pressure checked using a vacuum pump and gauge, as shown in Figure 3-31. Any loss of pressure will indicate a leaky valve that will need to be remachined.

Head Resurfacing

If your engine suffered from a pulled or broken head stud, then it might have incurred some damage to the head/cylinder mating surface (Figure 3-32). Often when studs break or become loose, they cause an exhaust leak at this interface. This exhaust leak eats away at the metal and causes both the head and the cylinder to become damaged. It's possible that the cylinder head gasket can become loose and then disintegrate as it is smashed repeatedly into the head and cylinder by the combustion cycle of the engine.

3-30 If there is enough margin left on the valve, then it can be reground to match the valve seats. The process is performed on a valve grinder that can be set to match the angle of the valve to the angle of the valve seat.

3-31 After performing all head work, including a valve and seat regrind, the sealing surfaces are checked by pulling a vacuum on each port. This vacuum test will indicate if there are any burrs left on the valve or the seat from the machining process and is the last and final quality control step to ensure that the head will function perfectly in your rebuilt engine. An alternative test would be to fill the combustion chamber of the assembled head with paint thinner and see if any leaks out into the ports.

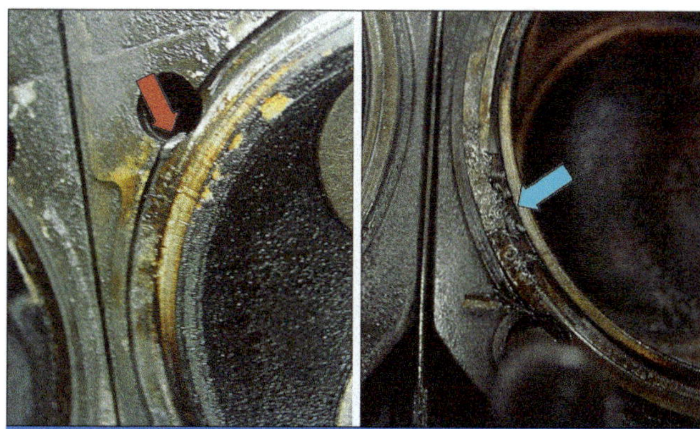

3-32 Shown here are a head and cylinder that have been damaged from an exhaust leak. The cylinder head gasket has been mashed into many little pieces and crushed against both the head (red arrow) and the cylinder (blue arrow). It is important to note that this car was driven for only about 40 miles with this exhaust leak. The head was damaged beyond repair and had to be replaced with a good used one.

The solution is to fly cut the heads in order to smooth out the cylinder head mating surface. All of the heads need to be cut the same amount (at least the ones used on the same side of the engine) to ensure that the entire assembly has the same clearances and heights all around. If your heads have been cut before, then you may run into trouble, as removing too much material will cause your combustion chamber volume to shrink. This in turn increases the danger that your pistons may hit your valves. Further discussion of this tolerance buildup is detailed at the end of this chapter.

CAMSHAFTS

Camshafts require a different type of attention when rebuilding your engine. Depending upon what type of engine you are rebuilding, then you may want to replace your camshafts with new ones, or have them reground to a more aggressive profile. Either way, you should carefully inspect your camshafts for wear when you remove them from the camshaft housings.

Camshaft Wear

Camshafts can experience wear on their cam lobes and bearing surfaces, as shown in Figure 3-33. Camshafts are not typically serviced by a Porsche machine shop, but instead should be sent directly to a shop that specializes in cam reconditioning and regrinding. They will have the expertise and knowledge to precision grind and reharden your camshaft to original specs. Webcam and Elgin are two excellent camshaft reconditioning shops.

When you remove your cams, you should carefully check the cam lobes. Mild discoloration on the lobes is typical for engines that have sat for a few years. This is a mere oil stain and doesn't indicate any significant wear. However, the cam lobes can show signs of pitting and wear on the upper side of one or more of the lobes. Typically, dirty oil plays a part in premature cam lobe wear. You can also see the effects of dirty oil on the bearing surfaces of the cam and inside the bearing journals of the camshaft housing. The good news is that camshafts can easily be rewelded, reground, and rehardened to original specifications, or to a more aggressive profile. Most good cam manufactures will be able to regrind your cams to just about any profile that you choose. More detail on this is available in Chapter 4, Section 3—Performance Enhancements.

Camshafts have a tendency to run for a very long time with little or no wear. However, once the wear begins, it rapidly increases. This is because the camshafts are surface hardened. Once the rocker and cam lobe wear through the thin hardening layer, the softer metal below tends to wear rapidly. Worn camshafts result in noisy valves and poor performance as the valves will no longer follow the desired camshaft profile.

Reconditioning Camshafts

Worn camshafts are rewelded and then reground to the profile that you specify. After they are reground, they are surface hardened to original specifications (Figure 3-34). Reworked camshafts offer comparable performance to brand-new ones, and can result in significant savings on the bottom line as well. If you are planning to have your camshafts reconditioned, then you should have your rockers reconditioned as well. New or reconditioned rockers should always be mated with new or reconditioned camshafts. The reasoning behind this is that both the rockers and the camshafts are hardened, and if one is new and the other is older, then one will wear out much faster than the other. You always want to keep the rockers and the camshafts matched together.

Feel free to take your camshaft to your Porsche-expert machine shop, or have a specialty camshaft house inspect it for you. They will be able to advise you on whether it will need reconditioning. If you are going to reuse your camshaft, then you should install your rockers back into the same locations they came from. You want to keep the wear patterns the same on the camshaft and the rockers. If you mix and match the rockers and the camshafts, then you will have a mismatch of worn hardened areas on the cam lobes meeting worn areas on the rockers. As a result your camshaft and rockers will wear prematurely. The important thing to remember here is that you want to mark and label

3-33 *Camshaft wear comes in two varieties—cam lobe wear and bearing wear. The scratches seen on this camshaft bearing (orange arrow) are the result of an engine being run with dirty oil. Although this particular camshaft is fine to reuse in a rebuild, any more damage to the bearing surface would probably render it scrap. The cam lobe wear shown here (red arrow) is typical when the hardened portion of the camshaft is worn away. This pitting is completely repairable if sent to a proper camshaft repair shop. The shop can weld and repair any pitting on the lobes.*

3-34 *Here is the camshaft from Figure 3-33 after it has come back from the shop. The cam lobes have been welded, reground, and rehardened for use with brand-new rocker shafts.*

all of your rockers as you remove them from your camshaft housings, otherwise you will be forced to recondition both, even if they aren't showing signs of wear.

In Chapter 4, I discuss a technique for determining your camshaft profile. You may find that the camshafts have been reground to a different profile, and that the original Porsche part number does not reflect the true nature of the camshaft. This is of course a moot point if you are having your camshafts reground and reconditioned. It's a smart idea to know what cam profile you have been running in your engine so that you can replicate or improve upon its performance.

CAMSHAFT HOUSINGS & ROCKERS

The camshaft housings are cast out of aluminum and are generally very robust. The camshaft rides on a thin layer of engine oil over bare aluminum within the camshaft housing. There are only three areas where the camshaft housings typically need attention—the cam bearing surface, the rocker shaft mounting surfaces, and the oil squirter tubes.

Camshaft Bore Wear

The cam bearing surface should be visually inspected when you remove the camshaft. Deep gouging or grooves are symptomatic of running the engine with dirty oil, as shown in Figure 3-35. In general, slight scratching of the camshaft housing inner bore surfaces are okay, but any significant gouges or grooves mean that the camshaft housing should be scrapped and replaced with a good used one. If you happen to have a good dial-bore gauge, you can measure the inside of the bearing bores and check them against the allowable dimensions (See Appendix A for the exact dimensions). The camshafts also have an axial play and runout specification, but due to the relatively low forces imposed on the camshafts, they are almost never out of spec with respect to these two measurements.

Rocker Bore Damage

The other area of the camshaft housings that need inspection is the rocker shaft bores. The rocker shaft bore does not act as a bearing surface, as the rockers rotate on the shaft itself. However, if the rockers were not removed properly or were stuck in their bores, then they might be badly scored inside the rocker shaft bore. Any significant scratches or grooves in the bore can cause oil leaks when the engine is reassembled.

Both the camshaft bearing surface and the rocker arm surface wear are somewhat subjective measurements—particularly when there are a lot of scratches on the inside of the bore. There is no easy specification that would be able to tell you easily whether you can reuse your camshaft housings. The best idea is to send them out to a Porsche machine shop and have them professionally cleaned and

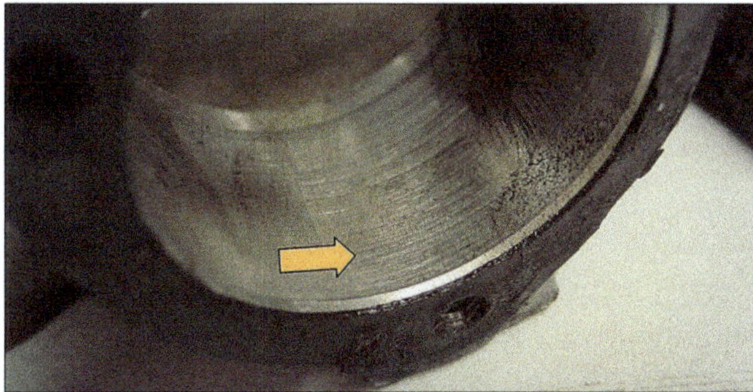

3-35 *As seen on the camshaft itself, the camshaft housing has similar scratches from using dirty oil (orange arrow). This type of wear is almost exclusively caused by running the engine with dirty oil. This particular camshaft housing can be reused again, but any more damage would necessitate replacement. When you send your camshaft housings off to your machine shop for cleaning, they should be able to tell you whether or not you should reuse them in your rebuild.*

checked. Your machinist should have years of experience and should be able to tell you whether or not you should reuse your camshaft housings. Of course, if the bearing and rocker mount surfaces are spotless and have no scratches or grooves, then it's likely that your camshaft housings can be successfully reused in your rebuild. If your bores are slightly scored, there is a fix available—a rocker arm seal that was originally used on the 911 RSR. This seal fits in the rocker shaft groove and helps to prevent oil leakage if the bore is damaged (part number 911.099.103.52).

Oil Squirter Tubes

The third area you need to pay attention to is the oil squirter tubes. These spray a stream of oil onto the rockers and the camshaft. The oil is supplied by the camshaft housing oil lines, which are connected to the engine case. Particularly with engines that ran with dirty oil, or with engines that may have had a catastrophic failure, these oil tubes can become clogged. In most cases a good high-pressure cleaning in a parts cleaner will unclog and clean the passages; however, there may be material or gunk stuck down the tube, and it may need to be removed or replaced. Try running a high-pressured stream of parts cleaner down the tubes. If this doesn't work then your Porsche machine shop should be able to clean and replace the tubes if necessary.

Cleaning

The camshaft housings need to be cleaned thoroughly before being reused in your rebuilt engine. You should clean them in parts cleaner or have your machine shop carefully wash them in their parts tank. Of particular importance is the surface where the camshaft housing and head mate. This is a gasket-free surface and is very susceptible to oil leaks if it is not cleaned properly. The camshaft housings should not be bead-blasted, so there is a distinct chance that some of the sealant will remain on this surface. Using a Scotch-Brite or similarly non-destructive pad, carefully scrub this surface until it is perfectly clean and smooth. Make sure that you don't use any materials that might gouge, scrape, or scratch the surface. Clean the inside of the bearing surfaces with carburetor cleaner, and also make sure that you use clean, lint-free cloths to dry off everything. When you are finished, wrap the camshaft housings in plastic and store them in a cool, dry place.

Three-Bearing vs. Four-Bearing

In 1978, Porsche revised the design of the camshafts and camshaft housings to reflect a four-bearing design instead of the previous three-bearing design (Figure 3-36). The bearing diameter of the four-bearing camshafts is larger than the three-bearing ones. In general, this design improvement helps to eliminate any camshaft bending and reduces the stress placed on it during normal operation. Racers often convert their camshaft setup to the later style for increased reliability under harsh racing conditions. However, for the average street engine, there really is no difference in performance or reliability between the three- and four-bearing designs. Four-bearing camshafts also allow for larger lift, because the bearings are a wider diameter

Rocker Reconditioning

As mentioned previously, if you replace your camshaft, you should have your rockers reground and rehardened. If they have already been reground a few times, they may have had too much material removed, in which case you'll need to purchase new ones. Rocker reconditioning involves the grinding and rehardening of the surface that rides against the camshaft and the replacement and honing of the bronze rocker arm bushing. Typically, the rocker arm shafts do not require any machining work because the

3-36 *Shown here are the three and four-bearing cams. Although some racers like to upgrade to the later style four-bearing camshafts and housings, this is not necessary for the average street engine. The three-bearing camshafts rarely suffer from bending problems and the bearings themselves seldom wear out.*

rocker arm bushing is manufactured out of a soft bronze material that wears much faster than the steel rocker arm shaft. However, using dirty oil may accelerate the wear process. Your machinist should be able to inspect your rocker arms and shafts and help you decide if they can be reconditioned or need to be replaced. The rocker arm bushing part number is 901.105.043.98.

Inspect the rocker arm adjustment screws before you reuse them. Although they don't suffer from the same type of wear that their VW brethren are known for, they can become damaged. Particularly if they are backed out into the rocker arm too much, the small floating head can be forced off of the end of the screw.

In the early years, Porsche used forged rocker arms. The forging process creates a much stronger part than casting does. In later years, Porsche stopped forging the rocker arms and switched to cast rockers. The reason behind this was not to reduce costs, but to reduce the strength of the rockers. If a piston ever hits the valves, the force will very often break the rocker arm. This typically stops the valves from bending and reduces the damage to an easily replaceable rocker arm. This unfortunately does not work on the CIS or Motronic pistons, since the tops of the pistons would hit the valves at an angle.

TIMING CHAIN AND TENSIONERS

The timing chain and tensioner system are two of the most important components of the 911 engine. Failed chain tensioners almost always result in a complete engine rebuild. Loose chains can result in a loss of timing, which is particularly dangerous in a high-compression engine.

The timing chain should be replaced during a rebuild. They will stretch over years of use, and eventually get to the point where they are so loose, they will rattle around inside the engine. Likewise, the chain ramps should always be replaced. Early engines had chain ramps manufactured out of rubber. The later style ramps are made out of a hard, tough plastic that is less prone to wear.

Chain tensioners can be rebuilt; however, I strongly advise against it. The best upgrade for your car is the Carrera pressure-fed chain tensioners. These are discussed in detail in Chapter 4. If for some reason you do decide to use spring-loaded tensioners, I recommend that you use the later style Turbo tensioners (930.105.053.00), which are less prone to failure than the earlier ones. Also important is the use of a safety collar around the shaft of the tensioner. If the tensioner should happen to fail, the collar will act as a stop-gap measure and prevent catastrophic engine failure.

You also need to inspect your chain tensioner idler arms. These will have a tendency to wear on their inner shaft and also on the contact patch that rides against the tensioner shaft, as shown in Figure 3-37. I recommend replacing these idler arms with the late-style upgrade discussed in Chapter 4.

3-37 *The chain tensioner idler arms have a tendency to wear—particularly if they are the early style arms. The later style arms incorporate a bronze bushing in the base to reduce binding and wear on the shaft. The photo on the left shows the inside bore of a severely worn early style idler shaft. The deep scratches and score marks indicate that this engine was run with very dirty oil. Replacement with the newer style idler arm is recommended. The photo on the right shows the idler arm where it mates with the shaft of the tensioner. This also shows some significant wear and is another indicator that the arms should be replaced.*

BALANCING

Balancing an engine is one of the most important tasks that you can perform while you have all your engine parts disassembled. A well-balanced engine runs smoother, revs higher, and generally places less wear on the internal components. From the factory, 911 engines have a natural balance by design—the horizontally opposed 6-cylinder boxer configuration is naturally balanced, whereas a standard V-8 is not. In addition, all engines from the Porsche factory were well balanced when delivered. Rebuilding the engine and replacing worn-out parts throws off this balance somewhat. Rebalancing a rebuilt engine usually costs around $300, and the benefits from a smoother running engine will indeed pay off when you drive your 911.

What is balancing, and how is it achieved? Balancing means that all of the reciprocating components in the engine are machined and weighed to create a circular mass that is evenly balanced on all sides. In layman's terms, it means that the engine will be counterweighted with all of its components. Imagine taking a full pail of water in your left hand and spinning around in a circle. Both you and the water will want to fly off into the distance as your rotational speed increases. However, if you have a pail of water that is of equal weight and held in each hand, you will be balanced on both sides and be able to spin more easily without falling out of balance. In the same manner, a perfectly balanced engine will run smoother, and actually have a greater efficiency because energy will not be wasted trying to keep the engine parts on their proper track.

There are five separate categories of parts that need to be balanced. These consist of the crankshaft, flywheel & ring gear, the pressure plate, pistons & piston pins, and rods. If you wish to have your engine balanced, you should send all of these parts to your machine shop, and they will be able to balance them all together.

Crankshaft

Let's talk first about balancing your crankshaft. This is performed on a balance machine that spins the crankshaft under a strobe light, shown in Figure 3-38. An out-of-balance crankshaft will begin to rock up and down on the spinning axis. Sensors track this motion and trigger the strobe light when the crank moves up or down. If the crankshaft is imbalanced, then the strobe will shine on a specific spot on the crank. You may have noticed that your crankshaft sometimes has some odd markings on it when you get it back from the machine shop. This is from the balancing process (they actually should be cleaned off by the shop), and they tell the machinist exactly where the crankshaft is imbalanced. To correct the imbalance, the machinist needs to remove some material from one or more of the flanges on the crank. Then he tests the crank again to see if it's balanced. The process is repeated until the crank shows no imbalance. Although the process and use of the machinery is a bit more complicated than I've described here, overall it's not a complicated task.

One thing to remember is that all 911 cranks are very well balanced from the factory. If you have a crank that has not been reground or altered in any way, then chances are that it is still well balanced. The factory performed the balancing process as a standard operating procedure when assembling the engine. If your crank has been reground, then theoretically, it should still be perfectly balanced. If performed properly, the regrinding process will remove an equal amount of material from all sides of the crank. If the regrind process is not performed too precisely, this will show up as an imbalanced crankshaft.

3-38 *Shown here is a crank that is ready to be balanced. The balancer rotates the crank using a small rubber belt (not shown in photo) and measures the resulting vibrations from the crank using sensors attached to the base of the balancer (red arrow). As the crank rotates, it vibrates up and down, triggering the sensor, which is attached to a strobe lamp. The strobe lamp signals the location where material needs to be removed while the crank is rotated by the machine.*

Flywheel & Pressure Plate

After the crankshaft is balanced, then the flywheel is balanced. It's important to send your flywheel ring gear with your flywheel, so that they can be balanced together. Also, be sure to include your clutch pressure plate and crankshaft pulley. The ring gear must be indexed to the flywheel and balanced as an assembly. This means that you must reassemble the ring gear onto the flywheel in the same position when you assemble the engine as when you balanced them together. Failure to do so will lead to an unbalanced engine.

The flywheel is balanced while attached to the crankshaft. Even if your crankshaft is perfectly balanced and doesn't need any modifications, you will still need to supply it to use as a mount for balancing the flywheel. The pressure plate is balanced in a similar manner; however, the typical Sachs clutch pressure plates are usually balanced from the factory and often do not require any modifications.

Pistons & Rods

So how are the pistons and rods balanced? Well, unlike a V-8 engine, the 911 engine is horizontally opposed in what is called a boxer configuration. This configuration uses a crankshaft that is perfectly balanced by itself—the only crankshafts that were not counterweighted were the early "T" crankshafts. Therefore, in order to balance the pistons and rods, they simply must have their overall total weights equalized. For balancing the rods, this means that their weights should be within 3 grams or less of each other. To adjust this weight, a small amount of material is removed from the rods in areas that will not damage or alter the structural integrity of the rod. In addition, the rod should be balanced end-for-end. This means that all of the small ends of the rod should weigh the same, and all of the big ends of the rod should weigh the same as well.

Pistons are a different story. The pistons should be balanced by removing material from the piston pins (Figure 3-39). Both the piston and its specific piston pin should be matched together and together weigh the same as each of the other piston/pin assemblies. The inside edge of each piston pin bore is the spot where you can safely remove material to balance them so that they all have the same weight. The removal should be tapered and leave no sharp corners or edges that can introduce stress concentrations to the material. Often, you can get very close to the final weights without removing any material, simply by weighing and swapping piston pins and pistons—couple the heavier pistons with the lighter pins.

CLEANING AND BEAD-BLASTING

Aside from the tasks mentioned above, there are some other very useful tasks that your machine shop can perform for you. For about $150 to$200, the machine shop can clean or bead-blast every part on your engine. This has

always seemed cheap to me, as I once tried to sand my sheet metal by hand. Two hours later, I had one big case of hand-cramp and only one piece of sheet metal stripped. Needless to say, having your parts blasted and cleaned is a very smart thing to do.

Bead-blasting uses small plastic pellets to remove oil, paint, and surface corrosion, whereas sandblasting uses sand. I prefer to have my parts bead-blasted, as the blasting material is less likely than sand to get stuck in small crevices. The finish that you get from bead-blasting is also a tad bit finer than with sandblasting. For hard-to-remove paint or powder coating, sand's abrasive properties are slightly better. I usually have my exhaust components sandblasted prior to painting or Jet-Hot coating. Most bead-blasting is done inside of a relatively small cabinet, which is not big enough for large exhaust components (Figure 3-40).

In most cases, it's uneconomical to ship all your parts off to your Porsche-expert machine shop for cleaning and blasting. The best approach is to take it to a local shop that can perform these relatively simple tasks themselves. However, there are some parts that should be cleaned only in a parts cleaner and some that can (and should) be bead-blasted.

It is important to note that all the parts are washed first before they are bead-blasted. If you take your parts to a professional machine shop that is familiar with Porsche 911 engines, then they should have no problem determining which parts need to be washed, versus which ones need to be bead-blasted. However, if you have any doubts, refer to the chart on the next page.

When you get the call from your machine shop that your parts are ready, be prepared to pick them up immediately. Bare steel will begin to rust in a matter of days, so you

3-39 *When balancing the pistons, the machinist will remove material from the piston pin (blue arrow) not the piston itself. In fact, you can often get very close to balancing the piston and pin assembly simply by mixing and matching the heavier pistons with the lighter piston pins.*

want to make sure that you paint it right away. If for some reason you can't paint the parts right away (you should really plan ahead here), then make sure that you take them home, wrap them with newspaper, carefully place them in boxes, and store them in a very dry place. I like to use the back of a closet inside the house—not the garage. Closets have a tendency to be very dry places and the newspaper will absorb moisture as well to help reduce rusting.

Another popular option is to have your sheet metal powder coated. Powder coating is a tough, durable paint-like finish that is baked onto the sheet metal. Typically, places that powder coat sheet metal will sand or bead-blast the parts first. Although powder coating is more expensive than painting it yourself, the added benefit of durability usually outweighs the costs.

A good rule of thumb is to avoid blasting parts that come in contact with engine oil. This will reduce the chances that any leftover particulate will contaminate and damage your engine. I heard of a 356 owner who had the oil reservoir tank completely blasted and powder coated—inside and out. The blasting process left some small sand or grit in the oil tank, which then contaminated the newly rebuilt engine. The entire engine was basically destroyed after only a few miles of driving.

There are some exceptions to the above rule of thumb. Valve covers don't typically have passages where grit can hide. Most machine shops will sand and bead-blast cylinder heads. If the part doesn't have any passages where left-over blasting material can hide, blasting can be an acceptable solution. Have the head stud nuts and washers blasted if they are rusty–rust on the threads can affect the final torque valve for the head studs. Store the blasted hardware in a jar filled with motor oil to prevent them from rusting.

It's also important to carefully inspect and clean all of the blasted parts when they return from the machine shop.

Parts that can be cleaned and/or bead-blasted.
- All engine sheet metal
- Timing chain housings
- Fan and fan housing
- Intermediate plate cover
- Front pulley
- Pressure plate
- Flywheel and ring gear
- Engine mount and bar
- Pistons (blast tops only, not sides)
- Cylinder heads and valves (disassemble first, and place bolts in valve guides to protect them from the blasting process)
- Case mounting hardware (through-bolts)
- Cylinder head nuts
- Valve covers
- CIS intake manifolds
- Rods
- Heat exchangers
- Muffler
- Fan strap

Parts that need to be washed–not blasted
- Crankshaft
- Cylinders
- Camshaft housings
- Fiberglass fan shroud
- Accelerator linkage mount
- Chain sprockets and supports
- Rocker arms and shafts
- Oil pump
- Intermediate shaft and oil pump connector
- Engine case
- Oil cooler (washed and pressure tested)
- Thermostat
- Number-eight bearing
- Camshafts
- Muffler strap
- Head studs

The blasting process can be somewhat messy and, in some instances, will leave blasting residue in tiny cracks and crevices in your parts. Clean all the parts carefully with carburetor or brake cleaner before you assemble them into your engine. This will help to reduce the chances that any residual blasting media will end up inside your engine.

Keep in mind that some parts are plated from the factory so that they will not rust. Very often, the bead-blasting process will remove this plating. The front pulley, the fan strap, the head stud barrel nuts, and much of the hardware used on the engine falls into this category. For this reason, you might want to have these parts cleaned but not blasted, as they will tend to rust if you don't paint or re-plate them. In general, it's a bad idea to paint fastening hardware. It's also very difficult to get good results by painting objects that are designed to bend, like the fan strap or the muffler straps. It's best just to clean these very well, replace them with new ones, or have them powder coated, which is better for flexible parts.

3-41 *Shown here is the timing chain housing after returning from being bead-blasted. The protective factory coating on the rear has been partially blasted off. It's best to remove the remainder of the coating and reapply a thick coat of JB Weld to the surface. The JB Weld makes for a nice sealant against oil leaks and closely resembles the original factory material.*

If you decide to sandblast your exhaust, make sure that you use a high-temp paint when repainting them. If your exhaust isn't manufactured out of stainless steel, then I suggest that you have the whole system Jet-Hot coated. This will place a ceramic-like layer of protection on your exhaust that will make it almost as durable as stainless steel. Total cost on this procedure would be about $300 to $400, depending upon the size of the exhaust system.

Another problem with blasting exhaust is the potential for particles to fall into the engine when you are assembling it. You typically install the heat exchangers when the engine is upside down. If there is leftover sand or bead material in the exhaust pipes, there is the potential to contaminate your newly rebuilt engine. If your exhaust has been blasted, I recommend that you install the exchangers with the engine on its side—to reduce the chance that any excess material may fall into your engine. Also make sure that the hot air passages used to heat the passenger compartment are free of leftover material. Otherwise you may end up blowing sand or grit into your passenger compartment when you turn the heat on.

The bead-blasting process has a tendency to remove the sealant that the factory uses on the engine case and timing chain housings. Specifically, this material is used to help seal the plugs on the engine cases and also the backsides of the shafts that are pressed into the timing chain housings. I recommend using a bit of JB Weld to reseal these surfaces and ensure that they don't leak oil (Figure 3-41). The JB Weld is very similar to the type of material used by the factory originally to seal these surfaces.

A lot of people like to paint and coat their fan and fan housing. If you want to do this, make sure that you use a process that bakes the paint on with heat. Normal engine paint has a tendency to flake off. Polishing the magnesium fan will also produce results that will fade over time. There is a technical article written by Tom Sharpes on this proce-

dure on the website at www.pelicanparts.com. He painted his fan using special paint that he baked and cured at high temperature in his kitchen oven. The finish on his fan has remained beautiful to this day.

MACHINE SHOP PET PEEVES AND PRICES

Sometime in the past, you may have heard the old joke, "it will cost you $100 to fix it, or $300 if you've already tried to fix it yourself." The same principle sometimes applies to your machine shop. In many cases, it's not necessary to tear down your parts to the most basic level. The crank gear does not need to be removed, unless you are replacing or cleaning it. The cylinder heads usually do not need to be disassembled, as most shops include this in their labor. Rods should be shipped with their old rod nuts and bolts attached. The case should have everything removed from it, but you don't need to clean it. Pistons and their cylinders should be packaged together in pairs.

Don't go overboard tearing down your engine. It's not necessary to disassemble the oil pump or the alternator. Don't ship your parts to your machine shop without first putting them in plastic bags. Oil can leak out and make a messy, if not suspicious-looking, box. Don't use Styrofoam peanuts without first placing the parts in plastic bags—the peanuts have a tendency to break up and clog just about everything. Don't clean the parts yourself, and don't sandblast anything that needs to be sent to the machine shop for reconditioning.

Another item to mention here is that you don't want to purchase your main or rod bearings until you have had all of your machine work completed. If your crank, case or rods

3-42 *Your best asset in rebuilding your engine is your machinist. Look for one who doesn't mind answering your questions. I would also recommend finding one who is an expert in Porsche 911 engines and has done extensive Porsche machine work before. Beware of those who insist that they know what's best without explaining why. Sometimes the cheapest machine shop isn't the best bet. Try to find one with machinists who take pride in their work. Ask around, as stories of bad shops tend to spread quite easily from the mouths of disgruntled customers. I also have a recommended list of machine shops and suppliers on the official website for this book: www.101projects.com.*

need undersized/oversized bearings, you won't know that until your machinist inspects your parts and tells you the results.

The following table shows the current pricing at Competition Engineering, which should be comparable to any top-notch Porsche-specialty machine shop. Prices and labor rates vary, and these prices are only current as of 2003.

MACHINE SHOP LABOR COSTS
Task Cost (pp = plus parts)

Line Boring

Spot face through bolt holes	$145
Line bore 911 case	$250
Resurface and line bore 911 case to Std.	$495 pp
Ream '69 911 case for 2nd countershaft bearing	$175

Case & Case-Savers

Inspect & evaluate case	$50 pp
Insert chain box studs	$150 pp
Bore out for larger 911 cylinder kit	$175
Install anti-shuffle pins	$350 pp
Boat tailing (streamline mains)	$350
Install 911 case-savers	
(includes resizing cylinder spigots & resurfacing)	$300 pp
Case-Savers Install, if studs removed	$285 pp
Remove old helicoils or Time-Serts	
& install proper inserts	$350 pp

Oil System

Remove and replace galley plugs 911 case	$275
Install piston squirter nozzles in 911 case	$250 pp
Clean & test piston squirters	$50
Modify 911 case for late oil pump bypass	$130
Sleeve 911 bypass bore for worn oil pistons	$175 pp
Modify 911 case for 964 oil pump, etc.	$125

Crank & Rod Labor

Inspect & evaluate crank	$ 35
Grind 6-cylinder	$275
Chemical flush 911 crank	$45
Remove and replace oil galley plugs	
& clean 911 crank	$225
Polish 6-cylinder crankshaft	$75
Magnaflux inspection	$50
Harden 6-cylinder crank	$ 225

Engine Balance & Pin

Balance & pin 6-cylinder	$300
Balance pistons & pins	$12 each
Balance flywheel only	$85
Balance flywheel & pressure plate	$95
Balance flywheel & pressure plate, 911 Turbo	$175
Balance pulley only	$30
Balance crankshaft only	$90
Balance connecting rods	$18 each

Intermediate Shaft Repair

Recondition early 2.0-liter	
intermediate shafts thru 1968	$250 pp
Recondition late 911 intermediate shafts	$150 pp

Camshaft Labor

Grind & harden 911 cams	$410
Weld & grind 911 Race cams	$750
Grind race cams	$175

Piston & Cylinder Repair

Inspect & evaluate pistons & cylinders	$35
Bore cylinders in full sets	$50 each
Bore cylinder in less than full set	$60 each
Hone cylinder only or deglaze	$18 each
Machine piston valve pockets (deeper, larger, or both)	$20 each
Machine 911 cylinders for Ni-Resist fire rings	$195 pp

Head Labor

Disassemble, clean & inspect heads	$50
Resurface cylinder heads	$40 each
Modify C2-C4 heads for update	$250 set/6
Install one valve seat	$48 pp
Install two or more 911 seats	$30 each, pp
Install all Porsche guides	$17 each, pp
Grind valves only	$10 each
6-cylinder precision valve job	$350 pp
Grind valve seats only	$15 each
Rebuild 911 rocker arm (rebush & grind radius)	$19 each, pp
Regrind rocker tip only	$12 each, pp
Repair crack in port at valve guide boss	$150
Install spark plug helicoil	$25
Install 8mm or 10mm misc. helicoil	$10
R & R broken/damaged exhaust studs (original)	$18 each, pp
R & R broken/damaged exhaust studs	
(if previously repaired)	$25 each, pp
Modify 911 heads for dual spark plugs	
(includes drilling lower valve covers)	$400
Weld up original 14mm plug holes	
and machine for dual 12mm spark plugs	$750
Machine 911 heads for Ni-Resist fire rings	$200 pp
Bore & blend intake only	$350 set
Bore & blend intake & exhaust	$400 set
Street port	$500 set
Race port	$700 set
Port & match manifolds	$250
Manifold match only	$100
Port & match Turbo blocks & plenum	$400

Flywheels

Install new ring gear on one-piece flywheel	$145
Street lightened flywheel (1/2-lb. removal)	$80
Race lightened flywheel (maximum material	
removal)	$125

Engine Assembly

Short block, 911	$500 pp
Long block, 911	$1,450 pp
911 engine complete (fuel injection & exhaust)	$2,500 pp
Short block, 911 Turbo	$600 pp
Long block, 911 Turbo	$1,500 pp
911 Turbo engine complete (fuel injection & exhaust)	$3,500 pp

TOLERANCE BUILDUP

With all this machining work that you are having performed on your engine, you must be aware of tolerance buildup. The 911 engine is a very precise machine that requires tight clearances and tolerances to be met prior to assembly. With a rebuilt engine, it is often impossible to achieve these original factory measurements. However, if you do it right, you should be able to build it better than original factory specs. In most cases, additional tolerance buildups will not affect the longevity or power of your rebuilt engine; however, they need to be checked prior to assembly in order to make sure that you will not have piston-to-valve interference problems.

Many major machining processes remove material that affects the piston-to-cylinder head clearance. Most people aren't even aware of how much material each machining task can remove. The following is a list of tasks that change some important distances in the combustion chamber:

Resizing the center bearing bore of the case. This moves the cylinder and cylinder heads slightly closer to the center of the engine. Since the rod length doesn't change, the piston at maximum travel is closer to the head. It is important to note that this is affected only by the case resizing technique discussed previously. It does not apply to cases that are simply align-bored to a larger bore.

Replaning the cylinder mounting surfaces on the case. This moves the cylinders and cylinder heads closer to the center of the engine, like the previous example.

Refinishing the surface of the heads. This brings the combustion chamber closer to the top of the cylinder. This means that the valves will be closer to the pistons.

Replacing valve seats. Installation of new seats will bring the starting position of the valves back to their original specifications. If the seats were previously cut deeply, this will bring the valves closer to the pistons.

Installing new valves. New valves that haven't been ground have a much larger margin on their face angle. This means that they sit slightly higher on the valve seat, and thus are closer to the pistons.

Reconditioning camshaft. Worn cam lobes mean that the valves are not achieving their maximum lift during operation. Reconditioning the cams means that valve lift will be brought back to original specifications, possibly bringing the valves closer to the pistons.

It is very important to keep these tolerance changes in mind when you are designing your engine. Using high-compression pistons with a high-lift cam may work on paper. However, after all the machining is performed on the case, you may find that you have piston-to-cylinder head clearance problems. You must maintain a minimum of 1.5mm (0.060 inches) clearance for the intake valve, and 2.0mm (.080 inches) for the exhaust valve at all times during the rotation of the crankshaft.

You can easily perform the check for piston-to-valve clearance by setting the engine at a specific point and then adjusting the valve adjustment screws until the valve just touches the top of the piston. Since each full turn of the screw moves it 1mm closer to the head, you can determine your exact valve-to-piston clearance at that particular point. This procedure is elaborated in further detail in Chapter 5.

You may also have a problem with your chain being too loose, if you don't perform some basic measurements. The stock chain tensioners can handle a significant amount of slop in the chain, but once you get to a certain point then you may have problems with a loose chain. One solution is to replace your chain idler sprocket with an aftermarket one that is sized a bit larger than the stock one. Having a chain that is too loose is a rare occurrence, as the deck height measurement you perform during preassembly will indicate if the camshaft housings are too close to the engine case. You can then compensate by placing thicker shims at the base of the cylinders. The deck height measurement is also further detailed in Chapter 5.

The machining tasks mentioned above will have a tendency to raise your compression ratio by removing volume from the combustion chamber. While this is not necessarily a bad thing, you do need to be aware of how it will affect your performance. If you're running a turbo or supercharger, it may increase your compression ratio beyond acceptable limits. There are a few methods to reduce the increase in compression ratio caused by this tolerance buildup. One method is to reduce the length of the rods. The piston pin bushing is quite thick and can be offset bored to reduce the overall throw of the rod. You can also add thicker shims underneath the cylinders.

If you are indeed concerned about changes in your compression ratio, then you need to "cc" the heads and the pistons—that is, check their volume in cubic centimeters. This will give you an accurate calculation of what your compression ratio is going to be in each cylinder. Unless you are building a very high compression ratio engine, checking the compression ratio on each cylinder is not necessary. Specifically, if your cylinder spigots are machined flat, your heads are fly cut and assembled in matched sets of three, and the deck height is properly measured and adjusted, then you should have no problems with compression ratio changes. The *Porsche 911 Performance Handbook*, by Bruce Anderson, details the process of calculating your compression ratio.

REPLACEMENT PARTS, RELIABILITY UPGRADES, & PERFORMANCE ENHANCEMENTS

I get asked this question a lot: "I'm rebuilding my 911 engine, and I want to know what I can do to it while it's apart to give me more power and greater reliability." While nothing in this world is free, there are many upgrades and enhancements that you can build into your 911 engine to make it run smoother, more reliably and with more horsepower.

Of course, just about everything in this world has a trade-off between price and performance. This is also true with the 911 engine. You can go wild adding high-performance options at the expense of your wallet and potential engine reliability. Or, you can spend modestly to increase and enhance your engine within a somewhat reasonable budget.

I've purposely divided this chapter into three separate sections. Section 1 list the parts that you absolutely need to replace when rebuilding your engine. Basically, if you don't replace these parts, you really shouldn't bother with the rebuilding process at all. Section 2 details and documents which upgrades and modifications I would recommend when rebuilding your 911 engine. Almost all of these are reasonably low-cost, and will increase the reliability of your 911 engine. If you're going to do the job right then I would suggest you implement all of these recommendations. A good example would be adding Carrera chain tensioners, or replacing Dilavar head studs. Following my suggestions detailed in Section II will yield a stronger, more reliable engine.

In Section 3, I discuss what you can do on an unlimited budget. Here is the exciting stuff that may cost a small fortune, and give you more horsepower. But it's all worth it for the increased throttle response at the track or on the street. Some examples include running high-compression pistons, twin-plugging, or installing a supercharger.

SECTION 1 — MUST-REPLACE PARTS & COMPONENTS

For this section, I've created an extensive table that lists all of the parts that should be replaced in your engine. With the exception of one or two items, all of these are parts that wear out and need to be replaced in order to guarantee optimum performance, and an oil-leak-free engine. Almost all of the gaskets will be contained with a standard gasket set that you can purchase from a reliable supplier like Pelican Parts. Also check the official website for this book (www.101projects.com) for places where you can purchase engine rebuild kits.

In addition to the list of must-replace items, I also have some recommendations for items on your car that should be inspected and replaced if necessary while your engine is out. Refer to specific replacement procedures in the book, *101 Projects for Your Porsche 911*.

Bearings, Lines and Hardware

Main bearings	These are the bearings that support the crankshaft. If your crankshaft needs to be reground, or your case needs to be align-bored, you must use undersized bearings, or use a different case or crankshaft.
Rod bearings	Rod bearings are similar to the main bearings and need to be replaced. These bearings can be replaced without splitting the case halves.
Rod nuts and bolts	Both the rod nuts and bolts are designed to yield and deform when they are tightened to their final torque. Reusing rod nuts or bolts may result in them becoming loose during the normal operation of the engine. When assembling the rods on the crank during final assembly, always use red Loctite on the threads of the rod bolts.
Rod bushings	These bushings wrap around the piston wrist pins. Replacement is performed at the machine shop, where new bushings are pressed into place, and reamed to the correct inner diameter.

PARTS, UPGRADES & ENHANCEMENTS

Intermediate shaft bearings	Although the early engines (thru 1969) did not have these bearings, they need to be replaced on the later model engines.
Piston rings	Piston rings are among the parts seeing greatest wear and need to be replaced. Each piston has three rings—two compression rings and one oil seal ring.
Camshaft oil lines (left and right)	Although these small lines that feed the camshaft can be reused, they have a tendency to leak, especially after being disturbed. The rubber-to-metal connection is the most common failure point, and breaks down after years of vibration.
Oil pressure switch	This tiny, five-dollar part can cause a huge headache if it leaks. It can often become damaged if it is removed and tightened improperly. I recommend replacing it while the engine is out and it is readily accessible.
Chain ramps	All six chain ramps are manufactured out of plastic and can become hard and brittle with age. Replace all of them even if they look like they are in perfect condition. You cannot tell if they have become brittle or not, and you also don't typically have any idea how old they are.
Timing chain	Chains stretch over time. You need to replace your chain in order to ensure that your chain will be tight at all times. If you are not splitting the case, you can install a master-link chain as a replacement instead.
Sheet metal screws, fan-housing screws	Although you can technically reuse your older sheet metal screws, new ones are inexpensive and improve the looks of your finished engine.
Inner and outer valve springs (12 pairs)	Springs are one of the basic wear items on the engine. Although 911 springs are very robust, over time they can fatigue and lose their tension. In addition, as they get old they can sometimes break, which can cause major engine problems.
Valve guides (6 intake, 6 exhaust)	Valve guides are one of the principal wear points in the engine and need to be replaced. Newer technology has produced replacement valve guides that will last much longer than factory originals.
Flywheel bolts	Like the rod bolts, these are designed to stretch when tightened to their proper torque. They should only be used once.
Flywheel pilot bearing	It's a wise idea to replace your pilot bearing while you're working in the clutch area.
Fan belt	One of the most important parts on the engine—finish off your newly rebuilt engine with a new fan belt.
Oil pressure relief piston springs (2)	As with any spring, constant use and age will contribute to a change in its mechanical properties. Renewing these will ensure proper oil pressure in your engine. (Replace pistons if performing oil-pump bypass modification.)
Spark plugs	Your new engine should be treated to a set of new plugs.
Distributor cap & rotor	Start off fresh with a new cap and rotor. Install new points and a new condenser on the early 911s (1965-68).
Air filter and fuel filter (smog pump filter if required.)	Don't let any dirt enter your newly rebuilt engine.
Engine oil cooler	If your engine has suffered catastrophic failure, you should not reuse the engine oil cooler. The oil from the cooler does not get filtered before it goes through the engine bearings. It is nearly impossible to remove all of the metal chips from the cooler, and they will become loose and destroy your bearings after you have rebuilt the engine. This applies to finned external oil coolers as well.

Engine Gaskets

Oil pump and passage o-rings	These are the four thick o-rings that mate with the case halves and the oil pump.
Oil strainer gaskets (2) **& drain plug gasket**	Make sure that you use two new oil strainer gaskets and a new drain plug gasket. Don't install the sump plate with the drain plug right underneath the oil pickup—this can interfere with the pump's operation.
Flywheel seal	The flywheel seal wraps around the flywheel-end of the crank. Install this seal before you mate the two case halves.

Pulley seal	The pulley seal fits inside the number eight nose bearing.
Number eight o-ring	The number eight bearing has an o-ring that wraps around it, and prevents oil from seeping out of the case.
Crankcase breather gasket	This small gasket prevents oil from seeping out past the breather cover.
Cylinder thru-bolt o-rings (24)	The bolts that clamp each case half together also are exposed to the flow of oil through the case. As a result, they can leak if they don't have these small o-rings placed under each beveled washer. It's also a wise idea to place a small bit of black silicone around the o-ring to sure up the seal.
Intermediate shaft cover o-ring or gasket	Early cars (thru 1983) use a gasket; later cars use an o-ring. Whichever one you have, it needs to be replaced.
Oil pressure relief valve aluminum gaskets (2)	The two oil pressure relief valves inside the engine have small circular aluminum sealing rings that need to be replaced.
Thermostat o-ring	The engine thermostat is sealed to the case with an o-ring. Replacing this o-ring is vital, as the thermostat can be very difficult to reach once the engine is installed in the car.
Temperature sensor	Depending upon the year of your car, you may have one, two, or three of these sensors. They are mounted on the rear of the engine either to the lower right of the fan, or on either side of the timing chain covers.
Oil return tube o-rings	Whether or not you replace your oil return tubes (recommended), you need to replace the seals on each end.
Carrera chain tensioner o-ring (2)	Don't overlook this tiny o-ring that seals the Carrera chain tensioner to the chain housing cover.
Carrera chain tensioner sealing ring (4)	The small metal line that feeds the chain tensioner requires two sealing rings per side.
Chain housing gaskets (4 total)	There are two gaskets for each side of the engine – one seals the chain housing cover, and the other seals the housing to the engine case.
Cam oil line aluminum gaskets (4)	Along with the cam lines, you should replace the o-rings that seal them to the camshaft housings.
Valve cover gaskets & mounting hardware	A very common source of leaks, the valve cover gaskets need to be replaced. Most kits come complete with new mounting hardware.
Rocker shaft seals (24)	Your engine may or may not have had these installed when you tore it down. As added insurance, I suggest adding these small seals at the end of each rocker shaft.
Camshaft-to-chain housing gasket & o-ring	At the interface between the camshaft and the chain housing, there is a paper gasket that mates the chain housing with the camshaft housing, and also an o-ring that seals the cam from the inside part of the chain housing.
Cylinder base gasket (6)	This is the thin copper gasket that seals each cylinder to the case.
Distributor shaft o-ring	This small seal prevents oil from seeping up past the base of the distributor.
Oil cooler seals (3 total)	Three seals keep the oil cooler from leaking where it mates with the engine.

4-1 *Shown here are the complete contents of a typical engine gasket set. It includes 24/25-valve cover gaskets (2 intake, 2 exhaust), 27-cylinder head gaskets (6), 1-cylinder base gaskets (6), 3-oil return tube seals (8), 4/5-oil cooler/oil pump seals (5 small + 1 large), 2-camshaft thrust plate o-rings (2), 7-fuel injector seals (6), 23-crankcase breather cover gasket (1), 24-oil sump plate gaskets (2), 21-camshaft housing-to-chain housing gaskets (2), 19-exhaust gaskets (6), 20-muffler gaskets (2), 17-flywheel seal, 16-pulley seal, 18-chain housing-to-case gaskets (2), 13-chain housing cover gaskets (2), 15-intermediate cover plate gasket, 14-intake manifold gaskets, 12-thermostat O-ring, 10-number eight bearing o-ring, valve stem seals, 11-through bolt O-rings, 9-valve cover washers, 8-assorted aluminum and copper sealing rings. Be careful not to confuse the hardened aluminum sealing washers with the aluminum sealing rings. The sealing rings are typically smaller in ring width than the washers.*

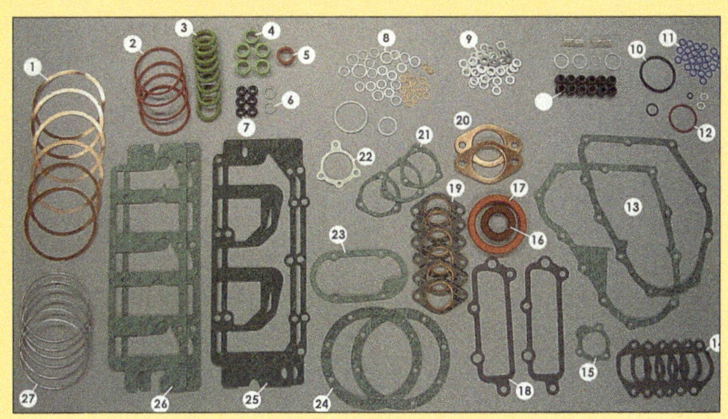

PARTS, UPGRADES & ENHANCEMENTS

Oil pressure sensor sealing rings	Depending upon which year car you have, the oil pressure sender may be mounted in different places. Either way, you need to replace its one or two aluminum sealing gaskets.
Cylinder exhaust gaskets (6)	These are the small copper gaskets that mate the heads to the heat exchangers or headers.
Exhaust/muffler gaskets	Different exhaust systems use unique gaskets – make sure that you have a complete set for your engine when you reassemble the exhaust system. It's also wise to replace old, rusty exhaust hardware as well.

Engine Fastening Hardware

Sheet metal screws	These screws come complete with encapsulated washers. Replace with new, cad-plated screws to give your engine a clean, polished look.
Case parting line and valve covers	Use new M8 self-locking nuts and washers for the exterior of the case. These nuts are typically cad-plated, and should be installed with hardened aluminum washers underneath. These washers help prevent electrolysis and corrosion. Most valve cover gasket kits come complete with new M8 self-locking nuts and washers.
Timing chain housings	Use new M6 self-locking nuts and washers.
Chain ramp bolts	Okay to reuse old hardware—use new sealing rings from your gasket set.
Case through-bolts	Okay to reuse old bolts, nuts, and washers. Use new o-rings from your gasket set.
Cylinder head studs	Reuse only if steel (see Chapter 1 and Chapter 4). Okay to reuse the cylinder head studs and washers only if they are clean and not rusty.
Camshaft housing	Use new M8 hardware to attach the camshaft housing to the heads. Okay to reuse small barrel nuts.
Rocker arms	Okay to reuse center bolt, conical bushing and conical nut.
Camshaft sprocket	Okay to reuse all hardware for the camshaft sprocket assembly.
Chain tensioner & housing	Use new M8 nuts and washers to attach the housing, and to secure the chain tensioner. Use self-locking hardware on the studs external to the engine, and use oblong-shaped nuts on the studs internal to the engine.
Cam oil line hollow bolts	Okay to reuse the hollow bolts and caps for the camshaft housings, and the Carrera pressure-fed chain tensioners.
Sump plate	Use new M6 self-locking nuts and washers.
Oil cooler	Use new M8 self-locking nuts and washers.
Distributor	Use new M8 nut and washer.
Intermediate shaft cover	Use new M6 self-locking nuts and washers.
Exhaust nuts	Use M8 exhaust nuts, and M8 barrel nuts.
Pressure plate	Use new pressure plate bolts and lock washers.

In addition to the list of must-replace items. I also have some recommendations fpr items on your car that should be inspected and replaced if necessary while your engine is out. Refer to specific replacement procedures in the book, *101 Projects for Your Porsche 911*.

Heater hoses	These are high-temperature hoses that connect the heat exchangers with the car chassis. Also inspect the heater flapper boxes for rust damage (Project 43 in *101 Projects…*).
Engine and transmission mounts	Manufactured out of both metal and rubber, these deteriorate over time. Inspect and replace if needed (Project 27 in *101 Projects…*).
Clutch	It's a good time to replace your clutch disc, pressure plate and throw-out bearing if you think that they might fail in the near future (Project 8 in *101 Projects…*).
Transmission input shaft seal	This seal is very difficult to get to unless the transmission is out of the car. It's an easy replacement that should be done if you have easy access to it.
Alternator	Inspection and replacement of the brushes is a wise idea when you have easy access to the alternator (Project 20 in *101 Projects…*).

Fuel system	Never a time like the present to rebuild your carburetors, or replace those cracked intake manifold hoses on your fuel injection system (Projects 28 through 35 in *101 Projects...*).
Transmission	If you've been grinding gears a lot, you might want to have your transmission rebuilt while you have it out of the car. The transmission cannot be removed from the car without removing the engine as well (Project 39 in *101 Projects...*).
Rear shocks	These are much easier to reach without the engine installed (Project 63 in *101 Projects...*).
Rear torsion bars/lowering	Access to the rear torsion bars for replacement is much easier with the engine out of the car (see Project 64 & 55 of 101 Projects...).
Rear wheel bearing	The difficult process of removing and installing new rear wheel bearings is easiest without the engine in the way.
High-torque starter	With the engine out, this upgrade is made significantly easier. (See Project 87 of *101 Projects...*).
Engine compartment seal	An important component of air flow in your engine compartment, make sure this seal is in good condition before you reinstall the engine. Replacing a hard, cracked engine compartment seal keeps the engine running cooler.
Engine sound pad	This pad insulates the passenger compartment from engine noise. The foam pad breaks down after many years, and is often in need of replacement (Project 65 in *101 Projects...*).

Chain Ramps

Another item on the must-replace list are the chain ramps. It's common to find pieces of an old plastic chain ramp in the bottom of your oil sump. If pieces break off, they will usually find their way there. Chain ramps with missing pieces can cause the chain to flap around and sag, or even worse, to skip on the timing sprocket. The newer style chain ramps are manufactured out of tough plastic, and are manufactured to perform better than the ones used on the early cars.

Two odd-shaped bolts that pass through the case create the mounts for each of the chain ramps. There are also two different types of chain ramps—use the black ones everywhere except on the lower right of the engine case, which uses a slightly different brown ramp. Make sure that you don't install the ramps backward—the four inboard chain ramps closest to the crankshaft point with their longer end toward the crankshaft; the two outboard ones point their longer ends out toward the wheels. The chain ramps pull off of their mounting posts, and the new ones simply snap on. You can reuse the old chain-ramp bolts, but make sure that you use new aluminum sealing rings under each bolt.

Timing Chain

It's very important that you replace the timing chain as well. Despite the fact that it looks a lot tougher than a typical rubber timing belt, the chain can stretch significantly over time. Replacing the chain ensures that your chain tensioners will keep the proper tension on the chain. As the chain stretches with age, the tension on it will decrease, increasing the likelihood of chain flapping, which can cause engine failure.

There is a type of chain called the master-link chain. This chain allows you to split the loop and attach it around the intermediate shaft without splitting the case. I do not recommend using a master-link chain unless you decide not to overhaul the bottom end of the engine. In this case, I do recommend replacing the chain with a master-link chain—it's your only real option to renew the chain. A brand-new master-link chain is far better than an older, stretched one-piece chain.

Intermediate Shaft

The intermediate shaft is mounted in the center of the case and drives both the timing chains and the oil pump. In most cases, the intermediate shaft is in good condition and doesn't need to be replaced. However, it is possible that the large aluminum gear has worn—especially if there was a catastrophic

4-2 *It is very important that you inspect your intermediate shaft gear for damage. The gear is manufactured out of aluminum, and the teeth can become marred if there are bits of metal floating around in your engine. Replace the intermediate shaft gear with one that is the same size (size indicated by green arrow). They are matched to each individual engine case.*

PARTS, UPGRADES & ENHANCEMENTS

engine failure and small pieces of metal have been circulating around the inside of the case. As with the camshaft gear in 4-cylinder Porsche engines, the intermediate shaft gear is matched to the engine case. Slight changes and variations in different cases can lead to gaps and backlash between the crankshaft gear and the intermediate shaft gear. If at all possible, it's a wise idea to keep the intermediate shaft with the case that it was originally installed in. If not, then you will have to test the intermediate shaft that you use to make sure that it fits properly inside the case (more on this in Chapter 5). Intermediate shafts are currently available in size 0 and size 1 (Figure 4-2). The engine cases have their associated intermediate gear number stamped on the side of the engine case. Too much backlash can lead to premature gear wear.

SECTION 2 — BASIC RELIABILITY UPGRADES

The overall design of the 911 engine has endured without any major changes from 1965 through 1989. Even the Carrera 3.6 motor introduced in 1989 with the C4 has its roots closely tied to the earlier engines. One of the benefits arising from this relatively unchanged design is the fact that many of the parts and upgrades to the design over the years are interchangeable. It's quite a testament to the 911 engine design that the original 1965 version closely resembles its 25-year younger brother of 1989. Even more surprising is the fact that some of the parts originally used in the 1965 version have the same part numbers on the 1989 Carrera 3.2 motor.

This significant overlap throughout the years allows for the rebuilder to add the late-model upgrades to many of the older models. In this section, I'll detail each individual major component of the engine, and what can be done to upgrade its reliability. We'll start at the bottom end of the engine with oil pump modifications.

OIL PUMPS

There are quite a few oil pumps that have been used on the 911 (Figure 4-3). From 1965-75, the oil pumps were basically the same, the only major difference being that the very early pump housings were manufactured out of aluminum. In 1976, the oil pump was modified to increase the output of the pressure side of the pump. The scavenge side (the side that sucks oil from the bottom of the engine) was reduced slightly so that the oil pump housing would maintain the same external dimensions.

The two pumps are very similar in appearance, but there is a trick to distinguishing the two. The 1976 and later pumps have four vertical lines on the right side of their housing. The early pumps only have three. Because the design change was subtle, and the outside dimensions of the oil pump remained the same, it's very easy to confuse the two types without looking for these identifying marks.

Along with this new oil pump, Porsche also made a change to the engine case. The scavenge side of the oil pump was decreased in size as a result of increasing the pressure side. This resulted in decreased capacity on the scavenge side, which is responsible for removing excess oil from the bottom sump of the engine. The oil bypass update performed on the engine case now routed excess oil back to the pressure side of the pump, instead of dumping it in the sump. This decreased the workload of the scavenge pump, allowing for a design that incorporated a smaller scavenge pump and a larger pressure pump.

A very common update to the early cases is the installation of this later-style oil pump, and the corresponding modification of the case. This is known as the oil bypass modification. This modification routes excess oil bled off by the pressure relief valve to the pressure pump inlet, instead of into the bottom of the crankcase. The oil bypass modification was a good upgrade that improved the flow of oil throughout the 911 engine. Even if you don't upgrade to the later style oil pump, you should have this modification performed on your case when it's being cleaned and machined.

A very important point to make here is that you need to replace your oil bypass pistons if you make the oil pump bypass modification to your case. Accidentally using the older style pistons will have the effect of producing no oil pressure in your case. The older style pistons have holes in them, whereas the newer styles do not (see Figure 3-36 in Chapter 5). This of course would be a very bad occurrence as you start your 911 engine for the first time after its rebuild.

Porsche changed the pump design again in mid 1983, when the factory updated and changed the engine case. This alteration occurred mid-year (March), and started with engine number 64 D 3717. The new version (called the Carrera oil pump) was similar in size, yet had the oil pump screen built in. The supply of brand-new older style pumps has since been exhausted, and now you can only purchase the later style pumps. If you find that your oil pump is worn out or damaged, then you will need to replace it with one of these later style pumps or a good used pump from post-1976. No modifications to the case are necessary. However, you must upgrade to the later style engine sump plate in order for the pump to fit (Figure 4-4). The primary disadvantage to this is that the new sump plate lacks an oil drain plug. However, you can simply empty the oil by removing the entire engine sump plate cover.

As mentioned previously, the 1976 oil pump upgrade is one that should be performed on all early engines. If you cannot find one of these oil pumps, the later style Carrera oil pump with the fixed sump screen will also bolt in without

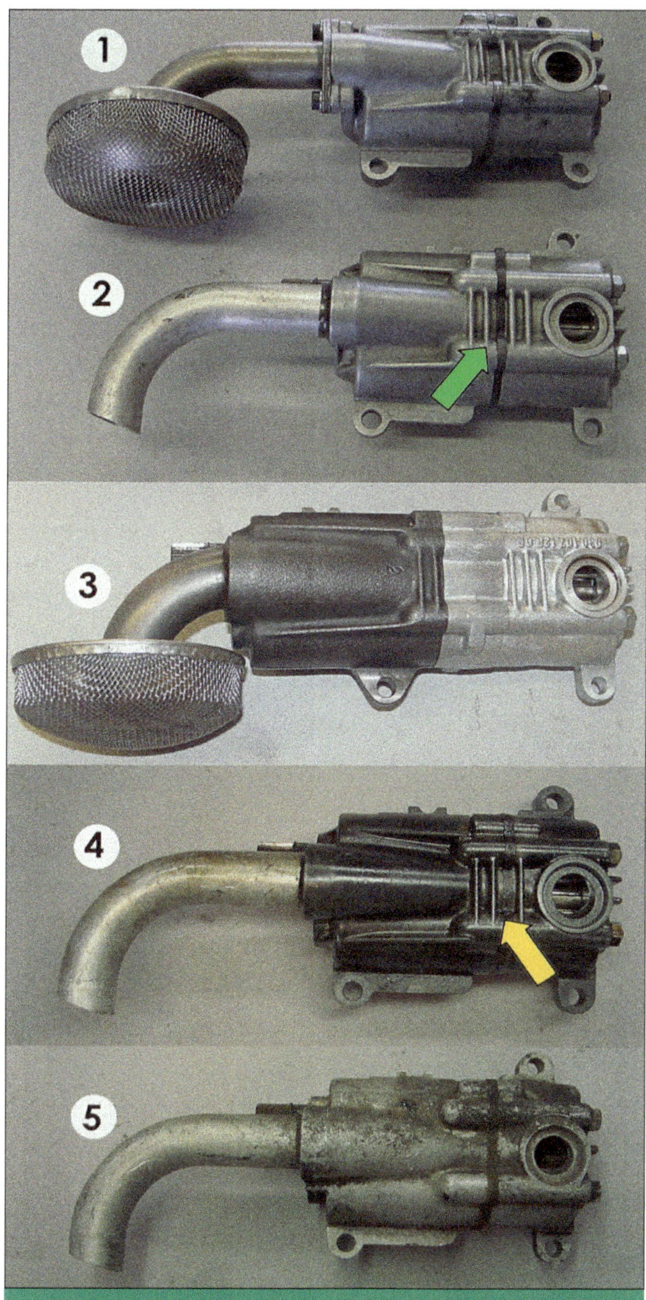

cast-iron. The Turbo pump can easily be adapted to any engine case from 1965, simply by machining the case. The bottom of the main bearing webs need to have some material removed in order to attain the proper clearance for the pump. The turbo pump has a larger pressure side than the other pumps, and the scavenge side is much bigger. Larger scavenge pumps are required for engines with greater cooling and lubrication requirements to prevent oil from collecting in the bottom sump of the engine. If the scavenge side of the pump is too small, then oil may build up in the bottom of the engine—starving the oil tank and engine bearings.

Another important note to mention here is that every 911 engine should be equipped with an external oil cooler. Most engines up to 1977 were not so equipped, and have a tendency to suffer from overheating problems. One instance of overheating can permanently damage your engine, so it's very important to make sure that this does not happen. For more information on installing an external oil cooler in the 911, see Project 26 in the book, *101 Projects for Your Porsche 911*.

CHAIN TENSIONERS

The 911 engine incorporates a single overhead cam system that is driven by timing chains that are driven by the intermediate shaft. One of the weak points of 911 motors through 1983 is the sealed spring-loaded tensioners that maintain the tension and accuracy of the chains. After many years of faithful service, these tensioners have a tendency to fail. It's only a matter of when, not if, they will fail. If a chain tensioner fails, then there is the distinct likelihood that the chain will become loose and flap around, or even jump off of

any case modifications. For high-performance, high-displacement engines, I recommend installing the heavier duty Turbo oil pump. This is the largest of any of the production pumps, and manufactured out of aluminum and

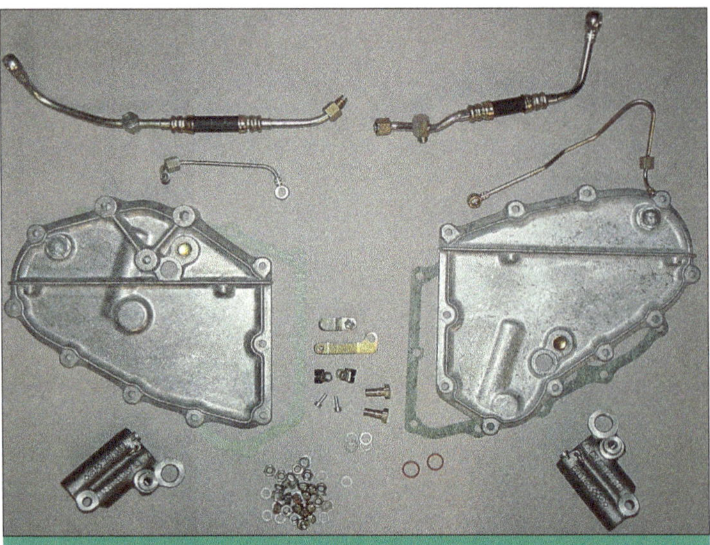

4-5 *The Carrera chain tensioner kit comes complete with just about everything that you need to perform the upgrade. Shown here are the new chain housing covers, the tensioners, the mounting hardware, two flexible oil lines, and two small hard oil lines that together replace your standard camshaft housing oil lines. The new chain housing covers are universal and should fit all 911s from 1969 thru 1983. The kit comes complete with all the mounting hardware that you need.*

the sprocket. The result can be catastrophic failure as the pistons can hit the valves, resulting in a minimum of a top-end engine rebuild and a hefty repair bill. As a result of early chain tensioner failures, Porsche actually redesigned the rocker arms to make them weaker. This was so a valve hitting a piston crown would snap the rocker, resulting in a much cheaper repair than if the valve was bent by the piston.

In 1984, Porsche developed a better tensioner, often referred to as the Carrera pressure-fed chain tensioner. This newly designed tensioner was driven both hydraulically by oil pressure and also by a standard mechanical spring. This design was a big improvement over the original style and as a result, the reliability of the chain timing system increased significantly. With the introduction of the new chain tensioners, Porsche also developed a bolt-on kit that could easily be retrofitted to all of the early cars from 1968 to 1983 (Figure 4-5). Engines from 1965-67 cannot use the bolt-in upgrade because the camshaft housing lines attach differently. If you rebuild your early 1965-67 engine and use a late-style chain housing and cover, you can then use the newer chain tensioners. Smog pumps from the 1968 engines will not fit unless the left cover is slightly machined as well.

The kit comes complete with everything that you need to perform the job on 1973-1983 cars with CIS (Continuous Injection System). Pre-1974 cars need an oil line adapter, because the location of the oil pressure sending unit changed in 1974. The 1973 911 Ts with CIS fuel injection are a special case. They need a special adapter because they use a smaller thread size for the cam lines than the 1974 and later cars.

If you do decide to retain your original-style tensioners, then I recommend that you install the late style "930" spring-loaded chain tensioners (Figure 4-6). I also recommend using what are known as tensioner collars on them. These small collars clamp around the shaft of the tensioner and act as a last barrier to tensioner failure. If the tensioners should fail and release tension on the chain, the collars will stop them from releasing completely. The result is that your engine will suddenly become very noisy; however, your engine will not suffer from the pistons hitting the tops of the valves. You would only want to use the spring-loaded tensioners if you wanted to keep your engine's appearance similar to the stock look. The spring-loaded tensioner combined with the collar is also a good solution for 1967 and earlier cars.

Before redesigning the chain tensioners in 1984, Porsche used to provide rebuild kits for the early mechanical tensioners. These kits are now difficult to find, as the factory strongly recommends that you upgrade to the hydraulic tensioners. I don't recommend messing around with rebuilding your tensioners, even if you can locate a rebuild kit. The newer style tensioners are much more reliable, and it's really not worth taking a chance with rebuilding your old ones.

Unfortunately, there have been some recent reports of Carrera chain tensioner failures. These reported failures occur almost exclusively when starting up the engine right after

4-6 *The old-style sealed, mechanical, spring-loaded chain tensioners were prone to failure. An inexpensive alternative to installing the pressure-fed Carrera chain tensioners is to add a safety collar around the shaft of the tensioner (not shown in photo). While not as good as a pure replacement, the safety collar can provide some emergency help when tensioners fail. A potential pitfall is that it is not easy to detect tensioner failure, and the repeated pounding of the collar may cause it to wear and begin to lodge metal bits inside your engine. The collar is only for use on the early sealed tensioners, and not the pressure-fed ones. Install the collar so that there is about 1/8th of an inch between the top and the bottom of the collar and the top of the chain tensioner housing.*

performing the upgrade. The chain tensioners appear to tension the chain incorrectly, which can lead to a lot of chain noise, and the possibility of having the valves hit the piston. At the time of this writing, this issue is still being investigated; however, I have gained some important information regarding this issue that should help to mitigate tensioner failures.

As co-owner of Pelican Parts, and moderator of the 911 Bulletin Board Forum on the Pelican Parts website, I have come across a lot of discussion about these chain tensioners. Upon hearing about a few failures, both on the bulletin board and also from our customers, I contacted our chief supplier. They responded with some useful information.

First of all, there is only one supplier for these tensioners. Whether your Carrera chain tensioners come from Porsche or an aftermarket supplier, they will be manufactured by the same company, in the same factory. The design and quality are exactly the same. Secondly, Porsche never released an installation Tech Bulletin specifically for those updated tensioners. The most common method is to bolt them in and then run the engine until oil pressure builds up. Instead, I recommend that you prime the tensioners by first submerging them in oil. More information on this procedure is provided in the chain tensioner installation section of Chapter 5.

If for some reason you wish to continue using the early spring-loaded chain tensioners, it's important to note that the 1965-80 chain tensioners have been superceded by the 911 Turbo-style ones (1980-83). These are designed to be used with the later style idler arms (see next subheading), and need either the updated arms or a special retrofit spacer (930.105.513.00) to run on older cars.

In early 1987, Porsche realized that the oil lines that feed the Carrera pressure-fed chain tensioners were beginning to show signs of failure. Excess vibration from normal engine operation was causing the lines to crack and break. As a fix, they added a set of brackets to secure and constrain the oil lines, and prevent them from vibrating. These brackets are included as standard equipment in the Carrera chain tensioner upgrade kit, and should also be retrofitted to cars manufactured before 1987.

IDLER ARMS

In 1980, Porsche also changed the design of the chain tensioning system in response to idler-arm failures. The original idler arms had too small a bearing surface, and were binding on their shaft, which helped to increase tensioner failures. Porsche solved this problem by increasing the length of the

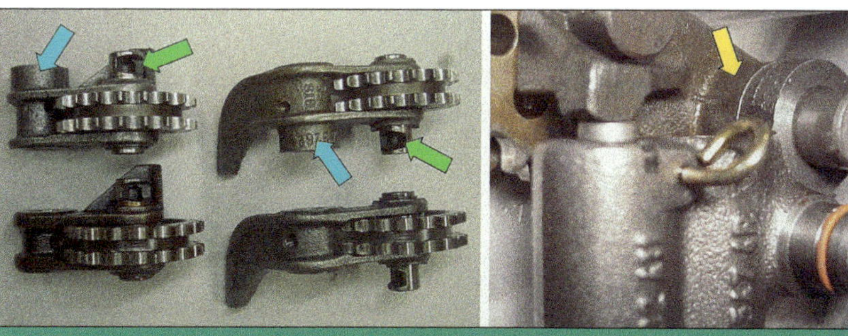

4-7 In 1980 Porsche upgraded the idler arms with a newer style that had an increased bearing surface around the idler pulley shaft (shown with blue arrow). I recommend that you upgrade to these idler arms as well (about $135 for the pair). The photo on the right shows the updated idler arms with the additional thick flange (yellow arrow). If you don't use these later style idlers, the thicker flange will be missing, and a special spacer will be required between the new pressure-fed chain tensioner and the older style idler (See Photo 7-15 in Chapter 5). When you upgrade to the new sprocket idler arms, you can use the old sprocket wheels. Remove the wheel by pressing out the small roll pin. Installation onto the new shafts is straightforward, but make sure that the open edge of the sprocket shaft is installed facing up in order to catch oil for the lubrication of the idler sprocket bearing (green arrow).

idler arm bearing surface, and decreasing the width of the chain tensioner, as shown in Figure 4-7. It was also theorized that loose and wobbly idler arms may have placed significant side loads on the chain tensioner shafts, contributing to chain tensioner failure.

If you upgrade to the Carrera chain tensioners (as I recommend you do), then you should also install the late-style idler arms as well. The Carrera chain tensioners are not the same width as the early tensioners and will leave a large gap between the tensioner and the idler arm on pre-1980 engines. You can purchase a spacer that fits in this gap, but this still leaves the potential for the idler arm to bind on its shaft.

These updated idler arms were installed on engines after serial number 640 0450 (1980). The updated idler arm part numbers are 930.105.509.00 for the left and 930.105.510.00 for the right. Each of these arms has a wider base and two separate bushings where they mount on the shaft in the timing housing. The new design reduces the likelihood of the idler arm binding on its shaft, which can cause premature chain tensioner failure.

ELEVEN-BLADE FAN

In 1976, Porsche implemented a five-blade fan instead of the normal eleven-blade one on all the 911 motors. The purpose of this fan was to provide less cooling to the engine, forcing it to run hotter. This was accomplished solely for the task of meeting emissions requirements. Running the engine hotter helped the thermal reactors work better and fewer emissions were produced. I have also heard the fan was changed to allow the alternator to run faster. However, the use of this smaller fan didn't help the longevity of the engine. These engines overheated more easily, and generally required rebuilding significantly sooner than their predecessors. One upgrade that should

4-8 *The 11-blade fan is an upgrade that should be performed on every 2.7L engine that is equipped with the 5-blade fan. The upgrade is required to restore adequate cooling to the cylinder heads. The early-style 11-blade fan fits directly inside the original 2.7L engine fan housing.*

be performed on every 2.7-liter motor is to replace the original five-blade fan with an eleven-blade one, shown in Figure 4-8. The two fans are interchangeable, and can be switched when replacing or removing the alternator. The only other part that may need to be replaced is the pulley half—it must be matched specifically to the size of the fan. Also, different sized fans and pulleys used different length belts—make sure that you get the one that's appropriate for your setup.

The 1976 fan housing is the same size as the one used in previous years. Therefore, the 1974 and earlier fans will fit into the 1976-77 fan housing. The part number for this eleven-blade fan replacement is 901.106.010.03. It is important to note that the fan housing and fan changed to a

different eleven-blade design in 1978-79, and as a result, the 1978-79 fans will not work with the 1976-77 fan housings. Fans from 1980 and later reverted back to the earlier style and can be used to update the 1976-77 engines. The 1974 pulley half that mates with the early fan is 901.603.421.01. If you are still running smog equipment on your car, you will need the 1975 pulley half instead (911.106.207.00, or in California only, 911.106.207.02).

AIR BLOCK-OFF PLATE

The 911 engine is an air-cooled engine. As such, it receives much of its cooling via the flow of air from the large upright fan mounted on the engine. Improving the flow of the air helps to keep the engine running cooler, which translates into increased longevity. Since the 911 uses its fan to supply air for the passenger compartment heating system, some of this air is diverted away from cooling the engine. With air-cooled cars, the passenger compartment heat comes from air blown through sheet metal passages that surround the exhaust headers.

If the heater in your 911 is not working or is disabled, then you might want to install what is commonly known as an air block-off plate on the side of the engine fan (Figure 4-9). Toward the left side of the engine, there is an air outlet that drives the heating system for the car. On the early cars, this flow of air was the only mechanism to push air into the passenger compartment. This arrangement didn't provide adequate warm airflow, and in later years Porsche installed an additional blower motor in the engine compartment. If your heater system is not working or is disabled (as it usually is on a track car), then a good upgrade is to replace your heater airflow plate with a block-off plate. This block-off plate does exactly what its name implies. It blocks the flow of air, and thus diverts it back over the cylinders, where it can cool the car.

4-9 *If your heater system is disabled, or you simply haven't installed it yet, block off the air outlet from the engine fan. There are aftermarket block-off plates available for this purpose (green arrows). Duct tape is a good temporary substitute if you are still working on the engine, and don't want the hoses and other heater equipment to get in your way.*

Along the same lines, you should never drive the car without the heater system hooked up properly, or without the airflow blocked off. Allowing the fan to blow air into the engine compartment from an opening in the heater system will rob the cylinders of precious air that is needed to cool them. Hooking up the heater system or blocking it off will create back pressure against the airflow that will force it back over the cylinders.

After reinstalling the engine, it's common for people to leave their heater system temporarily apart during the break-in period. This is because the heater system typically gets in the way of valve adjustments, visual oil-leak checks, and the tightening of the head studs. If you don't hook up your heater system, make sure that you at least use some tape to temporarily block off the flow of air from the left-side air duct.

ENGINE AIR BAFFLES MODIFICATION

In 1977, Porsche made a modification to the engine air baffles between the cylinders, resulting in the air cooling becoming more evenly spread between the cylinders. Previous tests had indicated that hot spots in the center cylinders might have been contributing to overheating problems experienced on the late-model 2.7-liter engines. The modification involved removing about 1 inch of material from each end of the four middle sheet metal pieces. Although you can easily use the sheet metal from a 1977-89 engine, the easiest approach is to cut the sheet metal

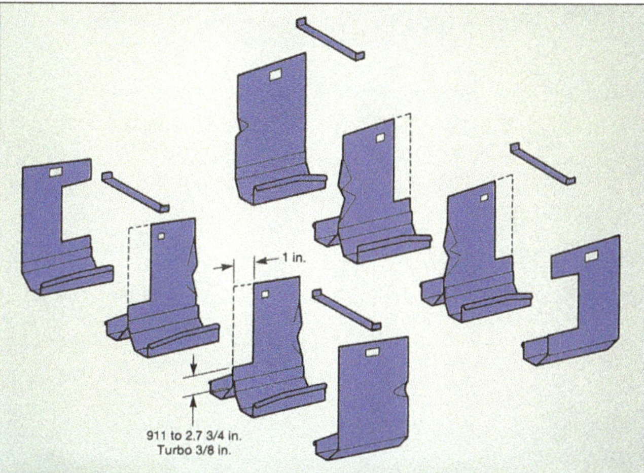

4-10 *Beginning in March 1977, Porsche introduced a modification to the cylinder air deflectors that fit between and under each cylinder. The four inner sections were made about 1 inch narrower than on the earlier engines. The reasoning behind this change was to equalize the air-cooling effect over all of the cylinders. This drawing shows the air deflectors, and the modifications that can be made with a good set of tin snips. Make sure that you make the cuts before you repaint the sheet metal. The Porsche factory claims that this modification drops the operating temperature by 10 to 15 degrees farenheit. See the technical article by Gill Paszek on the Pelican Parts website for exact instructions. Bruce Anderson, Porsche 911 Performance Handbook*

yourself with a good set of tin snips. Figure 4-10 shows you where you should make the cuts.

This modification was made for all 911s and 911 Turbos, and should be implemented on all the early cars as well. The modification of these air deflectors is said to have a significant effect on engine operating temperatures, sometimes dropping them by 10 to 15 degrees Fahrenheit. Being such a simple fix, there is no reason not to implement it in your pre-1977 engine.

Also worth noting is the fact that Porsche added another engine air guide beginning with the 3.0-liter engines. This extra piece fit over the top of the cylinder base and funnelled more air towards the hotter part of the cylinder, located near the head. For additional cooling benefit, this air baffle can be retrofitted to the earlier engines. See Appendix B-Engine Air Guides, for details.

TURBO VALVE COVERS

One of the most popular upgrades to the 911 engine is Turbo valve covers. The stock valve covers on almost all 911s from 1968 through 1977 were manufactured out of magnesium. The magnesium was originally used to cut down on the overall weight of the engine. Unfortunately, the magnesium covers were a poor match for the 911 engine and its stressful environment. It is very common for the magnesium valve covers to warp and then leak after many years of temperature cycling in the normal operation of the engine.

As the valve covers leak, the oil will spill onto the tops of the heat exchangers, causing the car to smoke a bit when driving. As original equipment, the magnesium valve covers were bolted to the aluminum camshaft housings of the engine. No one can quite agree on what causes the warping; however, this inevitably leads to the valve covers leaking. While replacing the valve cover gaskets with better silicone beaded ones may help the problem, the best solution is to replace the covers entirely with what have come to be known as the 911 Turbo valve covers (Figure 4-11).

First used on the 911 Turbo (930), these covers are made entirely of aluminum. The aluminum covers are stronger and less likely to corrode than their magnesium counterparts. Additionally, the late-model lower Turbo valve covers are reinforced with aluminum ribs that stiffen and support the structure of the cover, further decreasing the likelihood of warpage.

If your 1968 and later engine is equipped with the original magnesium covers, then you should definitely upgrade both the upper and lower covers to the later style Turbo aluminum covers. For cars manufactured after 1978, I recommend that you replace your lower valve covers with the reinforced Turbo ones. The upper valve covers on these 911s were already cast out of aluminum.

To check to see if your original magnesium covers (darker in color than the aluminum ones) are warped,

4-11 *Stiffening ribs on the Turbo valve covers strengthen the lower valve covers and reduce the chance of warping. The additional heat from the engine's exhaust system necessitates this additional stiffness. Have the valve covers' mating surface milled flat at your machine shop if you suspect that the covers might be warped from the machining process, or flatten the valve covers using the glass-plate technique documented in Chapter 5.*

place them on a flat surface (e.g., a glass table) and see if they rock back and forth. If they do, then you should most certainly replace them with the improved aluminum "Turbo" valve covers.

If your car still leaks from the valve covers even with the installation of the Turbo valve covers, you might want to take them to your local machine shop and have them milled flat. Sometimes the casting process used in manufacturing the covers can leave them slightly deformed. Milling the mating surface assures that they will be completely flat when bolted to the car. This can also work to resurrect the early 1965-67 aluminum valve covers as well. Or, you can lap the covers flat using the same technique detailed for the timing chain housing covers in Chapter 5.

ROD BOLTS
Carrera (1984-89)
911 Turbo (1978-89)

In 1984, with the release of the 3.2L engine, Porsche reduced the size of the rod bolts to 9mm from the 10mm used on previous engines. Using the crankshaft and rods from the 1978-89 Turbo 3.3-liter engine increased the displacement to 3.2 liter. Unfortunately, the rod bolt diameter is too small for the large loads that these engines place on the rods. A number of failures in the 911 Carrera and 911 Turbo engines have been traced to the rod bolts failing to maintain their proper tightness. Figure 4-12 shows some of the carnage from failed rod bolts.

The failure occurs when the engine is consistently revved at the high end of its RPM range. The stock rod bolts are designed to

stretch and permanently deform when tightened down to their final torque values. At RPMs of 6,700 or higher, the rotating mass on the end of each rod (namely the piston and the mass of the rod itself) has a tendency to stretch the rod bolt further. Repeated stretching of the rod bolts causes them to deform and loosen up, which can result in rod separation and complete engine failure.

While all engines for all years need to have their rod bolts replaced during a rebuild, the remedy for these particular engines is aftermarket performance rod bolts. Quality hardware from RaceWare (part number RTE-4004) or ARP are two very good substitutes for the original rod bolts. In the meantime, if you have a stock 3.2-liter engine, one remedy is to make sure that you do not rev the engine over a safe range like 6,300 rpm. This risk of failure applies to both the 3.3-liter 911 Turbo engines, and the 3.2-liter Carrera engines.

CAMSHAFT HOUSING OIL PRESSURE RESTRICTORS

A relatively recent upgrade has been identified by Lee Rice and Steve Grosekemper of the Porsche Club of America. All of the 911 Porsche engines from 1966 through 1989 use the same cam oil line adapter to connect the oil lines to the camshaft housings (part number 901.105.361.00). In 1991, the factory replaced this adapter on the 911 Turbo with a new updated part that had a greatly reduced center orifice. This new part (901.105.361.01) has a circumferential groove around the adapter to differentiate it from the original adapter (Figure 4-13).

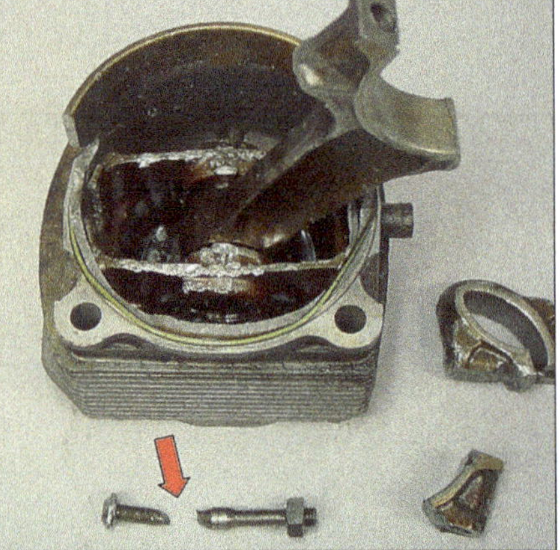

4-12 *The right half of this photo shows the result of a rod bolt failure (red arrow) in one of the later style engines (1977-89 Turbo and 1984-94 911). The rod bolt failed, and the end-cap of the rod twisted off. The rod then smashed a hole in the side of the engine case, basically destroying the entire engine. The photo on the upper left shows the carnage that resulted from a valve head falling off of a 2.7L engine. A possible cause of this failure is valve guides that were so worn that they did not dissipate heat away from the head of the valve. This caused the head to overheat and snap off. The two rods in the lower left are from the same engine.*

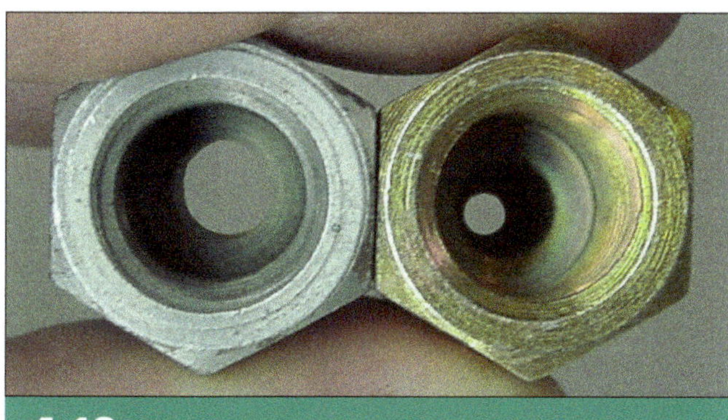

4-13 *A recently discovered upgrade is the installation of the 911 Turbo camshaft housing oil line restrictors. The factory replaced these original restrictors with ones that reduce excess oil flow into the bottom of the engine case. The side effect of these restrictors is increased oil pressure—particularly at idle.*

This change was supposedly adopted to address oil foaming problems in the crankcase. This foaming occurs when there is excess oil in the crankcase, which becomes whipped up into a foam by the rotating internal components. The cause of this excess oil is too much oil being fed to the camshaft housings. Excess oil drops from the rockers to the bottom of the camshaft housings, where it returns to the bottom of the engine crankcase.

The restrictor adapter provides a few benefits to the oil system of your 911 engine. It decreases the amount of potential foaming in the engine by reducing the flow of excess oil to the bottom of the crankcase. This decrease in excess oil and reduction of foaming allows the scavenge side of the oil pump to transfer oil out of the crankcase to the oil tank significantly faster. This maintains greater consistency in the oil tank level and generates more accurate oil level gauge readings. Reduced foaming also reduces oil losses through the crankcase breather system.

In addition, the restrictors increase oil pressure throughout the system, without reducing the oil flow feeding the camshaft housings to inadequate levels. Oil pressure is higher at the main bearings, the rod bearings, the piston squirters, and also the pressure-fed Carrera chain tensioners. Engines that normally read low or near-zero oil pressure at warm idle will show increases of 10 to 20 psi after installing the flow restrictors.

CYLINDER HEAD STUDS

In Chapter 1, I discussed the issue of head studs, and whether your engine may have issues with them. Without a doubt, they have been one of the major problems in the design of the 911 engine, and have contributed to more than their fair share of engine rebuilds. So what can you do to cure yourself of head stud woes? First, we'll talk about the magnesium cases (1968-1/2–77), and then we'll discuss the issues with the aluminum cases (1978-89).

If you've already read Chapter 1, then you know the problem with the head studs in the magnesium cases stems from the weaknesses of the case itself. Chapter 3 shows you the detail of the repair that is required in the machine shop. Case-savers are required in order to make the magnesium case strong again. Don't bother rebuilding your 2.7-liter engine without installing them. Also, don't bother performing a top-end rebuild without installing the case-savers either— just about every 2.7 liter top-end job performed without installing the case-savers will suffer studs that pull out.

So what about the earlier magnesium cases? Even though the 2.7-liter engines are most known for this infamous problem, it is possible for the 2.4-liter, 2.2-liter, and even 2.0-liter cases to experience the same problem. If you're rebuilding your engine, it's a very wise idea to have the case-savers installed. It will also increase the resale value of your car, as any savvy 911 buyer will ask whether you've installed them if the engine has a magnesium case.

Moving onto the 1978-89 aluminum cases (which also includes the 1976-89 911 Turbo and 1976-77 European Carrera) presents us with an entirely different head stud problem. The aluminum cases are very strong, and don't tend to be the failure point for the head stud problem. As discussed in Chapter 1, the stock head studs were manufactured out of Dilavar, which was designed to match the strength of steel with the thermal expansion properties of aluminum. These head studs performed well when new; however, they are susceptible to age and the elements, and have a tendency to break.

How can you tell if the studs you are using are Dilavar? From the factory, Dilavar studs were only installed on the lower, exhaust cylinder head studs, except on the 911 Turbo, which had them installed on both the upper and lower rows. One simple way to tell if your studs are Dilavar or not is to use a magnet. The Dilavar studs are a non-magnetic steel alloy, whereas the standard steel studs are magnetic. In addition to the original Dilavar studs, there are the late-style studs, commonly used on the 993. These studs are not shanked (thinner on the shaft, and thicker on the threads) like the earlier studs, but instead are threaded all the way across the length of the stud. These studs are also non-magnetic. The collection of head studs used on the 911 is shown in Figure 4-14.

One often asked question is, "what do I replace my head studs with?" The common consensus in the Porsche aftermarket industry is that you should replace the lower Dilavar studs with the standard original steel studs that have been used for years on the earlier cars. Doing so seems to have resulted in no problems, and has also solved the Dilavar stud snapping problem. In the past the quality control on the Dilavar studs was so bad that there were many stories about Dilavar studs snapping when they were tightened down at rebuild time to factory specifications. Needless to say, the

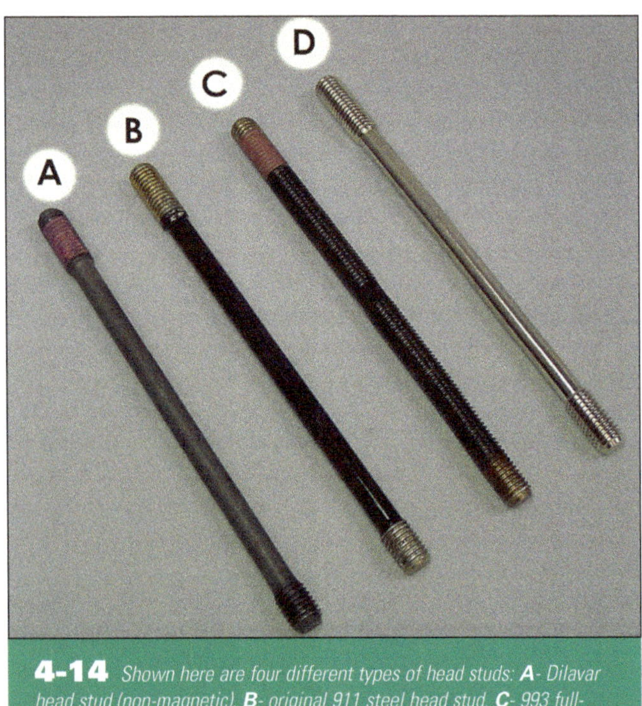

4-14 *Shown here are four different types of head studs:* **A**- *Dilavar head stud (non-magnetic),* **B**- *original 911 steel head stud,* **C**- *993 full-threaded head stud (non-magnetic),* **D**- *RaceWare aftermarket head stud.*

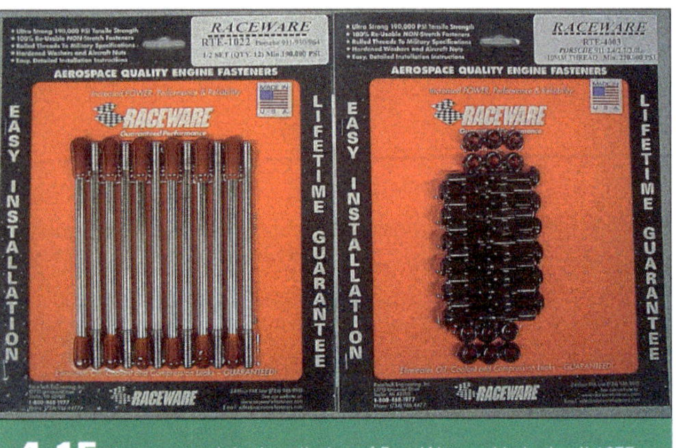

4-15 *I recommend the installation of RaceWare rod bolts in all 1977-89 911 Turbos, and 1984-1994 911 engines. The factory rod bolts were prone to failures at high RPM, and should not be used in these engines. Shown here are RaceWare brand head studs and nuts.*

risk of installing Dilavar studs seems to be much higher than I personally would feel comfortable with. My recommendation is to stay away from these and use the early steel studs for both upper and lower rows for all engines from 1965-89.

There is, however, another alternative to the original steel studs. A company in Michigan called Race-Tech Engineering manufactures RaceWare head studs, shown in Figure 4-15. These studs are well-known for their aerospace quality and construction, and have a reputation for being bulletproof. Their major downside is that they are very expensive—almost double the cost of the plain steel head studs. If you have a somewhat unlimited 911 engine rebuild

budget, then I would use the RaceWare head studs. If not, then the original steel studs should work fine. How do you know if you have RaceWare studs installed in your engine? They should have an "RTE" stamped on the end of each stud. ARP also makes a very high quality aftermarket head stud that can be used in place of the factory studs. Figure 4-16 shows aftermarket studs installed on the 911 engine.

One small item to note here is that the installation procedure for the RaceWare studs is slightly different from that for the standard steel studs. Whereas the steel studs should be installed with red Loctite on their threads, the RaceWare studs should be installed with anti-seize compund on the threads.

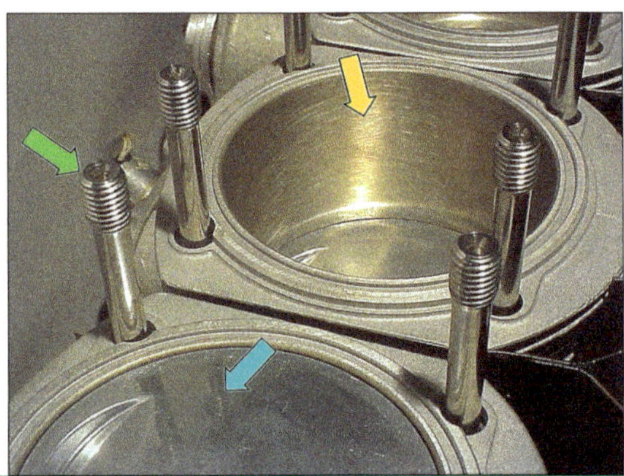

4-16 *This photo shows the use of aftermarket cylinder head studs (green arrow). These studs are well manufactured, and have been proven time and again on the racetrack. You can also see a good honing pattern on the inside surface of the cylinder (yellow arrow). This cross-hatch pattern helps the rings to seat with the sides of the cylinders. Finally, the piston domes have been polished smooth to aid airflow, and also to help reduce carbon buildup (blue arrow).*

DISTRIBUTOR

The pre-1974 engines used two different distributors from two manufacturers: Bosch and Marelli. Unfortunately, distributor caps and rotors are no longer available for the early Marelli distributors. The only viable alternative is to upgrade your distributor to one manufactured by Bosch. These Bosch distributors have the same centrifugal advance curves as the Marelli ones and are still available new. In addition, the caps, rotors, and points for these distributors are still readily available. Upgrading to the Bosch distributor is a good reliability upgrade, because it will enable you to replace your cap, rotor, and points at regular intervals.

Another good distributor upgrade is the Pertronix Ignitor breakerless ignition system. The Ignitor replaces the points system used on all 911s from 1965-77, and is more reliable and less susceptible to mechanical failure.

You should also check your distributor shaft end play while you have it out and available for inspection. Excessive end play can lead to erratic timing problems.

OIL SQUIRTERS

As discussed in Chapter Three, the engine cases manufactured through 1970 did not have the piston squirters installed. These squirters should reduce piston temperatures significantly. It's an excellent upgrade that should be performed on any early case when it's sent to the machine shop for work. Another useful upgrade is the installation of the larger 911 Turbo squirters. These provide more oil spray to the backsides of the pistons and provide further cooling on high-performance engines. Oil squirters must be installed if you are using Nikasil cylinders.

EXTERNAL OIL COOLERS

Every 911 engine should be equipped with an external oil cooler. Although some of the early engines appear to run fine without them, the external oil cooler can only help to increase the longevity of the engine. Decreasing operating temperatures helps to keep all of the critical tolerances inside your engine within optimal specifications. On warm days, most 911 engines will tend to run hotter than ideal. Adding an external oil cooler helps to bring down temperatures and protect the engine from overheating. If you are spending the money on rebuilding your engine, I recommend that you install an external oil cooler at the same time. For more information on installing the late-model Carrera oil cooler, see Project 26 in *101 Projects for Your Porsche 911*.

SECTION 3 PERFORMANCE IMPROVEMENTS

Okay, we've talked about the standard stuff. Now let's turn to the big question: "how can I squeeze more horsepower out of my engine?" The answer lies in how much you're willing to spend, and how much horsepower your original engine case can stand. Early magnesium cases are good for engines with displacements up to about 2.9 liters. The later style aluminum cases have almost an unlimited amount of potential, as these were originally designed for the 800-plus horsepower engines of the factory's 935 Turbo race cars.

Before you begin dreaming about your ideal motor, it's important to stress that the engine is a complete system that needs to be designed with all components in mind, from induction to exhaust. The most powerful engine will not perform well if it has an exhaust system that is too restrictive. Likewise, a large displacement engine will be weak on power if its carburetors are jetted incorrectly. Conversely, a small-displacement engine will also run poorly if too large of a carburetor is used for fuel delivery. The important thing to remember is that you need to consider *all* the elements of the engine prior to deciding which upgrades and performance modifications you wish to install.

In addition to reading the material presented here, I suggest that you pick up a copy of Bruce Anderson's *Porsche 911 Performance Handbook* (ISBN 0-7603-0033-X). In that book, Bruce touches on many topics that I did not have space to include in this chapter. These include the history of the 911 engine, from detailed discussions of high-performance race engines down to explanations of formulas for calculating your compression ratio. It's a great complement to this book, as I have purposely tried not to duplicate information that has already been published in the *Porsche 911 Performance Handbook*.

CAMSHAFTS

More than any other part on the engine, the camshafts determine the engine's overall "personality." You cannot increase the performance of your 911 engine without at least considering your camshaft profile and how it will interact with the other modifications that you are implementing at the same time.

When deciding which camshaft to run in your car, you need to take into consideration how you'll primarily be driving the car. Early "S" engines had high-lift, long duration cams that were designed primarily for the track. As a result, off-the-line performance of an early "S" car is often characterized as weak, when compared to a more standard "E" engine. Low-end torque is limited with the "S" cams as they begin to enter their high power band at around the 5,000-rpm range. Many people don't like the drivability of the "S" cars for this reason. I would suggest that you drive both an "E" engine and an "S" engine before you decide which cam to use.

The "T" and "E"-spec cars have a tendency to drop off their power in the higher RPM range. When deciding which camshaft to run, unless you're building a track car, drivability should be the overriding objective. Many people don't realize that more peak horsepower output is not very useful if it's available at the wrong RPM range. When rebuilding your engine, tailor any performance modifications to suit your specific needs—along with the other components you're using in the rebuild.

Your camshaft profile must also be matched to your engine displacement in order to achieve the desired results. The same camshaft may give entirely different performance characteristics when placed in a larger or smaller displacement engine. One good example is the early "S" cams. When installed in their native 2.2-liter or 2.4-liter engine, they produce torque and power in the very high RPM range, which is good for long tracks, but less desirable for normal street driving. The same camshaft installed in a larger displacement engine (for example a stock 3.2 or big bore 3.4) gives a more even power band, with none of the "peakiness" produced in the earlier engines. The larger displacement changes the feel and personality of the camshaft to the point where the valve overlap and lift work more smoothly across a wide range of RPMs than with the much smaller displacement sizes.

The type of fuel intake system you run is vital to your choice of camshafts. The early 911s had camshafts specifically designed for use with Solex carburetors; they were very similar to the 911 "S" cams but without as much duration and lift. The CIS injection system is not necessarily a high-performance system, and was primarily designed to meet stricter emissions regulations. The CIS irregularly shaped pistons will cause an interference conflict if used with a high-lift, high-duration camshaft, like the early "S" cams. In addition, the pistons themselves aren't optimized for any other injection system besides CIS. High-overlap camshafts, with their propensity to produce excess vibration, also interfere with the CIS metering system. Since the intake valve on a high-overlap camshaft is open at the same time the exhaust valve is, there tends to be exhaust vibrations from the combustion chamber that create significant sensor plate pulsations.

Mechanical Fuel Injection (MFI) systems utilize an injection pump that is synchronized with the camshafts. The three-dimensional cam (space-cam) inside the MFI pump controls the timing, speed and volume of fuel squirted into the combustion chamber. In order to gain the most horsepower and efficiency from your engine, the space-cam inside the MFI pump must be matched to the camshafts in the engine, and vice-versa. You can have your engine camshafts reground, and your MFI pump shaft reground and calibrated to match. Although it's certainly possible to design your own configuration for the camshafts and the pump, it's best to work with profiles that have been used and proven in the past (like the 2.7-liter Carrera RS camshafts and 2.7-liter MFI pump). For raw, unadulterated horsepower with a touch of nostalgia, my favorite choice is to run MFI.

Carburetors are perhaps the easiest fuel system to configure for a custom camshaft. Although the techniques associated with proper jetting of the carburetors are somewhat of an art, less complexity in the entire system makes relatively small changes easy to make. If your car is not going to be subjected to any smog or emissions testing, then carburetors are a safe bet for a non-standard engine combination.

With both the Motronic system and aftermarket engine management systems, you will have to reprogram them to take full advantage of any camshaft upgrades you install. The Motronic system requires a chip to change the fuel/timing map, so it's usually best to go with a manufacturer who will sell you the camshafts and the upgraded chip as a package. Aftermarket engine management systems can be custom programmed—they offer the best chance of squeezing every available horsepower out of your engine.

Another point to mention is that high-overlap camshafts have a tendency to cause what is commonly called reversion. On a high-overlap camshaft, the intake valve continues to remain open as the piston passes bottom dead center (BDC) and starts to compress the air mixture. At lower RPMs, this can push a small amount of the air mixture back out of the combustion chamber before the valve closes all the way. This mixture gets pushed back up into the injection system and creates a reversion "cloud" of air and fuel in the intake. At higher RPMs, this effect disappears because the momentum of the air-fuel mixture entering the cylinder is greater, and is not as easily overcome by the pushing back of the piston. A longer duration, high-overlap cam allows the engine to use the full effect of the intake mixture momentum at higher engine speeds, but with the cost of increased reversion at lower RPMs. Reversion causes reduced low-end power and rough idling—all downsides to running an aggressive camshaft.

So, how are cams described, and what do their specification numbers mean exactly? Figure 4-17 shows a typical camshaft profile for the 911 SC engine, and how the intake and exhaust valves interact with each other. Each camshaft lobe that controls a valve is characterized by its lift and duration. The lift of a valve is simple—it's the total maximum height of the valve off of its valve seat during each cycle. Lift is typically measured in inches or millimeters. Duration is a measurement of how long the valve stays open during each

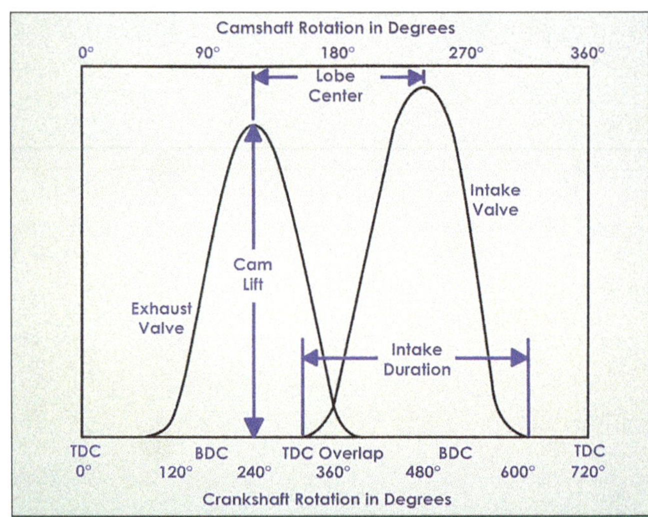

4-17 *Camshaft characteristics are best explained with a diagram. The lift of a cam refers to the maximum valve lift (typically of the intake valve) during a complete combustion cycle. The duration, expressed in degrees of the crankshaft, expresses how long the valve will be open. The lobe center is expressed in degrees of the camshaft, and indicates the angular distance on the cam between peak intake valve lift and peak exhaust valve lift.*

combustion cycle, and is typically measured in crankshaft degrees. The normal combustion cycle encompasses 720 degrees of crankshaft rotation, and the camshaft itself rotates once for every two crankshaft rotations.

Another important camshaft measurement is the difference between the lobe centers. This is the amount of camshaft rotation that exists between the high points (maximum lift) of each camshaft lobe. The smaller the angular difference, and the larger the duration and lift, the greater the overlap between the intake and exhaust valves. For example, the 906 camshaft has a mere 95 degrees between its two lobe centers, whereas the 911 SC CIS camshafts have a relatively large 113 degrees between lobe centers, which means that there is very little overlap between the two valves.

Why is it that the "S" engines lack significant power on the low end? The answer lies mostly with the significant valve lift overlap that we touched upon in Chapter 1, while discussing compression tests. In the same manner that the compression test gives a lower reading for high-overlap cams, the compression in the combustion chamber is reduced at lower RPMs when the car is operating. The overlap between the valves means that at times the intake and exhaust valves are open at the same time. This means that some of the effective compression of the engine is lost due to an open valve. This lower compression at lower RPMs accounts for the reduced power in these RPM ranges.

The significant valve overlap and high lift increases power on the higher RPM range by keeping the intake valves open farther and longer, allowing more air-fuel mixture to be drawn into the cylinder. The longer duration for the intake valve means that the cylinder will achieve the correct amount of air drawn into the cylinder at higher RPM, and will be able to deliver its full power range. The tradeoff is that power is reduced at the lower RPM range due to the lower compression in this range. For the early 911 S engines, the tradeoff point is about 5,000 rpm. This is where the high-RPM advantages of a high-lift, long-duration camshaft really begin to kick in. Below this 5,000 rpm level, the engine's power is weaker because the high-lift, high-duration camshaft produces weaker low-RPM compression.

One way around this problem is to increase your compression ratio. Doing so will help to counteract the power loss at lower RPMs. Increasing the compression ratio will increase the overall compression in the cylinder, and bring the effective compression at lower RPMs back up to a more acceptable range. The downside to this, of course, is that as the engine runs in its higher RPM range, it will have very high compression, and all of the issues that are associated with it.

For high-compression engines like these (10:1 or greater), twin-plug ignition is highly recommended, as is the use of high octane gasoline. You must be careful to make sure that the engine you design can run on pump gasoline, available in your neighborhood. West Coast gasoline with all of its environmental additives and unique formulations, is typically some of the worst octane gas you can buy (yet some of the most expensive). If you install a high-performance camshaft, you should always check the total advance at 6,000 rpm to make sure that the engine is not going to detonate. As you increase the compression in the cylinder, the total spark advance should be reduced to minimize detonation. Since detonation is more likely at low RPMs than at high RPMs, you can often get away with the higher compression ratio because the cam generates poor cylinder filling (and reduced compression pressure) at lower RPMs.

You must also make sure that your camshaft is properly matched to your piston domes. High-lift, extended-duration cams like the early "S" cams create a tighter piston-to-valve clearance inside the combustion chamber. The greater the valve lift, the more air-fuel mixture will be drawn into the combustion chamber. However, the greater the valve lift, the more likely a collision between piston and valve becomes, particularly at higher RPMs. You must account for this when designing your engine, otherwise you may experience a piston to valve collision in this high RPM range. On high-performance pistons, you will notice that the piston has two relief areas in the crown to create clearances for the valves. A 911 "S" camshaft would not work at all in an engine equipped with "E", "T", CIS or Motronic pistons. These pistons must be swapped out for ones that have these proper valve indentations or ones that have been properly modified (see Figure 4-21).

One problem many people encounter is determining exactly which cams they have in their car. While most cams have their original Porsche part number stamped on the side, they may have been rewelded and reground to a completely different profile. Often, you can find telltale signs of a reground camshaft, such as the machine shop's part number stamped into the end of the cam. The only true method to determine exactly which camshaft you have is to measure it. Most camshaft specialists have a machine that is known as the "Cam Doctor." This computer-controlled machine rotates and maps the camshaft and precisely determines the profile of the camshaft. Hands down, this is the best way to identify your camshaft.

If you are taking the engine apart, then I recommend that you simply send the camshafts out to your local cam shop—they will be able to determine what profiles you have very easily. However, if you would like to measure your camshaft profile with the engine still in the car, you can do it by placing a dial indicator on either the intake or exhaust valve while rotating the engine through its full compression and combustion cycle, which is 720 degrees. Set the engine at TDC for the cylinder that you are checking, and place a small degree wheel on the crankshaft. You can use double-sided sticky tape to temporarily attach the wheel to the crankshaft pulley. Set the dial indicator up against the valve in the same manner as you would if you were setting the cam timing (see Chapter 5). With the dial indicator resting on the edge of the valve retainer, turn the crankshaft at 5-degree intervals, and record the values on the dial indicator. Do this for two complete turns of the crankshaft. Repeat this procedure for the exhaust valve.

If you graph the angle of crankshaft rotation with respect to the amount of valve lift on a piece of paper, or on the computer, you will end up with a graph similar to Figure 4-17. From this diagram, you can then calculate the lift and duration of the cam. Using this technique, you can roughly determine which camshaft profile you have in your engine. It is important to note that you only need to record values for one cylinder, as the profile is the same for all six cylinders.

So which camshaft do you need? I've listed my compilations of good engine combinations at the end of this chapter. It's no secret that higher revving engines produce more horsepower per liter of displacement. Basically, if you are planning on racing the car on a track, you should probably design in as much high-end valve lift, duration, and overlap as you can stand to live with. Keep in mind that all the high-end power in the world is worthless if you're trying to pull out of a slow corner with a high power band camshaft. This is the reason why you will find that some very expensive production cars (like some 12-cylinder Ferraris) may not be able to match your 911 through the "twisties," but will blow you away on the straights. It's also important to mention that some high-performance (like the 906 and RSR) engines will not run well with the restrictions of a street muffler.

Running too high a compression ratio engine with a mild cam may also yield too much overall compression at low RPMs and actually cause the starter to kick back when turning over. On very high compression engines, you may need to install a high-torque starter. Despite their peaky performance, the early "S" cams are a popular choice—nearly everyone I know who has built engines using them loves their performance and responsiveness.

If you're looking for a good, drivable street car, then make sure you don't run too aggressive a cam. Get your power elsewhere (displacement upgrade, exhaust modifications) so that you're not going to be beaten off the line by a Dodge minivan. One last thing to remember: if you're located in a state with strict environmental regulations (like California), an aggressive camshaft may give you a lot of trouble if you're trying to pass a smog test. It's a very smart idea to find out if the configuration that you're considering building has been tested and passed the current smog tests in your state.

CYLINDER HEADS

Like many other components of the 911 engine, cylinder heads have remained largely unchanged throughout the 1965-89 time period. The biggest change was in 1976 when the 3.0L Turbo and European Carrera engines moved to a larger cylinder head stud spacing. Still, there have been some important changes to the heads that give some advantages over the others when it comes to performance.

All of the 911 heads can be modified to accommodate larger displacement engines. Polishing the internal intake and exhaust passages helps to increase air flow, and decrease friction. Porting is the art of modifying intake and exhaust ports to increase the airflow in and out of the combustion chamber. I call it an art, because there really are no tried and true rules when it comes to porting 911 heads. It's easy to over-port your heads and cause a reduction in power, in a similar way that using larger diameter exhaust pipes sap power. For a high-performance race engine, it's best to talk with someone who has experience in the particular configuration that you are looking at designing before you start porting your heads.

The early 911 cylinder head suffers from a restrictive design that limits its high-performance capabilities. This head has a relatively deep internal combustion chamber and valve angles that are relatively steep (Figure 4-18). This means that high-compression pistons with their high domes have a tendency to split the chamber into two halves. This

4-18 *In this photo, you can see the differences between the early 2.0-liter (top) and later 2.7-liter heads (bottom). The 2.0L heads have a sharper angle on the valves. This has the unfortunate effect of splitting the combustion chamber, and making it increasingly difficult for the flame front to propagate evenly across the chamber. The 2.2/2.4/2.7 heads are all very similar. The valve angles were changed from the 2.0L orientation to give the combustion chamber a flatter profile.*

creates a physical barrier to flame propagation, and limits the efficiency of combustion. As a result, high-compression 2.0L motors are increasingly prone to detonation and pre-ignition problems.

The next major head redesign occurred in 1970, and was used all the way through 1977 with the 2.7-liter engines. Minor changes in the port sizes and cylinder diameters were the only major difference between the heads. They all used the same valves and port sizes across the 2.2, 2.4 and 2.7-liter engines. The angle between the valves was reduced to give more of a flat, shallow combustion chamber. The pistons were changed as well to match the new profile of the heads. When used with the higher compression pistons, these heads perform very well and resist detonation problems. They can be ported and opened up to accommodate engine sizes up to 2.9 liters. If you are building a high-performance 2.0-liter engine, I recommend that you use a later model 2.2- or 2.4-liter head instead. The shallower head design is much improved over the 2.0 liter versions and should help to reduce detonation over the earlier version.

In 1978, Porsche increased the sizes of the valves and ports to correspond to the displacement upgrade to 3.0 liter. In 1980, they reduced the intake port size to match the change in the CIS fuel injection system. For high performance 3.0-liter engines not running CIS, the preferred heads are the 1978-79 ones with the larger ports. For high-compression performance engines, the ports in both heads can be enlarged beyond the original stock configuration.

In 1984, with the introduction of the 3.2-liter engine, Porsche designers enlarged the ports once more, yet kept the same valve sizes as the 911 SC 3.0-liter engine. The 3.2-liter head is probably the best head to start with for a performance engine, as it has the largest valves and largest ports. The ports can be enlarged even further for bigger displacement racing engines, and if unavailable, the same type of head can be created simply by porting out a 911 SC head. The intake runners cast into the 3.2 heads were also reduced in size.

Bigger isn't necessarily better, as larger valves have their own share of headaches. The larger valves create a heavier moving mass in the head, and tend to float more often at very high RPMs. This only happens at very high RPMs (above 6,800 rpm) where the speed of the engine is so fast that the valve spring doesn't have enough spring to force the valve to accurately follow the camshaft lobe. Too much valve float means that your engine will risk piston-to-valve contact, which can bend the valves. Accidental over-revs (which do happen occasionally with missed shifts) are almost guaranteed to destroy your valve train if you have a motor with significant valve float.

There are a few things that can be done to reduce valve float. Don't use very large valves unless you absolutely need them to match an increase in displacement. Objects in motion tend to stay in motion, and the momentum from a larger valve is more difficult to reverse than that of a smaller one. Stronger valve springs will also help the problem, although these springs typically place more wear on the rockers and the camshafts because of the higher forces required to actuate them. Stiffer springs also rob the engine of some horsepower, as the engine must work harder to lift the valves. Reducing the mass of the valve is another good method to reduce valve float. The use of lightweight titanium spring retainers (Figure 4-20), lightweight rocker arms, or lighter stainless steel or titanium valves is another solution. In general, Porsche 911 engines are not very prone to valve float except at very high RPMs with high-performance engines.

Let's talk for a moment about porting. Porting the heads is a type of black magic in the Porsche engine industry. A lot of people know a lot of information about porting, but tend to keep it to themselves as internal trade secrets. Individual porting jobs will vary greatly with the machinist's level of experience. Make sure that anyone you send your heads to for porting knows exactly what you are trying to achieve, and has previously performed quality porting on similar engine configurations.

Porting helps airflow by smoothing out sharp corners, reducing and smoothing the valve guide bosses, smoothing the area directly behind the valves (pocket porting), matching intake manifold ports to the head ports, opening up the combustion chamber where the valves are shrouded, and widening restrictive areas (often found in the port area around the valve guides). In its original design, the 911 has hemispherical heads with well-designed ports. The intake port is essentially a straight shot to the back of the valve. The exhaust port is almost as good. Straight from the factory, there are no sharp corners or restrictive areas in the ports. The hemispherical head ensures there is zero valve shrouding. In other words, there is only a small amount of additional performance that can be gained from the heads without enlarging the ports. A general rule of thumb on Porsche 911 heads is that the intake ports can all be increased. the exhaust ports are typically already quite large.

So, why not just enlarge the port diameter for improved airflow? Well, you can. This is exactly what the Porsche factory did on their 911 S model and racing engines. For example, the intake port diameter of a 2.0-liter 1969 911 T is 32mm. The 1969 911 S has a 36mm intake port, and the racing 906 engine (also 2.0 liter) has a 38mm port. Power ratings for these engines arc 110, 170, and 210 DIN horsepower, respectively. The problem here is large ports slow down the incoming air-fuel charge, so the cylinders fill less efficiently at low RPMs, resulting in poor torque at low engine speeds. At high RPM, the intake charge has greater momentum, and the open ports offer an advantage in reduced restriction. The result is more horsepower at high engine speeds. The 906 engine produces maximum torque at 6,200 rpm, a full 2,000 rpm above the 911 T's torque

4-19 *Here is an example of a ported and polished head. Note that the intake port of the head has not been polished to a mirror finish, but instead has a somewhat rough finish. This finish creates slight turbulence in the airflow, prevents fuel droplets from collecting and beading up in the intake runners, and helps the air and fuel to mix better when passing through the port. The inside of the combustion chamber has been completely polished to a mirror finish. This helps air flow in and out of the chamber, will help to reduce carbon buildup, and also reduces heat absorption.*

peak. This makes the 906 fine on the racetrack yet difficult to drive on the street. You might be able to help 911 airflow slightly by matching manifold ports to the head ports, and smoothing the valve guide bosses.

So what about polishing? Common sense would suggest that you want the smoothest finish possible wherever there is airflow, in order to achieve the maximum velocity with a minimal amount of friction. For the most part, this is correct, with the exception of the intake side of the heads. You don't want to create a mirror-finish on the inside of the intake because you want the air to swirl around in the chamber and mix effectively with the fuel. Leaving what is known as a semi-rough "swirl" finish on the inside of the intakes is usually best to create the ideal environment for atomization of the fuel mixture (Figure 4-19).

The inside of the combustion chamber should be as smooth as possible. Polish the heads, the valves, and the piston domes as smooth as you can get them. In addition, polish the exhaust ports. It's a real shame that all of this work and beauty will be hidden deep inside the engine, but it should be worth it in the long run. Reduced friction in the airflow means that the engine will breathe easier. You aren't going to gain 50 horsepower from the polish, but every little bit will help.

All things being equal, a lot of horsepower can be gained from tweaking the cylinder heads. For racers trying to compete in limited displacement classes, the cylinder heads probably offer the best area for horsepower gains. Unfortunately, cylinder head modification is very complicated, and is somewhat of an art. It really takes an expert who is experienced with the particular engine configuration you're building to pull the maximum horsepower out of the cylinder heads.

PISTONS & CYLINDERS

The tried and true rule of thumb is that displacement is king when it comes to power increases. You can tweak the compression ratio and perform a host of other engine modifications, but nothing buys you more horsepower than increasing your displacement. Changing the crank and rods can change the stroke and displacement, but usually will also require a change in pistons. While you have your engine apart, it's a great time to upgrade to pistons and cylinders specifically matched to the performance that you are looking for (Figure 4-21). Very often, you will find that your pistons or cylinders have seen better days, and cannot be reused. Use this blessing-in-disguise as a chance to increase your displacement or improve your compression ratio and incrementally increase your horsepower, torque and throttle response.

If you happen to design a high-compression engine (greater than 10:1), it's almost a requirement that you install a twin-plug ignition system (Figure 4-22). In addition, large bore cylinders (98mm and larger) typically benefit from a dual-ignition system because their outer diameter

4-20 *Every little bit counts! Using titanium valve keepers, or removing material from the keepers themselves, helps to minimize the reciprocating mass of the valve assembly. The lighter the assembly, the less likely that valve float will occur at high RPMs.*

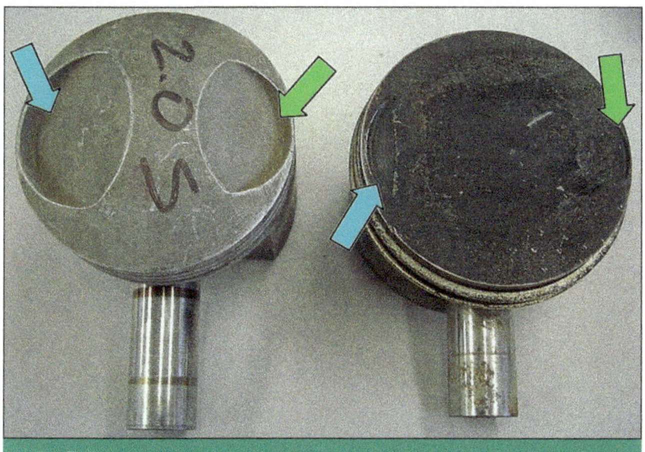

4-21 *Shown side-by-side are the early 911 S pistons and the early T pistons. Although they both have relief indentations cut into the piston dome for the valves, you can easily see the deep indentations on the 'S' piston (blue arrow for intake, green arrow for exhaust). These indentations are required for use with the high-lift 'S' camshaft. If you use a 'T' or 'E' piston with an 'S' camshaft, then you will encounter potential piston-to-valve clearance problems.*

4-22 *Shown here is the most radical of piston designs – a 2.8 911 RSR piston. You can easily see that the face of the piston has been cut very deeply for the huge valves of the RSR heads (blue arrow for intake, green arrow for exhaust). In addition, this high-compression piston travels so close to the heads that clearance pockets are required for both spark plugs to avoid hitting the top of the piston (yellow arrow).*

Whereas MFI systems squirt fuel down into the chambers in tune with the opening of the valves, the CIS continuously supply fuel to the intake manifold. On a microscopic scale, the fuel will pool at the bottom of the intake until it is ready to be opened again (this doesn't happen exactly like this, but it's a good visualization). The MFI systems have great atomization of the fuel in the intake (high injection pressures and pulsed injection with the valve open); the CIS engines do not. As a result, the atomization of the fuel occurs inside the combustion chamber itself. The dome on the pistons helps to swirl the fuel around and mix it with the air.

Although the Motronic system on 1984-89 cars is indeed pulsed injection, the pulsing is not a true sequential injection system. This means that the injectors do not fire individually, but as a group. The injectors fire in unison on each side of the engine (cylinders 1-2-3 fire together as do cylinders 4-5-6). A quick glance at the electrical diagrams for the Motronic system will confirm this. As a result, the

4-23 *Shown here is a 3.2L Motronic piston (left) and a CIS piston (right). They both have a similar half-dome shape in the top of the piston to aid in the swirling and atomization of fuel when it enters the combustion chamber. Because this dome sits high on the piston, these pistons cannot be used with high-lift camshafts.*

Motronic system encounters some of the "pooling" characteristics of the CIS engines. This is one of the reasons why the pistons on the Motronic 3.2-liter engine are similar in shape to the earlier CIS pistons.

As mentioned previously, JE pistons can be used in place of original pistons. With the ability to custom-design just about any piston shape, you can effectively dial-in and blueprint your exact compression ratio to just about any value you choose. These pistons can be used with the same clearances as their Mahle counterparts, and have proven themselves to be equally strong. Using these pistons in your high-performance engine opens up the door to nearly unlimited engine combinations.

An often-overlooked point to mention here is that all 911 cylinders are very similar. All the cylinders from 1965-89 have the same overall height. Up until the introduction of the 3.0 liter in 1976 (Euro/Turbo), the cylinder head

has increased the distance that the ignition flame front needs to travel across the entire combustion chamber. See Twin-Plugging later in this section.

As discussed in Chapter 3, Porsche used four different types of cylinders in the 911 engine: cast iron, biral, Nikasil, and Alusil. All 911 cylinder heights have been the same from 1965-89. Since Alusil cylinders cannot be reliably honed, they are often scrapped and exchanged for the Mahle Nikasil cylinders. The best pistons and cylinders you can use in your rebuild are these Mahle Nikasil ones. Most configurations are still available, and Mahle also offers aftermarket sets for big bore engines, like 98mm and 100mm bores.

The CIS pistons are shaped differently from earlier ones because this is a non-pulsed injection system (Figure 4-23).

stud spacing was exactly the same for all the cylinders. The only difference was the diameter of the inner bore. As a result, you can mix and match any size up to 2.7 on any case from 2.0 to 2.7 liters. For example, the 2.0-liter engines can use the later 2.2-liter cylinders, or even the 2.7 cylinders if you bore out the cylinder spigots. Another popular option is the installation of the 2.2 'S' pistons on the 2.4-liter engine. This creates a higher compression engine with more power and torque throughout the entire power band (compression ratio changes to about 9.6:1). There are many, many options, and I've documented many of them in my "Wayne's Top Engine Picks" table at the end of this chapter.

There are a few other high-performance upgrades that you can perform on your pistons and cylinders. Many people decide to coat the sides of their pistons with a dry-film lubricant. Dry-film lubricants are bonded to metal surfaces first by cleaning and etching the target surface. Then the material is applied and heated to a temperature where the material melts and adheres to the roughened surfaces. The dry-film lubricant process lowers friction between the piston and the cylinder and reduces overall wear. This process is not a requirement during a rebuild, but it is an extra option that helps to reduce friction—particularly during cold starts when oil hasn't reached all of the operating areas of the engine quite yet.

Another piston upgrade involves applying a ceramic coating to the piston domes, shown in Figure 4-24. This coating helps to reduce piston temperatures by creating a thermal barrier to the heat of the combustion chamber. The ceramic coating helps considerably to protect your high-compression or forced-induction engine from damage caused by detonation. The coating can take some of the beating caused by detonation and give you a few more sec-

ond chances before you damage your piston. I have however heard conflicting opinions on these ceramic coatings though. Some experts contend that the coatings interfere with the balance and maintenance of proper cylinder head temperatures.

Another option is to apply thermal displacement coatings on the outside of the cylinders. These coatings act as a thermal conductor and help to disperse the heat uniformly around the outside of the cylinder. The coatings help to reduce cylinder wall hotspots that can cause damage and increase friction inside the cylinder.

CRANK, RODS, CASE AND FLYWHEEL

Another way to squeeze more performance out of your engine is to install titanium rods, a lightweight flywheel (Figure 4-25), or aftermarket lightweight performance rods from companies like Pauter Engineering or Carrillo. The main advantage to lightweight components is that they reduce the rotational mass of the engine. While reducing this weight will not buy you any more horsepower, it can increase your engine's response and acceleration. The reasoning behind this is that the rotational mass of the engine takes time to "spin up" when you accelerate. Decreasing the rotational mass allows for quicker response times when accelerating. This is because more energy from the engine is being used to accelerate the mass of the car, instead of accelerating the mass of the engine components. In addition, reducing the mass of rotating engine components has a two-fold benefit in performance—you not only make the engine quicker, but you also reduce your car's total weight. This is discussed further in the section "Weight Reduction."

4-24 *Shown here are two 2.7L RSR pistons from JE Pistons. The piston on the left has been treated with a dry-film lubricant, as shown by its darker color on the sides. The top of the piston has also been treated with a ceramic coating that acts as a heat barrier to help isolate the piston from the heat of the combustion chamber. The piston on the right is an untreated one.*

4-25 *Shown here is a lightened race flywheel, with material removed from three sections (yellow arrows). These flywheels are good for race applications but are less desirable for street driving. Their reduced inertial mass means that the engine will rev up faster, and will also spin down faster when the accelerator is released. This makes for somewhat difficult street driving.*

The flywheel and other rotational components, such as the rods, pistons, and wrist pins, serve to raise the rotational or angular momentum of the engine so that it continues to turn smoothly until the next compression stroke. Adding lightweight components allows you to adjust engine RPMs much quicker. Note that this applies not only to acceleration, but also deceleration when you let off of the throttle. This often makes the car difficult to drive on the street in day-to-day traffic conditions.

In general, you should only add lightened engine components if your particular application supports it. High RPM race cars with close-ratio transmission don't benefit greatly from a lightened flywheel (other than the weight loss on the total weight of the engine) because they operate primarily in a narrow power band. Lightened components are best used on race engines, where engine response time is crucial.

As discussed in Chapter 3, modifications to the engine cases are usually required for performance upgrades. Particularly with the 2.7 magnesium cases, they need to be updated and reinforced before you can consider increasing horsepower. The early 2.0L sand-cast aluminum cases make an excellent starting point for a performance engine, and are usually the racer's first choice for engines under 3.0L. You will need to find an intermediate shaft for the case, install the piston squirters, and perform the oil bypass modification in order to prep the case. In addition, the cylinder spigots will have to be enlarged to accept the size cylinders that you wish to use.

Shuffle-pinning (shown in Figure 4-26) is an excellent reliability upgrade for racing engines. The process involves placing dowel pins on either side of the main bearing webs. These dowel pins constrain the bearing webs in position and prevent them from deforming under high loads. This modification is only necessary for high-horsepower race engines. Shuffle-pinning aluminum cases is not recommended, because the stiffened structure can place too much stress on the main bearing webs, causing them to crack.

The 3.0/3.2/Turbo 3.3 aluminum cases are basically all the same, and based on the design that Porsche used in their 800-horsepower 935 (Figure 4-27). As a result, you can safely modify any of these cases to build an engine with an incredible amount of horsepower. You can mix and match crankshafts with these cases to build almost any displacement engine.

For endurance racers, another upgrade is the installation of a serpentine fan belt, shown in Figure 4-28. The original V-belt design can be less than 100 percent reliable under harsh endurance racing conditions. Even owners of street-driven cars who are not com-fortable with the V-belt design can upgrade to a serpentine belt for peace of mind. The belt setup uses a thick rubber belt that is tightened with an idler pulley. Clewett Engineering of Manhattan Beach, California, manufactures a custom serpentine belt setup for the 911 engine that is designed to be robust and reliable under the harshest conditions.

Another good upgrade is to have your rods shot peened. This process places a somewhat grainy surface finish on your rods. This finish helps to reduce surface cracks by reducing stress concentration points.

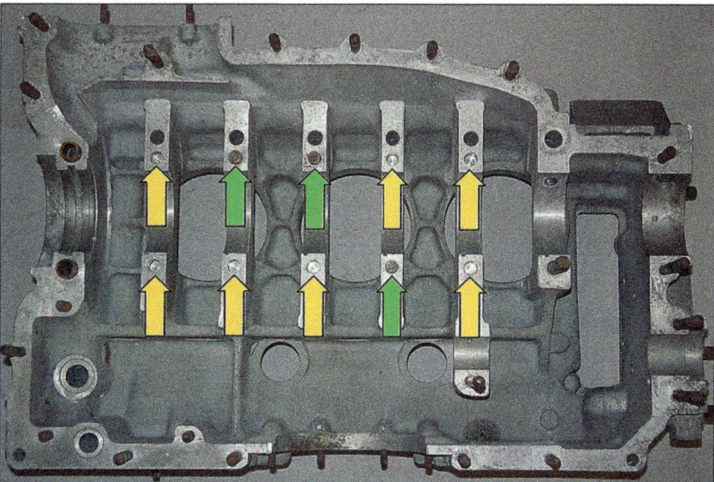

4-26 *Shuffle-pinning involves installing small dowel pins along each side of the main bearing webs. This prevents the case from "sliding" back and forth under high-stress conditions. The result is that the main bearings are firmly supported and do not deform under stress. The dowel pins are shown by the green arrows, and their mating holes are shown by the yellow arrows.*

4-27 *One of the gold standards of Porsche racing, the 911 Turbo engine case was originally designed to support the 800-horsepower loads of the venerable 935. The stock 3.0L engine case is based on the design of the Turbo case and, as a result, can also be used as the base for very high-horsepower engines.*

PARTS, UPGRADES & ENHANCEMENTS

4-28 *For endurance racers, the serpentine fan belt is a must. The typical V-belt arrangement found on the stock 911 engines can sometimes fail. This belt setup is much more reliable, and easier to tighten as well.*

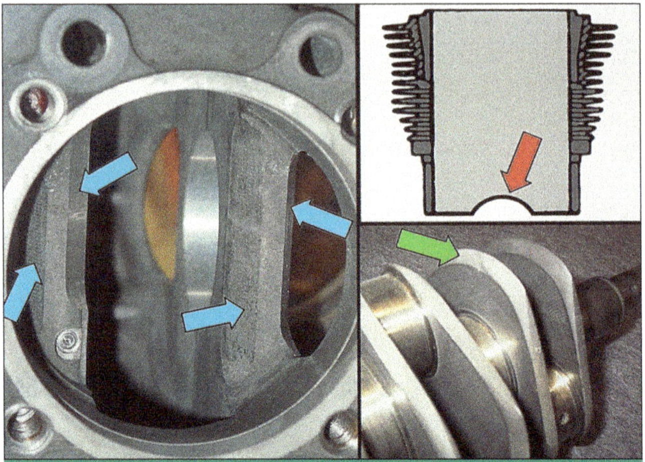

4-29 *This collection of photos shows some race-type modifications that can be performed on your engine in order to extract that last little bit of horsepower. On the left, you can see that the case is boat-tailed to allow for better airflow around the main bearing webs. The arrows show where material has been removed to create a profile that is similar to an airplane wing. In the upper right, these cylinders have been "mooned" out to allow for air to escape out the sides when the piston is pushed back towards the crankshaft. On the lower right, this crankshaft has had its counterweights knife-edged. This allows it to rotate through the air inside the case with reduced air resistance. Photo: Juan E. López-Santini, S-Car-Go Racing*

BOAT-TAILING, KNIFE-EDGING, AND CYLINDER MOONING

The inside of your engine case is a tumultuous place when the engine is running. Like your car when you're driving down the highway, the engine can encounter great air resistance inside the crankcase. As the pistons move back toward the center of the case, they draw air in from the outside via the intake manifolds. In a similar manner inside the case, the pistons push air around the internals of the case, past the crank and into other chambers. This pushing of air back and forth saps energy from the engine, and reduces its overall horsepower.

On a stock 911 engine, this loss due to internal air friction is minimal and does not play a large part in overall horsepower output. However, on a high-performance engine where you're trying to squeeze every ounce of power out of the engine, optimizing airflow inside the case can make a five to ten horsepower difference. There are three primary methods for reducing the airflow inside the engine: boat-tailing, knife-edging the crank, and cylinder mooning.

Boat-tailing is the relatively simple process of rounding off the edges of the main bearing support webs in the case (Figure 4-29). The theory behind this is that air pushed out by the piston as it makes its way toward the crank will encounter high resistance passing around the square edges of the bearing webs. Rounding off the edges of the main bearing webs creates a more aerodynamic profile that will allow air to pass by it more freely. Don't go overboard and file your main bearing webs so that they become a structural liability. Remove only the material that you need to to create a smooth flow of air around the support. Your machine shop should be able to perform this procedure on your 911 engine case.

Knife-edging the crank involves taking the counterweights and rounding each of them to a relatively sharp point. In this manner, as the crankshaft spins through the air inside the case it will act more like a fan blade, and less like a large brick with respect to aerodynamics. The air inside the crankcase is usually a very dense mixture of air and oil. Knife-edging can add a few horsepower to the engine by reducing the energy needed for the crankshaft to cut through this air-oil mixture.

Cylinder mooning involves machining a moon-shaped cut on each side of the cylinders. This small cut will allow air to escape from behind the piston as it moves toward the crankshaft.

FUEL INTAKE SYSTEMS

No discussion of performance options can be made without considering the fuel system that you will be running on your 911 engine. The fuel system should be decided first, or at least in close connection with your upgrades. Fuel intake systems and the engine go hand in hand. The limitations of some systems have to be considered when designing your engine; otherwise you may have a mismatched system that will deliver far lower performance than you would expect.

Carburetors

Without a doubt, a set of carburetors has always been a good, relatively inexpensive fuel induction system for the 911 engine. Perhaps more than any other intake system, carburetors allow you the ease and flexibility to adapt to just about any displacement and camshaft profile. In addition, it's easy to change jets and venturis in carburetors and mix and match combinations that work well for your engine. Good reliability and easy customization are the hallmarks of carburetors—the only downside being reduced fuel economy and problems with emissions testing.

The early 911 engines used three different carburetors from three different manufacturers: Solex, Zenith, and Weber. Unless you're running your car in a vintage racing class that requires an authentic original intake system, I don't recommend the Solex or Zenith carburetors. The Solex carburetors were never a top choice for the 911 engine, having a somewhat unusual fuel flow design that contributed to an infamous flat-spot on the performance curve. Although adequately designed for the stock 1970-71 2.2-liter engines, the Zenith carburetors are designed with relatively small 27mm venturis, and are not well equipped for high-horsepower applications where increased fuel delivery is required. In addition, Zenith jets and other replacement parts can be more difficult to locate.

Hands down, the best carburetor used on the 911 was the Weber triple throat IDA 3C series, shown in Figure 4-30. Before moving to Mechanical Fuel Injection, Porsche used Weber carburetors almost exclusively on their high-performance race engines—for example, the 46mm ones used on the 906. Needless to say, Weber carburetors have had a loyal following. Throughout the years, Weber carburetors in good condition have become increasingly difficult to find, as people have snatched them up for engine upgrades.

While they have a great reputation for performance and adaptability, the Weber carburetors are not without their own set of problems. They must be used with extremely clean fuel, as the jets and tiny fuel passages tend to get clogged very easily by debris. I recommend installing four fuel filters on your car if you're running a set of Weber carburetors—one filter back by the pump, one in the usual spot in the engine compartment, and two tiny filters directly in front of the fuel inlet to each carburetor. This seems to give the best protection against clogging in the inside passages. You must reset the float levels carefully when rebuilding the carburetors—throttle response and drivability suffer if they are incorrectly set. For more information, see Project 28, Carburetor Rebuild, in the book, *101 Projects for Your Porsche 911*.

You also don't want to use too high a fuel pressure to supply your carburetors. The Weber float valves can be sensitive to too much fuel pressure. Use a fuel pressure regulator and set it between 3.5 and 4.0 psi. Don't let your pump run directly into the carburetors—this is a common mistake that can stress the float valves, and possibly make them leak.

Building upon the excellent engineering of the Weber carburetor, a company named PMO has built a high-quality

4-30 *Webers are the carburetors of choice for the early 911 engines. Their excellent performance, good reliability, and adaptability make them a very popular choice for custom 911 engine configurations. Shown here are 46mm Weber carburetors on a 3.5L engine.*

replacement carburetor, shown in Figure 4-31. This unit is a completely new design based on the Weber 2-barrel 48 IDA carburetor, with improvements that fix some of the problems associated with the original design. In the past few years, PMO has redeveloped their carburetor into a superior replacement for the original Webers. The PMO carburetors contain a sight glass in the float chambers that allow you to monitor the fuel levels inside.

The PMO carburetors are also available in different sizes: 40mm, 46mm, and a 50mm that was never available in the original Weber configurations. One of the major failure points on original Weber carburetors is the throttle shaft bushings. As these bushings become worn the butterfly valves can rattle, and wear a groove in the throttle body. If the shafts are loose and the bushings aren't replaced, then the throttle valves will most likely permanently damage the throttle body in the very near future. The PMO carburetors solved this problem by using ball-bearing throttle shafts instead of the original bronze bushings.

So which venturis and jets do you need to run in order to achieve maximum performance? That's a good question that is mostly determined by your engine's configuration. Head flow, displacement, camshaft profiles, and a host of other factors affect the venturi and jet sizes required. However, the information provided here is a good point

4-31 *Richard Parr of PMO has updated the Weber design with his new PMO carburetors. These elegant beauties are a completely new carburetor based upon the track-proven design of the Weber carburetor. They are available in 40, 46, and even a 50mm size. PMO can supply and configure these carburetors for just about any normally aspirated 911 engine configuration you can design. photo: PMO*

from which to start. The following table gives a small breakdown of some suggested jets and venturis for the more popular 911 engine configurations. See also the book, *The Sports Car Engine*, by Colin Campbell, for more information on sizing venturis. Steve Weiner of Rennsport Systems in Portland created this table of recommended carburetor and venturi sizes for a range of popular engines:

Displacement	Camshaft	Carb Size	Venturi Size
2.0 to 2.2	S	40mm Webers	32mm
2.4 to 2.7	S	40mm Webers	34mm or 36mm
2.8	S	40mm Webers	36mm
2.8	RSR	46mm Webers	38mm or 42mm
3.0	S	40mm Webers	36mm
3.0 RSR	RSR	46mm Webers	42mm
3.2	S	46mm Webers	38mm
3.5	S	46mm Webers	42mm
3.5 RSR	RSR	46mm Webers	42mm (not really enough)
3.5	GE60 or 906	46mm Webers	42mm
3.8	GE80	50mm PMOs	46mm venturis (or larger)

Some additional performance options for carburetors include tall secondary venturis that funnel the air better when being drawn into the engine and give more mid-range power. Also useful are the tall manifolds that raise the carburetors' height above the heads. This additional height helps to reduce the effect of intake reversion that can occur with aggressive camshafts with significant intake and exhaust valve overlap.

The conclusion? Carburetors are an excellent choice for custom-designed 911 engines. Their flexibility in venturis and jets makes them adaptable to just about any engine. If they are calibrated, set up, and tuned properly, then they

can be extremely reliable. If you can find a good used set of Weber carburetors, they will make a great addition to your engine. The PMO carburetors, though more expensive than a good used set of Weber carburetors, go one step further in performance and reliability. The key is to use clean fuel, and to make sure that they are balanced and that your floats are set properly. For more information on balancing your carburetors, see Project 29 in *101 Projects for Your Porsche 911*. Also see *Weber Carburetors* by John Passini or *Weber Carburetors* by Pat Braden for detailed information on jet sizing and configuration.

Mechanical Fuel Injection (1969-73)

In 1966 Porsche used a Mechanical Fuel Injection (MFI) system on the 2.0-liter, 225-horsepower Carrera 906 (Figure 4-32). This engine was later installed in the legendary 911 R. The advantage of an MFI system is that the fuel delivery is metered to the RPM of the engine. In general, the system supplies fuel to the cylinders in a more precise and aggressive manner than carburetors can deliver. Because the system was designed with a closed, non-vented fuel supply, the emissions were also much better than with carburetors. MFI systems utilize a very high fuel pressure when injecting the fuel mixture into the cylinders. Fuel is squirted out of the injectors at a remarkably high 220 to 250 psi. This high pressure aids in the atomization of the fuel, which in turn increases the total surface area of the fuel droplets in the air-fuel mixture. This results in a more efficient and complete burn of the fuel.

The entire goal of any fuel injection system is to provide the proper mixture of air and fuel to the engine, and

4-32 *A rebuilt engine equipped with Mechanical Fuel Injection (MFI). My favorite of the vintage fuel delivery systems, MFI delivers raw unadulterated power by injecting large amounts of high-pressure fuel into the cylinder ports. Foreshadowing advanced electronic fuel injection systems, MFI is a true sequential system, meaning that it injects fuel into the intake in close coordination with the opening of the valve. Mechanical correction systems for altitude, engine speed and coasting help to correct and meter the fuel.*

to control manifold pressure through the throttle. The MFI system uses the injection pump to coordinate the amount and injection of the fuel with the opening of the intake valve. The velocity stacks and throttle bodies mounted to the top of the heads channel and regulate the airflow into the cylinders. In order to achieve the ideal air-fuel ratio, these two systems must be carefully coordinated. There is a lot that can go wrong with the MFI system, but when it is working it performs very well.

The fuel pump section of the injection pump works in close coordination with the valvetrain in the engine. A small three-dimensional cam inside the pump rotates and pushes on small cylinders. These cylinders act as plungers that push fuel through the lines to each engine cylinder. As the engine rotates, the 3D cam pushes the small fuel pistons up and down as each valve is opened. Close synchronization with the timing of the engine is required to get the process just right. In a similar manner to the method in which the ignition system is timed to piston position, the injection pump pushes fuel through the lines to each cylinder in a timed and controlled manner. When the fuel reaches the cylinder, it exits through an injector embedded in the cylinder heads. The injection pump is lubricated with oil fed from the engine. Two oil lines that connect to the top of the engine provide an oil supply and return for the internal mechanicals of the pump.

In addition to providing spurts of fuel that pulse with the speed of the engine, the injection pump also regulates the amount of fuel pushed during each spurt. In order to accomplish this, the plungers themselves are designed with a corkscrew-like groove cut into their side. The plungers are allowed to rotate about a half-turn in their bores. As the plunger turns, this corkscrew effect allows more fuel to enter each plunger. The rotation of these plungers is coordinated with the throttle position. The greater the throttle is opened, the more the pistons will turn, and the more fuel will be delivered.

To recap, the up and down motion of the fuel pistons occurs in time with the RPM of the engine. The rotation of the fuel pistons is connected to the position of the throttle. While this relationship is fine for many operating conditions, to maintain the ideal air-fuel mixture ratio, the engine must be supplied with different quantities of fuel under varying engine speeds and loads. Internal to the injection pump, a centrifugal governor works in conjunction with the throttle position lever to meter the fuel fed into the system. In addition, a barometric compensator is used to adjust to changes in altitude or ambient air pressure that might affect the air-fuel ratio. A warm-up thermostat linked to the heat exchangers senses when the car needs a richer mixture upon cold startup. Finally, a shut-off solenoid reduces fuel delivery to the injection system when the throttle is closed, and the engine is coasting in gear.

Because each pump's injection volume and timing is designed to work with a specific engine displacement and camshaft, swapping pumps from one engine configuration to another is not a wise idea, as the car will probably never run correctly. The pump, distributor, and camshafts of the engines must be matched for the MFI system to operate properly.

In many ways, the MFI system combines elements of the modern fuel injection systems and the older style carbureted systems. Like carburetors, the MFI system uses a set of throttle bodies to meter and control the airflow intake into the system. Since the entire goal of the fuel injection system is to maintain the proper air-fuel mixture, the throttle bodies must be properly synchronized with the fuel injection pump.

MFI pumps can be recalibrated to nearly any size engine displacement and camshaft. Two excellent MFI rebuilders are Pacific Fuel Injection of San Francisco and Eurometrix in Boston. One of the most popular engine modifications is to convert the engine's camshafts and pistons to 2.7 Carrera RS-spec with the pump modified to match. The throttle bodies and high-velocity stacks are the same ones used for the 911 S 2.4-liter engine. In addition, the history surrounding the MFI system is so well known that there have been many custom solutions designed for increased performance. High butterfly stacks and slide valve throttle bodies like the ones originally used in the 911 R can add proven performance. The slide valves are useful only for racing use, as dirt from everyday use can easily jam the mechanism.

The main drawback of the MFI system is its relative complexity. When MFI systems are running correctly they

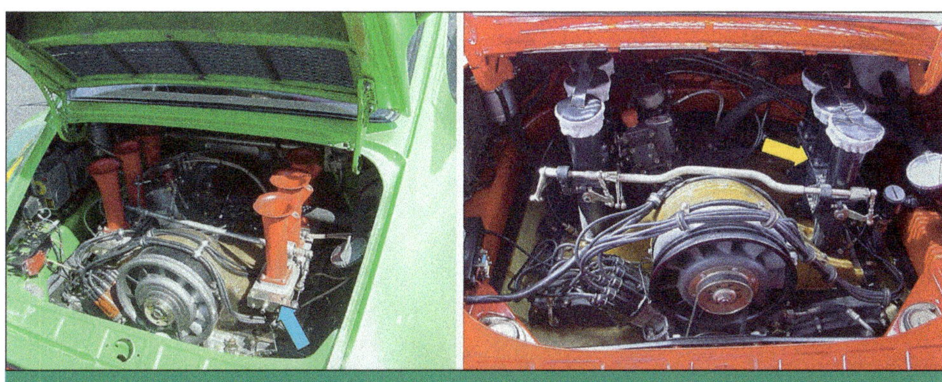

4-33 Here are two examples of high-performance Mechanical Fuel Injection systems. The 911 engine pictured on the left has tall velocity stacks combined with a slide-valve throttle mechanism (blue arrow). The tall stacks help to counter fuel reversion, and the slide-valve mechanism offers less restriction when fully open. The RSR engine on the right has the standard butterfly throttle bodies (yellow arrow).

run great, with good power and great throttle response (Figure 4-33). When they are out of adjustment, they can be very tricky to fix. Special Porsche protractor tools are required to align the throttle rods accurately, and the mixture can be very difficult to adjust correctly. For more information on the MFI systems, see Project 30 in *101 Projects for Your Porsche 911* or check out www.pelicanparts.com, where there is a rather extensive archive of MFI information no longer available elsewhere.

Bosch CIS / K-Jetronic
(911 1973–1/2-83, 911 Turbo 1976-89)

For more than ten years, Porsche used the Bosch K-Jetronic Continuous Injection System (CIS) on all production 911s. The system in general is very reliable, and was only bested in 1984 by the introduction of the Motronic engine management system that integrates ignition and fuel injection together.

CIS meters the amount of fuel provided to the cylinders as a function of the air drawn into the engine. The CIS airflow sensor plate measures this airflow and alters fuel pressures to control fuel delivery. This sensor plate is attached to a fuel distributor that evenly meters the amount of pressurized fuel sent to each injector. The system doesn't differentiate among the six injectors—it sends the same amount of fuel to each of them at all times. Unlike pulsed-injection systems like Motronic or even the earlier Mechanical Fuel Injection system, the CIS injectors distribute fuel to all of the cylinders at all times. With CIS, the opening and closing of the intake valves is the only mechanism that controls the flow of fuel into and out of the combustion chamber.

Through 1979, CIS was a semi-open-looped system, which means that it didn't monitor the output gases from the engine to see if the air-fuel mixture was set at the appropriate levels. In 1980, emissions requirements forced Porsche to add an oxygen sensor to the system, which helped the engine to regulate the air-fuel mixture level.

The CIS system does not lend itself well to modifications in the name of increased horsepower. The system is best suited to meeting emissions restrictions, and was developed for the 911 engine with this in mind. There are several obstacles that stand in the way of modifying CIS systems. The fuel injection system forces the air to follow a somewhat convoluted path before it reaches the cylinders. The pistons are dome shaped to aid in atomization and cannot be used with high-lift camshafts. Even if you swapped out the pistons, aggressive camshaft grinds also produce significantly more valve overlap than mild cams, and allow air pressure pulses to travel up the intake system and vibrate the CIS sensor plate. These pulses interrupt the precise measurement of airflow that controls the adjustment of the air-fuel mixture. Despite these limitations,

there are a few upgrades that can increase power and throttle response with the basic CIS system.. We'll talk about those later in the "Wayne's Top Engine Picks" section.

Motronic (DME) (1984-89)

The Motronic system (also called Digital Motor Electronics or DME) is hands-down the best overall fuel injection system for the 3.2-liter engine that you can use when you consider price and performance. Ignition timing and fuel delivery are all controlled by a digital map that is recorded in a removable chip within the main fuel injection (DME) computer. The computer takes input from a variety of engine sensors that measure cylinder head temperature, altitude (ambient air pressure), crank angle, throttle position, exhaust gas oxygen (mixture), ambient air temperature, and mass airflow. The DME chip is programmed from the factory with certain performance characteristics (mostly conservative) so that the engine will react well under a host of varying conditions. Major changes to the engine (including the addition of different camshafts) require an updated chip map to take full advantage of these modifications. When modifying mechanical components in your engine, a failure to update the Motronic system may actually result in a decrease in performance, as the original system is finely tuned to supply the correct timing and fuel injection values for a specific stock engine configuration.

Each system is matched directly to a specific engine configuration. Because of the proprietary nature of the Motronic system, there aren't a whole lot of changes that you can perform without updating the DME chip. Major changes to the engine (different camshafts, increased displacement) will not work well with the stock Motronic system because the computer chip is designed to deliver the proper amount of fuel and spark only for a stock engine. To gain the maximum benefit from engine modifications, you need to either upgrade your DME chip or install a programmable aftermarket engine management system (discussed in the next section).

There are a few things that can be done to improve the performance of the stock Motronic system. The 3.2 intake runners suffer from a poor design that results in uneven airflow into the cylinder heads. Intake flows in the runners can vary from a high of 290 cubic feet per minute (cfm) to a low of 180 cfm. Ideally, the cylinders should receive exactly equal amounts of air. The intake manifolds can be extrude honed to increase airflow and even it out to about 300 to 330 cfm across all cylinders.

The Motronic system is generally very reliable—its main failure point being the sensors that send data back to the DME computer. Another odd failure point appears to be the DME relay. Corroded contacts appear to cause this mission-critical part to fail somewhat intermittently. I have had many customers claim that their car runs much better right after they have replaced the DME relay. While I don't have any empirical data to back this up, there are a lot of people who will swear by replacing their DME relay once every two years. I do recommend that you carry a spare one, as well as a spare cylinder head temperature sensor, as the failure of either of these can potentially leave you stranded on the side of the road.

In addition, you can add a larger throttle body for increased airflow. The stock 3.2-liter system is somewhat limited in its airflow characteristics, so there are a few aftermarket throttle bodies out there that you can bolt on to increase airflow. Generally speaking, these do not require an upgrade to the DME chip to offer an improvement in performance. Adding a freer-flowing exhaust system will give you additional performance as well.

If you are running a stock 3.2-liter engine with the stock Motronic injection and exhaust, the best upgrade you can perform is to install an aftermarket DME chip. As stated previously, the factory programmed the original chip to compensate for a wide variety of driving characteristics. These days, you can find chips that will elevate the rev-limiter, advance your timing, and generally run the engine with less conservatism than the factory chip. The only downside to running a more aggressive chip is that sometimes the timing curves are a bit too advanced and may cause detonation on low-octane pump gas (as provided in California). It's best to find a chip manufacturer that offers a few different levels of performance and will guarantee your satisfaction with the system.

The most performance increases you can gain on the 3.2-liter engines come from replacing the exhaust (if legally permissable—see Exhaust Systems later in this Chapter). One note of caution needs to be considered when modifying 3.2-liter engines, the stock Motronic system has no knock sensor and no mechanism to advance or retard the timing. If you run too high of a compression, then your engine may knock and detonate. The only fix in this case is to tear down the engine, replace the Motronic system, or use expensive octane boosting additives everytime you visit a gas pump.

ENGINE MANAGEMENT SYSTEMS

Similar to the Motronic system, there are a host of complete engine management systems that integrate both fuel delivery and ignition system control. Electromotive and Motec manufacture two of the most popular systems for the 911. While you will be able to get the maximum amount of performance out of your engine with one of these systems, they are not for the faint of heart, are technically challenging, and also cost a pretty penny. But they are without a doubt the most flexible of any system, and will enable you to extract every ounce of power from your engine if you want to spend the time tweaking them. Most are programmable from a laptop computer, and can even interact both ways, giving you performance data and feedback from the engine as you run it through its paces. These systems typically cost anywhere from $3,000 to $10,000; however, they are usable on nearly any size 911 engine in any configuration.

With the option of complete engine control, the possibility for total power optimization becomes a reality. The latest engine management system from Electromotive is the TEC-3 (Total Engine Control, Version 3), shown in Figure 4-34. The total cost for a single-plug system is about $2,500. This system is far more advanced than previous versions and offers an almost unlimited amount of flexibility when designing your fuel and ignition systems.

The TEC-3 system has a proportional air-to-fuel ratio table that allows you to systematically control the mixture from idle to full throttle. According to modern fuel injection theory, fuel and air combustion achieves its maximum efficiency at a ratio of 14.67:1. Although this ratio may be optimum for good fuel economy, it's not best for maximizing power. On a normally aspirated engine at full throttle, maximum power is achieved with an air-fuel ratio set at about 14.2:1 to 14.3:1. On boosted engines this maximum power ratio is more in the range of 12.2:1 to 12.4:1. Using the variable fuel ratio characteristics of the TEC-3, you can create one set of programs for the track where optimum performance is key, and another set for the street, where maximum fuel mileage is desired. However, because the TEC-3 system senses engine load via a manifold absolute pressure sensor, the system can determine whether you're cruising on the highway or driving on the track. One single program can also be designed for both applications.

The system consists of a separate electronic control unit (ECU) and ignition coil packs. These coil packs or direct-fire units (DFUs) deliver a full-charge spark up to 15,000 rpm. On a single-plug 911 engine, you use a three coil assembly. Each coil fires a spark for two cylinders that are opposite

4-34 *The TEC-3 engine management system consists of the ECU and the coil packs. Previous versions had these two components integrated together. The coil pack needs to be mounted in the engine compartment, relatively near the spark plugs. The ECU can now be mounted up near the cockpit, for easy access.*

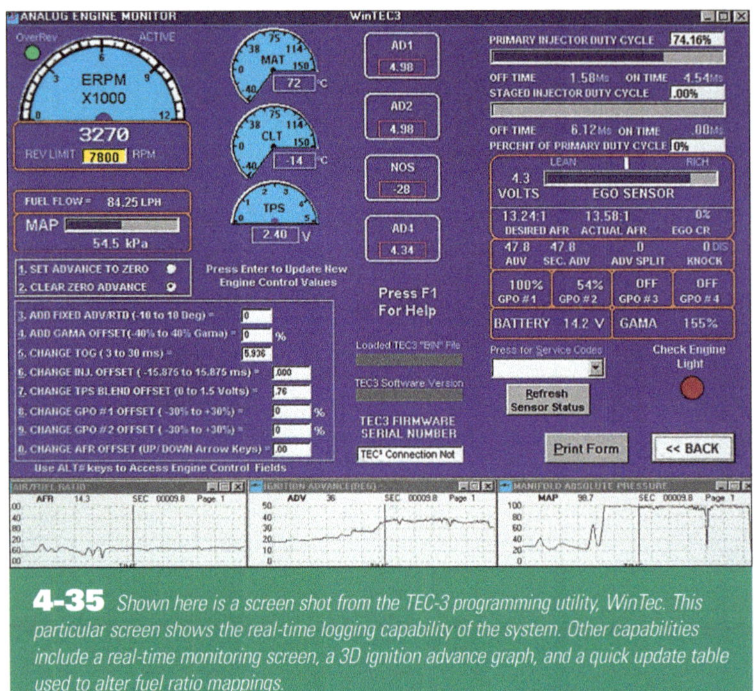

4-35 *Shown here is a screen shot from the TEC-3 programming utility, WinTec. This particular screen shows the real-time logging capability of the system. Other capabilities include a real-time monitoring screen, a 3D ignition advance graph, and a quick update table used to alter fuel ratio mappings.*

from each other in the firing order. By using a separate ignition coil for each pair of companion cylinders, the time available to recharge the coils increases by a factor of three (on the six-cylinder 911 engine). This configuration produces full spark energy while delivering a spark duration up to 2 milliseconds at 6,000 rpm. This duration is more than twenty times longer than most capacitive discharge units, and directly translates into better combustion and more power.

Each coil pack is wired into two cylinders that are opposite of each other in the firing order (i.e., 1 & 4, 6 & 3, 2 & 5). The ignition portion of the TEC-3 system is wired so that both companion cylinders fire at the same time. Each coil fires a plug on the compression stroke for one cylinder and on the exhaust stroke for the companion cylinder. This produces what is known as a "waste spark" on the exhaust stroke of the companion cylinder. The cylinder that has compressed the air-fuel mixture is delivered a higher voltage spark than its companion cylinder because the mixture creates an environment around the spark plug that offers a path of more resistance. Because the resistance inside the compressed cylinder is more than the resistance inside the cylinder on its exhaust stroke, the majority of spark energy is delivered to the compressed cylinder. A small amount of spark voltage is directed to the cylinder on its exhaust stroke. This waste spark has no effect at all on the performance of the engine. The electrical curcuit is completed through the waste spark, meaning all the energy is sent back through the opposite coil wire-not the chassis ground. Unplugging one coil wire will therefore disable two cylinders. Direct connection from the coil to each of the

cylinders eliminates sending the spark through the distributor cap and rotor, which can sometimes cause cross-firing and other distributor-related performance problems. In addition, computer-controlled custom advance/retard curves eliminate any potential mechanical problems that may occur with centrifugal or vacuum timing adjustment.

The TEC-3 ECU is dynamically programmed with easy-to-use software that comes with the system. The "Tuning Wizard" found in the WinTec 3.0 software allows you to create an instant engine profile in just a few steps (Figure 4-35). By inputting all of the parameters of your engine, you can get started with a good base profile from which you can make modifications. Mapped programs are easily downloaded into the ECU via a computer serial cable, and can be updated, changed or restored at any time. The base programs can be tweaked to get about 90 percent of the full potential power out of your engine. To achieve the final 10 percent, you will have to do extensive track testing, or run your engine on a dyno.

The system works by sampling the values from sensors in the engine, and then comparing them to various lookup tables that control fuel delivery and ignition timing. These sensors consist of the following:

- Oxygen sensor (measures mixture by measuring the exhaust gases)
- Manifold absolute pressure sensor (measures pressure, while compensating for altitude changes. You can also substitute a mass airflow sensor instead of the MAP)
- Knock sensor (detects and measures detonation caused by poor fuels, or too much timing advance)
- Crank angle sensor (measures RPM and crank location)
- Throttle position sensor (measures position for idle control and how quickly the peddle is depressed for fuel enrichments or deceleration cut-off)
- Cam angle sensor (detects cam timing for true sequential mode fuel injection)

All of these sensors work in conjunction to measure engine conditions at any one point in time. The ECU takes all of these sensor readings and translates them into formulas for delivering fuel and firing sparks. Using the advanced data-logging features, all of these sensor readings and the results of the ECU changes are recorded, snapping a picture of the engine functions at any one point in time. The data can be recalled for analysis and used as a reference for future ECU programming.

The TEC-3 can operate in either phased sequential or true sequential mode. Phased sequential means that the fuel injectors are activated multiple times per crankshaft cycle, once on an open valve and once on a closed valve. The 3.2-liter Carrera engine's Motronic fuel injection is an example of a phased injection system. For example, the fuel injectors on the left bank of the 3.2-liter engine all open and close together. They share the same wiring harness, and are electrically controlled as a group. True sequential injection means that each injector is activated in close coordination with that cylinder's ignition cycle. Fuel is squirted out of the injector in precise coordination with the opening and closing of the intake valve. Fuel is notinjected into the cylinder head when the valve is closed. The 3.6-liter 964 motors have true sequential injection, as did the early mechanical fuel injection engines. The mechanical fuel injection pump only pumps an injector when the intake valve is open, in precise synchronization with the complete combustion cycle of the engine. The TEC-3 operating in true sequential mode smooths out the engine idle and creates a cleaner running engine. At higher RPMs, phased sequential and true sequential modes show virtually identical performance, as the injectors are firing almost continuously when the engine is running at high RPMs.

Another advantage to the TEC-3 system is its flexibility; it can be used on just about any engine. Its ability to run engines up to 12 cylinders means that it can be moved from one engine to another as you upgrade. It's a very worthy investment that will be able to grow with you even if you upgrade your engine or your car.

The TEC-3 is also an excellent choice for running twin-plugged systems. The twin-plugged ECU unit is only about $150 more than the standard single-plug unit. To run twin-plug ignition, all you will need is an additional coil pack. You need not worry about adapting a 964 distributor, or the cost and expense of an original RSR distributor or one that has been modified to use the expensive RSR cap and rotor ($800 at the time of this writing). When you factor in the cost savings in mechanical hardware, it makes the total cost of the TEC-3 system increasingly affordable. Compared to the potential costs associated with implementing a mechanical twin-plugged system, the TEC-3 makes sense.

Pushing the limits of ultra-high performance, the TEC-3 also has four general output parameters (GPO) that can be controlled by any number of engine conditions. For instance, the system can automatically turn on cooling fans or open electric thermostats if the engine temperature or RPM increases past a certain threshold, or provide the driver with a custom-designed shift light on the dashboard. In what could be the ultimate performance system, the TEC-3 can control a variable turbo boost valve coupled with a knock sensor. This would allow you to run the maximum possible boost on a turbo or supercharged engine while actively monitoring and correcting for detonation. The engine management system can control this boost pressure, engine timing, and a host of other variables to achieve the highest possible boost without inflicting collateral damage. This system would be able to compensate dynamically for any octane fuel—automatically adjusting the timing and air-fuel ratio to squeeze the most power out of the engine.

The TEC-3 system can also run in an open or closed-loop configuration with respect to air-fuel mixture measurement. Open-loop mode is useful for racers who run leaded race fuels that cannot be used in conjunction with an oxygen sensor. In this mode, the system reads measurements from its sensors, and then compares the readings to its internal program maps. Spark and fuel-mixture are controlled using these maps without correcting for changes that would normally be measured by the oxygen sensor.

Another useful feature of the TEC-3 is its ability to self-diagnose problems that you are having with your engine's sensors. The ECU has a "check engine" warning lamp that will indicate if any of the engine's sensors are producing faulty signals. The error codes isolating the exact problem can be quickly downloaded from the ECU for diagnosing the problem.

The TEC-3 is not specifically designed for the 911 and thus requires some special adaptation to fit on the 911 engine. You can use custom manifolds specifically designed for aftermarket engine management systems, or adapt the Motronic 3.2 manifolds and throttle plate for the task. Clewett Engineering of Manhattan Beach, California, is an excellent source for custom-made adapters and sensors required to use the TEC-3 and other Electromotive systems with the 911 engine (Figure 4-36). The Electromotive systems have earned a great reputation with 911 tuners.

Needless to say, if you want to design the ultimate engine, you need to install some type of engine management system.

4-36 *Special sensor adapters are required to install and use the TEC-3 engine management system. Clewett Engineering of Manhattan Beach, Calif., manufactures a variety of adapters and sensors specifically for use with the TEC-3 and the HPX systems from Electromotive. Shown here is a crankshaft sensor, which consists of the actual sensor (yellow arrow), and a toothed wheel that is installed behind a specially designed crankshaft pulley (blue arrow). The sensor is mounted using two studs: the same stud that would normally hold the distributor and a stud mounted in the distributor bore plug.*

PARTS, UPGRADES & ENHANCEMENTS

The bottom line is that with a system like this, you can design and build any engine combination that you want. Whether it's a twin turbo-charged boosted engine, or a super high 12:1 compression ratio engine that runs on pump gas, the engine management systems will be able to control and optimize it. The possibilities are truly endless and unbounded.

IGNITION SYSTEMS

Although technically not an integral part of the engine re-build process, your engine's ignition system has a significant effect on its performance. The early 911 engines from 1965-68 use a standard coil, points, and condenser system. Although this system is very reliable and was used for years on the 356, the system proved a bit too weak for the richer running Weber carburetors, and had a tendency to foul the plugs quite often. On these older inductive systems, the coil must step up the voltage and store the electrical charge between each firing. When the RPM of the engine increases, the coil doesn't have enough time between firings to ramp up to its maximum voltage. This results in a weaker spark and a loss of power at higher RPMs.

In 1969, Porsche introduced a capacitive discharge (CD) system on the 911. With capacitive discharge, the ignition system contains a large capacitor that can be charged much more quickly (less than one millisecond) than the inductive coil. With a capacitive discharge system, the voltage sent to the coil is always at full strength, minimizing the risk of fouled plugs even when the engine is running at high RPM. The spark is triggered by the points, which now pass very little current. This CD system basically remained the same until 1978, when Porsche installed a breakerless pickup system that replaced the standard set of ignition points. Then in 1984, the Motronic engine management system integrated fuel injection and ignition, eliminating the need for the CD box.

So what can be done to upgrade the system? Aside from twin-plugging it, the two most common upgrades are a breakerless ignition trigger, and an upgraded CD system. The early 1965-69 cars can use the very reliable Allison-Crane XR700 unit to eliminate the use of points. The later style cars with the Bosch distributor (typically 1972-77) can use either the XR700 unit, or the Pertronix Ignitor. Both approaches increase reliability and eliminate the problems often associated with ignition points.

Installing an upgraded CD system can improve the performance of your 911. The MSD 6AL or Allison-Crane Hi-6 are two relatively inexpensive, high-quality units (Figure 4-37). In addition to the standard benefits of the capacitive discharge system, the MSD unit fires more than one spark per cycle. During the course of an ignition stroke, the MSD unit rapidly fires full-power sparks over 20 degrees of crankshaft rotation. This multiple spark firing aids in the combustion process and helps the fuel burn more completely, resulting in more power and less emissions. The number of

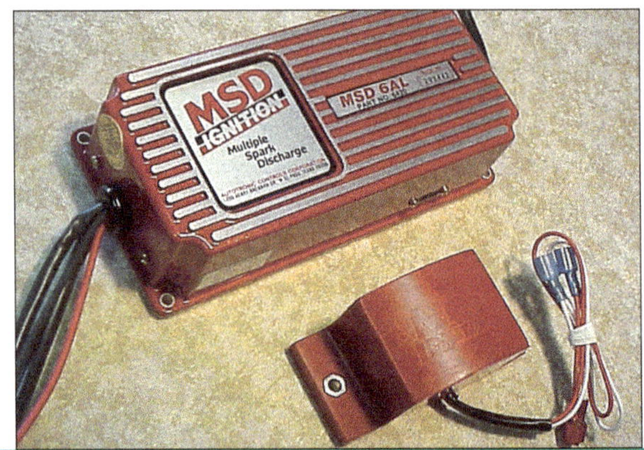

4-37 *A standard among automotive enthusiasts everywhere, the MSD ignition system is an excellent choice for replacing a worn-out or faulty original CD box. The MSD system is an affordable upgrade that will give you better combustion, particularly below 3,000 RPM. Two MSD units are an excellent choice for running dual-ignition systems, and I have also heard of people using one MSD box to fire two independent coils.*

sparks fired per power stroke decreases as the engine RPMs increase, and above 3,000 rpm, the MSD system only has enough time in the ignition cycle to fire a single high-powered spark. Above 3,000 rpm, the performance of the MSD system is comparable to the stock Bosch CD system. The MSD system also incorporates a rev limiter within the ignition system. Some of the early cars had a rev-limiting rotor that performs a similar purpose, and the later 911s (1978-89) had a rev-limiting function built into the CD box or Motronic ECU. The MSD system allows you to adjust this RPM level by plugging modules into the unit. Installing a CD unit can help improve the performance of engines with aggressive cams and rich-running fuel systems. The improved system helps reduce plug fouling and rough idling often associated with engines running Weber carburetors or MFI. This type of system also helps with higher compression engines. Higher compression results in a denser mixture that creates more resistance around the spark plug. This means the spark doesn't fire as easily.

The TEC-3 engine management system mentioned in the previous section integrates ignition and fuel control in a single programmable unit. Electromotive Engine Controls also produces a system that includes just the ignition components of the TEC-3. The HPX crank-triggered direct fire multiple coil ignition system has all of the advantages of the ignition segment of the engine management system and can be easily integrated into any 911 engine. The distributor is replaced with a crank-mounted, toothed wheel, and the CD system is completely removed. The crank-fire system uses the same three coil packs as the TEC-3 and provides enhanced spark duration times and programmable advance/retard curves. The HPX system is also an excellent alternative to replacing an expensive and difficult-to-find original distributor.

On some of the early cars, Porsche installed a distributor manufactured by Marelli. These distributors are no longer available—the supply of original caps, rotors, and points has been exhausted. IKAR, an aftermarket company that makes a lot of Mercedes parts, carries replacement points that fit Marelli distributors. The part number is 911.602.960.00. However, caps and rotors for the Marelli unit are nowhere to be found. The only practical solution is to upgrade to the Bosch distributor, which has an identical curve. This Bosch distributor is still available, and so are the basic tune-up parts. The cost of the distributor is around $700 for a new one, and used ones are very difficult to find because everyone is looking for them to replace their old Marelli distributor. If you have one of these older distributors, you will eventually have to upgrade it to the Bosch one. The good news is that the Bosch distributor is a drop-in replacement for the Marelli one and requires no modifications to the engine.

It is important to note that you cannot swap distributors from one engine to another. The advance and retard characteristics must be matched to a particular engine configuration. For example, installing a 911 T distributor on a 911 S engine will produce a different advance curve that will reduce the overall performance of the engine. You should plan on having your distributor recurved if you are building a custom or modified engine.

TWIN PLUG IGNITION

Twin plugging or twin ignition is an upgrade that is usually best installed along with an increase in the compression ratio. It's a common misconception that simply adding two plugs to the combustion chamber will generate an instant increase in power. In fact, the factory stated that twin-plugging by iteself typically added less than 3% more horsepower. Twin plugging is actually a modification that works in parallel with other engine modifications that increase the overall compression ratio.

To reduce cylinder head temperatures and reduce detonation, I recommend that a twin-plug ignition system be installed if your compression ratio is higher than 10:1. In addition, twin-plug ignition systems should be installed on engines with piston diameters greater than or equal to 98mm. In cylinders in this size range, it takes too long for the ignition flame front to propagate across the combustion chamber. This adversely affects combustion, and can lead to reduced performance. Usually minor horsepower gains can be expected from engines with less than a 10:1 compression ratio. Engines with compression ratios higher than 10:1 gain the most from twin plugging, including increased overall power and reduced detonation.

On a side note, I think it's worthy to mention that fuel octane additives really only serve to increase the effective octane of your tank of gas by about one point. This makes a very expensive option for reducing detonation—blending race fuel with pump gas is typically more econmical.

The 911 cylinder head does not lend itself to ideal, uniform ignition. The two valves in the center of the head take up the majority of the room, forcing the spark plug to be located off to the side. The ideal place for the spark plug would be in the center of the cylinder head, slightly offset to the exhaust side, which is the hottest part of the head. When the spark is fired and the mixture is ignited, the flame front expands across the combustion chamber. Installing two plugs per cylinder increases combustion efficiency and reduces the time it takes for complete combustion to occur. Having this ideal combustion also means that the ignition timing advance can be reduced, because the spark can be fired closer to top dead center. Reducing the ignition-timing advance can reduce the operating temperatures of high-compression engines. Most twin-plug engines will achieve their peak horsepower output at about 23 to 24 degrees of total advance, compared with the typical 30 to 35 degrees required for single-plugged engines. Because the combustion process is more efficient, it doesn't need to be ignited as early.

The high-domed pistons that are typically used in the 911 engine to increase compression ratio have the unfortunate side effect of splitting the combustion chamber in half. On a typical single-plug head, the flame front will start from one side of the combustion chamber and travel across the center of the head to the opposite side. This delay in complete combustion means that the ignition timing must be advanced so that complete combustion can occur by the time the piston is about 25 to 35 degrees past TDC. For more information on flame-fronts and detonation, see Chapter 2 of *The Sports Car* by Colin Campbell.

With two plugs per cylinder, the combustion process is initiated on both sides of the cylinder head. This accelerates the ignition process and allows you to retard the ignition timing by 10 degrees or more at higher RPMs. An engine produces power when the combustion process exerts force on the piston right after the piston has passed TDC. A pressure increase that occurs before the cylinder has reached TDC pushes back on the cylinder as its compressing the mixture—doing negative work and possibly causing knocking in the engine. The accelerated ignition sequence from twin plugging gives a net power increase because there is less energy wasted on pushing back the piston while it's approaching TDC. The gases in the combustion chamber expand later in the power stroke, and allow all of the pressure that is built up to act upon the piston during its downward stroke.

On an engine with a compression ratio of less than 10:1, twin plugging really doesn't have too much effect, primarily because these engines are not running at unusually high compression. However, on a race or high-compression street engine, the twin-plug system can increase horsepower pri-

4-38 *This distributor is probably the most impressive-looking upgrade that you can place on your engine. Originally used on the RSR and the venerable 917, this distributor is the ultimate vintage accessory for twin-plugging your 911 engine. Also noteworthy on this engine is the central-feed oiling system for the camshafts (blue arrow). This race-worthy setup supplies oil down the center of the camshaft to feed the camshaft housings. This system was also found on the very early 901 engines.*

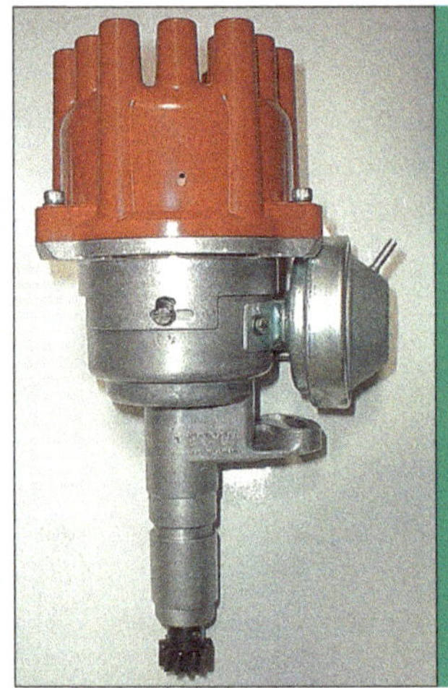

4-39 *Andial of Santa Ana, Calif., modified this 911 SC distributor to accept the 911 RSR cap and rotor. Although a more economical solution to installing the actual RSR distributor, you will still need to purchase caps and rotors, which can be very expensive ($700 or greater).*

marily in the high RPM range by creating more efficient and quicker combustion in conjunction with the increase in compression. In basic terms, twin plugging is used to gain the maximum effect of increasing the compression ratio. Without a twin-plug system, a high-compression motor may encounter significant detonation at mid-range RPM with an open throttle. Adding the twin-plug system decreases detonation, decreases your cylinder head temperatures, and also will decrease the octane requirements of higher compression engines. In order for your car to fully utilize another set of engine modifications that increase the compression ratio, you typically must add twin-plug ignition.

There are three common implementations of the twin-plug system: twin-plug distributors, dual-distributors, and crank-fire ignition or engine management systems. One such implementation uses a 12-plug RSR/917 distributor, shown in Figure 4-38. While RSR distributors have long been in the "unobtainium" class of parts, they can be located for about $2,000 to $4,000 each. If you happen to come across one of these distributors, make sure that it will suit your application. The engine pictured on the cover of this book has a 12-plug distributor installed on it; however, this distributor is originally from a 935, and contains no centrifugal advance mechanism. The 935 race car operated in a narrow RPM band and was tuned to this range. As a result, it didn't need the addition of the centrifugal advance. Such a distributor would be difficult to use on a street engine that needs a broad power band across its entire RPM range.

In addition to the potential $4,000 price tag for the bare distributor, the cost of a distributor cap typically runs about $700 each—not for the faint of heart. It's important to keep this in mind when you choose your method of twin-plugging.

An alternative to the genuine RSR/917 distributor is to have a standard distributor modified to accept the 12-plug RSR cap and rotor. The distributor is modified by mounting an adapter ring to its top and cutting the center shaft to accept the larger RSR rotor. Andial of Santa Ana, California, sells an excellent quality 12-plug distributor that is converted in this manner (Andial part number AND 602 033, shown in Figure 4-39). The manufacturing process is difficult, as the cap and ring must be aligned properly, and the distributor advance curve needs to be modified to match your individual engine's requirements. With a setup like this, it's usually wise to convert to a breakerless system like the Pertronix Ignitor. This is often the preferred method of twin plugging for the 911 Turbos because it is possible to keep the proper distributor curve (centrifugal retard on boost) that is required for smooth engine operation.

A second alternative to the expensive RSR solution is to install a 964 distributor (Figure 4-40). Starting with the 1989 Carrera 4, the 911 engine used a dual distributor configuration that is connected with a small-toothed timing belt. This distributor will fit, unmodified, into a 2.4 liter or later engine case. To use the 964 dual-distributor on pre-1984 and Turbo engines, you will need to change the crankshaft distributor drive gear to the later style gear from the 3.2-liter engine (part number 930.102.112.00). Machining costs for using the 964 distributor are modest, yet the cost of the actual distributor can be several hundred dollars. The major problem with using the 964 distributor is that you need to implement a method for adjusting the initial timing setting on the distributor. The 964 engine uses the Motronic Engine Management system, which controls timing advance and retard using the fuel injection computer. Therefore, its distributor was mounted to the engine with no ability to rotate it and adjust the initial timing or advance curves. Therefore, no adjustability exists within the 964 distributor itself.

The 964 distributor does contain a centrifugal advance mechanism. However, it provides only a crude method for

the lower spark plug wiring harness. This would be an expensive option to add to a stock Motronic 3.2 engine, with minimal horsepower gains unless the compression ratio of the engine is increased.

Both of the above solutions can be used with complete, independent ignition firing systems. You can install a pair of OEM Bosch capacitive discharge units (CD boxes), or run two aftermarket systems like the Permatune or the MSD 6AL units with Bosch blue coils.

The third solution is to install a crank-fire distributorless dual-ignition system. Although complicated, these aftermarket ignition systems can eliminate your distributor, and allow you to custom-design your ignition advance to suit your specific application. Another advantage is that you don't need to keep purchasing new caps, rotors, or points—with the RSR solution, the distributor cap has the potential to cost more than the entire crank-fire system. The best-known systems are the Electromotive HPV-1, TEC-II engine management systems, and the systems from MoTec. Setting up and installing these systems is difficult and usually requires

moving the rotor closer to the fining point on the ditributor cap as the DME computer advances the spark timing. This is incorporated so that the 964 distributor can use a thin rotor and a small distributor cap.

You also need to devise a pickup method for triggering the ignition system. The best solution that I have seen is to remove the internals from a 2.7-liter distributor and install them in the primary 964 distributor. You can then attach a Pertronix breakerless ignition system and trigger the spark electronically. Running this setup with an MSD unit that has an adjustable advance/retard curve eliminates the need for a vacuum canister or a mechanical centrifugal advance mechanism. Some of the newer MSD systems also allow you to adjust the basic spark timing of the system, solving the problem of the non-adjustable distributor. You can have the distributor modified to accept a 3.0L pickup mechanism as well. Running a crank-fire ignition system with the 964 distributor is also a good option.

Unfortunately, it is difficult to make this particular 964 distributor configuration work with the 911 Turbos because the turbo plumbing has a tendency to interfere with the two distributors. Depending upon your engine's configuration, the 964 solution may also require a slightly modified oil cam line to bypass the larger distributor assembly.

The Motronic 3.2-liter engines can be adapted to use twin-plug ignition with the 964 distributor using a splitter specifically designed for this purpose. This splitter is available from Andial (part number AND 903 950 02), and the triggering for the ignition comes from the stock Motronic flywheel sensor. The 964 distributor merely distributes the spark to each cylinder, much as it does on the actual 964 engine. All that is required is a second ignition coil, and

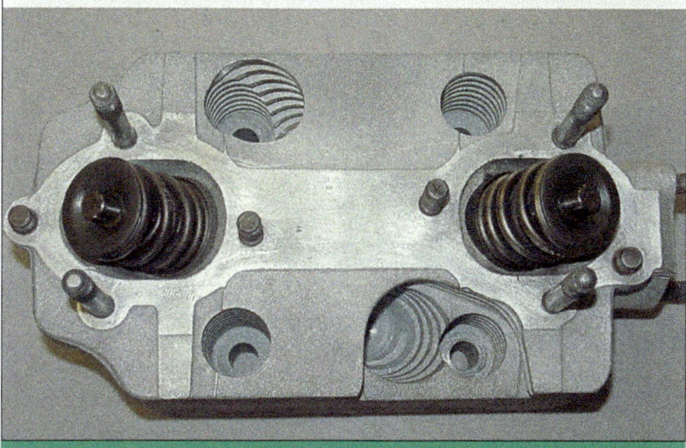

the help of an experienced installer. Clewett Engineering is the foremost designer and installer of the Electromotive single and twin-plug ignition systems, and a good source for 911 engine-specific adapters and components.

Regardless of your choice of distributors, you will need to modify the heads for the second set of spark plugs, as shown in Figure 4-41. The best time to do this machine work, of course, is when the engine is out of the car and you are overhauling the top end, or rebuilding the entire engine. Adding a second spark plug does not significantly weaken the heads, and the cost of the actual machining is a small percentage of the total cost of the dual-plug system.

In addition to the obvious machining to the heads (drill and tap holes for the spark plugs), you will also need to have clearance holes cut in the engine sheet metal so the wires can pass through to the lower valve covers. The lower valve covers (Turbo valve covers recommended) need to be machined for clearance holes for the spark plugs (Figure 4-42). Like the upper valve covers, these holes are drilled in the lower dry areas of the camshaft housing so oil leaks are not a concern. It's also common to install lower retaining brackets for the plug wires to reduce the chance that they will loosen with engine vibrations. In addition, on the 2.7 -liter and earlier engines, the lower head nuts on 2.7-liter and earlier engines have a tendency to interfere with the lower plug wires, connectors, and sometimes the plug socket used to install them. One solution to this problem

is to use low-profile 10mm nuts with smaller outside diameters. Typical 10mm barrel nuts on 2.7-liter and ealier engines have an outside diameter of 18mm, and a height of 18mm as well. The low-profile aftermarket nuts from RaceWare or ARP have a 14mm outer diameter and a height of 11mm (RaceWare part number RTE-5001).

The conclusion on twin plugging? Obviously, there is much more to the story than I can put into this section. The 964 distributor option is a bit less expensive than the RSR setup, and also reduces the requirement for expensive replacement distributor caps. The distributorless solutions are great if you are thinking of running an aftermarket ignition system, as the twin-plug, crank-fire systems are only slightly more expensive than the single-plug systems. As stated previously, twin plugging won't necessarily buy you any performance increase on its own—to take full advantage, you need to combine it with an engine modification that increases the compression ratio.

EXHAUST SYSTEMS

A free-flowing fuel intake system is very important to your 911's performance. Equally important is the flow of exhaust gases out of the engine. Since the days of the 1967 911 S, Porsche has used a very good exhaust header system, which has doubled as the car's heat exchangers. This system was used on all the production cars from 1968 through 1974, until it was replaced with a performance-robbing system designed to meet stricter emissions standards and noise regulations. These regulations have hampered the 911 ever since, to the point where none of the late-model exhaust systems have been as good for performance as the early ones.

In particular, the 1975-77 911s have an exhaust system that reduces engine longevity. The thermal reactors on these cars raise engine operating temperatures, which translates into greater stress and wear. If smog laws permit it, I recommend replacing these thermal reactors with the pre-1974 system.

One of the most popular 911 upgrades is to backdate the exhaust system and install the 1974 and earlier heat exchangers and muffler, shown in Figure 4-43. This approach, however, violates many state and federal laws that make it illegal to tamper with or remove any exhaust components between the engine and the catalytic converter. A legal alternative is to install a freer-flowing catalytic converter. The technology used in these units has improved over the past 20 years, and a new aftermarket catalytic converter flows almost as free as a cat-bypass pipe. The exhaust backdate modification can legally be performed only on 911s that are raced at the track. For a track car, I would recommend installing headers instead of the stock OEM or aftermarket

4-42 *To set up your engine for twin ignition, you will need to have your lower valve covers machined for the spark plug holes (yellow arrows). These holes are drilled in the dry section of the lower camshaft housings. A separate set of lower spark plug wires also needs to be routed to each of the lower cylinders.*

4-43 *A very popular upgrade for 1975 and later 911s is to backdate the exhaust to the 1974 and earlier style. Shown here are stainless steel heat exchangers from SSI, combined with a Dansk stainless steel muffler. Be aware that modifying your exhaust is only legal for track use—most states prohibit the tampering with exhaust systems and removal of catalytic converters. photo: Kurt Williams*

stainless steel heat exchangers, primarily because headers will reduce the weight of the car.

There are two aftermarket stainless steel heat exchangers that I recommend. Both are well-made units and will perform nearly identically. The two manufacturers are OEM muffler manufacturer Dansk, and longtime stainless steel manufacturer SSI. You can use the standard stock 911 dual-inlet, single-outlet muffler with either of these systems, and the result will be significantly less restriction on any post-1974 car. Backdating the exhaust is usually good for 15 to 20 extra horsepower, depending upon your engine.

For maximum horsepower, I prefer to run a dual-outlet sport muffler. Not only do these look sharp and have a loud, aggressive sound, but they also flow much better than the stock units. Also very good are the aftermarket mufflers manufactured by GHL and the OEM replica units made by Dansk.

As mentioned previously, removing the heat exchangers and installing headers reduces the weight of the car. When you remove the heating system, make sure that you install the air block-off plate described in Section 2. Power gains can vary from engine to engine and depend a lot on displacement, the camshaft overlap, and cylinder head flow characteristics. Picking the right header for your engine is not an exact science.

One of the biggest mistakes that you can make is installing too large a diameter header on your engine. Unfortunately, there are no hard and fast rules regarding header size. Bigger is not necessarily better. If your header is oversized, then your engine will suffer from a lack of back pressure. Street engines in particular tend to run at lower RPM, where the muffler works the best. Race engines that typically run in higher RPM

range benefit mostly from straight pipes or megaphones. As a result of using too large a header, the lower-end power band of the engine will suffer greatly and midlevel RPM power may decrease as well. It would be a shame to spend all that time, energy, and money on tuning and customizing your engine, only to place extra large headers on it that rob its power. (The contrary is true as well—smaller diameter pipes can create a restrictive flow for the exhaust at higher RPMs.)

Despite the potential loss of low-end power, 911 owners have a tendency to install oversized headers on their engines. In addition to the pipe diameter, the layout and overall length is important as well. All of the pipe lengths from the engine should be equal, so that each cylinder experiences the same amount of back pressure. If the pipes are too short, it can have the same effect as having pipe diameters that are too large—reduced low-end performance due to inadequate back pressure. A good reference on the subject is the book, *Scientific Design of Exhaust & Intake Systems*, by Philip H. Smith.

Header and exhaust design is not an exact science, and unfortunately there are a lot of myths and mistruths out there. For race cars, you must balance a number of parameters, including cost, noise level, flow characteristics, volumetric flow capacity and overall weight, to gain the optimum performance.

The following diagram shows recommended header sizes as a function of displacement. The chart should be used only as a starting point for choosing headers. Ideal header primary pipe diameter depends on factors like peak RPM and total flow, not just displacement. In general, it's better to err on the side of too small versus too big. For race applications where a more aggressive cam is used, install a slightly larger header. On street applications, it's a good bet to go with one size smaller. At this moment, the previously mentioned stainless steel (and stock OEM heat exchangers) are available in a maximum 1 5/8-inch pipe diameter, so their usefulness is limited on engines with displacements over 3.2 liters.

Engine	Header
2.0	$1\frac{1}{2}$" or $1\frac{5}{8}$"
2.2	$1\frac{1}{2}$" or $1\frac{5}{8}$"
2.4	$1\frac{1}{2}$" or $1\frac{5}{8}$"
2.5	$1\frac{5}{8}$"
2.7	$1\frac{5}{8}$"
2.8	$1\frac{5}{8}$"
3.0	$1\frac{5}{8}$" or $1\frac{1}{2}$"
3.2	$1\frac{5}{8}$" or $1\frac{1}{2}$"
3.4 to 3.5	$1\frac{3}{4}$"
3.6 to 3.8	$1\frac{3}{4}$" or $1\frac{7}{8}$"

TURBOS & SUPERCHARGERS

A lot of people incorrectly think that turbocharging and supercharging are the holy grail of power increases. They assume that because the factory turbocharged the 911, then any aftermarket turbocharger tossed on a 911 engine will instantly generate horsepower. As with any good, reliable means of generating horsepower, the addition of a turbo or supercharger needs to be carefully coordinated with your engine's design—as you keep in mind your desired performance characteristics.

Turbocharging and supercharging are methods of forced induction. Forced induction assists the engine in filling the combustion chamber with air-fuel mixture. On a normally aspirated engine, the maximum manifold pressure is atmospheric pressure (14.7 psi). On a forced induction engine, manifold pressure is increased by the supercharger (or turbocharger) above 14.7 psi. The result is a greater mass of air and fuel injected into the combustion chamber, resulting in more power.

Both a turbocharger and supercharger are very similar in principle. Both use a compressor/blower to increase the overall pressure of gases inserted into the combustion chamber (cold side). This increase in pressure results in an air-fuel mixture that is more compressed. When this denser mixture is ignited, it generates a more powerful stroke. The supercharger is powered by a pulley that attaches to the crankshaft. The turbocharger is powered by exhaust gases (on the hot side) that spin up the turbine, which is connected to the compressor. Both the turbo and the supercharger perform similarly, but have different characteristics based on their setup and configuration. Forced induction systems often make use of an intercooler as well. As the air from the turbine is compressed, it will heat up. This hot air is cycled through a large intercooler that cools the air before it is injected into the intake manifold. The cooler air helps to reduce detonation, and also increases the density of the air-fuel mixture.

The turbocharger unit drives its compressor from the excess exhaust given off by the engine. Although the back pressure on the exhaust may rob a small amount of power from the engine, the boost from the turbo is generally thought of as free boost. Whereas the turbo runs off of the exhaust system, a supercharger takes power from the engine crankshaft to run the blower. All things being equal, superchargers sap more power (40 to 50 horsepower to spin the blower to full boost) from the engine to run the compressor than turbochargers.

Many people wrongly believe that a larger turbocharger will generate more boost and horsepower. In reality, this is not necessarily true. You need to make other important changes to the engine when installing a larger turbocharger. The turbocharger generates compressed air known as boost when the blower is spun up to operating speed by the exhaust. This compressed air is then fed into the engine's intake system. Maximum boost pressure is limited by a pressure relief valve called the wastegate. The wastegate acts to release exhaust gas pressure, slowing the turbine so the engine doesn't suffer from too much boost. Installing a larger turbocharger without making adjustments to the wastegate will result in no increase in maximum boost levels.

How does the size of the turbocharger affect performance? Porsche has used a wide variety of turbochargers in their production and race engines. Some of these model numbers include K24, K26, K27, K29, and K31. The numeric portion usually corresponds to the actual size of the turbo exhaust fan wheel, or turbine wheel, inside the turbocharger. In addition, there is the compressor wheel on the intake (cold side) that compresses the air to create the actual boost. By changing the sizes of the two wheels you can alter the overall personality of the turbocharger to tailor the turbo response to your specific application.

For example, a small turbine wheel in the exhaust combined with a small impeller wheel on the compressor side

4-44 *A very impressive supercharger installation is shown here, performed by Mark Hargett. The motor base is a 1978 911 SC with 3.2L Nikasil cylinders, 8.5:1 JE pistons, Hastings piston rings, ARP case studs and rod bolts, 993 Super Sport camshaft profile, high-performance valve springs, twin-plug ignition with crank-fire, Haltech engine management system, Eaton M62 supercharger running 2:1 overdrive ratio (8 lbs. adjustable boost), custom induction system and intercooler, and stainless steel SSI heat exchangers with a Powertune muffler.*

4-45 *This twin turbo conversion is rightly dubbed the monster by owner/designer Stephen Kaspar of Imagine Auto. The engine is a normally aspirated 993 with 3.6, 7.5:1 Mahle pistons and cylinders, knife-edged crankshaft, boat-tailed case, oil shedding crankshaft, RaceWare head studs and rod bolts, Carrillo rods, pistons dry-lubed and ceramic coated on top, six-angle valve grinds, full port and smoothing, titanium valve retainers, Vmax valve springs, 993 Sport Cams, bored and polished Turbo 'S' throttle body, GT2 twin turbos, modified twin turbo intercooler, twin-plug ignition and a TEC-1 engine management system. The monster generates 607 horsepower at 1 bar of boost on the dyno, with full boost coming online at around 2400 rpm.*

will spin the turbo up quickly, and generate a quick throttle response, but power will also tend to drop off on the top end. A small turbine in the exhaust with a large blower will generate a good compromise between throttle response and top-end power. To obtain the best top-end performance, combine a large turbo wheel with a large blower wheel. The downside is that throttle-response will suffer.

A smaller turbine wheel in the exhaust will spin up much faster than a larger one. The ideal turbo configuration for everyday street driving is to have a smaller turbine on the hot side, and a larger blower turbine on the cold side. This configuration offers a good compromise between low-end throttle response and high-end power. The downside to this setup is that it takes a certain level of exhaust pressure at a minimum RPM to spin up the exhaust (hot-side) turbine to the point where it can begin to have an effect on the intake pressures. The lack of boost during the spin-up period is commonly known as turbo lag.

Turbo engines are specially designed to accommodate the additional stresses placed on them by the turbo boost. Turbo engines usually have very low compression ratios to compensate for the added pressures when the car is operating under full boost. These low compression ratios exacer-

bate the turbo-lag problem, because without the boost from the turbocharger, they are relatively low-power engines. A stock 911 Turbo engine with its turbo removed and carburetors installed would be a very poor performer because its overall compression ratio would be very low. The bottom line is that you can generate more horsepower from maximizing the boost from the turbo than you can with higher compression. If you run higher compression, then you will be forced to run with less boost at the higher end to avoid destroying your engine. You want to design your engine to have low compression, so that you can run higher boost at higher RPMs, and generate more horsepower.

There are a few ways to solve the turbo-lag dilemma. If you have an unlimited budget, you can install two sequential turbochargers to give the engine a broad-based boost across the entire power band. The first turbocharger has a very small turbine on the hot side, and a small wheel on the cold side. This gives the car quick response in the low-end. At about 4,300 rpm, a valve opens and brings the second turbocharger online—it has been partially brought up to speed by a portion of the exhaust gases from the first turbocharger. The result is that the two turbochargers deliver a strong boost across nearly the whole RPM range. This type of system was pioneered on the 959 and was later used in the 911 Twin Turbo.

If you have a somewhat more limited budget, there are a couple of upgrades that will go a long way toward reducing lag. Installing an aftermarket header system like the ones from GHL or B&B can reduce the start of the turbo boost range from 3,000 rpm to 1,700 rpm. The aftermarket systems perform a better job at funneling the exhaust gases directly into the turbocharger.

Swapping the turbocharger with a one that's a different size can change your turbo engine's characteristics. You can install a K27-29 turbocharger that delivers a little bit quicker response with more boost, and more power on the top end of the RPM range. There are numerous options for turbochargers—each one changes the performance characteristics in slightly different ways from the next. Perform some research and drive as many turbocharged 911s as you can before you spend a large amount of money on a new turbocharger. Adding an intercooler, or upgrading your existing one, will also increase your overall performance. Finally, increasing the compression in your engine will give you more low-end power. You need to make sure, however, that you don't deliver too much boost from the turbo with your higher compression engine. For more information on turbocharging, see the book, *Turbochargers*, by Hugh MacInnes, or *Supercharging, Turbocharging & Nitrous Oxide Performance Handbook*, by Earl and Diane Perkins-Davis.

So what about supercharging? Superchargers don't typically suffer from turbo lag because they're always spinning whenever the engine is running; they are already spinning at 1,000 rpm or so when the engine is idling. For the street, they offer good throttle response, and excellent drivability, with a power range over a wide RPM range. Superchargers typically generate less power than turbochargers because they are powered off of the crankshaft, which creates a more direct power drain than utilizing exhaust gases. The primary disadvantages of using a supercharger on the 911 are the difficulties in finding room to mount the unit, and the 40 to 50 horsepower they require from the engine to power the blower. Another overlooked element is that the factory performed a tremendous amount of research on turbocharging as part of their race program. This body of factory-derived information on which turbocharging systems work best for the 911 engine doesn't exist for supercharging.

So what can you do to improve the response of your turbocharged 911? Obviously, a set of sequential turbochargers configured to offer uniform boost across the entire power band is ideal. However, this arrangement can become extremely expensive to build and configure. Simply dialing in more boost from the turbocharger (by changing the wastegate relief valve spring) can give you an immediate performance improvement. However, this can be extremely hazardous to your engine. Severe detonation from poor quality gas can cause pistons to overheat, and the engine can literally blow itself apart. Adding or enlarging your intercooler is another good option for generating more power.

Unfortunately, the stock Porsche CIS does not help with the turbo-lag effect. In addition, the power on CIS turbo engines begins to fade at about 6,300 rpm. If you wish to have better low-end throttle response off the line, then my suggestion would be to decrease the size of the hot side turbine. This, however, will pull power away from the top end. In the end, it really depends upon the conditions under which you are going to drive the car, and how much turbo lag you can tolerate.

You can also run 964 or 911 SC camshafts in the 911 Turbo. This has the effect of increasing performance on the low end. You can also raise the compression ratio by stretching the rods or fly cutting the heads. Stock engines are designed at a low 6.5:1. You can safely increase this to 7.5:1 or 8:1 if you watch your total boost, timing advance, and use high-octane gasoline. There are also many aftermarket exhaust systems that provide better flow to the Turbo than the stock system. These systems channel the exhaust directly into the turbocharger, resulting in reduced turbo lag. Running a TEC-3 engine management system is also a good choice for improving power over the stock CIS.

TRANSMISSION GEAR RATIOS

Another thought to consider is your choice of transmission gears. A poorly matched transmission can make the most powerful engine seem sluggish. If your engine has a high-RPM power band (like the early 911 S), then you will probably want a transmission with very close ratio gears. This will allow you to maintain your optimum power band, and maximize the power output to the wheels. It's not uncommon to find Porsche race cars specifically designed for long tracks and rolling starts that have a "tall" first gear. This basically allows the racers to use first gear on the track, which effectively creates a true five-speed transmission for racing. Such a car would be very difficult to drive on the street, because off-the-line performance would be quite sluggish. However, on the track is where the drivetrain would shine, delivering peak power in a narrow power band closely matched to the transmission and the type of racetrack. For more information on choosing gear ratios, see Chapter 9 in the book, *Gearing and Differentials in Race Car Engineering & Mechanics*, by Paul Van Valkenburgh.

WEIGHT REDUCTION

A chapter on performance options would not be complete without discussing the option of placing your car on a diet. As mentioned previously, the benefits from weight reductions to rotational components in the engine are twofold—they not only reduce the rotational mass that the engine needs to spin up, but they also reduce the total weight of the car. These rotational components exist all over the car—not just in the engine. All of the rotational drivetrain components (wheels, transmission gears, axles, brake discs, etc.) have a significant effect on your car's overall performance. Using lighter weight wheels, for example, will have a similar effect to reducing the weight of your flywheel—the drivetrain will accelerate faster, and the total mass of the car will be reduced as well. Again, the gain is twofold. It is for this reason that most racers try to remove as much mass as possible from drivetrain components when lightening their chassis.

While reducing the mass of drivetrain components can produce the most efficient gains, you can go only so far. This is because the drivetrain is responsible for delivering power to the wheels and accelerating the car. You can only remove so much weight—you don't want to weaken the drivetrain to the point where it is going to fail. The second best thing to do is to remove weight from the chassis of the car. Theoretically, a 10 percent reduction in weight is equivalent to a 10 percent increase in equivalent horsepower. On a 200 horsepower, 3,000-pound car, it may be far more practical to remove 300 pounds than it would be to produce 20 more horsepower from your engine.

So what can you do to reduce weight? There are a couple of rules of thumb. The first place you should remove weight is from "unsprung" components. These are the parts of the car that are not supported by the suspension. Examples include trailing arms, A-arms, brake discs, wheels, etc. The next best place to remove weight is from the highest points on the car (sunroofs, windscreens, etc.). Removing weight here helps to lower the car's center of gravity. Next, you want to target the rear of the car. This is because the 911 is already tail-heavy due to the rearward mounting of the engine.

If your goal is pure performance, you can lighten your car significantly simply by removing or replacing the following on the car:

- Remove air conditioning systems
- Remove window regulators/support braces in doors
- Replace glass with Lexan
- Replace decklids and doors with fiberglass
- Remove most interior components (especially the rear seats)
- Remove undercoating on the chassis
- Replace the driver's/passenger seat with a lightweight one
- Move or replace the battery with a lighter one
- Remove any unnecessary components from the front trunk (spare, jack, etc.)
- Remove the DOT bumpers and replace them with fiberglass
- Remove stereo system
- Remove the sunroof and replace with fiberglass
- Drill brake rotors
- Remove power mirrors

Of course, any weight removal must be balanced with the practicalities of daily driving. If you enjoy air conditioning and a good stereo, then you probably won't want to sacrifice these amenities for improved performance. However, if your mission is to maximize performance, you might be surprised at how much of a difference weight removal can make.

ENGINE SWAPS

As chief technical writer for Pelican Parts, I often get asked about engine swaps as an alternative to engine rebuilds. Many 911 owners mistakenly assume that swapping in a late model 3.0L or 3.2L engine for their worn-out 2.4L is a good economic decision. While the conversion process for these engines is not too difficult, the costs can be more than you bargained for.

Most of the 3.0 and 3.2 liter engines that are coming up for sale these days are being pulled out of cars because they are tired and worn out. The newest 3.2-liter engine is now 13 years old, and undoubtedly has seals that are beginning to dry out and leak. If you decide to purchase a replacement engine, you may be stuck with a whole host of new problems. The 3.0-liter engine, for example, suffers from broken head stud problems. The 3.2-liter engines have both the head stud problems/valve guide wear problems, and the catastrophic rod bolt failures. The bottom line is that you may spend $7,000 on a replacement engine, only to find that you have to rebuild it in the very near future. Used motors come with added risks.

If you decide to perform an engine swap, make sure that you consider the consequences for resale as well. Most buyers are wary of engine swaps—if not performed correctly, they can be a world of trouble. An engine swap may increase the value of your car, but it will also deter some potential buyers if you do decide to sell it. Also important are current smog law restrictions. In California, if the car is a 1974 model or later and the engine is newer, the car must pass all of the emissions requirements for the year that the engine was manufactured. This usually means that you need to install the exhaust and fuel injection systems that were stock equipment on the newer engine.

In general, the 1965-89 911 can be easily adapted to fit any engine from this time period. The 1990 and later 3.6 engines are significantly different from the early ones and require a great deal of conversion work to fit and run properly in an earlier 911.

WAYNE'S TOP ENGINE PICKS

Okay, you've read this Chapter and you're all excited about rebuilding your 911 engine and extracting some more performance. However, you're still confused as to exactly what you need to do to get the engine performance that you want. In this subsection, I have polled quite a few Porsche engine rebuilding experts, and have generated the following table of engine recommendations, based upon the performance characteristics you may wish to extract out of your 911 engine.

Keep in mind that these recommendations only represent a small subset of what you can do. With a custom camshaft regrind, custom-designed JE pistons, or a custom-programmed engine management system, there really is no limit to the number of variations that you can achieve. If you are looking for a solution that is somewhat "outside of the box" then I suggest you consult with an expert in the Porsche rebuilding community. Check the official website for this book (http://www.101projects.com) for my current suggestions of top engine rebuilders.

This section contains my recommended picks. These are the proven designs that deliver good performance increases over the stock engines.

Wayne's Top Engine Picks

Case	Crank	Pistons	Cylinders	Cam	Fuel	Heads	Disp	Ratio
2.0	2.0/2.2 (66mm)	1969 S	2.0 (81mm)	E	40 Weber Carb	2.0L	2.0	9.8:1

2.0L S-Piston E-Cam Engine - This is a good street engine, although not too easy to drive at the low end. A good combination, but not as responsive or cost-effective as the 2.2 conversion (below). 'S' cams are not recommened (no low-end torque, requires high-octane gas, power is limited to high end of RPM range.

Case	Crank	Pistons	Cylinders	Cam	Fuel	Heads	Disp	Ratio
2.0	2.0/2.2 (66mm)	S	2.2 (84mm)	Solex	44 Weber Carb	2.2/2.4	2.2L	9.8:1

2.0 -> 2.2 Upgrade - The 2.0 and 2.2 share the same crank, so bolting in the 2.2 pistons is a simple upgrade. The heads need to be matched to the pistons. The 2.0L heads are not well designed, so you will want to use 2.2 or 2.4 heads.

Case	Crank	Pistons	Cylinders	Cam	Fuel	Heads	Disp	Ratio
2.0L Aluminum	2.0/2.2 (66mm)	11:1 Mahle High Dome	81mm Mahle	RSR	40 Weber 36mm Venturis	1969 S 36mm Port	2.0	11:1

2.0L HSR-spec Race Engine. Shuffle-pinned, boat-tailed, cylinders mooned, crank is knife-edged. Pauter lightweight rods, RSR cams in 4-bearing cam towers (originally 3.3 Turbo cams reground to RSR specs). Lightweight flywheel & puck-type clutch. Tall Weber manifolds, racing headers and megaphones. Engine makes 180-200 HP in the 6000-8000 rpm range. Race gas only.

Case	Crank	Pistons	Cylinders	Cam	Fuel	Heads	Disp	Ratio
2.2	2.4/2.7 (70.4mm)	E	2.2 (84mm)	E	Carbs or MFI	2.2	2.4L	10:1

2.2 -> 2.4 Upgrade - This is the best upgrade for the 2.2 engines, as it essentially turns them into a 2.4L displacement. The 2.4 and 2.7 share the same crank, so these cranks are easy to find out of junk 2.7 motors. Using the shorter stroke 2.2 pistons means that the compression ratio is elevated to about 10:1. This engine runs fine on pump gas without twin-plugging.

Case	Crank	Pistons	Cylinders	Cam	Fuel	Heads	Disp	Ratio
2.2/2.4	2.0/2.2 (66mm)	2.2 S High Dome	2.2L (84mm)	S	Carbs or MFI (2.2)	2.2/2.4 36mm	2.2L	9.8:1

2.2L S-Spec Engine - This engine is good for about 180 HP, and is one of the best small-displacement engines that you can build. Not a tremendous amount of torque on the low end, but should be good for the earlier, lighter-weight 911s. Avoid using the 2.2 T crankshaft, as it is not counterweighted.

Case	Crank	Pistons	Cylinders	Cam	Fuel	Heads	Disp	Ratio
2.2/2.4	2.4/2.7 (70.4mm)	2.2 S High Dome	2.2L (84mm)	S	Carbs or MFI (2.2)	2.2/2.4 36mm	2.4L	9.6:1

Stock 2.4S with 2.2 Pistons - Same engine as above, but with the 2.4/2.7 crankshaft (bolts together with no mofications). The increase in compression is worth about 10 more horsepower, and a boost in torque at the lower end. You will need to have your MFI pump recalibrated, or your carburetor jets changed to accomodate the change in compression. This is the same as a stock 2.4L that has had the pistons replaced with the 2.2L pistons (results in a significant increase in horsepower from the stock 2.4 liter, and does not need the case bored).

Case	Crank	Pistons	Cylinders	Cam	Fuel	Heads	Disp	Ratio
2.7	2.4/2.7 (70.4mm)	RS	2.7 (90mm)	S	Carbs or MFI	2.7	2.7L	8.5:1

2.7 RS Spec - This is the specification for the venerable 911 RS Carrera. It's no typo; the 8.5 compression is the original configuration. The RS cams and the early 911 'S' cams were also identical. This engine will run very well with an RS-spec MFI pump or with 40mm Weber carburetors with 34 or 35mm venturis. Power band starts at about 5000 rpm and pushes all the way up to 7300.

Case	Crank	Pistons	Cylinders	Cam	Fuel	Heads	Disp	Ratio
2.7	2.4/2.7 (70.4mm)	RS or JE	2.7 (90mm)	S	MFI	2.7	2.7L	9.8:1

2.7 RS Spec High Compression - This engine is the same as the RS spec, except that we've increased the compression ratio. The original RS-spec engine had suprisingly low compression. You can perform an increase in compression by running JE high-compression 2.7 RS pistons, stretching the rods, or fly cutting the heads. May require a rejetting of carburetors, but should remain the same for MFI.

Case	Crank	Pistons	Cylinders	Cam	Fuel	Heads	Disp	Ratio
3.0 Turbo	2.4/2.7 (70.4mm)	95mm High Dome	3.0L (Nikasil)	RSR	46 Carbs / high butterfly	3.0L Heads (1978-79)	3.0L	10.3:1

911 RSR-Spec Use JE pistons in combination with 3.0L Nikasil cylinders. This case accepts the 2.4/2.7 crankshaft, but also has the cylinder spacing for the 3.0L cylinders and heads. Twin-plug ignition recommended. You can also use the 1976-77 European Carrera aluminum engine case.

Case	Crank	Pistons	Cylinders	Cam	Fuel	Heads	Disp	Ratio
3.0 Turbo	2.0/2.2 (66mm)	95mm High Dome	3.0L (Nikasil)	RSR/GE80/ 906	46 Carbs/ high butterfly	3.0L (1978-79)	2.8L	11.0:1

Short Stroke 2.8L - This is a very rare and unusual engine. Because it uses the 3.0L Turbo case (Euro Carrera), you can use the short-stroke 2.0/2.2 crankshaft. The short stroke combined with the big pistons creates a very quick revving, high-RPM engine (8000-9000), with very little low-end torque. This would be an excellent engine for track use only. Use a high-lift, high-duration camshaft like the RSR, GE80 or 906.

Case	Crank	Pistons	Cylinders	Cam	Fuel	Heads	Disp	Ratio
3.0 SC	3.0L (70.4mm)	JE Pistons (95mm)	3.0L (Nikasil)	964	CIS	3.0L	3.0L	9.8:1

Upgraded 3.0L CIS Engine - This is a good upgrade for owners who wish to get a little bit more horsepower out of their stock 3.0L engine. You can use the high compression JE pistons, or you can use the 1980-83 CIS pistons, which have 9.3:1 compression. Installing a set of SSI heat exchangers on this engine will give a total increase of about 30-50 horsepower over the stock configuration.

Case	Crank	Pistons	Cylinders	Cam	Fuel	Heads	Disp	Ratio
2.7L	2.4/2.7 (70.4mm)	JE Pistons (90mm)	2.7L (Nikasil)	964	CIS	2.4/2.7	2.7L	9.8:1

Upgraded 2.7L CIS Engine - Same as the 3.0L configuration above, except with the stock 2.7L engine. Some people will argue that the 2.7L is an overall quicker engine and has better response than the 3.0L despite the increase in displacement.

Case	Crank	Pistons	Cylinders	Cam	Fuel	Heads	Disp	Ratio
3.0 SC	3.0L (70.4mm)	JE Pistons (95mm)	3.0L (Nikasil)	S	Carburetors	3.0L 36mm Ports	3.0L	10:1

High Performance 3.0L - Removing the CIS injection allows you to increase the horsepower of the 3.0L engine considerably. Replacing the CIS pistons with high-compression JE pistons and running the early 'S' cam, gives an engine that is very strong, with lots of power both on the low end and the top end. You can dial-in any compression ratio you desire with custom pistons from JE. Top it off with a set of SSIs and a sport muffler, and you'll have an engine that's good for the street, and great for the track.

Case	Crank	Pistons	Cylinders	Cam	Fuel	Heads	Disp	Ratio
3.2	3.0L (70.4mm)	98mm Mahle	98mm Mahle	S	46 Carb	3.0/3.2	3.2L	10.3:1

Short-Stroke 3.2L - This is what is known as the 3.2 short-stroke configuration. This is a 3.0L engine with bigger pistons. The stock 3.2L engine has the same diameter pistons as the stock 3.0-liter engine but with a longer-stroke crank. The GE80 cams are a good choice for this engine as well.

Case	Crank	Pistons	Cylinders	Cam	Fuel	Heads	Disp	Ratio
3.2	3.2/3.3 (74.4mm)	95mm European	95mm Mahle	Motronic	Motronic	3.2	3.2	10.3:1

3.2L Euro Upgrade - Increases total horsepower to about 231 simply by using the European pistons and cylinders. Increases compression ratio from 9.5 to 10.3:1. Does not require any additional modifications for this upgrade (use stock Motronic and exhaust). Best option for rebuilding a stock 3.2L engine.

Case	Crank	Pistons	Cylinders	Cam	Fuel	Heads	Disp	Ratio
3.2	3.2/3.3 (74.4mm)	98mm Mahle	98mm Mahle	S	46 Carb	3.2	3.4L	9.8:1

3.4L Upgrade - Adds an increase in displacement from using the aftermarket 98mm Mahle pistons and cylinders. Can be used with the stock Motronic fuel injection, but to gain the maximum in performance, use an engine management system, or carburetors. Bolt-on solution— no case mods necessary.

Case	Crank	Pistons	Cylinders	Cam	Fuel	Heads	Disp	Ratio
3.2/3.3	3.2/3.3 (74.4mm)	100mm Mahle	100mm Mahle	S/GE60 /GE80	46 Weber	3.2	3.5L	11-12:1

3.5L Upgrade - This is one of the best normally aspirated engines you can build. The 100mm Mahle pistons will create a compression in the 11-12 range, with about 325-350 hp. Start with a Turbo case and oil pump as a good platform. Using the S cams on this high-displacement engine will give it a very good response across the power band. Requires twin-plug ignition.

Case	Crank	Pistons	Cylinders	Cam	Fuel	Heads	Disp	Ratio
3.0 SC	3.2/3.3 (74.4mm)	Andial (104 mm)	Andial (104 mm)	964	CIS	3.0L (1978-79)	3.7L	10:1

High Performance 3.7L CIS - This experimental engine was developed at Andial and later sold to a Pelican Parts customer. It uses the 1978-79 3.0L CIS injection with a few tweaks and modifications to compensate for the added displacement. A 3.2L crank combined with huge 104mm pistons give this engine plenty of displacement and horsepower. While the CIS system is not the best for high-performance engines, the large displacement of this motor makes up for its shortcomings. Includes a 3.0L distributor that has been adapted for twin-plug ignition. Power is estimated at about 280-300 hp.

Case	Crank	Pistons	Cylinders	Cam	Fuel	Heads	Disp	Ratio
3.2/3.3 Turbo	3.2/3.3 (74.4mm)	Mahle Turbo (98 mm)	Mahle (98 mm)	Stock Turbo	Stock CIS	Stock Turbo	3.4L	8.0:1

3.4 Turbo Upgrade - For 3.3 Turbo owners, this is a bolt-on upgrade. The 98mm Mahle pistons are specific to the 911 3.3 Turbo and are constructed with a flat top. No additional modifications are necessary.

Case	Crank	Pistons	Cylinders	Cam	Fuel	Heads	Disp	Ratio
3.2/3.3 Turbo	3.2/3.3 (74.4mm)	Mahle Turbo (100 mm)	Mahle (100 mm)	Stock Turbo	Stock CIS	Stock Turbo	3.5L	8.0:1

3.5 Turbo Upgrade - Identical to the previous combination, except that the pistons are slightly larger in diameter. The cylinder heads and case must be modified to accept the larger cylinders.

CHAPTER 5

ENGINE ASSEMBLY

Now it's time for the exciting part. You've just gotten your parts back from the machine shop, and you've checked them over carefully to make sure that your engine is going to go together properly and precisely. You should have all the gaskets, bolts, hardware, and new parts that you need to assemble your 911 engine. Before you begin your assembly, you'll also want to have all the sealants and tools that are required for the job. Nothing is more frustrating than to get halfway through a project, only to find that you need to special-order a tool from your favorite Porsche parts house on the opposite coast. The only exception to this is the cylinder base gaskets—you won't know the correct size that you need until you measure the deck height of the half-assembled engine.

I've broken this chapter down into ten separate sections, each corresponding to a portion of the rebuild. At the start of each section, I've summarized the parts, tools, fastening hardware, and total time required to complete each section. Most people reading this book are not professionals, and will not have contiguous days to devote to rebuilding their engine. In each section, I've detailed how long a particular task should take, and also outlined the steps that need to be performed together. This way, you can plan ahead and allow ample time to complete the task.

SECTION 1 PREPARATION & CLEANING

OVERVIEW

The 911 engine is a particularly challenging engine to rebuild. It's not like a typical small-block Chevy motor that can be bolted together in an afternoon. A lot of attention to detail, coupled with obsessive-compulsive cleaning of parts, will yield a leak-free motor that will provide you with years of reliable power. Taking shortcuts in the process can result in a less-than-desirable end result—the worst-case scenario being a destroyed motor. This section details the basic tools, cleaners, materials, and any other resources that you will need for your rebuild.

TOOLS

Without a doubt, the most useful tools in your assembly arsenal are a pair of good-quality torque wrenches. A precise, accurate torque wrench is absolutely essential to proper assembly. For the 911 engine, you will need to tighten bolts ranging from 8 Nm (5.9 ft-lbs.) to more than 170 Nm (125 ft-lbs.) on some models. I don't personally know of any torque wrench capable of accurately spanning this range, so you will have to purchase two of them. I recommend purchasing one from a company like Snap-On that can accurately torque from 15 to 135 Nm (11 to 99 ft-lbs.), and another one that is accurate from at least 45 to about 265 Nm (33 to 195 ft-lbs.) or so. I also own a small torque wrench that can accurately measure from 0 to 14 Nm (0 to 10 ft-lbs.) This is useful for nuts that don't require too much torque. Overtightening a fastener can sometimes be worse than undertightening it.

There are three basic types of torque wrenches. The beam style wrench uses a long rod of metal that bends to apply the torque. This wrench rarely goes out of calibration because there are no moving parts, and the material properties of the beam don't change. You can expect these torque wrenches to stay accurate within 2 to 5 percent over their lifetime. The dial gauge torque wrench has a small dial mounted on the handle that indicates the amount of torque applied on the gauge. These are quite accurate over time, although they should be periodically calibrated.

The most popular torque wrench is the click-style one. With this style, you set the torque value and then turn the fastener until the wrench clicks. It's important to stop at that so that you don't overtighten the fastener. In addition, these torque wrenches have a tendency to become significantly uncalibrated over time. This affects all click-style torque wrenches, regardless of manufacturer or quality. If you do decide to use this type of torque wrench for your rebuild, I recommend that you have it calibrated prior to assembly. Most specialty tool shops will be able to recalibrate your torque wrench for you. Failing to properly torque an important fastener like one of the rod bolts can result in catastrophic engine failure. In this case, an inch-ounce of prevention is well worth the foot-pound of cure.

It's very important that your nuts and bolts get tightened to their proper torque. There is a right way and a wrong way to torque a fastener up to its final value. The correct method is to use what I call "nonstatic torque." As you begin to tighten the fastener, keep moving it in a steady constant motion until you hear the torque wrench click. Do not stop moving the wrench until you hear this click. If you do stop, or run out of working room, then loosen the nut and retighten again (except in the case of rod nuts/bolts and flywheel bolts).

Using this nonstatic torque method will give you the most accurate torque values on your fasteners. The wrong way of tightening fasteners is to use short strokes, stopping and starting until you reach final torque. This can lead to torque values that are less than the required specification. This is because static friction helps to keep the nut from moving. If you place a torque wrench on a nut, tighten it,

ENGINE ASSEMBLY

and it does not move, then you cannot be assured that it tightened to the value that the wrench is set to.

Along the same lines of thought, the condition of the fastener is very important to achieving the proper torque. Threads on the nut or stud that have been galled and damaged are more likely to show a higher torque value.

With small nuts and bolts, holding proper torque is very important, and you can damage fasteners and studs if you overtighten them. When you are finished using your torque wrench at the end of the day, make sure that you set it to its lowest setting. This will help to keep the internal springs inside the torque wrench from deforming and will help it keep its accuracy over time. Always use the torque wrench to tighten everything, and never use an impact wrench during the assembly procedure.

Another important item to take note of is that you should avoid using long ratchet extensions with a torque wrench. Using an extension does not change the final torque value as long as the extension remains perfectly perpendicular to the surface of the nut. The danger here is that the torque wrench will be cocked when you tighten the nut. This will change the final torque value. The rule of thumb is to avoid using extensions with torque wrenches, as they will have a tendency to skew the final torque value.

If you were able to use an impact wrench in the disassembly process, then you may have skipped over using a flywheel lock. For the assembly process, such a lock is vital. You can use the flywheel lock that works with the engine yoke, or you can use the small homemade one described in Chapter 3. Either way, you will need to hold the flywheel steady for a few assembly tasks.

For assembling the pistons into the cylinders, you will need a ring compressor. With so much room for error in this process, I do not recommend purchasing a cheap ring compressor. Placing the pistons in your cylinders is a very delicate process, and if performed incorrectly can easily lead to a broken ring, which will result in yet another teardown of the engine. There are three-dollar pieces of sheet steel for sale out there that are sold as ring compressors. I do not recommend using these, as it adds one more element of difficulty to the equation. A good-quality ring compressor will cost about $20 to $35 and will include a specially designed set of pliers whose specific purpose is to latch onto and compress the steel ring band. This type of compressor is much easier to use than the simple band one and will reduce the chances that you will break a ring. Since the tool is relatively inexpensive when compared to the risks involved, I fully recommend that you purchase a good one.

A clutch alignment tool is another often overlooked tool. This tool costs about three dollars, and is available at just about any Porsche parts house. A simple plastic one will do fine. However, make sure that you get the appropriate one that matches the transmission—not the engine. The mainshaft of the transmission contains splines that will mate with the grooves in the clutch disc when you reinstall the engine in the car. The tool aligns the clutch disc with

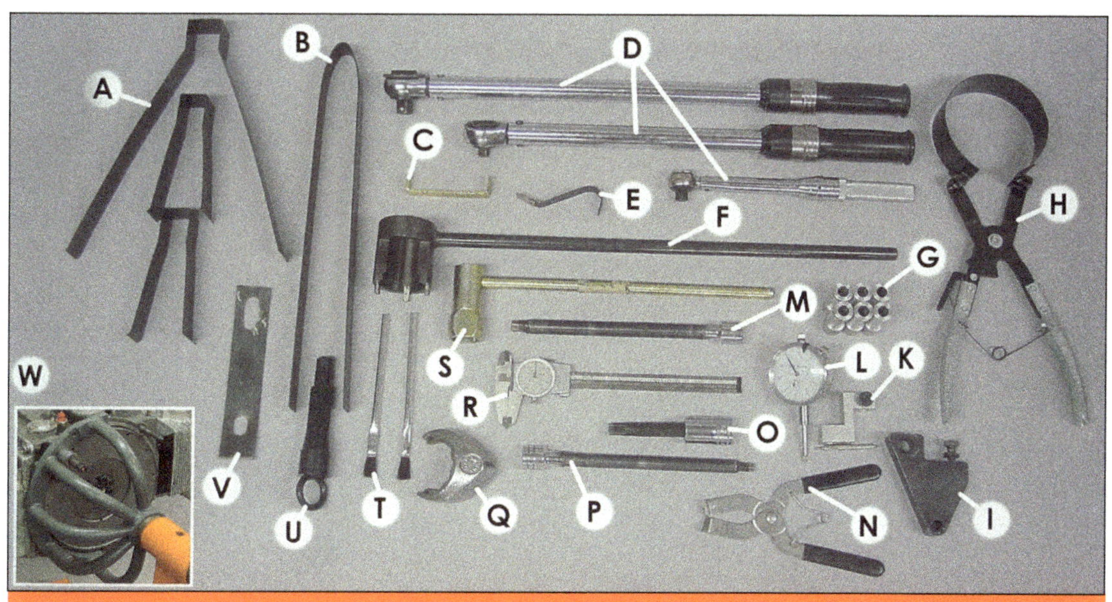

1-1 *Shown here are some special tools that are required to rebuild your engine:*
A - Rod holders, B - Chain holder, C - Chain tensioner tool (for early-style tensioners), D - Torque wrenches, E - Valve adjust tool,
F - Camshaft tool (9191) & socket (1980 1/2 and later), G - Porsche tool P140, used to hold the cylinders, H - Ring compressor, I -
Mechanical chain tensioner, K - Z-block for dial indicator, L - Dial indicator, M - Head stud tool, N - Ring expander, O - Flywheel bolt
tool, P - Exhaust nut tool, Q - Crowfoot wrench (up to 1980 1/2), R - Vernier caliper, S - Camshaft tool P202 (up to 1980 1/2), T -
Acid brushes, U - Clutch alignment tool, V - Flywheel lock, W - P201 Engine mount, Straightedge (not shown)

the crankshaft so that the transmission and engine can be easily mated together.

For timing the cams and measuring backlash and run-out, a good-quality dial indicator is an indispensable tool. There are several different styles available, including the bottom plunger, back plunger, and dovetail. To further confuse the issue, there are also a variety of different mounting systems (backs) and hundreds of attachments, holders, and tips. Prices range from $20 to over $300, not including extras. I would recommend starting with an indicator with a metric dial; however, a standard English one will suffice as long as you remember to convert the units to metric. You should also purchase the small Z-block fixture used for properly holding the gauge to the camshaft housings of the engine.

Figure 1-1 shows just about all of the special tools that I recommend you acquire for performing your engine rebuild. Some of the specialized tools are discussed in further detail in the upcoming sections in this chapter.

ASSEMBLY LUBE AND SEALANTS

You will need a tube of engine assembly lube. You can use just about any brand, but I personally like LiquiMoly Engine Assembly Lube (LM-3010). It comes in a 3.5-ounce tube, and one of these should be more than enough for a single 911 engine rebuild. You will also need a small tube of red Loctite Stud & Bearing Mount (271) for some of the critical studs and bolts that absolutely must not come loose.

You will also need to pick up a good case sealant. There are a number of choices out there, and I have heard recommendations from reputable sources recommending Dow Corning RTV 730 Fluorosilicone sealant and Permatex 3H for sealing metal-to-metal surfaces. However, my own personal choice is Loctite 573 or Loctite 574 Flange Sealant.

This is also what the factory recommends, and what they used originally, for assembly. A 50ml bottle should be sufficient for the entire assembly job. I would also pick up a set of acid brushes so that you can easily apply the sealant to the metal surfaces of your parts. Make sure that you get a good quality set from an art or automotive shop, because you don't want bristles from the brushes falling off into your gasket sealant. Although the factory manuals specifically show the use of Loctite 573 for sealing gasket surfaces, most engine rebuilders tend to use the Loctite 574. According to product specification information available from Loctite, the primary difference between the two sealants is the cure time, which is faster for the Loctite 574.

The Loctite 574 sealant is an orange goo that cures in the absence of air. When you assemble your case and mate the case halves, you will have some squeeze-out that will collect along the seam. If you leave this excess sealant exposed to the air, you will find that it will not harden. While this may cause you some head scratching, you shouldn't be concerned, as the sealant is designed to seal within tight clearances and between metal surfaces. Despite the fact that it appears that the Loctite 574 is not curing because the squeeze-out has not hardened, it has in fact properly sealed between your two case halves.

I use a few other multi-purpose sealants and materials during the assembly process. Good, clean, non-synthetic motor oil is very useful for pre-lubing some of the seals that are installed on the engine. Any good motor oil is suitable for this task, as long as it's clean. Curil-T is a good, thin sealant that I use as an extra precaution against oil leaks when installing some seals. Black Permatex high-temp silicone is useful for sealing the small O-rings on the case through-bolts. Loctite 271 or Permatex Thread-Locker is required for the rod bolts and head studs. JB Weld is an excellent heavy-duty epoxy that can be used to replace the dabs of factory epoxy that help seal some areas of the case and chain housings. All these sealants are shown in Figure 1-2.

CLEANERS

Carburetor and brake cleaner in compressed cans make excellent heavy-duty cleaners. These will be the workhorses of

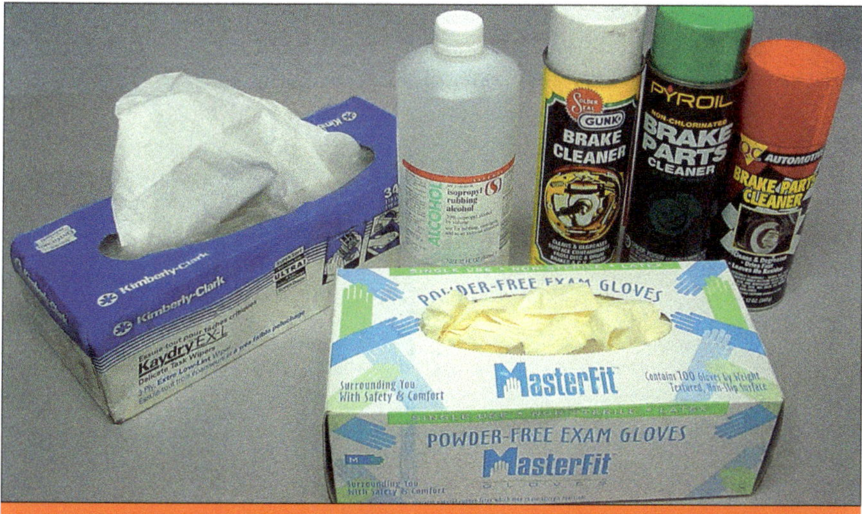

1-3 *One of the best-kept secrets in my opinion is Kimwipes. I was first introduced to these when I was designing satellites for Hughes Space and Communications. We used these all the time in the clean room atmospheres where the satellites were assembled. Their low lint content creates the perfect wipe for cleaning engine parts. I also like to use isopropyl alcohol (also used at Hughes), as it evaporates very quickly, and won't make you keel over from the fumes. In the heavy-duty cleaner department are brake and carburetor cleaner—the workhorses of your case and housing cleaning. Finally, powder-free latex gloves keep your hands and your parts clean.*

your cleaning process. One of the most important tasks for a quality rebuild is proper cleaning. Years of motor oil, dirt, and grime inside your engine can be difficult to remove. For getting all of the crud out of your old engine case, you will have to hit it with some pretty powerful cleaning agents. Just about any brand of brake or carburetor cleaner will do—I don't have any personal favorites. Wear chemical-resistant gloves during this process and work outdoors. Use some hard plastic brushes to get inside crevices where you can't normally reach with a towel.

Scrub every nook and cranny of the case, camshaft housings, chain housings, and any other parts that you are going to be reusing. Blue heavy-duty shop towels are pretty good for this cleaning task. Introducing dirt and grit into your new rebuild is just about the worst thing that you can do. Some professional engine rebuilders spend upward of ten hours carefully cleaning all the engine parts—you should do the same.

Don't count on your machine shop to adequately clean your case. They will clean it enough so that it will be able to be machined, but most of the time you will need to go over it many more times with your cans of brake or carburetor cleaner. The machine shops will dip and wash your case and parts in a large industrial washer that will remove most of the oil, but will not adequately remove the crud on the inside of the engine parts. Only heavy-duty cleaners and manual brushing will remove this grime.

In some situations, you may be able to bead-blast certain parts in order to clean them. For example, heads are usually blasted but not engine cases. There are too many small oil passages in the case that can be clogged with leftover grit from the blasting process. In general, the chain housings, sprockets, and external engine parts can be blasted.

Another useful item is clean-room cleaning cloths. When I used to work at Hughes Space and Communi-cations in their satellite division, we used these all the time. They are lint-free and dust-free and will not leave any fibers that can clog tiny oil passages. I highly recommend picking up a box of these clean-room wipes and also a bottle of isopropyl alcohol. At Hughes we cleaned each and every part meticulously before it was mated together. The 911 engine can only be improved by such close attention to cleanliness and detail. Before each part is assembled, wipe it down one last time with isopropyl alcohol to remove any dust or dirt. I prefer to use the brand Kimwipes from Kimberly-Clark, as they are easy to obtain and relatively inexpensive. A box of 100 large Kimwipes costs around $12 and should be good for the entire assembly job. Refer to the official website for this book www.101projects.com) for places where you can easily purchase these special wipes. Figure 1-3 shows a collection of cleaners that would be suitable for use with your engine rebuild.

I also recommend that you pick up some thick plastic sheeting that you can use to cover the engine when you are not working on it. The poor man's substitute for the plastic

1-4 *No matter how much you trust your machinist, don't depend upon him to send your parts back clean. You should take it upon yourself to carefully inspect and clean all your parts before assembly. This includes all of the new parts as well. Just because they came in a neat wrapper or box doesn't mean that they are clean enough to install in your engine. Shown on the left is a rod with small metal debris on the bearing surface—direct from the machine shop. On the right, you can see machining debris in the bearing journal of the rod.*

sheet is a large household garbage bag. Thick three-or-five mil drop cloths can be found at most hardware stores, and you can cut them into smaller sections that then can be used to cover your engine. You want to keep the entire engine as clean as possible when you are not working on it.

Powderless latex gloves are also very good for use during an engine rebuild. Regular latex gloves often have a powder placed inside the glove to ease putting them on. This can get messy, and get caught in engine assembly lube. Change gloves often, as the oils on your engine parts can attack and dissolve the latex in the gloves.

PARTS CLEANING

It's very common for people to assume that their parts come back from the machine shop spotlessly clean. In reality, this is not true, and this one assumption alone can ruin your rebuild. When you get parts back from the shop, you should always carefully inspect and thoroughly clean them. Figure 1-4 illustrates this point clearly, showing parts direct from the machine shop with significant amounts of debris on the bearing surfaces. Cleaning every passage, nook, and cranny with carburetor or brake cleaner is a necessity, and shouldn't be rushed or overlooked. Make sure that you use the clean-room wipes, or at best, a lint-free cloth. The small cloth fibers from a regular towel can clog the tiny oil passages inside the engine.

Another commonly overlooked step is the cleaning of parts that are brand new. Just because they come sealed in a package directly from Germany doesn't mean that they are clean enough to be placed in your engine. Take every part and clean it with carburetor cleaner or brake cleaner. Then use your clean-room wipes and isopropyl alcohol for a final cleaning. If the parts are pre-assembled like pistons and cylinders, separate them and clean each piston, ring, and cylinder. You're spending hundreds of hours on this rebuild—you don't want to simply trust that the parts are clean.

In addition to cleaning your parts, you should also carefully clean your assembly workspace. Organize it so that you don't have any clutter, and make sure that you have at least two tables (at least 6ft x 2ft) so that you can lay out your parts and tools prior to assembly. Vacuum the entire area, and make sure that any dust is removed from the air. The 911 engine is a finicky engine indeed, and any dirt, dust, or debris that gets inside the engine can lead to messy and annoying oil leaks. The bottom line is that you cannot be too clean when rebuilding your engine. Make sure that your hands are clean, and if you use a pumice-based hand cleaner, make sure that you also wash with soap and water afterward. The pumice is very abrasive, like sand, and you don't want it getting on any of the parts that you are handling.

PARTS STORAGE

Most people don't rebuild their engine the day after they receive their parts back from the machine shop. If your parts are going to be sitting for more than a few days, then you will need to protect them from rust and corrosion. Magnesium and aluminum parts like the engine case, camshaft housings, and timing chain housings will not rust and don't need to be protected. Exposed steel parts will rust if they are not adequately protected. A simple refrigerator magnet will stick to steel parts and help you determine which ones need protection.

The best method I have found for protecting steel parts is simply to coat them with clean, nonsynthetic 20W-50 motor oil. The motor oil will prevent the parts from rusting and shouldn't evaporate or require recoating. To protect your crankshaft, simply spread motor oil over all of the surfaces and then place it on a shelf in your garage. As an added layer of protection, you can place small parts into plastic bags.

If you send your external steel engine parts out to be bead-blasted (like the engine sheet metal) it's best to paint them immediately. They will begin to rust in your trunk on the way home from the blasting shop. However, if you cannot quickly spray a coat of primer on them, then you should carefully wrap them in newspaper and place them in the driest possible place.

PARTS INSPECTION

Even if your machinist is a close family relative, you should not trust him blindly with your rebuild. Double check everything that comes back from the shop. People are human and do make mistakes. It only takes a few moments to make a few measurements. Such assurance is cheap

1-5 *This photo shows the standard that all amateur engine rebuilders should strive to reach. The sparkling clean workshop of Competition Engineering represents owner Walt Watson's impeccable attention to detail during the assembly process. Day-in and day-out, the assembly area is cleaned, and all the parts required for each assembly step are carefully laid out on trays, as if for a surgeon preparing to operate. Brand-new oil-drip pans make excellent trays for gathering all your parts together on your bench.*

when compared to the total cost of repairing a faulty rebuild. You can perform every step in the assembly process correctly and meticulously, yet your engine may seize or leak oil if your machinist happened to have a bad day and made a mistake.

In a similar manner, all of your new replacement parts should be inspected carefully. I'm sure that at least once in your life, you've had to return something to the store because it was broken and didn't work. What if a new part used in your rebuild was defective? You'd hate to find out the hard way when your engine fails or leaks oil. New parts manufactured in Germany are of very high quality. However, there are more than 300 or so new parts or gaskets used in your rebuild. Even if the failure rate was as low as one-third of one percent, that would leave you with one bad part in your engine rebuild. The point here is to check over all your parts very carefully. Inspect and measure them. Clean them thoroughly. By diligently doing so, you increase the odds of having a successful rebuild.

PREPARATION

Enough cannot be said about preparation. Most mistakes in engine rebuilding are made because the initial preparation was sloppy or lacking in detail. Lay out all the parts on your table before you begin each section. I've provided pictures of every part, tool, and material that you will need for each step of the rebuild. Compare your table to the one in the photos to make sure that you haven't missed anything. Really good engine builders do this all the time—don't think that this part of the process is only for beginners. See Figure 1-5 for a photo of Competition Engineering's assembly area on a typical day. Removing parts one at a time from your pre-setup table will help you to keep organized, and will ensure that you won't leave out or forget a step. If something is left over you will see it on your table and not forget to install it on your engine.

PATIENCE

Finally, the last thing that you need is patience. Budget about thirty to sixty hours to assemble your engine. Sure, you can probably slap it together in a few hours, but chances are you will make a mistake or forget to check a critical clearance. A lot of people assume that rebuilding a 911 engine is similar to slapping together a domestic V-8 engine. In reality, there are many nuances and subtleties that make the assembly of a 911 engine a lot more difficult. Like a finely tuned Swiss watch, the 911 engine is a meticulously designed machine that requires care and precision when assembling it. It is not forgiving of mistakes and errors. If you overtighten something, assemble it in the wrong order, or even accidentally leave a speck of dust on an important mating surface, the engine will repay you with an oil leak or, even worse, a dire mechanical problem. Take your time, double-and-triple check all clearances, and make sure that all your parts are of the highest quality before you assemble them.

SECTION 2 CRANKSHAFT ASSEMBLY

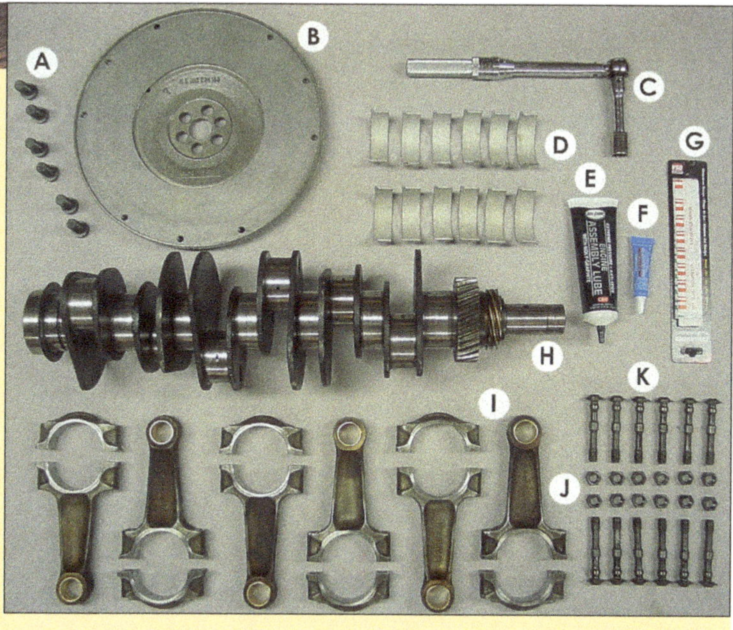

TOOLS: Crankshaft holding fixture, or flywheel with two flywheel bolts (**A & B**), torque wrench (**C**), 14mm socket (**C**), Plastigauge (**G**).

MATERIALS: Clean wipes and isopropyl alcohol, assembly lube (**E**), Loctite 271 or (**F**) Permatex Red Threadlocker.

PARTS: Crankshaft (**H**), rods (**I**), rod bearings (**D**), if not installed by machine shop: crankshaft gear, distributor drive gear, spacer, circlip.

HARDWARE: Brand-new rod bolts (**K**) and nuts. (**J**)

SEALS: none.

TIME: 4 hours.

TIP: Check to make sure the rods fall by their own weight after you have tightened the rod nuts.

OVERVIEW

You will begin your engine assembly with the crankshaft. This section details the cleaning, inspection, and assembly of the crankshaft and rods. This is a good, easy first step to get you acclimated to working on your engine.

You will need a crankshaft assembly stand to hold the crank while you work on it. There are commercial ones out there that will hold the crank and fit into your engine stand. This will allow you to hold the crank vertical, which makes it much easier to work with. However, simply mounting the flywheel to your crank and then standing it on a table makes a nice alternative. Hand tighten two flywheel bolts onto the crank (don't torque them down), and place the flywheel on a sturdy table.

CLEANING

Your crankshaft and rods should be thoroughly cleaned prior to assembly. Grit and grime from the polishing process can get trapped in the oil passages inside the crankshaft. Use carburetor cleaner or brake cleaner and spray the inside of the crankshaft, making sure that it flows out of the oil holes. Scrub the inside oil passages with a rifle bore brush to clean them out. Then spray the cleaner through the passages again. Use compressed air (either from your air compressor or air-in-a-can) to blow the excess cleaner out of the internal passages. Using your clean-room wipes and isopropyl alcohol, gently wipe down all of the outer surfaces of the crankshaft and the rods. The alcohol will quickly evaporate and won't leave any residue. Don't use a parts cleaner tank to clean any of the parts, as this will only serve to recycle dirty cleaner back onto the parts. Keep everything perfectly clean, as this will be the last time that the parts are cleaned prior to assembly.

CLEARANCE CHECKS

Before you assemble your rods onto your crankshaft, you will want to check the clearances of your rod bearing journals. No matter how much you trust your machinist, you don't know if his assistant or drunken partner actually did the machine work on your parts. Checking the clearances guarantees that the parts will go together correctly and perform admirably.

The material used for checking these clearances is called Plastigage. You can find it at most local automotive stores, and you want to make sure that you purchase the green type that can measure .001- to .003-inch clearances. Plastigage is a thin strip of wax-like material (like dental floss) that you can use to measure tight clearances. To check the rod bearing clearances, take a small piece of Plastigage and extend it across the width of the crank bearing journal, as shown in Figure 2-2. (The Plastigage should be used at the sides of the rods, not in the middle. The rods stretch when under load, and you want to measure the clearances at the sides.) Now, take one of the rods and carefully wipe down both bearing

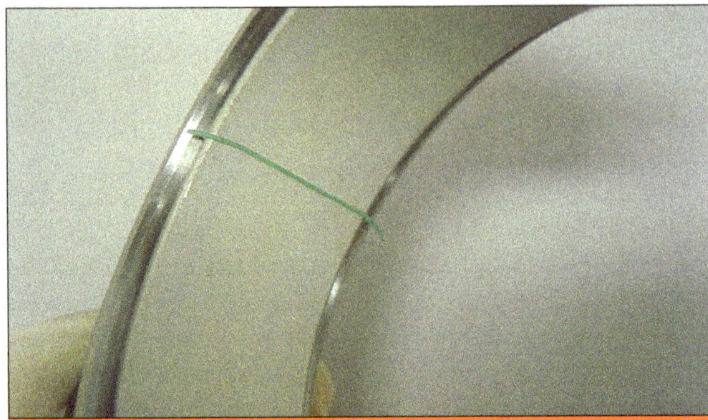

2-2 To measure the clearance between the rod bearing and the crankshaft, you can use what is known as Plastigage. Lay the wax out across the bearing surface as shown here. After tightening the rod nuts and bolts to their final torque values (using only old rod bolts and nuts), the wax will be flattened out. Compare the width of the wax to the measurement scale enclosed with the Plastigauge to obtain an accurate reading of the clearances.

surfaces with one of your clean-room wipes, wetting the cloth a bit first with some isopropyl alcohol. Remove the rod bearing from its packaging and install the front and back inside the rod. Don't use any assembly lube or oil at this point—just lay them in dry.

Take the rod with the bearings attached and carefully place it around the crank. Make sure that you don't bump or move the rod or you will smear the Plastigage, rendering it useless. This is one of those tasks that is easier to perform if the rods are hanging straight down, instead of horizontal as when the crank is standing upright on a table attached to the flywheel.

Using the original rod nuts and bolts from your engine, tighten up the rods. Tighten the old rod bolts according to the specification and procedure indicated in Appendix A. Again, make sure that you don't rotate the rod while you are tightening up the nuts. Also, make sure that you only use the original rod nuts and bolts that you removed from the rods when you disassembled the engine. Your brand-new rod nuts and bolts are designed only to be used once, and stretch when they are tightened to their final torque setting.

When the rod nuts have been tightened to their final torque setting, carefully loosen them up and remove the rod end cap. The Plastigage should be squeezed out into a wider, thinner line. Leaving the wax strip on the bearing, compare it to the chart that comes with the kit. This should give you an accurate measurement of the rod bearing oil clearance. Compare this to the specification numbers in Appendix A to determine if your clearances are within spec. Repeat this for each crank rod journal and each connecting rod. The goal here is to double-check that the rods were machined properly and that your crank wasn't ground or polished too much. Again, patience and perseverance here will indeed pay off in a long-lasting, smooth-running engine.

2-3 *Check all clearances when your parts come back from the shop. The crankshaft journals can be checked with a micrometer. The inner rod bores can be spot checked with a simple vernier caliper for roundness and proper diameter. The total rod length can be checked by measuring from the top of the piston pin bore to the bottom of the rod bore and subtracting half the diameter of the piston pin bore and half the diameter of the rod bore.*

Typical clearances are around .05mm, with the standard limits being between .030mm and .088mm. If the Plastigage readings are two small or too big, even after several different tests, then you may need to revisit your machine shop and investigate why the rods or crankshaft are out of spec and what remedies can bring them back to acceptable clearances.

Although I know of many engine rebuilders who have been using Plastigage for many years without problems, one point of concern was recently raised to me by an expert 911 engine rebuilder. This rebuilder does not use Plastigage on the premise that the rod bearings deform when tightened down. The theory is that tightening and then loosening the bearings permanently deforms them, and makes them more likely to spin in the rod. Although this theory is very debatable, I thought it worthy of mentioning here.

Now is also a good time to check your rod side-clearance tolerances with a feeler gauge. This is the distance between each rod and the crank sidewall. Typically this is a large clearance, and you should not encounter a problem. However, if the clearance here exceeds the values indicated in Appendix A, then you either have a tolerance problem with the crank or that particular rod.

Using a micrometer, carefully inspect the rod and main bearing journals on your crankshaft, as shown in Figure 2-3. They should be within the specifications indicated in Appendix A for your particular year 911. Verify that the crankshaft has been correctly ground, if this task was performed. Using a dial indicator or a bore gauge, measure the inside of the rods. Check them to make sure that they are

perfectly round and not oblong. Inspect the piston pin bushing for roundness and dimensional accuracy. Place the rod cap on the end of the rod, and measure the distance from the bottom of the end cap bore to the top of the piston pin bore. Subtracting one-half of the diameter of the piston pin bushing, and one-half of the diameter of the rod bearing bore should give you the total length of the rod. Compare this to the specification tables in Appendix A. Any change in the length of the rod can seriously affect the clearances in the engine and may increase the risk of the pistons hitting the valves. Your machine shop should perform all of these measurements before your parts are sent back to you; however, it's always good to double-check.

If you are building an engine that does not have its original crankshaft, intermediate shaft, and case all matched together, then I would suggest that you skip ahead to Section 3 and perform the backlash check between the crankshaft and the intermediate shaft. I normally prefer to perform this check after the crank/rods assembly, and intermediate shaft assembly are already installed in the case (Section 3). Almost all of the time, you will find that you will not encounter a problem with the backlash in the case. However, if the crankshaft, intermediate shaft, and engine case didn't all come out of the same engine, then the chances that there may be a problem are higher. Backlash problems sometimes occur if you replace your worn-out intermediate shaft gear with a new one. Either way, if you find a problem later on, the fix is to replace your intermediate shaft gear, which is not a terribly difficult task.

DRIVE GEAR & SPACER

Once you have checked to make sure that all clearances are within spec, you can now install the crankshaft drive gear. In most cases, your machine shop will be able to determine whether you need to remove this gear. Many times the shop

2-4 *The crankshaft timing gear can be installed on the crankshaft only after being submerged in a bath of hot oil. Take the gear and place it in a tin of hot oil and heat it in your kitchen oven until it reaches about 300° F. Using heavy-duty gloves and a piece of bent wire, quickly remove the gear and slide it onto the crankshaft. You will only have a few seconds to work with the gear before it will get stuck on the crankshaft.*

will just leave it on while reconditioning the crankshaft. Check for any raised edges around the keyway on the crankshaft, and file them down. Also check the woodruff key for damage.

Insert the woodruff key onto the tip of the crankshaft. Make sure that this woodruff key is installed snug and flat. You will not have too much time to adjust it when you install the crankshaft gear, as the gear is installed hot.

Take the crankshaft gear, and place it in a metal pot full of clean motor oil. Make sure that your pot is extremely clean before you fill it with oil. Without telling your wife, take the gear, place it in the pot of oil, and place it in your kitchen oven. Heat the pot up to about 150°C (300°F). Take the pot back to your engine, and carefully install the gear onto the crankshaft. It goes without saying that you should use waterproof, thermally isolated gloves when handling the very hot gear, as shown in Figure 2-4. Fish the gear out of the hot oil with a piece of stiff wire. Install the gear on the crankshaft with the shoulder on the gear facing in toward the rods. You won't have too much time to work with the gear—as soon as it hits the crankshaft it will cool and become stuck on the crank. If you don't work quickly enough, you will have to pull the gear off again with a gear puller.

DISTRIBUTOR DRIVE GEAR

With the drive gear installed, place the gear spacer on the crankshaft with its bevel facing the pulley end, and install the distributor drive gear. Heat it up in an oil bath in a manner similar to the drive gear, but this time at 100°C (212°F). Make sure that you install the distributor drive gear with the marks on the gear facing away from the rods (so that you can read them). Motronic engines (1984 and later non-Turbo) have a drive gear marked with an "X" on their end. This mark must face the pulley end or the distributor will not be properly lined up with TDC on the crankshaft.

With the two gears and the spacer installed on the crank, install the large circlip into the groove on the crank. Beginning in 1978, this circlip became available in various thicknesses in order to achieve the narrowest clearance. If your crank assembly is the same one that you disassembled earlier, then chances are that the circlip fits correctly. However, if you had to swap drive gears, spacers, or the distributor drive gear, then you may need an alternatively sized circlip. The circlip size should be stamped on its side. Use the following table to determine which circlip you may need when reassembling your crankshaft:

Part Number	Circlip thickness
901.102.148.00 (stock used from 1965-77)	2.4mm
901.102.148.01	2.3mm
901.102.148.02	2.2mm
901.102.148.03	2.1mm

2-5 *The distributor drive gear (yellow arrow) is installed in a manner similar to the crankshaft timing gear. Heat it up in a bath of oil (212°F), and slip it onto the crankshaft when hot. Make sure that you have the proper distributor drive gear for your application—Turbo and 911 SC distributor drive gears turn in the opposite direction from all other models.*

This particular circlip can be very difficult to attach and remove. Seeing how it doesn't have any holes on each end for a standard circlip tool to attach to, you will need a special circlip tool. Make sure that you wear safety glasses when removing this circlip, as I have had it spring off and fly across the room on occasion. The crankshaft with the two gears, the spacer, and the circlip installed is shown in Figure 2-5.

ROD INSTALLATION

With all of the gears attached to the crankshaft, it's time to install the rods permanently. Mount the crankshaft in its holding tool, or attach it temporarily to your flywheel, as shown in Figure 2-6. Using a clean-room wipe and some isopropyl alcohol, carefully clean the rod and each rod bearing, as shown in Figure 2-7. Install each bearing half into the rod cap and rod half. All of the rod bearing halves are the same—it doesn't matter which end of the rod they are inserted into.

2-6 *The best solution for assembling the crankshaft is to use a tool that will allow the crank to be placed horizontally. However, a good alternative is to bolt it to the flywheel and stand it on its end. The flywheel makes a good, sturdy stand that you can use during the assembly process. You only need to put the flywheel bolts on hand-tight.*

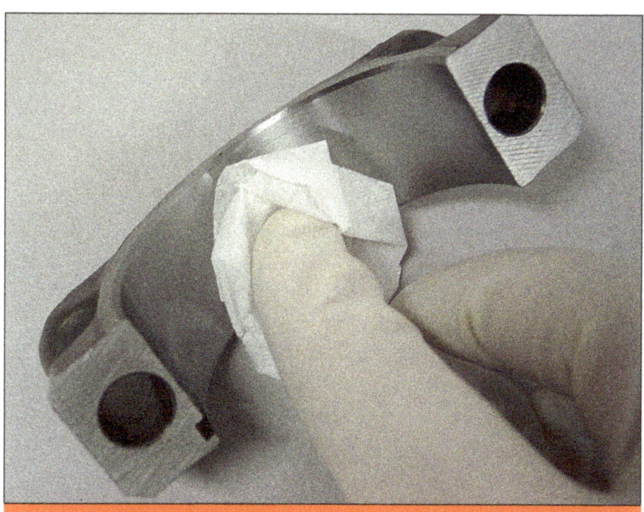

2-7 *Perhaps the most important task in the whole assembly process is proper cleaning. The entire rod should first be cleaned with brake or carburetor cleaner. Then take one of your clean-room wipes and spread some alcohol on it. Gently wipe the surface of the bearing, and also the bearing journal of the rod. Wipe down the crankshaft in its entirety and double check to make sure that there is no dirt anywhere on the assembly.*

2-10 *Make sure that you don't mix and match the rod end caps. They have numbers stamped on them to help keep them properly oriented with respect to the rod. The edges with the numbers on them should line up when bolting the rods together.*

2-8 *The head of the rod bolts will butt up against the side of the rod cap (green arrow) and prevent the bolt from rotating in the shaft. When you install the bolt in the rod cap, be sure the end of the bolt is securely seated against the side of the rod. The bolts have a close tolerance in the rod bolt bore. They should require a few taps with a hammer to be inserted into the rod. If not, the rod is worn and should be replaced.*

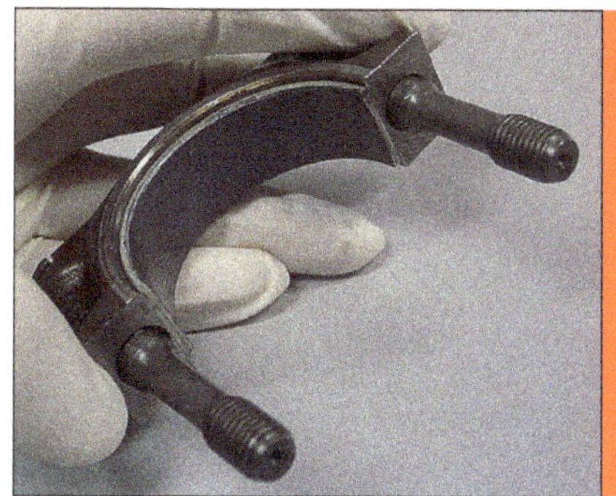

2-9 *Using your finger while wearing a powder-free latex glove, gently spread a thin layer of assembly lube on the inside surface of each bearing. Don't gob it on, but spread it evenly across the bearing surface.*

Using a clean-room wipe and some isopropyl alcohol, clean all oil and residue off of the rod bolts and nuts. Install the new rod bolts into the cap. The rod bolts will seat into their hole and the flat spot on each bolt will mate with the side of the rod, as shown in Figure 2-8. Take your assembly lube and apply a generous but even layer of assembly lube to the rod bearing. Spread the assembly lube across the rod bearing with your finger while wearing powder-free latex gloves, as displayed in Figure 2-9. If you're not using gloves, wash your hands first with nonpumice soft-soap and make sure they are clean of any dirt or debris. Lubricate both bearing halves and wipe a small amount around the sides of the big end of the rod. This will help lubricate any side contact that the rod and crankshaft might see before adequate oil pressure is achieved.

Each rod is stamped with a unique number, and rods and their matching caps must be kept together. Make sure that the numbers stamped in the rod butt up against each other, as indicated in Figure 2-10. If you have the cap aligned correctly with the numbers lining up, then the two sides of the bearings with tangs on them will also butt up against each other. Place a thin line of red Loctite 271 or Permatex red Threadlocker on each rod bolt before you tighten them up, as shown in Figure 2-11. Torque the bolts in the same manner and sequence that you did when you were checking the clearances with the Plastigage (Figure 2-12). Double check that you have properly lubed all the bearings and lined up the rods with their matching caps before you begin to torque the rod nuts to their final value. Again, it is important to note that the stock rod nuts and bolts can

2-11 *Place a thin strip of red Loctite 271 or Permatex Threadlocker on the threads of the rod bolts before you torque them.*

2-12 *Torque the bolts to their final torque values using the nonstatic torque method. If you are using aftermarket rod bolts and nuts from RaceWare or ARP, follow their specific instructions for tightening the bolts. They are different from the procedure used to tighten the stock rod bolts.*

only be torqued down once. Once they are tightened, they are permanently deformed, and cannot be reused.

On some other types of engines, the rods need to be placed in a certain orientation on the crankshaft. With the 911 engine, the rods can be placed on the crankshaft with either the numbers facing up or facing down. Flipping them upside down does not make a difference in the performance of the engine. The rods are symmetrical and are not offset like in other types of engines.

INSTALLATION CHECK

When the rods are all tightened, slowly rotate them around and check to see if there are any hang-ups or sticky spots. This could be a sign of a small piece of dirt or grime stuck in the bearing. You will want to remove this rod and investigate why there is a problem. Make sure that you don't reuse the rod bolt, as you can only torque them once. Another useful trick is to hold the crank sideways and let the rods fall freely by their own weight. The assembly lube will slow their fall, and you can tell if any fall faster or slower than the others in the group. Figure 2-13 shows this test in action. If one rod is out of spec, then this somewhat unscientific test may give you a hint.

2-13 *With the rods properly installed, take the crankshaft and rotate it sideways, letting the rods fall under their own weight. Check all the rods, and make sure that they are loose and smooth as you rotate them around the crankshaft.*

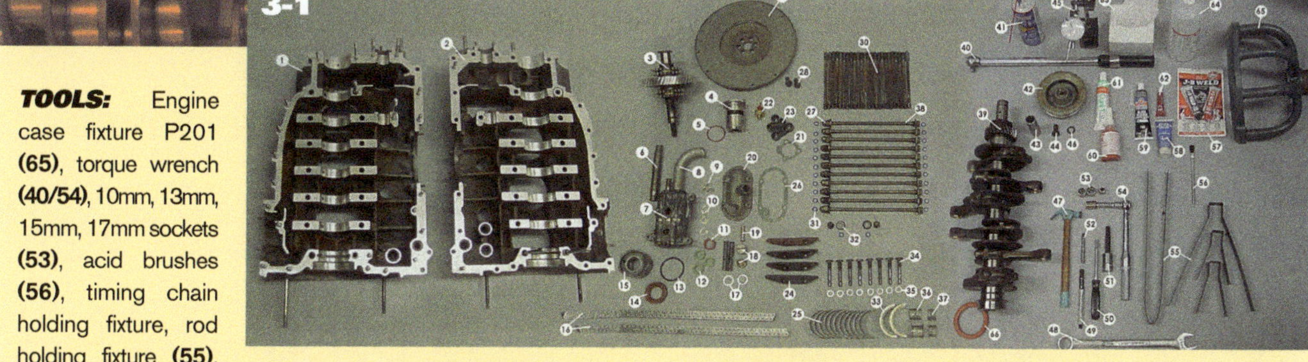

3-1

TOOLS: Engine case fixture P201 **(65)**, torque wrench **(40/54)**, 10mm, 13mm, 15mm, 17mm sockets **(53)**, acid brushes **(56)**, timing chain holding fixture, rod holding fixture **(55)**, M10x1.5 tap **(52)**, small hammer **(47)**, screwdriver **(50)**, stud installer, permanent marker or pen **(49)**, flywheel lock, flywheel bolt tool **(51)**, 17mm or 19mm deep socket for front pulley **(43)**, dial indicator and fixture **(45)**, 24mm wrench for oil pressure switch **(48)**

MATERIALS: Clean wipes **(63)** and isopropyl alcohol **(64)**, Loctite 271 or Permatex Red Threadlocker **(62)**, Loctite 574 case sealant **(60)**, Curil-T sealant **(61)**, Black Silicone Sealant **(59)**, can of compressed air **(41)**, assembly lube **(58)**, JB Weld epoxy **(57)**

PARTS: left **(2)** and right **(1)** case halves, crankshaft assembly **(39)**, oil pump **(7)**, oil pump shaft **(6)**, intermediate shaft assembly **(3)**, 2 timing chains **(16)**, main bearings set **(25/33)**, intermediate shaft bearings set **(36/37)**, number eight bearing **(15)**, flywheel **(29)**, thermostat **(4)**, oil switch **(22)**, crankcase breather cover **(20)**, oil pressure pistons (not shown) and springs, oil pressure spring piston guide **(19)**, chain ramps **(24)**, intermediate shaft cover plate **(23)**, pulley **(42)**.

HARDWARE: 11 Case through-bolts **(38)**, 13 cap nuts **(27)** and 24 beveled washers **(32)**, 22 13mm locking nuts and washers, 15mm nut, 24 cylinder head studs **(30)**, 3 oil pump lock tabs **(10)**, 3 oil pump mounting nuts **(9)**, qty 6 or 9 flywheel bolts **(28)**, 2 oil pressure relief caps **(18)**, Pulley nut **(44)**, Pulley nut washer **(46)**, 8 Chain ramp bolts **(34)**

SEALS: 3 Oil pump to left case half seals/case half seal **(12)**, oil pump to right case half seal **(11)**, flywheel seal **(66)**, pulley seal **(14)**, number eight o-ring **(13)**, 24 through-bolt o-rings **(31)**, thermostat o-ring **(5)**, crankcase breather cover gasket **(26)**, sealing ring for oil pressure switch, 8 sealing rings for chain ramp bolts **(35)**, 2 sealing rings for oil pressure pistons **(17)** intermediate shaft cover plate seal **(21)**.

TIME: 8 hours

TIP: Work quickly once you apply the sealant and attach the two case halves.

OVERVIEW

In Section 3, you will completely assemble the bottom end of your engine. The crankshaft and rods will be fitted into the engine case, along with the oil pump and intermediate shaft and timing chains. Then you will apply case sealant and bolt the two halves together. Finally, you will install the flywheel and a few other accessories that go on the outside of the case.

CLEANING

Once your crankshaft is completely assembled, set it aside and wrap it carefully in clean plastic if you aren't going to be installing it into the crankcase right away. Mount the right side of the crankcase (cylinders four through six) to the engine yoke as described in Chapter 3, and install it on your engine stand. Use brake or carburetor cleaner if you need a heavier duty cleaner to remove caked-on debris from the inside of the case. Just because the case was cleaned in a tank at your machine shop doesn't mean that it's ready for

3-2 I cannot stress enough how important cleaning the case is to achieving a clean, leak-free 911 engine. Dust or debris can clog tiny oil passages, or cause sealing surfaces to leak oil when the engine is running. Using non-abrasive pads like Scotch-brite, gently clean and scrub the parting line surface until it is 100% clean. If your case was machined on both of these surfaces, then it will usually be extremely clean and will only require some cursory cleaning with clean-room wipes and isopropyl alcohol. Attention to detail here, during the rebuilding stage, will translate into thousands of leak-free miles later on. Have patience here.

your rebuild. If you haven't spent at least three to four hours cleaning your case, it's probably still too dirty. Figure 3-2 shows an engine case that was cleaned at the machine shop before it was machined. As you can see, there is still a lot of dirt and grime stuck to the inside surface of the case. Clean the case until you can eat off of it.

Even if you have previously cleaned your case, it has probably been sitting around your garage for some time, and has more than likely acquired its share of dust and dirt. Clean every passage, nook, and cranny that you can reach. Oil is going to be passing through the case and will end up right on your bearings, along with any dust or dirt inside of the case. Don't hold back—clean until you think you're ready and then clean the case some more.

Another important thing to check is the oil relief pistons. Make sure that the bores are clean, and that pistons are not currently stuck in them. Good machine shops will remove these for you; however, if they don't stuck pistons may end up robbing your newly rebuilt engine of oil pressure when you start it up.

At this point, you should carefully inspect all of the case mating surfaces. These are the flat surfaces that you will be applying the case sealant to. It's extremely important that no dirt, grime, or residue remains on these mating surfaces, otherwise you may end up with a leaky motor. If your case was properly cleaned and machined by your machine shop, then this surface should be free of dings or raised edges. Using Figure 3-23 as a guide, carefully examine each and

3-3 *There are several spots on the case where the original bonding agent was placed. These are the places where a factory dowel pin or plug has been inserted into the case. These photos show the exact locations of the spots that need to be checked and rebonded. You should also JB Weld the spots on your timing chain housing while you have the epoxy out and ready (see Figure 6-2 later on in this chapter).*

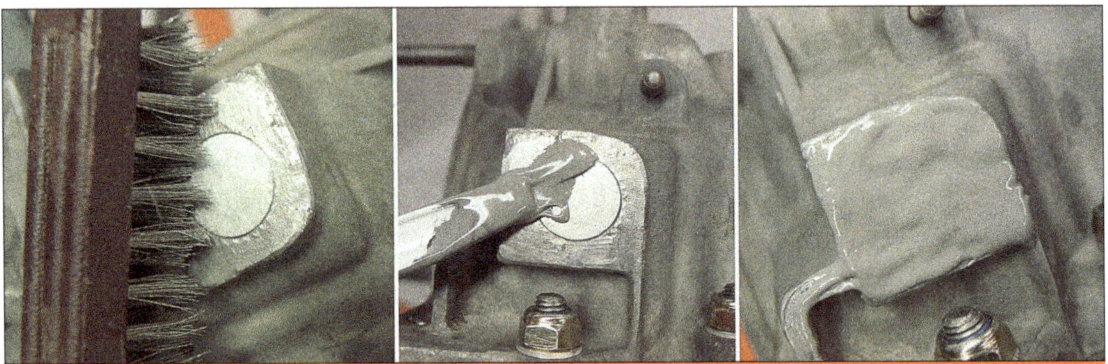

3-4 *This sequence of photos shows the proper method for applying the JB Weld material to the case. Use a wire brush to remove the old material, then wipe the area with a clean-room wipe and some brake cleaner. Apply the JB Weld with a spatula and spread it out evenly over the entire area of the plug. Make sure that the epoxy doesn't drip when it's drying—it has a tendency to creep slowly.*

every surface, and meticulously clean them with a clean-room cloth and isopropyl alcohol. If there is any old sealant still remaining on the case, carefully scrape it off with your fingernail, a plastic scraper, or a Scotch-Brite plastic sponge. Make sure that you only remove the sealant, and do not scratch or scrape the case-mating surface.

Examine all of the surfaces shown in the photo, including the ones located inside the case. You will apply case sealant to these surfaces as well so that the bonding agent is a uniform thickness throughout when you tighten up the case. Again, cleanliness cannot be emphasized enough. Failure to clean the case parting line meticulously will result in a leaky engine.

Also inspect the areas where the factory used a bonding agent. These areas, shown in Figure 3-3, are located throughout the case where there are plugs installed. This agent was an epoxy-type substance that is similar to JB Weld. Scrape off all of the older areas that had the original factory coating, clean it with brake cleaner, and replace it with a thick layer of the JB Weld epoxy, as detailed in Figure 3-4. This material acts both to seal the plugs from oil leaks and also to help hold the plugs secure. When you're finished with the brake cleaner, go over the case once more with a clean-room wipe and your bottle of isopropyl alcohol.

If you removed the head studs to replace them, then you will need to clean out the threads in the case with a tap. Take an M10x1.50 tap and carefully thread and remove it from each of the head stud holes. Don't force the tap, as you don't want to damage the existing threads. The goal of chasing the threads with the tap is to remove any old Loctite or Threadlocker that may still remain in the case. The threads should be perfectly clean before you install the head studs. Clean them using a Q-tip soaked in lacquer thinner or brake cleaner. Repeat the process until the Q-tip comes out perfectly clean. Blow each one out with some compressed air after you clean them. Use air from a shop air compressor, or you can use the disposable air-in-a-can that is normally used to blow dust out of computer equipment. Now is the time to do this cleaning—when the engine is half assembled, you don't want metal chips from the tap falling into the engine case. If you have an early case with the baffle screen in the bottom of the case, check to make sure it's clean and securely fastened.

INTERMEDIATE SHAFT BEARINGS

In your package of intermediate shaft bearings, you should have a total of four bearings. Remove two and place them into the right case half after you carefully clean both them and the bearing journal in the case. The bearing with the small oil hole in the center fits into the inside journal, and the bearing with the large lip on the side fits on the outside journal. With the tabs in their correct orientation, it's impossible to install them incorrectly. Start with the tang

aligned in its slot and gently push the bearing down into its bore on the right-side case half. Double check that the oil passage holes in the bearings line up with those in the case. With your finger, spread an even coat of assembly lube on the full surface of each bearing, as shown in Figure 3-5. If you have a stock early case (1965-69), then the intermediate shaft rides directly in the metal of the case. For these early cases, simply wipe down and clean the bearing journal where the shaft rides in the case, and apply the assembly lube directly to the journal. Move your attention to the left case half, and repeat the procedure.

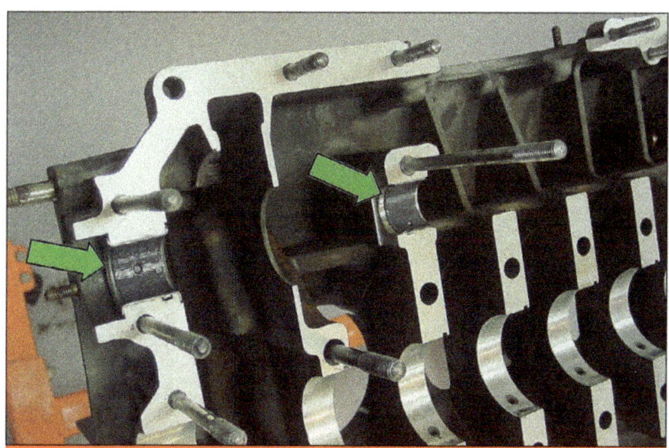

3-5 *Install the intermediate shaft bearings in the case in the same manner as the main and rod bearings (green arrows). Coat each with a bit of assembly lube, and check that the oil holes in the bearings line up with the oil holes in the case. For 1965-1968 1/2 aluminum engine cases, simply lubricate the surface where the intermediate shaft rides.*

OIL PUMP & INTERMEDIATE SHAFT TEST FIT

Prior to installation, clean your oil pump one more time. Dirt and debris in the pump can easily damage the precision gears. Take the intermediate shaft assembly and clean it as well. If you forgot to clean the center of the intermediate shaft, do it now. Also clean the center of the oil pump driveshaft. Take the oil pump and squeeze a small amount of your engine assembly lube into the inside gears on both the left and right sides of the pump. Mate the oil pump with the oil pump driveshaft and intermediate shaft and place them on your workbench, as shown in Figure 3-6.

Now, take the assembly and place it into the engine case, as displayed in Figure 3-7. You are performing a test fit on the assembly to make sure that it turns freely. Rotate the intermediate shaft, checking for any hang-ups or resistance. If you find any resistance, remove the assembly and disconnect the intermediate shaft. Rotate the shaft a quarter turn, and re-insert it into the oil pump driveshaft, making sure that you mate the shaft with different splines in the driveshaft. This should resolve any amount of resistance that you might encounter from the shafts being slightly

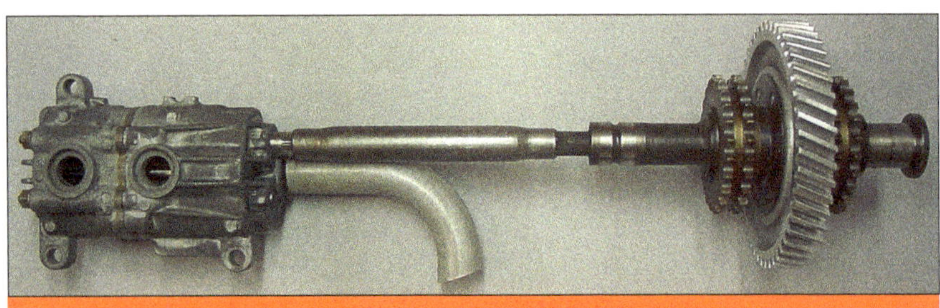

3-6 *Preassemble the oil pump, oil pump drive shaft, and intermediate shaft assembly on your workbench. Make sure that you clean the inside of the intermediate shaft assembly and the oil pump drive shaft as well.*

3-7 *Test-fit the oil pump and intermediate shaft assembly into the case. Rotate the shaft many times and check for binding or spots where the rotation doesn't feel smooth. In some cases, the intermediate shaft will not mate well with a particular spline on the oil pump shaft. If the assembly does not turn smoothly and evenly, remove the entire assembly, disconnect the oil pump drive shaft, and reposition it using different splines on the oil pump and intermediate shaft.*

misaligned. Once you have confirmed that the assembly fits well, remove it and place it on your workbench.

CRANKSHAFT INSTALLATION

Now open your box of new main bearings. Carefully inspect each one to make sure that there are no scratches or manufacturing defects and each one is the correct size. After cleaning both the bearing and the case bores (Figure 3-8), insert each of the main bearings into its respective bore on the right-side case half (Figure 3-9). The small tangs on the bearings should make it impossible to insert the wrong way. Visually confirm that the oil passage hole in the bearing lines up with the oil inlet from the case in the bearing bore. In 1975, the factory switched the location of the tangs on the bearings, and these special-order bearings can be difficult to locate. If you have a 1975-77 case, make sure that the bearings you have line up perfectly with the oil holes in the case. Repeat the process for the left case half on your workbench.

Now take your number eight nose bearing and lay it gently into its mating location in the right crankcase half. There is a small dowel pin in the case that will mate with the hole in the bearing. Double check to make sure that this dowel pin is there. Without the o-ring installed on the bearing, lay it in the engine case and use a felt-tip marker to draw a small line where the bearing meets the case parting line (Figure 3-

10). The number eight nose bearing can be difficult to line up when you're positioning the crankshaft in the case, and this line will give you an easy visual reference to use. Make sure that you have lined up only the small hole in the number eight bearing with the dowel pin—not the larger oil passage hole. If you install the bearing with this oil passage hole blocked, then you will starve your number eight bearing of oil.

Remove the bearing and bring it over to your workbench where you can install the pulley seal. The seal is very similar to the flywheel seal and is simply pushed into the center of the bearing. Take a small piece of sandpaper and lightly deburr the edge of the bearing where the seal is installed. This will reduce the chance of a sharp bearing edge damaging the seal. Spread some Curil-T sealant around the outer edge of the seal before you install it, as shown in Figure 3-11. Take a small amount of assembly lube and place it around the nose of the crankshaft. Take the bearing and slide it onto the end of the crankshaft (Figure 3-12). The seal should give you a little resistance as it slides around the tip of the crankshaft. Now, disconnect your crank from its stand and slip on the flywheel seal over the other end of the crank. Lubricate the outer diameter of the flywheel mounting flange on the crankshaft with a very light coat of assembly lube before slipping on the seal. Install the o-ring onto the bearing.

Now, turn your attention to the right case half and apply a smooth layer of assembly lube to the surface of each bearing (Figure 3-13), in the same manner as you did with the

3-8 *Use isopropyl alcohol and clean-room wipes to clean the surfaces and backs of each bearing half before you place them in the engine case.*

ENGINE ASSEMBLY

128

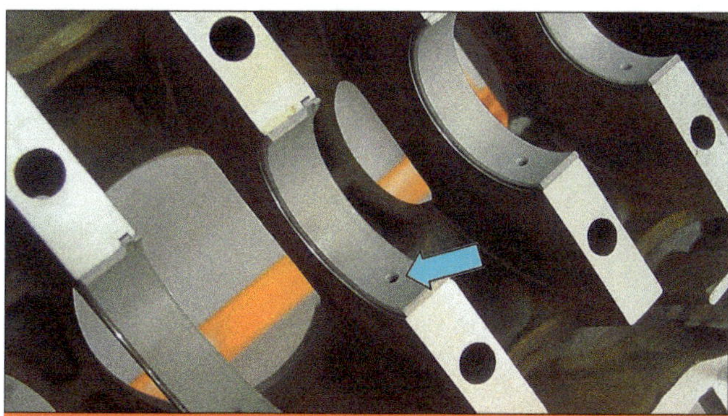

rod bearings. Also apply a very thin layer of assembly lube to the crankshaft bearing journals. Apply a thin layer of Curil-T to the surface where the flywheel seal will mate with the case (Figure 3-14). When complete, inspect the case and the crankshaft for any debris or dirt. When everything is clean, take the crankshaft and lower it into the right case half. You may have to jiggle and reposition the rods so that they fit properly in their respective case spigots (4, 5, and 6 should be pointing downward). Line up the number eight nose bearing with the line you previously marked, and the crankshaft should simply fit into place.

Once the crankshaft is installed, check the nose bearing to make sure it is firmly seated (Figure 3-15), and also rotate the crankshaft back and forth slightly to check for any resistance or interference. Also verify that your flywheel seal is properly positioned in the bore of the case, and didn't get pushed out when you were installing the crankshaft.

There is a set of special tools (P221) that are used to support the weight of the connecting rods, and keep them

3-14 *Take a small amount of the Curil-T sealant and apply it to the area of the case where the flywheel seal is going to mount. The sealant will provide extra assurance against oil leaks.*

3-15 *Install the crankshaft in the case simply by lowering it onto the main bearings. Let the rods for cylinders 4/5/6 hang down through the cylinder spigots. Line up the number eight nose bearing in the case using the line that you drew when you previously test-fit the bearing. At this point, the line cast into the bearing will be directly opposite from the dowel pin in the case (red arrow). Rock the crankshaft back and forth a bit to ensure that it has properly seated in the case.*

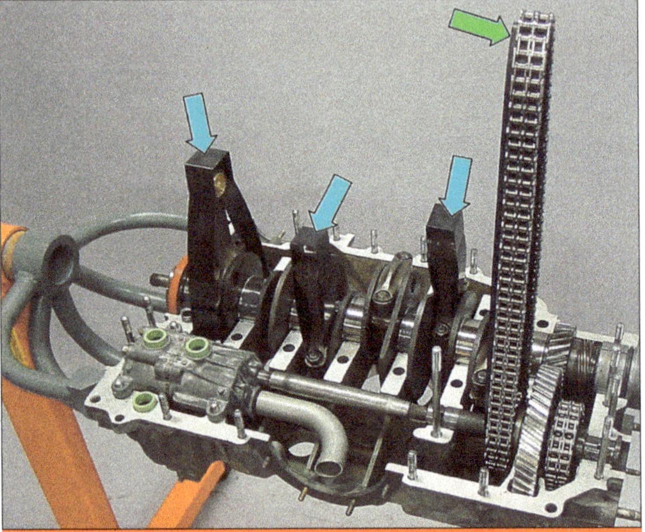

3-16 *Shown here are the rod support tools (P221 – blue arrows) and the chain support tool (P222 – green arrow). The three rod supports hold the rods up in the air and prevent them from touching the inside surfaces of the case. The chain support tool is most useful when you are installing the left case half—it will hold up the chain and keep it out of the way while you are maneuvering the two halves together.*

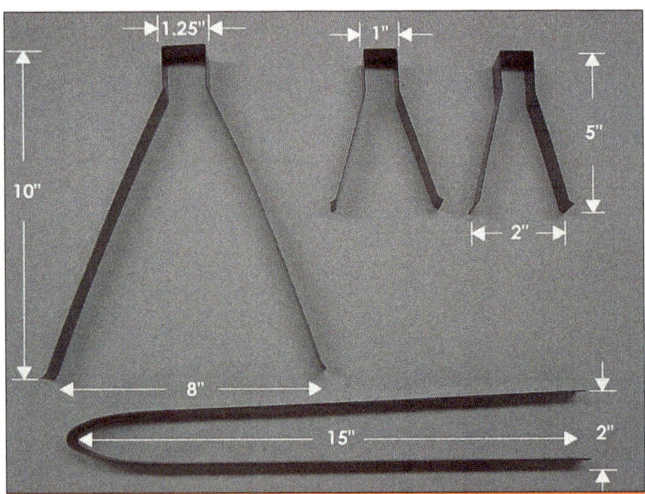

3-17 *Shown here are templates that can be used to make your own tools. These simple tools can be purchased from most Porsche supply shops for around $25, or can be simply manufactured out of sheet metal that you can find at your local hardware store.*

pointed up into the air, as shown in Figure 3-16. I suggest that you obtain these tools (they're not expensive), or make your own out of some flat strips of metal available at any good hardware store. Simply cut and bend the metal to fit the shape of the tools shown in Figure 3-17. Also fabricate a chain support tool (P222) while you have the sheet metal snips handy. Be sure to clean the tools thoroughly before you use them inside your case.

OIL PUMP & INTERMEDIATE SHAFT INSTALLATION

In your gasket kit, locate the one large and three small round seals that mate the oil pump and the two case halves together. Install two of these o-ring seals into the case—one smaller one on the case parting line, and the other larger one at the interface where the oil pump will attach, as shown in Figure 3-18.

Seals have a tendency to seat and seal better when they have been installed with some lubricant on them. However, when you are working with the bottom end of the engine case, it is very important that you do not get any motor oil or lubricants on the mating surfaces between the two case halves. It is for this reason that I do not recommend using any motor oil to prelube the seals or the oil pump before putting the two case halves together. Some rebuilders recommend filling the oil pump with motor oil after placing it in the case. While in general this is good practice, I don't recommend it for 911 engines because the motor oil can drip out of the pump and onto the mating surfaces of the case. Besides, when the engine is filled with oil, the oil will flow down directly into the oil pump from the oil tank. There is no need to prelube the oil pump with motor oil.

Open up your package of new timing chains, spray them down with carburetor cleaner, and wipe them with clean-room wipes. Don't assume that they are clean just because they are new. Take the larger, thick o-ring and place it in the engine case where the oil pump will sit. Take the oil pump and squeeze a small amount of your engine assembly lube into the inside gears on both the left and right sides of the pump.

Using the two brand-new timing chains, wrap each one around the two chain sprockets on the intermediate shaft. Forgetting to install the chains before sealing up the case halves is a common mistake. The good news is that you can

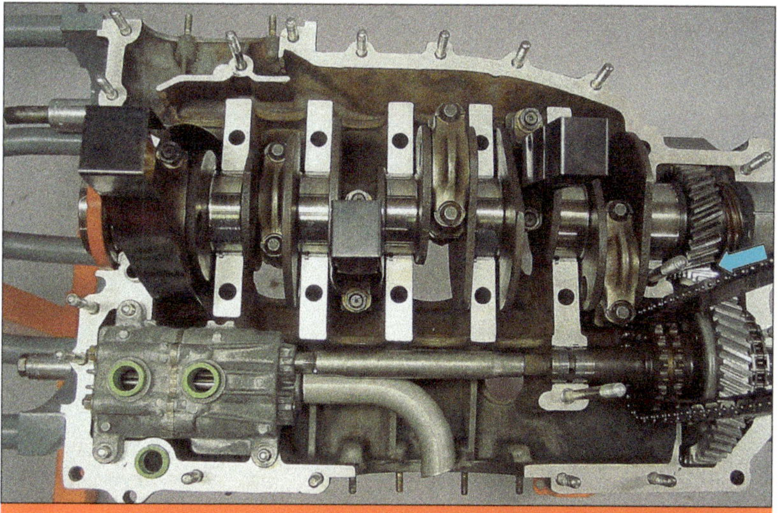

3-19 Using two hands, lower the oil pump/intermediate shaft assembly into the case. You may have to wiggle both the pump and the intermediate shaft gear in order to get the assembly to mate with the case and the crankshaft timing gear (blue arrow). This photo shows the internals of the engine installed, along with the rod and chain holders.

3-20 After you have placed the oil pump in the case, install the three oil pump lock tabs. One side of each tab is pushed down against the pump housing (blue arrow), and the opposite side is pushed up against the nut (yellow arrow) in order to prevent it from turning. Use a small hammer to tap the tabs into place.

3-18 Shown here is the large o-ring that mates the oil pump with the right half of the engine case (red). When you attach the oil pump to the case, make sure that this o-ring is seated properly and is not crushed or deformed. Also shown is the seal that connects the two case halves (green). You can also see the brass plug from the oil bypass modification that was made to this case.

always install a master link chain after the case is sealed. By this time, you have inspected your intermediate shaft for wear and have replaced it if necessary with a similarly sized gear (see Chapter 4).

Take the pump/intermediate shaft/timing chain assembly and lower it into the right crankcase half. The pump should mate with its mounting studs after a bit of wiggling. The intermediate shaft should also easily mate with the crankshaft gear after wiggling the two a bit. You may let the left chain drape over the side of the case while you are working on it—the right-side chain should simply drop down into the chain housing area. Keep a lookout for the large o-ring that mates to the opposite side of the oil pump (right side of the case). This o-ring should fit nicely into its respective counterbore on the opposite side of the oil pump.

Using the same thin sheet metal that you used to make the rod holders, you can also fabricate a tool to support the weight of the timing chain while you're working on the engine (Porsche tool P222). As an alternative, you can tie a piece of string to the chain and support it from a point on your ceiling, directly above the engine. Figure 3-19 shows the internals of the engine with the rod holders and chain holder installed.

With the oil pump in the case, install new oil pump locking tabs on the three studs—they are not typically included in the engine gasket kits. Bend the tabs upward with a small screwdriver to ensure that the nuts will not become loose, as shown in Figure 3-20. Attach three new 13mm nuts to the studs, and torque them down to 25 Nm (18.4 ft-lbs.). Install the two seals that fit into the oil pump, and check that you have already installed the one that joins the oil passages across the case halves. Don't forget this important seal between the case halves—you will have erratic oil pressure problems later on if you do. These three seals (these ones are green) can be seen in Figure 3-16.

BACKLASH CHECK

If your intermediate shaft, crankshaft, and case are not all from the same original engine, then you should have performed the backlash check before the assembly of the crank and rods. Most of the time the backlash measurement will be within specifications.

Intermediate shaft backlash is very difficult to measure without a somewhat complicated setup of tools and measuring devices. The backlash is measured as the amount that the intermediate shaft moves before it connects with the crankshaft gear. Note that this is, and should be, a very small distance and is very difficult to measure. Using a dial gauge indicator (like the one that you will need for the cam timing) set the indicator against the outer edge of the intermediate shaft, resting on one of the teeth on the gear, as shown in Figure 3-21. While holding the crankshaft steady, gently rock the intermediate shaft gear back and forth. The correct backlash measurement is typically between 0.017mm and 0.049mm. Needless to say, this is not an easy measurement to take with the dial gauge indicator.

Most engine rebuilders do not actually measure the amount of backlash, but instead simply confirm that it is actually there. Rocking the intermediate shaft back and forth should produce a very slight click as you feel the backlash. In general, you should hardly feel any movement. The important thing to remember with the backlash is that you need some minimal amount of backlash in the gears—you don't want the two gears to be too tight. This will create a stressful condition inside the case when it's

3-21 *It's not easy to set up the dial gauge to measure backlash. You will need a very flexible dial gauge holder and a bit of patience. Place the dial gauge indicator perpendicular to the intermediate shaft gear and rock the gear slightly to obtain the measurement. This particular photo shows the setup with the chain and rod holders installed. Remove them before performing any backlash measurements.*

bolted together, and could cause premature bearing and gear wear. With this particular situation, too loose is better than too tight. The rule of thumb is to rock the gears back and forth. If you can feel a tiny bit of play between the two of them, then your crank gear and intermediate shaft gear are matched up fine. Too much backlash can also be a problem—it can cause gear and timing problems.

MATING THE CASE HALVES

Once you have confirmed that the backlash setting is correct, it's time to mate the two case halves. Take the left case half to your workbench and carefully clean it with clean-room wipes and isopropyl alcohol. Apply a smooth layer of assembly lube to each bearing surface, in a manner similar to how you prepared the right case half (Figure 3-22). Carefully apply a very light coat of Curil-T to the outer diameter of the flywheel seal that is visible. This is extra insurance against oil leaks.

At this point this case should be sterile enough to perform surgery on and you can start mating the case halves. Before you start, make sure that you have enough time (you will need about 45 minutes or so) to completely finish sealing and tightening up the case. Check that you have all of your fasteners ready and waiting—you don't want to have to look for any while the sealant is curing. Liberally apply the Loctite 574 case sealant to the engine case mating surfaces shown in Figure 3-23. Use the 574 bottle, and squeeze out a nice thick bead onto all of the mating surfaces, including those located inside the center of the case. After you have applied the bead of sealant, carefully use an acid brush to spread the sealant across each of the mating surfaces so that you have a nice even coat across the case parting line (Figure 3-24). Make sure that you cover every surface that mates with the left-side half, and be careful

3-22 *In a manner similar to that used on the right case half, spread a thin layer of assembly lube on the main and intermediate bearings while the left case half is resting on your workbench.*

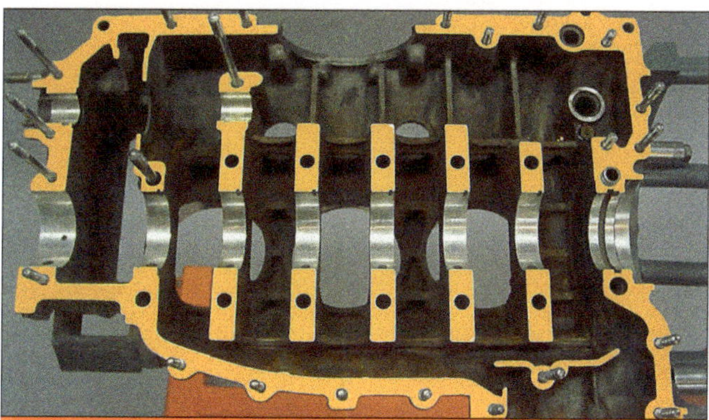

3-23 *This photo shows all of the areas where the Loctite 574 case sealant should be spread (orange areas). It is important to spread an even coat along all mating surfaces on the right-side case half only. This will ensure that your case will have a thin, even layer throughout, and will not bend in the areas where there is no sealant. This photo applies only to the application of the Loctite 574 sealant. This sealant will only bond on metal-to-metal contact—oil will wash away the excess sealant inside the case. If using a sealant other than the loctite sealant (such as the Dow Corning 730 flouro-silicone sealant), place a thin bead around the outside mating surfaces. If using the Dow Corning 730, apply it to the left case half—carefully avoiding the oil relief circular area surrounding the top left through-bolt hole (visible in Figure 3-22).*

3-24 *Spread the Loctite 574 evenly on the right case half only. The coat should be uniform and smooth across all of the mating surfaces. Be careful not to get the sealant on the surface of the crankshaft journals (red arrow) when you are spreading it across the surface.*

3-25 *The through-bolts for the 911 engine fit through areas of the case that also serve as pressurized oil passages. Therefore, you need to install o-rings on the end of each through-bolt in order to seal against oil leaks (top). The o-ring sits in a small bevel inside the large washers that press against the engine case. As an added protection against oil leaks, I recommend spreading a thin layer of black RTV silicone sealant around the outside of each o-ring (bottom). The excess sealant can be trimmed off after it has dried, and doesn't leave any visible residue.*

that the brush doesn't drop any bristles into your sealant. One missed bristle can lead to an oil leak at the case parting line. Apply the 574 sealant to the right-side case half only—not both case halves.

After you have a nice layer of sealant laid down, carefully place the left case half down onto the right side. The rod and chain holders should slip easily into the holes in the left side of the engine case—remove them after the left case half is lowered. Gently tap the cases together with a soft rubber mallet. The main bearings and intermediate bearings should not fall out of the left case half when you lower it onto the right half. If they do, then you probably have a problem with the bearing bore in your case; you should then take your case back to your machine shop for inspection. A loose bearing bore has the potential to cause all sorts of problems when the engine is running.

Now is the time to move really quickly. The sealant is beginning to harden, and you only have about 45 minutes to tighten down the entire case. Begin preparing the case studs with the two encapsulated studs in the oil cooler housing. These studs, like the case through-bolts, are exposed to the oil pressures that are inside the case. To prevent oil from leaking from these fasteners, the nuts have a special beveled washer and o-ring that fits under each nut. These small o-rings should be included with your engine gasket set. Take the small o-ring and place it on the stud. In order to ensure that your case absolutely will not leak from these bolts, I recommend applying a generous helping of silicone sealant around the o-ring, as shown in Figure 3-25. For this purpose I recommend the Permatex Ultra-Black

3-26 *With the increase in displacement to 2.7 liters in 1974, Porsche beveled the washers used on the through-bolts. The earlier engines can use either the thick washers (yellow arrow) or the beveled ones (green arrow); however, engines with displacements larger than 2.7 liters require the use of the beveled washers.*

3-27 *Don't forget the 15mm nut that is hidden in the left timing chain housing (blue arrow). Torque this nut to its final value before tightening up the outer case nuts.*

Hi-Temp RTV Silicone. The black color of the sealant will blend into the color of the engine case, and you won't even be able to see any after you trim off the excess. After you have applied the silicone, install the capped nut (also called an acorn nut), lightly hand-tighten.

The case through-bolts are very similar to the previous two studs, except that they use o-rings on both ends of the bolts, under a washer. Install them in the case so that the nuts are located on the left side of the engine. I doubt that this makes any difference, but this is the orientation that is shown in the Porsche factory manuals. Liberally apply the sealant to each of the o-rings (there are two o-rings per bolt) and lightly hand tighten each bolt.

The early engines used a flat, thick washer with the crankcase through-bolts. With the introduction of the 2.7-liter engine in 1974, these washers were updated to include a bevel on the outside edge. This bevel is machined into the washer to prevent any interference problems with the larger 2.7L cylinders. When rebuilding your engine, make sure that you use these beveled washers for cylinders 2.7L and larger. The earlier engines (2.4L and smaller), can use either the beveled washers or the early thick, flat ones. The difference between the two washers is shown in Figure 3-26.

After the through-bolts are installed, attach the one 10mm nut in the timing chain housing area on the left side of the engine (see Figure 3-27). Lightly hand-tighten it up. Attach the remaining M8 nuts around the perimeter of the

case housing. Lightly hand-tighten them as well. Use only new nuts and washers.

At this point, you will want to quickly check to make sure that everything looks perfect. Check things very quickly though, as the sealant is beginning to harden. The crank should rotate freely in the engine case, and there should be no sticky spots or obvious resistance. Check that all the fasteners are attached, and that the number eight nose bearing is properly seated. Check the case parting line—you should see significant squeeze-out of the orange Loctite 574 case sealant. Check that you have the timing chains installed—I have heard of more than one time when someone made this mistake.

When everything checks over, start tightening the case through-bolts. Begin with one of the four bolts that is located in the center spigot. Tighten it to its final torque value. Then

3-28 *Tighten the through-bolts using the crisscross pattern shown here. This will provide you with uniform compression of the case sealant on the case mating surfaces.*

134

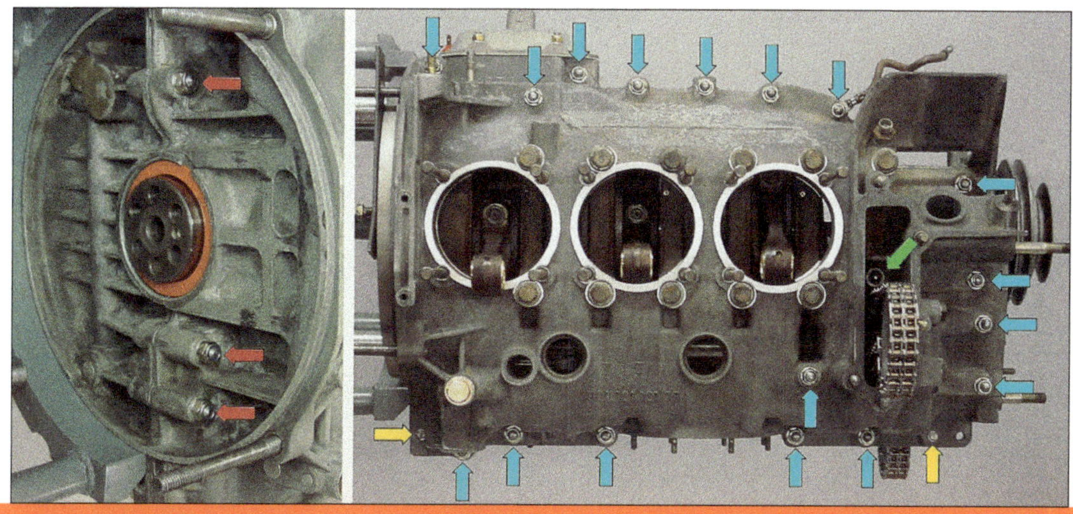

crisscross the cylinder spigot, and tighten the through-bolt that is located diagonally opposite. Start working quickly now, as the sealant has begun to cure, and you want to get the case torqued down before it hardens. Continue in this pattern (see Figure 3-28), tightening each one to its final value. Then tighten the two nuts located in the oil cooler housing to their final torque value. Tighten all of the nuts to their final value using the nonstatic torque method (described in Section 1 of this chapter). This torque value is very important because it is what determines the bearing clearances. Too tight will decrease the bearing clearances; too loose will increase the clearances.

When the case through-bolts are all tight, torque down the nut in the timing chain housing to its final value. Now, tighten down each of the outer perimeter case fasteners to their final torque, working your way around the outside of the case. There are 22 of these self-locking nuts, and they should be fastened to their final torque with washers under each one. The location of these nuts is shown in Figure 3-29. This part of the job must be completed in 45 minutes or less from the time that you first place the case halves together or the Loctite 574 sealant will begin to harden.

When finished, go back and double check all of the fasteners to make sure that they are all tightened to their final values. Double check to make sure that you have squeeze-out of the Loctite 574 at all of the seams of the case (Figure 3-30). If you don't have squeeze out in a particular section, then there is a likelihood that you did not apply enough material, or something is preventing the case from being completely tightened at that point. Rotate the crankshaft and make sure that it doesn't bind or hang up anywhere. It should turn freely and smoothly. Now would be a good time

ENGINE ASSEMBLY

3-32 *The procedure for adjusting the intermediate shaft end play applies only to the 1965-1968 1/2 aluminum 2.0-liter cases. Measure the amount of intermediate shaft overhang beyond the crankcase housing (green arrow). Compensate for the variations in the intermediate shaft location by installing gaskets underneath the intermediate shaft cover (inset).*

3-33 *Place a thin bead of Loctite 271 or Permatex Threadlocker on the head studs as you insert them into the case. Pay careful attention to the instructions included with the RaceWare or ARP studs, as the installation procedure is different. You can use two nuts twisted together to grab the end of the stud. Then turn the stud using a small socket and driver. Make sure the two nuts don't slip, as you may end up damaging the threads on the stud during the installation process. If the studs are too tight and require too much force, then use the Snap-On stud tool to install the studs in the case. Do not overtighten the stud; it should just bottom-out in its hole.*

to clean up the squeeze-out along the parting line and the excess black silicone from the through-bolts (Figure 3-31).

At this time, most people take a step back and admire the job that they have done so far. It is indeed a great feeling of accomplishment at this point. If you are building a performance engine and you are not using the original distributor that was disassembled with the engine, then I suggest that you quickly perform a test fit now. I have heard a few tales of woe from customers who assembled their entire engine, and then went to install the distributor, only to find that they had the wrong distributor drive gear installed on the crankshaft. There were a total of three different distributor drive gears used from 1965-89. The drive gear must match the distributor year-for-year. Test fit your distributor into the case and slightly rotate the crankshaft clockwise from the pulley end of the engine case. The distributor should turn in the required direction. You should perform this check especially if you are using a crankshaft of unknown origin—it's difficult to tell which distributor drive gear is on the crankshaft simply by looking at it.

INTERMEDIATE SHAFT END PLAY

With the crankcase assembled, you can now check the intermediate shaft end play. This only applies to the 1965-68 1/2 aluminum engine cases. When the intermediate shaft is installed, it is designed to stick out past the front surface of the crankcase. The small cover that fits over the end of the intermediate shaft needs to have paper gaskets or the later-style metal shims placed under it to compensate for variations in the amount of intermediate shaft protrusion from the case.

You adjust the end play on the shaft by adding paper gaskets underneath the intermediate shaft cover plate. These paper gaskets or metal shims are typically available in

varying thicknesses to compensate for the variations in the intermediate shaft's location in the case. Measure the initial amount of overhang of the intermediate shaft beyond the surface of the crankcase. This will give you an initial idea of which thickness shims you need.

Since the paper gaskets will compress to varying thicknesses, the only true way to determine which gaskets are needed is to tighten the assembly down and measure it with a dial gauge. Porsche tool P220 is designed to bolt onto the front of the engine case and secure a standard dial gauge. Start with the estimated amount of shims and install the dial gauge and tool P220. Use a long screwdriver inserted into the recess of the crankcase chain housing to push the intermediate shaft back and forth and measure the amount of travel on the dial gauge. The total travel, or backlash, should be 0.08mm to 0.12mm (0.003 to 0.005 inch). If your backlash is not within this range, then remove the shims and replace them with thinner or thicker ones. When you're finished, remove the P220 tool, and place the paper gaskets and end cover aside for later assembly.

HEAD STUD INSTALLATION

If you removed any of your head studs either to replace them or to strengthen the case with case-savers, now is the time to reinstall them. Each head stud should be carefully inspected for damage. Clean each one with a wire brush—using a brush on a grinder works well. Then go over the stud with isopropyl alcohol and a clean-room wipe, paying extra attention to the threads. There may be remains from the Loctite on the threads of the studs. If so, then you may wish to chase the ends of each stud with an M10x1.5 die to clean them out. Make sure that you don't damage the threads with the die, and if any head stud threads offer a lot of resistance, then replace them. Sometimes simply screwing on a head stud barrel nut will do the trick to clean out the threads as well.

It is important to note that you do not want to use Dilavar studs on your engine rebuild. See Section 2 in Chapter 4 for more information on which head studs to use in your rebuild. If you are using RaceWare or ARP studs, make sure that you follow the installation instructions that are specific to these studs. RaceWare does not recommend using Loctite on the stud threads unless you are using Time-Serts, which have a slightly larger thread than the original threads used in the standard Porsche cases. I also don't recommend using Loctite on RaceWare studs when used with case-savers.

The Snap-On stud remover tool discussed in Chapter 2 is a good tool for installing head studs in the case. Lacking one of these, you can use two nuts locked together on the stud. The nuts will grab the stud and allow you to screw it into the case without turning on the threads. Don't use too much force, and don't let the nuts slip on the threads, as you may damage the head stud threads. The book, *Carroll Smith's Nuts, Bolts, Fasteners, and Plumbing Handbook*, is an excellent resource for information on the physics behind nuts and fasteners.

Place a thin bead of Loctite 271 on the threads of each stud before you install it in the case (Figure 3-33). All head studs should be installed so that their total height above the case is 135mm (5.315 inches). Check the installation height (Figure 3-34) right after you have installed the stud because the Loctite 271 will begin to harden and bond immediately.

3-34 *All of the studs should be 135mm (5.315 inches) above the flange of the case. You can perform the measurement with a simple metal ruler—you don't need any precision measuring tools for this step. This height is important because the 10mm Allen-head stud tool won't seat in the head barrel nuts if the studs are too long.*

CRANKCASE BREATHER, THERMOSTAT, OIL PRESSURE SWITCH

Now, move to the top of the engine. Install the crankcase breather housing with four new locking nuts. Use the new gasket that should be included in your gasket kit, and install

it dry. Examine the gasket carefully—it is possible to install it backwards, which will result in a major oil leak later on. Next, find the o-ring that fits around the internal oil cooler thermostat. Wet this with a bit of clean motor oil and install it around the thermostat. It's also a wise idea to check the thermostat—place it on a hot plate and make sure the internal mechanism opens when it gets hot.

Clean both the inside of the thermostat mounting hole and the thermostat itself with some wipes and alcohol before you install the thermostat. A few light taps with a rubber mallet should ease the thermostat into the case. Tighten it down with two new self-locking fasteners. Also, reattach your oil pressure switch or sending unit (depending upon which year engine you have) after you have installed the thermostat. Teflon pipe thread sealing tape is also a good guard against oil leaks. Wrap the threads of the oil pressure switch with one layer of the tape and then tighten it down. Use a new aluminum sealing ring to prevent oil leaks. Do not overtighten the oil pressure switch as it is fragile, and can break off in the case. Figure 3-35 shows these three components installed in the top of the case.

3-35 *When you have finished tightening the case halves together, you can install the crankcase breather cover (yellow arrow), the thermostat (green arrow) ,and the oil pressure switch (blue arrow). Use a new sealing ring and a new oil pressure switch—old ones have a bad habit of leaking when reused.*

OIL PRESSURE RELIEF PISTONS

Toward the oil pump area of the case there are holes bored for the oil pressure relief pistons and springs. Install these two assemblies in the case, using new springs, new pistons, and new aluminum sealing rings. If you have performed the oil bypass modification, you must use the late-style oil pressure pistons. The older style ones are not compatible with the bypass modification and will rob your engine of oil pressure when you start it up. The main pressure relief valve is located on the bottom of the engine, and contains a small

3-36 *Shown here are the newer style oil pressure relief pistons (left) and the older style (right). The updated style pistons and springs are required if you had the oil pump bypass modification performed on your engine case. If you use the wrong pistons, you can starve your engine of oil when you go to start it up.*

3-37 *The oil pressure piston and spring assembly that goes into the bottom of the engine requires the longer spring, and the spring guide. Assemble them in the bottom of the engine as shown in this photo. Use the shorter spring without the spring guide for the relief valve that screws into the side of the case.*

3-38 *Lift the chains above the ramps so that they ride on top of the ramps (green arrows). It's easy to install the chain ramps while forgetting to position the chain properly around them. Double-check to make sure that the chains have not slipped off the intermediate shaft sproket.*

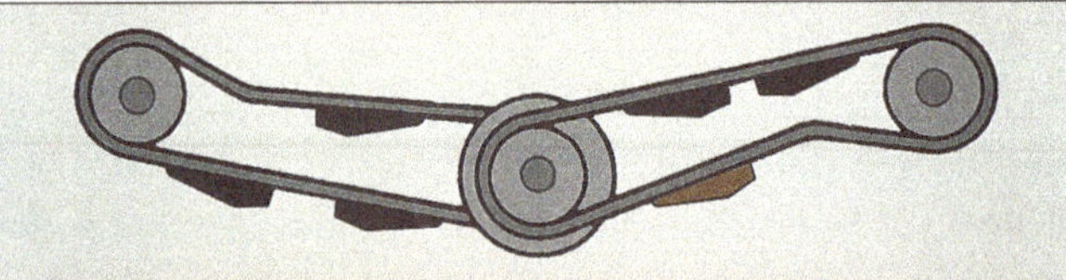

3-39 *This diagram shows the location and orientation of the chain ramps in your case. The four inner chain ramps have their longer ends pointing toward the center of the case. All the chain ramps are black with the exception of the lower inboard right ramp, which is brown. The brown ramp supports the chain at a slightly different height than the black ramps.*

piston that uses the longer spring. A handy upgrade is to replace your early-style flathead oil pressure relief cap with the later style 17mm one (part number 999.064.026.02). If you purchase the updated spring and piston kit to use with the oil bypass modification, these newer 17mm caps are usually included with the updated kit. The springs don't seem to wear out often, but it's a good idea to replace them with new ones when you're rebuilding your engine. The new and old kits are shown side-by-side in Figure 3-36.

Install the oil pressure piston and spring assemblies, following Figure 3-37. Coat the pistons with a thin layer of assembly lube before you install them. The bottom pressure assembly uses the spring guide and the longer spring. The relief piston assembly that fits into the side of the case uses the shorter spring with no guide. For cases without the oil pump bypass modification, the spring lengths are equal. Verify that the oil pressure pistons move smoothly in their bores. It is possible that a loose plug can interfere with the travel of the plug. Proper operation of both pistons is vital—a loss of oil pressure can result if they do not operate properly.

INBOARD CHAIN RAMPS

At this point, you can install the four inboard chain ramps. The newer style chain ramps are manufactured out of tough plastic, and are known to stand up better than the black soft plastic ones used on the early cars. Two odd-shaped bolts that pass through the case create the mounts for the chain ramps. Place each ramp inside the case and hold it there as you thread in the chain ramp bolts. The proper installation of the chain ramps is shown in Figure 3-38.

Push the bolts through the center of the holes in the ramps. Make sure that you don't install the ramps backwards—the four inboard chain ramps closest to the crankshaft point with their longer end towards the crankshaft; the two outboard ones point their longer ends out towards the outside of the engine (see Figure 3-39). Also be careful not to drop the ramps inside the engine, or you may have difficulty fishing them out. There are also two different types of chain ramps—use the black ones everywhere except in the lower right position where you install the slightly different brown ramp. Use a new aluminum sealing ring for each chain ramp bolt, and tighten to its specified torque setting (Appendix A). Don't install the upper chain ramps without lifting up the chain so that it rests over them. Otherwise, you will have to remove the ramps later on and correct this mistake. Verify that the ramps have properly snapped onto their mounting bolts.

FLYWHEEL & CRANKSHAFT PULLEY

I recommend that you install your flywheel at this time, as you will need to hold the crankshaft steady before you can attach and tighten the front crankshaft pulley. Make sure the flywheel seal is properly seated, the crankshaft threads are perfectly clean, and test fit your flywheel to the engine. If you have an early engine (up through early 1979), press out the old flywheel pilot bearing before you begin. Gently tap the new pilot bearing straight in until it is flush with the top surface (Figure 3-40), taking care that you don't damage the outer housing of the bearing as you press it into the flywheel. A small hand press is ideal, but some gentle taps with a soft mallet will also suffice. Tap it in straight until the

pilot bearing housing is flush with the top surface. The 915 pilot bearing (for 911s from late 1979-86) bolts onto the flywheel itself.

Don't forget to install the flywheel bolt washer (through 1977) directly underneath the bolts if you have the six-bolt flywheel. As you may remember from the teardown section, the flywheel bolts are a potential problem if you don't use the proper tool to attach them. Fasten your flywheel lock, as shown in Figure 3-41. Apply a very small drop of Loctite 271 to the flywheel bolt threads. Start tightening with one bolt, and then move across the center to one on the opposite side. Set your torque wrench at about 20 Nm (15 ft-lbs.) to start, and torque down all the bolts. Then repeat the process after increasing the wrench torque value by about 20 Nm (15 ft-lbs.). Don't tighten the bolts in a circle; crisscross your pattern. Final torque value for the 1965-77 911s is 150 Nm (110 ft-lbs.) and for the 1978-89 911s is 90 Nm

3-40 *The early pilot bearings are gently pressed or tapped into the flywheel. The later style ones are screwed directly onto the crankshaft. Remove your old one and gently press in the new one using a small mallet or press.*

3-41 *Although you can purchase a flywheel lock that specifically works with your engine stand, I prefer the simpler approach. A thin, flat piece of steel with two holes in it has worked well for me for many, many years. Simply slide one hole onto a stud in the case, and another hole on a bolt that you can screw into one of the holes on the flywheel.*

3-42 *If you have the correct engine stand, you should be able to tighten the flywheel bolts with the engine still on the stand. Only use the proper tightening tool, as the flywheel bolts need to be torqued down to very high values. Make sure that you install the flywheel washer under the bolts if you have a 1977 or earlier car.*

3-43 *With the flywheel lock still in place, attach and tighten the front pulley. Make sure that you torque it down to the final value—it's bad practice to tighten the pulley only slightly, as it's too easy to forget to torque it later on. In general, that's also a good rule to follow for any fastener that doesn't get special treatment, as discussed in this book. Don't tighten it down unless you torque it fully. Racing pulleys may be indexed differently—verify that the pulley's 'Z1' mark lines up with the case parting line at Top Dead Center (TDC).*

(66.3 ft-lbs.). Figure 3-42 shows the process of tightening up the flywheel bolts.

If you're performing a 914-6 conversion, you should scribe the timing marks on the edge of your flywheel. Original 914-6 flywheels had timing marks on them that could be seen through an access hole in the engine compartment.

After your flywheel is attached, then you can easily install the crankshaft pulley. Install your flywheel lock onto the flywheel. The pulley attaches to the rear of the crankshaft and is indexed with the crank using a small dowel pin. Line up the dowel pin and torque the pulley bolt to its specified torque value, as shown in Figure 3-43.

Depending upon the size and design of your flywheel bolt tool, the engine stand, and your torque wrench, you may have difficultly tightening the flywheel with the engine on its stand. If this is the case, then lower the engine off of the stand to attach the flywheel. Alternatively, you can also install two flywheel bolts in the crankshaft and use a pry bar to hold the flywheel steady while you torque the crankshaft pulley. I don't recommend that you temporarily attach the pulley because it's too easy to forget to tighten it up to its final torque value later on. If you're going to install it, make sure that it's tightened up properly.

Congratulations, the short block is complete! The completed short block assembly is shown in Figure 3-44.

3-44 *The completed short block is indeed a fantastic sight. Use your two chain sprockets to hold the chains downwards. In the following sections when you need to rotate the crankshaft, simply let one chain and sprocket hang down, while holding the other one up in the air. This will help you when turning the engine over—the chains will not become snagged or tangled.*

SECTION 4 PISTONS & CYLINDERS

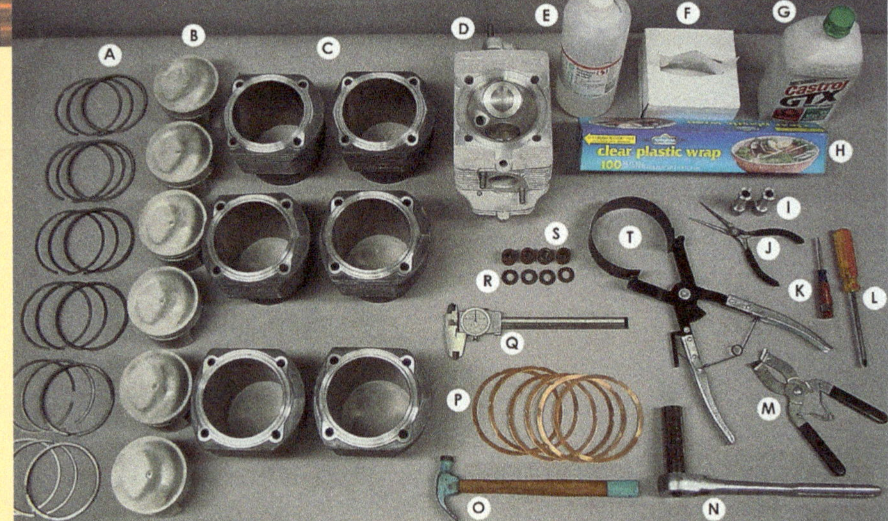

TOOLS: Needle-nose pliers **(J)**, small flathead screwdriver **(K)**, piston ring compressor **(T)**, piston ring installer/separator **(M)**, medium sized screwdriver **(L)** and small hammer **(O)**, Porsche tool P241 **(I)** or appropriate deep socket/head stud combination, vernier caliper **(Q)**, 19mm socket **(N)**, plastic hammer.

MATERIALS: Clean wipes **(F)** and isopropyl alcohol **(E)**, 30-weight motor oil **(G)**, plastic sandwich wrap **(H)**, hollow acid-core solder.

PARTS: 6 Pistons **(B)**, 6 cylinders **(C)**, piston ring set **(A)**, 6 piston pins, one cylinder head **(D)**

HARDWARE: 4 Cylinder head stud barrel nuts and washers **(S/R)**, piston pin circlips (12).

SEALS: 6 cylinder base gaskets **(P)**, cylinder-to-head gasket (qty 1, for 2.0-liter engines only)

TIME: 2 to 4 hours.

TIP: Don't forget to install the cylinder base gasket before placing the cylinder on the engine.

OVERVIEW

In this section, you'll be assembling parts of the engine and then taking them apart again as you check, measure, and adjust the cylinder deck height. It's important to follow the order of instructions carefully, otherwise you may end up repeating some steps that you don't need to perform. In this section, you will install all of the pistons into the cylinders. Then you will install one piston/cylinder assembly on each side of the engine and measure the deck height of the cylinder. The deck height changes due to the tolerance buildup discussed in Chapter 4. All of the machining tasks on the engine tend to remove material that brings the pistons closer to the heads. Measuring the deck height during installation allows you to adjust for this tolerance buildup by using thicker shims at the cylinder base. After you have confirmed and corrected your configuration to achieve the proper deck height, you will install the remaining pistons and cylinders.

CLEANING

With the crankcase assembled, it's now time to install the pistons and cylinders on each of the rods. As in the previous sections, cleaning is of paramount importance. Using your clean-room wipes and isopropyl alcohol, carefully clean each piston and cylinder completely. Just because your pistons and cylinders came out of a brand-new box doesn't mean that they are clean enough to be placed in your engine.

I recommend that you remove the pistons from the cylinders, and also remove the rings from the pistons and clean them thoroughly, as shown in Figure 4-2. Place the piston rings carefully on your workbench, and take notes of how they were installed in your cylinder. Orientation is important—you don't want to install a ring upside down. Most rings have their top side appropriately marked; however, this is not always the case. Although they may look similar, the two top compression rings on the pistons are different, and must not be mixed up. Some have different markings on

them and some do not. I like to mark them with a black permanent marker if there is no clear indication which ring is the top ring.

Make sure the inner cylinder bores are completely dry and have all dirt and debris from any machining processes removed. Use brake cleaner and shop towels to remove any excess grit left over from the honing process. Carefully clean between the internal passages of the ring grooves. Don't use any tools that may potentially damage the ring groove—use only your fingernails, a plastic scraper or toothbrush and the clean-room wipes. It's best to clean these parts right before you install them. However, if you cannot, make sure that you store the pistons and cylinders in sealed plastic bags. Spray them down with a bit of oil (regular motor oil works fine) to protect them from corrosion.

The only exception to this rule is if you are reusing your low-mileage Alusil pistons and cylinders and you simply removed them from your engine as an assembly with pistons, cylinders, and rings intact. With this situation, it's best to just leave the entire piston/ring/cylinder assembly alone and bolt it back onto the engine. However, you should still clean the outside surfaces that you can reach.

RING GAP CHECK

If you're using pistons and cylinders from a brand-new set, it's typically not necessary to check the ring gap. However, if you are mixing and matching components, then I would recommend it. With no rings installed on one piston, place it inside a cylinder. It will act as a backstop for the ring and keep it perpendicular while you are performing the measurement. Then insert the ring into the cylinder taking care not to damage the ring or scratch the cylinder. Using a feeler gauge, measure the gap that exists between the two ends of the ring. Compare it to the allowable tolerances listed in Appendix A. If the gap is too large or too small, then either the ring is defective or the cylinder diameter is too large.

PRE-INSTALLATION

There are two different methods that you can use to install the pistons and cylinders. One method is to install the pistons on the rods and then install the cylinder on the piston. The other method involves mating the pistons and cylinders on your workbench and then installing each one on your engine. While the factory workshop manuals distinctly show the first method for installing the pistons, I don't recommend it. It can be difficult to install the cylinders over the rings when the head studs are in your way. It can also be difficult to hold the piston at the proper angle, and position the engine stand in an easily accessible position. The factory manuals also show all of the pistons installed on the engine at the same time, without the cylinders installed. While this is fine for disassembling the engine, this orientation creates too much opportunity to damage the pistons or your new rings.

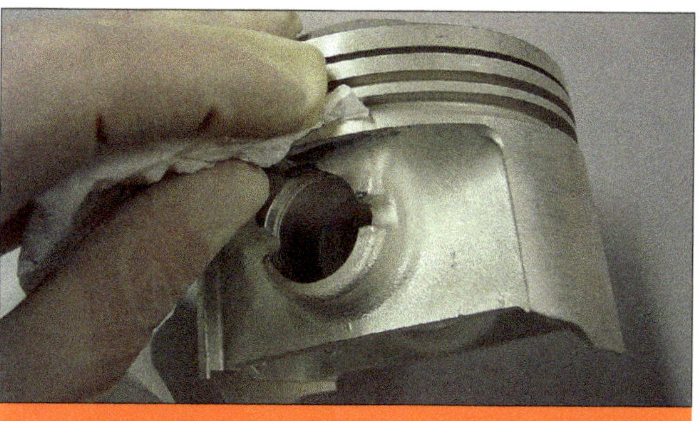

4-2 *Don't assume that your pistons and cylinders are clean, just because they came from a brand-new box. Don't trust your machine shop to clean them either. Use your brake cleaner first, and then clean-room wipes and isopropyl alcohol to carefully clean each groove and crevice.*

You must rotate the engine in order to move each piston to top dead center for installation. Rotating the engine with the pistons hanging out of the case spigots is an easy way for the rings to catch on the side of the case and break. I believe that the factory installed the pistons in this manner because the earlier pistons had to be heated prior to inserting the piston wrist pin. Later piston sets do not require this. Either way, even if you choose to install the pistons on the rods first, make sure that you install each piston and cylinder assembly one at a time, so that the pistons are not hanging out of the case. I recommend that you mate your pistons and cylinders on the bench, and then install them on the engine.

RING INSTALLATION

When you are satisfied that your pistons, cylinders, rings, and piston pins are as clean as they can possibly be, you can begin the process of installing the pistons and cylinders on your engine. Start on your worktable by installing the piston rings on the pistons. Each piston has three rings—two for sealing compression and one for sealing oil from the crankcase. Extreme care must be given to the process of ring installation, otherwise you can easily end up with a broken, cracked, or damaged ring. This will result in a low-compression, smoking engine and will require another complete teardown. Needless to say, don't rush through this section — perform each task gently and carefully. The rings themselves are manufactured out of a tough, yet brittle metal alloy. Too much bending or stress can cause them to crack and break. When you install the rings on the pistons, you are stretching them close to their breaking point. It's important to only bend and open the rings as far as they need to be stretched for installation. Improper installation can also cause them to break.

When you're ready to assemble your pistons and cylinders, start with the piston rings. If you purchased a set brand new, then these should already be pre-installed on the pistons. I personally like to use the OEM Goetz rings, as they have been used as the standard replacement rings in 911 engines for many years, with very few problems. However, aftermarket companies like Deves or Hastings also make very high-quality replacements on par with the German rings.

When installing your rings, make sure that you carefully read the instructions that accompany them. There are two compression rings that look very similar to each other. In reality, the bevel on the inside edges of the rings is different, and the rings must be installed in their specific ring groove or they will fail to work properly. They must also be installed with the proper side facing up, otherwise the bevel on the outside of the ring will be pointing in the wrong direction. Look for small dots on the side of the rings, or the word TOP, as shown in Figure 4-3. This will be printed on the top of the ring that must face the piston crown (the outside of the engine, away from the crankshaft). If the ring is installed upside down, then it will not seal, and the engine will not achieve adequate compression in that cylinder.

Piston rings can be installed by hand or by using a simple ring expander. Be careful using the expander though, as hand tools sometimes have lots of leverage that you can't feel with your fingers. Carelessly using a ring expander with such fragile components as piston rings can lead to scratched, cracked, or broken rings. Your own fingers make the best "feelers" for how much force you are using to stretch and bend each ring. If you haven't done this before, I recommend that you take one of your old rings and see how much force it takes to break it. You will then get a feel for how little margin for error there is when installing the rings on the pistons.

4-4 *The oil seal ring is the most fragile of the three rings. Here you can see the thin cross section of the ring. Because the spring runs inside of the ring, the ring must be "hollow" on the inside, which further weakens it. I have found that oil rings are the easiest to break when installing the pistons.*

4-3 *The rings are marked with the words 'TOP' or a few small dots to signal which side of the ring goes towards the piston crown. In this photo, you can also see the beveled edge of the ring, which is important for achieving a proper seal against the cylinder wall.*

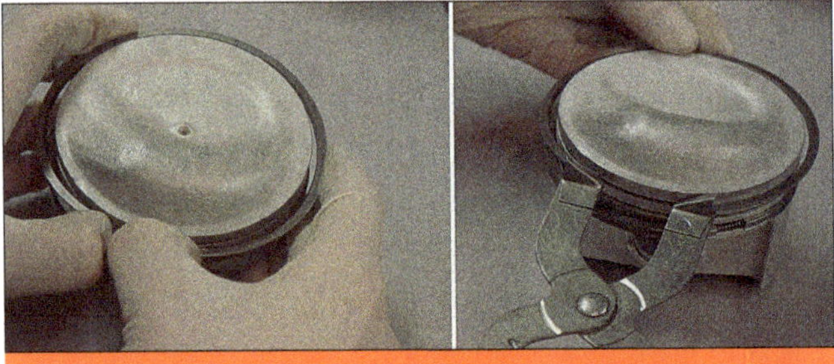

4-5 *You can use either your fingers or a ring expander tool to install the rings. Although the tool is easier on your fingers, you won't get as good a feeling for how much force you are applying to the rings. If you do choose to use the tool, make sure that you don't overextend the gap on the rings—you can damage and break them very easily.*

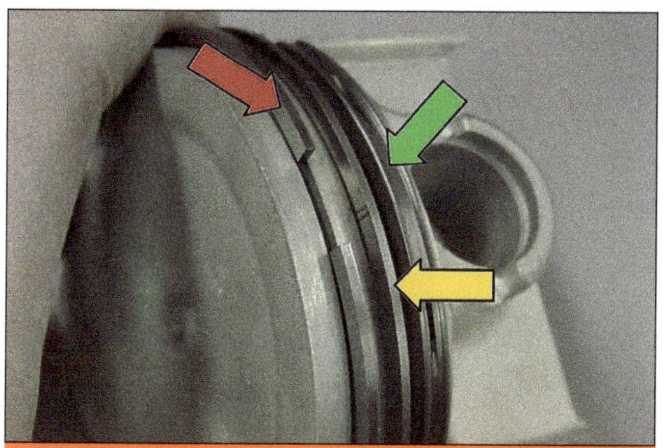

4-6 *Shown here is a piston with all three rings installed properly. Rotate them around to ensure that the ring doesn't bind or catch inside the ring groove. The red arrow indicates the top compression ring, the yellow arrow shows the middle compression ring and the green arrow shows the oil ring.*

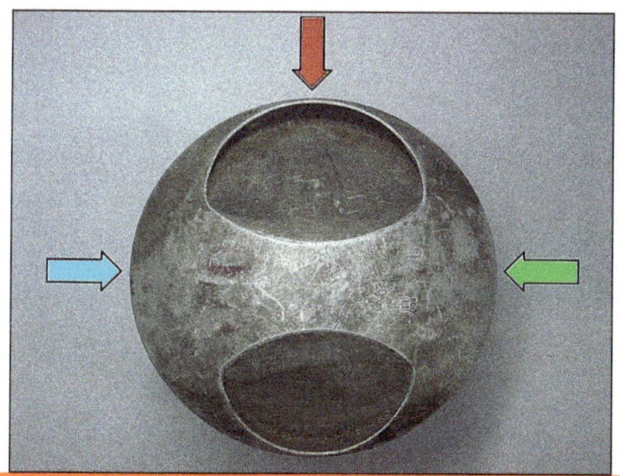

4-7 *The top two compression ring gaps should be oriented 180° from each other (blue and green arrows). This will help to achieve maximum compression. The oil ring should be rotated so that the gap faces the top of the piston (red arrow). This is done to prevent excess oil from leaking past this gap when the engine is not running.*

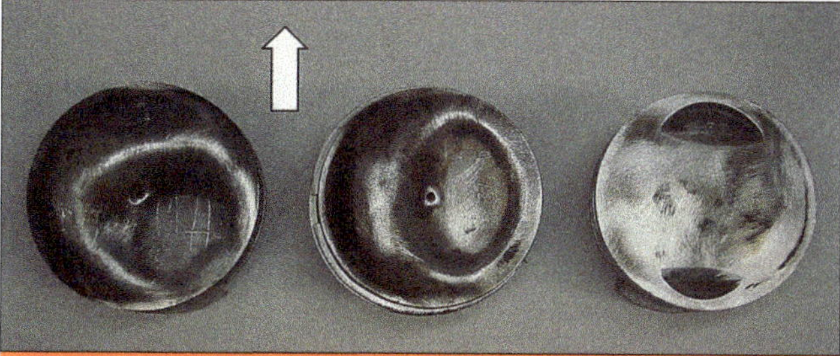

4-8 *It's very important to install the pistons and cylinders in their correct orientation. The cylinders must be installed with their longer fins facing down, toward the bottom of the engine. CIS (1973 1/2 -83 middle) and Motronic (1984-89, left) pistons must be installed with their large domes facing upward and off to the left of the piston. Earlier pistons (right) must be installed with the larger valve indentation (for the intake valve) facing upward.*

Install the larger oil seal ring first. This is the more complicated ring with the internal spring. Install this inside spring expander in the ring before you install it on the piston. Because of the very thin outer structure of the ring, this is also the easiest one to break (see Figure 4-4). Start the installation by expanding the ring so that it can just reach over the crown of the piston. Gently slide the ring down the piston, while expanding it with your fingers. Make sure that you don't scratch the side of the piston with the ring, but don't expand it too much that it snaps. Do this very slowly and very carefully. Double-check the orientation of the ring to make sure that it is facing the right direction. Carefully snap the ring into its ring groove. Rotate the ring around the piston and confirm that it is correctly installed in the ring groove. This process is shown in Figure 4-5. Repeat the process for the two upper compression rings. Install all the rings on all your pistons at the same time. When you are finished, carefully inspect all of the rings for cracks or breaks. The proper installation of the rings is shown in Figure 4-6.

After you have installed the rings on all your pistons, rotate them so that they are oriented correctly. The gaps in the two compression rings should be located roughly opposite from each other on the piston, and not lined up with the piston wrist pin. The oil seal ring should be oriented with its gap facing up toward the top of the engine. This correct orientation is shown in Figure 4-7. The top of the piston has the larger valve relief cutout for the intake valve. On CIS and Motronic engines, the large dome of the piston is located toward the left if you are looking straight at the dome. Refer to Figure 4-8 for more details. Rotating the rings in this manner is done to minimize the oil that collects at the bottom of the cylinder from leaking through the gap. The orientation of these rings need not be precise, as it will change with time as vibration from the engine rotates them around.

PISTON INSTALLATION

Now it's time for the difficult part. You must take special care and consideration during this step to avoid breaking one of your rings. Using a good-quality ring-compressor like the one shown in Figure 4-9 will help safeguard against broken rings. The worst-case scenario is that you break a ring and don't even realize it. On one engine that I rebuilt a few years ago, I had difficulty getting one piston to fit in its cylinder. I encountered some resistance and then, all of a sudden, the piston slipped in. Seeing how this piston had behaved differently from the other five, and not wanting to take any chances, I removed the piston and discovered a broken oil ring, which is shown in Figure 4-10. If I had not investigated the situation, then it would have meant a complete teardown and rebuild in the very near future.

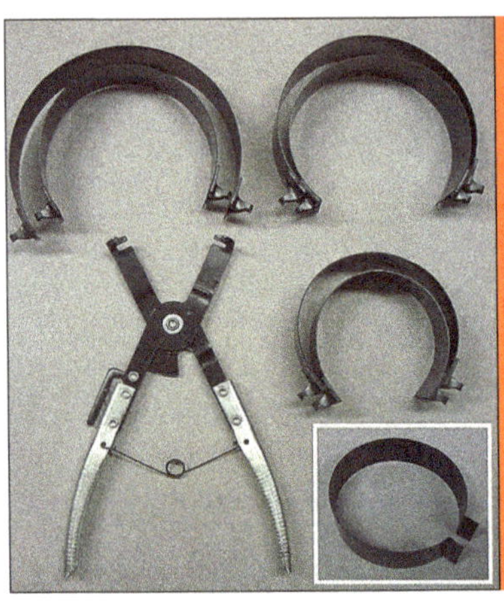

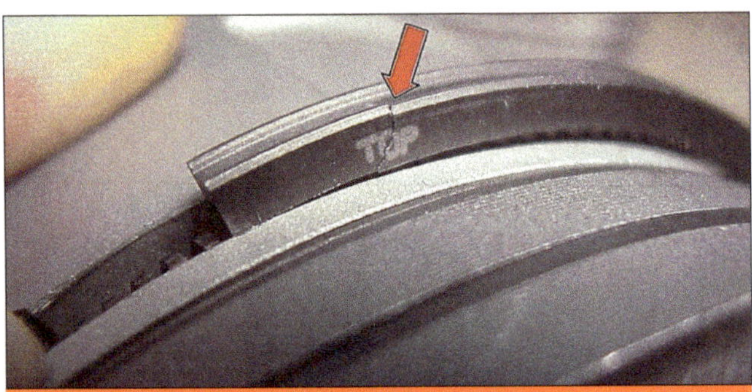

4-9 *The process of installing the pistons in the cylinders is so tricky that you want to make sure that you use the proper tool here. Cheap ring compressors (shown in photo inset) may cost only a few dollars; however, the risks involved with using them outweigh any cost savings. I recommend that you spend the $25 to $35 and purchase a good-quality ring compressor like the one shown here.*

4-10 *This is what happens when an oil ring catches on the side of the cylinder. This ring was broken without my knowledge. Because I had difficulty getting the piston into the cylinder, I decided to pull it out and check it—just to make sure. Sure enough, the ring was broken, and would have resulted in a costly teardown of the engine if I hadn't inspected it when I did. What's the lesson here? Check your rings if you think that one wasn't installed properly—it might have broken during the process.*

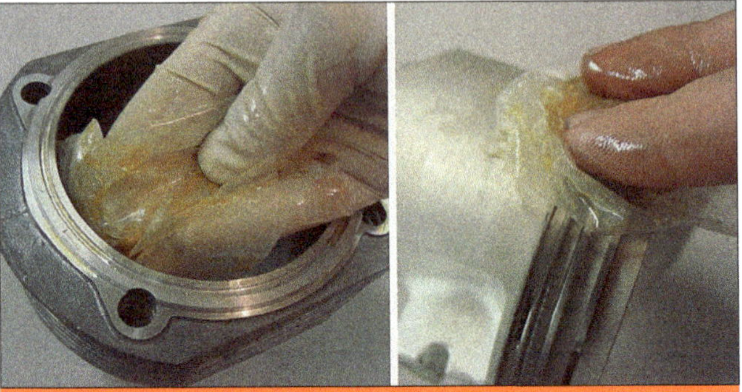

4-11 *Lightly coat the inside of the cylinders with motor oil prior to installing the pistons. Also liberally coat the rings. This will help you to install the pistons in the cylinders, and will help reduce the chances of breaking a ring.*

4-12 *This is the tricky part—carefully compress the rings and press the piston down into the cylinder. Confirm that the cylinder is oriented properly before you install the piston. If you encounter any resistance, stop what you are doing and check the rings to see if any are caught on the edge of the cylinder.*

4-13 *This is what happens if the ring slips out of the ring compressor tool. It will get caught on the edge of the cylinder, as shown by the red arrow. This can be caused by letting the ring compressor rise off of the base of the cylinder. Repeated pushing on the piston in this orientation will most certainly result in a broken ring. This ring is a compression ring, and will take quite a bit more force to break than the oil seal rings. If you encounter any resistance during the installation process, stop and check to make sure that the rings are properly compressed.*

Begin by liberally coating the inside of the cylinder with 20W-50 motor oil. Spread the oil around with your fingers (wear your powder-free latex gloves) and coat the entire inside of the cylinder. Then coat all three rings with a liberal supply of motor oil as well. This is detailed in Figure 4-11. Make sure that you use new, clean oil, and that your assembly environment is free of dust and debris.

Making sure that you have the correct cylinder matched with its proper piston, place the cylinder face down on your clean work surface. Place the piston in the cylinder, and make sure the piston and cylinder both are placed in their proper orientation. On a balanced engine, piston pins are matched to their respective pistons—don't mix them up while you're working on them. Cylinders on the 911 engine must be oriented with their longer fins facing the bottom of the engine. Pistons must be installed with the correct side facing up. On the CIS and Motronic engines, the flat surface of the piston faces right. On early pistons, the larger relief cutout in the piston is aligned with the intake valve, and must be pointed up. Refer to Figure 4-8 again for greater clarity on which way the piston should be oriented. Failing to install the pistons properly in their correct orientation can result in the valves hitting the pistons when the engine turns over.

Now you will install the pistons in the cylinders. Place a small dab of assembly lube on the piston skirts. Using your ring compressor, gently squeeze the piston so that the rings are compressed to the same outside diameter as the piston. Be careful that you don't catch a corner of the ring on one of the grooves as you are compressing it. Don't let the gap on the piston ring compressor line up with any of the ring gaps—this can pinch the ring when you're compressing it. With the rings compressed, gently push the piston into the cylinder. Make sure the piston is oriented so that the top of the piston is inserted into the top of the cylinder. Also be sure to keep the ring compressor seated perfectly on the base of the cylinder while you are pushing the piston. Push the piston into the cylinder only so far so that you can still insert the piston pin into the side of the piston later on. This process is detailed in Figure 4-12.

If you encounter any resistance, STOP! It is very easy to have a ring snap out from underneath the compressor and get caught on the top side of the piston, as is shown in Figure 4-13. It is important to note that you cannot easily see this happen, as the ring compressor is blocking your view. If you encounter any resistance, then slowly remove the piston from the cylinder and try again. This resistance is caused when the ring compressor accidentally gets lifted off of the bottom surface of the cylinder.

Install all of the pistons in their cylinders all at the same time on your workbench. Work slowly and carefully. If one piston seems to put up more of a fight than a previous one, stop and investigate. Chances are that something is wrong, and you might break a ring if you continue to proceed.

DECK HEIGHT CHECK

In this section, you will check the deck height of the piston with respect to the cylinder. The deck height is defined as the distance from the flat top of the piston to the top of the cylinder when the piston is at top dead center (TDC). See Figure 4-14 for a diagram of the deck height measurement.

As discussed in Chapter Four, machining the case, fly cutting the heads or the addition of different pistons and cylinders can lead to a tolerance buildup that brings the pistons closer to the heads. When you check the deck height, you are measuring this tolerance buildup, and will compensate for it by using thicker shims at the cylinder base. This is a necessary step for rebuilding your engine, and should not be skipped, especially if you are rebuilding an engine with a magnesium case. The deck height is a particularly important measurement for any magnesium case that has any significant machining performed on it—especially the 2.7-liter engines. In severe cases, an incorrectly set deck height can cause the pistons to impact the heads.

The measurement of deck height is vital to ensuring that your pistons will not impact the valves or cylinder head. This measurement, combined with the piston-to-valve clearance measurement performed in Section 8, will guarantee you that your engine will not have any interference problems.

There are two different methods for checking deck height. The first method is quite easy and involves a simple measurement. However, you can only easily measure the deck height of flat-topped pistons. The second method uses a technique pioneered by Competition Engineering and is useful for measuring deck height on high-domed pistons.

Begin the procedure for deck height measurement by temporarily installing one of the piston/cylinder assemblies on the engine. Achieving the proper deck height requires that you install one or more copper cylinder base gaskets. Each of the copper gaskets in your gasket kit is 0.25mm

4-15 An often-overlooked step is the installation of the cylinder base gasket. Place the base gaskets on all of the cylinders before you install the piston pins.

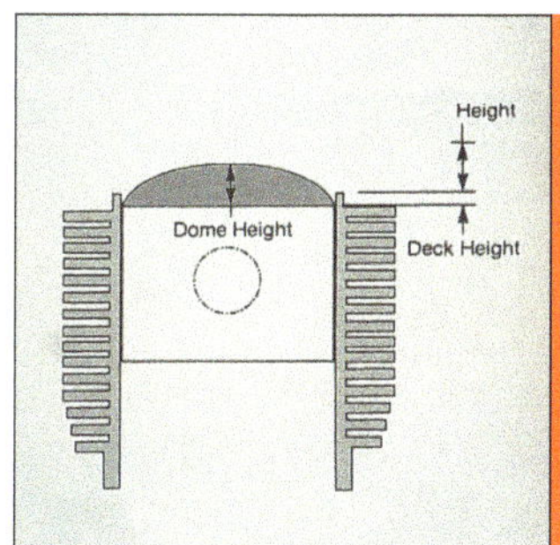

4-14 This photo shows where the deck height measurement is made with respect to the piston and cylinder. The deck height is defined as the difference between the flat top of the piston and the top of the cylinder. This distance is easy to measure on flat-top pistons, but can be more difficult with high-domed pistons. B. Anderson

4-16 Don't forget to prelube the rod bushing before you install the piston pin. Apply assembly lube to the bushing only—don't apply any to the piston pin itself. If you place it on the piston pin, it will get smeared away when you install it in the camshaft housing.

4-17 *Install the circlip on the right side of the piston, while the assembly is located on your workbench. I recommend that you install them all at the same time so that you don't forget later on. Use the needle-nose pliers and small screwdriver to maneuver the circlip into its groove. Also insert the piston pin temporarily to use as a backstop for the circlip. Don't bend the circlips too much as you can permanently deform them.*

4-18 *Place the piston/cylinder assembly on the engine and line it up with the hole in the rod. This step seems like it takes about three or four hands, but it can be done with some careful maneuvering.*

4-19 *Line up the piston with the bushing in the rod. When the piston pin is recessed into the piston, use the plastic end of a small screwdriver, and gently tap it with a small hammer until it presses up against the circlip on the opposite side.*

thick. You will need to use multiple gaskets to achieve the proper deck height if your case was machined or if your heads were cut. For example, if your heads were fly cut 0.25mm then you will need to start with two copper gaskets on the base of the cylinder instead of one.

Place one of the copper cylinder base gaskets onto the base of the cylinder, as shown in Figure 4-15. Place a bit of assembly lube on the rod bushing before you install the piston (Figure 4-16). You begin the deck height measurement by installing a piston/cylinder assembly on rod number one. This is the one located toward the left rear of the engine. Using the nut on the crankshaft pulley, carefully rotate the crankshaft until the top of the number one rod is at its highest point (TDC). Install one of the wrist pin circlips in the right side of the piston, as shown in Figure 4-17. Temporarily install the piston pin in the piston when you try to install the circlip. Having the piston pin as a backstop for the circlip eases installation. With the circlip installed, push the wrist pin out so that it is only inserted about a half-inch into the left side of the piston.

Carefully clean the inside cylinder spigots on the engine case, including the lip that the cylinder sits on. Looking in from the side, line up the rod bushing with the wrist pin that is installed halfway into the piston (Figure 4-18). When they are lined up, gently tap the wrist pin into the rod using a plastic hammer or the handle end of a screwdriver, until it touches the circlip on the opposite side (Figure 4-19). Once you have the piston pin in place, gently push the cylinder down until it lightly compresses the copper gasket against the case and seats in the case spigot.

For flat-top pistons, the measurement is easy. Take a vernier caliper and place it against the top of the piston and the side of the cylinder, as shown in Figure 4-20. You are directly measuring the distance from the top of the piston to the top of the cylinder wall. On 2.0-liter engines, there is a thick gasket that is also included in the measurement process. The 2.2-liter and later engines do not have a gasket that adds any thickness between the cylinder and the head.

To check the deck height on high-domed pistons, I like to use a method pioneered by Walt Watson at Competition Engineering. Walt uses a preassembly technique that accu-

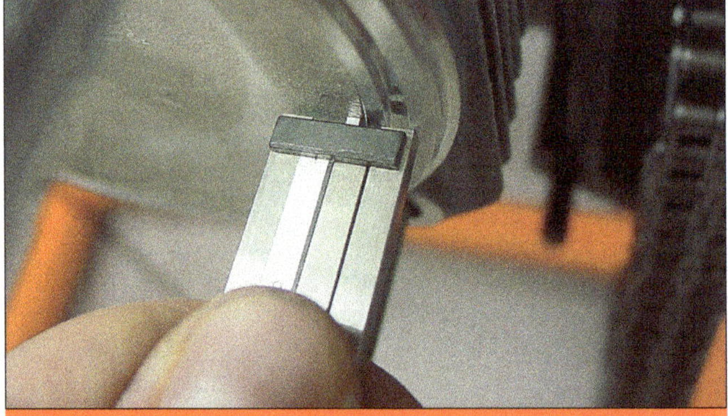

4-20 *A simple vernier caliper can be used to measure the deck height on pistons with flat tops. These include the early "T" pistons, and the CIS and Motronic pistons. The deck height on most high-domed pistons cannot be measured in this particular manner; you need to use the solder method.*

rately measures the deck height while the cylinder is bolted to the head. Measuring the deck height in this manner compensates for changes in dimensions that may have occurred when the heads were fly cut and resurfaced. This method technically measures not the deck height, but the height to the top of the combustion chamber.

Walt's technique involves the use of acid-core solder to record measurements in the combustion chamber. The reason you want to use acid core solder instead of a softer material like clay is that the clay is typically too soft to yield an accurate measurement. Acid core solder is large in diameter (about 3mm), which allows you to make a wide range of measurements. It is also widely available at hardware stores. Once the inner acid core of the solder is removed, it becomes hollow and crushes quite easily, yet maintains its shape for accurate measurement.

Using the pulley nut, turn the crankshaft until the piston is positioned just a few millimeters below top dead center. Clip two pieces of solder, each about 1 inch long. Use a sharp blade to cut both ends, as you want them to be perfectly square, not pinched. Remove the acid flux that is contained in the inside of the solder core by pushing it out with a small piece of wire or by using some compressed air. Make sure that you wear safety glasses, as the flux acid core is indeed acid and will burn your eyes if it gets into them.

Using a small dab of the Curil-T sealant to hold them in place, orient the pieces of solder on your piston as shown in Figure 4-21. They should be placed parallel to the crankshaft, avoiding any valve pockets. This will help avoid any cocking of the piston in the cylinder. The ends of the solder pieces should touch the inside of the cylinder walls. On high-domed pistons, you may have to bend the solder to fit the profile so that it doesn't roll off when it's crushed.

Now, take one of your reconditioned cylinder heads and install it on the top of the piston. If your engine uses a cylinder-to-head gasket (all 2.0-liter engines), install this as well, as it will affect the deck height measurement. Use the four barrel nuts to tighten the head to the cylinder. Install the thick washers underneath the barrel nuts; otherwise the stud will poke up out of the barrel nut and will be difficult to tighten with your 10mm Allen tool. Tighten them down to about 32 Nm (23.5 ft-lbs.) as is shown in Figure 4-22.

With the heads firmly attached to the cylinder, turn the crankshaft so that it reaches past TDC and crushes the solder. The solder should not require too much effort to crush. Competition Engineering has used this technique for more

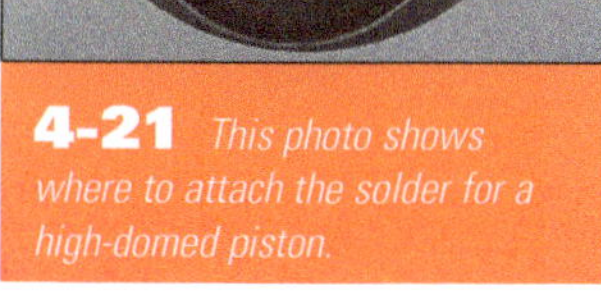

4-21 *This photo shows where to attach the solder for a high-domed piston.*

4-22 *This photo shows the cylinder head attached to one cylinder for the sole purpose of checking the deck height. Make sure that you use the cylinder head stud washers, and tighten them down to 32 Nm (23.5 ft-lbs.).*

than 15 years to measure deck height and has never damaged a piston. However, if you feel any resistance—don't push it. If you have 0.050-inch deck height or less, there is potential to damage your (expensive) piston. Instead, simply remove the piston/cylinder assembly and add another 0.25mm thick copper gasket to the base of the cylinder.

After you have crushed the solder, remove the cylinder head and pluck off the solder pieces. They should still be attached to the piston. Using a vernier caliper, measure the thinnest portion of the solder, as shown in Figure 4-23. This thickness will be the deck height. If the two solder pieces give slightly different measurements, it means that the piston may have been slightly cocked in the cylinder. Take the average of the two measurements as your deck height measurement.

So what do you do with this measurement? On stock Porsche engines, Competition Engineering recommends a deck height between 1.25mm and 1.5mm. For high-performance engines, you can run a thinner deck height as tight as 1mm if you are trying to achieve high compression. So, if you measure 0.45mm for your deck height, you will need to add a second 1mm shim that will give you a total deck

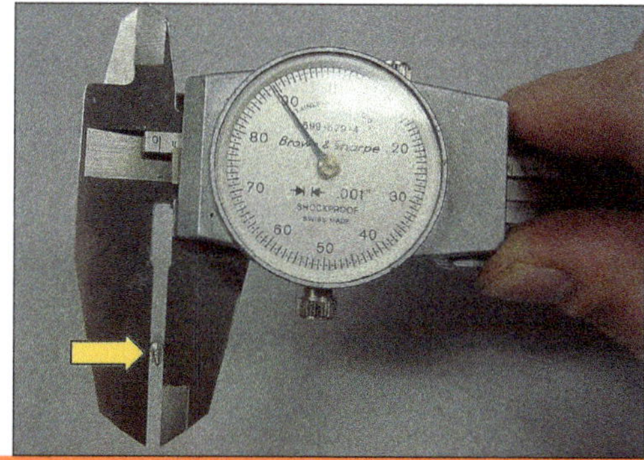

4-23 *The thickness of the crushed solder will give you the deck height for the cylinder. Perform the measurement with a vernier caliper, and measure the thinnest spot on the solder (yellow arrow). If the operation was performed correctly, this should be the tip of the solder that was closest to the cylinder wall.*

height of 1.45mm. For a bit more compression, you can remove the original 0.25mm shim and run a deck height of 1.3mm. Anything less than 1.3mm on a stock engine is pushing the tolerance limits. Keep in mind that these measurements are being performed when the engine is stone cold. When the 911 engine heats up, it can expand up to an eighth of an inch across the width of the entire engine. Keeping adequate clearance in your tolerances means that you will have a margin of safety when the engine is warm. When installing big bore kits, it's very important to check the deck height. Larger pistons need increased clearance so that they won't accidentally impact the head. You may find that you need to chamfer or bevel the edge of the head where the cylinder mounts.

Theoretically, the cylinders, heads, and case should all be the same on both the left and right sides of the engine case. However, I always like to double-check the deck height on both sides of the engine. Repeat the entire deck height measurement process for cylinder number four, which is located in the rear right of the engine. This measurement should be very similar to the opposite side. If it's not, then you will have to compensate by using thicker cylinder base gaskets.

Some engine rebuilders like to stack shims underneath the cylinders, although I don't recommend this approach. Instead I recommend using one shim that has been machined to the proper thickness. You can purchase shims of various thicknesses from most Porsche performance shops for just about any displacement piston. The problem with using these shims is that you don't know which size you will need until you perform the deck height measurement. So, you will have to wait a day or two for the shims to arrive before you can proceed to the next step and assemble all of your pistons and cylinders on the engine. When you get your new shims/gaskets, install them on the cylinder and perform the measurement one more time, just to make sure that everything fits.

On some high-performance engines, you may want to "cc" the head and cylinder. This process effectively measures the combustion chamber volume. This is important in high-compression engines because you want all of the cylinders to be exactly the same size and compression. If one cylinder is slightly smaller than another, you may risk detonation when the engine is running. For detailed procedures and formulas on measuring and checking the combustion chamber size, see the official web site for this book, or see the *Porsche 911 Performance Handbook* by Bruce Anderson. In general, the compression ratio (CR) of all six combustion chambers should be within .1 point of each other. Typically, variances in CR are caused by valve seats being recessed too deeply into the head. For most stock engines, it is not necessary to measure the combustion chamber size. If your machine shop has properly machined your case, you should have no problems—the

chamber sizes on each side of the engine should all be exactly the same. The only differences that you may encounter are variations from side to side. These can be compensated for by your choice of cylinder base gaskets.

CYLINDER ASSEMBLY INSTALLATION

When you are finished, it's time to install the cylinder assemblies onto the rods. Start on the left side of the engine, with piston number one. This is the cylinder closest to the distributor. Using a liberal amount of assembly lube, coat the inside of the wrist pin bushing located on the rod.

Install one of the piston circlips in the right side of the piston. For the number one piston, this is the side that is closest to the rear of the engine. Install the piston on the rod in the same manner as when you performed the deck height measurement. It's important to follow the order of assembly here for installing the pistons, otherwise you may have difficulty installing the circlips on the pistons. For example, you cannot install cylinders number one and number three without installing number two first, as you cannot reach the circlips to attach piston number two to its rod. I recommend that you install all six circlips in the right side of all six cylinders at the same time, so that you won't forget this step later on.

Now, take a sheet of plastic (I like to use clear plastic sandwich wrap) and cover the openings in the cases for cylinders four, five, and six, as shown in Figure 4-24. The reason for this is that you don't want to accidentally drop the wrist pin circlip down into your engine while you're installing it. Another solution is to rotate the engine so that the piston is parallel to the ground. Either way, dropping a circlip into your engine can result in many frustrating

4-24 *Take some of your plastic sandwich wrap and cover all of the cylinder spigots. This is to prevent the circlip from flying into the recesses of the engine. Don't skip this step, as you will soon find that precaution is necessary. There is a very good chance that you will drop the circlip while trying to install it.*

4-25 *Shown here is the completed cylinder installation. The cylinder can now be held in place using the official Porsche tool (P140), or you can create a makeshift holder out of some old half-inch sockets and an extra head stud nut (inset). You only need one of these on each cylinder—tighten them only finger-tight.*

hours of hunting and fishing as there are plenty of places for it to hide. Even if you tilt the engine so that gravity works in your favor, the springy circlip can sometimes go flying into the recesses of the engine case. Use the plastic covering and be on the safe side. Also wear safety glasses when installing these spring circlips.

Install the circlip for piston number one before installing cylinder number two. Otherwise you will not be able to reach it because cylinder number two will be blocking your path. Once you have the circlip in place, gently push the

cylinder down until it lightly compresses the copper gasket against the case. There is a set of special Porsche tools (P140) to hold the cylinder in place while you turn the engine over; however, you can simply use an extra half-inch socket and head stud nut to achieve the same results (Figure 4-25). Affix the socket and nut to hold the cylinder in place—you only need to hand-tighten the nuts.

With cylinder number one installed, repeat the process for number two and number three, in that order, as shown in Figure 4-26. Install the right-side circlip while the piston is on your workbench—you won't be able to reach it on the engine. Don't forget the copper base gaskets, and also be sure to place the first circlip on the right side of both pistons. When you're finished with each cylinder, clamp it down with the socket and head stud nut combination or the P140 tool mentioned previously.

When the left side is completed, rotate the engine on the stand over to the opposite side and repeat the installation process, beginning this time with cylinder number six. As with the left side, install the right-side circlip first. Work toward the rear of the engine, installing cylinder number four last. Tie all of the cylinders down with the P140 tool or your makeshift socket-and-head-stud-nut combination.

With all of the pistons and cylinders installed on the right side, alternate rotating the crank so that each piston is at its bottom most position (BDC). Using the clean-room wipes, carefully wipe off all of the excess oil from the walls of the cylinders (Figure 4-27). Rotate the engine and repeat this several times for each of the cylinders to remove as much of the oil as possible. Wiping off this oil will help the rings seat when you break in the engine.

4-26 *Use this diagram as a guide for installing the cylinders. If you install them out of order, you may find yourself having to remove one cylinder in order to install the one next to it. Installing them in this order will ensure that you will have adequate access to install all of the circlips.*

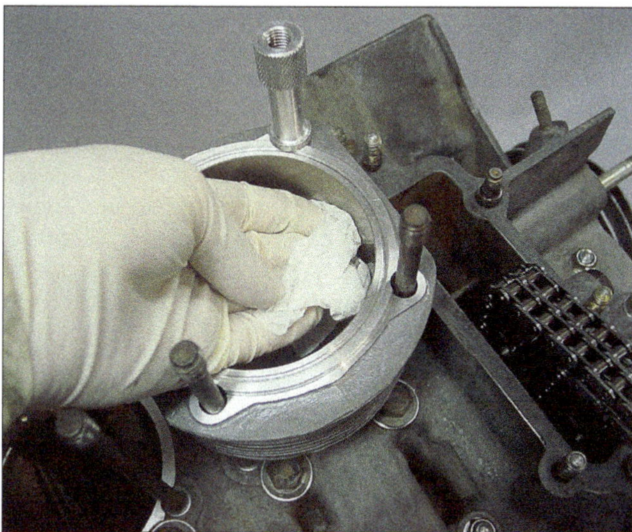

4-27 *With all of the cylinders installed and secured on one side of the engine, rotate the crankshaft, and clean out the excess motor oil from each cylinder. Repeat this procedure a few times so that you can remove as much excess oil as possible.*

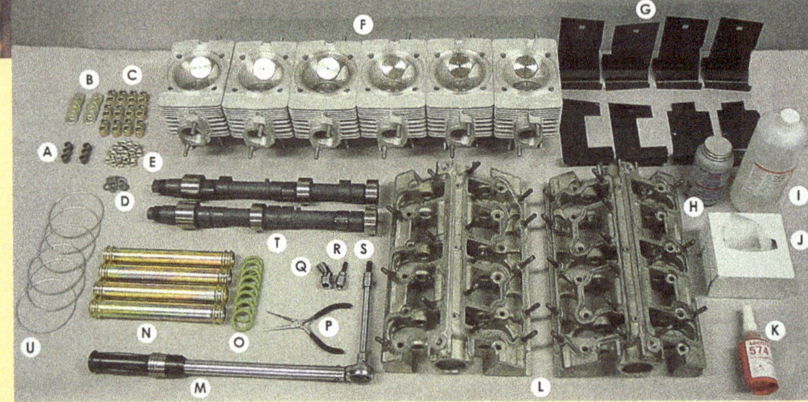

TOOLS: 10mm **(R)** and 8mm **(S)** Allen-head tool, 13mm socket and torque wrench **(Q/M)**, needle-nose pliers **(P)**

MATERIALS: Loctite 574 sealant **(K)**, motor oil, Optimoly HT lube or anti-seize compound **(H)**, Isopropyl alcohol **(I)**, clean-room wipes **(J)**

PARTS: Engine cylinder sheet metal **(G)**, 4 oil return tubes **(N)**, 6 cylinder heads **(F)**, 2 camshaft housings **(L)**, camshafts (left and right) **(T)**.

HARDWARE: 24 Cylinder head washers **(B)**, 6 camshaft housing mounting barrel nuts **(A)**, 24 cylinder head mounting nuts **(C)**, qty 30 13mm nuts **(E)**, 30 thin cylinder head mounting washers **(D)**.

SEALS: 8 Oil return tube o-rings **(O)**, 6 cylinder to head gaskets **(U)**.

TIME: 8 hours.

TIP: Thoroughly clean the surfaces where the heads and the camshaft housings mate, as the engine can easily leak at this junction

ENGINE ASSEMBLY

PRE-ASSEMBLE OR NOT?

Before you dive into this section, you need to consider the next measurement that needs to be made on the 911 engine. You will need to check the valve-to-piston clearance at top dead center. The only way to measure this distance accurately is to pre-assemble the entire engine without using any sealants, set the cam timing, and then take the measurement while you turn the crankshaft. Then you will have to tear the engine back down to the cylinders and reassemble it using all the proper gaskets and sealants. Obviously this takes quite a bit of time.

So the question is, when can this preassembly be avoided, and when will the engine have a good chance of passing the valve-to-piston clearance test? If you are designing a new engine or are changing any major components in the engine (crank/rods, heads, pistons, cylinders, camshafts), then I suggest you perform the pre-assembly operation and check the valve-to-piston clearance. On stock engines that have not been modified, you will have a good chance of finding that this clearance value is large enough to continue.

The piston-to-valve clearance is a function of the deck height clearance, the piston valve reliefs, the camshaft timing, the total camshaft lift, the size of the valves, and the amount of resurfacing that has been done to the heads. It is affected by changing the copper shims/gasket under the cylinders. If the deck height is set correctly, and you haven't made any major changes to the pistons, case, or heads, then it is unlikely you will have a problem with your pistons coming too close to your valves. Of course, all bets are off if you are using custom pistons with a custom-grind camshaft. I would definitely recommend a dry assembly and pre-check of all the clearances if you are going to be rebuilding an engine that could be dubbed "experimental."

So what happens if you decide to seal everything up during the next three steps, and you find that your piston-to-cylinder clearance is too small? Then you will have to tear down the engine completely, and clean all of your sealant off of your camshaft housings and heads. Not a great prospect, but also not the end of the world.

If you do decide to perform the pre-assembly check, then proceed through the next three sections without applying any case sealant to the camshaft housings, and don't use any assembly lube on the rocker shafts as it will get very messy when you remove them. Torque all fasteners down to their specified values, and pre-assemble both sides of the engine. Perform the piston-to-cylinder head clearance test described in Section 8, and then tear the engine back down to the starting point of this section. Reassemble it, this time sealing and lubricating all of the surfaces according to the instructions.

OVERVIEW

In this section, you will install the heads and the camshaft housings. It's important to work quickly when you apply the sealant so that you torque down the heads while the sealant is still curing. Plan ahead and make sure that you have plenty of time to complete the tasks—it takes about 45 minutes for the sealant to cure. Start with the right side of the engine (cylinders 4-6) and then move on to the left side. Both sides of the engine need not be assembled in the same evening; however, I recommend it if time permits.

SHEET METAL INSTALLATION

Start this section by working on the right side of the engine. With all of the pistons and cylinders installed, you can install the four sheet metal baffles that channel airflow around the cylinders. Install them according to the orientation displayed in Figure 5-2, taking care not to reverse and install them backwards. Incorrectly installed sheet metal can lead to inadequate cooling and seized pistons. You must correctly install the sheet metal now, as you will not be able to fit it around the cylinders after you have installed the camshaft housings and oil return tubes. If you haven't done so already, now would be a good time to modify your sheet metal according to the 1977 Porsche factory upgrade. See Section 2 of Chapter 4 for more details on this modification.

On 3.0-liter and later aluminum block engines, there is an additional sheet metal baffle that fits on top of each bank of cylinders, right where the top row of head studs enter the case. This baffle needs to be in place before you install the spring clips that hold the four baffles that fit between the cylinders. It's also important to note that the 3.0/3.2/3.3 cylinder sheet metal is different and non-compatible with the earlier engines.

PREPARATION, CLEANING & INSPECTION

With the sheet metal in place, remove each of the temporary cylinder hold-down nuts and sockets. Take each of the head nuts and washers and lightly lubricate them with Optimoly HT or anti-seize compound. Also lubricate the threads of the head

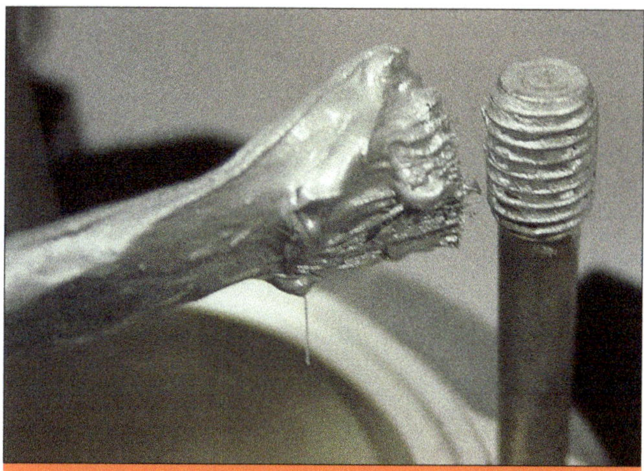

5-3 *Use Optimoly HT lube, or anti-seize compound on the head studs and washers. Lubricating the studs, nuts and washers is a factory-recommended procedure that helps to ensure that the proper torque is being applied to the head studs.*

5-2 *This photo shows the four baffles that fit between the cylinders and are required for proper air cooling. The photo on the bottom shows the baffle that is installed on the 3.0-liter and later engines.*

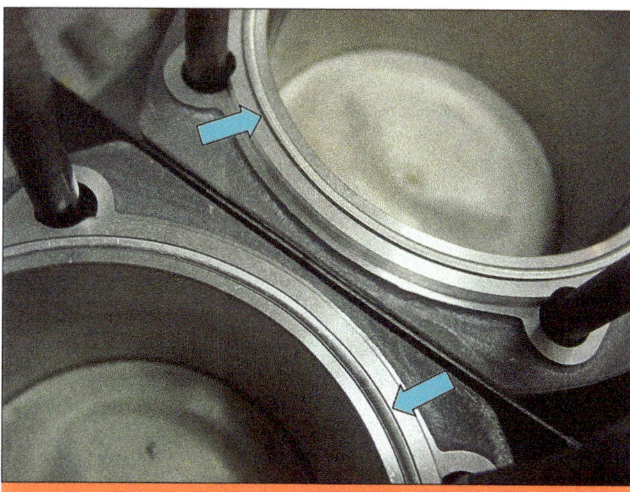

5-4 *Install the cylinder-to-head gasket in the small groove that is located in the top of the cylinder. The 2.0-liter engines use a gasket that actually sits between the entire cylinder and head and doesn't use a groove.*

151

studs, as shown in Figure 5-3. This is done to eliminate as much friction in the threads as possible and to ensure that the nuts are torqued as closely as possible to their desired values.

At this time, remove the cylinder-to-head sealing ring from your gasket kit and place it on the top of the cylinder, as shown in Figure 5-4. The 3.2-liter and 3.3-liter Turbo engines do not have cylinder head gaskets. Take three of your previously prepared cylinder heads and check that you have not missed anything up to this point. Here is a brief checklist to help you ensure that you haven't made any mistakes up to this point:

- Pistons installed in their correct orientation.
- Cylinders installed with long fins down.
- Cylinder copper base gasket installed.
- Cylinder head gasket installed.
- Sheet metal baffles installed between cylinders.
- Sheet metal baffles above cylinders (3.0L and later).
- Deck height measurement checked and adjusted.

At this time, you will want to inspect and clean your heads and your camshaft housings. Other than the case parting line surface, I cannot think of another surface on the 911 engine that is more susceptible to dirt and debris than the surface between the camshaft housings and the heads. Like the case parting line interface, the surfaces between the camshaft housings and the heads do not use a gasket. You

5-5 *The mating surface between the heads and the camshaft housings does not use a gasket. Therefore the cleanliness of this surface is essential to assembling a leak-free engine. Clean all residue off of the surfaces before applying any sealant.*

must make sure that this surface is 100 percent clean on both the heads and the camshaft housings. Clean them, and then clean them again. Use brake and carburetor cleaner first and then use isopropyl alcohol. Any traces of old sealant must be cleaned and removed in a manner similar to how you cleaned the case parting line. This is a delicate bond between these two, and if improperly prepared it is very susceptible to leaks. If the engine leaks at the junction between the heads and the camshaft housings, then your only recourse is to tear down the entire top of the engine to reseal it. Needless to say, you want to pay attention to detail here, and be as clean as humanly possible. The cleanliness of your camshaft housings should resemble the ones shown in Figure 5-5.

Clean the inside of the combustion chamber and the opposite side of the head. Use your clean-room wipes and isopropyl alcohol on the valve stems, springs and seals. Make sure that all debris from the machining process has been removed. Clean the chambers inside the camshaft housings where the rockers sit. Double check the cleanliness of each of the rocker arm bores, and pay special attention to the bearing surfaces that the camshafts ride on. Any dirt here will easily scratch and score the soft aluminum. Also spray brake cleaner into the spray bars in the camshaft housings and make sure that the squirter holes are not clogged.

CYLINDER TO CASE GASKET SEALANT

For your final installation, I recommend coating both sides of the cylinder base copper gasket with the Loctite 574 case sealant. This will create a nice, oil-tight seal with the case and help to prevent leaks. The Loctite 574 on the cylinder base gaskets is not absolutely required, but it certainly cannot hurt. On each side of the case, remove your cylinder hold-down tools, and slide each cylinder up about one-and-a-half inches. Then reach in and coat each side of the copper gasket with the Loctite 574 sealant. Press each

5-6 *Install the heads on the cylinders in preparation for attaching the camshaft housings. Don't tighten the head studs firmly—lightly tighten them up at this point.*

of the cylinders back down into the case, crushing the gasket. At this point, the 574 has begun to cure, so you need to work quickly through the remaining sections so that you get all of the heads and camshaft housings attached for this side of the engine. Plan ahead—don't put the sealant on the copper gaskets until all of the heads and the camshaft housing are cleaned and ready for installation.

CYLINDER HEAD INSTALLATION

With your parts fully cleaned, place each of the three cylinder heads on top of the cylinders, as shown in Figure 5-6. Install them with the intake port on top. The intake valve for the intake port is larger than the exhaust valve. Lightly lubricate the washers before you put them on the studs. Place all the washers around a long screwdriver and use it as a guide to drop a washer on each of the head studs. Use only the specified washer for the head stud, as they are manufactured to a specific thickness. Using the same screwdriver technique, carefully place a head stud barrel nut on each of the studs and use a 10mm Allen-head tool to lightly tighten them. At this point, you want to tighten these nuts only hand-tight. Do not torque them down. The heads should come back from the machine shop completely assembled and ready to install. If you wish to disassemble the heads and check the tolerances and spring heights, see the instructions at this book's official web site: http://www.101projects.com.

OIL RETURN TUBES

Grab two of your new oil return tubes and place new o-rings on the end of each one. Lightly lubricate the o-rings with motor oil before you install them, as shown in Figure 5-7. This will help them to seal in the engine case and camshaft housings. Press the tubes into their bores in the engine case, gently using a rubber mallet if they offer significant resistance. When installed, they should stick upward of their own accord, as displayed in Figure 5-8.

At this point, perform one last inspection on the camshaft housing. Although the camshaft housings themselves are technically interchangeable, the plugs, adapters, and hardware on each one makes them non-symmetrical. Each camshaft housing will always have the open bore for the camshaft facing the rear of the engine. Make sure that you have the correct side camshaft housing cleaned and ready for installation. Clean the mating surfaces one more time with clean-room wipes and isopropyl alcohol. Make sure once again that any previous case sealant is completely removed.

CAMSHAFT HOUSING INSTALLATION

Once you are confident that your camshaft housings and your heads are spotlessly clean, take your bottle of Loctite 574 and spread a thick bead on all surfaces where the

5-7 Prelube the oil return tube o-rings before you install them on the tubes. This will help you insert them into the case, and also help them seal with the case and the camshaft housings.

5-8 Shown here are the oil return tubes installed in the base of the case. Make sure that they are firmly seated—tap them in with a rubber mallet if necessary.

heads and the camshaft housings mate. Refer to Figure 5-9 for the locations of these specific areas. Spread the sealant

5-9 Shown here are all the surfaces that should have the sealant applied to them. Use an acid brush, and make sure that you don't lose any paintbrush bristles in the sealant, or you might create an oil leak. Again, make sure that this mating surface is 100% clean, and apply the sealant only to the camshaft housing surface.

evenly with an acid brush, watching for any bristles that may happen to fall off into the sealant. Make sure that every surface and mounting hole is surrounded by the sealant. Apply the sealant to the surface of the camshaft housings only, not the surface of the heads. Careful attention to detail during this step will help prevent oil leaks.

With the Loctite 574 evenly spread, take the camshaft housing and place it on top of the heads. You will need to adjust the oil return tubes so they mate with their respective holes in the camshaft housing. There are dowel pins located inside the heads that must mate with the camshaft housings—you may have to jiggle the heads slightly in order to get them to mate properly

in the camshaft housing. Stuff a rag or paper towel into the ends of the oil return tubes—small nuts and washers have a habit of finding their way down the tubes and into the case when dropped. Install and torque down the fifteen M8 13mm nuts and the three M8 8mm barrel nuts that attach the heads to the camshaft housing, shown in Figure 5-10. Torque the nuts in a crisscross pattern, as shown in Figure 5-11. Start with the low-torque value listed in Appendix A, and then repeat the pattern at the full-torque value.

Now tighten down the barrel nuts on the head studs. Use the 10mm Allen-head tool and follow the pattern shown in Figure 5-12 for tightening them down. Tighten them all to

5-10 Use the small 8mm barrel nuts where the camshaft housing sidewall clearance is too thin to fit a normal sized nut (orange arrow).

5-12 When you have torqued down the camshaft housings to the heads, use this diagram to torque down the entire assembly to the engine.

5-11 This photo clearly shows the torque down order for the camshaft housing bolts. Tightening the assembly in this crisscross pattern will ensure even tightening, and also a consistent bond with the surface of the heads underneath. Improper mating of this assembly can lead to messy oil leaks later.

75 percent of their final value, and then go back and repeat the process, tightening them to 100 percent of their final torque value. Do not exceed the final torque values for these fasteners. When the engine has been fully assembled and run for 1,000 miles, you will retorque the heads again.

When you have finished tightening the nuts, test-fit the right-side camshaft into the camshaft housing, as shown in Figure 5-13. If you look at this camshaft down its axis, the lobes will be spaced about 120 degrees apart. The lobes on the right-side camshaft are spaced more closely together in a V-shape. Refer to Figure 6-5 in the next section for more clarification. The camshaft should turn freely with minimal resistance. If the camshaft is unable to turn freely, it may indicate that the heads have been torqued unevenly. Loosen up the nuts and retighten them, slightly altering the pattern. Keep the same general pattern by starting in the middle, but begin with a different corner of each cylinder head stud. For example, if you started with the upper left hand corner of the center cylinder, then start now with the lower right, and then move across diagonally to the upper left. When finished, check the camshaft in the camshaft housings again.

With the right side of the engine completed with pistons, cylinders, heads, and camshaft housings, you can now move on to the left side. The procedure is nearly identical for the left side, with the only change being the use of the left-side camshaft and camshaft housing. If you have an engine with mechanical fuel injection, then you will need to install the pump gear seal on the rear of the camshaft. This seal is nearly identical to the pulley seal, and can be installed

5-13 *Check the rotation of the camshaft in the camshaft housings. If the heads were slightly cocked while they were torqued down, you will have difficulty turning the camshaft in the camshaft housings, or may not be able to insert it at all. If this happens, loosen everything up, and repeat the process again, slightly altering the torque-down pattern.*

simply by pushing it squarely into the rear of the camshaft housing. The seals for some of the specialized pumps on the Turbo engines are similar as well.

The engine is actually beginning to look like it did when you first took it apart! You're about halfway through the whole process, and you should be feeling very good about yourself and your accomplishments at this time. Figure 5-14 shows the completed assembly up to this point.

5-14 *Shown here is the engine with the camshaft housings and heads installed. It's finally beginning to look like a 911 engine again!*

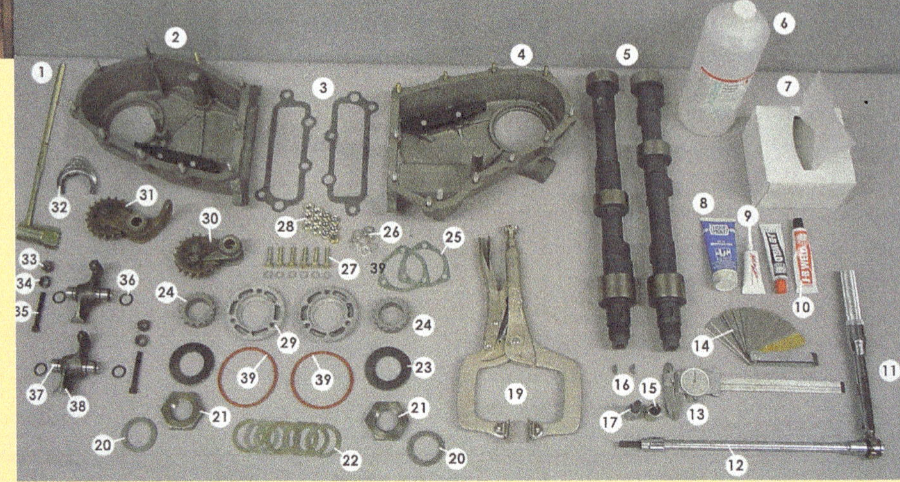

TOOLS: 13mm socket (15) and torque wrench (11), 3-ft. straightedge or sprocket alignment tool, vernier caliper (13), small dish or pot, c-clamp vise-grips (19), chain tensioner clamp tool, snap-ring pliers, 5mm Allen tool (17), 8mm Allen tool, 3/8" 12" long extension (12), small hammer, feeler gauge (14), P202 camshaft tool (1) & 46mm crowfoot wrench (32) (up thru 1980 1/2) or P9191 (1980 1/2 and later.)

MATERIALS: Assembly lube (8/9), motor oil, JB Weld (10), cotton swabs, isopropyl alcohol (6), clean-room wipes (7).

PARTS: Camshaft sprocket shims (22), (left and right) camshafts (5), 2 camshaft cover plates (29), 2 inner sprockets / adjustment flange (24), chain ramps (2 black), left and right idler arms w/sprockets (31 and 30), 2 cam sprockets, left and right timing chain housings (2 and 4), rocker arm (38), rocker arm shaft (37)

HARDWARE: 6 self locking 13mm nuts and washers (28/26), 2 inner camshaft washers (20), 2 camshaft woodruff keys (16), camshaft spring washers (23), camshaft nuts (21), (qty 2 46mm, thru 1980 1/2) or camshaft bolt (qty 2 M12x1.5x50mm, from 1980 1/2), camshaft end cover bolts (27), rocker arm bolt (35), rocker arm bushing (34) rocker arm nut (33) washers (26)

SEALS: 2 Camshaft o-rings (39), camshaft housing-to-chain tensioner housing gasket (25), chain housing-to-case gaskets (3), rocker arm seals (36) (2 per rocker arm).

TIME: 6 hours.

TIP: Install the chain sprocket idler arms with the oil-catch opening facing upwards.

ENGINE ASSEMBLY

OVERVIEW

In this section, you'll be assembling the timing chain components that are located at the rear of the engine. If you are using updated idler arms, you will convert these arms over to the newer style. Then you will assemble all of the chains and sprockets and perform the chain sprocket alignment measurement. This measurement is required before you can time the camshafts. After you have verified the correct alignment, you will then install rocker arms for the number one and four intake valves in preparation for your camshaft timing procedure.

TIMING CHAIN HOUSINGS

Begin this section by installing the timing chain housings. If you haven't already, turn the chain housings over to the reverse side and apply some JB Weld to the backsides of the housings where the idler arm shaft is inserted into the housing, as shown in Figure 6-2. The JB Weld epoxy is very similar to the original material used by the factory to seal this area. Scrape off all of the older material, clean it with brake cleaner, and apply a relatively thick spread of JB

Weld epoxy. You should let the JB weld set for about 24 hours before continuing with the assembly process.

Using new gaskets from your gasket set, install the chain housings on the engine case. Install them with the gaskets dry. Use self-locking fasteners for the two nuts on the bottom, and the single nut on top. Use the factory 13mm nuts

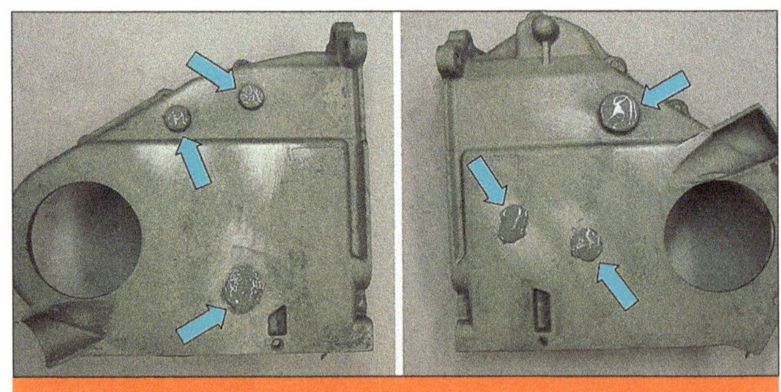

6-2 *JB Weld is a good substitute for the original material that was used in the factory. Clean off all of the original material and spread a generous coat of JB Weld over the area where the shafts are pressed into the housing. This will help prevent oil leaks.*

on the studs that protrude into the inside of the timing chain housing. These are egg-shaped locknuts that resist vibration and were used on the 3.2-liter and later engines. Tighten the five nuts that hold the housing to their specified torque (see Appendix A).

If a lot of material was removed when the case and heads were resized, replaned, and resurfaced, you may find the chain housing is now too far away from the engine case. You can machine the timing chain housing or simply remove the thin gasket between the housing and the case and install it with a small layer of Loctite 574 instead. Maximum float of the camshaft thrust plate in the chain housing should be 0.5mm. Adjust the housing location if the two are off-center by more than this value. In general, the housing can be slightly longer than the cylinder/head/camshaft housing assembly because it will not expand as much when the engine gets hot.

CHAIN RAMPS

With the chain stretched out inside the chain housing, install the two chain ramps on their respective posts. For these two chain ramps, the long end points toward the outside of the engine (see Figure 3-39 in Section 3 of this chapter). Both of these chain ramps should be black in color as well. The ramps simply snap onto the posts embedded in the timing chain housings. On the left side of the engine, the lower loop of the chain rests on top of the chain ramp, and on the right side the top loop of the chain rests on top of the chain ramp. The proper chain orientations are shown in Figure 6-3.

6-3 *This photo shows the left and right chain housings installed on the engine. The two chain ramps have also been installed at this point. Note how the chain is resting on top of the chain ramps, and how they are oriented with their longer section pointing outward.*

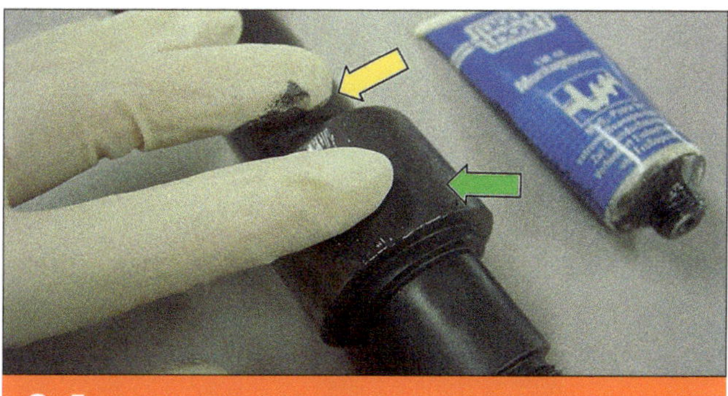

6-4 *Coat the bearing surfaces (green arrow) and the camshaft lobes (yellow arrow) with assembly lube before you install the camshaft.*

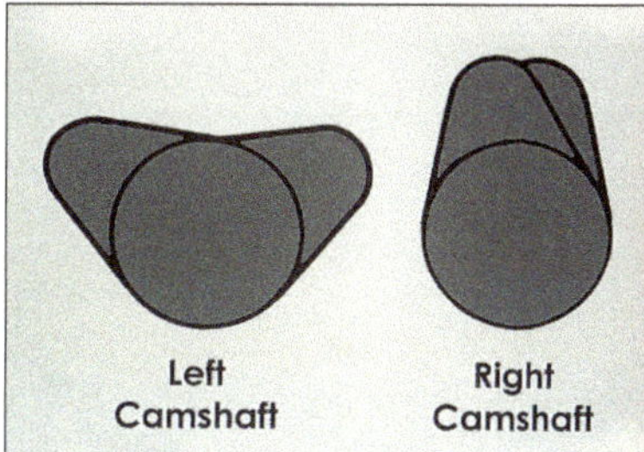

6-5 *This photo demonstrates the difference between the left and right camshafts. The left shaft is shaped more like a wide "V", whereas the right-side camshaft is angled more acutely in a very tight "V" orientation.*

CAMSHAFTS

At this point, install the two camshafts in their respective camshaft housings. Spread a thin layer of assembly lube on the inside of the bearing journals located in each of the two camshaft housings, and on each lobe and bearing surface on the camshaft (Figure 6-4). The left and right camshafts are different, so make sure that you don't confuse them, otherwise your engine will not turn over when you try to start it. The easy way to tell the difference between the two camshafts is that the left-side camshaft makes a wide "V" if you look down the axis of the camshaft. The right-side camshaft has more of a tight "V" shape to it. Refer to Figure 6-5 for more details. After both camshafts are installed, use a cotton swab to remove the excess assembly lube that will squeeze out into the area of the timing chain cover.

SPROCKET ASSEMBLY

With the camshafts installed, you can begin to install the camshaft sprocket assembly. Install a new o-ring on the outside of each of the two camshaft end cover plates. Place a thin layer of Curil-T on all sides of the o-ring to guard against oil leaks. Place a new camshaft housing/chain housing gasket onto each side surface of the camshaft end cover plate. This gasket should be installed against the end plate with some Curil-T spread on both sides. This will help prevent leaks at this interface. This gasket will have three holes in it that will line up with the three holes in the end of the camshaft housing. Using the three camshaft end cover bolts (it's fine to reuse these), and three thin washers, pass them through the camshaft end covers, and thread

6-6 *This photo sequence shows the proper installation of the sprocket assembly.* **Frame A** *shows the paper gasket that mates with the camshaft housing. Spread some Curil-T on these mating surfaces to guard against leaks.* **Frame B** *shows the camshaft housing end plate (thrust plate) with the outer o-ring installed in the camshaft housing.* **Frame C** *shows the large washer (underneath) installed against the camshaft. Install the beveled edge of the washer facing the camshaft.* **Frame D** *shows the alignment shims installed.* **Frame E** *shows the sprocket flange that is used for adjusting the camshaft timing. The woodruff key is installed in the camshaft before installing the sprocket flange.* **Frame F** *shows the cam sprocket correctly installed for the left side of the engine.* **Frame G** *shows the sprocket installed with the large spring washer and 46mm nut (911s up to 1980 1/2).* **Frame H** *shows the left-side camshaft sprocket assembly, where the cam sprocket is flipped around so its concave edge is facing outward. Inspect both the thrust washer and flange prior to assembly—both have a tendency to wear out.*

them into the tapped holes in the end of the camshaft housings. With the bolts attached and acting as a guide, press each camshaft end cover into the timing chain housings. They will require just a bit of force to seat properly because the o-ring will be squeezed in the process. Torque the three bolts on each side down to their specified torque value. Install the thick camshaft washer (also called a thrust plate) onto the shaft of the camshaft, resting up against the camshaft end plate. The washer must be installed with the bevel facing in toward the cylinders. The sequence for this installation is displayed in Figure 6-6.

When you disassembled the engine, you should have kept track of how many sprocket shims were used on each side. Reinstall those shims now in the same quantity as were there when you removed them. If they were missing, or you are building your engine from a stack of unrelated parts, install three shims on the left side, and four shims on the right side to start. Install the camshaft sprocket flange against the shims on each side of the engine.

The camshaft sprockets can be used on either the left or right side of the engine, but their orientation needs to be correct. The left side of the engine has the dish on the

6-7 *The two camshaft sprockets are identical; however, they are installed in different orientations. The left side is installed with the cup of the sprocket facing outward (green arrow). The right side is installed with the flat side of the sprocket facing outward (yellow arrow).*

6-8 *Using the 46mm crowfoot wrench and Porsche tool P202 (left) or the P9191 tool (right), tighten the sprocket onto the camshaft. Use the appropriate tools for tightening the sprocket—failure to do so can damage your engine components.*

sprocket facing toward the rear. On the right side, this dish is facing the front of the engine. The correct orientation of these sprockets is shown in Figure 6-7. Inspect the sprockets for wear before you install them. They have a tendency to wear on the edges of the gears, making them pointy and smooth. A loose chain or a misaligned chain sprocket often causes this type of wear. Install the two sprockets without hooking the chain to them. Place the large spring washer onto each sprocket and then torque down the sprocket retaining nut (through 1980) to 150 Nm (110 ft-lbs.) or the sprocket bolt (post 1980) to 120 Nm (88.4 ft-lbs.), as shown in Figure 6-8.

SPROCKET ALIGNMENT

Both the left and right chain sprockets must be precisely aligned with the corresponding sprockets on the intermediate shaft. If there is a misalignment, then the chain will be adversely stressed, which may lead to premature sprocket wear, or worse, a chain failure. The alignment check is a very important step, and shouldn't be overlooked or skipped. Failure to confirm and set this alignment can lead to total engine destruction in future years.

You can use either a three-foot-long straightedge to perform your measurements or a special tool available from Stomski Racing for about $85. This tool bolts onto the front of your engine case and allows you to make more accurate measurements than are possible with a standard straightedge. It's not a requirement, but it will make the alignment process more accurate and simpler.

Place your three-foot-long straightedge against the front flanges of the case. The first measurement you will be taking will be the distance from the front of the case to a spot on the intermediate shaft. On the early cases (1965-1983 1/2) there is an access hole that allows you to measure from the case flange down to the top surface of the rearmost sprocket on the intermediate shaft. On later cars (1983 1/2-1989), you will need to measure the distance from the flange of the case to the end flange of the intermediate shaft. These two measurement points are shown in Figure 6-9. Record this measurement.

Next, you will check the alignment of the right-side sprocket. Measure the distance between your right-side sprocket and the straightedge, as shown in Figure 6-10. Make sure you take the measurement from the edge of the sprocket. On the right side you should have a nice, wide flange to measure this distance. Write this number down. For the early cases, it should be very similar in value to the previous measurement

If you have an early case (1965-1983 1/2) then this right-side measurement should be the same as the first measurement that you took. For the later cars, add 43.27mm to the first measurement and compare it to the right-side measurement. The maximum difference between these two

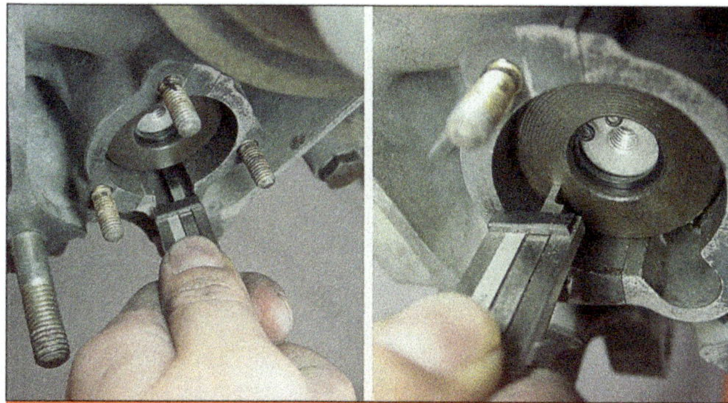

6-9 *The photo on the left shows the measurement of the intermediate shaft dimension on the early cases (1965-1983 1/2). The photo on the right shows how to perform this measurement for the later-style cases (1983 1/2-1989).*

6-10 *The measurement from your straightedge to the camshaft sprockets is made to the outer edge of the sprocket surface. On the sprocket on the left side, this is a very thin flange. On the right side, the flange is much thicker.*

measurements should be 0.25mm. If your two measurements are off by more than that amount, then you will need to change the number of shims underneath the right-side sprocket flange. Remove the sprocket assembly, and add shims to decrease the second measurement or remove shims to increase it. Each shim is 0.25mm thick, so you can easily calculate how many shims you will need to achieve the desired measurement. Tighten up the sprocket assembly and perform the measurement again. Repeat the procedure until the two measurements are within 0.25mm of each other.

The measurement of the left side is very similar. Measure the distance from your straightedge to the left sprocket flange, again shown in Figure 6-10. Make sure that you take the measurement from the outside flange of the sprocket. It should be a very thin flange at this point. Write this measurement down and add 54.8mm to the value. This value should now be equal to your first measurement (for the early cases), or equal to your first measurement plus 43.27mm (for the later cases). You can adjust this value in a manner similar to the right side—simply add or remove the 0.25mm shims to move the sprocket forward or backward.

With the two sprockets properly aligned (Figure 6-11), and the correct number of shims calculated, remove the camshaft nut or bolt from the camshaft. Place the small woodruff keys in

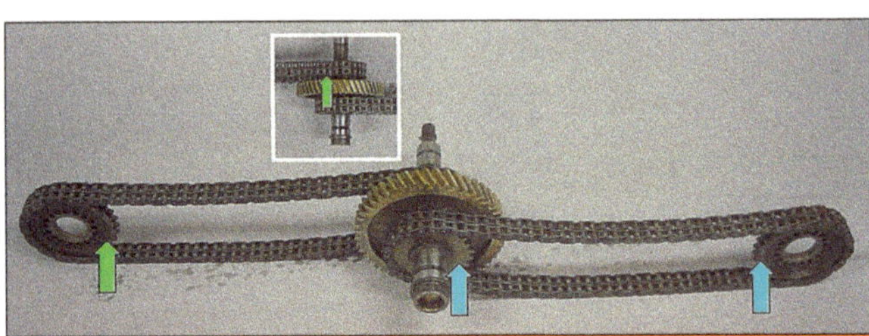

6-11 *This diagram shows the relation of the two sprockets and the measurements that you need to make in order to achieve proper alignment. Looking at the 911 engine from above, you can easily visualize why the chain sprocket alignment is so important. The chain will be stressed and twisted in an '"S" shape if the sprockets are not aligned.*

6-12 *Inspect your idler arms carefully. The original-style idler arms shown on the left show significant wear from dirty oil (red arrow), and may contribute to premature tensioner failure if reinstalled in the engine. The later style ones shown on the right also show a lot of wear on their inside bushings (green arrow). Have these arms rebushed if you find wear patterns like these.*

the channel of each camshaft. Now, reinstall the sprocket with the chain wrapped around it. Install the nut/bolt on the shaft finger-tight to keep the sprocket from falling off.

IDLER ARM INSTALLATION

As mentioned in Chapter 4, Porsche discovered that the relatively small bearing surface used in the chain tensioner idler arms was causing them to bind and contribute to chain tensioner failure. On the idler arms that I removed from the 2.7L engine featured in this book, I found evidence of signifcant scoring and wear (Figure 6-12). The factory has hinted that this binding was one of the contributors to premature chain tensioner failure. The solution is to upgrade your idler arms to the later style ones, which have a wider bearing surface to distribute the load. In addition, these updated idler arms also have bronze bushing inserts.

If you are upgrading your idler arms, you will need to reuse your idler arm sprockets. The sprockets are held onto the idler shafts with a small circlip. Before you remove this circlip, observe how the sprocket shaft is oriented with respect to the idler arm. The sprocket bearing is lubricated by oil that sloshes around inside the timing chain housing. On the sprocket shaft there is a little cup that must be facing up when the idler arm is installed in the engine, as shown in Figure 6-13. This little cup catches the oil that lubricates the bearing.

If you are swapping out your sprockets, I recommend spreading a little bit of assembly lube on the inside of the shaft bearings before you install the sprockets on the new idler arms. If you are simply swapping them from one motor to another, put a few drops of motor oil in the small catch bucket on the idler arms. Spread a little bit of assembly lube on the shaft inside the timing chain housing as well. Install the idler arm by simply placing it on this shaft in the housing. It's pretty difficult to mix up left and right sprockets—refer to Figure 6-14 for the proper orientations.

I cannot stress enough that the correct way to rebuild your engine involves the installation of the later style idler

6-13 *The idler sprockets are attached with a small circlip. Remove this circlip, and transfer the sprockets to the new idler arms. Make sure that you install them with the small oil cup facing upwards (red arrow)—otherwise the idlers may run dry and freeze on the shaft. Prelube the shafts with a bit of assembly lube.*

6-14 *This photo shows the left and right idler arms installed in the timing chain housings.*

arms and the Carrera chain tensioners. To rebuild your engine without performing this reliability upgrade would be foolish. Don't shortchange your rebuild—do it right.

For the process of timing the camshafts (Section 7), you need to have the chain tensioners removed from the engine in order to maintain the highest level of tension on the chain. For this purpose, you will hold off on installing the chain tensioners until after the camshaft timing is completed.

ROCKER SHAFT INSTALLATION

I'll now discuss the installation of the rocker arms. In the next two sections, you will need to install some of the rocker arms in order to perform critical measurements. I'll discuss the proper installation procedure for all of the rocker arms here, and then you can refer back to this particular section when you need to install an individual rocker arm or two.

It is important to note that you will not be installing all of your rocker arms at this point in the assembly process—only the intake rockers for cylinders one and four. Do not install the remaining rocker arms until you need to.

The rocker arm shafts fit tightly in their bores in the aluminum camshaft housings. The rocker arm shafts themselves are hollow, and are flanked on each end by a conical 8mm nut and a conical bushing. A disassembled rocker arm is shown in Figure 6-15. A 5mm hex bolt runs down the center of the rocker arm shaft. When this bolt is tightened, the bolt pulls the nut and the bushing together, squeezing the shaft against its aluminum bore, as shown in Figure 6-16. This has the effect of sealing the shaft in the aluminum, and prevents it from leaking oil.

In order to prevent the compression of the conical nut and bushing from having an effect on the diameter of the shaft where the rocker arm rides, there are two grooves cut into the shaft. These two cuts isolate the inner part of the

shaft from the two outer sections that deform when compressed. On the RSR race cars, Porsche used special seals that fit inside these two grooves. Although they were never used on a production car, they work very well for preventing leaks, and I recommend that you install them on your rocker arm shafts as an added precaution. If you are planning on using the RSR rocker arm seals (recommended), then install them in each side of the rocker shaft as shown in Figure 6-17.

When the appropriate time in the installation procedure arrives, installation of a rocker arm and shaft is relatively simple. Begin by installing the two RSR seals on the rocker shaft. Then assemble the shaft, bushing, bolt, and nut together. Take one of your rocker arms and lightly apply assembly lube to the inside of the bronze bushing, as shown in Figure 6-18. Also apply a thin layer of assembly lube to the contact area where the rocker meets the camshaft lobe. If you are using new valve adjustment screws, install them now. If you are reusing your camshafts and rockers without having them reconditioned, place your rocker arms into exactly the same locations that they previously occupied in the camshaft housing. If you look carefully at your camshaft housing, you will see that each rocker arm location has both a thin and thick flange on either side. For example, intake rocker number one has the thick flange located on the right, and the thinner flange on the left. When you install a rocker

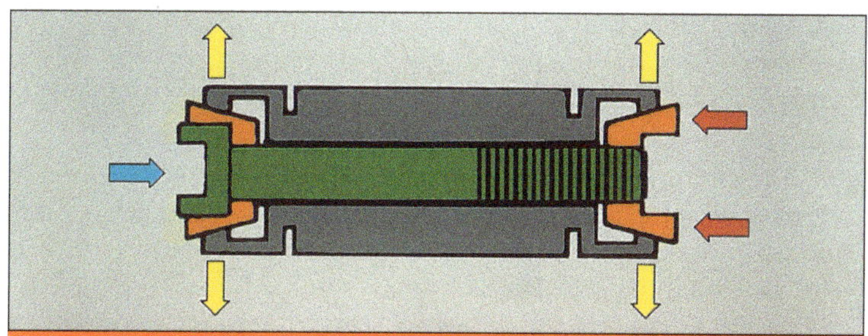

6-16 *As the center bolt is tightened down around the shaft (blue arrow), the conical nut (red arrow) and bushing spread out the shaft into the surface of the camshaft housing (yellow arrows). The assembly works to deform the shaft and seal it against the aluminum camshaft housing. Always install the shaft without the screw, nut, or bushing installed.*

6-15 *The rocker arm assembly consists of the rocker arm (E), shaft (B), a long bolt (H), a conical bushing (F), and a conical nut (A). The RSR rocker arm seals (G) were never a production-car part, but I recommend their use to guard against rocker arm shaft oil leaks. Also shown are the valve adjustment screw (D) and retaining nut (C).*

6-17 *The RSR rocker shaft seal simply slides into the small groove in the rocker arm shaft (blue arrow).*

arm, insert the shaft from the thinner side. The head of the bolt should be facing one of the center sections of the camshaft housings, as shown in Figure 6-19. This will make it easier to remove a rocker shafts if necessary when the engine is assembled. Install the rocker shafts without the screw, nut, or conical bushing installed. Tapping on the end of the shaft with these installed may cause them to expand, potentially damaging the camshaft housing.

Tap the rocker arm shaft into the bore in the thinner flange until just before it begins to peek out the opposite side. Then slip in the rocker arm. Using a small hammer and a 12-inch-long 3/8-inch socket extension, gently tap the rocker shaft into the rocker arm. A handy trick described in the factory manuals is to use a feeler gauge between the rocker arm and opposite edge of the camshaft housing. Tap the rocker arm shaft in until you can sense the feeler gauge touch either the seal or the groove in the shaft, as shown in Figure 6-20. Then tap in the shaft about 1.5mm more. Hold the rocker arm shaft in this position,

install the screw, nut, and conical bushing and then tighten the Allen-head bolt to the value indicated in Appendix A while holding the nut steady, as shown in Figure 6-21.

Some precautions are necessary here, as you can make a few mistakes when installing the rocker arms. First of all, don't center the rocker arm shaft in the center of the space between the flanges. The flanges are different thicknesses on each side and centering the rocker arm shaft will put it in the incorrect position. Depending upon which side of the engine you are working on, the thin and thick flanges of the camshaft housings may be on different sides. The important fact to remember is that the edge of the rocker arm shaft should be very close to being flush with the outer edge of the thinner flange. Don't ever turn the large 8mm nut on the end of the shaft. Instead, use the smaller 5mm bolt to tighten up the rocker arm shaft. Turning the conical nut will cause the nut to turn in its beveled groove, which can damage this surface.

6-18 *Apply a generous coat of assembly lube to the rocker arm bushing before you install it in the camshaft housing. Walt Watson of Competition Engineering has an alternative method of installing rockers that supposedly helps reduce rocker arm leaks. Instead of spreading assembly lube on the rocker bushing, install the rocker arms dry. Then insert serveral drops of oil through the holes in either side of the rocker. This way, you're not smearing assembly lube across your sealing surfaces.*

6-20 *Slide your feeler gauge between the rocker arm and the flange of the camshaft housing (yellow arrow). When you can feel the gauge grab on the seal or the groove, then push in the rocker shaft (green arrow) about 1.5mm and tighten to the specified torque value. Although it is not shown in this photo, you should always install the rocker shaft without the screw, conical nut, or bushing installed.*

6-19 *The orientation of the rocker arm in the camshaft housing is important. One side of the rocker shaft should be almost flush with the thinner flange in the housing (blue arrow).*

6-21 *Holding the 8mm nut steady (green arrow), carefully torque the bolt down to its final torque value (blue arrow). Do not turn the nut—only turn the screw to tighten the assembly in the housing.*

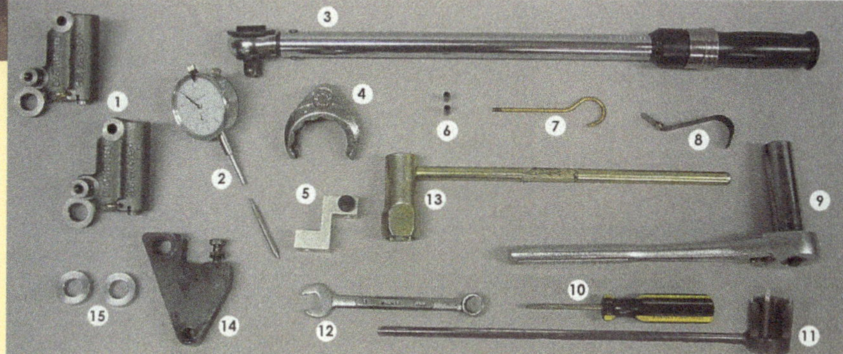

TOOLS: Pin removal tool (7) (or old spark plug), dial gauge (2), dial gauge Z-block (5), valve adjustment feeler gauge (8), torque wrench (3), flathead screwdriver (10), 13mm wrench (12), 19mm deep socket and driver (9), vise-grips, oil pan, bench vise, P202 camshaft tool (13) & 46mm crowfoot wrench (4) (up thru 1980 1/2) or P9191, (11) (1980 1/2 and later), P214 (for use with early-style chain tensioners), Mechanical chain tensioner (14)

MATERIALS: Motor oil

PARTS: 2 Chain tensioners (1), Spacers for use with pre-1980 tensioners (15)

HARDWARE: dowel pins (6) (qty 2- 8x14mm), intake rocker arms, 13mm nuts & washers (2 each)

TIME: 6 hours.

TIP: Take your time and work slowly in this section. Double check your timing.

OVERVIEW

The adjustment and setting of the camshaft timing is one of the more difficult tasks in the rebuild process. Complicating the situation is the fact that Porsche changed the method by which the camshafts are timed when the factory started using the reduced-lift, short-duration camshafts in the CIS and Motronic engines. In this section, you will perform the procedure for timing the camshafts and then install the chain tensioners.

SETUP

Begin the process by turning the crankshaft so that the pulley marked "Z1" is lined up with the case parting line, as shown in Figure 7-2. This will indicate top dead center for cylinder number one on the engine. Double check that you have torqued your crankshaft pulley bolt to its final torque.

You'll start the camshaft timing process with the left side of the engine. Take a large pair of vise-grips and clamp the top of the tensioner idler arm to the side of the timing chain housing, as illustrated in Figure 7-3. The goal here is to increase the tension on the chain and to minimize any backlash or slop that may be in the chain. This will ensure that you will achieve accurate measurements and the correct timing configuration. Wrap the ends of your vise-grip tool with duct tape to avoid damaging any of the surfaces that you may clamp down on.

7-2 *Start the camshaft timing process with the "Z1" mark on the crankshaft pulley aligned with the case parting line (green arrow). This will be the starting point for top dead center for cylinder number one.*

7-3 *Clamp down the vise-grips between the idler arm (red arrow) and the side of the timing chain housing. This will keep maximum tension on the chain, and will allow you to achieve the most precise reading.*

7-4 Using the camshaft tool, turn the camshaft until the small dot, "930" mark, or keyway is facing directly up. This is the basic setting of ignition TDC for cylinder number one.

With the engine at TDC, use your camshaft tool to rotate both the left-side and right-side camshaft until the small dot on the camshaft is facing up. Late-model engines will have a "930" stamped into the end of the camshaft instead of the dot. Some camshafts may not have either marking. In this case, use the keyway for the woodruff key on the camshafts, and make sure that it is pointing upward. The correct orientation for the camshaft is shown in Figure 7-4.

ROCKER ADJUSTMENT

Now you will install the rocker shaft for intake valve number one. Refer to the rocker arm installation procedure in the previous section for details on the proper alignment, torque, and orientation for the rocker arm and shaft. The intake rocker arm is shown installed in Figure 7-5.

The next step is to make sure that the intake valve for cylinder number one is adjusted properly. This is a very important step, and if the valve clearance is even slightly

7-5 Install the rocker arm for cylinder number one according to the installation instructions detailed in the previous section.

off, it will affect the timing setting that you will dial in for the cams. Double check that your camshaft is in the correct orientation (keyway, "930" mark, or small dot facing upward) before you begin to adjust the valve clearance.

Begin by loosening the 13mm retaining nut around the adjustment screw and turn the screw counterclockwise. Now, place your valve adjustment tool (feeler gauge) between the valve and the swivel-foot screw and tighten down the screw. The feeler gauge should move freely between the valve and the swivel foot, with a light drag when you move it around. When the feeler gauge has been properly compressed, tighten up the retaining screw while holding the adjustment screw steady using a screwdriver (Figure 7-6). Don't overtighten the retaining nut—this can damage the threads on the screw and make future adjustments difficult. Remove and replace the feeler gauge and recheck the clearance as the screw has a tendency to move when the retaining nut is retightened. The clearance on the number one intake valve should be 0.10mm (0.004 inch). Double-and triple-check this clearance, as it will severely affect your camshaft timing if it's even slightly off.

7-6 Adjust the valve clearance to 0.1mm (.004 inch) using the special valve adjustment feeler gauge (red arrow). This measurement is very important, as it will affect the valve timing if not properly set.

DIAL INDICATOR SETUP

Once you are assured that the number one intake valve is set at its proper clearance, you need to attach a dial indicator gauge to the cylinder number one intake valve in order to read the amount of valve lift. Make sure you properly convert all the measurements to metric units if you don't happen to use a metric dial gauge (25.4mm = 1 inch). The gauge should be mounted to one of the studs located on the camshaft housing. There is a specific Porsche tool for this process, typically called a dial gauge Z-block. It mounts to one of the studs on the camshaft housing and positions the dial gauge at the exact correct angle for measuring the valve

164

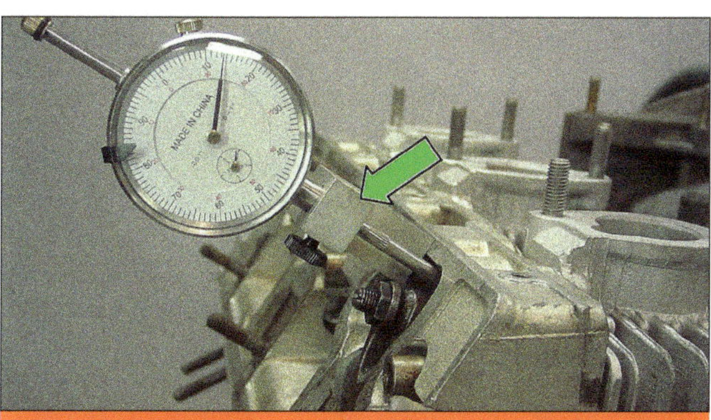

7-7 *Use the proper Z-block tool to mount the dial gauge (green arrow). The Z-block allows you to mount the gauge easily on one of the studs attached to the camshaft housing. Using the Z-block ensures that the gauge will be exactly parallel with the motion of the valve.*

7-8 *Set the dial indicator tip to sit on top of the valve spring retaining collar (green arrow). The indicator needs to measure exact valve lift, so make sure that it doesn't slip, and is firmly mounted. Also make sure that it has enough play to measure the entire lift of the valve.*

lift, as shown in Figure 7-7. Make sure that the dial gauge tip is perfectly parallel to the valve stem and positioned exactly on the edge of the spring retaining collar, illustrated in Figure 7-8. Adjust the dial gauge so that the indicator arm is depressed at least 10mm (about 0.4 inch). This will provide enough preload clearance for the dial indicator arm to travel as the valve moves up and down.

It is important to familiarize yourself with your dial indicator before you begin the timing process. Some gauges have what is known as a counter on the gauge face. On precision gauges, the large needle will sweep around the outer dial once for every 1mm. When timing high-lift camshafts like the 911 S cam, this means that the indicator will sweep around five times before arriving at the specified value of 5.2mm. You must be attentive and watch the dial indicator when timing your camshafts. It's a common mistake for beginners to accidentally time the camshafts to an incorrect value because they weren't carefully watching how many turns the dial indicator rotated.

TIMING METHODS

Here is where the procedure begins to diverge for the two different types of camshafts used. The reduced-lift, short-duration camshafts, like the ones used on the CIS and Motronic engines, make the cam timing procedure a bit easier than the procedure used to time the high-lift, long-duration camshafts found on the earlier engines.

Camshaft timing adjustment is set at a point where the intake and exhaust valves are open at the same time. For each engine configuration, there is a value called "*intake valve stroke in overlapping TDC with 0.1mm valve clearance.*" This value is different for each camshaft configuration, and is listed in Appendix A for most 911s. If you have a custom-grind camshaft, then you should check with the manufacturer for the optimum value. The basic rule of thumb here is that you can use the CIS and Motronic method of timing the camshafts if the *intake valve stroke in overlapping TDC with 0.1mm valve clearance* is less than 2mm. If it's greater than 2mm, then you need to use the second method, which is similar, yet subtly different. Use this second method for all engines with high-lift, high-duration camshafts, like the early T, E, and S engines that used carburetors or mechanical fuel injection. If you have a high-lift camshaft, skip the following sub-section and move on to **High-Lift, High-Duration Camshaft Timing.**

CIS & MOTRONIC CAMSHAFT TIMING

With the camshaft dot, 930 symbol, or keyway properly facing upwards install the small dowel pin that couples the camshaft sprocket and flange together. In this TDC position, one of the alignment holes of the camshaft sprocket will line up with one of the spaces in the sprocket flange, located just behind the sprocket. They are slightly offset in order to give a significant degree of adjustment. Using Porsche tool P212, or the screw tip on an old spark plug, place the pin in the only hole that is lined up with the sprocket. You can look through the camshaft sprocket and

7-9 *When placing the small alignment pin in the camshaft sprocket, it will line up with only one hole of the sprocket mounting flange (orange arrow). The holes in the two flanges are angularly offset to allow a slight degree of adjustment when setting the timing. Place the alignment pin in the hole and then unscrew the tool—the pin shouldn't fall out.*

it will be obvious which hole the pin needs to go into. See Figure 7-9 for additional clarity. Simply place the pin in there and unscrew the tool—the pin will not fall out. Insert the pin on the right-side camshaft sprocket as well.

Now, tighten the 46mm camshaft nut (thru 1980 1/2) or the camshaft bolt (from 1980 1/2). You do not need to tighten it down to its final torque value, but you should tighten it with your camshaft tools so that it is snug. Tighten up the right-side camshaft nut or bolt only hand-tight. Now, slowly turn the crankshaft about one revolution (360 degrees) in a clockwise rotation, all the while keeping an eye on your dial indicator. After turning the crankshaft for a while, you will notice that the dial indicator will begin to move. Turn the crankshaft until the dial indicator shows that the valve has moved the amount indicated for the *intake valve stroke in overlapping TDC with 0.1mm valve clearance*. This value as given by Porsche is actually a range, and can be found in Appendix A, for all stock Porsche camshafts. For example, on a 911 SC type 930/10 engine, this *intake valve stroke in overlapping TDC with 0.1mm valve clearance* should be set between 0.9mm and 1.1mm. Turn the crankshaft until your dial indicator reads the value in between these two numbers, as shown in Figure 7-10. With the 911 SC, you would turn the crankshaft until the value on the dial gauge reads 1.0mm. It is important to note that you will not turn the crankshaft a full 360 degrees before reaching the proper value on the dial indicator. The dial indicator should reach its desired value just before the "Z1" mark is lined up with the case parting line.

At this point, loosen up and remove the camshaft nut and washer, and remove the small threaded dowel pin. Then turn the crankshaft clockwise until the Z1 mark lines up with the parting line of the case. This should be a very minor correction. Reinstall the pin in the sprocket and tighten down the camshaft sprocket, keeping an eye on the dial indicator as you do so. Using the crowfoot wrench and P202 camshaft tool (or 19mm deep socket and tool P9191 for engines after 1980 1/2), hold the camshaft steady as you tighten it to make

sure that it doesn't move, and tighten it to its final torque value. This is the tricky part, as the dial indicator will want to move as the camshaft is tightened. Tighten down the nut to its final torque value (Appendix A), all the while confirming that the dial indicator has not moved.

When everything is tight, rotate the engine 720 degrees. The crankshaft should have the Z1 lined up with the case parting line, and the dial indicator should read right in middle of the range for your *intake valve stroke in overlapping TDC with 0.1mm valve clearance*. For example, on a 911 SC type 930/10 engine the desired value would be 1.0 mm (0.040 inch), right in the middle of the range. If the value is out of the specification range, then you need to loosen up the camshaft sprocket and repeat the process. If the value is correct, you can move on to set the camshaft timing for the right side of the engine.

If you just checked your left-side timing by rotating the crankshaft 720 degrees, then you should be at the proper crankshaft location for timing the right side. If you are unsure, you can check simply by looking at the intake valve for cylinder number one. The engine will be at the proper location if the Z1 mark on the pulley lines up with the case parting line, and the intake valve on cylinder number one has begun to open. The clearance gap between the valve and the adjustment screw will be zero, and you will not be able to rock the rocker arm back and forth with your fingers (Figure 7-11).

The right-side chain is more difficult to keep tight due to its orientation in the timing chain housing. For the purpose of timing the right side of the engine, I recommend using a mechanical chain tensioner. This tool is a block of metal the size of a regular chain tensioner with a screw on the top, shown installed in Figure 7-12. You can adjust the screw to increase the tension on the chain while you're timing the

7-10 *Watch the dial indicator as you tighten down the nut or bolt. Make sure that the specified value on the dial indicator does not change while you are tightening to the final torque value.*

7-11 *You can check for top dead center on cylinder number four by confirming that the "Z1" mark is lined up with the case parting halves, and the intake valve for cylinder number four can be rocked back and forth slightly. There should be a small gap between the adjustment screw and the end of the valve (yellow arrow). You should also not be able to rock the intake rocker arm for cylinder number one when the valve is in this orientation.*

7-12 *When setting the right-side timing, you will need to use a mechanical chain tensioner tool (green arrow). This tool is shaped like a standard chain tensioner and allows you to keep high tension on the timing chain while you are setting the camshaft timing.*

camshafts. Again, the goal is to keep a lot of tension on the chain when you are timing the camshafts.

Install the rocker arm for intake valve number four, using the installation technique detailed in the previous section. Adjust the valve clearance to be 0.10mm (0.004 inch) in the same manner as you did with the left side. Move the dial gauge to the right side of the engine, and set the tip against the valve keeper for intake valve number four. Set the dial gauge to have 10mm of preload on the dial.

The basic process for timing the right camshaft is very similar to the left side from this point on. Confirm that the camshaft dot, 930 mark, or keyway is facing downward (the same way that the left side is facing). Tighten up the large nut or bolt on the camshaft with your camshaft tightening tools. Again, there is no need to torque it to the final value—just make it snug. Rotate the crankshaft clockwise until the dial gauge reads the value for the *intake valve stroke in overlapping TDC with 0.1mm valve clearance.* Try to set it to the same value that you set for the left-side camshaft. Then remove the nut or bolt that holds the camshaft sprocket and remove the small pin. Turn the crankshaft clockwise until the Z1 mark lines up with the case parting line. Then reinstall the pin in the camshaft sprocket, lining it up with the sprocket flange underneath. Tighten up the nut or bolt to its final torque value.

Double check the measurement when you are finished by rotating the crankshaft 720 degrees. A neat trick is to use two dial gauges mounted on both sides of the engine so that you can check and verify that the timing is correctly set to the same value for both camshafts. Setting the timing on one camshaft does not affect the timing on the opposite camshaft, but it's nice to verify them both at the same time. In addition, using two gauges makes it easy to set the values at exactly the same amount for both sides of

the engine. For example, if the right side is set at 0.95mm, the left side should be set as close to that value as possible. Using two dial gauges avoids having to switch gauges back and forth to check both camshafts.

On the 911 SCs, some people advocate advancing the timing slightly; however, dyno tests have failed to reveal any significant increase in power from doing so. I recommend setting your timing values to the factory settings for your camshafts, and looking for horsepower increases elsewhere.

When you have completed the timing and checked both camshafts, skip the next subsection on timing high-lift camshafts and move directly to **Chain Tensioner Installation.**

HIGH-LIFT, HIGH-DURATION CAMSHAFT TIMING

With the camshaft dot or keyway facing upward and the Z1 mark on the pulley lined up with the engine case halves, install the small dowel pin that couples the camshaft sprocket and flange together. In this TDC position, one of the alignment holes of the camshaft sprocket will line up with one of the spaces in the sprocket flange, located just behind the sprocket. They are slightly offset in order to give a significant degree of adjustment. Using Porsche tool P212, or the screw tip on an old spark plug, place the pin in the only hole that is lined up with the sprocket. You can look through the camshaft sprocket and it will be obvious which hole the pin needs to go into. See Figure 7-9 for additional clarity. Simply place the pin in there and unscrew the tool—the pin will not fall out. Insert the pin on the right-side camshaft sprocket as well.

Tighten the camshaft nut to its final torque value (see Appendix A). It is important to note that the original spec books for the early cars indicated that the large 46mm nut should be torqued down to 100 Nm (72 ft-lbs.). This was later changed to the current value of 150 Nm (110 ft-lbs.). For the camshaft timing procedure, torque down the 46mm nut on all pre-1980 cars to 150 Nm (110 ft-lbs.). Tighten the right-side camshaft nut only hand-tight.

Now, rotate the crankshaft clockwise exactly 360 degrees so that the Z1 mark is again lined up with the case parting line. After turning the crankshaft for a while, you will notice that the dial indicator will begin to move. Take note of how far the dial gauge moves when you finish the rotation. If your indicator rotates around multiple times, make sure that you carefully count the total number of turns. At this point in the procedure, the camshaft should be rotated 180 degrees and the dot or keyway should be facing downward.

With the camshaft tool securely holding the camshaft in place, loosen and remove the camshaft nut. While holding the camshaft steady with your camshaft tool, carefully remove the small threaded dowel pin. Do not let go of the camshaft or it will rotate from the force of the intake valve

ENGINE ASSEMBLY

spring acting on the cam lobe. Now rotate the camshaft until the dial indicator shows that the valve has moved the amount indicated for the *intake valve stroke in overlapping TDC with 0.1mm valve clearance,* as shown in Figure 7-10. This value as given by Porsche is actually a range, and can be found in Appendix A, for all stock Porsche camshafts. For example, on a 1970 911 S type 911/02 engine, this intake valve stroke in overlapping TDC with 0.1mm valve clearance should be set between 5.00mm and 5.40mm. Turn the camshaft until your dial indicator reads the value in between these two numbers. With the 1970 911 S, you would turn the crankshaft until the value on the dial gauge reads 5.20mm.

While holding the camshaft steady at that value, insert the small threaded pin into the hole in the sprocket that lines up with the cup in the sprocket flange. Now you can let go of the camshaft—the pin connects the camshaft flange to the camshaft sprocket and should keep them from moving. Now, take the camshaft tool and rock the camshaft back and forth. This is the backlash in the pin/sprocket assembly—confirm that the values on the dial gauge are within the range of specification for the *intake valve stroke in overlapping TDC with 0.1mm valve clearance* given for your particular camshaft. If the range of motion in the backlash moves the dial indicator far out of range, then you need to remove the pin and place it in another location in the sprocket flange that will come closer to meeting this specification.

With the pin installed, you can now tighten down the camshaft nut to its final torque value. Hold the camshaft steady and watch the dial indicator. You need to keep the dial indicator pegged on the desired value while you are tightening it down. This is the tricky part, as the dial indicator will want to move as the camshaft is tightened. Tighten down the nut to its final torque value using the crowfoot wrench and the P202 camshaft holder, all the while confirming that the dial indicator has not moved.

When everything is tight, rotate the engine 720 degrees. The crankshaft should have the Z1 lined up with the case parting line, and the dial indicator should read right in middle of the range for your *intake valve stroke in overlapping TDC with 0.1mm valve clearance.* For example, on a 1970 911 S type 911/02 engine, the desired value would be 5.2mm (0.20 inch), right in the middle of the range. If the value is off, then you need to loosen up the camshaft sprocket, and repeat the process. If the value is correct, you can move on to set the camshaft timing for the right side of the engine.

If you just checked your left-side timing by rotating the crankshaft 720 degrees, then you should be at the proper crankshaft location for timing the right side. If you are unsure, you can check simply by looking at the intake valve for cylinder number one. The engine will be at the proper location if the Z1 mark on the pulley lines up with the case parting line,

and the intake valve on cylinder number one has begun to open. The clearance between the valve and the adjustment screw will be zero, and you will not be able to rock the rocker arm back and forth with your fingers (Figure 7-11).

The right-side chain is more difficult to keep tight due to its orientation in the timing chain housing. For the purpose of timing the right side of the engine, I recommend using a mechanical chain tensioner. This tool is a block of metal the size of a regular chain tensioner with a screw on the top, shown installed in Figure 7-12. You can adjust the screw to increase the tension on the chain while you're timing the camshafts. Again, the goal is to keep a lot of tension on the chain when you are timing the camshafts.

Install the rocker arm for intake valve number four, using the installation technique detailed in the previous section. Adjust the valve clearance to be 0.1mm (.004 inch) in the same manner as you did with the left side. Move the dial gauge to the right side of the engine and set the tip against the valve keeper for intake valve number four. Set the dial gauge to have 10mm of preload on the dial.

The basic process for timing the right camshaft is very similar to the left side from this point on. Confirm that the dot, 930 mark, or keyway is facing downward (the same way that the left side is facing). Tighten the nut on the camshaft to 150 Nm (110 ft-lbs.). Rotate the crankshaft until the Z1 mark lines up again with the case parting line. While holding the camshaft steady with your camshaft holder, remove the nut or bolt that holds the camshaft sprocket and remove the small pin. Turn the camshaft until the dial gauge reads the value for the *intake valve stroke in overlapping TDC with 0.1mm valve clearance.* Try to set it to the same value that you set for the left-side camshaft. Then reinstall the pin in the camshaft sprocket, lining it up with the sprocket flange underneath. Let go of the camshaft and then rock it back and forth. Verify that the backlash in the pin/sprocket interface is within the desired range on the dial indicator. Tighten up the nut or bolt to its final torque value, all the while holding the camshaft and watching to make sure that the dial indicator does not move from the proper value.

Double-check the measurement when you are finished by rotating the crankshaft 720 degrees. A neat trick is to use two dial gauges mounted on both sides of the engine so that you can check and verify that the timing is correctly set for both camshafts at the same time. Setting the timing on one camshaft does not affect the timing on the opposite camshaft, but it's nice to verify them both at the same time. In addition, using two gauges makes it easy to set the values at exactly the same amount for both sides of the engine. For example, if the right side is set at 5.10mm, the left side should be set as close to that value as possible. Using two dial gauges avoids having to switch gauges back and forth to check both camshafts.

7-13 *The differences between setting the camshaft timing on the CIS/Motronic engines and the earlier engines are subtle, but important. With the CIS/Motronic camshafts, you turn the crankshaft to the overlap value, and then adjust the crankshaft to the Z1 mark. With the high-lift camshafts, you set the crankshaft to the Z1 mark and then rotate the camshaft until it reaches its proper value.*

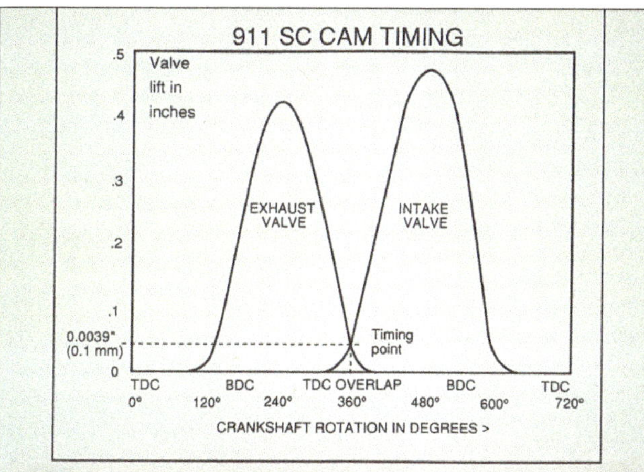

7-14 *This diagram clearly shows the relation of valve lift to crankshaft rotation. The 911 crankshaft turns exactly two full rotations for every one rotation of the camshafts. The process of setting the timing involves synchronizing the rotation of the camshafts to the rotation of the main crankshaft. At the point dubbed "top dead center overlap," the crankshaft has completed its first rotation (pushing exhaust gases out of the cylinder), and is now beginning to open the intake valve. At this point, both the intake and exhaust valves are slightly open. The exact distance that they are open is what is measured when setting the timing. When the engine reaches the specified value for "intake valve lift at overlap TDC with 0.1 mm (0.004 inch) valve clearance," the crankshaft should be set at the Z1 mark on the pulley, or exactly 360 degrees off from TDC for cylinder number one. Advancing or retarding the cam timing setting will result in the exhaust and intake profiles being moved either to the left or the right on the diagram. It is important to note that this is very different from the ignition timing, which controls firing of the spark with respect to the crankshaft. Bruce Anderson*

CHAIN TENSIONER INSTALLATION

As mentioned in Chapter 4, the best upgrade I can recommend for any pre-1984 911 engine is the installation of the pressure-fed Carrera chain tensioners. More than any other upgrade, these tensioners will increase the reliability of your engine. The old-style tensioners will fail—it's just a matter of when. They can be rebuilt with new components, but if you are rebuilding your engine and doing it right, you should definitely upgrade to the later style tensioners.

If you are not going to upgrade your idler arms, but still are going to install the chain tensioner kit, then you will need to install spacers (930.105.513.00) that fit between the tensioner and the older style idler arm. The newer style chain tensioners (from 1980) all have a thinner flange that is designed to mate with the late-style idler arms. The small spacer fills this gap when the early idler arms are used, and is shown in Figure 7-15. As mentioned in Chapter 4, I don't recommend using this older style idler arm and spacer combination in your rebuild.

The most commonly accepted installation procedure for the updated pressure-fed chain tensioners has been simply to bolt them on and then run the engine until oil pressure builds up. Although most mechanics have used this method and have been doing so for years, air pockets in the tensioner can occur, causing uneven oil pressure. The resulting rattling noises that come from the timing

7-15 *If you decide to reuse your old-style idler arms (not recommended) with the Carrera chain tensioner upgrade, then you need to install a small spacer in between the tensioner and the old-style idler arm (blue arrow).*

7-16 *Submerge the tensioner completely in oil and pump it up with either your fingers or a set of C-clamp vise-grips. Prime the tensioner until no more air bubbles exit the oil supply hole.*

chain housing upon startup will appear to indicate a weak and faulty tensioner, when in fact it is symptomatic of a faulty installation.

Although there was never a factory technical bulletin released on the subject, there is a procedure that you can perform to help prime the tensioners. This procedure involves first submerging the tensioner completely in motor oil. Grab a small, clean dish or tub, and fill it with motor oil. With the tensioner completely submerged in this oil, pull the small pin located in the side of the tensioner. This will release the tensioner piston, while sucking oil into the internals of the tensioner. With the tensioner completely submerged in oil, pump the piston of the tensioner with your hand until no more air bubbles come out of the oil inlet, as shown in Figure 7-16. Remove it from the oil and place it on a paper towel on your bench.

With the tensioner primed in this manner, you have removed any excess air bubbles in the tensioner, and filled it with clean motor oil. You may need some assistance from a C-clamp-shaped pair of vise-grips if your fingers aren't strong enough to pump the tensioner when it's submerged in oil. Carefully inspect your tensioner at this time as well (Figure 7-17), as some chain tensioners have been known to have damaged bleed valves or faulty plugs that look like they are going to fall out.

After you have primed the tensioner, place it in your vise and compress the piston down far enough so that you can reinsert the small holding pin (Figure 7-18). Wrap both sides of the vise with duct tape so that you don't damage the piston pin or the bottom housing of the chain tensioner. The pin will hold the piston of the tensioner closed so that you can easily install it in the engine. If you are reusing your old pressure-fed chain tensioners, then simply compress them in a vise and insert the pin to hold the piston. If you don't have the original pins from the chain tensioner, a thick nail will suffice.

As you compress the tensioner in your vise, you will find that it requires a lot of force to move the piston. This is because the tensioner is bleeding oil out of a relief valve. If you remove the tensioner from the vise after pushing the

7-18 *If you are reusing your tensioner, then you will probably have to compress it in a vise in order to be able to place the small retaining pin in to hold it (blue arrow). Compress slowly, as the oil will bleed out of the tensioner slowly.*

piston all the way down, you should find that you can now easily compress it with your fingers. This is not the sign of a failed tensioner—it simply means that the tensioner does not have any oil trapped inside.

The tensioner works in a manner similar to the original spring-loaded tensioners, with an additional oil piston that helps to dampen and support the mechanical spring. Excess oil from the tensioner is bled out of the relief hole in the top, as you may have seen when you compressed it in your vise. If the tensioner is primed properly with oil before it is installed, it should stiffen up quickly when the engine supplies it with oil pressure.

Although I have not personally witnessed a failed pressure-fed chain tensioner, a small number of my Pelican Parts customers have. The failure seems to appear when the car is first started, and results in a very loud rattling noise coming from the timing chain housings. The consensus is that the tensioners either work or they don't. I have not heard of a single report of these tensioners failing after many successful miles in the engine. The bottom line is that you need to prime the tensioners and listen closely for problems when you start up your engine. Even with these recent problems, the newer chain tensioners are much more reliable than the older styles. Jerry Woods of Jerry Woods Enterprises has developed a novel method to install emergency retaining collars on these new hydraulic chain tensioners. Unfortunately, I learned of this too late to incorporate the modification procedure here. See http://www.101projects.com for more information on this upgrade.

There are three types of early-style spring-loaded chain tensioners. The first two generations are the least reliable and should be replaced if you are rebuilding your engine. The third generation is marked with a part number that will begin in 930, and this style is considerably more reliable than the earlier spring-loaded tensioners (see photo 4-7 in Chapter 4). No spring-loaded tensioners are as reliable as the pressure-fed Carrera chain tensioners described above. If for some reason you need to install the spring-loaded tensioners in your engine, I recommend that you use brand-new later style 930-type tensioners. There are rebuild kits available for spring-loaded ten-

7-17 *Inspect your tensioners carefully before you install them into your engine. Some tensioners suffer from defective pressure relief valves (green arrow)—check them for broken components before use. Also check the small plug on the side of the tensioner (yellow arrow) to ensure that it is securely attached.*

sioners but I do not recommend them. There are just too many things that can go wrong with these extremely vital engine components.

The actual installation of the chain tensioners is quite easy. The most important thing to remember is that you want to keep constant tension on the chain at all times. Do this by making sure that the idler arm is held tight all the time. Do not let go of the idler arm and do not let *any* slack into the chain. Do not let the chain go slack at all; otherwise, you may lose your cam timing positioning. If this happens, you may have a catastrophic failure when you go to start the engine. The valves may hit the pistons, and you will be forced to tear down and rebuild your engine again. Do not make this mistake—keep tension on the chain at all times.

In the past, I have had customers who have bent their valves doing a Carrera chain tensioner upgrade. Even though they swear that the chain never came off of the cam sprockets, they did let some slack into the chain. Although it's difficult to figure out what went wrong during the upgrade, the end result was a complete teardown and top-end rebuild of the engine. The rule of thumb is to keep tension on the chain via the idler arms at all times.

Holding the chain tight, simply place the tensioner onto the shaft, and tighten up the 13mm nut that secures it. If you are installing the Carrera chain tensioners, use a new small inlet o-ring on each of the tensioners. With everything tightened down, pull the small pin on the Carrera chain tensioner. The piston should snap into place against the idler arm and hold the chain tight. Keep ten-

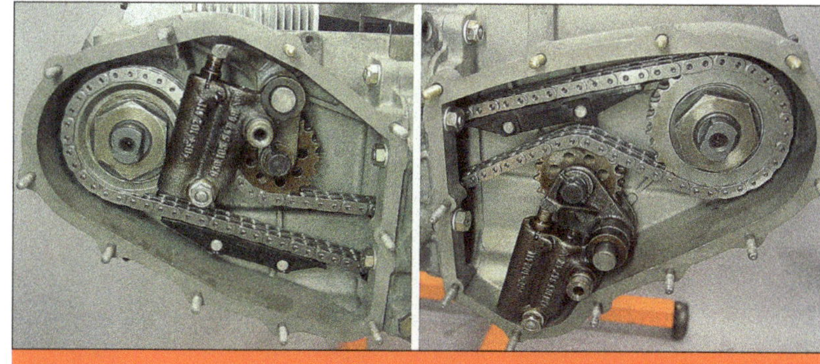

7-19 *This photo shows the entire timing chain assembly completely installed. Note the proper orientation of the chains, idler arms and chain tensioners.*

sion on the chain at all times and don't ever let it go slack. Remember to install the tensioner spacers if you haven't upgraded your idler arms. Repeat the installation process for the chain tensioner on the opposite side.

If you are installing a very early-style chain tensioner (not recommended), you need to compress it and hold it with a chain tensioner tool (P214). This will make it easier to fit the idler arms on the engine. Compress the tensioner in a vise and slide on the tensioner-clamping tool. Then install the tensioner on the engine. The later style 930 spring-loaded tensioners have a small snap-ring that holds the piston in a contracted position. Install the tensioner on the engine and then remove the small snap-ring. The chain tensioner piston will snap into place.

With the tensioners installed, your engine will be timed, and ready for the important valve-to-piston clearance check. Figure 7-19 clearly shows how both sides of your timing chain housings should look after the installation.

SECTION 8 PISTON/VALVE CLEARANCE CHECK

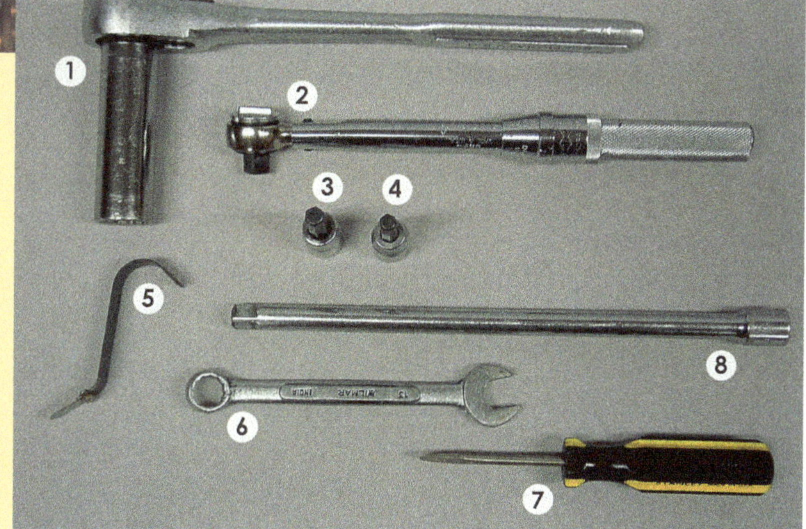

TOOLS: Flathead screwdriver (7), 13mm wrench (6), 19mm deep socket and driver (1), feeler gauge (5), 5mm and 8mm Allen-head tool (4/3), torque wrench (2), 12" extension (8)

PARTS: 2 Rocker arm assemblies

SEALS: 4 Rocker arm seals

MATERIALS: white chalk.

TIME: 3 to 5 hours.

TIP: Look through the intake port and the spark plug holes to see where the pistons come closest to the valves.

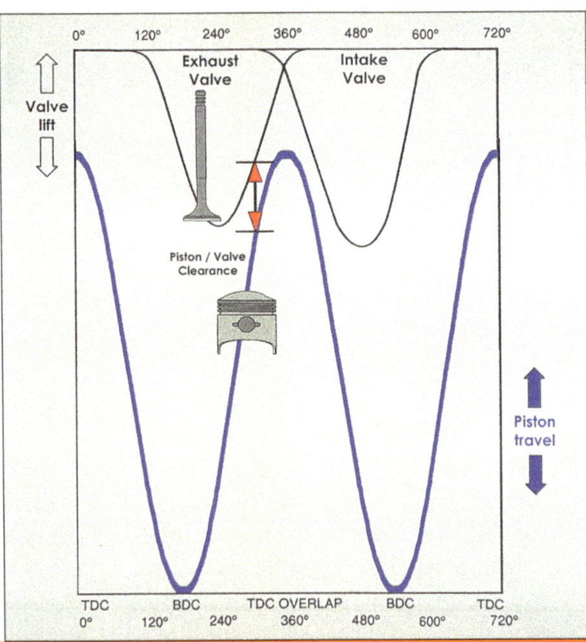

8-2 *In this diagram, I've recreated a view of the cylinders and valves as the engine runs through an entire 4-stroke cycle (720 degrees). The blue line represents the sinusoidal path that the pistons travel during each cycle. The curve at the top of this diagram represents the paths traveled by both the intake and exhaust valves. It is a common misconception to assume that the pistons and valves are closest to each other when the piston is at the end of its travel (top dead center). In reality, the piston is closest to the valves as it is rising to meet them. This is because the valves are open at this point. The closest interaction between the piston and the valve occurs somewhere along this path, and is indicated by the distance marked with the red arrows.*

8-3 *The procedure for checking the piston-to-valve clearance involves measuring both the exhaust and intake valve profiles on both sides of the engine. As a result, you will need to install the two lower exhaust rockers for cylinders number one and four (yellow arrow).*

OVERVIEW

The piston-to-valve clearance check is one of the most important measurements that you need to perform on your 911 engine. It's a tedious task, but it will guarantee you success in your rebuild. In this section, you will be measuring the distance between the pistons and the valves for the entire profile of both the intake and the exhaust valves, on both sides of the engine. Adequate clearance must exist, because the engine expands when hot, rods stretch at high RPMs, and valves can float in this upper range as well. Without this clearance, the pistons and valves may collide under severe operating conditions.

BACKGROUND

One of the most important checks you can perform is the measurement of the valve-to-piston clearance when the valves are opening. If your case or heads have been machined, or you are using a different camshaft or pistons, then the valve-to-piston clearance will change. Failure to perform this check at this point may lead to some significant damage, as your valves may hit your pistons when the engine is running. Even stock 911 engine configurations may experience some problems if there has been extensive machine work performed on the case or the heads.

Different camshaft profiles will yield vastly different interactions between your valves and pistons. It is important to test valve-to-piston clearance over the entire range of the camshaft profile, for both intake and exhaust valves. The procedure is time-consuming and tedious, but absolutely necessary in order to guarantee that you don't have any interference problems in your engine. Therefore, when performing this valve-to-piston clearance, you must take careful measurements across the entire lobe of the camshaft. See Figure 8-2 for a graph and explanation of the piston-to-valve interaction.

It is important to note that this check can only be performed after the deck height has been set and the camshafts have been timed. The piston-to-valve clearance must also be performed on both sides of the engine. It is not unheard of to have your machinist remove 0.15mm of material from the heads on one side of the engine, while removing 0.25mm on the other side. Because of this potential mismatch, you need to make sure that you perform the measurement on both the left and right sides.

8-4 *Adjust the rocker arm so that you have zero clearance between the valve and the swivel foot (blue arrow). This will allow you to measure how far you are opening up your valve when you turn the adjustment screw.*

EXHAUST ROCKER ARMS

You will be measuring clearances on both the left and right side of the engine, with both the intake and exhaust valves. Therefore, you will need to install the rocker arm shafts for the exhaust valves on cylinders number one and four (Figure 8-3). Perform the installation of the rocker arms according to the procedure indicated in Section 6. When you are finished, you should have both the intake and exhaust rocker arms installed for cylinders one and four.

CLEARANCE CHECK

Start with the intake valve on cylinder number one. Rotate the crankshaft until it is at TDC for cylinder number one. This is when the Z1 mark is lined up with the case parting line, and both valves are closed on cylinder number one. This valve should be adjusted with a 0.10mm (0.004 inch) clearance from the previous section, where you adjusted the cam timing. The intake rocker will have a slight clearance gap, and you should be able to rock it back and forth very slightly.

Once you have verified that you have the engine at TDC for cylinder number one, back out the retaining nut all the way on the valve adjustment screw and rotate the screw in until it touches the tip of the valve, as shown in Figure 8-4. You have effectively reduced the valve adjustment clearance to zero. Do not install or tighten the retaining nut on the screw.

The thread pitch of the adjustment screw is exactly 1mm. This means that for every full turn of the adjustment screw (360-degree rotation), the screw will open the valve exactly 1mm. By turning the screw and counting the turns until the valve rests up against the piston, you can determine the clearance between the two at any one position of the camshaft. One turn of the screw equals 1 mm (.040 inch).

One might naturally think that the position where the valves are closest to the pistons would be at overlapping TDC. This is the point where you took the measurement for the camshaft timing. At this point, the piston will be closest to the heads. However, because the valves are mostly closed at this moment, this point may not be the

location where you will have the minimum piston-to-valve clearance. As the valves open, they open quicker than the piston can retreat back into the engine case. Depending upon your camshaft profile, piston-to-valve impact may occur at almost any point along this path.

The bottom line is that you really need to take measurements across the entire lobe of the cam, for each of the four valves that you are testing (intake and exhaust for one and four). It is important to perform this measurement on both the left and right side. As mentioned previously, it's not uncommon to have varying amounts of clearances on opposite sides of the engine from machining operations. The piston-to-valve clearance must be kept within a minimum range (1.5mm for the intake valves and 2mm for the exhaust); otherwise, you will risk a piston-to-valve collision.

Again, I cannot stress how important it is to make this measurement, even if you are using a mild camshaft like the ones used with CIS injection. Extensive machining of the heads or case can result in dangerously close clearances between the valves and the pistons. It's important to note that

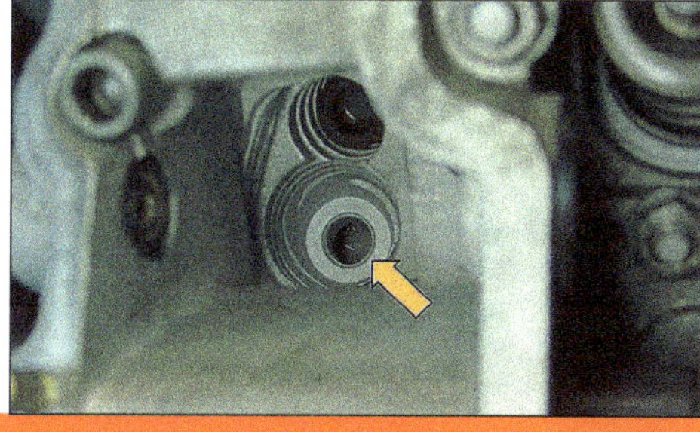

this procedure is not documented in the factory manuals, simply because the engines that were assembled in the early days did not have any machining work done to them. Rebuilding, or more appropriately, restoring your engine requires this machine work, which can then skew the tolerances and clearances that would otherwise be perfectly fine on a brand-new engine.

Begin the measurement process by turning over the crankshaft to top dead center for cylinder number one. At this point, the Z1 mark on the crankshaft pulley will be at the case parting line, and the intake and exhaust valves for cylinder number one will be completely closed. Now turn the crankshaft until you see the intake rocker arm begin to move. At this point, the camshaft is acting on the rocker, and beginning to open the valve (Figure 8-6).

Now you can shine a flashlight down the spark plug hole and see the piston and valve move as you turn the crankshaft, as shown in Figure 8-7. Looking down the hole will give you an idea of when the piston-to-valve clearance is very close. You can save yourself some time by visually verifying where the closest clearances exist, and then carefully taking measurements around that point. Unfortunately, you can't see the exhaust valve from the spark plug hole, but you can see where the piston begins to rise up toward the valves. You can figure out from watching the piston exactly when you need to pay close attention to the measurements.

When you've rotated the crankshaft so that the valve appears closer to the piston, use a screwdriver and carefully turn the adjustment screw. You will be opening the valve farther into the combustion chamber. Turn the screw at least one and a half turns. If you suddenly feel any resistance while you are turning, then stop immediately, as the valve has touched the top of the piston. On the other hand, don't tighten the screw so far down that it is about to fall out of the rocker arm. Remember that the minimum valve-to-piston clearance that you need to maintain is 1.5mm for the intake and 2mm for the exhaust. When you are turning your adjustment screw, if you find that you surpass 2 turns on the screw, then you are assured that you have enough clearance, and can proceed to the next measurement.

Take a small piece of chalk and mark the pulley at the point where it intersects the case parting line (Figure 8-5). This will indicate that you have already taken this measurement at this location of the crankshaft. Now, turn the engine back toward TDC until the camshaft is no longer acting on the rocker arm. Readjust the screw so that it is just resting against the tip of the valve again. Turn the crankshaft until it reaches your chalk mark, and then turn it about 10 degrees more. This would be about 1cm on the edge of the pulley. Repeat the measurement process for this point on the crankshaft.

Repeat the measurement process until you reach the other side of the camshaft lobe, or you can visually observe that the piston is no longer near the valve. If any of your measurements of the valve-to-piston clearance are very close to the limits (1.5mm intake, 2.0mm exhaust), then you will want to go back and take additional measurements. If two measurements indicate that the valve is very close to the piston, then go back and measure the point directly between those two chalk marks on the pulley.

When you've finished with the intake valve, erase the chalk marks from the pulley and repeat the entire process for the exhaust valve. Watch the camshaft movement in the same manner, and calculate the distance between the exhaust valve and the piston. When complete, repeat the entire process for both the intake and exhaust valve on cylinder number four.

A quick short-cut on this whole process can be made by simply turning the valve screws in and carefully rotating the crankshaft 720 degrees. If you don't proceed very carefully, however, you may damage your valves by having them touch the pistons. Proceed slowly and with caution.

RESULTS

When you're finished, you should have a pretty good map of the valve-to-piston clearances in your engine. If your piston-to-valve clearances have exceeded the allowable limits, then you will need to tear down your engine and fix the problem. This is not a trivial problem, and will cause you major damage later on if you don't fix it now. Tight tolerances between the pistons and valves will result in contact—especially at high RPM. If you over-rev or miss a shift while driving, you can basically guarantee yourself a new rebuild. Do it right and address the problem while you still have easy access to the engine.

So what can you do if your clearances are too small? If you're running a high-compression engine, the best solution is to increase the depth of the relief cutouts in the tops of the pistons. A basic rule of thumb is that almost all Porsche pistons can be cut down about 1mm from their stock height. Don't cut them so that the thickness of the piston is less than 5mm. This is the most common solution to this clearance problem. You can also choose not to run a high-lift, long-duration camshaft, instead opting for a milder one.

An example of a typical potential valve-to-piston clearance problem occurs when you combine "E" pistons with an "S" camshaft. This combination will yield pistons that come very close to the valves during normal operation. Depending upon how much machine work was performed on your heads and your case, this configuration may or may not work. With such an engine, the piston-to-valve clearance check is absolutely essential.

Most engines running CIS or Motronic camshafts will have no problems with the piston-to-valve clearances, but they need to be checked regardless. If the piston-to-valve clearances all look within spec, then you can breathe a sigh of relief and move on to the next section.

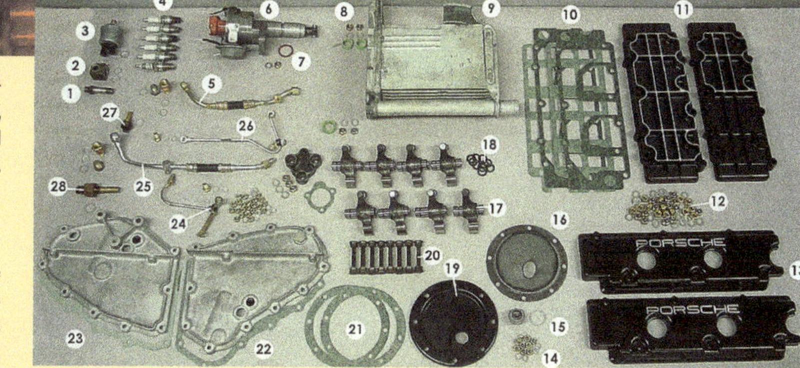

TOOLS: 5mm and 8mm Allen-head tool, valve adjustment tool, torque wrench, feeler gauge, 10mm, 13mm sockets, 12mm open-end wrench (cam oil lines), 17mm socket (cam oil lines), spark plug socket.

MATERIALS: Assembly lube, motor oil.

PARTS: Rocker assemblies (17), oil cooler (9), valve covers (11/13), distributor, points, rotor (6), cam oil lines (5/25), chain tensioner oil lines—Carrera chain tensioners only (24/26), spark plugs (4), oil pressure sender (3), sender block (2), sender connector (1), temperature sensors (27/28), timing chain covers (22/23), engine sump cover (19), engine sump screen (16), sump drain pug (15), Intermediate plate cover (22/23), 2 Carrera chain tensioner o-rings (7), distributor o-ring (8), RSR rocker arm seals (18), intermediate plate gasket, drain plug sealing ring (15), hollow bolt sealing rings

HARDWARE: Distributor nut (7), valve cover hardware (12), chain cover hardware, oil cooler mount hardware (8), sump hardware (14), rocker arm hardware (20)

SEALS: Sump gaskets (21), oil cooler seals (8) (2 small, 1 large), valve cover gaskets (10) (2 upper, 2 lower), chain housing cover gaskets

TIME: 5 hours.

TIP: Take your time and don't rush at this stage—there are plenty of little items that are easy to forget.

OVERVIEW

By this point, you've timed your camshafts and checked your piston-to-valve clearances. Just about all of the tough tasks are complete. In this section, you'll complete the assembly of the long block and finish up the installation of some external components. First, you will seal up the front timing chain covers, then install the remaining rockers and adjust all of the valves. Then, you'll install the cam oil lines and spark plugs and attach the valve covers. Following that will be the installation of the oil cooler, sump plate, and the front engine mount and bar.

TIMING CHAIN COVERS

Verify that your engine is back at TDC for cylinder number one. The Z1 mark should be at the case parting line and the dot, 930 mark, or camshaft keyways on both camshafts should be facing up. Also check that you have a bit of clearance in your number one intake and exhaust valve rockers. You will set the engine at TDC for cylinder number one, and leave it there while you close up the front timing chain covers. Immediately afterward, you can install your distributor, knowing that you are correctly located at TDC.

Check that everything looks good inside your timing chain housings. If you have installed the Carrera chain tensioners, verify that you have removed the pin from the tensioner and that the chain is sufficiently tight. Also verify that the o-ring on the inlet to each Carrera chain tensioner is installed (Figure 9-2). In your gasket kit there should be two very thin gaskets that fit on the left and right sides. Install these gaskets dry.

9-2 *A common mistake is to forget the small o-ring on the end of the Carrera chain tensioner. This o-ring is not included in the gasket kit for cars before 1984 and needs to be ordered separately if your early car has had the chain tensioners upgraded.*

Before you install the timing chain housings, check to make sure that they are flat. Place them on a piece of flat glass with a piece of fine sandpaper (120 or 180 grit) in between. Place the smooth side of the sandpaper against the glass and flood the paper with some WD-40 as a lubricant. Press down gently in the center of the case and rub in a circular direction until the entire mating surface has been sanded to a uniform matte finish. The mating surface is now flat. Then place the timing chain housing covers on each side. Place a bit of assembly lube on the o-ring that is located on the Carrera chain tensioners. Even with the lube, you

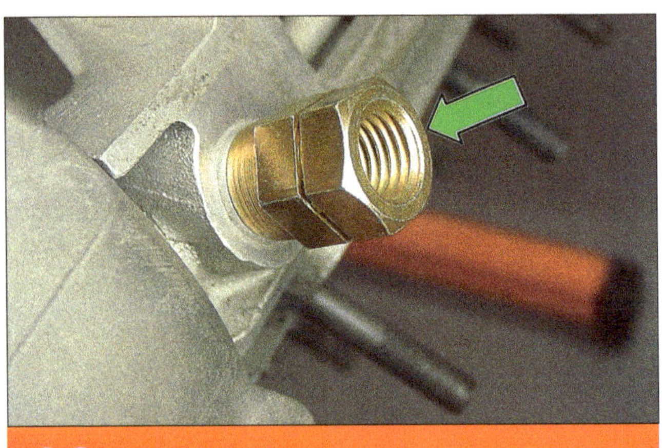

9-3 Install the oil line restrictor in your camshaft housing. I recommend that you use the newer, updated style discussed in Chapter Four. Also use a new sealing washer between the restrictor and the camshaft housing base.

9-4 The banjo fitting can sometimes interfere with the valve covers. Test fit the covers before tightening down the fitting. If there is a clearance issue, then simply rotate the end of the oil line until it no longer interferes with the attachment of the valve cover.

9-5 Don't forget to install the camshaft housing plug at the front of each camshaft housing. Use a new sealing ring from your gasket set.

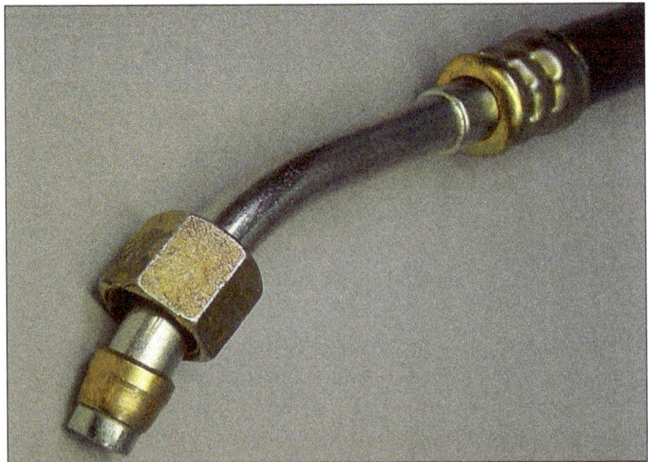

9-6 The inside fittings for the cam oil lines have a nut/ferrule compression fitting that mates into an adapter in the case. Assemble the fitting according to the photo, and don't tighten it down too much, as it can strip the fitting.

might have to use just a little bit of force to get the o-ring on the tensioner through the inlet hole in the cover.

The small locking nuts that are used to secure the covers should only be torqued to 10 Nm (7.4 ft-lbs.). These are very small 6mm nuts and can easily be overtightened by a zealous wrench. For small nuts like these, I usually use a small, quarter-inch ratchet. The small tool will help to prevent you from cranking down too hard on these nuts. If you have a 911 with an early mechanical fuel pump, mount it to the front of your timing chain housing.

CAM OIL LINES

After you have reattached the two chain cover housings, you need to install the new camshaft housing oil lines. Lay them out on your workbench and make sure you have all the fittings, brackets, gaskets, and washers that you need. The lines have both banjo fittings and straight-line fittings with aluminum sealing rings (from your gasket set) that fit under a hex cap cover. Install the oil line restrictor/adapter first, using a new sealing ring from your gasket kit (Figure 9-3). As mentioned in Chapter 4, I recommend upgrading to the late-style 911 Turbo adapters, which have a smaller restrictor hole.

After the adapter is installed, you can now install the oil line. The oil line is attached with a banjo fitting. A hollow bolt attaches the line to the adapter and allows oil to pass through the shaft of the bolt and out two small access holes in the side of the bolt. When you install this fitting, take your upper valve cover and test fit it onto the camshaft housing. It is possible for the cam oil line to interfere with the proper fit of the valve covers. If there is a fitment problem, then rotate the cam oil line slightly on the banjo fitting until there is enough clearance. Use two new sealing rings and tighten down the banjo fitting, as shown in Figure 9-4. At this time you should install the camshaft housing plug on the opposite side of the camshaft housing. Use a new sealing ring for this plug, as shown in Figure 9-5.

ENGINE ASSEMBLY

176

Attachment of the outboard oil-line fittings is straightforward, but the inboard ones are a bit trickier. They involve a ferrule-type fitting that must be assembled according to Figure 9-6. Make sure that you have the inboard straight oil lines placed exactly square into the inboard fittings, and the tapered sealing rings have their small edge pointing downward. Do not use too much force on any of the fittings—they will seal perfectly if installed properly. It is quite easy to strip the edge of the line if you tighten down too tightly, so proceed with caution here. You can always tighten it up a bit more later on if it does happen to leak. The correctly installed fitting shown in Figure 9-7.

If you are using the pressure-fed Carrera chain tensioners, install the tensioner supply lines now. They run from the middle of the cam oil lines to the inlet hole in the chain housing cover. The lines are attached to the chain tensioner inlet by a banjo fitting that is smaller than the one used with the cam oil lines. Use two new sealing rings on both sides of the hollow bolt, as shown in Figure 9-8.

If you are using Carrera chain tensioners, install the small support brackets in place. The factory updated the

kit sometime in the late 1980s to include a set of small brackets that support the chain tensioner oil lines. These brackets are a requirement for all cars that are using the Carrera chain tensioners. Excess vibration from the engine was found to have weakened the stiff oil lines—if you don't have these brackets, you need to install them on your engine. Figuring out the exact installation locations of the brackets can be tricky—refer to Figure 9-9 as a guide for assembling the bracket hardware.

The right-side line also supports and connects to the oil pressure sender. If you have a new one, install it into its mounting block (Figure 9-10). Tighten it from the nut on the bottom of the adapter piece—not by gripping the housing. These housings are weak, and can separate and leak oil if you tighten them by using your hand.

DISTRIBUTOR INSTALLATION

After the front timing chain covers have been installed and the cam lines attached, you can now install the distributor. The 911 engines before 1978 all have a mechanical points

9-11 *The inside view of the Bosch distributor shows the points and the gap that needs to be set prior to setting the timing. The arrow points to the gap that should be set initially using a feeler gauge. This is the same Bosch distributor that is the upgrade for the Marelli distributor for the 1969-71 911s.*

9-13 *The tip on the rotor should be pointing directly to the small notch on the distributor housing (blue arrow). This will ensure that the distributor is installed at top dead center for cylinder number one.*

system to trigger the ignition spark. If you haven't already, install a new set of points in the distributor and set the points gap using a feeler gauge, as shown in Figure 9-11. The 1965-68 911s have an initial points gap of 0.016 inch, and 1969-77 cars with the capacitive discharge ignition system should have an initial gap of 0.012 inch.

Install a new ignition rotor, place a new o-ring on the base of the distributor, and apply some assembly lube to both the o-ring and the distributor gear. When you place the distributor into the engine (Figure 9-12), the distributor drive gear on the crankshaft will mesh with the gear on the distributor and rotate it slightly. You also might encounter a bit of resistance as the o-ring grips the inside of the distributor bore. Check the distributor shaft end play before installation—too much play can cause the timing to change and become erratic.

9-12 *Install the distributor with a little bit of assembly lube on the o-ring (green arrow). This will help it to seal easier in the engine case. Confirm that the distributor rotor is properly lined up with the top dead center mark on the outside of the distributor housing.*

You need to install the distributor in the engine so that the tip of the rotor lines up with the small notch in the side of the distributor. The distributor may rotate in either direction depending upon which engine you are rebuilding (1978-89 Turbo and 911 SC distributors rotated counterclockwise—in the opposite direction). It may take a little bit of trial and error in order to get the distributor to properly line up with the mark on the housing. Look at the distributor straight down from above the rotor to determine if it's installed correctly, as shown in Figure 9-13. It's easy to install it slightly cocked if you look at it from an odd angle. Tighten the nut that holds the distributor hand-tight.

Now would be a great time to upgrade your early 911 Marelli distributor to a brand-new Bosch one. The older Marelli caps and rotors are no longer available, and the upgrade to the Bosch distributor is really the only viable option for your rebuild. Another good upgrade at this time would be to a breakerless ignition system like the Pertronix Ignitor. These systems have been proven to be more reliable and require less maintenance than the original points ignition system used on the early 911s.

ROCKER ARM INSTALLATION

In Section 6, I documented the procedure for the proper installation of the rocker arms. At this point, you should have both the intake and exhaust rockers installed for cylinders number one and four. Now you will complete the rest of the camshaft housings and install the rocker arms for cylinders 2, 3, 5, and 6. The complete set of rocker arms is shown installed in Figure 9-14. Refer back to Section 6 for the specifics of the installation process. Remember to torque them down to the proper amount (17.5 Nm, 13 ft-lbs.), and only turn the long bolt, not the conical nut. Also make sure that you orient them so that the long bolt faces one of the

9-14 *Install the remaining rocker arms according to the instructions detailed in Section 6. Orient the heads of the bolts so that they point inward toward a center section of the camshaft housing. Only turn the bolt—don't ever turn the large conical nut on the end of the rocker arm shaft.*

center sections of the camshaft housings. This allows you to remove them easily if necessary when the engine is installed in the car.

When installing the rocker arms, you may have to rotate the engine in order to get the camshaft oriented at a spot where it is easy to install them. The camshaft must not be in a position to act on the rocker arms if you are installing them. If you find this is the case, simply rotate the engine until a flat spot on the cam is facing outward. At this point in the assembly process, you should only turn the engine clockwise. Turning in the opposite direction can cause the chain to hang up.

VALVE ADJUSTMENT

After the rockers have all been installed, you need to set the engine at top dead center for piston number one. Rotate the engine to the point where the Z1 mark on the crankshaft engine pulley lines up with the split in the case, and the valves for cylinder number one are completely closed. At this point, the distributor will be pointing to the notch on the side of its housing.

When the engine is at TDC for cylinder number one, it's time to adjust the valves for that cylinder. Both the intake and the exhaust valves can be adjusted at the same time. For each valve, you'll perform the same procedure that you used when you adjusted the number one and number four intake valves for performing the cam timing.

Begin by loosening the 13mm retaining nut around the adjustment screw, and turn the screw counter-clockwise. Now, place your valve adjustment tool (feeler gauge) between the valve and the swivel-foot

screw, and tighten down the screw. The feeler gauge should move freely between the valve and the swivel foot, with a light drag when you move it around. When the feeler gauge has been properly compressed, tighten up the retaining nut while holding the adjustment screw steady using a screwdriver. Remove the feeler gauge and recheck the clearance as the screw has a tendency to move when the retaining nut is retightened. The clearance on both the intake and exhaust valve should be 0.10mm (0.004 inch).

Now, rotate the engine crankshaft 120 degrees clockwise using the crankshaft pulley. There is a mark on the crankshaft engine pulley that will indicate the 120-degree position. Repeat the adjustment procedure for cylinder number six. When finished, rotate the engine another 120 degrees and adjust the valves for cylinder number two. Repeat the rotation and adjustment procedures for the remaining valves following the engine firing order 1-6-2-4-3-5 (Figure 9-15).

When you are finished, rotate the engine back to TDC for cylinder number one. Again, this is when the Z1 mark will line up with the case parting line, and the distributor is pointing at the notch in its housing. Now go back through the rotation procedure and check the clearance of all the valves using the feeler gauge. If any feel too tight or too loose, then repeat the adjustment procedure for that valve.

9-15 *Shown here is the firing order of the 911 engine (completed long block shown here). Adjust the valves by starting with cylinder number one, and then following the firing order, 1-6-2-4-3-5. Turning the crank 120 degrees clockwise will move the engine into position to adjust the next set of valves.*

9-17 *Install new valve cover gaskets from your gasket kit.*

The valve adjustment procedure is much easier than when the engine is in the car. You will discover this when you readjust your valves after the engine has been run in for about 500 miles. When you're finished checking your clearances, rotate the engine forward to TDC for cylinder number one. If you've just finished adjusting cylinder number five, you should only have to rotate the engine 120 degrees.

SPARK PLUGS

Now is a good time to install your new spark plugs. Measure and set the gap on each plug, and install them in the cylinder heads without using any anti-seize compound (Figure 9-16). Torque the spark plugs to 25 to 30 Nm (18.4 to 22 ft-lbs.). Porsche doesn't recommend the use of anti-seize compound, as detailed in Porsche Technical Bulletin 9102, Group 2, identifier 2870. The bulletin applies retroactively to all Porsche models and the theory is that the anti-seize tends to act as an electrical insulator between the plug and the cylinder head. This could have detrimental effect on the firing of the spark due to the loss of a good, consistent ground connection. For more information on chosing spark plugs for your engine, see this book's official web site: http://www.101projects.com.

VALVE COVERS

Finally, you can seal up the valve covers. Use the sanding method you performed on the chain housing covers to ensure that your valve covers are flat. Use the new gaskets from your gasket kit (Figure 9-17), and attach the valve covers with new 13mm hardware. If you don't already have them, I recommend upgrading to the Turbo valve covers—see Section 4 for more details.

The valve covers are notorious for being overtightened. The nuts should only be tightened to 8 Nm (5.9 ft-lbs.). If you overtighten them, then you have the potential of warping and deforming them. This may cause leaks later on. Tighten them down to the specified torque. If you find that they are leaking later on, you can always tighten them up a bit more.

Many people like to paint their valve covers. It's a quick and easy way to dress up your engine. For this particular engine, I painted the aluminum Turbo valve covers with some medium-gloss, high-temperature engine paint, which is available at any good auto parts store. Then I took some sand

9-16 *Now is a good time to install your spark plugs. Use a torque wrench to tighten them up, and make sure that you don't use anti-seize compound on the threads. The compound can interfere with the proper grounding of the spark plug.*

9-18 *This is what your engine should look like with your valve covers installed. Use new mounting hardware on the valve covers, and only torque them down to 8 Nm (5.9 ft-lbs.). I dressed up the looks of my valve covers by painting them black with high-temperature engine paint, and then removing the paint on the "Porsche" script and the fins of the Turbo valve covers.*

9-19 *Install the two small seals at the top (yellow arrows), and the larger seal at the bottom of the oil cooler mount (red arrows), located on the right side of the engine case. Wet the seals with a dab of clean motor oil before installing them.*

paper and removed the paint from the raised 'PORSCHE' lettering on the upper covers, and the reinforcing fins on the lower covers. This is shown in Figure 9-18.

OIL COOLER

The engine oil cooler is attached to the right front of the engine. By this time, your oil cooler should have been cleaned and pressure-tested for leaks. Rotate the engine so that the right side is facing up. Then install the two small seals at the top of the oil cooler mount. The larger seal goes into the recess at the bottom of the oil cooler mount. All three seals are shown in Figure 9-19. I recommend wetting these seals first in a bit of clean motor oil—it should help them seal the cooler. The oil cooler is attached using four self-locking nuts. Place the cooler on the studs and torque the nuts down. The oil cooler is shown installed in Figure 9-20.

SUMP PLATE

Move now to the bottom of the engine case. It's a good idea to install the sump plate towards the end of the assembly process because you may accidentally drop something inside your engine, and you can sometimes fish it out of the bottom of the engine sump. Install the bottom crankcase oil sump screen and gaskets. There are two gaskets; one goes between the case and the strainer, and the other goes between the strainer and the sump plate cover. Refer to the photo sequence in Figure 9-21 for the proper assembly order. Be careful when you reinstall the bottom sump plate—it must be properly aligned in the recess of the suction plate; otherwise, it will interfere with proper oil pump operation. Use new hardware, and tighten the lower sump assembly nuts to their final torque values. Make sure that you don't position the drain plug under the oil pump pickup—it will interfere with the proper operation of the oil pump.

INTERMEDIATE PLATE COVER

Don't forget to install this small cover over the end of the intermediate shaft. A small gasket fits between the

9-20 *Shown here is the engine cooler properly installed. Two nuts on the top and bottom of the cooler mount it to the engine.*

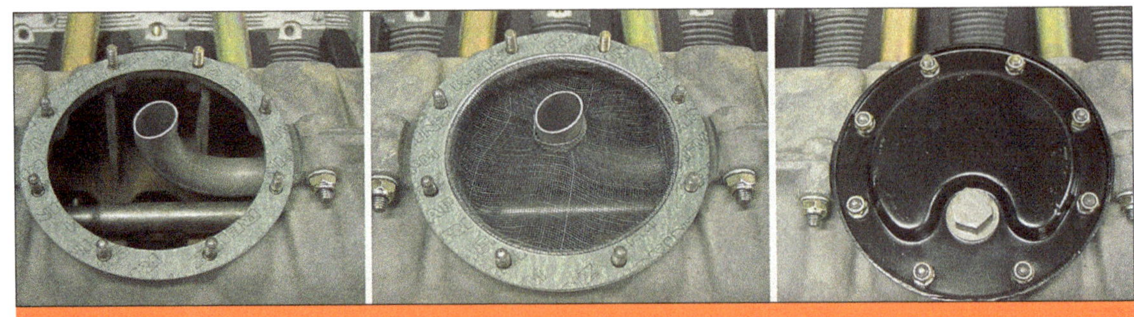

9-21 *Install the sump plate assembly on the bottom of the engine after you have completed all other tasks. The proper installation order is gasket (A), strainer plus gasket (B), and sump plate (C). The oil drain plug must not be placed under the pickup for the oil pump, as this will cause oil pump suction problems. Use two new gaskets and make sure that your screen is clean before reinstalling it.*

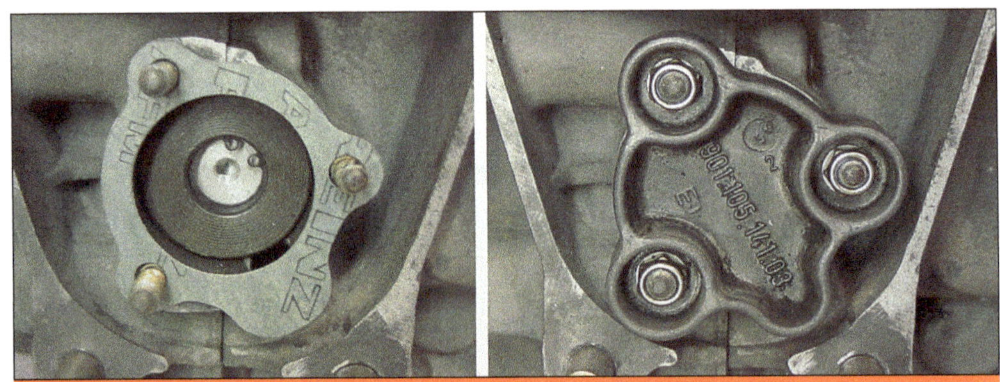

9-22 *Don't forget to install the small intermediate plate on the front of your engine. Later style cases used an o-ring instead of the gasket pictured here.*

cover and the case on early cars (thru mid-1983). Later cars used an o-ring and a plug to seal this interface. The gasket and cover for the early cars are shown in Figure 9-22.

LONG BLOCK COMPLETE

At this point, you have completed the assembly of your long block, shown in Figure 9-23. You have spent many hours in your garage, and I hope the spine of this book has been bent many times as it has been placed on top of your engine. You should feel quite proud of yourself—the hard part is over. There is still quite a bit of work to be done on the accessories, exhaust and fuel injection, but from this point on, it's smooth sailing.

9-23 *Shown here is a photo of the completed long block 2.7-liter engine. Take a few pictures of your engine at this point, as it never looks quite as good after you've installed it in the car.*

TOOLS: Sockets—engine mount bar, fan pulley wrench, fan strap, clutch alignment tool, fan belt tool.

MATERIALS: Anti-seize compound.

PARTS: Exhaust system, fuel injection, engine mount bar, fan assembly, sheet metal.

HARDWARE: Exhaust hardware, engine sheet metal screws, air guide screws, exhaust nut, barrel nut.

SEALS: Exhaust gaskets, intake manifold gaskets.

TIME: 5 hours.

TIP: Reinstall the exhaust and fuel injection according to the notes and photos that you took during the disassembly process.

OVERVIEW

In this section, you'll complete everything that needs to be done prior to mating the engine with the transmission and installing it in the car. First, you will install the engine mount bar. Then you will install the fan, housing, alternator, wiring harness, and fan shroud. Next you will rotate the engine over and install the exhaust system. Flipping the engine over once more, you will install the spark plug wires and the fuel injection system. Finally, you'll attach the outer sheet metal to complete your engine.

OIL LINE ADAPTER

Depending upon which year engine you are rebuilding, you may have an oil line adapter that fits into the side of the engine case. Install this adapter first, before you install the exhaust system. Figure 10-1 shows the location of this adapter. Make sure that you use a new sealing ring from your gasket kit to guard against any leaks.

AIR INJECTION PLUGS

If you are using cylinder heads from a 1975-79 engine and are not going to be using the smog pump or air injection equipment, then you will want to install these small plugs into your heads. Figure 10-2 shows them installed into 1975 heads used with a 1974 engine that doesn't have an air injection system. Install the plugs dry—the high heat from the cylinder heads will make standard compounds such as Loctite ineffective.

FRONT ENGINE MOUNT BAR

Now you should install the engine mount bar, as it makes for a good handle to rotate the engine around. Start by bolting the engine mount to the crankcase. Four large 17mm nuts and washers fasten the mount to the studs in the case. Use new hardware when attaching the motor mount to the case, as shown in Figure 10-3.

10-1 Install the oil line adapter that fits into the left side of the engine case. Use a new sealing ring from your gasket set. This particular fitting is an AN adapter for use with an aftermarket oil cooler setup

The rear engine support bar is also called the rear engine support leaf spring in the factory manuals. Although it doesn't appear to do much actual springing, it must be mounted exactly horizontal to the engine case. This is an easy task to perform with the help of your long straightedge. Simply attach the support bar to the motor mount using 17mm bolts and washers. Hand tighten each one so that you can still rotate the bar slightly. Then place the straightedge across the intake manifold, as shown in Figure 10-4. Measure the distance from the straightedge to the top of the engine mount bar. Repeat the measurement on the opposite side of the engine. Rotate and adjust the bar

until the two measurements are the same. When finished, tighten up each of the nuts.

EXHAUST SYSTEM

I recommend that you now place the exhaust system on the engine. It's not a wise idea to turn the engine upside down with your fuel injection installed. There is a chance that old fuel can leak out, and I have even heard of the CIS sensor plate becoming stuck open from being suspended upside down.

There are many different exhaust combinations that were used on the 911, so I will just cover the basic principles here. Assemble the system according to the notes and photos that you took during the disassembly process. Begin by attaching the heat exchangers or headers to the engine. Use the correct mounting hardware (six 13mm or 12mm nuts, and six small barrel nuts) and gaskets. Make sure that you have the proper gaskets for your year car—there were subtle differences, especially between the 1984-89 Carreras and the earlier cars.

The 1975-77 cars have thermal reactors and the 1975-79 cars have air injection pipes as well. Install these pipes before installing any other exhaust components. The 1975-77 exhaust system is somewhat unique and consists of thermal reactors in addition to heat exchangers. Refer to the notes and photos that you took when you disassembled the system.

With the engine turned upside down, install the gaskets on the bottom sides of the heads. Apply a liberal coat of anti-seize compound to the exhaust studs, as shown in Figure 10-5. Don't overlook this step—these nuts can be very difficult to remove if the anti-seize is not used.

A note of caution should be issued here. If you had your exhaust system recently sandblasted, then there is the distinct potential that some excess sand or blasting material may fall down into your newly rebuilt engine! The same is true if your heat exchangers are rusty or dirty. The safe rule of thumb is to not turn your engine upside down if you have recently had your heat exchangers blasted or cleaned, or if they appear to be quite dirty. Instead, turn it on its side so that no debris will fall into the exhaust ports. If you are installing brand

10-5 *Using a brush, apply a liberal amount of anti-seize compound to the exhaust studs. Without the compound, these studs often rust and become very difficult to remove.*

new units (as shown in the photos here) then you need not be concerned with contamination.

Now place the heat exchangers on the heads. Spin on the exhaust nuts with your hands so that the heat exchangers are still quite loose and can be moved around. Refer to Figure 10-6 for the best methods to attach and tighten the heat exchanger mounting hardware. Now attach the cross-over pipe (1978-89). You may have to wiggle the heat exchangers to insert the pipe.

Bolt on the catalytic converter and the muffler. You will want to check the condition of your catalytic converter before you reinstall it on the car. Shine a shop lamp in one end of the Cat. You should be able to see light coming out the

other end (it's reflected off of the right angle pipe in the converter). If the converter is clogged, then I suggest that you replace it. Doing so will increase performance by reducing exhaust restriction.

On the 1978-89 cars, the muffler bolts directly to the catalytic converter. Loosely attach the muffler to the converter, and then fasten the muffler straps around the engine mount. Don't let the muffler hang solely by the converter— make sure that it is adequately supported by the straps. Don't fully tighten up the straps yet—you want to make sure that you have everything in alignment before you tighten it up snug.

On the 1974 and earlier cars, the heat exchangers bolt directly to the muffler, as shown in Figure 10-7. Again, make sure that the muffler is properly supported by the muffler straps and not simply hanging by the heat exchangers. Refer to Figure 10-8 for the best method for installing the muffler straps.

The 911 Turbo owners have the most work. There are several oil lines and a complicated exhaust system that is integrated with the fuel injection. Install new gaskets on all the connections and refer to the pictures and notes that you took when you disassembled the system.

When you have everything assembled, tighten all of the nuts, bolts, and clamps. Make sure that all of the flanges seat properly. Tighten all the fasteners snug, and then go back and torque them down. This will ensure that you have reduced the amount of hidden stress contained in your exhaust assembly.

The final step will be to attach your muffler straps. This strap is very important, as it prevents the muffler from bouncing up and down while the car is moving. If the straps are left off, the muffler will hang on the end of the heat ex-

10-6 *Two types of nuts are used to mount the heat exchangers to the engine. Small 8mm barrel nuts are used where access is tight. For easier access, there are clearance holes that are manufactured into the heat exchangers. Using the long 8mm heat exchanger tool, you can tighten these barrel nuts while holding them with a set of long pliers. Where the barrel nuts are not used, you can use standard 13mm nuts. A swivel foot driver, like the one shown on the left, really helps the installation process.*

changers and could permanently damage either them or your cylinder heads. Figure 10-9 shows the completed exhaust system with the muffler properly attached to the engine mount.

FAN ASSEMBLY

Flip the engine right side up and take your newly cleaned or painted fan and place it on your workbench

10-7 *Here is a set of stainless steel heat exchangers installed on the engine. Truly a work of art, it's a shame they are mostly invisible when the engine is installed in the car.*

10-9 *This photo shows the complete installation of the stainless steel heat exchangers and a stainless steel muffler.*

10-8 *Installing the muffler strap is one of the tougher jobs. Start with a larger bolt, and thread it into the strap. Tighten down the strap until it is very tight. This will deform the strap and mold it into place. Then take a tie-wrap and tie the two ends of the clamp together. Remove the longer bolt, and replace it with the smaller one that comes with the clamp. Make sure that the clamp fits around the bracket on the engine mount (green arrow), and that the lip of the muffler is resting against this bracket (yellow arrow). When tight, clip and remove the tie-wrap.*

alongside the alternator. The fan needs to be pressed onto the shaft of the alternator. Line up the keyway on the fan with the one on the alternator and lightly tap the center shaft of the fan with a rubber mallet. You don't want to use too much force here, as you can damage either the fan or the alternator bearings. Don't bang on the blades of the fan, as they are weak and can easily break. If you are having problems mating the fan, check to make sure that the key isn't rotating in the keyway. You also might want to take it to your local machine shop and have them press it on.

With the fan and alternator assembled, spin the assembly a few times to check the bearings for smoothness. If you haven't already, remove the back panel of the alternator and check the brushes (for those models that have removable brushes). If the two brushes are very short (about an eighth of an inch long), then you should replace them with new ones, which are about a half-inch long. See Project 20 in *101 Projects for Your Porsche 911* for details on replacing the brushes.

When you're confident that your fan is properly mated with your alternator shaft, insert the assembly in the fan housing. Check the orientation of the alternator with respect to the housing, and make sure that it's aligned properly so that the alternator is facing up when the fan housing is properly lined up on the engine. It's a close fit and may require some tapping with your rubber mallet again. Make sure that the fan is seated properly in the housing. Spin the fan blades—none should touch the side of the housing. They should be very close, though. If there is some scraping, then you need to investigate why. Is the alternator pressed all the way into the housing? Is the fan mounted squarely on the alternator shaft? Sometimes painting or powder coating the fan will add just enough thickness to make the fan blades rub against the inside of the housing.

10-11 *Place the shroud and harness on the engine in preparation for attaching it permanently to the engine block. Reconnect all of the wires to the alternator and attach the alternator air guide. The fan strap is omitted from this photo for clarity.*

Grab your fan assembly strap and insert it between the two openings in the top of the case. If the distributor is in the way, then move the crankshaft to TDC for cylinder number one and temporarily remove it. Install the strap in the case, and then replace the distributor, making sure that the rotor is pointing to the notch on the outside of its housing. With the fan assembly ready, temporarily place it on the engine, as shown in Figure 10-10. The fan housing ring will line up with a small pin that is located in the top of the case. This pin can be seen in the top of Figure 8-5, located earlier in this chapter. This pin aligns the fan so that the timing mark on the fan housing lines up with the parting line of the case. Attach the alternator ground strap to the engine. Then gather your fan shroud and wiring harness. Carefully feed the alternator connections through the hole in the back of the fan shroud, as shown in Figure 10-11. Also feed the wires through the air deflector that mates to the back of the alternator. Following the notes, labels, and photos you made during disassembly, carefully reconnect all of the alternator wires. Once the alternator is wired correctly, attach the air guide to the fan housing. Double-check to make sure the alternator harness is not pinched by the fins of the air guide—this can cause an electrical fire. Don't tighten up the nuts too tightly, as you can crack and break the plastic air guide piece. Finally, connect the strap around the fan and tighten it up, as shown in Figure 10-12. Don't tighten it up too much— just let the bolts used with the strap slightly exit the captive nuts on the other side. Now, fasten down the fiberglass fan shroud using new hardware and attach the two side air guides as well.

10-10 *Assemble the alternator and fan together and place them on the engine. The assembly should fit well into the cup formed by the two engine case halves. This photo shows a test fit of the fan housing—you should install the fan strap first.*

10-12 *Install the left and right air deflectors, or block-off plates. Never run the engine without a hose attached, or the hole plugged.*

pieces of tape. If you do drop a washer down into the port, and it doesn't fall into the combustion chamber, rotate the engine until you are sure that the valve is completely closed. Then rotate the engine upside down and shake it loose.

FAN BELT

One of the most important tasks in maintaining your 911 is the proper replacement and tensioning of the fan belt. If the belt and pulley are not properly adjusted, the belt can come loose and stop the cooling action of the fan. If you don't happen to notice the temperature gauge or the alternator lamp illuminate, then you may overheat and destroy your engine! Needless to say, proper installation of the fan belt is very important.

Ironically, the fan belt is also one of the most misunderstood items on the car, and is often improperly tightened. The system works using a set of shims that regulate the thickness of the virtual pulley created by the pulley half and the fan. As you add more shims between the pulley half and the fan, the tension on the fan belt decreases because the pulley width is larger, and the belt rides lower in the valley. In the opposite manner, when the shims are removed from between the pulley half and the fan, it pinches the belt tighter. As a result, the belt will ride higher and farther toward the outside of the pulley, increasing the tension on the entire belt. The system is similar to the one used on the 356 and has worked well for many, many years.

Be careful when working around your open intake ports. It's very easy to get distracted and accidentally drop a small washer or screw into the inside of your engine. If this happens, and the valve is open, then you may have to tear down your engine completely in order to retrieve a tiny washer. Figure 10-13 shows an example of one such mistake. Try to keep the intake ports covered as much as possible with

The key to installing the belt properly is to follow a set procedure that will guarantee the proper seating of the pulley and the proper tensioning of the belt. Start by installing five shims on the inside of the pulley and one on the outside. It is very important to note that the pulley must always have a total of six shims on it, inside and out at all times, as shown in Figure 10-14. If you don't place the extra shims on the outside of the pulley, the nut will bottom out and the belt won't tighten properly. If you are missing some shims, get some and put them in right away.

Make sure that you tighten the pulley completely. To achieve this, tighten as much as you can, then turn the engine over a bit and then retighten. This will give the belt a chance to become unpinched from the pulley. You should be able to feel the point at which all the shims are tight against the fan and the outer pulley half—you won't be able to tighten any more no matter how hard you try. The final factory torque specification for this nut is 40 Nm (29 ft-lbs.).

10-13 *Don't let this happen to you! In this photo you can see where a small washer has fallen down the intake manifold. If the valve were opened all the way, the washer would have fallen into the combustion chamber. It's very hard to retrieve items once they are in the chamber, so keep the intake ports of the heads covered as much as possible.*

ENGINE ASSEMBLY

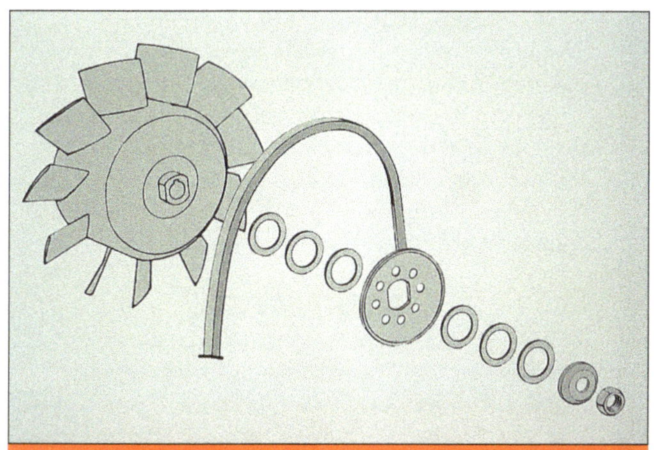

10-14 *The proper order of assembly for the fan hub. Start with five shims on the inside, and then move them to the outside as needed to obtain the proper tightness.*

The tension of the belt should be tight enough so that the belt can be deflected with your finger about 10 to 15mm at the halfway point between the two pulleys. If the belt is too tight, move some shims to the inside. If it's too loose, remove some from the inside and move them to the outside. At all times keep the total number of shims inside and outside of the pulley at six. Figure 10-15 shows the completed fan and belt assembly.

WIRING HARNESS

Now finish installing your wiring harness. Depending upon your year engine and your fuel injection system, there may be many connections that you cannot make just yet. Route the wiring harness around the engine so that it will run underneath the intake manifolds and be out of the way when you install the fuel injection system. If you have any connections that can be mated, or any tie-down points that the harness can be hooked to, connect them now. There is sometimes a ground wire that needs to be connected to a small bolt located behind the distributor. If the distributor is in the way, then move the crankshaft to TDC for cylinder number one and temporarily remove it. Install the ground wire and then replace the distributor, making sure that the rotor is pointing to the notch on the outside of its housing.

With the wiring harness installed, now attach the spark plug wires. Most wire sets have small rubber holders that will mate with a hole in the fiberglass fan shroud and hold the wires secure. Install a new cap on your distributor and attach the new wires. I typically like to leave the

cap on the ends of the wires when I remove them from the engine. If your cap is still attached, then it should make wiring up the connections very easy. If your wiring harness is loose at the distributor end, then use Figure 10-16 as a guide for where to plug your wires into the cap. Now, bolt your coil to the top of the fan housing, and attach the coil wire to the distributor. Also connect the positive and negative wires from the wiring harness to the coil.

FUEL INJECTION

Unfortunately, there are too many options in fuel injection systems to cover them all here. Install your fuel system according to the photos and notes that you created when you removed it. Replace rubber manifold hoses with new ones, and check fuel lines for leaks or cracks, prior to installation. Connect the remaining wiring harness connections to the fuel injection.

MECHANICAL FUEL INJECTION (MFI)

Once you have the MFI pump mounted on the engine, the toothed drive belt must be properly set in order to synchronize the pump with the main crankshaft. There is a mark located on the pulley hub of the MFI pump. Make sure that this mark is aligned with the small notch on the case of the pump. Then place the engine at TDC for cylinder number one. Then rotate the engine clockwise 360 degrees. The engine should now be at TDC for cylinder number four. Then rotate the engine until the FE mark on the crankshaft pulley aligns with the mark at the bottom of

10-15 *Install the fan belt according to the procedure documented in Project 3 of 101 Projects for Your Porsche 911. Never use less than six shims total on the fan belt (inside and out).*

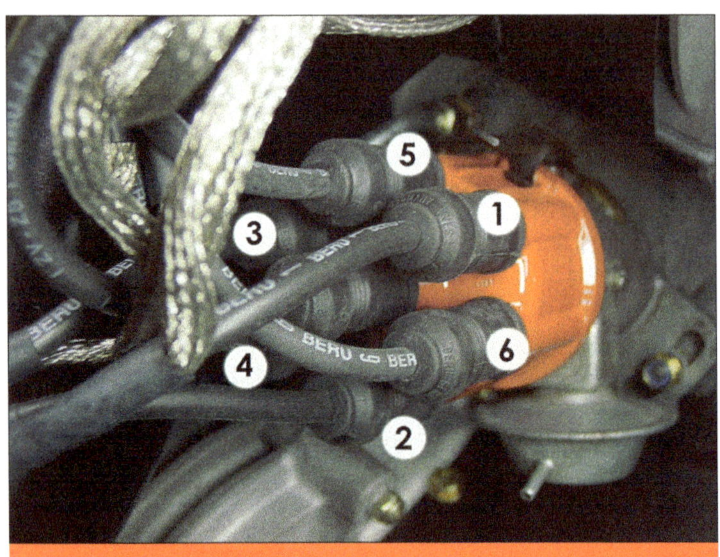

10-16 *If you are installing a new ignition wiring harness, refer to this figure for the locations of the ignition wires on the distributor. This photo shows the order for all 911s except the 911 SC and the 1978-89 Turbo. Swap plugs 6 and 5, along with plugs 3 and 2 for the SC and Turbo configuration.*

ACCELERATOR LINKAGE

The linkage setup is highly dependent upon the fuel injection setup that you are using. One note—don't forget the aluminum standoff that fits underneath the CIS injection accelerator linkage. Figure 10-17 shows the accelerator linkage installation for a typical CIS engine. Snap on the small linkage ball joints and connect them to your fuel injection system.

SHEET METAL

The sheet metal helps to cool and channel air around the engine when it's running. It's very important to install each piece carefully and in the right location. Use new hardware when you're fastening each piece and refer to Appendix B as a guide to where each piece is located.

HEATER SYSTEM

Each car has a slightly different heater system. Reconnect yours using the photos and notes that you created during disassembly. Use new heater hoses for all your connections, and make sure that you only use high-temp heater hose. The plastic air hoses that are commonly sold at hardware stores will melt when exposed to the high heat of the engine.

the fan housing. At this point, install the toothed belt. The pump should now be synchronized with the engine.

10-17 *Install the accelerator bracket on the engine. On CIS cars, there is a small support bracket that also attaches to the fuel injection air box.*

10-18 Center your clutch disc using the clutch alignment tool. Before you attach the pressure plate, make sure that you properly attach the throw-out bearing (for push-type clutches). Don't forget to install the flywheel starter ring. This is a somewhat common mistake to make.

CLUTCH

The clutch installation is described in further detail in Project 8 of *101 Projects for Your Porsche 911*. Begin by placing the clutch disc against the surface of the flywheel and support it there using the clutch alignment tool, as shown in Figure 10-18. The purpose of the tool is to keep the disc centered while you bolt down the pressure plate. If the disc is not centered, you will have great difficulty remounting the engine to the transmission.

If you have a 1972-86 911, you will need to install and attach the throw-out bearing to the pressure plate. Assemble the bearing according to how the old one was put together, and be careful to place all the rings and spacers in their correct orientation. If you have a 1965-69 car, you can just install the pressure plate on the flywheel—the throw-out bearing is installed on the transmission.

It is common not to fully install your heater system until the engine is completely run-in. If this is the case, then you should make sure that you cover the two side air channels that are attached to both sides of the fan housing. If these are left open, then the lack of back pressure will rob the cylinders of valuable cooling air.

If you have a mechanical fuel injection system, it's important that you attach the MFI pre-heat hose. This hose is connected to the heat exchangers and heats the element inside the pump to lean out the mixture. When the car is cold, the mixture is rich to aid in starting and warm up. If the hose is disconnected or damaged, then the element does not get heated and the pump is set to run rich all the time. Make sure that the hose on your car is firmly connected, and installed properly.

Install the pressure plate and bolt it down, pressing the clutch disc in place. Make sure you reinstall the starter ring on 1970-86 911s. When you are finished, you should be able to easily remove the alignment tool, and the clutch disc should not move at all.

Congratulations, your rebuilt engine is complete. Figure 10-19 shows the final assembly with the CIS fuel injection installed for a 1974 engine. For those of you who have removed the fuel injection, Figure 10-20 shows the same engine with a setup that utilizes dual Weber carburetors.

10-19 Shown here is the 1974 CIS engine, complete except for the engine sheet metal.

10-20 The same motor as in Figure 10-19 outfitted with a set of Weber carburetors.

Now it's time for the really exciting part. In this chapter, you'll reinstall the engine in your engine bay and start it up for the first time. There are a few very important break-in procedures that we'll cover in this chapter, along with a bonus section on dyno testing. An important note to remember during these final steps is not to rush. There is a potential to hurry in this section because you're excited about starting and running your engine. Keep it slow and safe—you don't want to ruin your fresh rebuild or, even worse, injure yourself or start a fire!

ENGINE INSTALLATION

It's tough to discuss engine installation here because all of the 911s have very many subtle differences that make each engine installation slightly different. My primary advice would be to perform all the steps very carefully and make sure that your gas lines are very snug and secure. If you have a 915 or G50 transmission, make sure that you properly mate the throw-out bearing with the clutch arm. Failure to do so will result in a clutch that doesn't work and an engine that needs to be removed again. See the official website for this book (www.101projects.com) for additional material that I did not have space to publish here.

ENGINE BREAK-IN

Careful attention to detail is required when you are running in your newly rebuilt engine. It's important to follow the guidelines detailed here, as many small parts in your engine are beginning to mesh and wear together. These first few moments of your engine's life are very important. Wear patterns are initiated in this break-in stage and must be started properly, otherwise your freshly rebuilt engine will wear out faster than you'd like.

What is Break-In?

Before we start discussing what you need to do and what you need to avoid when first starting your engine, let's talk for a moment about what exactly the break-in of your engine really means. The difference between your old engine and your newly rebuilt one is basically clearances. Aside from a few replaced seals, the only change that you made was to machine and replace parts that were out of tolerance. The newly rebuilt engine now has many parts that have been brought back to their original factory specifications.

The process of breaking in an engine involves all of the parts in the engine beginning to wear together and find their "grooves." The close-tolerance parts are going to wear and machine themselves into proper alignment with their counterparts as the engine begins to wear. Because a lot of

wear will occur at this very early stage, it's vital that the procedure for break-in be followed very closely and carefully. The pistons, cylinders, valve guides, and bearings will all begin to shape themselves to each other as you initially run the engine.

When you first start up the engine, you will run it at higher RPMs for a period of about twenty minutes. This is primarily so that you can get adequate lubrication to the camshafts and the rockers. Failure to do so will begin what is known as a wear pattern. Once a wear pattern begins between two metal surfaces, the wear accelerates quickly soon after. Running the engine at an elevated RPM means that your camshafts and rockers will not develop a destructive wear pattern.

The pistons, cylinders, and rings typically take a longer time to mate and seal properly with each other. Contrary to common belief, the rings don't necessarily seat themselves to the cylinder walls. They primarily seal between the top and bottom of the piston ring groove. Also, the force provided to seal the ring against the cylinder wall comes from combustion pressure—not the tension of the cylinder ring. Failure to obtain higher combustion forces in the early minutes of the engine's life can lead to rings taking much longer to seat.

Gas Tank

If your car has been sitting idle for more than 6 months or so, then I highly recommend that you empty the gas tank and use fresh fuel. Gasoline does not have a good shelf life, and after sitting in your tank for many months, the gas can deteriorate and become like varnish. This old gas doesn't burn well, leaves deposits in your new engine, and gums up carburetors and fuel injection systems. Use a small carburetor fuel pump available at your local auto parts store, and some long fuel line to pump the gasoline out of your tank and into a portable storage container. You should be able to evacuate almost all of the old gas from your car with this method. You would hate to have dirty, gummy gas end up in your freshly rebuilt carburetors.

Use at least three gallons of fresh fuel in your tank. Use the highest octane fuel that you can buy at the pump—this will guard against any pinging or detonation that may occur before you are able to tune the engine properly. The three gallons of gasoline will help dilute any old fuel still left in the tank. In addition, the CIS and Motronic fuel injection systems run fuel in a continuous loop—from engine to tank. These systems need a minimum amount of fuel to circulate in the system. Adding three gallons ensures that you will not run your fuel pump dry.

Motor Oil

Let's begin by talking about motor oil. With your engine completely dry, you should fill it up with a minimum of nine quarts. Check your owner's manual as well, as some years required a bit more or less. Add an extra quart of oil if you have an external oil cooler. When you fill the oil, it should empty directly from the oil tank into the inlet to the oil pump, lubricating the pump when you first start the engine. I recommend that you use standard non-synthetic 20W-50 motor oil. Don't use synthetic oils until the engine has been run-in for at least 1,000 miles. Buy at least 3 cases (36 quarts) of oil, as you will be changing it often. Non-detergent motor oils are not necessary—the engine will run-in and the rings will seat properly with the standard off-the-shelf motor oil.

Final Check

Before you turn the car over, it's good to make a final check of everything to be sure that you didn't make any silly mistakes. Here is a brief checklist:

- Transmission in neutral.
- Nine quarts of motor oil in engine.
- Plug wires attached in proper order.
- Three gallons of gas in tank.
- All fuel lines attached and properly seated.
- Lug-nuts tightened on wheels.
- Fire extinguisher handy (just in case).
- Static timing is set (Project 23 in *101 Projects for Your Porsche 911*).

Build Oil Pressure

Before you start the engine, you will turn it over with the starter so that you can build oil pressure. I know mechanics who claim that the oil pressure builds so fast in the 911 engine that this is not necessary. While the oil pressure may build fast, it's not good practice simply to fire up the engine. Turning over the engine until oil pressure is built up can prevent some costly damage. If you used the wrong pistons in your oil pump bypass modification, then you will see this when oil pressure doesn't build. If you have a leaky oil line, or one that you forgot to connect, then you will see this also.

In order to build oil pressure, you will need to disable the ignition system on the engine. I also like to disable the fuel system too, just in case there are any problems. On the CIS and earlier cars, you can pull out the small red fuel pump relay in the front fuse/relay box. Also disconnect the plug to the CD box on the left side of the engine compartment. For Motronic cars, all you need to do is pull out the DME relay, which is located under the driver's seat. An alternative to sitting in the driver's seat is to use what is known as a remote starter switch. This plugs into your starter terminals and has a trigger that you press to turn the car over. These are available at Sears for about fifteen dollars.

Place a battery charger on your battery, and set it to charge at ten amps. Don't set it any higher—you just want to give the battery a boost while you're cranking, and you also want to help it recharge in between turnover efforts.

With everything in place, turn over the engine with the starter key for exactly thirty seconds. This should start oil flowing around your engine. After thirty seconds, take a look at both the top and bottom of the engine. Look for oil spots, spray, or other indications of something gone horribly awry. After you have concluded that everything looks okay, get ready to crank the engine over again.

If you installed a high-compression engine, then you may find that your starter is having problems turning over the engine. High-torque starters are readily available and are lighter than the original ones used on the 911. For more information on installing one of these high-torque starters, see Project 87 in *101 Projects for Your Porsche 911*.

After letting the starter rest for about a minute or two, crank the engine over again. Let it turn over until the green oil pressure light on the dashboard goes off. This should take about thirty seconds. When the light goes out, stop cranking and rest the starter for about thirty seconds. Then, continue cranking the engine, and keep it going for about fifteen seconds after the light goes out. The oil pressure switches are set at very low values—just because the light has gone out doesn't necessarily mean that oil has reached all the areas of the engine. Just make sure that you don't crank the engine any more than thirty seconds at a time.

If the light doesn't go out then STOP! You now need to take a closer look at your engine to see what the problem is. Did you connect the oil pressure switch? Is it working properly? The cam housing oil lines are located at one of the high points of the engine—you may want to slightly loosen one of the lines while an assistant cranks over the engine. This will create a slightly messy oil leak, but will also give you a definitive answer as to whether your engine is receiving oil

6-1 *Crank the engine over for 30-second intervals until the oil pressure light goes out (yellow arrow). Don't crank for more than 30 seconds, and make sure that you give your starter a break of at least a minute in between crankings.*

or not. Check the pistons in your oil pressure relief valves, located on the side and bottom of the engine case. Is the piston securely seated? Sometimes a case plug will interfere with the proper operation of the piston. Are you using the correct pistons? Did you remember to use the spring guide with the longer spring?

Engines with low oil pressure may have problems with the oil pressure pistons in the bottom side of case—check them and verify that the pistons move freely in their bores. Typical oil pressure valves should be about 15 psi per 1000 RPM (10 psi per 1000 RPM minimum). At idle, oil pressure of 1-2 psi is considered normal. With low oil pressure engines, you can shim the bottom oil pressure spring with 6mm washers. Shim to a height of 4-5mm.

Sometimes your starter will not be able to turn your engine over fast enough to make the oil pressure light go out. If this is the case, you have a few options. First, you can remove the spark plugs from the engine. This will eliminate compression in the cylinders and enable the engine to spin a lot faster. An alternative is to start the engine, let it turn over only for a second or two, and then shut it off immediately. The oil pressure light should go out almost immediately. Don't run the engine for more than a few seconds. If the light doesn't go out, perform some of the checks outlined in the previous paragraph.

Start Engine

With the engine primed with motor oil, you can now reconnect the fuel and ignition systems and start the engine. Don't start the engine with the car in your garage—push it out into the driveway. It's also a wise idea not to start the engine outside late at night. Even though you have been working all day to get to this goal, it's probably best to wait until morning. You will be running the engine at high RPMs for quite a while, and your neighbors will have a fit if you subject them to this noise in the evening hours. Trust me—I have learned from experience on this one.

As soon as the engine is started, immediately raise the idle to about 1,800 to 2,000 rpm. Use an RPM meter hooked up to your spark plug wires if you think that your tachometer may not give you accurate readings. It is important that the engine not be at idle speed for any length of time. On the CIS cars, you can simply adjust the large spring-loaded screw on the side of the throttle body. For carbureted and MFI engines, turn the two idle adjustment screws on the ends of the throttle bodies. If your car is equipped with a hand throttle, simply pull it up until the idle reaches the desired level. For the Motronic engines, your best bet is to just sit in the car with your foot on the gas pedal, keeping the car within the proper RPM range.

Make sure that you take a stopwatch with you. This isn't an option, but a requirement. The reason is that after about five to ten minutes, you'll turn the engine off and swear it was twenty minutes. The twenty minutes will feel like forever, because the engine will be very loud, and you'll think that this treatment can't be good for a new engine. Never fear—it is. Running in the engine at this RPM raises oil pressure and oil flow volume so that all your new meshing parts in the engine are sure to get plenty of lubrication. The higher RPMs are best for forming the initial wear patterns between the rocker arms and the camshafts. At this RPM range, the engine is turning over just fast enough that the rockers begin to be thoroughly lubricated as they follow the camshaft lobes. The rockers begin to ride on a thin layer of oil, which separates them from direct contact with the cam lobe. At lower RPMs, the valve clearance gap comes into play as the rockers have a tendency to hammer the camshaft. You can hear this as you raise the RPM—the click-clack of the valves will subside somewhat.

It's a wise idea to have a helper during this stage. One person can turn the car over, and another can quickly adjust the idle up to the proper range. In addition, I always like to have at least one other person standing nearby with a fire extinguisher. Every time you work with fuel lines, there is always the possibility that you can make a mistake or a fuel connector can fail. If you see any gas leaks or smell significant amounts of fumes, then shut off the car immediately. Keep in mind that your carburetors will smell fumy under normal operation. Check the top and bottom of the engine for oil leaks. Working so many hours around the engine when it was on the stand may also give you a false sense of security around the engine. Be aware of the hot exhaust and especially the engine fan.

During the break-in, your engine will smell terrible. A sulfur-like smell is typical of the rings burning in. In addition, any coating, paint, or even manufacturers' stickers left on your exhaust will begin to burn off. If you painted your exhaust, then the paint will begin to cure at the high exhaust temperatures. Expect the car to smell strange for about 1,000 miles. It is for this reason that I don't recommend hooking up your heater system until after the engine is completely broken-in, and all the paint, dust, and fumes are gone.

What do you do if your engine doesn't start? There are a variety of reasons why you might have problems. There are a few common mistakes that will sometimes leave even the experts scratching their heads:

• If the starter spins and spins, and doesn't turn over the engine, then you probably forgot to install the flywheel ring gear.

• If the starter won't turn over and the engine is not spinning, then you may have a dead battery, or your engine may have too high a compression for your starter. Get a high-torque starter and make sure that your battery is fully charged.

• Strange engine electrical problems may also be caused

by accidentally leaving the transmission ground strap off of the engine. The engine is electrically isolated from the chassis via the rubber motor and transmission mounts. If the ground strap is disconnected, then the only ground return will be through the smaller cables in the engine harness. A clear indicator of this problem is weak performance from a starter that is known to be working properly. Check all of your cables and grounds.

• If your engine doesn't want to turn over, take a wrench and place it on the fan belt and try to turn over the engine slowly by hand. You want to make sure that there's nothing in the engine or transmission that is causing it to get stuck or caught.

• The car turns over and seems to fire on one or two cylinders only. This is a common mistake and can usually be traced back to an ignition problem. Either the distributor is not installed properly at TDC, or you may have installed the spark plug wires in the wrong order.

• The car turns over, but there is no sign of it firing. Make sure that you have both spark and fuel. Use a timing light clipped on the spark plug wires to determine if there is a spark signal going to the plug. If your timing light can detect a spark, then you know that you probably have either a fuel delivery problem or a timing problem. If you don't find a spark, then check your CD box (1969-83) to make sure that it's plugged in. It should make a faint high-pitched whine when it's working properly. Also check your ignition trigger points on the distributor. Check the dwell gap for systems that use points (1977 and earlier), and check to make sure all the sensors are plugged in on any breakerless ignition system (1978 and later).

• To check for fuel, pull out an injector and place it in a clear glass jar. Have an assistant crank over the car and check to make sure that you see fuel exiting the injector. Lift up on the CIS sensor plate located inside the large black plastic injection air box. You should hear a "meow" sound from the injectors as they begin to disperse fuel. If there is no fuel, check the fuel pressure in your fuel injection system. Check to make sure that none of the rubber fuel lines became kinked when you reinstalled the engine. Even if one or two injectors are clogged and not dispersing fuel, the engine will still try to fire on the remaining cylinders.

• If you have an MFI car, double-check to make sure that the pump is properly synchronized with the camshaft. Having a misaligned belt will cause the fuel to be delivered to the cylinders at the wrong time.

• If you have a Motronic 3.2-liter engine and you don't have spark or fuel, then there are a few things to check. Check to make sure that your DME relay is installed and working (located under the driver's seat). Also check the speed/reference sensor gap (should be about 0.8mm) at the flywheel, or the wires that connect the sensor to the harness. Also check that the fuel injector harness is plugged in properly.

• If you have both fuel and spark but the engine isn't firing, then you probably have a timing problem. The spark is being fired at the wrong time. Check your distributor orientation and also your spark plug wires.

Oil Change #1

When the engine has run for twenty minutes, turn it off, and immediately empty the oil. If you don't believe that an oil change is warranted after only twenty minutes, then simply look at the oil as it empties out of the engine. You will see millions of tiny metallic flakes in it. This is the evidence of all your new parts breaking in and beginning to mesh with one another. Empty the oil from the engine and the oil tank and replace the filter. Refill the engine with about eight or nine quarts of oil.

If your car is equipped with a front-mounted oil cooler, you should check to see if the thermostat has opened up the flow of oil to the cooler. Feel the oil cooler lines to see if they are warm. If the thermostat hasn't opened then you'll have to add about three quarts of oil after it opens up on your initial drives.

Now, restart the engine. Adjust the idle down to proper levels (800 to 900 rpm for most engines). Check the oil level in the tank with the engine at idle (it still should be warm at this point). Add a quart or two if the oil level appears low. Using your timing light, set the timing according to Project 23 in *101 Projects for Your Porsche 911*.

Initial Drives

You're now ready for that all-important first drive. Check the brakes and the clutch before you take the car out of your driveway. Take the car to a location where there isn't much traffic. You're going to be quite distracted listening to your engine and breaking it in—you don't want too many other cars around. Drive the car varying the load and the RPM range. Shift gears often and do not let the car stay in any one RPM range for very long. Don't let the RPMs go above 5,000 for this initial drive.

You want to vary the engine speeds because you want all the parts to wear and mesh at all RPMs. Running the engine at a constant 4,000 RPM or so will cause the rings to seat fine at that RPM, but not at other ranges. You want to wear the engine evenly and consistently, particularly on this first drive.

On your first drive, take it out for about a three- to five-mile drive. Stay close to your home base. You want to be able to return quickly to your garage and tools if you encounter a problem. After the first drive, return to your garage and check the oil lines, carburetors, oil temperature, etc. Make sure that nothing is amiss. Check the oil level— if your thermostat has opened up, you will find that your oil level is now probably about three quarts low. Check the oil using the dipstick, not the gauge, and only check it when the car is warm and running at idle.

On your second drive, take the car out for about eight to ten miles, then return home and check everything again. The third drive should be ten to twenty miles, and the fourth drive should be about fifty miles.

During your initial drives, vary the load and RPM from 1,000 to 5,000. Accelerate quickly and also decelerate with the car in gear. You want to increase pressure on both sides of the rings. Pressure on the cylinder head side of the ring is easy—simply accelerate to 5,000 rpm at about three-quarter throttle. To build pressure on the engine case side of the rings simply pick a long downhill stretch and coast from fifty-five down to about twenty miles per hour, with the engine in gear. This will increase vacuum in the engine case and help pull the rings in the opposite direction.

Don't venture too far from home on your first drive. Pull over every so often and check under the car and inside the engine compartment. Look for fuel and oil leaks, and also for burning, smoking oil. Take a flashlight with you just in case you need to look at something more closely. A cellular phone, halon fire extinguisher, and toolkit are good precautions against something going wrong as well.

When you get your 911 back home, while the car is still warm, empty the oil again. While you may think that all of these oil changes are superfluous, just look at the oil. Again, it will contain loads of bright specs of metal. Flushing the oil out of the engine at this stage is good for the car, as it will reduce the amount of metallic parts that will increase wear inside your engine. Also change the filter again.

THE NEXT DAY & BEYOND

After your initial drive, I recommend that you let the car sit and cool down completely overnight. This will give the seals and internal engine parts a good chance to go from cold to hot to cold again. You don't really want them going from cold to hot to warm to hot again, because it may not give them a good chance to completely seal within the engine.

Fill up the car again with oil, if you didn't already do that the previous evening—make a note to yourself if you left the car without oil. Then start the car and let it warm up by driving it around the neighborhood a bit. When the car is warm, you can then recheck the ignition timing and also adjust the carburetors. Detailed procedures for adjusting the timing and adjusting your carburetors or fuel injection can be found in the book, *101 Projects for Your Porsche 911*.

Drive the car for about 500 miles, and then change the oil again. At this time, you will want to adjust your valves (see *101 Projects*) and retighten your head stud nuts. You can reach the head studs with your head stud tool when the valve covers are off during your valve adjustment. The engines with aluminum crankcases typically don't require any additional tightening, but you will probably find that the magnesium case head stud nuts will turn at least a quarter turn before tightening up to their final torque. At

about 1,000 miles, change the oil again, readjust the valves, and tighten the head studs one more time. At this time, your engine should be completely broken in, and oil consumption should be down to about 1 quart per 1,000 miles. This is about the average amount for a newly rebuilt 911 engine.

A lot of people aren't really sure what motor oil to use in their car. Traditionally, the characteristics of motor oil were linked closely to their weight. Heavier weight oils protect well against heat. Lighter weight oils flow better in engines in cold environments. In general, if you live in a cold climate, you should use a 10W-40 or similar oil. This oil is a 10-weight oil that behaves and protects against heat like a 40-weight oil. In warmer climates, you should use a 20W-50 oil. This oil doesn't flow as well in the colder climates, but gives extra protection on the hotter end.

The question of whether to use synthetic or "dinosaur" oil often comes up among car buffs. Consumer Reports (July 1996) did an extensive test a few years ago on both types of oil, and after tearing apart engines and measuring wear, they couldn't find any discernable differences between the two. Still, some people swear by synthetic oil. In general, you should not use the synthetic oil if you have an older car with old seals in the engine. There have been many documented cases where the addition of synthetic oil has caused an otherwise dry car to start leaking. If you own an older 911 that doesn't have fresh seals in the engine, I would stick to the non-synthetics. However, since your engine seals should be brand new at this stage, the use of synthetics should be fine. I would recommend against using them for the first 1,000 miles of engine break-in, however.

Smog Testing

If you live in an environmentally conscious state like I do (California), then you are probably very familiar with the trials and tribunes associated with the dreaded smog test. Current law states that automobiles manufactured in 1974 or later must pass an increasingly strict set of emissions tests. Unfortunately, the tests have gotten more stringent over the years. Despite the "official" line from the California state government that cars are only tested to emissions standards that they would have passed when new, this is not entirely true. In the summer of 1998, California's Smog Check II program began testing vehicles on a dynamometer for three pollutants: oxides of nitrogen (NOx), carbon monoxide (CO), and hydrocarbons (HC). The 911 engine was never originally designed to meet the NOx standard, but thankfully, the engine typically runs clean enough to pass this standard.

A problem does exist for newly rebuilt engines. Since your 911 engine will not be fully broken-in until it is driven about 1,000 miles, if you take the car in for a smog check beforehand, then there is a chance it will fail. Since new engines burn lots of oil when they are breaking in their parts, you may even have your new engine tagged as a "gross polluter." This is not good, as it will permanently flag your car in the state-wide database as one that is likely to fail. Then, in order to pass the smog check, you will need to bring it to what is known as a test-only station. These stations are more likely to fail your car for any small infraction like an unplugged vacuum hose, and they are not authorized to make repairs to your car (like plugging in the hose to get you to pass). Needless to say, you want to avoid this situation at all costs.

If you have rebuilt your engine over a relatively short period of time, then you should have no problem, because your car is currently registered. However, a lot of 911 owners rebuilding engines have had the cars on non-operational status for a while. This means that the car is unregistered for driving on the road. As soon as the car hits the road, you are then required to register it and have the smog check performed. The catch-22 is that you need time to break-in the engine. If you have the car checked right away, it will certainly be flagged as a gross polluter.

The bottom line is that you need to drive the car on the road legally for about 1,000 miles before it is completely broken in. Check with your local government regarding the specific laws regulating the procedure for driving a car with a newly rebuilt engine. There are currently a few options available in the state of California, but the law changes all the time.

BONUS SECTION: DYNO TESTING

What performance engine rebuilding book would be complete without a section on dynamometer testing? One of the neatest trips you can make after you've rebuilt and broken in your engine (1,000-plus miles) is to your local dyno shop. For about $100, you can make a few runs on the dyno and actually measure the horsepower that is generated by your engine. The whole process is somewhat complicated, with varying degrees of detail and accuracy, but for the sake of this section, we'll just cover the basics.

What Is a Dyno?

Short for dynamometer, the dyno measures the horsepower output by your engine. There are two basic types of dynos, one that you bolt the engine up to and run, and one that measures horsepower at the rear wheels of your car. This is also called RWHP (rear wheel horsepower). Most modern dyno testing is performed on a rolling dyno that measures the power output at the wheels. You drive your car onto big rollers and accelerate at full throttle until you reach your rev limit. Then, you let the clutch pedal out and let the rollers spin down freely. Large fans and environmental controls aim to keep the test environment at a steady state so that you can compare dyno runs.

The dyno works by placing a load on the car, similar to how you would experience air friction as you were driving down the road at high speeds. By measuring this load, combined with the total RPM of the vehicle, a graph of the power output by the car can be derived.

Torque / Horsepower

The dyno actually measures the torque output by your rear wheels. Torque is a measurement of rotational force and is related to your engine's overall power output. The horsepower output by your engine is equivalent to the following formula, which is derived from an early English standard:

$$\text{Horsepower} = \text{Torque} \times \text{RPM} / 5252$$

This translates into a power relation such that horsepower is defined as 33,000 ft-lb. (force) per minute (or the power required to lift 33,000 pounds one foot in one minute). This is also the horsepower definition as defined by the Society of Automotive Engineers (SAE Horsepower).

You may have also seen other definitions for horsepower and wondered what they meant. European documentation often gives horsepower numbers in kilowatts. For reference, one horsepower equals 0.746 kilowatts. Porsche's ratings are often listed in the European standard of DIN HP. One DIN horsepower is rated as the power required to raise

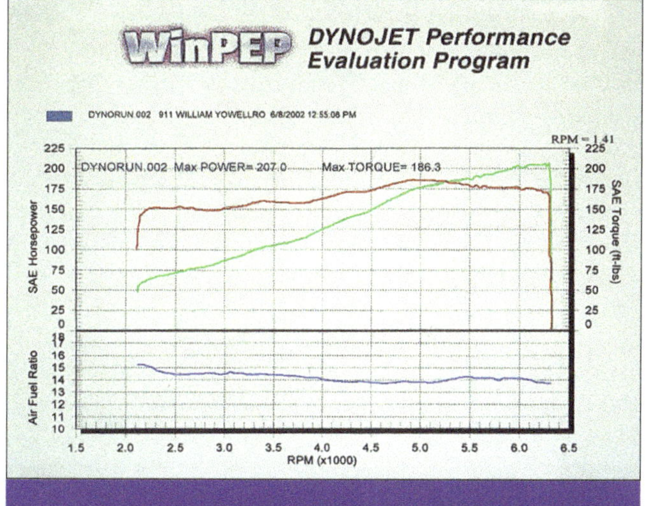

6-2 *A typical dyno graph for a 1985 911 Carrera with a 3.2L engine. The graph shows about 207 rear wheel horsepower. The minimum rating for this engine in its stock configuration is 207 hp at the flywheel. The owner of this car, Bill Yowell, has upgraded the engine with a Weltmeister chip, stainless steel exhaust, a Cat bypass test pipe, Magnecor ignition wires, and he has also removed the A/C system. This particular dyno also measures the air-fuel mixture, which can be an added benefit especially when tuning engine management systems. Note that as per the relationship between torque and horsepower, they are equal when the RPM has reached 5252. The test was performed with the car in fourth gear, and the rev limit of 6200 rpm was programmed into the dynamometer.*

450,000 kilograms one centimeter in one minute. The values of SAE and DIN horsepower are very similar, with 1 SAE HP being equal to .98629 DIN HP. For all practical purposes, you can think of them as the same.

You may have also heard the term brake horsepower (BHP). Brake horsepower is measured at the flywheel of the engine with no load from the chassis, without any electrical or mechanical accessories attached, under ideal fuel and timing conditions. In modern terms, the brake horsepower figure would be mostly associated with what is now called gross horsepower.

Factory HP Numbers

There is a common misconception when people talk about horsepower numbers released by the factory. Porsche has traditionally released minimum horsepower figures for their cars. Most manufactures release average horsepower numbers. Depending upon manufacturing tolerances between any of the thousands of parts in the 911 engine, you can have variations of up to ten to fifteen percent. For example, the 911 S engine rebuilt in this book is rated at 175 horsepower from the factory. This figure is the power output at the flywheel from the entire engine assembly. This would include required accessories like the alternator or the MFI pump. In reality, this horsepower figure is a minimum cutoff number. Any engines that did not meet 175 horsepower were discarded or reworked and not installed in 911s. As a result, when you dyno test your engine, you will often find that its output is slightly higher than you were expecting. This subtle difference is important if you are comparing different cars to one another. The point is that you should compare apples to apples when talking about Porsche horsepower figures.

Air-Fuel Measurement

In addition to measuring output torque and RPM, some dynos can also monitor your air-fuel mixture. This will allow you to adjust the mixture tables on an engine management system to match the power output. In other words, if you find that your engine is running lean at 4,500 rpm, you can adjust the fuel injection mixture to richen it up and produce more ideal combustion. This translates to more horsepower output from the engine.

Dyno Results

The dyno will generate a graph of horsepower versus RPM for the engine being tested. With this graph, you will be able to determine the engine's peak horsepower and peak torque. The graph will also show you the peak horsepower output from the engine. On a 911 engine, this will typi-

6-3 *This photo shows Kurt Williams' 911 RS clone on a rolling dynamometer. The car is driven slowly through its full RPM range on the dyno, while the machine carefully records all of the applicable data. Conditions are tightly controlled using fans and air temp/humidity measurement devices to ensure that the environment remains constant between dyno runs.*

cally be at the higher end of the RPM range, right near the redline. The engine will peak in horsepower, and then fall off dramatically as the rev-limiter in the engine cuts off the ignition system.

Comparing Results

An unfortunate downside to dyno tests is that they often cannot be accurately compared to one another. Environmental conditions play a large part in these variances, as well as the fact that the large dynos cannot be easily calibrated. As a result, tests from the same dyno with the same car on different days may produce different results. Even the manufacturers of some dynamometers admit that their dyno at one location may test five to ten percent differently from the same model dyno at another location. When you consider that the figure may become bigger when you include dynos from different manufacturers, the ability to compare results becomes significantly less useful.

An important issue to mention with respect to dyno figures is that the test is influenced heavily by environmental conditions. This includes temperature, humidity and altitude to name a few. Since conditions may change from day to day, dyno runs that span multiple days may produce different results.

Engine Optimization

As previously mentioned, dyno testing can be very subjective. Other than bragging rights, pure dyno numbers are not very useful. The true benefit of the dyno test comes when you are able to use it to optimize your engine. Particularly with engine management systems like the TEC-3, you really need extensive dyno testing in order to determine what your optimum operating parameters should be on the fuel ratio and ignition timing maps. The factory used the same type of procedure to optimize and program the Motronic factory chip used in the 3.2-liter engine.

In order to gain the most horsepower from your engine, you need to do several dyno runs while varying many different engine parameters (timing, mixture, advance curve, etc.). Only after carefully analyzing the data can you determine what the best values are for your engine management system map. In a similar manner, you can use the dyno runs to optimize MFI settings, or carburetor jetting. Measuring the power output of the engine will allow you to optimize your engine and get the peace of mind knowing that you are extracting the maximum horsepower that you possibly can.

Driveline Losses

Since the dyno testing is performed using rollers on your car, there are going to be forces that are going to slow down and reduce the power between the flywheel and the rear wheels. These driveline losses are the result of friction from the transmission, brake discs dragging slightly, and friction in the wheel bearings. On the 911, typical driveline losses are about eleven to twelve percent for the 901 transmission, and about fourteen percent for the 915 transmission. Through a complicated process of calculations that are computed by the dynamometer, you can figure out what your driveline loss is by the time it takes the dyno rollers to stop when you let out the clutch. Using these calculations, you can then estimate what your horsepower output is at the flywheel.

Transmission Gearing

One of the benefits of dyno testing is the ability to design your transmission ratios to meet the exact power characteristics of your engine. Depending upon where you want optimum performance, you can install taller or shorter gears in any of the five speeds on your transmission. For example, the 2.7-liter 911 S engine being rebuilt for this book has a significant rise in horsepower beginning at about 3000 rpm. In my 914-6, second gear at about thirty miles per hour places the engine exactly at 3000 rpm. As a result, acceleration to redline from thirty to about sixty-five in second gear is lightning quick. The results of the dyno test will give you specific horsepower numbers for each RPM range, and allow you to tailor your transmission gearing to suit your desires.

G-TECH

This handy gadget is what I call the poor man's dyno. It's an accelerometer that sits on your dashboard and measures the acceleration (or G-force) of your car. If you have an accurate measurement of the weight of your car, then you can get horsepower estimates from the acceleration recorded by the unit.

The G-Tech is a great concept. However, like the big roller dynos, the horsepower figures are somewhat subjective. Driving ability and habits can skew results on the G-Tech. As with the traditional dyno, the G-Tech is best viewed as a comparison and tuning tool. Although it has much less precision than a dyno, you can test your car indefinitely, and use it to determine if you're gaining any horsepower from minor modifications and tweaks. As with the big dyno, the results are tremendously dependent on environmental factors, so you should only really compare numbers from same-day runs. It's also highly dependent on the characteristics of your driving, including the speed at which you shift through the gears.

6-4 *What I dub the "poor man's dyno," the G-Tech is an interesting and unique device. It has a built-in accelerometer that will measure your total acceleration over a period of time. If you know the weight of your car, you can achieve a good estimate of the horsepower that your engine is putting out. Although the first version of this unit was somewhat primitive, at the time of this writing a newer, advanced version is about to be released (shown in photo). With a more readable display, and the ability to download your test data, the new G-Tech should be a great improvement on the original concept.*

Appendix A: Porsche 911 Engine Technical Specifications

In the following tables, I've compiled an extensive array of technical information that you may need to inspect and rebuild your 911 engine. The information contained in these tables was compiled from original factory resources. In many cases, I found inconsistencies and incorrect values in the original documentation. I have done my best to cross-reference all of the information contained in these tables to correct the errors and omissions that were contained in the original documentation. (All measurements are expressed in millimeters (mm) unless otherwise specified.)

Torque Specifications

Description	Threads	Torque	Chapter 5 Figure	Notes
Rod nuts	M10x1.25		2-12	Use red Loctite 271 on threads
1st step (initial torque)		20 Nm (14.7 ft-lbs.)		
2nd step (final torque)		90 degrees		Tighten to initial torque and then turn nut 90 +/- 2 degrees
Oil pump nuts	M8	25 Nm (18.4 ft-lbs.)	3-20	Use factory self-locking oblong nuts
Case through-bolts	M10	35 Nm (25.8 ft-lbs.)	3-28	Torque according to pattern in Figure 3-28 in Chapter 5
Studs in oil cooler housing	M10	35 Nm (25.8 ft-lbs.)	3-28	Same as above
Nut in left-side chain housing	M10	35 Nm (25.8 ft-lbs.)	3-27	Same as above
Outer perimeter nuts on crankcase	M8	25 Nm (18.4 ft-lbs.)	3-29	
Crankcase breather cover nuts	M6	11 Nm (8.1 ft-lbs.)	3-35	
Temperature sensor in crankcase breather cover		25 Nm (18.4 ft-lbs.)	3-35	
Thermostat nuts	M6	11 Nm (8.1 ft-lbs.)	3-35	
Oil pressure switch	M10x1	20 Nm max (14.7 ft-lbs.)	3-35	
Oil pressure relief valve plugs	M12x1.5	60 Nm (44.2 ft-lbs.)	3-37	On side and bottom of case
Chain ramp bolts		25 Nm (18.4 ft-lbs.)	3-38	Use sealing ring beneath bolt
Flywheel bolts (1965-77)	M12x1.5	150 Nm (110 ft-lbs.)	3-42	Make sure that flywheel washer is in place, use red Loctite 271
Flywheel bolts (1978-89)	M10x1.25	90 Nm (66.3 ft-lbs.)	3-42	Use red Loctite 271
Flywheel pilot bearing bolts	M6x12	10 Nm (7.4 ft-lbs.)		
Pressure plate bolts	M8	25 Nm (18.4 ft-lbs.)	10-18	
Crankshaft pulley bolt (without A/C)	M12x1.5	80 Nm (59 ft-lbs.)	3-44	Use spring washer underneath
Crankshaft pulley bolt (with A/C)	M12x1.5x22	170 Nm (125.3 ft-lbs.)	3-44	
Camshaft to cylinder head nuts	M8	25 Nm (18.4 ft-lbs.)	5-11	
Cylinder head nuts	M10		5-12	
1st step (initial torque)		10 Nm (7.4 ft-lbs.)		Use anti-seize compound, or Optimoly HT lube on both nuts and washers prior to performing the tightening process
2nd step (final torque)		32 Nm (23.5 ftl-lbs.)		
Timing chain housing to engine case	M8	25 Nm (18.4 ft-lbs.)	6-3	Use factory self-locking oblong nuts
Camshaft thrust plate to camshaft housing bolts	M6	10 Nm (7.4 ft-lbs.)	6-6A	
46mm camshaft nut (1965-82)	M27x2	150 Nm (110 ft-lbs.)	6-8	Original spec was superceded to this value for all 1965-82 911s
Camshaft bolt (1982-89)	M12x1.5	120 Nm (88.5 ft-lbs.)	6-8	
Chain tensioner nut	M8	25 Nm (18.4 ft-lbs.)	7-19	
Rocker arm shafts	M6	18 Nm (13.2 ft-lbs.)	6-21	Turn the bolt, not the conical nut, torque to 25 Nm if rockers leak
Camshaft housing oil line adapters		35 Nm (25.8 ft-lbs.)	9-3	
Camshaft housing oil line plug		35 Nm (25.8 ft-lbs.)	9-5	
Adapter for left side camshaft oil line		35 Nm (25.8 ft-lbs.)	9-7	
Adapter to crankcase (on neck for oil pressure sender)	M12x1.5	35 Nm (25.8 ft-lbs.)	9-10	Goes through the square block
Oil pressure sender to adapter	M18x1.5	35 Nm max (25.8 ft-lbs.)	9-10	Don't tighten using the fragile casing of the pressure sensor— use the built-in nut on the bottom instead
Crankcase oil temperature sender	M14x1.5	25 Nm max (18.4 ft-lbs.)	9-10	High pressure oil runs past this sensor
Hydraulic chain tensioner hollow bolt		10 Nm (7.4 ft-lbs.)	9-8	Tighten further if leakage occurs
Temperature sensors on chain housing covers		25 Nm (18.4 ft-lbs.)	9-9	Tighten further if leakage occurs
Distributor nut	M8	25 Nm (18.4 ft-lbs.)	9-12	
Spark plugs	M14x1.25	25-30 Nm (18.4-22 ft-lbs.)	9-16	Do not use anti-seize compound, as per Porsche tech bulletin 9102, Group 2, identifier 2870, see manufacturer's recommended torque specs
Valve cover nuts	M8	8 Nm (6 ft-lbs.)	9-18	Tighten further if leakage occurs
Oil cooler nuts	M8	25 Nm (18.4 ft-lbs.)	9-19	Use self-locking nylon nuts
Engine sump plate nuts	M6	11 Nm (8.1 ft-lbs.)	9-21	Tighten further if leakage occurs
Engine oil drain plug in sump (1965-83)	M22x1.5	42 Nm (31 ft-lbs.)	9-21	Drain plug must not be located under oil pump pickup
Engine oil drain plug in crankcase (1983-89)	M20x1.5	70 Nm (51.5 ft-lbs.)	9-21	Located on left side of engine cases from late 1983
Engine oil line adapter	M22x1	120 Nm (88.5 ft-lbs.)	9-21	Connects engine case and oil line that feeds external oil tank/cooler
Intermediate shaft cover plate	M6	10 Nm (7.4 ft-lbs.)	9-22	
Exhaust nuts	M8	25 Nm (18.4 ft-lbs.)	10-6	Retighten when cool, after first drive, use anti-seize
Air injection adapter on cylinder heads (1975-77)	M10x1	12 Nm (8.8 ft-lbs.)		
Air injection line to adapter (1975-77)	M14x1.5	23 Nm (17 ft-lbs.)		
Fan belt pulley nut	M16x1	40 Nm (30.2 ft-lbs.)	10-14	Use factory tool to hold pulley when tightening
Miscellaneous Nut (8.8 class, coarse thread)	M14	141 Nm (104 ft-lbs.)		Use this table to determine the torque values for miscellaneous fasteners located on your fuel injection and exhaust system.
Miscellaneous Nut (8.8 class, fine thread)	M14x1.5	150 Nm (110 ft-lbs.)		" " " "
Miscellaneous Nut (8.8 class, coarse thread)	M12	89 Nm (65.5 ft-lbs.)		" " " "
Miscellaneous Nut (8.8 class, fine thread)	M12x1.25	95 Nm (70 ft-lbs.)		" " " "
Miscellaneous Nut (8.8 class, coarse thread)	M10	51 Nm (37.2 ft-lbs.)		" " " "
Miscellaneous Nut (8.8 class, fine thread)	M10x1.25	52 Nm (28.3 ft-lbs.)		" " " "
Miscellaneous Nut (8.8 class, coarse thread)	M8	25 Nm (18.4 ft-lbs.)		" " " "
Miscellaneous Nut (8.8 class, fine thread)	M8x1	27 Nm (19.9 ft-lbs.)		" " " "
Miscellaneous Nut (8.8 class, coarse thread)	M6	11 Nm (8.1 ft-lbs.)		" " " "
Miscellaneous Nut (8.8 class, coarse thread)	M4	3.1 Nm (2.2 ft-lbs.)		" " " "

Notes:
- Use proper method for tightening fasteners. See Section 1 of Chapter 5.
- Figures refer to assembly photos located in Chapter 5.
- Rod bolt torque specification changed in later years. For all factory rod bolts, torque to initial amount, then rotate nut an additional 90 degrees. Original Porsche specification from 1965 was 50 Nm(36.2 ft-llbs) with no Loctite and thread and mating surfaces lubricated.

Engine Model Types and Data

Year	Engine	Type	Disp	Max HP/RPM	Max Torque/ RPM	Bore/ Stroke	Comp Ratio	Valves Int/Ex	Ports Int/Ex	Fuel System	Engine Serial #	Notes
1965	911	901/01	1991	130/6100	175/4200	80/66	9.0:1	39/35	32/32	Solex 40 PI	900 001	
	906	901/20	1991	210/8000	206/6200	80/66	10.3:1	45/39	38/38	Weber 46 IDA	N/A	
1966	911	901/01	1991	130/6100	175/4200	80/66	9.0:1	39/35	32/32	Solex 40 PI	903 551	
	911	901/05	1991	130/6100	175/4200	80/66	9.0:1	39/35	32/32	Weber 40 IDA	907 001	
	906E	901/21	1991	220/8000	206/6200	80/66	10.3:1	45/39	38/38	Mech Fuel Inj	N/A	Slide valve MFI
1967	911	901/05	1991	130/6100	175/4200	80/66	9.0:1	39/35	32/32	Weber 40 IDA	909 001	
	911	901/06	1991	130/6100	175/4200	80/66	9.0:1	39/35	32/32	Weber 40 IDA	911 001	With new heat exchangers
	911S	901/02	1991	160/6600	179/5200	80/66	9.8:1	42/38	36/35	Weber 40 IDS	960 001	
	911R	901/23	1991	220/8000	206/6200	80/66	10.3:1	45/39	38/38	Weber 46 IDA	N/A	
1968	911	901/14	1991	130/6100	175/4200	80/66	9.0:1	39/35	32/32	Weber 40 IDAP	328 0001	USA
	911	901/17	1991	130/6100	175/4200	80/66	9.0:1	39/35	32/32	Weber 40 IDAP	338 0001	USA
	911L	901/06	1991	130/6100	175/4200	80/66	9.0:1	39/35	32/32	Weber 40 IDA	308 0001	
	911L	901/07	1991	130/6100	175/4200	80/66	9.0:1	39/35	32/32	Weber 40 IDA	318 0001	
	911T	901/03	1991	110/5800	157/4200	80/66	8.6:1	42/38	32/32	Weber 40 IDT	208 0001	European model
	911T	901/13	1991	110/5800	157/4200	80/66	8.6:1	42/38	32/32	Weber 40 IDT	218 0001	
	911S	901/02	1991	160/6600	179/5200	80/66	9.8:1	42/38	36/35	Weber 40 IDS	408 0001	
	911S	901/08	1991	160/6600	179/5200	80/66	9.8:1	42/38	36/35	Weber 40 IDS	418 0001	
	911L	901/14	1991	130/6100	175/4200	80/66	9.0:1	39/35	32/32	Weber 40 IDAP	328 0001	USA
	911L	901/17	1991	130/6100	175/4200	80/66	9.0:1	39/35	32/32	Weber 40 IDAP	338 0001	USA
1969	911T	901/03	1991	110/5800	157/4200	80/66	8.6:1	42/38	32/32	Weber 40 IDT P	619 0001	
	911T	901/13	1991	110/5800	157/4200	80/66	8.6:1	42/38	32/32	Weber 40 IDT P	619 3001	Sportomatic
	911T	901/16	1991	110/5800	157/4200	80/66	8.6:1	42/38	32/32	Weber 40 IDT P	619 3297	USA
	911T	901/19	1991	110/5800	157/4200	80/66	8.6:1	42/38	32/32	Weber 40 IDT P	619 7292	USA- Sportomatic
	911E	901/09	1991	140/6500	175/4500	80/66	9.1:1	42/38	32/32	Mech Fuel Inj	629 0001	
	911E	901/11	1991	140/6500	175/4500	80/66	9.1:1	42/38	32/32	Mech Fuel Inj	629 8001	Sportomatic
	911S	901/10	1991	170/6800	181/5500	80/66	9.9:1	45/39	36/35	Mech Fuel Inj	639 0001	Also seen with 33mm exhaust ports
1970	911T-C	911/03	2195	125/5800	177/4200	84/66	8.6:1	46/40	32/32	Zenith 40 TIN	610 0001	
	911T-C	911/06	2195	125/5800	177/4200	84/66	8.6:1	46/40	32/32	Zenith 40 TIN	610 3001	Sportomatic
	911T-C	911/07	2195	125/5800	177/4200	84/66	8.6:1	46/40	32/32	Zenith 40 TIN	610 5001	USA
	911T-C	911/08	2195	125/5800	177/4200	84/66	8.6:1	46/40	32/32	Zenith 40 TIN	610 8001	USA- Sportomatic
	911E-C	911/01	2195	155/6200	191/4500	84/66	9.1:1	46/40	32/32	Mech Fuel Inj	620 0001	
	911E-C	911/04	2195	155/6200	191/4500	84/66	9.1:1	46/40	32/32	Mech Fuel Inj	620 8001	Sportomatic
	911S-C	911/02	2195	180/6500	199/5200	84/66	9.8:1	46/40	36/35	Mech Fuel Inj	630 0001	
	914-6	901/37	1991	110/5800	157/4200	80/66	8.6:1	42/38	32/32	Weber 40 IDA	640 0001	Also 901/37/38/39
1971	911T-C	911/03	2195	125/5800	177/4200	84/66	8.6:1	46/40	32/32	Zenith 40 TIN	611 0001	Or Weber 40 IDT P1
	911T-C	911/06	2195	125/5800	177/4200	84/66	8.6:1	46/40	32/32	Zenith 40 TIN	611 90	Sportomatic
	911T-C	911/07	2195	125/5800	177/4200	84/66	8.6:1	46/40	32/32	Zenith 40 TIN	611 4001	USA
	911T-C	911/08	2195	125/5800	177/4200	84/66	8.6:1	46/40	32/32	Zenith 40 TIN	611 9501	USA- Sportomatic
	911E-C	911/01	2195	155/6200	191/4500	84/66	9.1:1	46/40	32/32	Mech Fuel Inj	621 0001	
	911E-C	911/04	2195	155/6200	191/4500	84/66	9.1:1	46/40	32/32	Mech Fuel Inj	621 8001	Sportomatic
	911S-C	911/02	2195	180/6500	199/5200	84/66	9.8:1	46/40	36/35	Mech Fuel Inj	631 0001	
	911	911/21	2380	230/7800	230/6200	87.5/66	10.3:1	46/40	38/38	Mech Fuel Inj	N/A	911 factory race engine
	911	911/22	2247	250/7800	255/6200	85/66	10.3:1	46/40	38/38	Weber 46 IDA	N/A	911 factory race engine
	911	911/70	2492	270/8000	260/5300	86.7/70.4	10.3:1	46/40	41/41	Mech Fuel Inj	N/A	911 factory race engine
1972	911TV-E	911/57	2341	130/5600	196/4000	84/70.4	7.5:1	46/40	32/32	Carburetor	652 0001	Carb, also seen with 30mm intake/exhaust ports
	911TV-E	911/67	2341	140/5600	196/4000	84/70.4	7.5:1	46/40	32/32	Carburetor	652 9001	Carb- Sportomatic
	911T-E	911/51	2341	140/5600	196/4000	84/70.4	7.5:1	46/40	32/32	Mech Fuel Inj	612 0001	MFI- USA
	911T-E	911/61	2341	165/6200	196/4000	84/70.4	7.5:1	46/40	32/32	Mech Fuel Inj	612 9001	MFI- USA- Sportomatic
	911E-E	911/52	2341	165/6200	206/4500	84/70.4	8.0:1	46/40	32/32	Mech Fuel Inj	622 0001	MFI
	911E-E	911/62	2341	165/6200	206/4500	84/70.4	8.0:1	46/40	32/32	Mech Fuel Inj	662 9001	MFI- Sportomatic
	911S-E	911/53	2341	190/6500	216/5200	84/70.4	8.5:1	46/40	36/36	Mech Fuel Inj	632 0001	MFI
	911S-E	911/63	2341	190/6500	216/5200	84/70.4	8.5:1	46/40	36/36	Mech Fuel Inj	632 9001	MFI- Sportomatic
	911RSR	911/72	2808	308/8000	294/6200	92/70.4	10.3:1	49/41.5	43/43	Mech Fuel Inj	N/A	Factory RSR 2.8 race engine
1973	911TV-E	911/57	2341	130/5600	196/4000	84/70.4	7.5:1	46/40	32/32	Carburetor	653 0001	Carb
	911TV-E	911/67	2341	130/5600	196/4000	84/70.4	7.5:1	46/40	32/32	Carburetor	653 9001	Carb- Sportomatic
	911T-E	911/51	2341	140/5600	196/4000	84/70.4	7.5:1	46/40	32/32	Mech Fuel Inj	613 0001	MFI- USA
	911T-E	911/61	2341	140/5600	196/4000	84/70.4	7.5:1	46/40	32/32	Mech Fuel Inj	613 9001	MFI- USA- Sportomatic
	911E-E	911/52	2341	165/6200	206/4500	84/70.4	8.0:1	46/40	32/32	Mech Fuel Inj	623 0001	
	911E-E	911/62	2341	165/6200	206/4500	84/70.4	8.0:1	46/40	32/32	Mech Fuel Inj	623 9001	Sportomatic
	911S-E	911/53	2341	190/6500	216/5200	84/70.4	8.5:1	46/40	36/36	Mech Fuel Inj	633 0001	
	911S-E	911/63	2341	190/6500	216/5200	84/70.4	8.5:1	46/40	36/36	Mech Fuel Inj	633 9001	Sportomatic
	Carrera RS	911/83	2687	210/6300	255/5100	90/70.4	8.5:1	46/40	36/35	Mech Fuel Inj	663 0001	
1973 1/2	911T	911/91	2341	140/5600	201/4000	84/70.4	8.0:1	46/40	30/33	CIS Fuel Inj	613 3001	USA
	911T	911/96	2341	140/5600	207/4000	84/70.4	8.0:1	46/40	30/33	CIS Fuel Inj	613 9301	USA
1974	911	911/92	2687	150/5700	235/3800	90/70.4	8.0:1	46/40	32/33	CIS Fuel Inj	614 0001	Also seen with 30/32 intake/exhaust ports
	911	911/97	2687	150/5700	235/3800	90/70.4	8.0:1	46/40	32/33	CIS Fuel Inj	614 9001	Sportomatic. Also seen with 30/32 intake/exhaust ports
	911S	911/93	2687	175/5800	235/4000	90/70.4	8.5:1	46/40	35/35	CIS Fuel Inj	634 0001	Also Carrera
	911S	911/98	2687	175/5800	235/4000	90/70.4	8.5:1	46/40	35/35	CIS Fuel Inj	634 9001	Sportomatic
	911RSR	911/75	2994	315/8000	313/6500	95/70.4	10.3:1	49/41.5	43/43	Mech Fuel Inj	N/A	Slide valve MFI
	Carrera	911/83	2687	210/6300	255/5100	90/70.4	8.5:1	46/40	36/35	Mech Fuel Inj	665 0001	European Carrera RS MFI
1975	911	911/41	2687	150/5700	235/3800	90/70.4	8.0:1	46/40	32/32	CIS Fuel Inj	615 0001	
	911S	911/42	2687	175/5800	235/4000	90/70.4	8.5:1	46/40	35/35	CIS Fuel Inj	635 0001	
	911S/C	911/43	2687	165/5800	226/4000	90/70.4	8.5:1	46/40	35/35	CIS Fuel Inj	645 0001	USA
	911S/C	911/44	2687	160/5800	226/4000	90/70.4	8.5:1	46/40	35/35	CIS Fuel Inj	655 0001	California
	911	911/46	2687	150/5700	235/3800	90/70.4	8.0:1	46/40	32/32	CIS Fuel Inj	615 9001	Sportomatic
	911 S	911/47	2687	175/5800	235/4000	90/70.4	8.5:1	46/40	35/35	CIS Fuel Inj	635 9001	Sportomatic
	911 S	911/48	2687	165/5800	235/4000	90/70.4	8.5:1	46/40	35/35	CIS Fuel Inj	645 9001	USA- Sportomatic
	911 S/C	911/49	2687	160/5800	226/4000	90/70.4	8.5:1	46/40	35/35	CIS Fuel Inj	655 9001	Sportomatic- California
	Carrera	911/83	2687	210/6300	255/5100	90/70.4	8.5:1	46/40	36/35	Mech Fuel Inj	665 0001	European Carrera (RS) MFI
	Turbo	930/50	2993	260/5500	343/4000	95/70.4	6.5:1	49/41.5	32/36	CIS Fuel Inj	675 0001	European model only

Year	Engine	Type	Disp	Max HP/RPM	Max Torque/RPM	Bore/Stroke	Comp Ratio	Valves Int/Ex	Ports Int/Ex	Fuel System	Engine Serial #	Notes
1976	911	911/81	2687	165/5800	235/4000	90/70.4	8.5:1	46/40	35/35	CIS Fuel Inj	636 0001	
	911	911/86	2687	165/5800	235/4000	90/70.4	8.5:1	46/40	35/35	CIS Fuel Inj	636 9001	Sportomatic
	911S	911/82	2687	165/5800	255/4200	90/70.4	8.5:1	46/40	35/35	CIS Fuel Inj	646 0001	USA
	911S	911/84	2687	165/5800	255/4200	90/70.4	8.5:1	46/40	35/35	CIS Fuel Inj	656 0001	Calif
	911S	911/89	2687	165/5800	255/4200	90/70.4	8.5:1	46/40	35/35	CIS Fuel Inj	656 9001	USA/Calif Sportomatic
	Carrera	930/02	2993	200/6000	255/4200	95/70.4	8.5:1	49/41.5	39/35	CIS Fuel Inj	666 0001	
	Carrera	930/12	2993	200/6000	255/4200	95/70.4	8.5:1	49/41.5	39/35	CIS Fuel Inj	666 9001	Sportomatic
	Turbo	930/50	2993	260/5500	343/4000	95/70.4	6.5:1	49/41.5	32/36	CIS Fuel Inj	676 0001	
	Turbo	930/51	2993	245/5500	343/4000	95/70.4	6.5:1	49/41.5	32/36	CIS Fuel Inj	686 0001	USA
	934 Turbo	930/71	2994	530/7000	589/5400	95/70.4	6.5:1	49/41.5	41/41	CIS Fuel Inj	N/A	934 fact. turbo engine
	935 Turbo	930/72	2856	590/7900	594/5400	92.8/70.4	6.5:1	49/41.5	41/41	CIS Fuel Inj	N/A	935 fact. turbo engine
1977	911	911/81	2687	165/5800	235/4000	90/70.4	8.5:1	46/40	35/35	CIS Fuel Inj	637 0001	
	911	911/86	2687	165/5800	235/4000	90/70.4	8.5:1	46/40	35/35	CIS Fuel Inj	637 9001	Sportomatic
	911S	911/85	2687	165/5800	255/4200	90/70.4	8.5:1	46/40	35/35	CIS Fuel Inj	627 0001	USA
	911S	911/90	2687	165/5800	255/4200	90/70.4	8.5:1	46/40	35/35	CIS Fuel Inj	627 9001	USA Sportomatic
	Carrera	930/02	2993	200/6000	255/4200	95/70.4	8.5:1	49/41.5	39/35	CIS Fuel Inj	667 0001	
	Carrera	930/12	2993	200/6000	255/4200	95/70.4	8.5:1	49/41.5	39/35	CIS Fuel Inj	667 9001	Sportomatic
	Turbo	930/52	2993	260/5500	343/4000	95/70.4	6.5:1	49/41.5	32/36	CIS Fuel Inj	677 0001	
	Turbo	930/53	2993	245/5500	343/4000	95/70.4	6.5:1	49/41.5	32/36	CIS Fuel Inj	687 0001	USA
	Turbo	930/54	2993	245/5500	343/4000	95/70.4	6.5:1	49/41.5	32/36	CIS Fuel Inj	677 2001	Japan
1978	911 SC	930/03	2993	180/5500	265/4200	95/70.4	8.5:1	49/41.5	39/35	CIS Fuel Inj	638 0001	R.o.W.
	911 SC	930/13	2993	180/5500	265/4200	95/70.4	8.5:1	49/41.5	39/35	CIS Fuel Inj	638 9001	R.o.W. Spm.
	911 SC	930/04	2993	180/5500	245/4200	95/70.4	8.5:1	49/41.5	39/35	CIS Fuel Inj	628 0001	USA
	911 SC	930/05	2993	180/5500	245/4200	95/70.4	8.5:1	49/41.5	39/35	CIS Fuel Inj	618 0001	Japan
	911 SC	930/15	2993	180/5500	245/4200	95/70.4	8.5:1	49/41.5	39/35	CIS Fuel Inj	618 9001	Japan Spm.
	911 SC	930/06	2993	180/5500	245/4200	95/70.4	8.5:1	49/41.5	39/35	CIS Fuel Inj	658 0001	California
	911 Turbo	930/60	3299	300/5500	421/4000	97/74.4	7.0:1	49/41.5	32/34	CIS Fuel Inj	678 0001	R.o.W.
	911 Turbo	930/61	3299	265/5500	395/4000	97/74.4	7.0:1	49/41.5	32/34	CIS Fuel Inj	688 0001	USA
	911 Turbo	930/62	3299	265/5500	395/4000	97/74.4	7.0:1	49/41.5	32/34	CIS Fuel Inj	678 2001	Japan
	911 Turbo	930/63	3299	265/5500	395/4000	97/74.4	7.0:1	49/41.5	32/34	CIS Fuel Inj	688 1001	California
1979	911 SC	930/03	2993	180/5500	265/4200	95/70.4	8.5:1	49/41.5	39/35	CIS Fuel Inj	639 0001	R.o.W.
	911 SC	930/13	2993	180/5500	265/4200	95/70.4	8.5:1	49/41.5	39/35	CIS Fuel Inj	639 9001	R.o.W. Spm.
	911 SC	930/04	2993	180/5500	245/4200	95/70.4	8.5:1	49/41.5	39/35	CIS Fuel Inj	629 0001	USA
	911 SC	930/05	2993	180/5500	245/4200	95/70.4	8.5:1	49/41.5	39/35	CIS Fuel Inj	619 0001	Japan
	911 SC	930/15	2993	180/5500	245/4200	95/70.4	8.5:1	49/41.5	39/35	CIS Fuel Inj	619 9001	Japan Spm.
	911 SC	930/06	2993	180/5500	245/4200	95/70.4	8.5:1	49/41.5	39/35	CIS Fuel Inj	659 0001	California
	911 Turbo	930/60	3299	300/5500	421/4000	97/74.4	7.0:1	49/41.5	32/34	CIS Fuel Inj	679 0001	R.o.W.
	911 Turbo	930/64	3299	265/5500	395/4000	97/74.4	7.0:1	49/41.5	32/34	CIS Fuel Inj	689 0001	USA
	911 Turbo	930/65	3299	265/5500	395/4000	97/74.4	7.0:1	49/41.5	32/34	CIS Fuel Inj	679 1001	Japan
	911 Turbo	930/63	3299	265/5500	395/4000	97/74.4	7.0:1	49/41.5	32/34	CIS Fuel Inj	689 1001	California
1980	911 SC	930/07	2993	180/5500	245/4200	95/70.4	9.3:1	49/41.5	34/35	CIS Fuel Inj	640 0001	USA
	911 SC	930/08	2993	180/5500	245/4200	95/70.4	9.3:1	49/41.5	34/35	CIS Fuel Inj	630 8001	Japan
	911 SC	930/09	2993	188/5500	265/4200	95/70.4	8.6:1	49/41.5	34/35	CIS Fuel Inj	630 0001	R.o.W.
	911 Turbo	930/60	3299	300/5500	421/4000	97/74.4	7.0:1	49/41.5	32/34	CIS Fuel Inj	670 0001	R.o.W.
	911 Turbo	930/64	3299	265/5500	395/4000	97/74.4	7.0:1	49/41.5	32/34	CIS Fuel Inj		USA-Model not exported to US
	911 Turbo	930/65	3299	265/5500	395/4000	97/74.4	7.0:1	49/41.5	32/34	CIS Fuel Inj	670 8001	Japan
1981	911 SC	930/10	2993	204/5900	267/4300	95/70.4	9.8:1	49/41.5	34/35	CIS Fuel Inj	631 0001	R.o.W.
	911 SC	930/16	2993	180/5500	265/4200	95/70.4	9.3:1	49/41.5	34/35	CIS Fuel Inj	641 0001	USA
	911 SC	930/17	2993	180/5500	265/4200	95/70.4	9.3:1	49/41.5	34/35	CIS Fuel Inj	631 8001	Japan
	911 Turbo	930/60	3299	300/5500	421/4000	97/74.4	7.0:1	49/41.5	32/34	CIS Fuel Inj	671 0001	R.o.W. / Canada
1982	911 SC	930/10	2993	204/5900	267/4300	95/70.4	9.8:1	49/41.5	34/35	CIS Fuel Inj	63C 0001	R.o.W.
	911 SC	930/16	2993	180/5500	265/4200	95/70.4	9.3:1	49/41.5	34/35	CIS Fuel Inj	64C 0001	USA
	911 SC	930/17	2993	180/5500	265/4200	95/70.4	9.3:1	49/41.5	34/35	CIS Fuel Inj	63C 8001	Japan
	911 Turbo	930/60	3299	300/5500	421/4000	97/74.4	7.0:1	49/41.5	32/34	CIS Fuel Inj	67C 0001	R.o.W. / Canada
1983	911 SC	930/10	2993	204/5900	267/4300	95/70.4	9.8:1	49/41.5	34/35	CIS Fuel Inj	63D 0001	R.o.W.
	911 SC	930/16	2993	180/5500	265/4200	95/70.4	9.3:1	49/41.5	34/35	CIS Fuel Inj	64D 0001	USA
	911 SC	930/17	2993	180/5500	265/4200	95/70.4	9.3:1	49/41.5	34/35	CIS Fuel Inj	63D 8001	Japan
	911 Turbo	930/66	3299	300/5500	421/4000	97/74.4	7.0:1	49/41.5	32/34	CIS Fuel Inj	67D 0001	R.o.W. / Canada
	911SCRS	930/18	2993	255/7000	250/6500	95/70.4	10.3:1	49/41.5	43/43	Mech Fuel Inj	N/A	Factory RS race engine
1984	Carrera	930/20	3164	231/5900	284/4800	95/74.4	10.3:1	49/41.5	40/38	Motronic	63E 00001	R.o.W.
	Carrera	930/21	3164	207/5900	260/4800	95/74.4	9.5:1	49/41.5	40/38	Motronic	64E 00001	USA, Japan
	911 Turbo	930/66	3299	300/5500	430/4000	97/74.4	7.0:1	49/41.5	32/34	CIS Fuel Inj	67E 00001	R.o.W. and Canada
1985	Carrera	930/20	3164	231/5900	284/4800	95/74.4	10.3:1	49/41.5	40/38	Motronic	63F 00001	R.o.W.
	Carrera	930/21	3164	207/5900	260/4800	95/74.4	9.5:1	49/41.5	40/38	Motronic	64F 00001	USA
	Carrera	930/26	3164	231/5900	284/4800	95/74.4	10.3:1	49/41.5	40/38	Motronic	63F 10001	Switzerland/Sweden/Australia
	911 Turbo	930/66	3299	300/5500	430/4000	97/74.4	7.0:1	49/41.5	32/34	CIS Fuel Inj	67F 00001	R.o.W. and Canada
1986	Carrera	930/20	3164	231/5900	284/4800	95/74.4	10.3:1	49/41.5	40/38	Motronic	63G 00001	R.o.W.
	Carrera	930/21	3164	207/5900	260/4800	95/74.4	9.5:1	49/41.5	40/38	Motronic	64G 00001	USA, Japan
	Carrera	930/26	3164	231/5900	284/4800	95/74.4	10.3:1	49/41.5	40/38	Motronic	63G 10001	Switzerland/Sweden/Australia
	911 Turbo	930/66	3299	300/5500	430/4000	97/74.4	7.0:1	49/41.5	32/34	CIS Fuel Inj	67G 00001	R.o.W. and Canada
	911 Turbo	930/68	3299	282/5500	390/4000	97/74.4	7.0:1	49/41.5	32/34	CIS Fuel Inj	68G 00001	USA - first year imported since 1980
1987	Carrera	930/20	3164	231/5900	284/4800	95/74.4	10.3:1	49/41.5	40/38	Motronic	63H 00001	R.o.W.
	Carrera	930/25	3164	217/5900	265/4800	95/74.4	9.5:1	49/41.5	40/38	Motronic	64H 00001	USA/Austria/Switzerland/Japan and FRG with Cat. Conv. (M 298)
	Carrera	930/26	3164	231/5900	284/4800	95/74.4	10.3:1	49/41.5	40/38	Motronic	63H 10001	Sweden
	911 Turbo	930/66	3299	300/5500	430/4000	97/74.4	7.0:1	49/41.5	32/34	CIS Fuel Inj	67H 00001	R.o.W.
	911 Turbo	930/68	3299	282/5500	390/4000	97/74.4	7.0:1	49/41.5	32/34	CIS Fuel Inj	68H 00001	USA
1988	Carrera	930/20	3164	231/5900	284/4800	95/74.4	10.3:1	49/41.5	40/38	Motronic	63J 00001	R.o.W.
	Carrera	930/25	3164	217/5900	265/4800	95/74.4	9.5:1	49/41.5	40/38	Motronic	64J 00001	USA/Austria/Switzerland/Japan and FRG with Cat. Conv. (M 298)
	Carrera	930/26	3164	231/5900	284/4800	95/74.4	10.3:1	49/41.5	40/38	Motronic	63J 10001	Sweden
	911 Turbo	930/66	3299	300/5500	430/4000	97/74.4	7.0:1	49/41.5	32/34	CIS Fuel Inj	67J 00001	R.o.W.
	911 Turbo	930/68	3299	282/5500	390/4000	97/74.4	7.0:1	49/41.5	32/34	CIS Fuel Inj	68J 00001	USA / Canada
1989	Carrera	930/20	3164	231/5900	284/4800	95/74.4	10.3:1	49/41.5	40/38	Motronic	63K 00001	R.o.W.
	Carrera	930/25	3164	217/5900	265/4800	95/74.4	9.5:1	49/41.5	40/38	Motronic	64K 00001	Australia/Austria/Switzerland/Sweden/Japan with Cat. Conv. (M 298)
	911 Turbo	930/66	3299	300/5500	430/4000	97/74.4	7.0:1	49/41.5	32/34	CIS Fuel Inj	67K 00001	R.o.W.
	911 Turbo	930/68	3299	282/5500	390/4000	97/74.4	7.0:1	49/41.5	32/34	CIS Fuel Inj	68K 00001	USA / Canada

Notes:
- Engine serial number located on bottom left side of engine cooling fan housing. A169.
- For camshaft timing and specifications, please see the camshaft section in this Appendix.
- CIS = Continuous Injection System.
- R.o.W. = Rest of World.
- Bore, stroke, valve sizes, and port sizes are given in millimeters.
- Displacement is given in cubic centimeters.
- Horsepower is minimum HP rating (DIN 70020).
- Torque is measured in Newton-meters.
- Sportomatic = supplied with Sportomatic auto-clutch transmission.

202

Ignition Timing and CO % Measurements

Year	Model	Breaker Gap	Dwell Angle	Dynamic Timing	Spark Plugs	Plug Gap	Idle Speed	Idle CO % Level	Partial Load CO %	Total Advance / Timing check
1965-68	911/911L (901/01/05/06/07)	0.3 min	38° ± 3° (10)	30° BTDC @ 6000rpm (no load)	W 250 P 21	0.35	900 ± 50	N/A		32° BTDC @ 6000 rpm (w/load)
1965-68	911S (901/02/08)	0.3 min	38° ± 3° (10)	30° BTDC @ 6000 rpm	W 265 P 21	0.35	900 ± 50	N/A		see dynamic timing
1965-68	911T (901/03)	0.4 ± 0.03	40° ± 3° (10)	35° BTDC @ 6000rpm (no load)	W 230 T 30	0.6	900 ± 50	N/A		see dynamic timing
1965-68	911L (901/14/17 w/EECS)	0.3 min	38° ± 3° (10)	3° ATDC @ 850-950 rpm	W 250 P 21	0.35	900 ± 50	1.0-1.5		32° ± 2° BTDC @ 6000 rpm
1969	911T	0.3 min	38° ± 3° (10)	35° BTDC @ 6000 rpm	W 230 T 30	0.6	900 ± 50	3.5 ± 0.5		see dynamic timing
1969	911T - USA	0.3 min	38° ± 3° (10)	33°-35° BTDC @ 6000 rpm	W 250 P 21	0.6	900 ± 50	3.5 ± 0.5		see dynamic timing
1969	911E	0.3 min	38° ± 3° (10)	30° BTDC @ 6000 rpm	W 265 P 21	0.6	900 ± 50	3.0-4.0 (11)	2.3-3.3 (3,11)	see dynamic timing
1969	911E - USA	0.3 min	38° ± 3° (10)	29 - 31° BTDC @ 6000 rpm	W 265 P 21	0.6	900 ± 50	3.0-4.0 (11)	2.3-3.3 (3,11)	see dynamic timing
1969	911S	0.3 min	38° ± 3° (10)	30° BTDC @ 6000 rpm	W 265 P 21	0.6	900 ± 50	3.5-4.5 (11)	2.4-3.4 (3,11)	see dynamic timing
1969	911S - USA	0.3 min	38° ± 3° (10)	29 - 31° BTDC @ 6000 rpm	W 265 P 21	0.6	900 ± 50	3.5-4.5 (11)	2.4-3.4 (3,11)	see dynamic timing
1970-71	911T-C (carb)	0.3 min	38° ± 3° (10)	35° BTDC @ 6000 rpm	W 230 T 30	0.6	900 ± 50	3.5 ± 0.5		see dynamic timing
1970-71	911T-C - USA (carb)	0.3 min	38° ± 3° (10)	33 - 35° BTDC @ 6000 rpm	W 250 P 21	0.6	900 ± 50	3.5 ± 0.5		see dynamic timing
1970-71	911E-C	0.3 min	38° ± 3° (10)	30° BTDC @ 6000 rpm	W 265 P 21	0.6	900 ± 50	2.5-3.5 (11)	2.2-3.2 (3)	see dynamic timing
1970-71	911E-C - USA	0.3 min	38° ± 3° (10)	29 - 31° BTDC @ 6000 rpm	W 265 P 21	0.6	900 ± 50	2.5-3.5 (11)	2.2-3.2 (3)	see dynamic timing
1970-71	911S-C	0.3 min	38° ± 3° (10)	30° BTDC @ 6000 rpm	W 265 P 21	0.6	900 ± 50	3.1-4.1 (11)	1.2-2.2 (3)	see dynamic timing
1970-71	911S-C - USA	0.3 min	38° ± 3° (10)	29 - 31° BTDC @ 6000 rpm	W 265 P 21	0.6	900 ± 50	3.1-4.1 (11)	1.2-2.2 (3)	see dynamic timing
1972-73	911T-E (USA)	0.35	38° ± 3° (2)	5° ATDC @ 900 rpm (5)	W 235 P 21	0.55	900 ± 50	2.5 ± 0.5	1.5-2.0 (3)	38° BTDC @ 6000 rpm (5)
1972-73	911E-E (USA)	0.35	38° ± 3° (2)	5° ATDC @ 900 rpm (5)	W 265 P 21	0.55	900 ± 50	2.5 ± 0.5	2.0-2.5 (3)	38° BTDC @ 6000 rpm (5)
1972-73	911S-E (USA)	0.35	38° ± 3° (2)	5° ATDC @ 900 rpm (5)	W 265 P 21	0.55	900 ± 50	2.5 ± 0.5	2.0-2.5 (3)	38° BTDC @ 6000 rpm (5)
1972-73	911TV-E (Carb, Europe)	0.35	38° ± 3° (2)	5° ATDC @ 900 rpm (5)	W 230 T 30	0.7	900 ± 50	3.5 ± 0.5		38° BTDC @ 6000 rpm (5)
1972-73	911E-E (Europe)	0.35	38° ± 3° (2)	5° ATDC @ 900 rpm (5)	W 260 T 2	0.7	900 ± 50	3.0 ± 0.5	2.0-3.0 (3)	38° BTDC @ 6000 rpm (5)
1972-73	911S-E (Europe)	0.35	38° ± 3° (2)	5° ATDC @ 900 rpm (5)	W 260 T 2	0.7	900 ± 50	3.0 ± 0.5	2.0-3.0 (3)	38° BTDC @ 6000 rpm (5)
1973	911 Carrera RS (MFI)	0.35	38° ± 3° (2)	TDC	W 260 T 2	0.7	900 ± 50	2.5 ± 0.5	2.5-3.0 (3)	38° BTDC @ 6000 rpm (5)
1973 1/2	911T CIS	0.35	38° ± 3° (2)	5° ATDC @ 900 rpm (5)	W 235 P 21	0.55	900 ± 50	1.5-2.0		38° BTDC @ 6000 rpm (5)
1974	911	0.35	38° ± 3° (2)	5° ATDC @ 900 rpm (5)	W 215 P 21	0.55	900 ± 50	1.5-2.5		38° BTDC @ 6000 rpm (5)
1974	911S/Carrera (CIS)	0.35	38° ± 3° (2)	5° ATDC @ 900 rpm (5)	W 235 P 21	0.55	900 ± 50	1.5-2.5		38° BTDC @ 6000 rpm (5)
1974-75	Carrera (MFI)	0.35	38° ± 3° (2)	TDC	W 260 T 2	0.55	900 ± 50	2.5 ± 0.5	2.5-3.0 (3)	38° BTDC @ 6000 rpm (5)
1975	911	0.35	38° ± 3° (2)	5° ATDC @ 900 rpm (5)	W 215 T 30	0.7	900 ± 50	2.0-2.5		38° BTDC @ 6000 rpm (5)
1975	911S	0.35	38° ± 3° (2)	5° ATDC @ 900 rpm (5)	W 225 T 30	0.7	900 ± 50	2.0-2.5		38° BTDC @ 6000 rpm (5)
1975	911 S/C (USA Carrera)	0.35	38° ± 3° (2)	5° ATDC @ 900 rpm (5)	W 235 P 21	0.55	900 ± 50	1.5-2.0		38° BTDC @ 6000 rpm (5)
1976	911S (USA)	0.35	38° ± 3° (2)	5° ATDC @ 900 rpm (5)	W 225 T 30	0.7	900	2.0-4.0 (6)		
1976	911 Turbo			29° ± 2° BTDC @ 4000 rpm (4)	W 280 P 21	0.6	900 ± 50	2.0-2.5 (6)		TDC ± 4° BTDC @ 900-950 (5)
1976	911 Turbo (USA)			5° ± 3° ATDC @ 900-1000 rpm (5)	W 280 P 21	0.6	900 ± 50	1.0-3.0 (6)		26° ± 3° BTDC @ 4000 rpm (4)
1977	911S (USA)	0.35	38° ± 3° (2)	TDC ± 2° @ 950-1000 rpm (5)	W 225 T 30	0.7	950-1000	1.5-3.0 (6)		
1977	911S (California)	0.35	38° ± 3° (2)	15° ± 2° ATDC @ 1000 rpm (5)	W 225 T 30	0.7	950-1050	1.5-3.0 (6)		
1977	911S (Japan)	0.35	38° ± 3° (2)	15° ± 2° ATDC @ 950-1000 rpm (5)	W 225 T 30	0.7	950-1050	1.0-2.0 (6)		
1977	911 Turbo (USA)			7° ± 2° ATDC @ 950-1050 rpm (5)	W 280 P 21	0.6	950-1050	2.0-4.0 (6)		29° ± 3° BTDC @ 4000 rpm (4)
1977	911 Turbo			29° ± 2° BTDC @ 4000 rpm (4)	W 280 P 21	0.6	900 ± 50	2.0-4.0 (6)		TDC ± 4° BTDC @ 900-950 (5)
1976-77	911	0.35	38° ± 3° (2)	5° ATDC @ 900 rpm (5)	W 225 T 30	0.7	900 ± 50	1.0-1.5		
1976-77	Euro Carrera 3.0	0.35	38° ± 3° (2)	5° ATDC @ 900 rpm (5)	W 260 T 2	0.7	900 ± 50	1.0-1.5		
1978-79	911SC (Europe)			5° BTDC @ 900 ± 50 rpm (4)	W 5 D	0.8	900 ± 50	2.0-4.0 (6)		24°-31° BTDC @ 6000 (4)
1978-79	911SC (USA, Calif/Japan)			5° BTDC @ 900 ± 50 rpm (4)	W 8 D	0.8	950 ± 50	1.5-3.5 (6)		24°-28° BTDC @ 6000 (4)
1978-79	911SC (Australia/Sweden)			5° BTDC @ 900 ± 50 rpm (4)	W 5 D	0.8	900 ± 50	1.0-2.0 (6)		24°-31° BTDC @ 6000 (4)
1978-80	911 Turbo (Europe, R.o.W)			29° BTDC @ 4000 rpm (4)	W 3 DP	0.6	950 ± 50	2.0-4.0 (6)		0° ± 2° BTDC @ 1000 ± 50 (5)
1978-80	911 Turbo (Sweden)			29° BTDC @ 4000 rpm (4)	W 3 DP	0.6	1000 ± 50	1.5-2.5 (6)		0° ± 2° BTDC @ 1000 ± 50 (5)
1978-80	911 Turbo (USA)			10° ± 2° ATDC @ 1000 ± 50 (5)	W 3 DP	0.6	1000 ± 50	2.0-3.0 (6,7)		26° ± 4° BTDC @ 4000 (4)
1978-80	911 Turbo (California)			5° ± 1° ATDC @ 1000 ± 50 (5)	W 3 DP	0.6	1000 ± 50	2.0-3.0 (6,7)		31° ± 4° BTDC @ 4000 (4)
1978-80	911 Turbo (Japan)			5° ± 1° ATDC @ 1000 ± 50 (5)	W 3 DP	0.6	1000 ± 50	1.5-2.0 (6)		31° ± 4° BTDC @ 4000 (4)
1980	911SC			5° BTDC @ 900 ± 50 rpm (4)	W 4 C1	0.8	900 ± 50	1.5-2.5 (6)		23°-29° BTDC @ 6000 (4)
1980	911SC (Australia/Sweden)			5° BTDC @ 900 ± 50 rpm (4)	W 4 C1	0.8	900 ± 50	1.0-2.0 (6)		23°-29° BTDC @ 6000 (4)
1980-81	911SC (USA/Japan)			5° BTDC @ 900 ± 50 rpm (4)	W 5 D	0.8	900 ± 50	0.4-0.8 (6,7)		19°-25° BTDC @ 6000 (4)
1981	911 Turbo (Europe/Canada)			29° BTDC @ 4000 rpm (4)	W 3 DP	0.6	950 ± 50	1.5-2.5 (6)		0° ± 2° BTDC @ 1000 ± 50 (5)
1981	911SC			25° BTDC @ 4000 rpm (4)	W 4 C1	0.8	800-950 (8)	1.0-2.0 (6,8)		25° MAX BTDC @ 6000 (4)
1982-83	911SC (USA/Japan)			5° BTDC @ 900 ± 50 rpm (4)	WR5DC/WR5DP	0.7+0.1	900 ± 50	0.4-0.8 (7)		19°-25° BTDC @ 6000 (4)
1982-83	911SC			25° BTDC @ 4000 rpm (4)	WR3CC/WR3CP	0.7+0.1	800-950 (8)	1.0-2.0 (6,8)		25° MAX BTDC @ 6000 (4)
1982-83	911 Turbo (Europe, R.o.W)			29° BTDC @ 4000 rpm (4)	W3DP/W3DP0	0.6+0.1	950 ± 50	1.5-2.5 (6)		0° ± 2° BTDC @ 1000 ± 50 (5)
1984-87	Carrera (Europe)			3° ATDC @ 800 ± 40 rpm	WR4CC/WR4CP	0.7+0.1	800 ± 40	1.0-1.5 (7)		26° ± 2° BTDC @ 3800 ± 100
1984-87	Carrera (USA/Canada/Japan)			3° ATDC @ 800 ± 40 rpm	WR7DC/WR7DP	0.7+0.1	800 ± 40	0.6-1.0 (7)		26° ± 2° BTDC @ 3800 ± 100
1984-87	Carrera (Australia/Switz/Swed)			3° ATDC @ 800 ± 40 rpm	WR4CC/WR4CP	0.7+0.1	800 ± 40	0.5-1.0 (7)		26° ± 2° BTDC @ 3800 ± 100
1987-89	Carrera (Europe) (9)			3.5° ± 3° BTDC @ 880 ± 40 rpm	WR4CC/WR4CP	0.7+0.1	880 ± 40	1.0-1.5 (7)		26° ± 2° BTDC @ 3800 ± 100
1987-89	Carrera (USA/Canada/Japan) (9)			3.5° ± 3° BTDC @ 880 ± 40 rpm	WR7DC/WR7DP	0.7+0.1	880 ± 40	0.6-1.0 (7)		26° ± 2° BTDC @ 3800 ± 100
1987-89	Carrera (Australia/Switz/Swed) (9)			3.5° ± 3° BTDC @ 880 ± 40 rpm	WR4CC/WR4CP	0.7+0.1	880 ± 40	0.5-1.0 (7)		26° ± 2° BTDC @ 3800 ± 100
1984-86	911 Turbo (930/66)			29° ± 1° BTDC @ 4000 rpm (4)	W3DP/W3DP0	0.6+0.1	950 ± 50	1.5-2.5 (6)		2° ± 2° BTDC @ 900 ± 50 (5)
1987-89	911 Turbo (930/66)			29° ± 1° BTDC @ 4000 rpm (4)	W3DP/W3DP0	0.6+0.1	950 ± 50	1.5-2.0 (6)		2° ± 2° BTDC @ 900 ± 50 (5)
1984-89	911 Turbo (USA, 930/68)			26° ± 1° BTDC @ 4000 rpm (4)	W3DP/W3DP0	0.6+0.1	950 ± 50	0.6 ± 0.2 (6,7)		1° ± 2° ATDC @ 900 ± 50 (5)

Notes:

(1) Detach hose at aux air pump and plug, if checking or setting CO level.

(2) Dwell angle 37° ± 3° with Marelli distributor.

(3) Only for MFI cars. Measured under load on road or dyno. Exhaust measurements taken at partial load range with 9° throttle valve setting, 2,400 rpm, in 2nd gear.

(4) Check with distributor vacuum hose disconnected and plugged.

(5) Check with vacuum hose connected.

(6) Detach hose at aux air pump and plug, if checking/adjusting CO % level.

(7) From 1980, with cars that have catalytic converter, CO % levels must be measured before converter with oxygen sensor plug pulled off.

(8) For 1981 and later models, the lower values for both idle and CO % level are the ideal values.

(9) From 1987 models, used in conjunction with control unit 911.618.111.18 /.19/.20.

(10) Dwell angle 40° ± 3° with Marelli distributor.

(11) At intake temperature of 25° C.

- Set initial timing at TDC for all 911s except for 1965-68 911S (5° BTDC).

- 1984-89 911 ignition timing is controlled by the Motronic computer (DME).

- Warm car to 176° to 194° F (80° to 90°C) before making any measurements or adjustments.

- Cars with the Sportomatic transmission should have their idle adjusted to 950 ± 50.

- Spark plug part numbers are from manufacturer Bosch.

- 1973-75 R.o.W. Carrera came with 2.7 MFI engine installed. 1974-77 USA Carrera came with CIS engine identical to 911S.

Crankshaft

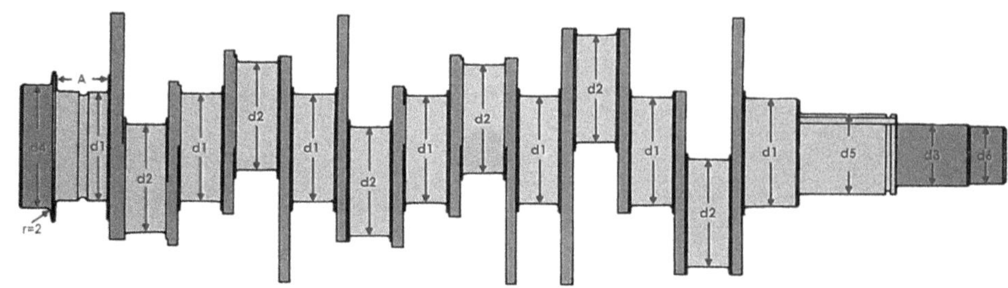

Tolerances and Wear Limits

All clearances are expressed in millimeters (mm) unless otherwise specified.

Models / Years	2.0/2.2 911 (1965-71)	2.4/2.7/3.0 Turbo 911 (1972-77) 911 Turbo (1976-77) Euro Carrera (1976-77)	3.0SC 911 (1978-83)	3.2/3.3 Turbo 911 (1984-89) 911 Turbo (1978-89)
Stroke	66mm	70.4mm	70.4mm	74.4mm
Flywheel Bolt Pattern	6-bolt	6-bolt	9-bolt	9-bolt
Main Bearings 1-7 (D1)				
Bore	57.010 - 57.059	57.020 - 57.059	60.020 - 60.059	60.020 - 60.059
Shaft	56.971 - 56.990	56.971 - 56.990	59.971 - 59.990	59.971 - 59.990
Clearances	from +0.030 to +0.088	from +0.010 to +0.072	from +0.010 to +0.072	from +0.010 to +0.072
Shaft Wear Limit	56.960	56.960	56.960	56.960
Crankshaft Bearing No. 8 (D3)				
Bore	31.041 - 31.084	31.041 - 31.084	31.041 - 31.084	31.041 - 31.084
Shaft	30.980 - 30.993	30.980 - 90.993	30.980 - 30.993	30.980 - 30.993
Clearances	from +0.048 to +0.104	from +0.048 to +0.104	from +0.048 to +0.104	from +0.048 to +0.104
Shaft Wear Limit	30.970	30.970	30.970	30.970
Rod Bearings (D2)				
Bore	57.020 - 57.059	52.020 - 52.059	53.020 - 53.059	55.020 - 55.059
Shaft	56.971 - 56.990	51.971 - 51.990	52.971 - 52.990	54.971 - 54.990
Clearances	from +0.030 to +0.088	from +0.030 to +0.088	from +0.030 to +0.088	from +0.030 to +0.088
Shaft Wear Limits	56.960	51.960	52.960	54.960
Crankshaft Runout	0.03 max	0.04 max	0.04 max	0.04 max
Crankshaft Unbalance (cmg)	10 max	10 max	10 max	10 max
Main Bearing Axial Play	+0.110 to + 0.195	+0.110 to +0.195	+0.110 to +0.195	+0.110 to +0.195
Wear limit	0.30	0.30	0.30	0.30
Timing Gear (D5)				
Bore	41.975 - 42.000	41.975 - 42.000	41.975 - 42.000	41.975 - 42.000
Shaft	42.002 - 42.013	42.002 - 42.013	42.002 - 42.013	42.002 - 42.013
Press Fit	from -0.002 to -0.038	from -0.002 to -0.038	from -0.002 to -0.038	from -0.002 to -0.038
Distributor Drive Gear (D5)				
Bore	41.975 - 42.000	41.975 - 42.000	41.975 - 42.000	41.975 - 42.000
Shaft	42.002 - 42.013	42.002 - 42.013	42.002 - 42.013	42.002 - 42.013
Press Fit	from -0.002 to -0.038	from -0.002 to -0.038	from -0.002 to -0.038	from -0.002 to -0.038
Flywheel (D4)				
Bore	65.000 - 65.030	65.000 - 65.030	90.000 - 90.030	90.000 - 90.030
Shaft	64.981 - 65.000	64.981 - 65.000	89.981 - 90.000	89.780 - 90.000
Clearances	from 0.0 to +0.049	from 0.0 to +0.049	from 0.0 to +0.049	from 0.0 to +0.049
Pulley (D6)				
Bore	30.000 - 30.033	30.000 - 30.033	30.000 - 30.033	30.000 - 30.033
Shaft	29.960 - 29.993	29.960 - 29.993	29.960 - 29.993	29.960 - 29.993
Clearances	from +0.007 to +0.073	from +0.007 to +0.073	from +0.007 to +0.073	from +0.007 to +0.073
Pulley Radial Runout	.015 max	.015 max	.015 max	.015 max
Pulley Lateral Runout	.20 max	.20 max	.20 max	.20 max

Bearing Sizes

	2.0/2.2 911 (1965-71)	2.4/2.7/3.0 Turbo 911 (1972-77) 911 Turbo (1976-77) Euro Carrera (1976-77)	3.0SC 911 (1978-83)	3.2/3.3 Turbo 911 (1984-89) 911 Turbo (1978-89)
Crankcase Diameter, Bearings 1-8				
Standard	62.000 - 62.019	62.000 - 62.019	65.000 - 65.019	65.000 - 65.019
Oversize	62.250 - 62.269	62.250 - 62.269	65.250 - 65.269	65.250 - 65.269
All Main Bearings (D1)				
Standard	56.971 - 56.990	56.971 - 56.990	59.971 - 59.990	59.971 - 59.990
-0.25mm	56.721 - 56.740	56.721 - 56.740	59.721 - 59.740	59.721 - 59.740
-0.50mm	56.471 - 56.490	56.471 - 56.490	59.471 - 59.490	59.471 - 59.490
-0.75mm	56.221 - 56.240	56.221 - 56.240	59.221 - 59.240	59.221 - 59.240
-1.00mm			58.971 - 58.990	58.971 - 58.990
Rod Bearings (D2)				
Standard	56.971 - 56.990	56.971 - 56.990	52.971 - 52.990	54.971 - 54.990
-0.25mm	56.721 - 56.740	56.721 - 56.740	52.721 - 52.740	54.721 - 54.740
-0.50mm	56.471 - 56.490	56.471 - 56.490	52.471 - 52.490	54.471 - 54.490
-0.75mm	56.221 - 56.240	56.221 - 56.240	52.221 - 52.240	54.221 - 54.240
-1.00mm			51.971 - 51.990	53.971 - 53.990
Number Eight Bearing (D3)				
Standard	30.980 - 30.993	30.980 - 30.993	30.980 - 30.993	30.980 - 30.993
-0.25mm	30.730 - 30.743	30.730 - 30.743	30.730 - 30.743	30.730 - 30.743
-0.50mm	30.480 - 30.493	30.480 - 30.493	30.480 - 30.493	30.480 - 30.493
-0.75mm	30.243 - 30.230	30.243 - 30.230	30.230 - 30.243	30.230 - 30.243
-1.00mm			29.980 - 29.993	29.980 - 29.993
Flywheel Seal Collar (D4)				
Standard	64.981 - 65.000	64.981 - 65.000	89.780 - 90.000	89.780 - 90.000
-0.50mm	64.310 - 64.500	64.310 - 64.500	89.280 - 89.500	89.280 - 89.500
Crankshaft Pulley Seat (D6)				
Standard	29.960 - 29.993	29.960 - 29.993	29.960 - 29.993	29.960 - 29.993
-0.50mm	29.370 - 29.500	29.370 - 29.500	29.370 - 29.500	29.370 - 29.500
Thrust Bearing (A)				
Standard	28.000 - 28.060	28.000 - 28.060	28.000 - 28.060	28.000 - 28.060

Notes

- There were four distinct crankshafts used on the 911 engine from 1965-89.
- Wear limits for bore are visual inspection only.
- Grind bearing surfaces for radial oil seals to 29.5mm and 89.5mm when scoring is deep.
- Repolish crank as necessary: 3 microns.
- Give oil bores a radius of 0.5mm after grinding.
- A 0.2 to 0.5 radius should be used to break all sharp edges.
- Harden crank according to spec Tenifer 90 W PN 1053.
- Do not straighten bearings 3 or 5 after treatment.
- Other main bearings may be straightened by stemming the radii.
- Color codes for repair sizes: blue paint dot (first repair size), green paint dot (second repair size), yellow paint dot (third repair size), white paint dot (fourth repair size).
- All 911 crankshafts were counterweighted except for the ones used in the 1969-71 911T.

Connecting Rods

Models / Years	2.0/22 911 (1965-71)	2.4/2.7/3.0 Turbo 911 (1972-77) 911 Turbo (1976-77) Euro Carrera (1976-77)	3.0SC 911 (1978-83)	3.2/3.3 Turbo 911 (1984-89) 911 Turbo (1978-89)

Rod Dimensions

	2.0/22 911 (1965-71)	2.4/2.7/3.0 Turbo 911 (1972-77)	3.0SC 911 (1978-83)	3.2/3.3 Turbo 911 (1984-89)
A - Center-to-Center Distance	130.00	127.80	127.75 - 127.80	126.95 - 127.00
B - Piston Pin Bushing Width	25.80 - 26.00	25.98 - 26.00	24.80 - 25.00	24.50 - 25.00
C - Rod Width at Big End	21.70 - 21.80	23.70 - 23.80	21.70 - 21.80	21.70 - 21.80 (1978-85)
				21.85 - 21.90 (1986-89)
Rod Width at Crankshaft with bearing	22.00 - 22.10	24.00 - 24.10	22.00 - 22.05	22.00 - 22.05
Clearances (rod / sidewall)	from +0.200 to +0.400	from +0.200 to +0.400	from +0.200 to +0.350	from +0.200 to +0.350 (1978-85)
				from +0.100 to +0.200 (1986-89)
D - Inside Rod Diameter at Big End	61.000 - 61.019	56.000 - 56.019	56.000 - 56.019	58.000 - 58.019
E - Inside Rod Diameter at Small End	25.000 - 25.021	25.000 - 25.021		
F - Piston Pin Bushing Outer Diameter (uninstalled)	25.035 - 25.055	25.035 - 25.055		
Press Fit	from -0.014 to -0.055	from -0.014 to -0.055		
G - Rod Bushing / Piston Pin Diameter	22.020 - 22.033	22.020 - 22.033	22.020 - 22.033	23.020 - 23.033
Piston Pin / Bushing Clearances	from +0.020 to +0.039	from +0.020 to +0.039	from +0.020 to +0.037	from +0.020 to +0.037
Wear Limit	0.055	0.055	0.055	0.055

Weight Groups

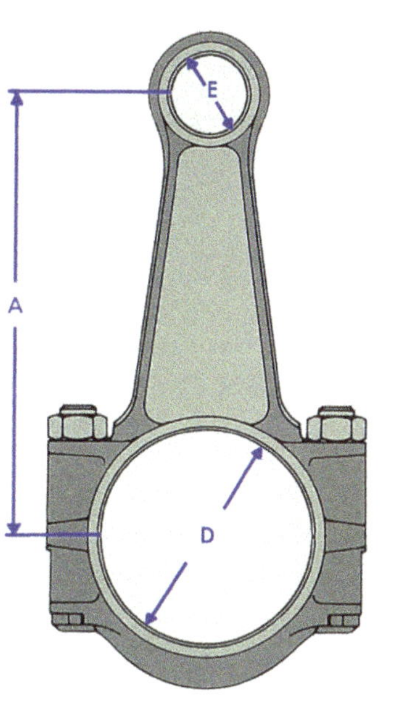

Weight Range	Weight Group	Part Number	Rod Code
2.0 - 911 (1965-69)			
551 - 560		901.103.011.21	21
560 - 569		901.103.011.22	22
569 - 578		901.103.011.23	23
578 - 587		901.103.011.24	24
587 - 596		901.103.011.25	25
596 - 605		901.103.011.26	26
605 - 614		901.103.011.27	27
614 - 623		901.103.011.28	28
623 - 632		901.103.011.29	29
632 - 641		901.103.011.30	30
641 - 650		901.103.011.31	31
650 - 659		901.103.011.32	32
2.2 - 911 (1970-71)			
700 - 709		911.103.013.21	21
709 - 718		911.103.013.22	22
718 - 727		911.103.013.23	23
727 - 736		911.103.013.24	24
736 - 745		911.103.013.25	25
745 - 754		911.103.013.26	26
754 - 763		911.103.013.27	27
763 - 772		911.103.013.28	28
2.4 / 2.7 / 3.0 - 911 / 911 Turbo (1972-77)			
645 - 654	1	911.103.015.31	31
654 - 663	2	911.103.015.32	32
663 - 672	3	911.103.015.33	33
672 - 681	4	911.103.015.34	34
681 - 690	5	911.103.015.35	35
690 - 699	6	911.103.015.36	36
699 - 708	7	911.103.015.37	37
708 - 717	8	911.103.015.38	38
718 - 727	9	911.103.015.39	39
3.0 911SC (1978-83)			
633 - 642	1	930.103.015.51	51
642 - 651	2	930.103.015.52	52
651 - 660	3	930.103.015.53	53
660 - 669	4	930.103.015.54	54
669 - 678	5	930.103.015.55	55
678 - 687	6	930.103.015.56	56
687 - 696	7	930.103.015.57	57
696 - 705	8	930.103.015.58	58
705 - 714	9	930.103.015.59	59
3.2 / 3.3 Carrera (1984-89), Turbo (1978-89)			
615 - 624	3	930.103.020.73	73
624 - 633	4	930.103.020.74	74
633 - 642	5	930.103.020.75	75
642 - 651	6	930.103.020.76	76
651 - 660	7	930.103.020.77	77
660 - 669	8	930.103.020.78	78
669 - 678	9	930.103.020.79	79
678 - 687	10	930.103.020.80	80
687 - 696	11	930.103.020.81	81

Notes

- Always use new rod nuts and rod bolts.
- Use RaceWare or ARP bolts for all 3.2L and 3.3L engines.
- Install rod bolts with red Loctite.
- See crankshaft table for rod bearing sizes and tolerances.
- Big end rod width changed on Carreras and Turbos in 1986.
- Connecting rods installed in an engine must not vary in weight by more than 9 grams without bearings installed.

Crankcase

Models / Years	2.0 911 (1965-68) Aluminum Case	2.0/2.2 911 (1968-71) Magnesium Case	2.4/2.7/3.0 Turbo 911 (1972-77) - Mag 911 Turbo (1976-77) - AL Euro Carrera (1976-77) - AL	3.0SC 911 (1978-83) Aluminum Case	3.2/3.3 Turbo 911 (1984-89) 911 Turbo (1978-89) Aluminum Case
Case Bore for Bearings 1-8					
Bore	62.000 - 62.019	62.000 - 62.019	62.000 - 62.019	65.000 - 65.019	65.000 - 65.019
Oversize		62.250 - 62.269	62.250 - 62.269	65.250 - 65.269	65.250 - 65.269
Case Bore for Intermediate Shaft					
Outer thrust bearing (bore)	29.800 - 29.821	27.500 - 27.521	27.500 - 27.521	27.500 - 27.521	27.500 - 27.521
Outer thrust bearing (shaft)	29.841 - 29.854	24.980 - 25.000	24.980 - 25.000	24.980 - 25.000	24.980 - 25.000
Inner bearing (bore)	24.000 - 24.021	26.500 - 26.521	26.500 - 26.521	26.500 - 26.521	26.500 - 26.521
Inner bearing (shaft)	23.967 - 23.980	23.967 - 23.980	23.967 - 23.980	23.967 - 23.980	23.967 - 23.980
Intermediate Shaft Clearance	from +0.020 to +0.054	from +0.030 to +0.084	from +0.030 to +0.084	from +0.030 to +0.084	from +0.030 to +0.084
Intermediate Shaft Axial Play	from +0.080 to +0.120	from +0.040 to +0.133	from +0.040 to +0.133	from +0.040 to +0.133	from +0.040 to +0.133
Wear Limit		0.16	0.16	0.16	0.16
Chain Ramp Bolt					
Bore	8.000 - 8.015	8.000 - 8.015	8.000 - 8.015	8.000 - 8.015	8.000 - 8.015
Shaft	7.822 - 7.837	7.822 - 7.837	7.822 - 7.837	7.822 - 7.837	7.822 - 7.837
Distributor Pinon to Shaft					
Bore	12.456 - 12.474	12.456 - 12.474	12.456 - 12.474	12.456 - 12.474	12.456 - 12.474
Shaft	12.444 - 12.455	12.444 - 12.455	12.444 - 12.455	12.444 - 12.455	12.444 - 12.455
Clearances	from +0.001 to +0.030	from +0.001 to +0.030	from +0.001 to +0.030	from +0.001 to +0.030	from +0.001 to +0.030
Distributor Shaft / Crankcase					
Bore	27.000 - 27.021	27.000 - 27.021	30.000 - 30.021	30.000 - 30.021	30.000 - 30.021
Shaft	26.947 - 26.980	26.947 - 26.980	29.947 - 29.980	29.947 - 29.980	29.947 - 29.980
Clearances	from +0.020 to +0.074	from +0.020 to +0.074	from +0.020 to +0.074	from +0.020 to +0.074	from +0.020 to +0.074
Safety Valve Spring (case side)					
Relaxed Length	70.00	70.00	70.00	70	69
Spring force at 52mm	104 N	104 N	104 N	104 N	104 N
Spring force at 46mm	138 N	138 N	138 N	138 N	138 N
Spring wire diameter	1.8mm	1.8mm	1.8	1.8	1.8
Pressure Relief Valve (case bottom)					
Relaxed Length	Same as above	Same as above	Same as above (see notes)	87 (use piston guide)	87 (use piston guide)
Spring force at 50.5mm				82.4 N	82.4 N
Spring wire diameter				1.5	1.5

Notes:

- Engine case changed from aluminum die-cast to magnesium pressure-cast on January 9, 1968.
- Engine case changed from separate sump to integrated sump in 1983 with engine # 64D3717.
- Oil pressure pistons changed in 1976 with the oil pump bypass modification. Use updated pistons if modification has been performed on case.

- Updated pistons use two different length pistons for safety valve and pressure relief.
- Use spring guide with 87mm pressure relief spring in bottom of case.
- From Engine # 901283, the 3.5mm thick aluminum ring has been discontinued—oil pressure relief valve bore changed accordingly.
- Distributor bore changed to 30mm in 1972 with the 2.4L engines.

Intermediate Shaft

Aluminum Shaft Gear (x)	
Wear limit - standard gear	136.50
Wear limit - size 1	136.55

Backlash Measurement	Centerline Dist	Case Code	Crank Gear Code	Intermediate Gear Code	Backlash
Ideal configuration	103.975 - 103.990	0	0	0	0.029 - 0.049
Installation still possible	103.975 - 103.990	0	1	0	0.016 - 0.042
Installation still possible	103.975 - 103.990	0	0	1	0.017 - 0.043
Ideal configuration	103.990 - 104.000	1	1	1	0.012 - 0.041
Installation still possible	103.990 - 104.000	1	0	1	0.025 - 0.049
Installation still possible	103.990 - 104.000	1	1	0	0.025 - 0.048

Notes:

- Measure intermediate shaft gear with two 4.5mm rollers placed exactly 180 degrees apart.
- Left side of crankcase should be marked with "0" or "1" below alternator support.
- Centerline distance is the distance between the center of the crankshaft and the center of the intermediate shaft.

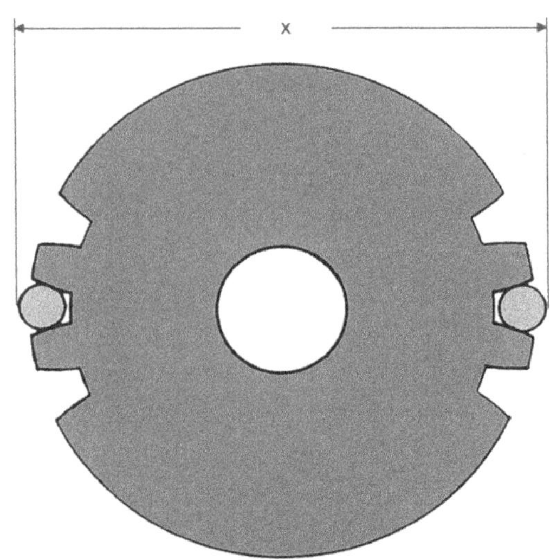

Camshafts

Stock Camshafts

Year	Engine	Model	Left Camshaft	Right Camshaft	Intake Valve Overlap	Cam Lift Intake	Cam Lift Exhaust	Intake Opens	Intake Closes	Exhaust Opens	Exhaust Closes
1965-68	911 Solex**	901/01 up to Eng # 903069**	901.105.109.01	901.105.110.01	4.2 - 4.6 (4.3)*	37.2	36.5	29° BTDC	39° ABDC	39° BBDC	19° ATDC
1965-68	911 Solex**	901/01 from Eng 903070 - 907000**	901.105.109.04	901.105.110.04	4.2 - 4.6 (4.3)*	37.2	36.5	29° BTDC	39° ABDC	39° BBDC	19° ATDC
1965-68	911S	901/02/08 from Eng # 960001	901.105.123.00	901.105.124.00	5.0 - 5.4 (5.2)*	37.2	36.3	38° BTDC	50° ABDC	40° BBDC	20° ATDC
1965-68	911T	901/03 from Eng # 2080001	901.105.133.00	901.105.134.00	2.3 - 2.7 (2.5)*	36.25	36.51	15° BTDC	29° ABDC	41° BBDC	5° ATDC
1965-68	911	901/05 from Eng # 907001 to 909927	901.105.109.04	901.105.110.04	4.2 - 4.6 (4.3)*	37.2	36.5	29° BTDC	39° ABDC	39° BBDC	19° ATDC
1965-68	911/911L	901/06/07 from Eng # 911001, 901/07	901.105.109.05	901.105.110.05	3.0 - 3.3 (3.15)*	36.5	36.2	20° BTDC	34° ABDC	40° BBDC	6° ATDC
1965	911/911R	901/20/22/23/30	901.105.103.00	901.105.104.00	6.7 - 6.9 (6.8)*	37.61	36.59	104° BTDC	104° ABDC	100° BBDC	80° ATDC
1968	911	901/14/17	901.105.139.00	901.105.110.05	3.0 - 3.3 (3.15)*	36.5	36.2	20° BTDC	34° ABDC	40° BBDC	6° ATDC
1969-71	911T	901/03/13/16/19, 911/03/06/07/08	901.105.133.00	901.105.134.00	2.30 - 2.70 (2.5)*	36.25	35.51	15° BTDC	29° ABDC	41° BBDC	5° BTDC
1969-71	911E	901/09/11, 911/01/04	901.105.181.00	901.105.110.05	3.0 - 3.3 (3.15)*	36.58	36.25	29° BTDC	39° ABDC	39° BBDC	19° ATDC
1969-71	911S	901/10, 911/02	901.105.167.00	901.105.168.00	5.0 - 5.4 (5.2)*	37.30	36.44	38° BTDC	50° ABDC	40° BBDC	20° ATDC
1972-73	911T	911/51/61	901.105.133.00	901.105.134.00	2.4 - 2.8 (2.6)*	36.25	35.51	16° BTDC	30° ABDC	42° BBDC	4° BTDC
1972-73	911E	911/52/62	901.105.181.00	901.105.110.05	2.70 - 3.10 (2.9)*	36.58	36.25	18° BTDC	36° ABDC	48° BBDC	8° BTDC
1972-73	911S/ Carrera	911/53/63/83	901.105.183.01	901.105.168.00	5.0 - 5.4 (5.2)*	37.30	36.44	38° BTDC	50° ABDC	40° BBDC	20° ATDC
1973 1/2	911T CLS	911/91/92	911.105.141.00	911.105.142.00	0.90 - 1.10 (1.0)*	38.00	37.48	TDC	32° ABDC	30° BBDC	10° BTDC
1974	911	911/92/97	911.105.141.00	911.105.142.00	0.70 - 0.90 (0.8)*	37.90	37.38	1° ATDC	35° ABDC	29° BBDC	7° BTDC
1975	911	911/41/46	911.105.141.00	911.105.142.00	0.5 - 0.7 (0.6)*			1° ATDC	35° ABDC	29° BBDC	7° BTDC
1974-77	911S/ Carrera CIS	911/42/47/43/44/48/49 911/81/82/84/86/89/85/93/97/98	911.105.143.00	911.105.144.00	0.40 - 0.54 (0.47)*			6° ATDC	50° ABDC	24° BBDC	2° BTDC
1974-75	Carrera MFI	911/83	901.105.183.01	901.105.168.00	5.00 - 5.40 (5.2)*			38° BTDC	50° ABDC	40° BBDC	20° ATDC
1975-76	Turbo	930/50	930.105.141.00	930.105.142.00	0.65 - 0.80 (0.73)*			3° ATDC	37° ABDC	29° BBDC	3° BTDC
1976	Carrera CIS	930/02/12	930.105.147.08	930.105.147.08	0.9 - 1.1 (1.0)*			1° BTDC	53° ABDC	43° BBDC	3° ATDC
1976-77	Turbo	930/51/52/53/54	930.105.143.00	930.105.142.00	0.65 - 0.80 (0.73)*			3° ATDC	37° ABDC	29° BBDC	3° BTDC
1978-83	911SC	930/04/05/15/06/10	930.105.147.08 or 930.105.147.10	930.105.148.08 or 930.105.148.10	0.9 - 1.1 (1.0)*			1° BTDC	53° ABDC	43° BBDC	3° ATDC
1978-83	911SC	930/03/13/07/08/09/19/16/17	930.105.147.08 or 930.105.147.10	930.105.148.08 or 930.105.148.10	1.4 - 1.7 (1.55)*			7° BTDC	47° ABDC	49° BBDC	3° BTDC
1978-83	Turbo	930/60/61/62/63/64/65/66	930.105.143.00 or 930.105.143.01	930.105.142.00 or 930.105.142.01	0.65 - 0.80 (0.73)*			3° ATDC	37° ABDC	27° BBDC	5° BTDC
1984-89	Carrera	930/20/25/26	930.105.147.10	930.105.148.10	1.1 - 1.4 (1.25)*			4° BTDC	50° ABDC	46° BBDC	TDC
1984-89	Turbo	930/66	930.105.143.01	930.105.142.01	0.65 - 0.80 (0.70)*			3° ATDC	37° ABDC	27° BBDC	5° BTDC
		930/68 from July 1984	930.105.143.03	930.105.142.03	0.65 - 0.80 (0.70)*			3° ATDC	37° ABDC	27° BBDC	5°BTDC
1989-94	964 3.6	M 64/01/02	964.105.247.07	964.105.246.09	1.16 - 1.36 (1.26)*			4° BTDC	65° ATDC	44° BTDC	4° ATDC

Performance Camshafts

	Intake Lift (mm)	Intake Duration (deg crank)	Exhaust Lift (mm)	Exhaust Duration (deg crank)	Lobe Center (deg camshaft)	Intake Valve Overlap
GE20	11.56	248	10.80	230	98	4.0 - 4.3 (4.15)*
GE40	11.94	256	11.18	238	102	4.2 - 4.5 (4.35)*
GE60	12.45	266	11.56	248	102	4.8 - 5.2 (5.0)*
GE80	12.70	274	11.94	256	100	6.0 - 6.3 (6.15)*
GE100	13.21	284	12.45	266	100	6.5 - 6.8 (6.65)*
RSR	11.79	278	11.43	267	101	6.1 - 6.3 (6.2)*
906	11.73	281	10.24	251	95	6.7 - 6.9 (6.8)*

Notes:

* Refers to the desired value for the intake valve stroke in overlapping TDC with 0.1 mm valve clearance.
** These camshafts are referred to as the Solex cams and come in two versions: the first with central lubrication, and the second with spray bar lubrication. Use the spray bar lubrication for all street engines after 1965.
- Solex Cams have a profile that is nearly identical to the early L camshafts and are in-between the performance of E and S cams.
- "Intake Valve Overlap" is "Intake valve stroke in overlapping TDC with 0.1 mm valve clearance." See Chapter 5, Section 7
- BTDC = Before Top Dead Center, ATDC = After Top Dead Center, BBDC = Before Bottom Dead Center, ABDC = After Bottom Dead Center.
- In 1982, the design of the camshafts changed from using a 46mm nut to secure the sprocket to a bolt. The camshaft profiles remained the same during this transition.

- Most camshaft speciality shops will provide specifications for timing with the camshafts supplied.
- Camshafts are often identified by their full or partial part numbers. Example: camshaft 911.105.141.00 would have "911.141.00" stamped on the side.
- Pre-1973 cannot be accurately identified by the numbers cast on the camshaft billet.
- The only accurate method to determine which camshaft is in your engine is to have it analyzed on a camshaft profiler (cam doctor).
- Early 911L camshafts are often referred to as the first generation of 911 E camshafts.
- Valve timing specs are listed according to the European standard of measuring valve action with a clearance of 1mm (.040"). For actual valve action with the 911 standard 0.1mm valve backlash, see Appendix B in the book, *Porsche 911 Story*, by Paul Frère.

Camshaft Housings

Models / Years	2.0/2.2/2.4/2.7/ 911 (1965-77)	3.0/3.2/3.3 Turbo / 911 (1978-89) 911 Turbo (1976-89) Euro Carrera (1976-77)
Housing Bearing Style	3-bearing	4-bearing
Camshaft Bearings		
Bore	46.967 - 46.992	48.967 - 48.992
Shaft	46.926 - 46.942	48.926 - 48.942
Clearances	from + 0.025 to +0.066	from + 0.025 to +0.066
Wear Limit	0.10	0.10
Camshaft Axial Play	from +0.150 to +0.200	from +0.150 to +0.200
Wear Limit	0.40	0.40
Camshaft Sprocket Flange		
Bore	30.000 - 30.013	30.000 - 30.013
Shaft	29.979 - 30.000	29.979 - 30.000
Clearances	from 0.000 to +0.034	from 0.000 to +0.034
Camshaft Runout (on center bearing)	0.02 max	0.02 max
Rocker Arm Shaft to Camshaft Housing		
Bore	18.000 - 18.018	18.000 - 18.018
Shaft	17.992 - 18.000	17.992 - 18.000
Clearances (untightened)	from 0.000 to +0.026	from 0.000 to +0.026
Rocker Arm Bushing to Rocker Arm Shaft		
Bore	18.016 - 18.027	18.016 - 18.027
Shaft	17.992 - 18.000	17.992 - 18.000
Clearances	from +0.016 to 0.035	from +0.016 to 0.035
Wear Limit	0.080	0.080
Rocker Arm Axial Play	from +0.100 to +0.350	from +0.100 to +0.350
Wear Limit	.50	.50

Notes:
- Mechanical Fuel Injection 911s as well as Turbo 911s have an additional gear that attaches to the left camshaft and exits out of the back of the camshaft housing.
- Four bearing camshafts and housings were introduced with the 1976 911 Turbo and used on all 911s beginning with the 911SC in 1978 (see Chapter 3, Figure 3-36).
- Camshaft housings may be used on either side of the engine. Hardware must be swapped from one end of the housing to the other.
- Use updated oil line restrictor for increased oil pressure (see Chapter 4, Figure 4-13).

Models / Years   911 / 911 Turbo (1965-89)

Chain Housing Shaft to Chain Tensioner

Bore	15.000 - 15.018
Shaft	14.973 - 14.984
Clearances	from +0.016 to +0.045

Chain Housing Shaft to Idler Arm

Bore	15.000 - 15.018
Shaft	14.973 - 14.984
Clearances	from +0.016 to +0.045

Idler Arm to Sprocket Center Pin

Bore	15.000 - 15.018
Shaft	14.989 - 15.000
Clearances	from 0.000 to +0.029

Sprocket Wheel to Sprocket Center Pin

Bore	15.032 - 15.050
Shaft	14.989 - 15.000
Clearances	from +0.032 to +0.610

Chain Ramp to Mounting Stud

Bore	8.000 - 8.015
Shaft	7.886 - 7.895
Clearances	from +0.105 to +0.129

Chain Ramp Mounting Stud to Timing Chain Housing

Bore	7.857 - 7.872
Shaft	7.886 - 7.895
Press fit	from -0.014 to -0.038

Notes:
- Parallel alignment of both sprockets cannot deviate by more than 0.25mm.
- Engines from #6400451 have improved idler arms with pressed bushings (recommended upgrade).

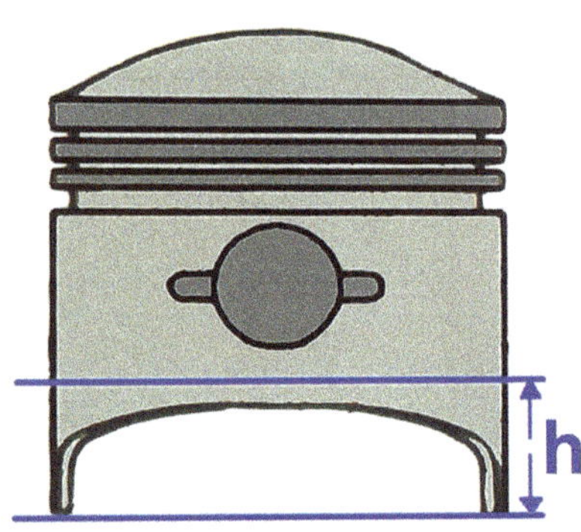

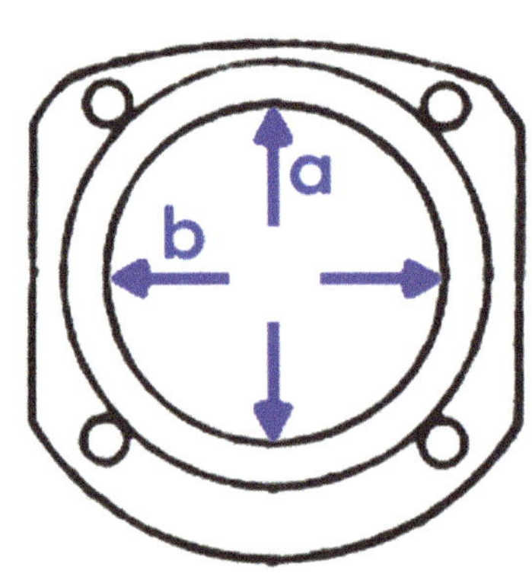

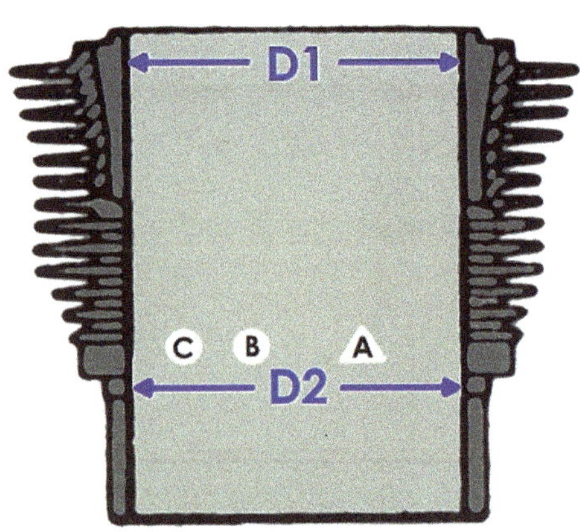

A = Tolerance group for cylinder height
B = Tolerance group for cylinder diameter
C = Manufacture's Identification

Pistons & Cylinders

Piston / Cylinder Internal Dimensions and Tolerances

	Standard Size 0	Standard Size 1	Standard Size 2	Standard Size 3	Dim h	Piston Weight	Piston / Cyl Clearance	Oversize Size 0	Oversize Size 1	Oversize Size 2
1965-67 911 2.0 (901/01/02/06)										
Cylinder Markings	-1	0	+1					-1 KD 1	0 KD 1	+1 KD 1
Nominal Diameter	80.000	80.010	80.000					80.500	80.500	80.500
Cylinder Diameter	79.990 - 80.000	80.000 - 80.010	80.010 - 80.020					80.490 - 80.500	80.500 - 80.510	80.510 - 80.520
911 2.0 Piston	79.925 - 79.935	79.935 - 79.945	79.945 - 79.955		11.5	364 ± 3	0.045 - 0.065	80.425 - 80.435	80.435 - 80.445	80.445 - 80.455
1968-69 911 2.0										
Cylinder Markings	0	1	2					0 KD 1	1 KD 1	2 KD 1
Nominal Diameter	80.000	80.000	80.000					80.500	80.500	80.500
Cylinder Diameter	80.000 - 80.010	80.010 - 80.020	80.020 - 80.030					80.050 - 80.510	80.510 - 80.520	80.520 - 80.530
911T 2.0 - KS Piston	79.953 - 79.966	79.963 - 79.976	79.973 - 79.986		21.0	366 ± 3	0.034 - 0.057	80.453 - 80.466	80.463 - 80.476	80.473 - 80.486
911T 2.0 - Mahle Piston	79.965 - 79.975	79.975 - 79.985	79.985 - 79.995		21.0	356 ± 3	0.025 - 0.045	80.465 - 80.475	80.475 - 80.485	80.485 - 80.495
911L/E 2.0 - Mahle Piston	79.955 - 79.965	79.965 - 79.975	79.975 - 79.985		15.5	371 ± 3	0.035 - 0.055	80.455 - 80.465	80.465 - 80.475	80.475 - 80.485
911S 2.0 - Mahle Piston	79.945 - 79.955	79.955 - 79.965	79.965 - 79.975		1.5	365 ± 3	0.045 - 0.065	80.455 - 80.455	80.455 - 80.465	80.465 - 80.475
1970-71 911 2.2										
Cylinder Markings	0	1	2					0 KD 1	1 KD 1	2 KD 1
Nominal Diameter	84.000	84.000	84.000					84.250	84.250	84.250
Cylinder Diameter	84.000 - 84.010	84.010 - 84.020	84.020 - 84.030					84.250 - 84.260	84.260 - 84.270	84.270 - 84.280
911T-C 2.2 - KS Piston	83.952 - 83.967	83.962 - 83.977	83.972 - 83.987		15.0	393 ± 4	0.033 - 0.058	84.212 - 84.217	84.212 - 84.227	84.222 - 84.237
911T-C 2.2 - Mahle Piston	83.965 - 83.975	83.975 - 83.985	83.985 - 83.995		11.5	380 ± 3	0.025 - 0.045	84.215 - 84.225	84.225 - 84.235	84.235 - 84.245
911E-C 2.2 - Mahle Piston	83.955 - 83.965	83.965 - 83.975	83.975 - 83.985		2.5	385 ± 3	0.035 - 0.055	84.205 - 84.215	84.215 - 84.225	84.225 - 84.235
911S-C 2.2 - Mahle Piston	83.945 - 83.955	83.955 - 83.965	83.965 - 83.975		2.5	375 ± 3	0.045 - 0.065	84.195 - 84.205	84.205 - 84.215	84.215 - 84.225
1972-73 911 2.4										
Cylinder Markings	0	1	2					0 KD 1	1 KD 1	2 KD 1
Nominal Diameter	84.000	84.000	84.000					84.250	84.250	84.250
Cylinder Diameter	84.000 - 84.010	84.010 - 84.020	84.020 - 84.030					84.250 - 84.260	84.260 - 84.270	84.270 - 84.280
911T-C 2.4 - KS Piston	83.962 - 83.977	83.972 - 83.987	83.982 - 83.997		12.5	375 ± 3	0.023 - 0.048	84.212 - 84.227	84.222 - 84.237	84.232 - 84.247
911T-C 2.4 - Mahle Piston	83.965 - 83.975	83.975 - 83.985	83.985 - 83.995		8.0	376 ± 3	0.025 - 0.045	84.215 - 84.225	84.225 - 84.235	84.235 - 84.245
911E-C 2.4 - Mahle Piston	83.965 - 83.975	83.975 - 83.985	83.985 - 83.995		2.5	371 ± 3	0.025 - 0.045	84.215 - 84.225	84.225 - 84.235	84.235 - 84.245
911S-C 2.4 - Mahle Piston	83.945 - 83.955	83.955 - 83.965	83.965 - 83.975		8.0	354 ± 3	0.045 - 0.065	84.195 - 84.205	84.205 - 84.215	84.215 - 84.225

Additional 2.4 Oversize Group Available:	2nd Oversize Size 0	2nd Oversize Size 1	2nd Oversize Size 2
Cylinder Markings	0 KD 2	1 KD 2	2 KD 2
Nominal Diameter	84.500	84.500	84.500
Cylinder Diameter	84.500 - 84.510	84.510 - 84.520	84.520 - 84.53
911T-C 2.2 - KS Piston	84.462 - 84.477	84.472 - 84.487	84.482 - 84.497
911T-C 2.2 - Mahle Piston	84.465 - 84.475	84.475 - 84.485	84.485 - 84.495
911E-C 2.2 - Mahle Piston	84.465 - 84.475	84.475 - 84.485	84.485 - 84.495
911S-C 2.2 - Mahle Piston	84.445 - 84.455	84.455 - 84.465	84.465 - 84.475

	Standard Size 0	Standard Size 1	Standard Size 2	Standard Size 3	Dim h	Piston Weight	Piston / Cyl Clearance
1973 911 Carrera 2.7							
Cylinder Markings	0	1	2				
Nominal Diameter	90.000	90.000	90.000				
Cylinder Diameter	90.000 - 90.010	90.010 - 90.020	90.020 - 90.030				
2.7 - Mahle Piston	89.945 - 89.955	89.955 - 89.965	89.965 - 89.975		2.5	392 ± 3	0.045 -0.065
1974-77 911 / 911S / Carrera							
Cylinder Markings	0	1	2				
Nominal Diameter	90.000	90.000	90.000				
Cylinder Diameter	90.000 - 90.010	90.010 - 90.020	90.020 - 90.030				
911 (1974-1977) Nikasil Piston	89.965 - 89.975	89.975 - 89.985	89.985 - 89.995		6.0	± 6 / set	0.025 - 0.045
911 (1974-1977) Alusil Piston	89.952 - 89.967	89.962 - 89.977	89.972 - 89.987		18.0	± 6 / set	0.035 - 0.060
911 (1974-1977) Carrera MFI - Nikasil	89.945 - 89.955	89.955 - 89.965	89.965 - 89.975		2.5	± 6 / set	0.025 - 0.045
1976-77 Euro Carrera 3.0							
Cylinder Markings	0	1	2	3			
Nominal Diameter	95.000	95.000	95.000	95.000			
Cylinder Diameter	95.000 - 95.007	95.007 - 90.014	95.014 - 95.021	95.021 - 95.028			
911 (1976-77) Nikasil Piston	94.963 - 94.977	94.970 - 94.984	94.977 - 94.991	94.984 - 94.998	See A	± 6 / set	0.023 - 0.044
1976-77 Turbo 3.0							
Cylinder Markings	0	1	2				
Nominal Diameter	95.000	95.000	95.000				
Cylinder Diameter	95.000 - 95.010	95.010 - 95.020	95.020 - 95.030				
3.0 Nikasil Piston	94.933 - 94.947	94.943 - 94.957	94.953 - 94.967		See A	± 6 / set	0.053 - 0.077
1978-89 Turbo 3.3							
Cylinder Markings	0	1	2	3			
Nominal Diameter	97.000	97.000	97.000	97.000			
Cylinder Diameter	97.000 - 97.007	97.007 - 97.014	97.014 - 97.021	97.021 - 97.028			
3.0 Nikasil Piston	96.960 - 96.970	96.967 - 96.977	96.974 - 96.984	96.981 - 96.991	See A	See B	0.030 - 0.047
1978-83 911SC 3.0							
Cylinder Markings	0	1	2	3			
Nominal Diameter	95.000	95.000	95.000	95.000			
Cylinder Diameter	95.000 - 95.007	95.007 - 95.014	95.014 - 95.021	95.021 - 95.028			
3.0 Nikasil Piston	94.965 - 94.975	94.972 - 94.982	94.979 - 94.989	94.986 - 94.996	See A	See B	0.025 - 0.042
3.0 Alusil Piston	94.963 - 94.977	94.970 - 94.984	94.977 - 94.991	94.984 - 94.998	See A	See B	0.023 - 0.044
1984-89 Carrera 3.2							
Cylinder Markings	0	1	2	3			
Nominal Diameter	95.000	95.000	95.000	95.000			
Cylinder Diameter - Nikasil	95.000 - 95.007	95.007 - 95.014	95.014 - 95.021	95.021 - 95.028			
3.0 Nikasil Piston	94.965 - 94.975	94.972 - 94.982	94.979 - 94.989	94.986 - 94.996	See A	See B	0.025 - 0.042
Cylinder Diameter - Alusil	95.000 - 95.005	95.005 - 95.010	95.010 - 95.015	95.015 - 95.020			
3.0 Alusil Piston	94.975 - 94.980	94.980 - 94.985	94.985 - 94.990	94.990 - 94.995	See A	See B	0.020 - 0.030

Notes:

A - From 1976, piston diameter is measured at the lower edge of the piston pin bore.

B - From 1980, weight classes are calculated according to the table in the following section.

- KS = manufacturer Kolbenschmidt
- Piston diameters are measured at a point that is a specific distance from the bottom of the piston. This distance is dimension h.
- For 1965-74 model years, replacement of pistons should occur when dimension measured at the wear point (given by dimension h in above table) is less than 0.1mm of the initial installation diameter.
- For 1975-89 model years, replacement of pistons and cylinders should occur when the running clearance between them exceeds 0.15mm (1975-81) or 0.12mm (1982-89).

- The measuring point for cylinder wear is 30mm below the upper edge (D1). A cylinder is worn if the dimension recorded is greater than the installation diameter by 0.1mm (1965-74) or 0.08mm (1975-89).
- Cylinder ovality is measured at dimension D1 and the level where the cylinder mates to the crankcase (at the level of the cylinder base gasket, D2). Ovality is determined by measuring the inside diameter of the cylinder across lines a and b. The dimensions recorded must be within 0.04mm of each other, or the cylinder needs to be replaced.
- Measurement D2 is where the piston ring gap measurement is performed.

Piston Weight Classes (1980-89)

	Weight Codes for Assembly of Engine (max weight difference = 4 grams)				Single Piston Replacement (max weight difference = 8 grams)	
	Code --	Code --	Code +	Code + +	Code -- or -	Code + or ++
911SC (1980)						
930/09 - Mahle Pistons	660 - 664	664 - 668	668 - 672	672 - 676	660 - 668	668 - 676
930/07/08 - Mahle Pistons	636 - 640	640 - 644	644 - 648	648 - 652	636 - 644	644 - 652
930/09 - KS Pistons	695 - 699	699 - 703	703 - 707	707 - 711	695 - 703	703 - 711
911SC (1981-83)						
930/10 (R.o.W) - Mahle	668 - 672	672 - 676	676 - 680	680 - 684	668 - 676	676 - 684
930/16/17 (USA/Japan) - Mahle	636 - 640	640 - 644	644 - 648	648 - 652	636 - 644	644 - 652
930/16/17 (USA/Japan) - KS	673 - 677	677 - 681	681 - 685	685 - 689	673 - 681	681 - 689
911 Turbo (1980-89)						
930/60/66/68 - Mahle	616 - 620	620 - 624	624 - 628	628 - 632	616 - 624	624 - 632
911 Carrera (1984-89)						
930/20/25/26 (R.o.W) - Mahle	618 - 622	622 - 626	626 - 630	630 - 634	618 - 626	626 - 634
930/21 (USA) - Mahle	613 - 617	617 - 621	621 - 625	625 - 629	613 - 621	621 - 629
930/21 (USA) - KS	650 - 654	654 - 658	658 - 662	662 - 666	654 - 662	662 - 670

Notes:

- Only install pistons of the same weight group into one engine
- Piston pins must be kept with their respective pistons upon disassembly, even if all pistons are within the same weight group. Exception: if the engine is going to be rebalanced at the machine shop, then the piston pins can be rematched to the pistons.
- KS Pistons, Manufacturer: Kolbenschmidt

- Pistons are weighed complete with piston pin, piston rings, and circlips.
- R.o.W. = Rest of World. Typically all models except USA and/or Japan.
- All pistons must belong to the same weight group when assembling the engine. When replacing a single piston, it is acceptable to locate one that is within 8 grams of the service group that is within the engine.
- See previous table for weight class information on 1965-79 engines.

Piston Ring & Outer Cylinder Wear Measurement

	2.2 (1965-69)	2.2 (1970-71)	2.4 (1972-73)	2.7 (1974)	2.7/3.0 Turbo (1975-77)	3.0/3.3 Turbo (1978-81)	3.0/3.2/3.3 Turbo (1982-89)
Piston Top Ring Side Clearance							
Groove	1.565 - 1.585	1.565 - 1.585	1.560 - 1.590	1.560 - 1.580	N/A	N/A	N/A
Ring	1.478 - 1.490	1.478 - 1.490	1.478 - 1.490	1.478 - 1.490	N/A	N/A	N/A
Clearances	+0.075 to +0.107	+0.075 to +0.107	+0.070 to +0.112	+0.070 to +0.102	+0.070 to +0.102	+0.070 to +0.102	+0.070 to +0.102
Wear Limit	0.20	0.20	0.20	0.20	0.20	0.20	0.20
Piston Middle Ring Side Clearance							
Groove	2.035 - 2.050	2.035 - 2.050	1.790 - 1.810	1.790 - 1.810	N/A	N/A	N/A
Ring	1.978 - 1.990	1.978 - 1.990	1.728 - 1.740	1.728 - 1.740	N/A	N/A	N/A
Clearances	+0.060 to +0.072	+0.060 to +0.072	+0.050 to +0.082	+0.050 to +0.082	+0.040 to +0.072	+0.040 to +0.072	+0.040 to +0.072
Wear Limit	0.20	0.20	0.20	0.20	0.20	0.20	0.20
Oil Seal Ring Side Clearance							
Groove	4.015 - 4.030	4.015 - 4.030	4.010 - 4.040	4.010 - 4.030	N/A	N/A	N/A
Ring	3.978 - 3.990	3.978 - 3.990	3.978 - 3.990	3.978 - 3.990	N/A	N/A	N/A
Clearances	+0.025 to +0.052	+0.025 to +0.052	+0.020 to +0.062	+0.020 to +0.052	+0.020 to +0.052	+0.020 to +0.052	+0.020 to +0.052
Wear Limit	0.20	0.20	0.20	0.20	0.10	0.10	0.10
Piston Ring Gaps							
Top Ring Gap	+0.15 to +0.45	+0.15 to +0.45	+0.15 to +0.45	+0.15 to +0.45	+0.10 to +0.20	+0.15 to +0.30	+0.20 to +0.40
Wear Limit	1.00	1.00	1.00	1.00	.80	.80	.80
Middle Ring Gap	+0.15 to 0.45	+0.15 to 0.45	+0.15 to 0.45	+0.15 to 0.45	+0.10 to 0.20	+0.15 to 0.30	+0.20 to 0.40
Wear Limit	1.00	1.00	1.00	1.00	.80	.80	1.00
Oil Seal Ring	+0.15 to +0.45	+0.15 to +0.45	+0.15 to +0.45	+0.15 to +0.45	+0.15 to +0.30	+0.15 to +0.30	+0.30 to +0.60
Wear Limit	1.00	1.00	1.00	1.00	1.00	1.00	2.00
Oil Seal Ring (3-piece 'LS' ring)					+0.40 to +1.40	+0.40 to +1.40	
Wear Limit					2.00	2.00	
Cylinder Outer Base Diameter to Crankcase							
Bore	92.072 - 92.159	92.072 - 92.159	92.072 - 92.159	97.072 - 97.152	97.072 - 97.152	N/A	N/A
Shaft	91.874 - 91.928	91.874 - 91.928	91.874 - 91.928	96.874 - 96.928	96.874 - 96.928	N/A	N/A
Clearances	+0.144 - +0.285	+0.144 - +0.285	+0.144 - +0.285	+0.144 - +0.285	+0.144 to +0.285	N/A	N/A
Cylinder Top Outer Diameter to Cylinder Head							
Bore	88.000 - 88.054	97.072 - 97.159	97.072 - 97.159	107.000 - 107.073	107.000 - 107.073	N/A	N/A
Shaft	87.874 - 87.928	96.874 - 96.928	96.874 - 96.928	106.893 - 106.928	106.893 - 106.928	N/A	N/A
Clearances	+0.072 to +0.180	+0.144 to -0.285	+0.144 to -0.285	+0.72 to -0.180	+0.72 to -0.180	N/A	N/A

Notes:

- N/A = Data not available.
- Piston ring gap measured at point D2 (See earlier diagram).

Piston & Cylinder Height Groups

	2.0 (1965-68)	2.0 (1969)	2.2/2.4 (1970-73)	911 (1974-89) Turbo(1976-77)	911Turbo (1978-89)
Height Group 5	82.200 - 82.225	82.200 - 82.225	85.400 - 85.425	85.400 - 85.425	85.600 - 85.625
Height Group 6	82.225 - 82.250	82.225 - 82.250	85.425 - 85.450	85.425 - 85.450	85.625 - 85.650
Height Group R5 (replacement)		81.950 - 81.975	85.150 - 85.175		
Height Group R6 (replacement)		81.975 - 82.000	85.175 - 85.200		

Notes:

- All cylinders installed onto one side of the engine must belong to the same height group.
- 1973 Carrera 2.7 indicated height groups via a color dot. Red = height group 5. Blue = height group 6.

Piston Pin Tolerances

	911 (1965-69)	911 (1970-75)	911 (1976-89)
Color Code White			
Bore	21.997 - 22.000	22.000 - 22.005	N/A
Shaft	22.000 - 22.003	21.996 - 22.000	N/A
Clearance Fit	0.000 to - 0.006	0.000 to +0.009	N/A
Color Code Black			
Bore	21.994 - 21.997		
Shaft	21.994 - 21.997		
Clearance Fit	-0.003 to +0.003		

Notes:

- N/A = Data not available.
- Early piston pins were press-fit into the piston. This required heating the piston prior to insertion.
- Color codes for piston pins discontinued after 1969.
- This technique is valid only for 1965-69 engines. Later style piston pins are a tight fit, but don't need to be heated

Valve, Guide, and Seat Dimensions/Tolerances

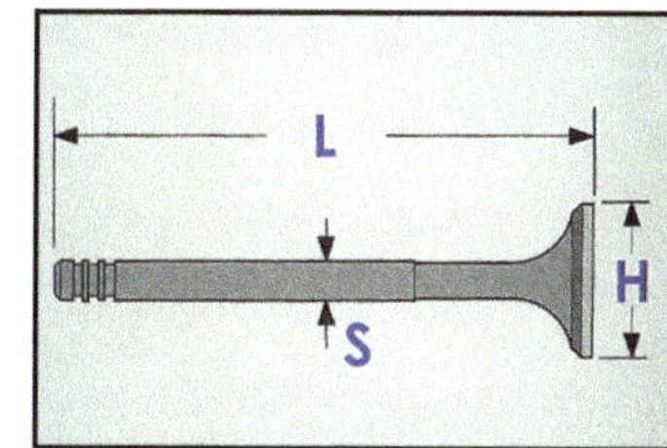

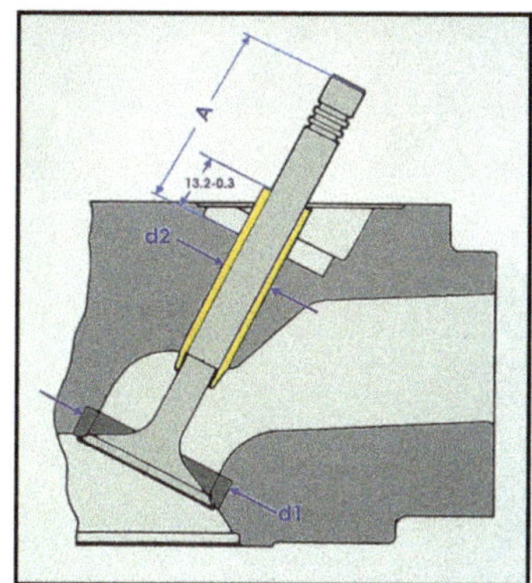

	911T/L (1965-68)*	911T/E (1969) 911S (1967-68)	911S (1969)	911/T/E/S (1970-77)	911 (1978-89) Turbo (1975-89)
Head Diameter (H)					
Intake	39.0 ± 0.1	42.0 ± 0.1	45.0 ± 0.1	46.0 ± 0.1	49.0 ± 0.1
Exhaust	35.0 ± 0.1	38.0 ± 0.1	39.0 ± 0.1	40.0 ± 0.1	41.5 ± 0.1
Valve Stem Diameter (S)					
Intake	8.958 - 8.970	8.958 - 8.970	8.958 - 8.970	8.958 - 8.970	8.958 - 8.970
Exhaust	8.938 - 8.950	8.938 - 8.950	8.938 - 8.950	8.938 - 8.950	8.938 - 8.950
Total Valve Length (L)					
Intake	111.15 ± 0.05	114.0 ± 0.1	113.3 ± 0.1	114.0 ± 0.1	110.1 ± 0.25
Exhaust	111.75 ± 0.05	113.5 ± 0.1	112.2 ± 0.1	113.3 ± 0.1	108.4 ± 0.25
Valve Height (distance A)**					
Intake / Exhaust	45.85 – 47.05	47.50 ± 0.60	47.50 ± 0.60	47.50 ± 0.60	46.00 ± 0.30
Intake Valve Seat - Std					
Bore (D1)	42.000 - 42.025	45.000 - 45.025	47.000 - 47.025	48.000 - 48.025	51.500 - 51.530
Shaft (d1)	42.180 - 42.164	45.180 - 45.164	47.180 - 47.164	48.180 - 48.164	51.680 - 51.661
Press Fit	-0.155 to -0.164	-0.155 to -0.164	-0.155 to -0.164	-0.155 to -0.164	-0.150 to -0.161
Intake Valve Seat - 1st Oversize					
Bore (D1)	42.320 - 42.345	45.320 - 45.345	47.320 - 47.345	48.320 - 48.345	51.820 - 51.850
Shaft (d1)	42.500 - 42.484	45.500 - 45.484	47.500 - 47.484	48.500 - 48.484	52.000 - 51.981
Press Fit	-0.155 to -0.164	-0.155 to -0.164	-0.155 to -0.164	-0.155 to -0.164	-0.150 to -0.161
Exhaust Valve Seat - Std					
Bore (D1)	38.000 - 38.025	41.000 - 41.025	41.000 - 41.025	42.000 - 42.025	44.000 - 44.025
Shaft (d1)	38.200 - 38.184	41.200 - 41.184	41.200 - 41.184	42.200 - 42.184	44.200 - 44.184
Press Fit	-0.175 to - 0.184	-0.175 to - 0.184	-0.175 to - 0.184	-0.175 to - 0.184	-0.175 to - 0.184
Exhaust Valve Seat - 1st Oversize					
Bore (D1)	38.560 - 38.585	41.560 - 41.585	41.560 - 41.585	42.560 - 42.585	44.560 - 44.585
Shaft (d1)	38.760 - 38.744	41.760 - 41.744	41.760 - 41.744	42.760 - 42.744	44.760 - 44.744
Press Fit	-0.175 to - 0.184	-0.175 to - 0.184	-0.175 to - 0.184	-0.175 to - 0.184	-0.175 to - 0.184

Notes:

* Oversized guides were listed as available for 1965-68 (13.260-13.249 and 13.460-13.449).

** Valve height data for SC and later 911s may require modifications to work with late-style heads.

- Includes European Carrera 3.0.
- Valve stem diameter must be within spec across the entire length of the valve.

- See main engine chart for port sizes.
- Dimension d1 references the outer dimension of the valve seat. Dimention D1 (not shown) represents the inside bore that the seat is pressed into.
- Dimension d2 references the outer dimension of the valve guide. Dimention D2 (not shown) represents the bore inside the cylinder head that the valve guide pressed into.

Valve Guide Tolerances

Cylinder Head to Valve Guide Interface - Standard Size

Bore (D2)	13.000 - 13.018
Shaft (d2)	13.049 - 13.060
Press Fit	-0.031 to -0.060

Cylinder Head to Valve Guide Interface - 1st Oversize

Bore (D2)	13.200 - 13.218
Shaft (d2)	13.249 - 13.260
Press Fit	-0.031 to -0.060

Cylinder Head to Valve Guide Interface - 2nd Oversize

Bore (D2)	13.400 - 13.418
Shaft (d2)	13.449 - 13.460
Press Fit	-0.031 to -0.060

Intake Valve Guide

Bore (D2)	9.000 - 9.015
Shaft (d2)	8.958 - 8.970
Clearances	+0.030 to +0.057
Wear Limit	0.15

Exhaust Valve Guide

Bore (D2)	9.000 - 9.015
Shaft (d2)	8.938 - 8.950
Clearances	+0.050 ± +0.077
Wear Limit	0.20

Installation Length of Valve Springs

	Intake	Exhaust
911 (1965-68), up to engine 911 001	36.0 ± 0.3	36.0 ± 0.3
911/L (1965-68), from engine 911 001	35.0 ± 0.3	35.0 ± 0.3
911S (1967-68)	35.0 ± 0.5	35.0 ± 0.3
911T (1968)	35.0 ± 0.3	35.0 ± 0.3
911T (1968), single spring*	40.75 ± 0.25	40.75 ± 0.25
911T (1969-71)	36.0 ± 0.3	36.0 ± 0.3
911E (1969-71)	35.5 ± 0.3	35.0 ± 0.3
911S (1969-71)	35.5 ± 0.3	34.5 ± 0.3
911T (1972-73)	35.0 ± 0.3	35.0 ± 0.3
911E (1972-73)	34.0 ± 0.3	34.0 ± 0.3
911S (1972-73)	35.5 ± 0.3	34.5 ± 0.3
Carrera RS (1973)	35.5 ± 0.3	34.5 ± 0.3
911/S/Carrera (1974)	35.0 ± 0.3	35.5 ± 0.3
911/911S (1975-77)	35.0 ± 0.3	35.5 ± 0.3
Carrera MFI (1974-75)	35.3 ± 0.3	34.5 ± 0.3
Turbo (1975)	33.5 ± 0.3	33.5 ± 0.3
Carrera 3.0 (1976-77)	34.5 ± 0.3	34.5 ± 0.3
911 Turbo (1976-89)	33.5 ± 0.3	33.5 ± 0.3
911 (1978-89)	34.35 ± 0.15	34.35 ± 0.15

–See diagram below.

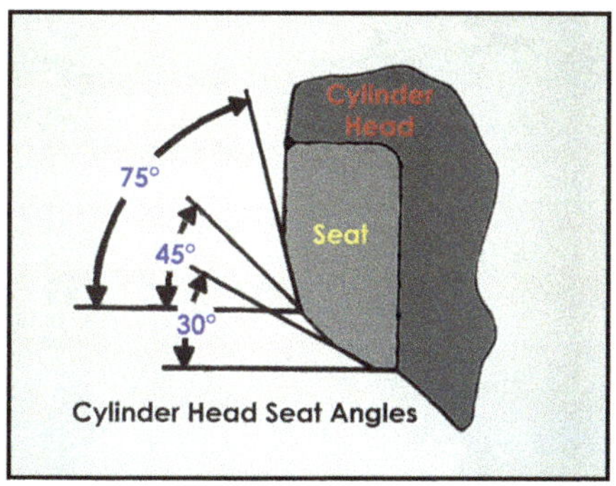

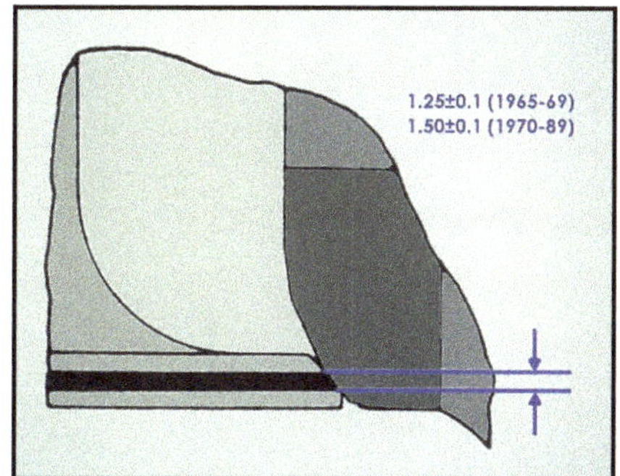

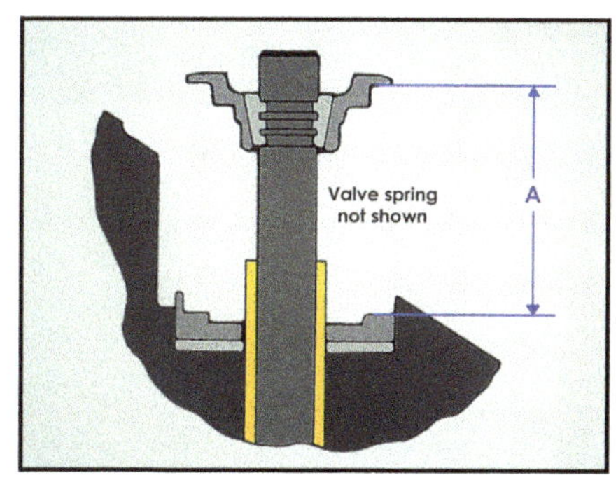

Spring Rate Checks

911 All (1965-89)	Compressed Length	Measured Force
Initial Pressure Check	42.0 - 42.5	20 kp
First Compression Check	30.5 - 31.0	80 kp
Second Compression Check	31.5 - 32.0	75 kp

Notes:
* Single spring installations have been superceded to standard dual spring configuration.
- Measured loading for used springs (not recommended) should not vary more than ± 5% from the values listed above.

Clutch Tolerances

	911T/L/S (1965-68)	911T/E/S (1969)	911T/E/S (1970-74)	911 (1975-86)	911 (1987-89)	911 Turbo (1975-88)	911 Sporto (1970-83)
Clutch Disc							
New Thickness	9.2 ± 0.2*	9.8 ± 0.4	8.1 ± 0.4	8.1 ± 0.3	10.1 ± 0.3	10.1 ± 0.3	7.3 ± 0.25
Wear Limit (symmetrical)	7.8 - 8.0	6.5	6.0	6.3	8.5	8.5	5.5
Max Lateral Runout	0.6 max	0.6 max	0.6 max	0.6 max	0.5 max	0.5 max	0.5 max
Diameter	215	215	225	225	240	240	190
Pressure Plate							
Contact Pressure (kp)**	N/A	500-560 (T/E) 530-590 (S)	600-670 (70-71) 715-785 (72-74) 720-780 (2.7RS)	795-866 715-785 (1975)	755-836	920-1020 (75-77) 1142-1233 (78-88)	800-880

Notes:
* Indicates compressed thickness. Free thickness 9.7-10.1.
** Indicates initial early specification. Most pressure plates have been superceded to later models that also fit the earlier cars.
- Rubber centered clutch discs are prone to sudden failure and have been discontinued. Replace with spring center disc.
- 1 kp = 9.8 Newton = 2.19 pound-force (lb).
- Clutch discs cannot be reconditioned and must be replaced when worn.
- Symmetrical wear limit is the even wear around the disc.

1965-68 Notes:
- Diaphragm springs must not be scored beyond 0.3mm.
- Pressure plates warped inward are still serviceable up to 0.3mm.
- 911S flywheel and pressure plate have 0.5-0.7mm thick bronze coating on the contact surfaces.
- Minimum thickness of clutch plate (5.5mm with 0.5 max runout).
- N/A = Information not available.

Flywheel Tolerances

	Dim when New	Machining Step 1	Machining Step 1	Machining Step 1	Tolerance
911 (1965), up to engine P 901 638					
Measuring Point a	22.5	22.5	-	-	± 0.2
Measuring Point b	44.6	44.2	43.8	43.4	± 0.2
Measuring Point	Worn out at 11.000mm				
911 (1965-69), from engine P 901 639					
Measuring Point a	22.5	22.5	-	-	± 0.2
Measuring Point b	39.0	38.6	38.2	37.8	± 0.2
Measuring Point c	Worn out at 11.000mm				

911/Turbo (1970-1983), 911 Turbo (1976-88)
Wear limit at point #1: 8.5mm (911), 9.9mm (911 Turbo)
Max runout 0.1mm at outer circumference of contact area
Make smallest possible cut at point #2

911 (1984-86)
Wear limit at point #1: 8.5mm (911)
Max runout 0.1mm at outer circumference of contact area
Make smallest possible cut at point #2

911 (1987-89)
Dual-mass flywheel not serviceable.
Release bearing could bear on the drive plate dampner depending upon the tolerances.

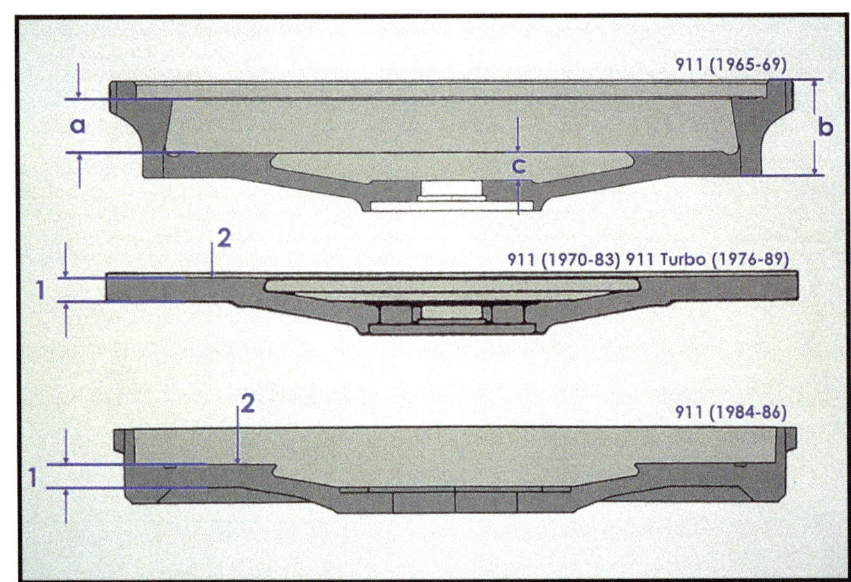

Appendix B: Engine Parts Listings (1974-89)

For this section, I've compiled a lengthy list of parts that are used on the 911 engine. All of the information here was compiled from various sources, all of which are no longer published. I have done my best to double-check the accuracy of this information. However, I have found several errors in original Porsche parts diagrams books, and sometimes they even contradict each other. In addition, some parts have been superceded to a later part number. Please use this information as a reference only, keeping in mind that Porsche may decide to supercede or change part numbers at any time.

Crankshaft & Rods

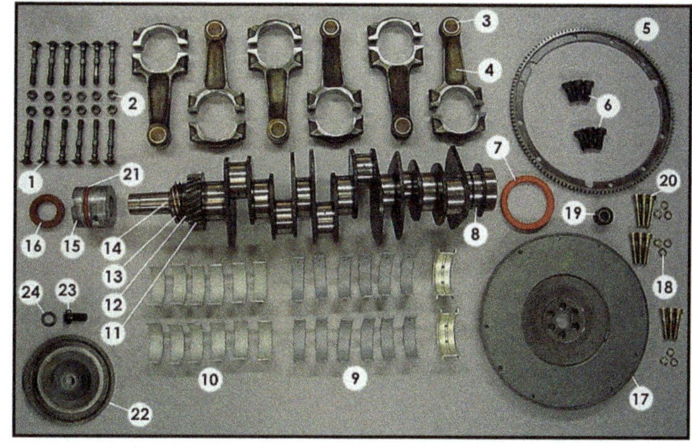

No.	Model / Engine / Years	Part Number	Description	Qty	Comments
1	911 (1974-83), Turbo (1976-77)	914.103.171.00	Rod Bolt	12	Use only new rod bolts
1	911 (1984-89), Turbo (1978-89)	930.103.176.00	Rod Bolt	12	NOT RECOMMENDED: Use RaceWare or ARP Rod bolts instead
2	911 (1974-83), Turbo (1976-77)	901.103.173.00	Rod Nut	12	Use only new rod nuts
2	911 (1984-89), Turbo (1978-89)	930.103.174.00	Rod Nut	12	NOT RECOMMENDED: Use RaceWare or ARP Rod nuts instead
3	911 (1974-83), Turbo (1976-77)	911.103.132.00	Rod Bushing	6	
3	911 (1984-89), Turbo (1978-89)	930.103.134.01	Rod Bushing	6	
4	911 (1974-77), Turbo (1976-77)	911.103.015.38	Rod	6	See rod weight
4	911 (1978-83)	930.103.015.57	Rod	6	groups in
4	911 (1984-89), Turbo (1978-89)	964.103.020.61	Rod	6	Appendix A

No.	Model / Engine / Years	Part Number	Description	Qty	Comments
5	911 (1974-86)	911.116.239.00	Flywheel Ring Gear	1	
5	911 (1987-89), Turbo (1989)	950.116.143.01	Flywheel Ring Gear	1	
5	911 Turbo (1976-77)	930.116.230.00	Flywheel Ring Gear	1	
5	911 Turbo (1978-88)	930.116.230.02	Flywheel Ring Gear	1	
6	911 / 911 Turbo (1974-77)	911.102.171.00	Flywheel Bolt	6	
6	911 / 911 Turbo (1978-89)	930.102.206.00	Flywheel Bolt	9	
	911 / 911 Turbo (1974-77)	901.102.162.04	Flywheel Washer	1	
7	911 / 911 Turbo (1974-77)	999.113.057.52	Flywheel Seal	1	Size: 65x85x10mm
7	911 / 911 Turbo (1974-77)	901.102.911.00	Flywheel Seal	1	Size: 64.5x85x10mm
7	911 / 911 Turbo (1978-89)	999.113.426.40	Flywheel Seal	1	Size: 90x110mm
8	911 / 911 Turbo (1974-77)	916.102.016.00	Crankshaft	1	
8	911 (1978-83)	930.102.015.05	Crankshaft	1	
8	911 (1984-89)	930.102.014.09	Crankshaft	1	
8	911 Turbo (1978-89)	930.102.014.10	Crankshaft	1	
9	911 (1974-75)	911.101.901.00	Crankshaft Main Bearing Set	1	Std/Std up to Engine # 6450388/6459030/655022/6559021
9	911 (1974-75)	911.101.901.60	Crankshaft Main Bearing Set	1	Standard inner diameter / .25mm outer diameter
9	911 (1974-75)	911.101.901.50	Crankshaft Main Bearing Set	1	25mm inner diameter / Std outer diameter
9	911 (1974-75)	911.101.901.70	Crankshaft Main Bearing Set	1	.25mm inner diameter / .25mm outer diameter
9	911 (1974-75)	911.101.901.55	Crankshaft Main Bearing Set	1	.50mm inner diameter / standard outer diameter
9	911 (1974-75)	911.101.901.75	Crankshaft Main Bearing Set	1	.50mm inner diameter / .25mm outer diameter
9	911 (1975-77)	911.101.902.00	Crankshaft Main Bearing Set	1	Std/Std from Engine # 6450389/6459031/6550023/6559022
9	911 (1975-77)	911.101.902.60	Crankshaft Main Bearing Set	1	Standard inner diameter / .25mm outer diameter
9	911 (1975-77)	911.101.902.50	Crankshaft Main Bearing Set	1	.25mm inner diameter / Std outer diameter
9	911 (1975-77)	911.101.902.70	Crankshaft Main Bearing Set	1	.25mm inner diameter / .25mm outer diameter
9	911 (1975-77)	911.101.902.55	Crankshaft Main Bearing Set	1	.50mm inner diameter / standard outer diameter
9	911 (1975-77)	911.101.902.75	Crankshaft Main Bearing Set	1	.50mm inner diameter / .25mm outer diameter
9	911 (1978-89)	964.101.901.00	Crankshaft Main Bearing Set	1	Standard inner/outer diameters
9	911 (1978-89)	964.101.901.61	Crankshaft Main Bearing Set	1	Standard inner diameter / .25mm outer diameter
9	911 (1978-89)	964.101.901.51	Crankshaft Main Bearing Set	1	.25mm inner diameter / Std outer diameter
9	911 (1978-89)	964.101.901.71	Crankshaft Main Bearing Set	1	.25mm inner diameter / .25mm outer diameter
9	911 (1978-89)	964.101.901.56	Crankshaft Main Bearing Set	1	.50mm inner diameter / standard outer diameter
9	911 (1978-89)	964.101.901.76	Crankshaft Main Bearing Set	1	.50mm inner diameter / .25mm outer diameter
10	911 / 911 Turbo (1974-77)	914.198.141.00	Rod Bearings - Std	1	
10	911 / 911 Turbo (1974-77)	914.198.141.50	Rod Bearings - .25mm Undersize	1	
10	911 / 911 Turbo (1974-77)	914.198.141.60	Rod Bearings - .50mm Undersize	1	
10	911 (1978-83)	930.198.148.00	Rod Bearings - Std	1	
10	911 (1978-83)	930.198.148.50	Rod Bearings - .25mm Undersize	1	
10	911 (1978-83)	930.198.148.60	Rod Bearings - .50mm Undersize	1	
10	911 (1984-89), Turbo (1978-89)	930.198.147.00	Rod Bearings - Std	1	
10	911 (1984-89), Turbo (1978-89)	930.198.147.50	Rod Bearings - .25mm Undersize	1	
10	911 (1984-89), Turbo (1978-89)	930.198.147.60	Rod Bearings - .50mm Undersize	1	
11	911 / 911 Turbo (1974-89)	901.102.111.00	Crankshaft Timing Gear - Size 0	1	
11	911 / 911 Turbo (1974-89)	901.102.111.10	Crankshaft Timing Gear - Size 1	1	
	911 / 911 Turbo (1974-89)	901.102.147.00	Woodruff Key	1	Indexes crankshaft and timing gear
12	911 / 911 Turbo (1974-89)	901.102.145.00	Crankshaft Gear Spacer	1	
13	911 (1974-77)	111.105.223	Distributor Drive Gear	1	
13	911 (1978-83), Turbo (1978-89)	930.102.115.01	Distributor Drive Gear	1	Runs in counter clockwise direction
13	911 (1984-89)	930.102.112.00	Distributor Drive Gear	1	
14	911 / 911 Turbo (1978-89)	901.102.148.00	Circlip - 2.4mm	1	
14	911 / 911 Turbo (1978-89)	901.102.148.01	Circlip - 2.3mm	1	
14	911 / 911 Turbo (1978-89)	901.102.148.02	Circlip - 2.2mm	1	
14	911 / 911 Turbo (1978-89)	901.102.148.03	Circlip - 2.1mm	1	
15	911 (1974-77), Turbo (1976-77)	901.101.138.03	Number Eight Nose Bearing	1	Standard size

No.	Model / Engine / Years	Part Number	Description	Qty	Comments
15	911 (1974-77), Turbo (1976-77)	901.101.138.53	Number Eight Nose Bearing	1	.25mm undersize
15	911 / 911 Turbo (1978-89)	964.101.138.01	Number Eight Nose Bearing	1	.Standard size
15	911 / 911 Turbo (1978-89)	964.101.138.53	Number Eight Nose Bearing	1	.25mm undersize
16	911 / 911 Turbo (1974-89)	999.113.465.40	Pulley Seal	1	Size: 30x50x10mm
16	911 / 911 Turbo (1974-89)	999.113.291.40	Pulley Seal	1	Undersize: 29.5x50x10mm
17	911 (1974-77)	911.102.201.11	Flywheel	1	Without ring gear
17	911 (1978-79)	930.102.204.00	Flywheel	1	Without ring gear, up to Engine #6292280/6591575
17	911 (1979-83)	930.102.215.00	Flywheel	1	Without ring gear, from Engine #6292281/6591576
17	911 (1984-86)	930.102.033.01	Flywheel	1	With ring gear
17	911 (1987-89)	930.102.033.03	Flywheel	1	With ring gear
17	911 Turbo (1976-77)	930.102.201.01	Flywheel	1	Without ring gear
17	911 Turbo (1978-79)	930.102.202.01	Flywheel	1	Without ring gear, up to Engine #6890504/6891231
17	911 Turbo (1979-88)	930.102.213.00	Flywheel	1	Without ring gear, from Engine #6890505/6891232
17	911 Turbo (1989)	930.102.027.00	Flywheel	1	Without ring gear
	911 (1974-77)	901.102.162.04	Flywheel Washer	1	Install under flywheel bolts
18	911 / Turbo (1974-86)	900.027.015.02	Pressure Plate Washer	9	
18	911 (1987-89), 911 Turbo (1989)	N 012.241.8	Pressure Plate Washer	1	
19	911 (1974-79)	901.102.025.01	Pilot Bearing	1	Pressed into flywheel, up to Engine # 6292280/6591575
19	911 Turbo (1976-79)	930.102.025.00	Pilot Bearing	1	Up to Engine # 6890504/6891231
19	911 (1979-86), Turbo (1979-88)	930.102.042.00	Pilot Bearing	1	From Engine # 6292281/6591576 or # 6890505/6891232 (Turbo)
19	911 (1987-89), 911 Turbo (1989)	931.102.111.00	Pilot Bearing	3	For use with G50 transmission
	911 (1979-89)	N 014.701.3	Pilot Bearing Bolt	9	For use with 930.102.042.00 or 931.102.111.00
20	911 (1974-86)	900.067.090.02	Pressure Plate Bolt	9	
20	911 Turbo (1976-88)	900.074.136.02	Pressure Plate Bolt	9	
20	911 (1987-89), Turbo (1989)	900.067.045.02	Pressure Plate Bolt	1	
21	911 / 911 Turbo (1974-77)	900.174.041.40	Nose Bearing O-ring	1	Size: 50 x 4mm
21	911 / 911 Turbo (1978-89)	999.707.285.40	Nose Bearing O-ring	1	Size: 51 x 4.5mm
22	911 (1974-75)	911.102.017.50	Crankshaft Pulley	1	Without Factory Air Conditioning
22	911 (1976-77)	911.102.017.04	Crankshaft Pulley	1	Without Factory Air Conditioning
22	911 (1978-79)	930.102.028.01	Crankshaft Pulley	1	Without Factory Air Conditioning
22	911 (1980-82)	930.102.128.04	Crankshaft Pulley	1	Without Factory Air Conditioning
22	911 (1983)	930.102.128.07	Crankshaft Pulley	1	Without Factory Air Conditioning
22	911 (1984-89)	930.102.028.08	Crankshaft Pulley	1	Without Factory Air Conditioning
22	911 Turbo (1976-77)	930.102.126.01	Crankshaft Pulley	1	Without Factory Air Conditioning
22	911 (1974-75)	911.102.015.50	Crankshaft Pulley	1	With Factory Air Conditioning
22	911 (1976-77)	911.102.022.01	Crankshaft Pulley	1	With Factory Air Conditioning
22	911 (1978-79)	930.102.023.01	Crankshaft Pulley	1	With Factory Air Conditioning
22	911 (1980-83)	930.102.023.03	Crankshaft Pulley	1	With Factory Air Conditioning
22	911 (1984-89)	930.102.024.03	Crankshaft Pulley	1	With Factory Air Conditioning
22	911 Turbo (1976-77)	930.102.017.02	Crankshaft Pulley	1	With Factory Air Conditioning
22	911 Turbo (1978-79)	930.102.017.04	Crankshaft Pulley	1	With Factory Air Conditioning
22	911 Turbo (1986-89)	930.102.024.04	Crankshaft Pulley	1	With Factory Air Conditioning
23	911/Turbo (1974-89)	999.093.005.02	Crankshaft Pulley Bolt	1	
24	911/Turbo (1974-89)	900.028.014.01	Spring Washer		

Inside Case

No.	Model / Engine / Years	Part Number	Description	Qty	Comments
1	911 / 911 Turbo (1974-83)	930.101.391.01	Sump Gasket	2	Up to Engine #64D3716
2	911 / 911 Turbo (1974-83)	900.028.008.02	Nuts	8	
	911 / 911 Turbo (1974-83)	900.076.010.02	Washers	8	
3	911 / 911 Turbo (1974-83)	930.107.314.00	Sump Strainer	1	Up to Engine #64D3716
4	911 / 911 Turbo (1974-83)	911.107.176.03	Drain Plug	1	Up to Engine #64D3716
5	911 / 911 Turbo (1974-83)	900.123.011.20	Drain Plug Seal	1	Sealing ring (Size: 22x27mm)
6	911 / 911 Turbo (1974-83)	901.101.386.00	Sump Cover	1	Up to Engine #64D3716
7	911 / 911 Turbo (1974-89)	900.076.025.02	Oil Pump Nuts	3	
8	911 / 911 Turbo (1974-89)	999.039.001.00	Oil Pump Lock Tabs	3	Always use new lock tabs
9	911 / 911 Turbo (1974-89)	999.704.172.50	Case Half / Oil Pump Seal	3	
10	911 (1974-75)	901.107.002.06	Oil Pump	1	Early style pump
10	911 (1976-83), Turbo (1976-77)	901.107.008.01	Oil Pump	1	New pumps no longer available, up to Engine # 64D3716

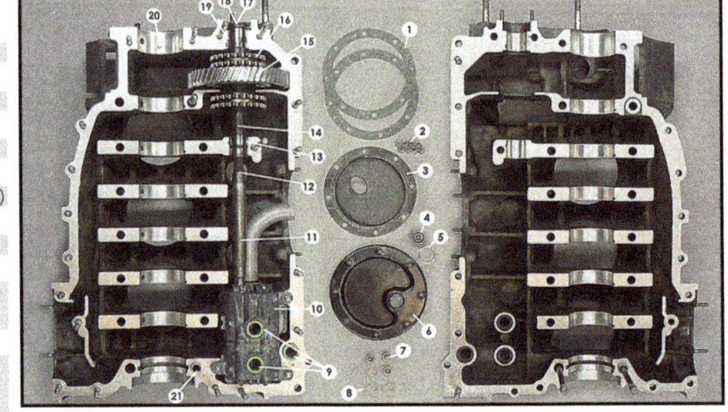

No.	Model / Engine / Years	Part Number	Description	Qty	Comments
10	911 (1983-89)	911.107.008.05	Oil Pump	1	Carrera oil pump, from Engine # 64D3717
10	911 Turbo (1978-89)	930.107.008.04	Oil Pump	1	Big Turbo pump - changed in 1983 to include embedded screen
11	911 (1974-89), Turbo (1976-77)	901.107.121.00	Oil Pump Shaft	1	
11	911 Turbo (1978-89)	930.107.143.01	Oil Pump Shaft	1	
12	911 / 911 Turbo (1974-89)	N 012.381.1	Circlip	1	
13	911 / 911 Turbo (1974-89)	993.101.135.00	Intermediate Shaft Inner Bearing	2	
14/15	911 / 911 Turbo (1974-89)	930.105.013.01	Intermediate Shaft Assy - Size 0	1	Match your intermediate shaft gear to the case and crankshaft timing gear
14/15	911 / 911 Turbo (1974-89)	930.105.013.11	Intermediate Shaft Assy - Size 1	1	
16	911 / 911 Turbo (1974-89)	901.105.125.04	Intermediate Shaft Sprocket	2	
17	911 / 911 Turbo (1974-89)	901.105.275.00	Intermediate Shaft Plug	1	
18	911 / 911 Turbo (1974-89)	N 012.296.1	Circlip	1	
19	911 / 911 Turbo (1974-89)	993.101.137.00	Intermediate Shaft Outer Bearing	2	
	911 / 911 Turbo (1974-89)	900.118.010.00	Woodruff Key	1	
20	911 / 911 Turbo (1974-89)	900.012.061.00	Dowel Pin	1	
21	911 / 911 Turbo (1974-89)	901.101.195.00	Locating Sleeve	2	

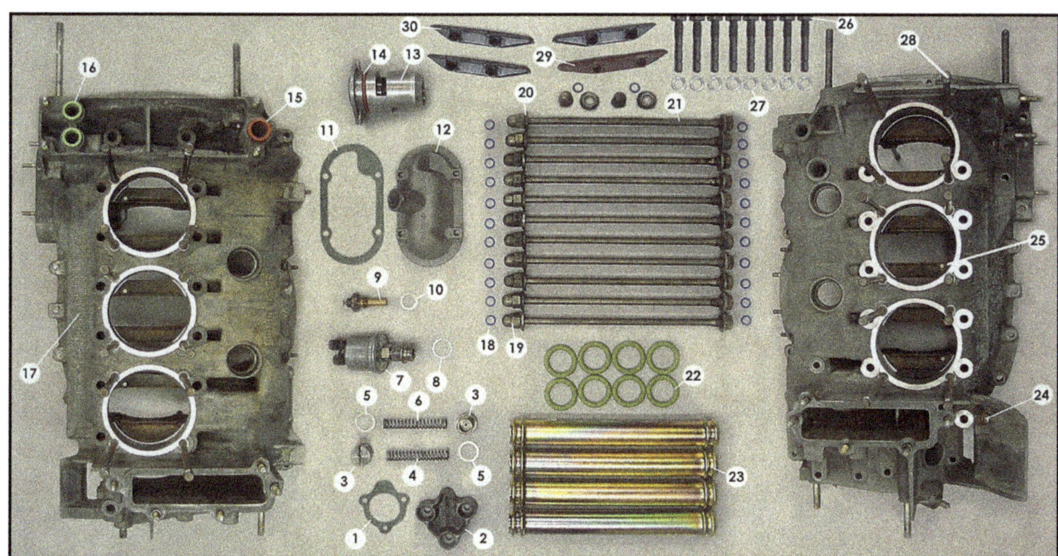

Outside Case

No.	Model / Engine / Years	Part Number	Description	Qty	Comments
1	911 / 911 Turbo (1974-83)	930.105.198.01	Intermediate Shaft Cover Gasket	1	Up to Engine # 64D3716
1	911 /911 Turbo (1983-89)	999.707.314.40	Intermediate Shaft Cover O-Ring	1	From Engine # 64D3717
2	911 / 911 Turbo (1974-83)	911.105.162.00	Intermediate Shaft Cover	1	Up to Engine # 64D3716
2	911 / 911 Turbo (1983-89)	930.105.165.00	Intermediate Shaft Cover	1	From Engine # 64D3717
3	911 / 911 Turbo (1974-89)	999.064.026.02	Oil Piston Cap	2	Use late-style plug as upgrade
4	911 / 911 Turbo (1974-89)	901.107.531.00	Oil Pressure Spring-side	2	Shorter of both springs
5	911 / 911 Turbo (1974-89)	900.123.106.30	Sealing Ring	2	
6	911 / 911 Turbo (1974-89)	930.107.531.00	Oil Pressure Spring-bottom	2	Longer of both springs
	911 / 911 Turbo (1974-89)	911.107.512.00	Oil Pressure Relief Piston	2	Late-style upgrade w/oil bypass modification
7	911 / 911 Turbo (1974-77)	911.606.111.00	Oil Pressure Sender	1	
7	911 / 911 Turbo (1978-83)	911.606.111.01	Oil Pressure Sender	1	
7	911 (1984-89), Turbo (1986-89)	911.606.135.00	Oil Pressure Sender	1	
8	911 / 911 Turbo (1974-89)	900.123.009.20	Sealing Ring	1	
9	911 (1981-83)	930.606.117.01	Oil Temperature Switch—Breather Housing	1	
9	911 (1984-89)	930.606.118.00	Oil Temperature Switch—Breather Housing	1	
9	911 Turbo (1986-89)	930.606.117.03	Oil Temperature Switch—Breather Housing	1	
10	911 / 911 Turbo (1978-89)	900.123.007.30	Sealing Ring	1	
11	911 / 911 Turbo (1978-89)	930.107.791.01	Breather Gasket	1	Double-check orientation on install
12	911 (1974-80), Turbo (1976-79)	901.107.073.02	Breather Cover	1	
12	911 (1981-89), Turbo 1986-89)	930.107.073.02	Breather Cover	1	
13	911 / 911 Turbo (1974-89)	930.107.765.00	Thermostat	1	
14	911 / 911 Turbo (1974-89)	999.707.314.40	Thermostat O-ring	1	
15	911 / 911 Turbo (1974-89)	999.704.017.50	Lower Oil Cooler Seal	1	
16	911 / 911 Turbo (1974-89)	999.704.172.50	Upper Oil Cooler Seal	2	
17	911 (1974-77)	911.101.915.00	Crankcase	1	Bearing tangs changed in mid-1975
17	911 (1978-83)	930.101.917.00	Crankcase	1	Up to Engine # 64D3716
17	911 (1983-89)	930.101.917.00	Crankcase	1	From Engine # 64D3717
17	911 Turbo (1976-77)	930.101.914.00	Crankcase	1	
17	911 Turbo (1978-89)	930.101.918.00	Crankcase	1	
18	911 / 911 Turbo (1974-89)	999.701.006.40	Through-bolt O-ring	24	Size: 8x2mm
19	911 (1974-77)	999.070.004.02	Cap Nut	13	
19	911 (1978-89), Turbo (1976-89)	930.101.172.01	Cap Nut	13	
20	911 / 911 Turbo (1974-89)	901.101.161.01	Washer (Beveled)	24	Use beveled washers on all engines 2.7 or larger
21	911 (1974-77)	901.101.173.00	Through-bolt	11	
	911 (1978-78), Turbo (1976-89)	930.101.173.02	Through-bolt	11	
22	911 / 911 Turbo (1974-89)	999.707.112.40	Oil Return Tube O-ring	8	
23	911 / 911 Turbo (1974-89)	901.107.351.01	Oil Return Tube	4	
24	911 / 911 Turbo (1974-89)	901.107.375.00	Camshaft Oil Line Adapter	1	
25	911 (1978-89)	911.101.011.01	Piston Squirters	6	
25	911 (1978-89)	911.101.011.51	Piston Squirters	6	Oversized
25	911 Turbo (1978-89)	930.101.015.00	Piston Squirters	6	Turbo squirters are good for case upgrades
25	911 Turbo (1978-89)	930.101.015.50	Piston Squirters	6	Oversized
26	911 / 911 Turbo (1978-89)	901.105.226.03	Chain Ramp Bolt	8	
27	911 / 911 Turbo (1978-89)	900.123.066.30	Sealing Ring	8	
28	911 (1974-89)	911.101.172.00	Cylinder Head Stud	24	Original steel head stud (upper)
28	911 (1978-89), Turbo (1976-89)	930.101.170.02	Dilavar Cylinder Head Stud	24	Turbo upper & lower - Dilavar not recommended
29	911 / 911 Turbo (1974-89)	911.105.222.05	Chain Ramp (Brown)	1	
30	911 / 911 Turbo (1974-89)	911.105.222.06	Chain Ramp (Black)	5	

Cylinder Heads & Pistons

No.	Model / Engine / Years	Part Number	Description	Qty	Comments
1	911 All (1974-77)	911.105.411.00	Intake Valve, 46mm	6	Used valves can
1	911 (1978-89)	930.105.409.13	Intake Valve, 49mm	6	be reground if
1	911 Turbo (1976-89)	964.105.409.06	Intake Valve, 49mm	6	there is enough
2	911 (1974-77)	911.105.415.50	Exhaust Valve, 40mm	6	material left on
2	911 (1978-89)	930.105.419.15	Exhaust Valve, 41.5mm	6	the head of the valve
2	911 Turbo (1976-89)	930.105.419.03	Exhaust Valve, 41.5mm	6	
3	911 / 911 Turbo (1974-89)	901.105.901.50	Inner and Outer Valve Spring Set	12	The 911 uses a dual spring setup to keep the valves against the seat
4/5	911 / 911 Turbo (1974-89)	901.105.421.03	Outer Valve Spring Seat / Retainer	12	
6	911 / 911 Turbo (1974-89)	901.105.463.00	Inner Valve Spring Seat	12	
7	911 / 911 Turbo (1974-89)	901.105.417.00	Valve Spring Keeper	24	Use 2 per each cylinder
8			Piston Pin	6	Not available separately
9	911 (1974-77)	911.198.939.00	Piston Ring Set	1	90mm - 2.7L Nikasil (1.5x1.75x4.0mm)
9	911 (1974-77)	911.198.956.00	Piston Ring Set	1	90mm - 2.7L 3pc Alusil Oil Ring (1.5x1.75x4.0mm)

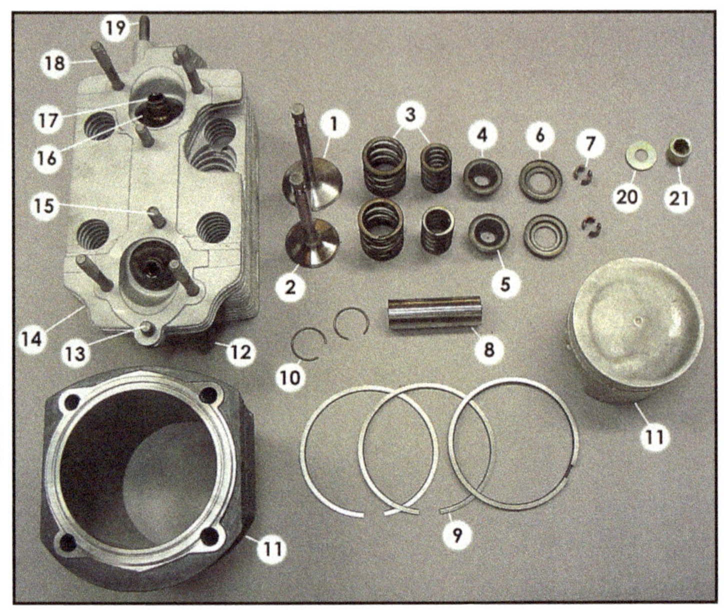

No.	Model / Engine / Years	Part Number	Description	Qty	Comments
9	911 (1978-79)	930.198.963.00	Piston Ring Set	1	95mm - 3.0L Mahle (1.5x1.75x4.0mm)
9	911 (1978-79)	930.198.967.00	Piston Ring Set	1	95mm - 3.0L Kolbenschmidt (1.5x1.75x4.0mm)
9	911 (1980-83), 911 (1984-89)	930.198.986.00	Piston Ring Set	1	95mm - 3.0L/3.2L Mahle (1.5x1.75x3.5mm)
9	911 (1980-83)	930.198.985.00	Piston Ring Set	1	95mm - 3.0L Kolbenschmidt (1.5x1.75x3.5mm)
9	911 (1987-89)	930.198.986.01	Piston Ring Set	1	95mm - 3.2L Kolbenschmidt (1.5x1.75x3.5mm)
9	911 Turbo (1976-77)	930.198.959.00	Piston Ring Set	1	95mm - 3.0L (1.5x1.5x4.0mm)
9	911 Turbo (1978-89)	930.198.968.00	Piston Ring Set	1	97mm - 3.3L (1.5x1.5x3.5mm)
10	911 (1974-83), Turbo (1976-77)	N 012.278.1	Piston Pin Circlip	12	
10	911 (1984-89), Turbo (1978-89)	900.908.019.00	Piston Pin Circlip	12	
11	911 (1974-77)	911.198.951.00	Piston & Cylinder Set	1	2.7L, 90mm, 8.0:1 CR
11	911S (1974-77)	911.198.949.00	Piston & Cylinder Set	1	2.7L, 90mm, 8.5:1 CR
11	911 (1978-79)	930.198.962.00	Piston & Cylinder Set	1	3.0L, 95mm, 8.5:1 CR
11	911 (1980-83)	930.198.977.00	Piston & Cylinder Set	1	3.0L, 95mm, 9.3:1 CR
11	911 (1984-89)	930.198.981.00	Piston & Cylinder Set	1	3.2L, 95mm, 9.3:1 CR
11	911 Turbo (1976-77)	930.198.958.00	Piston & Cylinder Set	1	3.0L, 95mm, 6.5:1 CR
11	911 Turbo (1978-89)	930.198.969.01	Piston & Cylinder Set	1	3.3L, 97mm, 7.0:1 CR
12	911 (1974-77)	999.062.006.02	Exhaust Stud M8X20	12	These have a tendency to harden from the heat given off by the exhaust system, and become very difficult to remove
12	911 Turbo (1976-77)	999.062.010.02	Exhaust Stud M8X35	12	
12	911 (1978-79), 911 Turbo (1978-79)	999.062.237.02	Exhaust Stud M8X35	12	
12	911 (1980-89), 911 Turbo (1986-89)	999.062.239.02	Exhaust Stud M8X30	12	
13	911 / 911 Turbo (1974-89)	999.012.006.00	Locating Dowell Pin	12	
14	911 (1974)	911.104.044.00	Bare Cylinder Head	6	Engines 911.92/97
14	911S (1974)	911.104.045.00	Bare Cylinder Head	6	Engines 911.93/98
14	911 (1975-76)	911.104.046.00	Bare Cylinder Head	6	Engines 911.43/48/82
14	911 (1975-77)	911.104.046.02	Bare Cylinder Head	6	Engines 911.44/49/84/85/89/90
14	911 (1978-79)	930.104.029.08	Bare Cylinder Head	6	Engines 930.04/06
14	911 (1980)	930.104.028.03	Bare Cylinder Head	6	Engine 930.07
14	911 (1981-83)	930.104.028.05	Bare Cylinder Head	6	Engine 930.16
14	911 (1984-89)	930.104.033.06	Bare Cylinder Head	6	Engines 930.21/25
14	911 Turbo (1976-77)	930.104.023.06	Bare Cylinder Head	6	Engines 930.51/53
14	911 Turbo (1978-86)	930.104.043.09	Bare Cylinder Head	6	Engines 930.61/63/64/68
14	911 Turbo (1987-89)	930.104.043.10	Bare Cylinder Head	6	Engine 930.68
	911 (1984-89)	930.606.915.00	Cylinder Head Temperature Sensor	1	For use only with the 1984-89 Motronic Engine Management System
15	911 / 911 Turbo (1974-89)	999.062.006.02	Cylinder to Cam Tower Stud M8X20	12	Usually not necessary to replace
16	911 / 911 Turbo (1974-89)	930.105.461.00	Spring Shim		As needed
17	911 / 911 Turbo (1974-89)	928.104.193.12	Valve Stem Seal	12	Intake or Exhaust
	911(1974-86), Turbo (1976-89)	930.104.321.50	Oversized Intake Valve Guide	6	
	911 (1987-89)	930.104.321.53	Oversized Intake Valve Guide	6	
	911 / 911 Turbo (1974-89)	930.104.321.50	Oversized Exhaust Valve Guide	24	Uses the same part number as the oversized intake valve guide
18	911 / 911 Turbo (1974-89)	999.062.041.02	Cylinder to Cam Tower Stud M8X50	12	Usually not necessary to replace
19	911 (1974)	999.062.007.02	Intake Stud M8X22	12	Only replace these if they are damaged
19	911 (1975-77), 911 (1980-83)	999.062.008.02	Intake Stud M8X25	12	
19	911 (1978-79)	999.062.009.02	Intake Stud M8X28	12	
19	911 Turbo (1976-89)	999.062.178.02	Intake Stud M8X120	12	
20	911 / 911 Turbo (1974-89)	999.031.091.01	Cylinder Head Nut Washer	24	Don't forget to install these when you mount your heads—they are very important for the proper mounting of the head stud nuts. Use only the factory washers—they are a specific thickness
21	911 / 911 Turbo (1974-89)	901.104.382.02	Cylinder Head Barrel Nut	24	When studs break off or pull out of the case, it's not uncommon to find these floating around in your cam towers

Camshaft Housings

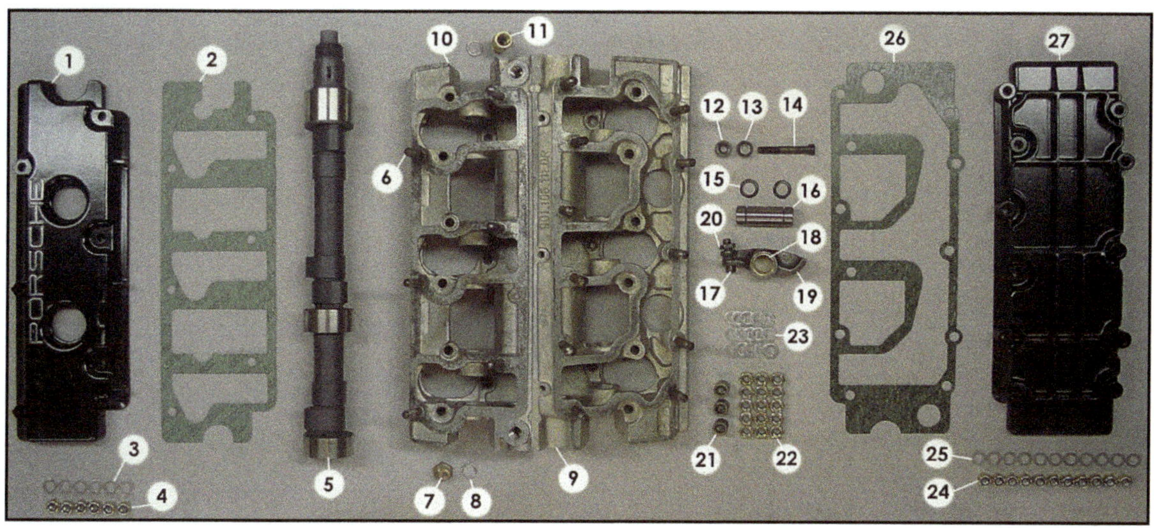

No.	Model / Engine / Years	Part Number	Description	Qty Req	Comments
1	911 / 911 Turbo (1974-89)	901.105.115.03	Upper Valve Cover	2	Verify that yours is manufactured out of aluminum, not magnesium.
2	911 / 911 Turbo (1974-89)	930.105.194.02	Upper Valve Cover Gasket	2	The valve cover gasket kit typically comes complete with two gaskets, and a complete set of brand-new mounting hardware.
3	911 / 911 Turbo (1974-89)	900.031.014.30	Upper Valve Cover Washers	12	
4	911 / 911 Turbo (1974-89)	900.084.004.02	Upper Valve Cover Nuts	12	
5	911 (1974)	911.105.141.00	Camshaft - Left	1	For engine 911.92/97
5	911S (1974-77)	911.105.143.00	Camshaft - Left	1	For engines 911.43/44/48/49/82/84/90/93/98
5	911 (1978-89)	930.105.147.10	Camshaft - Left	1	Camshaft changed in 1981 to use bolt instead of 46mm nut
5	911 Turbo (1976-89)	930.105.143.03	Camshaft - Left	1	Camshaft changed in 1981 to use bolt instead of 46mm nut
5	911 (1974)	911.105.142.00	Camshaft - Right	1	For engine 911.92/97
5	911S (1974-77)	911.105.144.00	Camshaft - Right	1	For engines 911.43/44/48/49/82/84/90/93/98
5	911 (1978-89)	930.105.148.10	Camshaft - Right	1	Camshaft changed in 1981 to use bolt instead of 46mm nut
5	911 Turbo (1976-89)	930.105.142.03	Camshaft - Right	1	Camshaft changed in 1981 to use bolt instead of 46mm nut
6	911 / 911 Turbo (1974-89)	999.062.009.02	Camshaft Housing Stud - Upper	34	Size: M8x28
6	911 / 911 Turbo (1974-89)	999.062.010.02	Camshaft Housing Stud -Lower	34	Size: M8x35
7	911 / 911 Turbo (1974-89)	901.105.374.00	Camshaft Housing Plug	2	
8	911 / 911 Turbo (1974-89)	900.123.005.00	Sealing Ring For Plug	6	
9	911 (1974-77)	901.105.161.01	Camshaft Housing End Plug	2	
9	911 (1978-89) / Turbo (1976-89)	930.105.161.00	Camshaft Housing End Plug	2	
10	911 (1974-77)	901.105.021.05	Camshaft Housing	2	3-Bearing camshaft housing
10	911 (1978-89) / Turbo (1976-89)	930.105.021.07	Camshaft Housing	2	4-Bearing camshaft housing
	911 (1974-77)	901.105.362.01	Oil Splash Tube	1	Replace the splash tube if yours is so badly clogged that it cannot be adequately cleaned.
	911 (1978-89) / Turbo (1976-89)	930.105.362.00	Oil Splash Tube	1	
	911 / 911 Turbo (1974-89)	901.105.379.00	Splash Tube Plug	2	
11	911 / 911 Turbo (1974-89)	901.105.361.01	Oil Line Adapter	2	This is the updated adapter with the narrower orifice
12	911 / 911 Turbo (1974-89)	901.105.376.02	Rocker Arm Nut	12	
13	911 / 911 Turbo (1974-89)	901.105.344.02	Rocker Arm Conical Bushing	12	
14	911 / 911 Turbo (1974-89)	999.067.008.00	Rocker Arm Bolt	12	Size: M7x48
15	911 / 911 Turbo (1974-89)	911.099.103.52	RSR Rocker Arm Seal	24	Used to guard against leaks through the rocker arm shafts
16	911 / 911 Turbo (1974-89)	901.105.342.04	Rocker Arm Shaft	12	
17	911 / 911 Turbo (1974-89)	901.105.370.02	Valve Adjustment Screw	12	Check the condition of this screw and verify that the foot is securely attached
18	911 / 911 Turbo (1974-89)	901.105.043.98	Rocker Arm Bushing	12	Replacement part number for the rocker arm bushing
19	911 / 911 Turbo (1974-89)	930.105.043.00	Rocker Arm	12	New rocker arms come complete with new bushings
20	911 / 911 Turbo (1974-89)	999.034.005.00	Valve Adjustment Nut	12	M8x1
21	911 / 911 Turbo (1974-89)	901.111.271.00	Camshaft Housing Barrel Nuts	6	Three of these barrel nuts are used in tight places on the camshaft housing
22	911 / 911 Turbo (1974-89)	N 011.008.13	Camshaft Housing Nuts	34	
23	911 / 911 Turbo (1974-89)	N 012.241.8	Camshaft Housing Washers	40	
24	911 / 911 Turbo (1974-89)	900.084.004.02	Lower Valve Cover Nuts	11	The valve cover gasket kit typically comes complete with two gaskets. and a complete set of brand-new mounting hardware.
25	911 / 911 Turbo (1974-89)	900.031.014.30	Lower Valve Cover Washers	11	
26	911 / 911 Turbo (1974-89)	930.105.195.06	Lower Valve Cover Gasket	1	
27	911 (1974-89)	930.105.116.00	Lower Valve Cover	1	
27	911 Turbo (1976-79)	930.105.116.00	Lower Valve Cover	1	This is the desired lower Turbo valve cover with the stiffening ribs
27	911 Turbo (1986-89)	930.105.116.00	Lower Valve Cover - Right	1	
27	911 Turbo (1986-89)	930.105.116.01	Lower Valve Cover - Left	1	

Timing Chain Housing

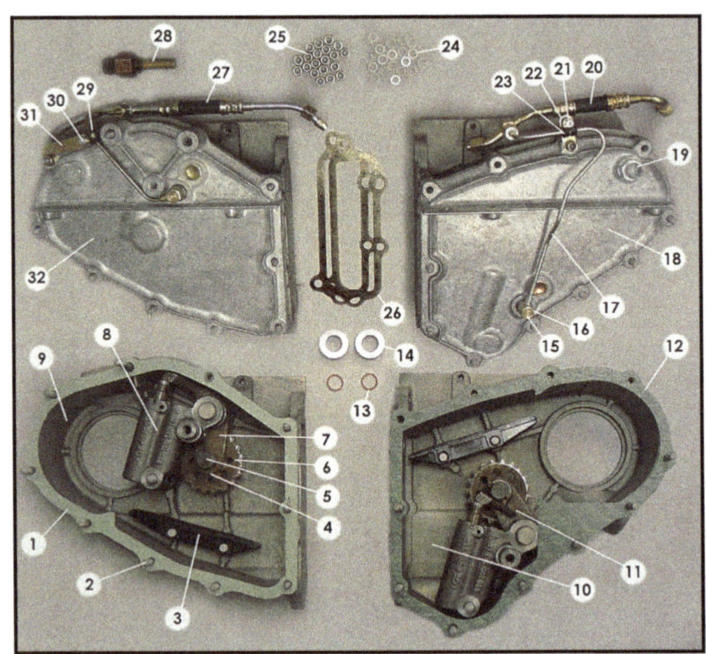

No.	Model / Engine / Years	Part Number	Description	Qty	Comments
1	911 / 911 Turbo (1974-89)	930.105.191.03	Left Chain Housing Gasket	1	
2	911 / 911 Turbo (1974-89)	999.062.102.02	Chain Housing Stud	19	May vary slightly with year. Size: M6x22
	911 / 911 Turbo (1974-89)	999.062.209.08	Chain Housing Stud	2	May vary slightly with year. Size: M8x60
3	911 / 911 Turbo (1974-89)	911.105.222.06	Chain Ramp	5	Total of five black chain ramps are used in the engine
4	911 / 911 Turbo (1974-89)	900.197.010.00	Chain Sprocket Pin	2	Used to hold the pin to the idler arm
	911 / 911 Turbo (1974-89)	N 012.415.1	Chain Sprocket Circlip	2	Used to hold the pin to the idler arm
5	911 / 911 Turbo (1974-89)	901.105.056.01	Chain Sprocket Shaft	2	Confirm that oul-catch bucket is facing upwards
6	911 / 911 Turbo (1974-89)	901.105.055.00	Chain Sprocket	2	Can be used on left or right side
7	911 / 911 Turbo (1974-80)	901.105.505.02	Left Idler Arm - Original (up to #6400450)	1	Requires spacer to be used with hydraulic tensioner
7	911 / 911 Turbo (1981-89)	930.105.509.00	Left Idler Arm - Updated (from 64D3717)	1	Recommended Upgrade
8	911 / 911 Turbo (1974-83)	930.105.053.00	Chain Tensioner - Spring Loaded	2	
8	911 / 911 Turbo (1984-89)	930.105.058.03	Chain Tensioner - Hydraulic	2	Recommended Upgrade

No.	Model / Engine / Years	Part Number	Description	Qty	Comments
9	911 / 911 Turbo (1974-89)	930.105.061.02	Left Chain Housing	1	
10	911 / 911 Turbo (1974-89)	930.105.062.01	Right Chain Housing	1	
11	911 / 911 Turbo (1974-80)	901.105.506.02	Right Idler Arm - Original (up to #6400450)	1	Requires spacer to be used with hydraulic tensioner
11	911 / 911 Turbo (1981-89)	930.105.510.00	Right Idler Arm - Updated (from 64D3717)	1	Recommended Upgrade
12	911 / 911 Turbo (1974-89)	930.105.192.03	Right Chain Housing Gasket	1	
13	911 / 911 Turbo (1984-89)	999.701.690.40	Hydraulic Chain Tensioner O-ring	2	Seals the chain tensioner to the chain housing cover
14	Needed for upgrade	930.105.513.00	Idler Arm Spacers	2	Required if upgrading to hydraulic tensioners without upgrading idler arms
15	911 / 911 Turbo (1984-89)	N 021.073.1	Hollow Bolt - Chain Tensioner Line	2	Attaches the oil line to the hydraulic chain tensioner
16	911 / 911 Turbo (1984-89)	900.123.115.30	Sealing Ring For Hollow Bolt	4	For use with hydraulic chain tensioners
17	911 / 911 Turbo (1984-89)	930.107.348.09	Right Chain Tensioner Oil Line	1	For use with hydraulic chain tensioners
	911 / 911 Turbo (1984-89)	930.107.347.06	Left Chain Tensioner Oil Line	1	
18	911 / 911 Turbo (1974-83)	930.105.064.02	Right Chain Housing Cover - Spring Tensioner	1	
18	911 / 911 Turbo (1984-89)	930.105.064.10	Right Chain Housing Cover - Hydraulic Tensioner	1	For use with hydraulic chain tensioners
19	911 / 911 Turbo (1974-89)	N 016.155.3	Plug	1	
	911 (1980-83) / Turbo (1986-89)	930.606.117.00	Temperature Sensor	1	
	911 / 911 Turbo (1974-89)	900.123.007.70	Seal For Plug / Temp Sensor	1	
20	911 / 911 Turbo (1974-83)	901.107.348.01	Right Camshaft Oil Line - Spring Tensioner	1	Always replace when rebuilding
20	911 / 911 Turbo (1984-89)	930.107.348.11	Right Camshaft Oil Line - Hydraulic Tensioner	1	Always replace when rebuilding
21	911 / 911 Turbo (1984-89)	900.119.059.02	Bolt For Bracket	1	Recommended upgrade for all cars with hydraulic tensioners, and 1984-87 cars manufacted prior to January 1987
22	911 / 911 Turbo (1984-89)	930.107.342.01	Right Side Oil Line Bracket	1	
23	911 / 911 Turbo (1984-89)	999.511.174.02	Clamp For Oil Line	1	
24	911 / 911 Turbo (1974-89)	900.031.011.30	Washers	19	
25	911 / 911 Turbo (1974-89)	N 011.183.11	Nuts	19	Use M6 self-locking nuts
26	911 / 911 Turbo (1974-89)	930.105.193.05	Chain Housing to Case Gasket	2	
27	911 / 911 Turbo (1974-83)	901.107.347.01	Left Camshaft Oil Line - Spring Tensioner	1	Always replace when rebuilding
27	911 / 911 Turbo (1984-89)	930.107.347.05	Left Camshaft Oil Line - Hydraulic Tensioner	1	Always replace when rebuilding
28	911 (1974-83) / Turbo (1976-79)	911.617.117.00	Temperature Sensor	1	Varies with fuel injection system
28	911 Turbo (1986-89)	930.617.118.00	Temperature Sensor	1	
29	911 / 911 Turbo (1984-89)	999.511.174.02	Clamp For Oil Line	1	Recommended upgrade for all cars with hydraulic tensioners, and 1984-87 cars manufacted prior to January 1987
30	911 / 911 Turbo (1984-89)	900.119.059.02	Bolt For Bracket	1	
31	911 / 911 Turbo (1984-89)	930.107.341.00	Left Side Oil Line Bracket	1	
32	911 / 911 Turbo (1974-83)	930.105.063.01	Left Chain Housing Cover - Spring Tensioner	1	
32	911 / 911 Turbo (1984-89)	930.105.063.08	Left Chain Housing Cover - Hydraulic Tensioner	1	

Timing Chain

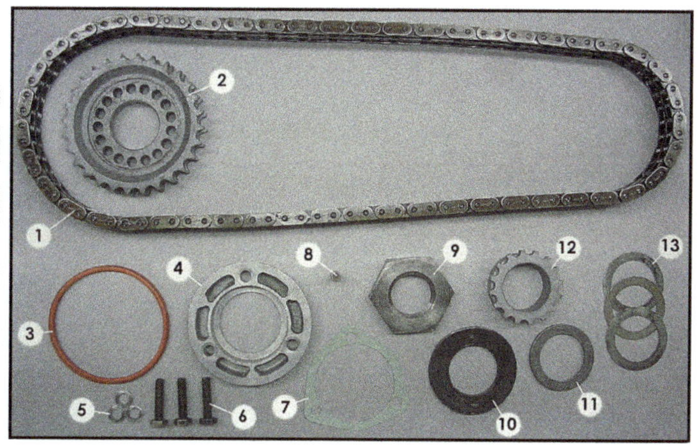

No.	Model / Engine / Years	Part Number	Description	Qty	Comments
1	911 / 911 Turbo (1974-89)	911.105.529.00	Timing Chain	2	Always replace when rebuilding
	911 / 911 Turbo (1974-89)	911.105.529.50	Timing Chain-Master Link		Use when not separating case halves
	911 / 911 Turbo (1974-89)	901.105.530.00	Master Link for chain		The small link used to join the chain together
2	911 / 911 Turbo (1974-89)	901.105.546.02	Camshaft Sprocket	2	Left and right sprockets are not installed in the same manner. See Chapter 5
3	911 / 911 Turbo (1974-89)	999.701.468.40	Cover Plate O-Ring	2	Included in gasket set. Use Curil-T for additional sealing. (Size: 6.75x75.4x4mm)
4	911 / 911 Turbo (1974-89)	930.105.196.00	Cover Plate	2	Don't pinch o-ring with plate when installing
5	911 / 911 Turbo (1974-89)	900.028.008.01	Cover Plate Washers	6	Washer is integrated with later-style bolts (below)
6	911 / 911 Turbo (1974-89)	900.075.341.02	Cover Plate Bolts	6	This newer-style bolt contains a captivated washer
7	911 / 911 Turbo (1974-89)	930.105.197.05	Camshaft Housing Gasket	2	Coat with Curil-T to guard against leaks

No.	Model / Engine / Years	Part Number	Description	Qty	Comments
8	911 / 911 Turbo (1974-89)	900.243.001.00	Dowel Pin	2	Used to align camshaft sprocket with adjustment flange
9	911 / 911 Turbo (1974-81)	901.105.172.00	Securing Nut	2	Used to secure camshaft (1965-81)
	911 / 911 Turbo (1982-89)	900.082.072.01	Securing Bolt	2	Used to secure camshaft (1982-89). Size M12x1.5x50mm
10	911 / 911 Turbo (1974-81)	900.028.021.02	Spring Washer	2	Fits under the large 46mm nut
	911 / 911 Turbo (1982-89)	930.105.163.00	Washer	2	Use with 1982-89 bolt
11	911 / 911 Turbo (1974-89)	901.105.562.00	Spacer	2	Install with bevel facing towards camshaft
12	911 / 911 Turbo (1974-89)	901.105.583.01	Adjustment Flange	2	Indexes the camshaft sprocket with the camshaft
13	911 / 911 Turbo (1974-89)	901.105.561.00	Spacer Shims		Install as needed to align the sprockets with the gears on the intermediate shaft
	911 / 911 Turbo (1974-89)	N 012.708.2	Woodruff Key	2	Secures the location of the adjustment flange on the camshaft

Engine Air Guides

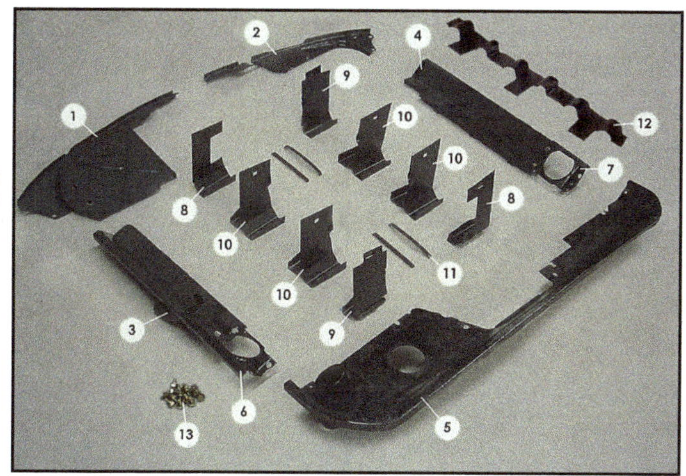

No.	Model / Engine/ Years	Part #	Description	Qty	Comments
1	911 / 911 Turbo	930.106.089.01	Rear left sheet metal	1	Part Numbers for 1985 USA Carrera only. There were literally hundreds of variations in the sheet metal over the 911 engine production period. Check your model for specific variations, such as year, air conditioning options, rest-of-world (ROW) designation, and Turbo-specific sheet metal.
2	911 / 911 Turbo	911.106.802.03	Rear right sheet metal	1	
3	911 / 911 Turbo	930.106.861.00	Left side sheet metal	1	
4	911 / 911 Turbo	930.106.862.00	Right side sheet metal	1	
5	911 / 911 Turbo	930.106.085.11	Front sheet metal	1	
6	911 / 911 Turbo	901.106.825.00	Left side hose guide	1	
7	911 / 911 Turbo	901.106.826.01	Right side hose guide	1	
8	911 (1974-77)	901.106.041.00	Cylinder air guide	2	
8	911 (1978-89), 911 Turbo (1976-77)	930.106.221.00	Cylinder air guide	2	It's important to install all of the cylinder air guides in the proper orientation. Failure to do so will severly reduce the cooling effect of the cylinders. Also be sure to modify the sheet metal to use the factory upgrade for increased cooling. See the modification instructions in Chapter Four (Figure 4-10) for more deatils.
8	911 Turbo (1978-89)	930.106.221.01	Cylinder air guide	2	
9	911 (1974-77)	901.106.039.01	Cylinder air guide	2	
9	911 (1978-89), 911 Turbo (1976-77)	930.106.222.00	Cylinder air guide	2	
9	911 Turbo (1978-89)	930.106.222.01	Cylinder air guide	2	
10	911 (1974-77)	901.106.035.01	Center cylinder air guide	4	
10	911 (1978-89), 911 Turbo (1976-77)	930.106.023.00	Center cylinder air guide	4	
10	911 Turbo (1978-89)	930.106.023.01	Center cylinder air guide	4	
11	911 (1974-77)	901.106.339.01	Guide retainer	4	
11	911 (1978-89), 911 Turbo (1976-89)	930.106.228.00	Guide retainer	4	
12	911 (1978-89, 911 Turbo (1976-89)	930.106.301.00	Late model cylinder cover plate	2	Only used on 3.0L engines and later (including all Turbos)
13	911 All	900.075.363.02	Cheese-head fastening screws	As Req	Total quantity required varies greatly from year to year. Qty 40 should cover all years

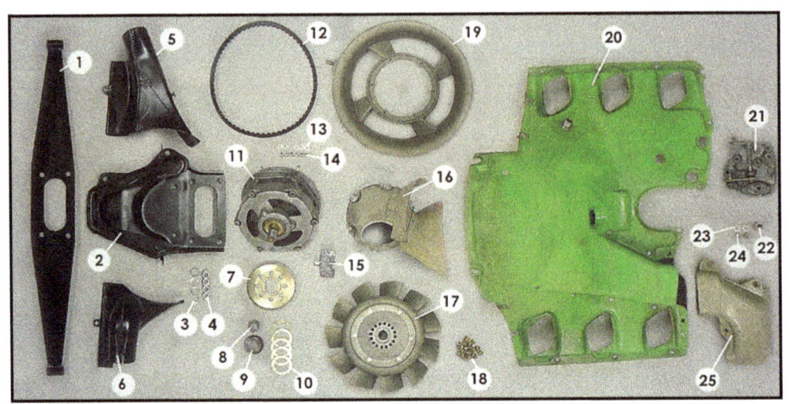

Fan Shroud & Accessories

No.	Model / Engine / Years	Part Number	Description	Qty	Comments
1	911 / 911 Turbo (1974-89)	911.375.043.00	Engine Mount Bar	1	Align according to procedures in Chapter 5
1	911 / 911 Turbo (1983-89)	911.375.043.07	Engine Mount Bar - Cabriolet	1	
2	911 / 911 Turbo		Engine Mount	1	Varies greatly with year, engine and A/C option
	911 / 911 Turbo (1983-89)	900.156.006.02	Bolts	6	
3	911 / 911 Turbo (1983-89)	N 012.242.3	Washers	6	
4	911 / 911 Turbo (1983-89)	N 011.133.4	Nuts	6	
5	911 (1974)	911.106.321.00	Left Air Guide	1	Keep this air guide completely closed off, if you're running the engine without the heater system connected.
5	911 (1975-83)	930.106.326.01	Left Air Guide	1	
5	911 (1984-89)	930.106.321.01	Left Air Guide	1	
6	911 (1974)	911.106.036.00	Right Air Guide	1	Plug this outlet if running the engine without the heater system attached.
6	911 (1975-89)	911.106.036.01	Right Air Guide	1	
7	911 (1974)	901.603.421.01	Fan Belt Outer Pulley Half	1	
7	911 (1975)	911.106.207.00	Fan Belt Outer Pulley Half	1	
7	911 (1975)	911.106.207.02	Fan Belt Outer Pulley Half	1	California cars only
7	911 (1976-79)	911.106.208.00	Fan Belt Outer Pulley Half	1	
7	911 (1980-89), Turbo (1976-89)	930.106.209.02	Fan Belt Outer Pulley Half	1	
8	911 / 911 Turbo (1974-81)	901.603.905.00	Fan Belt Nut	1	Size: M16x1
8	911 / 911 Turbo (1982-89)	928.603.904.00	Fan Belt Nut	1	Size: M17x1.5
8	911 / 911 Turbo (1982-89)	911.603.127.00	Fan Belt Nut Cover	1	
9	911 / 911 Turbo (1974-81)	901.603.428.00	Pulley Nut Flange	1	
9	911 (1975)	911.106.211.01	Pulley Nut Flange	1	California cars only
9	911 / 911 Turbo (1982-89)	911.603.428.01	Pulley Nut Flange	1	
10	911 (1974-75)	901.105.561.00	Pulley Shims	6	Always use a minimum of six shims at ALL times.
10	911 (1975)	911.106.212.00	Pulley Shims	6	
10	911 / 911 Turbo (1976-89)	930.106.564.00	Pulley Shims	6	
11	911 (1974)	911.603.120.06	Alternator	1	External regulator
11	911 / 911 Turbo (1975-83)	911.603.120.04	Alternator	1	External regulator
11	911 / 911 Turbo (1984-89)	911.603.120.05	Alternator	1	Internal regulator
12	911 (1974-75), 911 (1978-79)	999.192.097.50	Fan Belt	1	Fan Belt 9.5x725mm
12	911 (1976-77), 911 (1980-89), Turbo (1976-89)	999.192.176.50	Fan Belt	1	Fan Belt 9.5x710mm
13	911 / 911 Turbo (1974-89)	N 012.226.5	Washers	6	
14	911 / 911 Turbo (1974-89)	N 011.006.8	Nuts	6	Size: M6
15	911 (1974)	901.603.907.00	Alternator Brushes	1	
16	911 (1974)	911.106.033.01	Alternator Air Guide	1	
16	911 / Turbo (1975-83)	911.106.033.05	Alternator Air Guide	1	
16	911 / Turbo (1984-89)	911.106.055.01	Alternator Air Guide	1	
17	911 (1974-75)	901.106.010.03	Fan	1	Early 11-blade fan
17	911 (1976-77)	911.106.028.00	Fan	1	Five-blade fan—replace with early 1974-75 fan for upgrade
17	911 (1978-79)	930.106.011.01	Fan	1	11-blade fan
17	911 (1980-89), Turbo (1976-89)	930.106.012.00	Fan	1	11-blade fan
18	911 All	900.075.363.02	Cheese-head fastening screws	As Req	Total quantity required varies greatly from year to year. Qty 40 should cover all years
19	911 (1974)	901.106.011.00	Fan Housing	1	The fan housing must be matched to the fan used.
19	911 (1975-77)	911.106.008.00	Fan Housing	1	
19	911 (1978-79)	930.106.005.00	Fan Housing	1	
19	911 (1980-83), Turbo (1978-80)	930.106.006.00	Fan Housing	1	
19	911 (1984-89)	930.106.102.07	Fan Housing	1	
19	911 Turbo (1986-89)	930.106.006.06	Fan Housing	1	
19	911 / 911 Turbo (1974-89)	964.106.251.20	Fan Strap	1	
20	911 (1974-77)	911.106.901.05	Fan Shroud	1	Color: green
20	911 (1978-83)	930.106.041.04	Fan Shroud	1	Color: red
20	911 (1984-89)	930.106.041.09	Fan Shroud	1	Color: black
20	911 Turbo (1978-89)	930.106.041.13	Fan Shroud	1	Color: black
21	911 (1974-83)	911.110.234.10	Accelerator Bracket	1	
21	911 (1984-89)	911.110.091.07	Accelerator Bracket	1	
22	911 / 911 Turbo (1974-89)	901.110.236.00	Standoff	1	
23	911 / 911 Turbo (1974-89)	900.031.014.30	Washers	As Req	
24	911 / 911 Turbo (1974-89)	900.084.004.02	Nuts	As Req	
25	911 / 911 Turbo (1974)	911.106.036.00	Oil Cooler Air Guide	1	
25	911 / 911 Turbo (1975-89)	911.106.036.01	Oil Cooler Air Guide	1	

INDEX

www.ingramcontent.com/pod-product-compliance
Ingram Content Group UK Ltd.
Pitfield, Milton Keynes, MK11 3LW, UK
UKHW061321250126
467270UK00005B/59